FREE EXPRESSION & DEMOCRACY IN AMERICA

FREE EXPRESSION
and
DEMOCRACY
in America

—• A HISTORY •—

STEPHEN M. FELDMAN

THE UNIVERSITY OF CHICAGO PRESS   *Chicago and London*

The University of Chicago Press, Chicago 60637
The University of Chicago Press, Ltd., London
© 2008 by The University of Chicago
All rights reserved. Published 2008.
Paperback edition 2015
Printed in the United States of America

24 23 22 21 20 19 18 17 16 15   2 3 4 5 6

ISBN-13: 978-0-226-24066-4 (cloth)
ISBN-13: 978-0-226-33306-9 (paper)
ISBN-13: 978-0-226-24074-9 (e-book)
10.7208/chicago/9780226240749.001.0001

Library of Congress Cataloging-in-Publication Data

Feldman, Stephen M., 1955–
    Free expression and democracy in America: a history /
    Stephen M. Feldman.
        p.   cm.
    Includes index.
    Includes bibliographical references and index.
    ISBN-13: 978-0-226-24066-4 (cloth: alk. paper)
    ISBN-10: 0-226-24066-5 (cloth: alk. paper)
    1. Freedom of expression — United States — History.
    I. Title.
    KF4770.F45 2008
    342.7308'5—dc22
                                            2007053062

TO MY FAMILY, Laura, Mollie, and Samuel

The citizen under a free government has a right to think, to speak, to write, to print, and to publish freely, but with decency and truth, concerning public men, public bodies, and public measures.

JAMES WILSON, 1790–92

———•◆•———

I know of no country in which there is so little independence of mind and real freedom of discussion as in America.

ALEXIS DE TOCQUEVILLE, 1835

———•◆•———

If there is any fixed star in our constitutional constellation, it is that no official, high or petty, can prescribe what shall be orthodox in politics, nationalism, religion, or other matters of opinion or force citizens to confess by word or act their faith therein.

JUSTICE ROBERT JACKSON, 1943

———•◆•———

Contents

Acknowledgments

I developed and wrote this book over a number of years, and many people have contributed at different stages. I thank those individuals who have commented on the entire manuscript or its parts (including article manuscripts that I later developed into chapters of the book): Richard Delgado, Mark Tushnet, G. Edward White, Barry Friedman, Michael Kent Curtis, Eugene Volokh, Alan Chen, Deb Donahue, Frank Ravitch, and Lew Schlosser. I appreciate the comments of my colleagues at the University of Wyoming who participated in faculty colloquies related to this project. The Housel/Arnold endowment provided financial assistance for the work. And the librarians at the College of Law, including Tim Kearley, Susan Wozny, and Tawnya Plumb, helped in innumerable ways. I also thank the dean, Jerry Parkinson, for his support of my scholarship. Finally, I thank David Pervin of the University of Chicago Press for helping to usher the book through the publication process.

Articles that, to different degrees, served as the bases for various parts of the book include *The Theory and Politics of First-Amendment Protections: Why Does the Supreme Court Favor Free Expression Over Religious Freedom?*, 8 U. Pa. J. Const. L. 431 (2006); *Unenumerated Rights in Different Democratic Regimes*, 9 U. Pa. J. Const. L. 47 (2006); *Free Speech, World War I, and Republican Democracy: The Internal and External Holmes*, 6 First Amendment L. Rev. 192 (2008).

CHAPTER 1

Democracy and Free Expression

Does democracy require the protection of free expression?

In 1948, Alexander Meiklejohn wrote: "The principle of the freedom of speech springs from the necessities of the program of self-government. . . . It is a deduction from the basic American agreement that public issues shall be decided by universal suffrage." Ever since, a steady stream of jurists, constitutional scholars, and political theorists have repeated the maxim: free expression is a precondition for democracy. The people must be able to discuss political issues openly, without fear of governmental punishment, or democracy cannot exist.[1]

Yet, throughout American history, numerous presidents, congressional members, Supreme Court justices, and state and local officials have endorsed suppression, particularly of political speech and writing. If the connection between free expression and democracy were so obvious, so necessary, why would so many governmental leaders act in such a manner?

Consider flag desecration. In June 1904, Nebraska convicted Nicholas Halter and Harry Hayward for violating a state law proscribing desecration of the American flag. Halter and Hayward had sold bottled beer affixed with labels bearing the flag. In defense, they argued that the law violated their constitutional right to "personal liberty," encompassing freedom of expression. Rejecting their argument, the Nebraska Supreme Court reasoned: "Patriotism has ever been regarded as the highest civic virtue, and whatever tends to foster that virtue certainly makes for the common good." The U.S. Supreme Court agreed, upholding the convictions in *Halter v. Nebraska*, decided in 1907. "It is familiar law," Justice John Marshall Harlan wrote for an eight-justice majority, "[that] the rights inhering in personal liberty are subject, in their enjoyment, to such reasonable restraints as may be required for the general good." Harlan thus emphasized the expressive nature of the flag. "[T]o every true American the flag is the symbol of the nation's power, — the emblem of freedom in its truest, best sense." Exactly for that reason, Nebraska had enacted its law, which resembled those in two-thirds of the then forty-five states. As the Court concluded, "a duty rests upon each state . . . to encourage its people to love the Union with which the state is indissolubly connected." In short, the state legitimately pursued the common good by nurturing patriotism, even if doing so entailed restrictions on expression.[2]

Eighty years after Halter's and Hayward's convictions, Gregory Lee Johnson burned an American flag during the 1984 Republican National Convention in Dallas, Texas, to protest the policies of President Ronald Reagan's administration and certain Dallas-based corporations. Texas convicted Johnson for violating a state law prohibiting desecration of venerated objects, including the flag. The Texas Court of Criminal Appeals reversed, holding that the conviction violated Johnson's right to free expression. In *Texas v. Johnson,* decided in 1989, the U.S. Supreme Court affirmed, now finding that the first amendment protected flag desecration from governmental punishment. Like in *Halter,* the Court emphasized the expressive quality of the flag. "Pregnant with expressive content, the flag as readily signifies this Nation as does the combination of letters found in 'America,'" wrote Justice William J. Brennan for a five-justice majority. The *Johnson* Court recognized, again like in *Halter,* that the state enacted the law precisely because of the flag's symbolism. The state argued that the antidesecration statute would further its "interest in preserving the flag as a symbol of nationhood and national unity." This time, though, contrary to the *Halter* Court's reasoning, the Court found this very purpose problematic: the government's desire to promote patriotism by protecting an emblem, the flag, could not withstand first-amendment scrutiny. "If there is a bedrock principle underlying the First Amendment, it is that the government may not prohibit the expression of an idea simply because society finds the idea itself offensive or disagreeable."[3]

What happened? What can explain the seemingly inconsistent results of *Halter* and *Johnson?* Did the *Halter* justices betray our hallowed principle of free expression — even though the majority included Oliver Wendell Holmes, Jr., renowned as perhaps the greatest Supreme Court guardian of free expression in history? Did the *Johnson* justices sully our flag and debase the value of patriotism — even though the majority included Antonin Scalia, one of our most conservative justices? Didn't the *Johnson* Court, despite its ultimate conclusion, also celebrate the "cherished place" of the flag in American life? Had the Supreme Court justices over the years become, quite simply, more protective of free expression?[4]

These questions frame a central theme of this book. The free expression of the early-twentieth century, when the Court decided *Halter*, differed from that of the late-twentieth century, when the Court decided *Johnson*. What caused the concept of free expression to change? Democracy, more than anything else. As Meiklejohn and other first-amendment theorists have posited, free expression and democracy are integrally bound together. American democracy, however, has not remained static. During the 1920s and 1930s, cultural, social, and economic pressures caused the nation to transform from a republican democracy into a pluralist democracy. Under the republican regime, virtuous citizens and officials ostensibly pursued the common good. Free expression therefore always remained subordinate to the overarching communal goal of the common good — as *Halter* suggested. Under the pluralist regime, democratic processes structured supposedly fair and open political battles in which citizens sought to satisfy self-interest. Free expression became a crucial component of the pluralist processes and thus developed into a constitutional "lodestar" — as *Johnson* emphasized.[5]

DIMENSIONS OF FREE EXPRESSION

Many scholars equate free expression with the first-amendment legal doctrine emanating from the Supreme Court. If the Court pronounces that the government cannot punish political speech unless necessary to achieve a compelling purpose — a balancing test skewed to favor free expression — then the court, it appears, affords free speech an importance commensurate with the highest pantheon of constitutional rights. But Supreme Court legal doctrine tells only part of the story of free expression in the United States. Other institutions, particularly Congress, contribute to the formation and interpretation of legal doctrine. Equally important, one must go beyond legal doctrine, regardless of its sources, to appreciate the relevance of two competing traditions: dissent and suppression. The tradition of dissent recognizes an American ethos of speaking one's mind without fear of punishment. In the politically turbulent 1790s, courts had not yet developed strong doctrinal protections for expression, but Americans generally enjoyed a robust de facto liberty. Yet, alongside this American tradition of dissent, a countervailing tradition of suppression has always remained powerful. Whereas many Americans have reasonably expected to speak their minds without penalty, many (and often the same) Americans have simultaneously suppressed political outsiders, whether based on race, religion, or otherwise. Both traditions can be manifested officially—through a congressional statute, for instance—or unofficially—through nongovernmental actors. Mob violence, tar and feathering, and chasing outsiders from town have been common means for unofficially suppressing those who diverged too far from the mainstream. During the regime of republican democracy, legal doctrine harmonized more closely with the tradition of suppression, while during the pluralist regime, doctrine has shifted closer to the tradition of dissent. Even so, both traditions have persisted throughout the course of American history and have contributed to the experience and understanding of free expression.

One might envision legal doctrine, the tradition of dissent, and the tradition of suppression as three intersecting axes that together determine the degree of free expression at any particular time in history. Each axis represents a variable that specifies a component of free speech and writing. Consequently, for the year 1800, one can discuss the courts' doctrinal approaches to free expression, how strongly Americans manifested the tradition of dissent, and how strongly they manifested the tradition of suppression. The same could be done for 1850, for 1950, or for any other year (or for various eras). The three axes together provide a relatively complete picture of free expression. Despite this mathematical metaphor, though, I do not propose to identify a precise "quantity" of free expression for any point in time, as if one merely needed to identify the proper coordinates on a graph. Instead, I depict with something akin to a three-dimensional picture the American experience and understanding of free expression during different historical periods. Legal doctrine is important here, but it is not everything.[6]

Doctrine, dissent, and suppression are not independent of each other. Intense governmental suppression implemented through statutory laws might, for example, spark strong dissent. Likewise, expressions of dissent sometimes provoke in reaction both official and unofficial suppression. And judicial applications of apparently well-established legal doctrines can vary in accordance with the current magnitudes of the competing traditions. If, at a particular time, public opinion strongly supports suppression, then the Supreme Court justices will probably uphold governmental acts punishing unpopular speech and writing. Much depends on the contemporary political and cultural alignments. Moreover, doctrine, dissent, and suppression all interrelate not only with each other but also with democracy. In the courts, for instance, republican democracy engendered a methodology of judicial review: courts ensured that governmental actions promoted the common good rather than partial or private interests. Following from this general methodology, specific legal doctrines governing free expression subordinated speech and writing to the pursuit of the common good. The transition from republican to pluralist democracy, however, generated a concomitant change in judicial review. Instead of emphasizing a supposed distinction between the common good and partial or private interests, courts typically sought to police the functioning of pluralist democratic processes. Consequently, as a crucial component of those pluralist processes, free expression transmuted into a preeminent constitutional right. Yet, regardless of the niceties of legal doctrine — whether under republican or pluralist democracy — Americans have manifested the countervailing traditions of dissent and suppression. To take one illustration, during the pre–Civil War nineteenth century, elite white Southerners relied on republican democratic principles to justify both slavery and the suppression of abolitionist speech and writing. These white Southerners insisted that African Americans lacked the virtue requisite for liberty and free government and that abolitionist expression therefore contravened the common good. In response, abolitionists consistently proclaimed a traditional liberty to speak their minds, especially on an issue so central to free (republican) government. In the slavery-abolition battle, as well as in other disputes through American history, democracy provides the fundamental context for understanding the intertwined operations of doctrine, dissent, and suppression.

In recent years, we commonly hear talk of the "culture wars," but American culture wars are as old as the nation itself. Cultural battles, played out on the shifting fields of democracy, have been endemic to American history. During the framing era, Americans constructed republican democratic governments grounded on the assumed existence of a common good for a homogeneous people. But how did these Americans maintain homogeneity? By excluding other Americans from belonging to and participating in the polity. Yet, early outsiders — including women, indigents, African Americans, and Native Americans — and new ones in subsequent eras have fought to expand the political community so that they too might belong. During many of those battles, free expression has been a tool, sometimes a sword and sometimes a shield, as individuals and groups maneuvered for advantage. In the crucible of these cultural and political clashes, often literally fought to the death, Americans have forged democracy and free expression.[7]

THE ENGLISH AND COLONIAL BACKGROUND

Most American colonists considered themselves Englishmen, and as such, believed they had inherited the rights and liberties of all Englishmen. The first Charter for Virginia, issued in 1606, declared that the colonists "shall have and enjoy all Liberties, Franchises, and Immunities . . . to all Intents and Purposes, as if they had been abiding and born, within this our Realm of England." The English had long viewed themselves as the freest and most liberty-loving people in the world — to be "free-born" was an Englishman's "birthright." Those birthrights reached at least as far back as 1215 and the Magna Carta, in which the king agreed that "[n]o freeman shall be captured or imprisoned or disseised or outlawed or exiled or in any way destroyed . . . except by the lawful judgment of his peers or by the law of the land." As even the future King George III put it in the eighteenth century, shortly before he ascended to the throne, "The pride, the glory of Britain, and the direct end of its constitution, is political liberty."[8]

But to what extent was free expression, including speech and press, protected in England? Despite the Magna Carta, England had a lengthy history of restricting speech and writing — a tradition of suppression — often manifested through official (or governmental) actions. The overriding justification for restrictions was the preservation of society. The government constrained expression to protect public peace and social order, to maintain cultural and religious values, and to uphold the dignity of governmental officers. Given these goals, the chief legal mechanisms for controlling speech were initially the imposition of a licensing requirement on printers — preventing printers from disseminating information without prior governmental approval (the first printing press in England began operating around 1476) — and subsequently the criminal punishment of seditious libel — speech criticizing the government or its officials.[9]

England, though, endured a tumultuous seventeenth century. The country passed through a Civil War and interregnum, a Restoration of the monarchy, and a Glorious Revolution. The Civil War period of the 1640s and 1650s, in particular, was a time of social ferment in which the king, Charles I, was executed amid a struggle to establish an English republic grounded on the sovereignty of the people. Divisions within Christianity — particularly among Anglicans, Roman Catholics, and Puritans — splintered the English people. During this time, criticism of officials, whether governmental or religious, became pervasive and strident, and the traditional respect for authority diminished. Parliament abolished the Court of Star Chamber, a notorious royal tool of repression. Calls for freedom, including free expression, rang out. John Milton issued his *Areopagitica* in 1644 to protest against the licensing of printers and to plead for tolerance in the pursuit of truth: "And though all the winds of doctrine were let loose to play upon the earth, so truth be in the field, we do injuriously by licensing and prohibiting to misdoubt her strength. Let her and falsehood grapple; who ever knew truth put to the worse, in a free and open encounter?" As the Parliament and the king clashed in the years leading up to the Civil War, the House of Commons, led by Sir Edward Coke, protested James I's declaration that the Commons served merely at the king's "grace and permission." The Commons' Protestation asserted not only that Parliament's powers were an English birthright but that "every member of the House of Parliament hath, and of right ought to have, freedom of speech to propound, treat, reason, and bring to conclusion" issues within Parliament's jurisdiction.[10]

Regardless of this early claim to free speech and the challenge to authority embodied by the Civil War, English law continued to restrict expression, even during the interregnum. And after the Restoration of the monarchy in 1660, suppression intensified. Parliament enacted a law in 1662 that placed the licensing of printers on statutory ground, explaining that "by the general licentiousnes of the late times many evil disposed persons have been encouraged to print and sell heretical schismatical blasphemous seditious and treasonable Bookes Pamphlets and Papers." The laws, moreover, could be enforced with a vengeance, as the case of John Twyn gruesomely illustrates. In 1663, the government prosecuted Twyn for publishing a book that claimed the people had a right to rebel against the king. Although Twyn had printed but not actually written the book, his harsh sentence was executed: "You shall be hanged by the neck, and being alive, shall be cut down and your privy members shall be cut off, your entrails shall be taken from your body and you living, the same to be burnt before your eyes."[11]

In 1688 and 1689, William and Mary succeeded to the throne after the Glorious Revolution, a bloodless overthrow of James II. Under the new regime, England liberalized to a degree and shifted more to a parliamentary monarchy, established at the outset through an agreement memorialized in a 1689 parliamentary act, which came to be called the Bill of Rights. This English Bill of Rights provided "that the freedom of speech and debates or proceedings in parliament ought not to be impeached or questioned in any court or place out of parliament." Then, in 1695, Parliament ended the prior restraint of printers by allowing the 1662 licensing statute to expire, mostly for practical reasons related to the free flow of commerce and the difficulty of administration. John Locke, not incidentally, wrote many of his most important tracts on political theory, stressing individual rights and liberties, during the years before and after the Glorious Revolution. Nonetheless, the demise of licensing did not end suppression: the English government began prosecuting seditious libel as its primary means for controlling expression.[12]

By the time William Blackstone wrote in the 1760s, he could summarize the English law of free expression: "The liberty of the press is indeed essential to the nature of a free state: but this consists in laying no *previous* restraints upon publications, and not in freedom from censure for criminal matter when published. Every freeman has an undoubted right to lay what sentiments he pleases before the public: to forbid this, is to destroy the freedom of the press: but if he publishes what is improper, mischievous, or illegal, he must take the consequence of his own temerity." Blackstone, thus, celebrated the prohibition against prior restraints as the core of free expression while underscoring that the government retained the power to punish seditious libel. Expression criticizing public officials, he explained, disseminated "bad sentiments," had "a pernicious tendency," and disturbed "the public peace," and therefore was subject to criminal punishment regardless of whether "it be true or false." Blackstone reasoned that appropriate restrictions were crucial to sustain free expression itself. "So true will it be found," he wrote, "that to censure the licentiousness, is to maintain the liberty, of the press."[13]

Even with the continuing legal restrictions on expression, the Civil War era challenges to authority spawned a tradition of English dissent — countering the tradition of suppression. Sustained for decades, the tradition of dissent blossomed in the early-eighteenth century with the Country or Opposition ideology, which would (along with Lockean theory) subsequently prove influential in Revolutionary America. John Trenchard and Thomas Gordon wrote some of the most important Opposition tracts, published as "Cato's Letters" in the *London Journal* during the early 1720s. One letter, signed by Gordon and entitled "Of Freedom of Speech," declared: "Without freedom of thought, there can be no such thing as wisdom; and no such thing as publick liberty, without freedom of speech: Which is the right of every man, as far as by it he does not hurt and control the right of another." Free government, Cato continued, is impossible without free speech. Cato then invoked the bulwark-of-liberty phrasing that would later echo throughout America during the Revolutionary and framing eras: "Freedom of Speech is the great Bulwark of Liberty; they prosper and die together." But what of the legal protection of governmental officials, insulating them from criticism? "That men ought to speak well of their governors, is true,"

Cato admitted. But then he sharply qualified this admission: officials should be praised only if they "deserve to be well spoken of; but to do publick mischief, without hearing of it, is only the prerogative and felicity of tyranny: A free people will be shewing that they are so, by their freedom of speech." The tradition of dissent would survive despite legal restrictions.[14]

Tradition is rarely neat enough to be reduced to a single outlook or attitude. Neither the tradition of suppression nor the tradition of dissent was monolithic. To take one example, admirers typically celebrate Milton's *Areopagitica* for its advocacy of tolerance and freedom, but Milton sought freedom only for those who substantially agreed with his views, or in his own words, to "those [of] neighbouring differences, or rather indifferences." From the all-important religious vantage, Milton supported a Puritan form of Protestantism and expressly denied toleration to "popery, and open superstition, which as it extirpates all religions and civil supremacies, so itself should be extirpate." In Milton, the tradition of suppression ensnarled around the tradition of dissent. More generally, the law seemingly justified the criminal prosecution of any critic of the government and its officials, but the tradition of dissent could temper this potential. In 1742, David Hume summarized the English viewpoint on liberty of the press as follows: "Nothing is more apt to surprise a foreigner than the extreme liberty which we enjoy in this country of communicating whatever we please to the public and of openly censuring every measure entered into by the king or his ministers." If the government wanted war, Hume explained, then political writers demanded peace. If the government sought peace, then commentators breathed "nothing but war and devastation."[15]

THE AMERICAN COLONISTS inherited from the English the legal restrictions on expression, commensurate with a form of (English) republican government, as well as the traditions of dissent and suppression. Not only did the English law punishing speech apply in the colonies, but many colonies adopted additional laws to restrict expression. The second Lord Baltimore pronounced on April 15, 1637, that all Maryland colonists "honor, respect and obey him as they ought to do, upon pain of such punishment to be inflicted upon them, and every of them, as such high contempt shall deserve." The 1669 Fundamental Constitutions of Carolina, first framed by John Locke, provided: "Since multiplicity of comments, as well as of laws, have great inconveniences, and serve only to obscure and perplex; all manner of comments or expositions, on any part of these fundamental constitutions, or on any part of the common or statute laws of Carolina, are absolutely prohibited." Such restrictive laws were not dead letters. Colonial prosecutions for seditious expression were common, though less so toward the end of the seventeenth century. John Lee was convicted for calling the Massachusetts governor, John Winthrop, no more than "a lawyer's clerk," with the penalty being a fine and a whipping. A Virginia court convicted Richard Barnes for making "'detracting speeches'" about a prominent citizen and banished him from Jamestown after having "his tongue bored through with an awl."[16]

Confronting the legal suppression of expression, the American colonists, like many of their contemporaries in England, sought to memorialize the protection of rights and liberties through written documents. The first such document, the Maryland Act for the Liberties of the People, promulgated in 1639, echoed the law-of-the-land provision from the Magna Carta. Meanwhile, many of the Massachusetts Bay colonists had been struggling against a ruling oligarchy, including Governor Winthrop, to establish a greater degree of free government. Out of this dispute, the Massachusetts Body of Liberties emerged in 1641 just as England itself teetered on the brink of Civil War. The Body of Liberties contained a remarkably long list of protected rights and liberties, and given the nature of the underlying dispute, it unsurprisingly included a limited protection of speech and petition for the purpose of facilitating free government. "Every man whether Inhabitant or fforreiner, free or not free shall have libertie to come to any publique Court, Councel, or Towne meeting, and either by speech or writeing to move any lawfull, seasonable, and materiall question, or to present any necessary motion, complaint, petition, Bill or information, whereof that meeting hath proper cognizance, so it be done in convenient time, due order, and respective manner." With the adoption of the Body of Liberties, the colonies leapt past their English homeland in the legislative or written protection of individual rights and liberties. The Body of Liberties served as a model for similar lists of legal protections in other colonies, though not one other colony included an analogous explicit protection of a right to speech, print, or petition. Despite this paucity of explicit legal protections for expression — and despite the many legal mechanisms that authorized suppression — colonial officials, when compared with their brethren in England, displayed a greater leniency toward seditious speakers, particularly as the seventeenth century progressed. Correlatively, the interrelated diminution of respect for authority and increasing willingness to criticize officials were even more intense in the colonies than in England. The tradition of dissent grew stronger in America than in England.[17]

A variety of reasons led to this burgeoning American tradition. First, one should recall that English settlers established the North American colonies at the same time that England itself struggled through its Civil War, Restoration, and Glorious Revolution. One hundred and five colonists first came to Jamestown, Virginia, in 1607, while 102 Pilgrims fled England in 1620 hoping to establish a Puritan colony. Over the next decades, governmental officials in England were often so preoccupied with turmoil at home that they were inattentive to the colonies, which engendered sometimes unexpected freedoms for the colonists. Second, and closely related to the first reason, the ultimate source of official authority in the colonies was literally across an ocean. English governmental officials not only had their own worries at home in England, but they had to try to extend their authority all the way to the colonies at a time of slow travel and communication. True, colonists had to face local representatives of the crown, but they did not have to confront the full panoply of monarchical power, which remained in England. Third, as would often be the case in America, religion played an important role. Many colonists left England to escape religious persecution, but they rarely intended to protect religious freedom for all individuals in their new colonies. Instead, they sought to create governmental structures that would nurture and support their own religions. The Puritans of New England are a prime example, as their record of persecuting religious dissenters amply demonstrates. Roger Williams founded Rhode Island only after being banished from the Massachusetts Bay Colony for disseminating "newe & dangerous opinions." Even so, most American Protestant denominations were far less hierarchical than either the Catholic or Anglican Churches. This resistance to religious hierarchies, which intensified during a mid-eighteenth-century Protestant revivalist movement, the First Great Awakening, encouraged a questioning of authority that spread readily to nonreligious realms.[18]

By the end of the seventeenth century, prosecutions of seditious expression were less for preserving the general public peace, order, and dignity of governmental officials and more for protecting the government from "real, immediate danger." The American tradition of dissent strengthened, facilitating the criticism of officials; this tradition sowed the seeds for the Revolutionary sentiments of the 1770s. Moreover, the law bent, to some degree, to correspond more closely with contemporary social norms, as revealed in the trial of John Peter Zenger in 1735. The printer for the *New York Weekly Journal*, an Opposition newspaper that published copies of "Cato's Letters" on free expression, Zenger was prosecuted for seditious libel after criticizing William Cosby, the royal governor of New York. Zenger's attorney, the renowned Andrew Hamilton, admitted that Zenger had, in fact, printed material criticizing Cosby, but Hamilton insisted that the criticisms were true. Under the then current law of seditious libel, however, not only was truth not a defense, it was grounds for aggravation of the crime. The jury nevertheless ignored the judge's instructions and acquitted Zenger.[19]

How significant was the *Zenger* case? From one perspective, the result "was the product of a single-minded jury, determined to acquit a man whose only crime was exposing the venality of the governor." From another perspective, the idea that truth should be a defense to charges of seditious libel did not strike Andrew Hamilton like a bolt of lightning; rather the foundation for considering the truth of allegedly libelous statements had been building for a century in the colonies. From yet another perspective, the law of seditious libel, as a matter of abstract doctrine (rather than in its application), remained unchanged; the *Zenger* jury, after all, did not have the institutional power of a high court. Without any equivocation, Americans continued to believe that any liberty of expression was subordinate to the government's power to protect communal values. As explained in one Philadelphia newspaper, no irony intended, "every man has a privilege of declaring his sentiments with the utmost freedom; provided he does it with a proper decency and a just regard to the laws." Yet, *Zenger* shows the potential influence of the tradition of dissent on legal doctrine. "[I]f [*Zenger*] is not law, it is better than law," another Philadelphia paper celebrated, "it ought to be law, and will always be law wherever justice prevails." *Zenger* was well publicized, and after the decision, the colonies never again saw a successful criminal prosecution for seditious libel. During the Revolutionary period, a defendant could count on a jury to acquit if he was prosecuted for criticizing the Crown or its officials.[20]

While the colonies nurtured a vigorous tradition of dissent, the counter-tradition of suppression always remained extant. Dissent enjoyed popular support so long as the dissenting opinion was, well, popular. The people and their officials persecuted unpopular outsiders who sufficiently threatened the values and interests of the colonial mainstream. Suppression could be implemented through official or unofficial channels. While prosecutions for seditious libel diminished, colonial legislatures and executives asserted quasi-judicial powers and occasionally punished seditious statements. In at least twenty instances, colonial assemblies claimed that a power of legislative privilege allowed them to punish their critics. The tradition of suppression often was manifested in the religious realm. In the Massachusetts Bay Colony, Roger Williams did not suffer the only banishment due to religious beliefs and statements. Among the many others, Anne Hutchinson's expulsion underscores how sedition and heresy could overlap when government and religion closely intertwined. In the Massachusetts Bay of the mid-1630s, a minister's acceptance of an individual as a visible saint was prerequisite to that person's full citizenship and participation in civil and church matters. Hutchinson and her followers, however, charged that most of the Massachusetts Bay ministers were unqualified to determine whether an individual was touched by grace and was therefore a saint. To Hutchinson, the ministers had corrupted Puritanism by transforming the covenant of grace into a covenant of (this-worldly) works. The colonial government prosecuted and convicted Hutchinson for what amounted to sedition, rather than heresy, though the distinction was effectively irrelevant. Winthrop, who served as judge and prosecutor at Hutchinson's trial, explained: "Mrs. Hutchinson, you are called here as one of those that have troubled the peace of the commonwealth and the churches." Suppression of religious expression was most vigorous in (though not limited to) New England, particularly during the early- to mid-seventeenth century when prosecutions for heresy and blasphemy, for "reviling ministers, deriding church practices, and denouncing the tithe," were common. During the late-seventeenth and eighteenth centuries, the number of successful prosecutions diminished, but the sword of suppression still threatened. The infamous Salem, Massachusetts, witch trials resulted in the executions of nineteen individuals in 1692. Such incidences, no doubt, encouraged conformity.[21]

CHAPTER 2

Republican Democracy from the Revolution through the Civil War

Beginning with the earliest state constitutions, the American people and their elected officials, as well as political and legal theorists, developed a republican democratic system of government. The framers of the national Constitution refined the practice and theory of republican democracy, creating a remarkably pliant regime. Then, through the early-nineteenth century, the American people accommodated the constitutional structures to the nation's changing social, cultural, and economic practices. As the Civil War would demonstrate, however, some political disputes could be too vehement for even the flexible republican democratic system to withstand.[1]

ESTABLISHING THE PARAMETERS: THE REVOLUTION TO THE FRAMING

The Revolutionary era established republican democracy as the essence of American government. Steeped in the rhetoric of the Country or Opposition ideology that flourished among early- and mid-eighteenth-century English thinkers, Americans understood the British Constitution to be grounded on principles of civic virtue, the common good, and political liberty. But, Americans believed, British officials had for years been corrupt, acting contrary to those principles. As early as the mid-1760s, Americans protested that British tax laws violated their rights as "British subjects." "Freeborn American" wrote in the *Boston Gazette* that a "free people" can "consent" to laws only if they are "for the general good." In 1776, the Declaration of Independence drew upon these same republican concepts as well as John Locke's theoretical justification for resisting unjust rulers. According to the Revolutionaries, civic virtue legitimated, even demanded, resistance to governmental encroachments of republican liberties and principles, especially the failure to pursue the public good.[2]

Many Americans viewed themselves as uniquely suited for republican government. They not only lacked "the stifling and corrupting refinement of the Old World," but they also lived in a land of equality where "'almost every man is a freeholder.'" Widespread property ownership allowed many Americans to enjoy an independence and interest in the community that spurred a virtuous commitment to the common good. The early state constitutions reflected this popular conviction in the mutual compatibility of the American people and republican government. The Preamble to the Massachusetts Constitution of 1780 declared that the "body-politic is formed [so that the whole people] shall be governed by certain laws for the common good." Even with widespread landowning, "virtue" should be further encouraged, the 1776 Virginia Bill of Rights instructed, so as to preserve "free government" and "the blessings of liberty." What was the common good? While the state constitutions did not specify it in detail, they repeatedly distinguished the common good from "private and partial interests." According to the Massachusetts Constitution, "[g]overnment is instituted for the common good, for the protection, safety, prosperity of the people, and not for the profit, honor, or private interest of any one man, family, or class of men." Therefore, legislators — the people's representatives — were to be "disinterested men, who could have no interest of their own to seek." Legislation must benefit the people, the public good, not benefit some privileged segment of the population, whether an aristocracy or otherwise.[3]

One state constitution after another underscored that American republican government rested on the sovereignty of the people. Going back to Aristotle, civic republican theorists had defended government of the one, the few, and the many — a mixed government combining elements of a monarchy, an aristocracy, and a democracy. Blackstone had expressed the British view: constitutional (republican) government entailed the sovereignty of the legislature, so the Parliament's commands bound the people. But in the United States, government depended upon the consent of the governed, so sovereignty ultimately and always was grounded on the people. In the phrasing of the New Hampshire Constitution, "all government of right originates from the people, is founded in consent." The 1776 North Carolina Constitution declared, in its first sentence, that "all political power is vested in and derived from the people only." This was the democratic component of republican democracy. "By a democracy is meant, that form of government where the highest power of making laws is lodged in the common people, or persons chosen out from them," it was written in the *Providence Gazette* on August 9, 1777. "This is what by some is called a republic, a commonwealth, or free state."[4]

To be sure, state legislatures wielded the bulk of governmental power, but they supposedly represented the people's common good. Moreover, while states severely limited suffrage, mostly to white males who possessed property or similar wealth, state legislators were always popularly elected — given the limitations on the electorate. The early clarion call to revolution, after all, had been no taxation without representation. Thus, the Massachusetts Constitution stated that "[a]ll power residing originally in the people, and being derived from them, the several magistrates and officers of government . . . are the substitutes and agents, and are at all times accountable to them." Ultimately and crucially, though, the Americans did not view themselves as radically repudiating the English form of government. British officials had acted corruptly and contrary to republican principles, but Americans still admired the British governmental system. Americans merely needed to modify the British formula so they could participate directly in their own representative government.[5]

IN THEORY, STATE GOVERNMENTS would follow the tenets of republican democracy. Devoted to the common good, government would be "majoritarian" without pursuing the majority's "factious" interests. Unfortunately, the reality did not match the theory. Political experiences under the early state constitutions had revealed problems inherent to republican democracy — or at least so it seemed to those who met during the summer of 1787 in Philadelphia at the Constitutional Convention. One notorious breakdown in republican government occurred in 1785 and 1786 when an economic depression struck Massachusetts and brought foreclosures on many tracts of land. Town meetings produced demands for legislative reforms to protect the vulnerable landowners. When these demands went unrequited, a former militia captain, Daniel Shays, led a rebellion in central and western Massachusetts that disrupted court sessions and threatened an armory. The governor suppressed the insurrection, but in the next elections, the people chose a new governor, who pardoned Shays, and different legislators, who enacted many of the desired reforms. Such events led John Jay to write to George Washington: "Private rage for property suppresses public considerations, and personal rather than national interests have become the great objects of attention. Representative bodies will ever be faithful copies of their originals, and generally exhibit a checkered assemblage of virtue and vice, of abilities and weakness." From the framers' perspective, in other words, the people themselves often lacked civic virtue, so they in turn elected insufficiently virtuous governmental officials, who then used governmental power to pursue private interests rather than the common good.[6]

Under civic republican theory, liberty was the capacity to participate in government — so long as government was republican rather than despotic. The Americans had managed to shed the shackles of so-called virtual representation in the British Parliament, but direct participation in American free government, the election of representatives to American legislatures, had not produced a republican utopia. Now, the framers perceived that even under American republicanism, the people must be wary of their own government, of their own representatives, of their own majoritarian overreaching. Most state constitutions already contained bills of rights, lists of Lockean natural rights that theoretically preexisted government (the inconsistent degrees to which state constitutions protected free expression, in particular, is discussed in the next chapter). The 1776 Virginia Bill of Rights, for instance, provided that "all men are by nature equally free and independent, and have certain inherent rights . . . namely, the enjoyment of life and liberty, with the means of acquiring and possessing property, and pursuing and obtaining happiness and safety." The purpose of government was, in part, to protect the enjoyment of these preexisting rights. Nevertheless, given the experiences under the state constitutions during the 1780s, the framers had become more concerned with protecting individual rights and liberties *from* governmental encroachment. They therefore recast republican liberty to be as much a freedom from as a freedom in republican government.[7]

The 1780s, that is, had seen a shift in American political ideology toward a greater emphasis on Lockean (Enlightenment) liberalism vis-à-vis civic republicanism. John Locke had posited a state of nature in which each individual enjoys "perfect freedom," an "uncontrollable liberty to dispose of his person or possessions." Given the emerging English capitalism at the end of the seventeenth century, when Locke was writing, he emphasized possessions or property. Each individual, Locke explained, has a right to the "labor of his body and the work of his hands." When any individual takes an object from nature and mixes it with his or her labor, then that object or the resulting product becomes the "unquestionable property of the laborer." Yet, individuals in the state of nature live in fear of others, so they voluntarily agree to a social contract. They consent to join civil society for the "mutual preservation of their lives, liberties, and estates." Lockean liberalism thus stressed that individuals enter civil society for the very purpose of protecting their natural rights to liberty and property. Moreover, government stood, according to Locke, one step removed from civil society. Locke distinguished civil society from government, at least in theory if not in practice; the action of consenting to the formation of civil society theoretically preceded the formation of a specific form of government. Once individuals agreed to form a civil society, which had to be done unanimously, then their first order of business was to form a specific government, which could be accomplished by majority decision. From the Lockean standpoint, one could glean the contours of two conceptually separable (though not completely distinct and independent) realms: the private — that of civil society — and the public — that of government. Government (the public) derived from civil society (the private). Since civil society itself existed in order to protect individual life, liberty, and property, then it followed that government must do the same. This Lockean division of private and public realms, with a special concern for protecting liberty and property, was more evident in the framing of the national Constitution than it had been in the adoption of the earlier state constitutions. The framers had grown wary of the potential for legislative majorities to act for private or partial interests by taking property from one individual or group and giving it to another without a legitimate public purpose. Nonetheless, while the framers' political thought shifted in a Lockean direction, they modified without repudiating civic republicanism. Even Locke himself had insisted that the end of government was the "public good" or the "common good"; Lockean theory, properly understood, did not contravene civic republicanism.[8]

Despite the Lockean shift, then, the framers largely followed the governmental models embodied in the state constitutions. The framers sought to construct a new Constitution that would install a national republican democratic government — a representative government mixing civic republicanism and Lockean liberalism over a democratic base of popular sovereignty. With the words "We the People," the framers began with a ringing endorsement of popular sovereignty, the democratic component of the American republic. In the *Federalist, Number 39,* James Madison defined a republic as "a government which derives all its powers directly or indirectly from the great body of the people, and is administered by persons holding their offices during pleasure, for a limited period, or during good behavior." James Wilson, a prominent framer as well as "[t]he preeminent legal scholar of his generation," declared that the "one great principle, the vital principle I may well call it, . . . is this, that the supreme or sovereign power of the society resides in the citizens at large." Furthermore, the framers' "polyglotism," or conglomeration of political ideologies, produced a constitutional scheme that at least aimed for the ideals of civic republicanism. The constitutional Preamble explicitly declared that the aim of the national government was to "promote the general Welfare," while Publius in the *Federalist Papers* repeatedly proclaimed the ends of government to be the "public good" and the "common good." The citizens, Publius hoped, would display sufficient virtue to elect governmental officials who would have "enlightened views and virtuous sentiments" and therefore would naturally pursue the common good.[9]

Yet, the framers distrusted the democratic masses. For the most part, the framers were elitists who hoped that "speculative men" would be elected to be the "guardians" for "the mass of the citizens." Madison, Alexander Hamilton, and others worried exceedingly about factionalism. A faction, by definition, was any group of citizens, whether minority *or* majority, who were motivated by passion or interest to oppose the public good. At the Constitutional Convention, Madison explained: "What has been the source of those unjust laws complained of among ourselves? Has it not been the real or supposed interest of the major number? Debtors have defrauded their creditors. The landed interest has borne hard on the mercantile interest. The Holders of one species of property have thrown a disproportion of taxes on the holders of another species. The lesson we are to draw from the whole is that where a majority are united by a common sentiment and have an opportunity, the rights of the minor party become insecure."[10]

Consequently, a republican democratic government did not mechanically follow majoritarian sentiments. "There is no maxim," Madison insisted, "which is more liable to be misapplied, and which, therefore, more needs elucidation, than the current one, that the interest of the majority is the political standard of right and wrong. . . . In fact, it is only reestablishing, under another name and a more specious form, force as the measure of right." The common good could not be determined merely by aggregating the private interests of individual citizens. To the contrary, Publius characterized the public or common good as the "true interest" of the people and contrasted it against "private opinions and partial interests." For this reason, representative government was superior to direct democracy. Elected representatives would filter their constituents' raw interests:

"the public voice, pronounced by the representatives of the people, will be more consonant to the public good than if pronounced by the people themselves."[11]

BUT HOW COULD the new Constitution engender government for the public good? This was the framers' great conundrum, particularly given their conviction that the nonvirtuous would often be elected and that even the virtuous, once elected, might be tempted to chase private or partial interests. "The aim of every political constitution is, or ought to be," Madison wrote, "first to obtain for rulers men who possess most wisdom to discern, and most virtue to pursue, the common good of the society; and in the next place, to take the most effectual precautions for keeping them virtuous whilst they continue to hold their public trust." Despite these noble republican ideals, the framers did not attempt to eliminate the *causes* of factionalism. As a general matter, the framers viewed people as naturally "ambitious, vindictive, and rapacious." When people are granted liberty, they readily develop opposing interests and form into factional groups. "All kinds of experience show," according to John Adams, "that great numbers of individuals do oppress great numbers of other individuals; that parties often, if not always, oppress other parties, and majorities almost universally minorities." More specifically, the most powerful causes of factionalism were the inequalities emanating from the private realm or "civil society," especially the economic marketplace. "[T]he most common and durable source of factions has been the various and unequal distribution of property," Madison observed. "Those who hold and those who are without property have ever formed distinct interests in society." More than anything, then, the people needed to fear themselves, or more precisely, needed to fear their elected representatives in the legislature. Regardless, the framers unequivocally refused to attempt to control the liberties and inequalities of the private realm to diminish factionalism. To the contrary, manifesting their Lockean turn, the framers declared that government should seek not only to promote the public good but also to protect private interests. Even if property ownership induced factionalism, it was also the foundation of independence, equality, and political power. Freely alienable property and widespread ownership were, according to Noah Webster, "the whole basis of national freedom" and, in fact, "the very soul of a republic."[12]

Choosing not to disturb the causes of factionalism, the framers instead sought to control its *effects* through a variety of institutional mechanisms. The overarching idea was to capitalize on the very root of the republican problem: self-interest or factionalism. The new Constitution pitted "opposite and rival interests" against each other; in Madison's words, "[a]mbition must be made to counteract ambition." The constitutional system would disperse governmental power among so many officials and departments that the self-interested grasping of one would meet the self-interested grasping of another. "[T]he constant aim," Madison explained, "is to divide and arrange the several offices in such a manner as that each may be a check on the other — that the private interest of every individual may be a sentinel over the public rights." Madison, a diffident yet brilliant tactician of political diplomacy, realized that if people naturally devolved into factional interests, then the constitutional system should allow competing factions to strive and struggle so that, in the end, they would do no more than neutralize each other. Thus, despite the constitutional commitment to popular sovereignty, the framers constructed a variety of institutional mechanisms to control (the effects of) factional interests, including those of majorities. The Constitution purposefully shifted power from the state governments to the national government because, Madison argued, large republics — such as the nation — were more stable and less tyrannical than small republics — such as the states. In a larger republic, with a greater population and geographic area, the number of divergent interests would multiply. To Madison, the greater the number of interests, the more diverse their viewpoints, the greater the stability and justness of the republic. With so many diverse interests pitted against each other, the framers believed that agreement on governmental goals and policies would, most often, be reached only for the common good. Private or partial interests would counter other private and partial interests.[13]

Even as the framers shifted power from the states to the federal government, they simultaneously constrained the latter's ability to exercise its expanded powers. The crucial structural provisions of the Constitution — including separation of powers, checks and balances, bicameralism, and federalism — encumbered the national government's exercise of power by dispersing power among a multitude of departments and officials, each of which would have its own interests. Moreover, Congress supposedly could exercise only its constitutionally enumerated powers rather than a general or police power. The framers, in short, weakened the state governments yet constrained the national government, and in doing so, they enhanced the protection of the private realm of liberty and property. The national government, in Madison's words, would abstain "from measures which operate differently on different interests, and particularly such as favor one interest, at the expense of another." Put in different words, the law would treat all citizens equally. According to Madison, the law "violates equality" if it either subjects some citizens to "peculiar burdens" or grants others "peculiar exemptions." The government would act for the common good, or not act at all.[14]

IN SUM, THE FRAMERS still believed in civic virtue and the common good. They still hoped that citizens would act virtuously and would elect the most virtuous among them to official positions. They still hoped that virtuous governmental officials, once elected, would act disinterestedly and thus would pursue the common good. Largely for that reason, George Washington would be the unquestioned choice to be the first president. His willingness to resign his command of the Revolutionary army exemplified civic virtue. Yet, the framers were no longer optimistic that these ideals would be realized as a matter of course. There was only one George Washington. The framers were wary that governmental officials would represent factional interests and would therefore infringe on private liberties, particularly property rights, for pretextual reasons. Too often, the officials might claim to pursue the common good, but they might truly be favoring private or partial interests. The framers therefore structured the constitutional system so that it would, first, promote the election of virtuous governmental officials who would voluntarily pursue the common good. In the event, however, that officials were not sufficiently virtuous, the constitutional system would, second, seek to induce the officials to pursue the common good, despite their initial inclinations. Finally, if the officials still could not be induced to pursue the common good, then the constitutional system would, third, prevent those officials from using governmental power to favor partial or private interests.

"To secure the public good and private rights against the danger of . . . faction," Madison wrote, "and at the same time to preserve the spirit and the form of popular government, is then the great object to which our inquiries are directed." The government was not to infringe on individual liberty and property *unless* for a legitimate public purpose — that is, in pursuit of the common good. Clearly, republican democracy as understood at both the state and national levels did not entail laissez-faire capitalism, an economic marketplace free of governmental regulation. By the time of the framing, American political ideology had shifted to give greater protection for the Lockean rights of liberty and property. Yet, regardless of the niceties of Lockean political theory, American political thinkers did not view a private realm of natural rights as sacrosanct (except, perhaps, for the Protestant freedom of conscience). Instead, the contours of the private sphere — the protections afforded to private-sphere liberties — were determined through the operations of the public sphere. Specifically, government could always regulate and abridge individual liberties so long as the governmental action was for the public good rather than for partial or private interests. Madison, consequently, might in one breath celebrate the benefits of a free and open economic marketplace but in the next breath argue that the government should assist certain industries and agriculture. Moreover, under all but one of the state constitutions in effect in 1787, individual participation in the public realm of government was contingent on property ownership or an alternative showing of economic wealth. For example, Maryland extended suffrage only to those "freemen . . . having a freehold of fifty acres of land [or] having property in this State above the value of thirty pounds current money." The possession of property, an interest in the private sphere, supposedly established one's independence and gave one a sufficient "stake in society" — a concern for the common good — so as to justify the power to vote and to hold office. Prototypical citizens were property-owning small farmers and, to a lesser extent, tool-owning artisans. In short, while the public and private realms were conceptually separable, they were practically and integrally linked.[15]

REPUBLICAN DEMOCRACY
IN AMERICAN SOCIETY

How could the framers believe that a country as diverse as the United States would coalesce around a common good, especially when those same framers seemed so cognizant of the diverse interests motivating individuals? Because the framers, despite recognizing the diversity of interests, nonetheless viewed the American people as being remarkably homogeneous. "Providence has been pleased to give this one connected country to one united people," John Jay declared, "a people descended from the same ancestors, speaking the same language, professing the same religion, attached to the same principles of government, very similar in their manners and customs." On the importance of homogeneity, the Anti-Federalist opponents of the proposed Constitution agreed with the Federalist supporters: a homogeneous people was prerequisite for republican government. "In a republic," explained the Anti-Federalist Brutus, "the manners, sentiments, and interests of the people should be similar. If this be not the case, there will be a constant clashing of opinions; and the representatives of one part will be continually striving against those of the other." But the Anti-Federalists insisted that the proposed scheme of constitutional government would undermine the homogeneity of the American people. How, then, could the framers view the American people as not only being homogeneous but as likely to remain so, regardless of their diverse interests? The simple answer: exclusion. The framers saw homogeneity because they excluded or acquiesced in the exclusion of large segments of the population from the polity. Such exclusionary sentiments were common to republican thought, being evident all the way from the classical republicanism of Aristotle to the republican democracy of the early American state governments. The fact that only a small minority of Americans voted for the delegates to the state ratification conventions for the proposed Constitution was neither surprising nor accidental. The severe limits on suffrage in the states barred more than half the population from voting. Property and wealth requirements disqualified some white men, while states also typically excluded women, Native Americans, and African American slaves. With all these disqualifications, compounded by a low turnout among eligible voters, only approximately 4 percent of the population voted in the ratification elections! And once the appropriate people were excluded from the polity, who was left? White men. The American belief in homogeneity was, in a sense, grounded in reality.[16]

Other factors contributed to this sense and reality of homogeneity. As Americans had long recognized, the relatively widespread ownership of property presented them with a unique opportunity. In America, property was a material cause of equality. Ownership was not concentrated in a mere handful of feudal lords, but rather was spread throughout the community. The economy was thoroughly agrarian, not industrial; in 1800, 83 percent of the labor force worked in agriculture, with most free men owning land (or, if artisans, owning the tools of their respective trades). Not insignificantly, too, more land always remained available for the taking (so long as one was willing to take it from the Native American tribes, and many white men, supported by governmental policies, were more than willing to do so). Religion further cemented the society. From the time of the Revolution, several states had moved toward the official disestablishment of government-supported churches, and the national government had refrained from compelling religious adherence or support. Nonetheless, the nation was de facto Protestant. With 99 percent of Revolutionary era Americans being Protestant, confidence in the continuing Protestant nature of American society facilitated official disestablishment. For many Americans, governmental establishments became superfluous. True, Protestants themselves divided among numerous sects, but even so, the "vast majority of Americans assumed that theirs was a Christian, i.e. Protestant, country, and they automatically expected that government would uphold the commonly agreed on Protestant ethos and morality." Federalists and Anti-Federalists alike viewed Protestantism as a significant source of values fostering unity and republican government. Legislative measures and even constitutional provisions continued to bolster Protestantism in American society, regardless of official establishment or disestablishment. Governments often overtly burdened non-Christians with civil disabilities, such as prohibitions on voting and public office holding. Despite such legal inhibitions, some Anti-Federalists brooded that "[t]here is a door opened for the Jews, Turks, and Heathen to enter into publick office, and be seated at the head of the government of the United States." The Federalist response? Don't worry, we're (almost) all Protestants here. "But it is never to be supposed," the future Supreme Court Justice James Iredell assured, "that the people of America will trust their dearest rights to persons who have no religion at all, or a religion materially different from their own." The nation's de facto Protestantism only deepened during the first decades of the nineteenth century. By 1835, a remarkable 75 percent of the population regularly attended church, with official church memberships nearly doubling since 1800.[17]

The American perception and (at least partial) fact of homogeneity provided a crucial multifaceted foundation for republican democracy. Homogeneity contributed to a sense of political equality as well as to a sense of opportunity. In order to succeed, Americans did not need debtor relief laws or any other special governmental assistance; they just needed to work hard. The "cheapness" of available land in the United States, according to Madison, presented all the people with "unrivalled" advantages. Limited government, in this context, seemed to make sense. Government should not intrude into the private realm of liberty and property unless acting for the good of all. Homogeneity also contributed, most significantly, to an acceptance of the common good. The polity of white, Protestant, American men, with some modicum of wealth, shared a reasonable number of interests and values. "Public good is not a term opposed to the good of individuals," Thomas Paine could declare. "[O]n the contrary, it is the good of every individual collected. It is the good of all, because it is the good of everyone." Putting this in different words, the common good manifested the shared interests of "the People"—appropriately defined.[18] The United States—bereft of European feudal hierarchies—might have seemed the most republican, the most democratic, the most egalitarian nation in the world — plus, the nation ripest with economic prospects — at least from the perspective of white Protestant men. If one did not fall into this favored group, however, the country was ridged with hierarchies of its own — of race, gender, and religion — which generated grossly disparate opportunities for wealth and power.[19]

JUDICIAL REVIEW UNDER
REPUBLICAN DEMOCRACY

During the early years of the nation, two overarching factors contributed to the republican pursuit of the common good. First, the state and national constitutions were structured to produce government for the common good. Second, the homogeneity of the people — at least of the people admitted to the polity — contributed to the coalescence of the people around public goods. Even so, the identification of the common good in concrete situations was often problematic. The relatively homogeneous people, when faced with practical issues, did not always agree on which specific governmental course should be followed. Of course, this simple fact was no surprise. Despite their belief in the homogeneity of the people, the national framers were all too aware of the diversity of interests and values among those same people and how such diversity would likely foster factionalism.

While the occurrence of disputes about the common good was predictable, the intensity was less so. Some of the disputes during the 1790s, ranging from whether Congress had the power to incorporate a national bank to whether the United States should support England or France during war, were so unexpectedly vehement that many political leaders feared for the survival of the republic. As these disputes unfolded, the Federalists, led by Alexander Hamilton and John Adams, and the Republicans, led by Thomas Jefferson and James Madison, accused each other of intentionally plotting to undermine republican principles and destroy the nation. The various controversies culminated in the vindictive Federalist persecutions of the Republicans under the 1798 Alien and Sedition Acts, which not only triggered battles over free expression (discussed in chapter 4) but also backfired to spark Republican victories in the 1800 presidential and congressional elections.[20]

During these turbulent early national years, a partial solution for disputes about the common good began to emerge: judicial review. In some states, legislatures initially had performed judicial functions, even reviewing court decisions. But now, the courts were developing into the institution where disagreements regarding the propriety of governmental actions might be resolved, often with less of the partisan rancor that was otherwise poisoning the nation's lifeblood. Hamilton had suggested this institutional role for the federal courts in *The Federalist, Number 78,* when he wrote "that the courts were designed to be an intermediate body between the people and the legislature, in order, among other things, to keep the latter within the *limits* assigned to their authority." What was the limit on the legislative power? At a general level, it was the common good. The courts were to ensure that legislative actions were for public goods rather than for partial or private interests. Hamilton stressed that this power of the courts to judge the propriety of legislative actions did not place the judiciary above the legislature. Instead, the judicial power arose from the framers' recognition that the people needed to be wary of their own legislative representatives. The people and not their legislatures were sovereign. Thus, the judiciary would act as a sentinel guarding against the misuse of legislative power. The judiciary would enforce the people's virtuous desire for the common good, regardless of the partisan desires of the people's legislators — and regardless of the all-too-often partisan desires of the people themselves. By 1830, Madison acknowledged that even though he sometimes disapproved of judicial decisions, "[s]till it would seem that, with but few exceptions, the course of the judiciary has been hitherto sustained by the predominant sense of the nation." To Madison, the judiciary had become the most trustworthy governmental repository of civic virtue — "the only institution that came close to resembling an umpire, standing above the marketplace of competing interests and rendering impartial and disinterested decisions."[21]

Under this conceptualization of the courts' function in republican democracy, the courts began the seemingly endless task of "boundary pricking." Boundary pricking required the courts to resolve concrete disputes over the specification of the common good: was a particular legislative action in pursuit of the common good or merely a reflection of private or partial interests? The courts, in other words, needed to place various legislative actions in either the public-good category or the private-interest category. In doing so, the courts traced the boundary between the common good, on the one side, and partial and private interests, on the other side, by pricking one point (or case) at a time. In effect, this judicial boundary pricking identified the contours of a protected private realm of individual liberty (including property as well as free expression). Yet, given the nature of republican democracy, the courts did not focus on the definition of individual liberties and did not declare such liberties as beyond governmental reach. Instead, the courts focused on the legislative actions and purposes. In each case, the question became whether the legislature, in the eyes of the court, had acted for the common good. If the legislature had acted for the common good, then the court would uphold the government's action. If the legislature, though, had instead acted for the benefit of private or partial interests, then the court would invalidate the government's action. In the words of Chancellor James Kent, "private interest must be made subservient to the general interest of the community."[22]

This judicial function developed largely at the state level and entailed the application of common law concepts as much as constitutional guarantees. Even so, the U.S. Supreme Court provided a clear early statement of the judicial function under republican democracy in *Calder v. Bull,* decided in 1798. Justice Samuel Chase condemned any "law that takes property from A. and gives it to B." Such a law would favor one private or partial interest over another rather than benefiting the common good. "It is against all reason and justice, for a people to entrust a Legislature with such powers," Chase explained. "The genius, the nature, and the spirit, of our State Governments, amount to a prohibition of such acts of legislation; and the general principles of law and reason forbid them." Governmental power, in short, is limited. While legislative power is thus constrained, individual liberties, including property ownership and use, are always subordinate to the public welfare. "[T]he right of property," Chase wrote, "as well as the mode, or manner, of acquiring property, and of alienating or transferring, inheriting, or transmitting it, is conferred by society; is regulated by civil institution, and is always subject to the rules prescribed by positive law."[23]

Chase's phrasing of the prohibition against legislative actions that favored partial or private interests would be reiterated often, especially as the mid-nineteenth century approached. For instance, in a state case decided in 1822, Chief Justice Stephen Hosmer of Connecticut wrote: "If the legislature should enact a law, without any assignable reason, taking from A. his estate, and giving it to B., the injustice would be flagrant, and the act would produce a sensation of universal insecurity." In an 1848 New York decision, the trial court judge expressly grounded this prohibition against legislation favoring partial or private interests on the sovereignty of the people. "[I]f the title of A. can, without his fault, be transferred to B., it may as well be done without as with a consideration. . . . It is not to be presumed that such a power exists, and those who set it up should tell where it may be found. Under our form of government the legislature is not supreme. It is only one of the organs of that absolute sovereignty which resides in the whole body of the people."[24]

Of course, judges articulated the idea of limited government in many other diverse manners. Here is Chief Justice John Marshall in 1810: "It may well be doubted whether the nature of society and of government does not prescribe some limits to the legislative power; and, if any be prescribed, where are they to be found, if the property of an individual, fairly and honestly acquired, may be seized without compensation." Sometimes, cases involving the republican limits on legislative powers were adjudicated under state constitutional provisions requiring the government to follow the "due process of law" or the "law of the land." In an 1829 Tennessee Supreme Court case, Judge John Catron, who would eventually sit on the U.S. Supreme Court, explicitly linked the state's "law of the land" provision with the prohibition against legislating for partial or private interests. "The right to life, liberty and property, of every individual must stand or fall by the same rule or law that governs every other member of the body politic, or 'land,' under similar circumstances," according to Catron. "[E]very partial or private law, which directly proposes to destroy or affect individual rights, or does the same thing by affording remedies leading to similar consequences, is unconstitutional and void." Two years later, Catron's colleague, Judge Nathan Green, interpreted the state Constitution similarly in the case of *State Bank v. Cooper.* "[A]n edict in the form of a legislative enactment, taking the property of A, and giving it to B, might be regarded as the 'law of the land,' and not forbidden by the constitution," explained Green, "but such a proposition is too absurd to find a single advocate." Green elaborated how this limit on legislative power mandates equality or generality in the law. "Does it not seem conclusive . . . that this provision was intended to restrain the legislature from enacting any law affecting injuriously the rights of any citizen, unless at the same time the rights of all others in similar circumstances were equally affected by it?" Finally, Green underscored that equality assures that the minority will be protected from potential majoritarian overreaching. "If the law be general in its operation, affecting all alike, the minority are safe, because the majority, who make the law, are operated on by it equally with the others."[25]

Regardless of the precise phrasing by the various state and federal judges, the basic point was always the same: in a republican democracy grounded on the sovereignty of the people, the legislative power must be constrained. Nonetheless, besides consistently pronouncing the republican principle of limited government, the courts also insisted that individual liberties were subordinate to the legislative power to pass laws for the common good. "The sovereign power in a community . . . may, and ought to prescribe the manner of exercising individual rights over property," wrote Justice John

Woodworth of New York in 1827. "It is for the better protection and enjoyment of that absolute dominion which the individual claims. The power
rests on the implied right and duty of the supreme power to protect all by
statutory regulations, so that, on the whole, the benefit of all is promoted."
By 1851, Chief Justice Lemuel Shaw of Massachusetts could definitively formulate the legislative "police power": "the power vested in the legislature
by the constitution, to make, ordain and establish all manner of wholesome and reasonable laws, statutes and ordinances, . . . as they shall judge
to be for the good and welfare of the commonwealth, and of the subjects
of the same." Shaw explained how "the nature of [a] well ordered civil society" necessitates that individual liberties, including especially property
ownership, must be subordinated to public purposes. "All property in this
commonwealth [is] held subject to those general regulations, which are
necessary to the common good and general welfare." State courts often adverted to a maxim, *sic utere tuo*—"so use your own right, that you injure not
the rights of others"—to elucidate the proper demarcation between the
government's police power and individuals' rights and liberties. "This police power of the state extends to the protection of the lives, limbs, health,
comfort, and quiet of all persons, and the protection of all property within
the state," explained Chief Justice Isaac Redfield of Vermont. "According
to the maxim, *Sic utere tuo ut alienum non laedas,* which being of universal
application, it must of course, be within the range of legislative action to
define the mode and manner in which every one may so use his own as not
to injure others." Each individual, in other words, was obligated to exercise
his or her liberties so as not to harm others, and the legislature possessed
the power to regulate and to restrict an individual's liberties to ensure the
protection of others.[26]

Consequently, limited government did not equate with no government
or even minimal government. To the contrary, as a general matter, courts
readily found that public goods or purposes justified legislative actions.
For example, in 1828, Boston prosecuted Henry Vandine pursuant to a municipal bylaw prohibiting the removal of house dirt and offal from the city
without a license. Vandine challenged the bylaw as an illegal restraint of
trade. The court delineated the purview of governmental power in simple
terms: "If the regulation is unreasonable, it is void; if necessary for the good
government of the society, it is good." The court found that the city's purpose for enacting the law was to preserve the health of the inhabitants. If
not for the bylaw, the court reasoned, the carts carrying refuse would be
"breaking up the streets by their weight and poisoning the air with their
effluvia." Regardless of the city's interference with the economic market-

place, the court concluded that "the law is reasonable, and not only within the power of the government to prescribe, but well adapted to preserve the health of the city."[27]

In 1851, Shaw provided a partial yet lengthy list of appropriate police power regulations. "There are many cases in which such a power is exercised by all well ordered governments, and where its fitness is so obvious, that all well regulated minds will regard it as reasonable. Such are the laws to prohibit the use of warehouses for the storage of gunpowder near habitations or highways; to restrain the height to which wooden buildings may be erected in populous neighborhoods, and require them to be covered with slate or other incombustible material; to prohibit buildings from being used for hospitals for contagious diseases, or for the carrying on of noxious or offensive trades; to prohibit the raising of a dam, and causing stagnant water to spread over meadows, near inhabited villages, thereby raising noxious exhalations, injurious to health and dangerous to life." Four years later, Isaac Redfield noted that courts had even allowed "[t]he destruction of private property in cities and towns, to prevent the spread of conflagrations," which, according to Redfield, demonstrated "the subserviency of private rights to public security."[28]

Although courts readily upheld numerous governmental actions, the republican concept of limited government was not specious. The courts, in fact, occasionally invalidated legislative actions for not being in pursuit of the common good. Laws granting special privileges or subsidies to individuals or private businesses were struck down. In an 1826 Vermont case, the legislature passed a law that authorized inhabitants of Mountholly to pass along a turnpike without paying the ordinary toll. The court concluded that this action was contrary "to correct and just legislation, and of course void." In the case of *State Bank v. Cooper*, discussed above, Tennessee had enacted a law creating a special court that would operate with unusual procedures and that would hear only cases brought by the Bank of Tennessee. Judge Green concluded that this law was "partial"—it "only acts upon individual cases, and is the same in principle as if a law had been passed in favor of some one merchant." Therefore, the court held the law beyond "the limits of legislative authority." Ultimately, the courts were engaged in boundary pricking, tracing the border between public goods and partial or private interests, point by point, or case by case. The concept of the common good was the fulcrum for these many judicial decisions, which were made, for the most part, in a formalistic or categorical manner. Courts placed disputed legislative actions and purposes either into or out of the supposedly preexisting category, the common good. At least on the surface, courts did not engage in a balancing test, weighing the governmental interests against counter-vailing interests (which would become common in twentieth-century juris-prudence). Nevertheless, the categorization of disputed legislative actions and purposes was precisely the point where judges' political inclinations and cultural sentiments would most likely become apparent.[29]

CHANGING INTERPRETATIONS
OF REPUBLICAN DEMOCRACY

The United States experienced staggering social and cultural upheavals during the first part of the nineteenth century, yet the American commit-ment to republican democracy remained steadfast. Indeed, in some ways, republican democracy contributed to these massive shifts in the American social landscape. Meanwhile, interpretations of specific concepts, particu-larly virtue and the common good, transformed significantly in response to the social and cultural shifts. Overall, the broad parameters of republican democracy remained in place, but what Americans meant by virtue and the common good altered.

Republican democracy itself helped engender a changing definition of virtue. As envisioned by the framers, republican democracy had entailed a division between (private) society and (public) government. While the framers did not intend to create a laissez-faire economy, they nevertheless sought to construct a system that included a protected realm of liberty and property subject to governmental control only for the public good. Over time, then, the division between society and government facilitated the development of a new type of virtue, centered in the private realm. Besides encouraging republican "civic virtue"—the selfless pursuit of the common good—republican democracy also engendered a "social virtue"—a private-sphere virtue that celebrated independence and the pursuit of self-interest, albeit tempered by a benevolent and decent Protestant civil-ity. During the turmoil of the English Civil War, Thomas Hobbes had de-picted individual action without governmental control, in a state of nature, as inherently dangerous to others, but in the relatively stable and secure early-nineteenth-century America, individual choice and action in a private or nongovernmental realm often seemed beneficial and productive.[30]

Without doubt, in the public sphere, virtue remained tied to the pur-suit of the common good, and significantly, it would be so throughout the nineteenth century. Yet, even the understanding of public or civic virtue shifted. During the early national years, the framers' generation viewed factionalism or partisanship as contrary to civic virtue and thus as a detriment to republican government. Factionalism or partisanship might be inevitable, but it was to be avoided as much as possible and its effects were to be controlled. For this reason, during the 1790s, the Federalists accused the opposition — the Republicans led by Madison and Jefferson — of forming a political or factional party bent on corrupting the republican government, while the Republicans accused the Federalists of the same. When a new generation began to lead the nation, however, the perceived antagonism between partisanship and civic virtue faded. During the 1820s, Martin Van Buren began to champion organized political parties as a positive — as, in effect, contributing to the common good. A political party became a means for overcoming local interests or factions. In the late 1820s, the Jacksonian Democrats initiated the practice of organizing and applying systematic methods to appeal to the common man; the first campaign managers emerged. Political parties, from that time forward, sought to convince partisan voters to express support for their respective parties. Citizens no longer viewed partisanship as contrary to the virtuous pursuit of the common good; parties became integral to the rhetoric and practice of republican democracy. Looking back in 1884, the *Philadelphia Inquirer* commented on the strength of political partisanship: "[F]ifty years ago, in times of peace, and twenty years ago, in time of war, party lines were as strictly drawn as were the lines of religious sects. A man belonged to either the Democratic or the Whig party, to the Republican or the Democratic. He did not merely entertain opinions, he had convictions."[31]

Meanwhile, under earlier conceptualizations of republican government, many Americans had viewed economic wealth as a potential threat to civic virtue, though many had also believed a minimal degree of wealth established an individual's independence and stake in society. Large disparities of wealth, it had been feared, tended to breed divisive interests that would deter individuals from pursuing the common good. This fear had been central to the Anti-Federalists' opposition to the Constitution. For instance, "Cato" worried "that the progress of a commercial society begets luxury, the parent of inequality, the foe to virtue, and the enemy to restraint; and that ambition . . . will teach magistrates . . . to have separate and distinct interests from the people." As the nineteenth century dawned, however, Americans increasingly dwelled on private-sphere activities, particularly in the economic marketplace. Character and success were measured more in commercial than governmental activities. Hence, whereas self-interest had previously been understood to be antithetical to virtue, now the pursuit of self-interest, albeit conceptualized in terms of the Protestant work ethic, became a legitimate component of the admirable, forward-looking individual. As early as 1786, Benjamin Rush had explained that commerce was "next to religion in humanizing mankind." While the ownership of (a minimal amount of) property had previously been the source of disinterested civic virtue, wealth now became a goal for a private-sphere virtue. In his theoretical defense of democracy, written in 1841, George Sidney Camp emphasized the centrality of this capitalist-tinged private virtue for a self-governing society: "When you tell the plainest man that every one understands his own business best, that every one is the best guardian of his own interests, you appeal to acknowledged truths, which he has long since known to be of constant application in the daily affairs of common life."[32]

This changing conception of virtue contributed to but was also shaped by broad economic changes that swept the nation during the nineteenth century. The United States, during this time, began to transform economically from a thoroughly agricultural society to an increasingly commercial and industrial one. The transition began in the 1790s, when the Federalists, especially Hamilton, favored "mercantile and investing classes" and the Jeffersonian Republicans favored "landed interests." Even so, once the politically opportunistic yet evasive Jefferson took over the presidency, he largely maintained Hamilton's Federalist economic policies. Jefferson's 1807 Embargo Act and Madison's War of 1812 sparked commercial and industrial development by isolating the nation and thereby forcing Americans to begin manufacturing products they previously had imported. These economic sparks combined with the ever-increasing size of the nation — remember Jefferson's purchase of the Louisiana Territory in 1803 — to spur a growing concern for the improvement of the nation's infrastructure. Roads, canals, and railroads started to weave across the land, connecting together previously isolated peoples and generating new economic marketplaces. By the mid-1830s, Alexis de Tocqueville observed that Americans had already "joined the Hudson to the Mississippi and made the Atlantic Ocean communicate with the Gulf of Mexico, across a continent of more than five hundred leagues. . . . The longest railroads that have been constructed up to the present time are in America."[33]

James Kent, speaking at the 1821 New York state constitutional convention, envisioned the impending economic changes with a combination of enthusiasm and trepidation: "We stand this moment on the brink of fate, on the very edge of the precipice. . . . We are no longer to remain plain and simple republics of farmers, like New-England colonists, or the Dutch settlements on the Hudson. We are fast becoming a great nation, with great commerce, manufactures, population, wealth, luxuries, and with the vices and miseries that they engender." Then, little more than a decade later, Tocqueville declared that almost all Americans "are engaged in productive industry." American farmers, Tocqueville added, typically "combine some trade with agriculture; most of them make agriculture itself a trade." Most farmers, in other words, had turned at least partly from subsistence to commercial cash-crop agriculture. All in all, the American transition from a highly agricultural to a highly commercial and industrial nation happened with shocking speed. Whereas 83 percent of the labor force had been in agriculture in 1800, only 53 percent remained similarly occupied in 1860. During those first six decades of the nineteenth century, the gross national product (GNP) per capita more than doubled, significantly improving the standard of living of the average American family.[34]

One aspect of these economic changes, reflected in the changing concept of virtue, was an increasing degree of individualism. Each individual — or at least each white male, preferably Protestant — had a right to pursue wealth in the economic marketplace. In the 1830s, Tocqueville coined the term "individualism" and linked it to the American conception of government — that is, to republican democracy. To be sure, republican government stressed the common good and the subordination of private to public interests. Yet, American republican democracy was also firmly grounded on the sovereign people, and if power emanated from the people as a whole, then power would seem to originate ultimately in each person, in the dignity and desires of the individual. Even if the framers had not intended to stress this individualist potential in republican democracy, American society and culture developed in that direction. As early as 1800, Tunis Wortman had proclaimed that "[a]ll our prospects of improvement . . . depend upon the industry and exertion of individuals. It is almost impossible to conceive the extensive effects which may be produced by the agency of a single person." The growing individualist ethos intertwined with the increasing sense of equality that was spreading through American society. To an extent, Americans "were all alike, all seeking their own individual interests and happiness." The Lockean liberal component of republican democracy, one might say, was becoming increasingly important, as evident in President Andrew Jackson's message vetoing the recharter of the national bank in 1832. "Distinctions in society will always exist under every just government," Jackson explained. "Equality of talents, of education, or of wealth can not be produced by human institutions. [But in] the full enjoyment of the gifts of Heaven and the fruits of superior industry, economy, and virtue, every man is equally entitled to protection by law."[35]

This individualist and egalitarian orientation developed elsewhere in

American society and culture. In the first half of the nineteenth century, a distinctly American literature emerged, emphasizing individual independence, self-improvement, and an iconoclastic wariness toward authority. In his essay, "Self-Reliance," Ralph Waldo Emerson observed: "A foolish consistency is the hobgoblin of little minds, adored by little statesmen and philosophers and divines." This ethos blossomed nowhere more fully than in the religious realm. During this time, the Second Great Awakening swept across America. Like the First Great Awakening, of the mid-1700s, the Second Awakening strengthened the grip of Protestantism on America. Protestants founded new denominations and sects and readily switched from one to another. From 1800 to 1835, not only did church membership nearly double, but many other Americans attended churches without becoming official members. Even so, the doctrinal changes that the Second Great Awakening introduced into American Protestantism were at least as important as the swelling numbers. Before this time, many American Protestants had believed in the Calvinist doctrine of predestination: God supposedly had preselected a special few for salvation. Everyone else was doomed to damnation. The individual was powerless to change his or her own fate, whether prechosen for salvation or damnation. But during the Second Awakening, American Protestants widely rejected the doctrine of predestination. The ordinary individual, Protestants now believed, could *choose* salvation. Each and every individual could be saved, merely by declaring his or her belief in Christ. A Baptist confession, for instance, declared that "God has endowed man with power of free choice." Thus, "salvation is rendered equally possible to all; and if any fail of eternal life, the fault is wholly their own." According to the evangelical preacher Charles Grandison Finney, "all that was necessary [to receive salvation], was to get my own consent to give up my sins, and accept Christ."[36]

The religious changes that swept through America during the Awakening intertwined with another part of the transforming concept of virtue. Not only did virtue become more privatized and individualistic, but also the location or situs of virtue shifted. Where was virtue to be found, or in other words, who was virtuous? The Second Great Awakening amounted to a great populist movement in the religious realm. If each individual could choose to be saved — and could attain salvation merely by declaring faith in Christ — then the people no longer needed elite religious leaders. The Awakening, from this perspective, pushed the Protestant reaction against Catholicism to its extreme limits. The average Protestant neither needed nor wanted formally trained clergy to lead the religious flock. Common sense seemed more reliable "than the judgment of an educated few." Ordinary people could read the Protestant Bible without the benefit of officially sanctioned interpretation; the scriptures, one preacher insisted, "'were designed for the great mass of mankind and are in general adapted to their capacities.'" Nonetheless, even though the fastest-growing Protestant denominations, the Methodists and the Baptists, promised that salvation for each individual was "imminently accessible and immediately available," many Americans still were illiterate, especially in the more western states, like Kentucky and Tennessee. Consequently, Protestant revivalists could still help reveal to illiterate individuals the way to salvation. Revivalists most often were (or appeared to be) of the people; they were not so much learned educators as exemplars of religious intensity. Going from camp meeting to camp meeting, they appealed to the raw religious emotions of their audiences, encouraging individuals to declare their faith. "'[T]he power of God was strong upon me,'" thundered one Methodist minister. "'I turned . . . and losing sight of fear of man, I went through the house shouting and exhorting with all possible ecstasy and energy.'"[37]

This antielitist populism also crystallized in the political realm. The constitutional framers themselves had been, to a great extent, prominent men who hoped that virtuous elites (like themselves) would be elected to governmental offices. But in the 1790s, the Republicans frequently contrasted their populist sentiments against the Federalists' elitism. Republican lawyer and theorist Tunis Wortman explained that truth "is not a courtier whose residence is confined to palaces, nor is it always to be found in the solemn gravity of a deliberative assembly. [Truth] is to be discovered and ascertained by judgment; and judgment is a faculty possessed in common by mankind." Republican populism, to be sure, developed partly because wealthy Southern planters, resentful of Hamilton's favoring of northern commercial interests, aligned themselves with the multitude of small farmers. Regardless, as it turned out, the election of 1800 was the last in which candidates would seek national elective office while professing "hierarchical values or deferential political practices." After the framers' generation, intellectual elites would never again dominate national politics. Instead, a widespread antielitism — or anti-intellectualism — gradually took hold. There was a growing "belief in the superiority of inborn, intuitive, folkish wisdom over the cultivated oversophisticated, and self-interested knowledge of the literati and the well-to-do." In the late 1820s, President Andrew Jackson declared that the "duties of all public offices are . . . so plain and simple . . . [that] no one man has any more intrinsic right to official station than another."[38]

In other words, the situs of virtue gradually shifted from the elites to the common people. Correspondingly, the right of suffrage expanded to the point that, by 1825, every state but three (Rhode Island, Virginia, and Louisiana) had eliminated wealth or property requirements and had extended the franchise to all white males. "[M]y fervent prayers," Jackson solemnly pronounced, "are that our republican government may be perpetual, and the people alone by their Virtue, and independent exercise of their free suffrage can make it perpetual." In effect, then, the concept of popular sovereignty changed — the sovereign people had expanded. Perhaps just as important, not only did the number of eligible voters increase, but the percentage of eligible voters who exercised their franchise also increased dramatically. Spurred partly by the development of political parties, with their emphases on partisanship and getting out the vote, and spurred partly by ever-growing technological improvements in communication and transportation, the nineteenth century became a time of mass popular politics. Improved (steam-driven) printing presses, faster and more-extensive railroads, and the introduction of the telegraph, meant that information could be disseminated more quickly to far more people than ever before imaginable. In 1824, the percentage of eligible voters who cast their ballots in the presidential election was only 16.2 percent, but a short four years later, with the election of Andrew Jackson, the percentage had increased to 51.7 percent. The percentage of voter turnout continued to increase until 1840, when 77.5 percent of eligible voters cast ballots. After a slight falloff in the next two elections, the 1856 and 1860 elections saw the percentage rise again above 70 percent. Political success during these and subsequent decades required support from the common people. Elaborate campaign parades and rallies simultaneously generated and demonstrated such popular endorsement: the greater the spectacle, the greater the pageantry, the better for the candidate.[39]

Yet, the nineteenth century did not present a story of steady progress where "the People" expanded to encompass ever-increasing numbers of individuals. To the contrary, there were ebbs and flows. Through the Civil War era, African Americans, women, and Native Americans were denied most civil rights, including the franchise. The law deemed unmarried women "perpetual minors," for example, and married women's property automatically vested in their husbands. Slaves, of course, being literally owned by other human beings, were denied the most rudimentary of rights and liberties. Even Northern states denied free blacks rights to vote, to hold office, to serve on juries, and to testify as witnesses in cases involving whites. Struggles over suffrage would continue after the Civil War.[40]

Religion provides a useful lens for understanding the ambiguous quality of nineteenth-century social and cultural changes and their interrelationships with republican democracy. American Protestantism developed a new individualist and egalitarian ethos, yet this religious individualist egalitarianism did not extend to everyone. All were equal, one might say, but only if all were Protestant. Going back to the Massachusetts Bay Puritans, most Americans had viewed the country as de facto Protestant, a conviction reinforced by the Second Great Awakening. "In the United States," Tocqueville observed, "Christianity [read: Protestantism] itself is an established and irresistible fact." Yet, during the first half of the nineteenth century, Roman Catholic immigration to the United States, particularly from Ireland, accelerated exponentially. In the 1820s, Irish immigration numbered 54,388, but through the next decade, the number increased almost fourfold, partly because of falling transatlantic ticket prices. Then, a catastrophic famine in Ireland during the late 1840s caused immigration between 1841 and 1850 to soar to 780,719. The 1850s saw yet another increase, to 914,119. Consequently, at the same time that the American commitment to Protestantism was becoming deeper and wider, the American Catholic population was increasing rapidly. Given the traditional animosities between Protestants and Catholics, a Protestant American backlash against Catholic immigrants proved all too predictable. Protestant nativism appeared in a variety of forms. Violent attacks against Catholics and their property, including churches, were common; in one well-known instance from 1834, a Catholic convent near Boston was burned to the ground. Yet, nativism and anti-Catholicism could be manifested more subtly. The leaders of the public or common school movement of the mid-nineteenth century claimed to be nonsectarian, yet they were thoroughly Protestant in outlook. In New York City, to take one illustration, the public schools overtly inculcated specific religious views by having the children read from the Protestants' King James Bible, while the textbooks condemned Catholics "as deceitful, bigoted, and intolerant."[41]

Republican democracy also provided a ready outlet for nativist sentiments. From the nation's inception, republican democracy had contained an exclusionary component; large segments of the population had been carved out of the polity. While the right of suffrage generally expanded during the early-nineteenth century — given that many states had extended the franchise by eliminating property and wealth requirements — the idea that the people must be virtuous enough to pursue the common good in the public sphere still justified political exclusion. Protestant nativists readily condemned Catholics as "unfit for citizenship," as lacking the civic virtue necessary for participation in American republican institutions.

Catholicism contravened the Protestant vision of an American City of God and threatened to undermine the republic. A diary entry from 1838 denoted a typical American Protestant view. "It was enough to turn a man's stomach — to make a man abjure republicanism forever — to see the way [the Catholic immigrants] were naturalizing this morning at the Hall," wrote George Templeton Strong. "[T]he very scum and dregs of human nature filled the . . . office so completely that I was almost afraid of being poisoned by going in." Quite simply, as Samuel Morse explained in the 1830s, "'Protestantism favors Republicanism,' whereas 'Popery' supports 'Monarchical power.'"[42]

These nativist sentiments culminated in the Know-Nothing political movement of the 1850s. Its formative roots stretched back to the mid-1830s in the eastern cities, particularly New York, which harbored large immigrant populations. The so-called American or Native American party — or Know-Nothings — officially formed in 1849 as a secret society requiring members to be native-born white males with no personal or family connections to Catholicism. This society expanded with lightning speed to become a powerful political force comprised of one million members in 1854. Especially strong in the North, including New England, the Know-Nothings gained control of at least six state legislatures and won nine governorships in the 1854 and 1856 elections. While the specific Know-Nothing agendas varied in each state, the unifying force of the party was its nativism. "The grand work of the American party is the principle of nationality," declared a Know-Nothing journal. "[W]e must do something to protect and vindicate it. If we do not it will be destroyed." The Know-Nothings, in short, expressly encouraged religious and ethnic discrimination and denigrated the growing immigrant population. They sought especially to restrict voting and office holding by Catholic immigrants. In 1855, Abraham Lincoln lamented: "When the Know-Nothings get control, [the nation will practically claim that] 'all men are created equal, *except* negroes, and foreigners, and catholics.'"[43]

NOT ONLY DID the republican democratic concept of virtue change in definition and situs, but the concept of the common good also transformed. Through most of the eighteenth century, the economy was primarily a local affair. Given the poor infrastructure throughout the nation — the first improved road in America was built only in 1794 — there were, one might say, many local economies. The state and national governments rarely took actions to regulate or direct these economies. Management, in reality, was more a matter for the household than for the government. States did not have general incorporation laws, so a corporation could be created only if a legislature granted a special charter. Furthermore, states rarely granted such corporate charters because they extended exclusive privileges to the recipients. To many Americans, such exclusive grants prickled the republican democratic antagonism toward partial or private interests. The few corporate charters usually were for unequivocal public goods or purposes, such as transportation or banking. Before 1800, of the 335 state-granted corporate charters, 219 were for turnpikes, bridges, and canals, and 67 were for banks and insurance companies. Yet, even in such circumstances, the exclusivity of the charters tended to spark criticism. Justice John Hobart of New York explained: "All incorporations imply a privilege given to one order of citizens which others do not enjoy, and are so far destructive of that principle of equal liberty which should subsist in every community."[44]

But as the economy started to change in the early-nineteenth century, becoming more commercial and industrial, the government's role vis-à-vis the economy also changed. States began chartering literally hundreds of corporations. To compare, while states had chartered only 33 corporations from 1781 to 1790, they chartered almost 1,800 during the first eighteen years of the nineteenth century. The corporation transformed from an exceptional governmental device, exercised in rare circumstances, to a common and "convenient instrument of private enterprise." Whereas all of Europe still had maybe six corporations, New York alone "issued 220 corporate charters between 1800 and 1810." Consistent with the expanding importance of and respect for private sphere activities, the governmental support of private enterprise through the issuance of corporate charters itself became a manifestation of the common good. Governmental policy, whether through corporate charters or otherwise, became a means for the "release of individual creative energy."[45]

While the states were the key governmental players in the development of corporations, the U.S. Supreme Court decided two cases emblematic of the changing interpretations of the common good: *Dartmouth College v. Woodward* and *Charles River Bridge v. Warren Bridge Company*. *Dartmouth College*, decided in 1819, arose when the state of New Hampshire enacted legislation to amend the original eleemosynary charter incorporating the College. Marshall's opinion held that the initial corporate charter constituted a contract protected under the contract clause of the national Constitution. Moreover, Marshall reasoned, the attempted legislative amendment materially changed and therefore unconstitutionally impaired the charter-contract. The Court's opinion manifested an especial concern for

private-sphere activities in two ways. First, the Court broadened the definition of a contract that would fall within the scope of protection under the
contract clause. Given that contracting is a prototypical private-sphere activity, this part of Marshall's opinion effectively expanded the private realm
vis-à-vis the public realm. Second, the Court reiterated the framers' concern that factional groups not use legislative power to "take the property of
A and give it to B," as Justice Joseph Story stated in his concurrence. Even
so, *Dartmouth College* did not disparage the power of a state to regulate for
the common good. True, the Court reinforced the stability and security of
vested property rights, but simultaneously, as Story explained, the Court
left intact the legislative prerogatives under republican democracy. When
issuing a charter, a legislature could always reserve, either "expressly or implicitly," its power over the corporation, even to the extent of substantially
altering the terms of the charter. Many states did so explicitly. For example,
Massachusetts law stated: "Provided always, That the Legislature may . . .
upon due notice to any corporation, make further provisions, and regulations for the management of the business of the corporation, and for the
government thereof, or wholly to repeal any act, or part thereof, establishing any corporation as shall be deemed expedient."[46]

In 1837, the Supreme Court decided *Charles River Bridge*. The state of
Massachusetts in 1785 had enacted a corporate charter for the building
and operation of a toll bridge across the Charles River. In 1828, the state
legislature chartered a new corporation, the Warren Bridge Company, for
the purpose of building and operating a second bridge. This second bridge
caused the Charles River Bridge to lose much of its expected traffic and
toll income. Consequently, the Charles River Bridge Company, citing *Dartmouth College*, argued that its original charter had created a vested property
right protected by the contract clause. The Court disagreed. In an opinion
written by Chief Justice Roger B. Taney, the Court reasoned that legislative
actions, including the granting of corporate charters, were always presumed
to be for the common good. "While the rights of private property are sa-
credly guarded, we must not forget, that the community also have rights,
and that the happiness and well-being of every citizen depends on their
faithful preservation." Legislatures can encourage economic competition,
including in the construction of infrastructure such as bridges, because
doing so is for the public good. Taney explained: "[T]he object and end of
all government is to promote the happiness and prosperity of the community by which it is established. [I]n a country like ours, free, active and
enterprising, continually advancing in numbers and wealth, new channels
of communication are daily found necessary, both for travel and trade, and

are essential to the comfort, convenience and prosperity of the people. A state ought never to be presumed to surrender this power." *Charles River Bridge*, in sum, underscored that corporate charters now would rarely be interpreted as granting exclusive or monopolistic privileges.[47]

The same year that the Court decided *Charles River Bridge*, the state of Connecticut enacted the first general incorporation law, allowing corporations to form without procuring special legislative action. Other states followed suit over the next twenty years. These general incorporation laws reflected both the growing commercial excitement of that era and the perception that special corporate charters violated the republican democratic prohibition against private or partial legislation. And in fact, state legislators had all-too-often granted special corporate charters as rewards for their partisan supporters. Taken together, the two 1837 governmental actions — the national action embodied in the Court's *Charles River Bridge* decision and the state action of introducing general incorporation laws — further facilitated the "release of energy" by encouraging private competition and "creative change" in the economic marketplace.[48]

By the mid-nineteenth century, the conception of the common good had shifted. *Dartmouth College* afforded private-sphere economic liberties greater protection from governmental control, but *Charles River Bridge* and the general incorporation laws revealed that property and contract rights would not be protected from competition within the private sphere itself. To be sure, people contested shifts in the meaning of the common good. During this time, for instance, Whigs continued to maintain that the legislative granting of special privileges, such as a special corporate charter, could often be justified as conducive to the common good, while more radical Democrats, called Locofocos, insisted that any such special legislative actions were "inherently inequitable." Despite such disputes, the common good transformed. Partly for this reason, democracy helped unleash, according to Tocqueville, "an all-pervading and restless activity, a superabundant force, and an energy which is inseparable from it and which may, however unfavorable circumstances may be, produce wonders." The common good now encompassed the governmental encouragement of commercial enterprises and economic competition. As Theodore Sedgwick wrote, "all good laws tend to the production and just distribution of wealth; all good laws are good economy."[49]

Moreover, as the locus of the ever-expanding commercial activities was the economic marketplace — the private sphere — some mid-century Americans expected the government not only to facilitate but also increasingly to avoid interfering with market transactions. For these individuals, the common good had shifted so strongly toward private-sphere economic actions that any governmental interference had become at least questionable. For instance, a New York court in 1856 struck down a state liquor prohibition statute as violating due process. "In a government like ours, theories of public good or public necessity may be so plausible, or even so truthful, as to command popular majorities," the court admitted. "But whether truthful or plausible merely, and by whatever numbers they are assented to, there are some absolute private rights beyond their reach, and among these the constitution places the right of property." Although this judicial statement was extreme for its time, the courts and other governmental institutions were unquestionably becoming mechanisms for "delegating the public force in aid of private decision making." A Georgia court in 1853 offered a panegyric salute to the intertwined blessings of free-market commercialism and Christianity. "Free Trade is destined to become the predominant principle — the permanent and paramount policy of the world. And I rejoice that it is so. It is the forerunner, as well as the fruit, of the rapidly advancing civilization of the nineteenth century. It is the adjunct and handmaiden of Christianity. May these 'golden girdles' soon encircle the globe! Free Trade and the Bible, walking hand-in-hand together, will finally work out the problem of man's moral regeneration, and establish the reign of Peace on earth."[50]

Given such a growing focus on private activities in the economic marketplace, the disparities of wealth in America increased during the Jacksonian era and after. While an egalitarian ethos permeated American society — and all white Protestant men had an equal right to pursue wealth — this equality was more formal than substantive. In reality, certain families were accumulating immense quantities of wealth, enjoying lives of opulence in mansions of European grandeur, but the great majority of individuals and families owned little. Family farmers often struggled to survive, and working-class urban families lived in "dismal to abysmal" conditions. In Philadelphia, for example, fifty families might be squeezed into one tenement, with one room to a family, without "the accommodation of a privy for their use." Generally, in the large northeastern cities, "the top 1 percent of wealthholders owned about one fourth of the wealth in the mid-1820s and about half the property by midcentury." The same was true in other sections of the nation. In one Texas county, in 1850, a mere 5 percent of the adult male population owned greater than 50 percent of the property. In short, the rapid development of commercialism had generated new sources of wealth, but not all Americans shared equally in this new wealth, despite the widely accepted rhetoric of egalitarianism.[51]

DESPITE THE CHANGING conceptions of virtue, popular sovereignty, and the common good that emerged during the first part of the nineteenth century, the broad parameters of republican democracy always remained in place. One reason for the resiliency of republican democracy was the flexibility of its central concepts, which allowed governmental theory and practice to shift with the changing society and culture. That flexibility, moreover, facilitated the invocation of republican democratic principles in a multitude of political contexts. As the antebellum era drew to a violent close, the new Republican party fueled its emergence with a free labor, free soil ideology. Purposefully ambiguous so as to broaden the party's appeal, to attract supporters who had resisted the Garrisonians' more strident evangelical abolitionism, the Republicans' free labor ideology rested on the connections between economic independence and republican democratic citizenship. Free labor tied the private virtue of the marketplace to the public virtue of republican democratic politics. Free labor built on a man's "ambition, his enterprise, his capacity," wrote journalist and politician Horace Greeley. "In the constitution of human nature, the desire of bettering one's condition is the mainspring of effort." Slavery destroyed such desire, as the *New York Times* explained in 1856: "Slavery is an evil [that] depresses industry, impoverishes the soil, degrades labor, and injures fatally the society in which it takes root." More conservative Republicans stressed that slavery degraded and impoverished "White Labor," in particular. But whether focused solely on whites or not, Republicans insisted that slave labor corrupted republican democratic government, while free labor engendered "hardy, industrious, intelligent and free citizens." From the Republicans' vantage, moreover, "[i]nvoluntary servitude and free labor . . . cannot exist on the same soil"; slavery and free labor could not be mixed. All laborers within a particular state or territory must remain independent, and concomitantly, must retain the opportunity to acquire property or to become shop-owning artisans. Such economic independence cultivated the virtue of the republican citizen. A "free man" was never "fixed for life in the condition of a hired laborer," Abraham Lincoln declared. "Men, with their families . . . work for themselves on their farms, in their houses, and in their shops, taking the whole product to themselves, and asking no favors of capital on the one hand nor of hired laborers or slaves on the other." For this reason, the continued availability of free-soil land in the western territories — land bereft of slavery — provided continuing hope and opportunity for wage laborers.[52]

CHAPTER 3

Free Expression in the Early Years

Before the 1760s, newspaper printers and editors rarely proclaimed strong partisan views on political issues. Instead, authors would pay papers to print essays, sometimes criticizing and sometimes praising public policies and officials. The press believed it enjoyed liberty because it could remain neutral in controversies while allowing others to express their views. A young Benjamin Franklin, writing in his *Pennsylvania Gazette* in 1731, expressed the pragmatic business-oriented approach that typified many contemporary printers. Franklin explained that printers "chearfully serve all contending Writers that pay them well, without regarding on which side they are of the Question in Dispute." Yet, he encouraged printers to censor themselves by refusing to print "bad things," including "[t]hings as usually give Offence either to Church or State." Such American attitudes would shift, however, during the Revolutionary and framing periods, when the three components (or axes) constituting free expression — the tradition of dissent, the tradition of suppression, and the legal doctrine regarding a free press and free speech — would solidify with the emerging nation.[1]

THE REVOLUTIONARY PERIOD

In the Revolutionary era, a series of events induced the press to become increasingly partisan and opposed to the British Crown. In 1760, George III became king, and he set forth to rule aggressively, generating widespread dissatisfaction in England and America. No less a conservative than Edmund Burke became concerned with George's unscrupulous tactics. In

1763, George complained about "the spirit of fermentation and the excessive licence which prevails in England. It is essential to neglect nothing that can check that spirit." George became outraged when a member of Parliament, John Wilkes, published an article in the *North Briton*, number 45, claiming that George had lied in a public speech. Wilkes had groused that the king "can be brought to give the sanction of his sacred name to the most odious measures." Under an information for criminal libel, the government issued a general search warrant that led to the arrest of forty-nine people, including Wilkes, who were allegedly connected to the publication. Within a short time, George had impelled two hundred libel prosecutions, but his heavy-handed tactics proved disastrous. The attempted suppression of Wilkes and his writings — the Crown ordered *North Briton*, number 45, burned — only fanned Wilkes's popularity. The people reelected him to the House of Commons three times — doing so even while he was in prison. In both England and America, then, Wilkes became symbolic of the fight for liberty, especially for freedom of the press, in the face of a corrupt monarch. The widespread call was for "Wilkes and Liberty!"[2]

Shortly after the Wilkes fiasco began, George III blundered into another strategic error. In 1763, with American help, the British defeated the French in the expensive (and long) Seven Years' (French and Indian) War, which forced the French to relinquish their North American empire. George decided the Americans ought to begin contributing revenue for the further defense and maintenance of the British Empire, including the colonies. That decision led to the enactment of the Sugar Act of 1764 and the Stamp Act of 1765, which taxed most uses of "skin" or paper. Yet, not only were Americans likely to resent being directly taxed for the first time, but with the French exit from the continent, they were now less dependent on British military protection. The Stamp Act, in particular, engendered a swing in American sentiments, forged a sense of unity in opposition to the tax, and prompted the first American declarations of no taxation without representation. The British responded by insisting that members of Parliament virtually represented the Americans. Even when Parliament repealed the Stamp Tax in 1766, it simultaneously asserted the British power over the colonies in the Declaratory Act: "[Parliament] had, hath, and of right ought to have, full power and authority to make laws and statutes of sufficient force and vitality to bind the colonies and people of America . . . in all cases whatsoever." Moreover, of long-term significance, the Stamp Act before its repeal had threatened American printers with financial ruin and thus, rather suddenly, had motivated them to adopt a partisan stance in opposition to the British Crown.[3]

Over the next decade, relations between the British and the Americans worsened. Growing tensions over the imposition and payment of taxes led Parliament, in 1774, to enact a series of punitive laws, called the Intolerable Acts. For example, the Boston Port Act, passed as punishment for the Boston Tea Party (of December 16, 1773), closed the port of Boston until the town paid for the destroyed tea. The Intolerable Acts provoked widespread alarm throughout the colonies and stiffened the sense of unity against Britain. Before long, Americans called for the first Continental Congress, and on October 14, 1774, the Congress declared that the colonists were "entitled to life, liberty, and property, & they have never ceded to any sovereign power whatever, a right to dispose of either without their consent." The colonists were "entitled to all the rights, liberties, and immunities of free and natural-born subjects within the realm of England." Significantly, then, "the foundation of English liberty, and of all free government, is a right in the people to participate in their legislative council." Among other rights, the colonists "have a right peaceably to assemble, consider of their grievances, and petition the King." The Intolerable Acts, the Congress concluded, were "impolitic, unjust, and cruel, as well as unconstitutional, and most dangerous and destructive of American rights."[4]

As more and more Americans turned against the British before and during the Revolution, the press increasingly found that profit lay in patriotism. Neutrality or support for the Tories (or Loyalists) and the king was likely to end in economic disaster. American newspapers filled with denunciations of the British, with many attacks focused on prominent individuals. The *Massachusetts Spy* claimed that George III provided "sinecures for every dirty booby who was thought a convenient tool." A favorite target for American scorn was Thomas Hutchinson, who served in a variety of official positions in Massachusetts, including chief justice, lieutenant governor, and governor. The newspapers castigated Hutchinson as "the greatest of criminals — more worthy to be 'delivered into the hands of the executioner' than private robbers, assassins or murderers." Josiah Quincy, Jr., pronounced that Hutchinson was "degrading the highest station in the law to the lowest office of the inquisition. . . . [Hutchinson was] the first, the most malignant and insatiable enemy." Before long, Americans were sending ultimatums to the British through the newspapers. In the *Boston Gazette,* an anonymous author wrote that if Britain did not change its treatment of the colonies, the Americans "probably will . . . form a government of their own, similar to that of the United Provinces in Holland, and offer a free trade to all nations in Europe." Two months later, another anonymous writer declared: "If public measures be not speedily and diametrically changed, the people, quite weary of oppression and insult, will unite their force, like a torrent or hurricane, and drive their oppressors, from the face of the American world."[5]

Royal officials futilely attempted to prosecute their critics. Over and over again, Hutchinson tried and failed to garner indictments for seditious libel. "My repeated Charges to Grand Juries," Hutchinson groaned, "[are] so entirely neglected [that] I have no Hope of the ceasing of this atrocious Crime." These royalist efforts at suppression typically served to spark American encomiums to the glories of a free press. In the *Boston Gazette* in 1768, Samuel Adams echoed "Cato's Letters" by proclaiming freedom of the press the bulwark of liberty: "There is nothing so fretting and vexatious; nothing so justly terrible to tyrants, and their tools and abettors, as a free press. The reason is obvious; namely, because it is as it has been very justly observ'd in a spirited answer to a spirited speech, 'the bulwark of the People's Liberties.' For this reason, it is ever watched by those who are forming plans for the destruction of the people's liberties, with an envious and malignant eye." If the Americans did not resist British suppression of speech, Isaiah Thomas wrote in the *Massachusetts Spy* in 1772, then "[w]e may next expect padlocks on our lips, fetters on our legs, and only our hands left at liberty to slave for our worse than Egyptian task masters, *or—or—*FIGHT OUR WAY TO CONSTITUTIONAL FREEDOM!"[6]

Americans thus invigorated their tradition of dissent with a vengeance during the Revolutionary era. Yet, the same Americans who exercised and celebrated their free expression actively suppressed the views of Tories who sought to express their support for the British. The tradition of suppression was as alive and well as the tradition of dissent. Tories were scared into silence, driven out of town, or tarred and feathered. At the direction of the Continental Congress, Patriots created local Committees of Observation or Inspection to enforce a commercial boycott of Great Britain, but these Committees soon were monitoring the output of printers with the ominous vigor of an Orwellian Big Brother. When a Pennsylvania newspaper published an unsigned letter on February 11, 1775, insisting that "if the King's Standard were now erected, nine out of ten would repair to it," the Philadelphia Committee of Inspection went into action. The Committee discovered the author and compelled him to recant his "malignant insinuation" and to promise his future defense of "all the constitutional rights and privileges in America." In New York City, shortly before Americans declared independence, every printer was sent the following message: "Sir, if you print, or suffer to be printed in your press anything against the rights and liberties of America, or in favor of our inveterate foes, the King,

Ministry, and Parliament of Great Britain, death and destruction, ruin and perdition, shall be your portion." The message, which proved remarkably effective while New York remained under American dominion, was "Signed, by order of the Committee of tarring and feathering. Legion."[7]

Not only did the Americans actively suppress Tory speech, they also continued to accept the propriety of the long-standing British law on seditious libel. The Americans, it might be said, were either confused, ambivalent, or indifferent about free expression. At one instant, they celebrated free speech, and at the next instant, they suppressed it. At one instant, they denounced the British, and at the next instant, they willingly acquiesced to the British law on seditious libel. The best explanation for such inconsistencies is simple: the Americans were less concerned with political theory, including the abstract definition of free expression, than with the pressing and concrete political problems of their turbulent times. Revolutionary Americans knew that if they lost the war, they well might face British prosecutions for treason. This was the type of political problem that caught and held one's attention; conviction for treason could leave one dangling from a gallows rope. With their lives at stake, Americans were adamant about crushing any Tory voices that might weaken the war effort, not about conceiving or upholding some abstract principle of free expression (for Tories at least).[8]

The writings of "Freeborn American" in the *Boston Gazette* illustrate the American attitudes toward free expression. Hutchinson sought to prosecute Benjamin Edes and John Gill, publishers of the radical *Gazette*, because of their persistent polemical attacks on the British. The *Gazette* repeatedly reprinted "Cato's Letters," including "Of Freedom of Speech," and consistently celebrated the degree of free speech and press in England and America. Writing in the *Gazette*, "Freeborn American" agreed that free expression was a wondrous blessing necessary for good government, yet, when it came time to define the concept, "Freeborn American" wrote: "Man, in a state of nature, has undoubtedly a right to speak and act without controul. In a state of civil society, that right is limited by law — Political liberty consists in freedom of speech and action, so far as the laws of a community will permit, and no farther: all beyond is criminal, and tends to the destruction of Liberty itself." In other words, individuals might have a natural right to free expression, but once in civil society, that right is subordinate to the positive law of the political community. To allow any greater freedom would undermine liberty itself because it would be harmful to the community. In short, from the pages of the radical *Gazette*, denouncing the British and celebrating free expression, came the standard justification for the law of seditious libel: expression criticizing the government or its officials had a harmful or bad tendency or, that is, tended to undermine public peace and order.[9]

Naturally, Americans elicited the law and theory of seditious libel as legitimating their suppression of Tories. John Adams, invoking the customary distinction between liberty and licentiousness, condemned "the scandalous license of the tory presses." Francis Hopkinson of New Jersey, a member of the Continental Congress and a signer of the Declaration of Independence, elaborated: "[The liberty of the press] hath been justly held up as an important privilege of the people. . . . But when this privilege is manifestly abused, and the press becomes an engine for sowing the most dangerous dissensions, for spreading false alarms, and undermining the very foundations of government, ought not that government, upon the plain principles of self-preservation, to silence by its own authority, such a daring violator of its peace, and tear from its bosom the serpent that would sting it to death." Many Americans, though, advocated for a change in the law of seditious libel to correspond with the result of the *Zenger* case. Truth, it was argued, should be a defense to a charge of libel, and a jury should ultimately resolve whether the defendant had committed a criminal libel. Yet, even those Americans who advocated for this Zengerian liberalizing of the law did not think to suggest that the law of seditious libel should be totally wiped from the books. In the late-eighteenth century's leading American dissertation on free expression, William Bollan's 1766 *The Freedom of Speech and Writing upon Public Affairs, Considered, with an Historical View,* Bollan linked free government and free expression: "[T]he free examination of public measures, with a proper representation by speech or writing of the sense resulting from that examination, is the right of the members of a free state, and requisite for the preservation of their other rights." In prosecutions for seditious libel, Bollan argued that truth should be a defense and that a jury should determine the outcome. Beyond that, though, Bollan worried about the "licentious use of the press" perpetrated by "enemies of the public weal." The law of seditious libel, therefore, provided the government with a needed mechanism for keeping expression within "just and proper bounds."[10]

WHEN THE REVOLUTION finally began, Americans memorialized their attitudes toward free expression in their state constitutions and in newly enacted laws. Most striking in the early state constitutions is not the number of bold assertions of protected expressive liberties, but rather the ambivalence revealed by the inconsistencies among the various states. For instance, the Virginia Bill (or Declaration) of Rights, adopted on June 12, 1776, nearly a month before the Declaration of Independence, contained the very first written constitutional or legislative protection of a free press (again echoing the bulwark-of-liberty phrasing): "That the freedom of the press is one of the great bulwarks of liberty, and can never be restrained but by despotic governments." Yet, the Virginia Bill of Rights did not proffer any express protection for free speech or assembly. Pennsylvania soon followed Virginia's example by including the Declaration of the Rights of the Inhabitants of the State of Pennsylvania as part of its 1776 Constitution, but Pennsylvania went far beyond Virginia in the scope of its protections. Article XII of the Pennsylvania Constitution of 1776 provided: "That the people have a right to freedom of speech, and of writing, and publishing their sentiments; therefore the freedom of the press ought not to be restrained." Article XVI added: "That the people have a right to assemble together, to consult for their common good, to instruct their representatives, and to apply to the legislature for redress of grievances, by address, petition, or remonstrance." In fact, the Pennsylvania Constitution was the first to extend explicit protection to freedom of speech, though its use of the word "ought" ("the people have a right to freedom of speech, and . . . therefore the freedom of the press *ought* not to be restrained") sounds precatory rather than mandatory. Pennsylvania also included in the main body of its Constitution an additional protection of the press, relating it to the operation of free (republican) government: "The printing presses shall be free to every person who undertakes to examine the proceedings of the legislature, or any part of government."[11]

As it turned out, not one other state included constitutional protections of expression as wide ranging as those of Pennsylvania. The *only* other state to protect free speech explicitly (beyond speech and debate in the legislative forum) was Vermont, which framed its first constitution in 1777, even though it was not officially admitted into the Union until 1791. Article XIV of Vermont's Declaration of Rights followed Pennsylvania's Article XII word for word in its protection of the people's "right to freedom of speech." For the sake of comparison, while only Pennsylvania and Vermont protected free speech, twelve states protected freedom of conscience or the free exercise of religion. Yet, the lack of state constitutional provisions protecting free speech did not mean that Americans were "afraid to speak their minds." To the contrary, Americans continued to enjoy their tradition of dissent. States failed to protect free speech partly because concrete political disputes had not recently rendered free speech per se a live pressing issue and partly because constitutional protections mostly seemed unnecessary, at least for Americans supporting the Revolution. Unlike the Tories, patriotic Americans without compunction "habitually lambasted their leaders, excoriated public policies, and acted as if their governments were their servants." Pennsylvania newspapers, for instance, readily denounced governmental officials for "selling official honesty" and peddling "Official Blunders by the groce." As Alexander Hamilton would soon observe, individual rights and liberties depended far more on the people's sentiments than on written constitutional protections.[12]

Unsurprisingly, given the recent controversies over printing and the press, ten state constitutions protected freedom of the press explicitly. The First Continental Congress had earlier underscored the prominence of the press in America and anticipated the state constitutional provisions with its Address to the Inhabitants of Quebec, promulgated on October 26, 1774. The Continental Congress had already decided to adopt a radical stance vis-à-vis the Crown, so the Americans understood the potential strategic military importance of the French-Canadian population to the north, recently added to the British empire. In their Quebec Address, the Americans ostensibly advised the Canadians about their rights and privileges as English subjects, but the Address appeared to be little more than a propaganda statement "purely for export," oriented toward political advantage. Even so, the Americans chose to emphasize in their message only five of the "invaluable rights" of Englishmen, and "freedom of the press" was among them, albeit "last." The Americans explained: "The importance of this [freedom of the press] consists, besides the advancement of truth, science, morality, and arts in general, in its diffusion of liberal sentiments on the administration of Government, its ready communication of thoughts between subjects, and its consequential promotion of union among them, whereby oppressive officers are shamed or intimidated, into more honourable and just modes of conducting affairs." All in all, this part of the Quebec Address was surprisingly broad in its substance. Perhaps most important, the Americans asserted that freedom of the press facilitates free government, allowing "subjects" to communicate among themselves and with their representatives, thus discouraging the abuse of governmental power. Since, under civic republican theory, liberty generally meant the ability to participate in republican government, it followed that liberty of the press would be oriented toward such participation. Even further, the Americans asserted, freedom of the press contributes to the progress of "truth, science, morality, and arts in general." Yet, despite such aspirational breadth, one should remember that the Address did not mirror (in America or England) the current state of the law regarding expression, especially the law of seditious libel.[13]

The various state constitutional provisions on freedom of the press not only avoided explicit mandates but also tended to be far less precise than the Quebec Address. Delaware and Maryland both provided: "That the liberty of the press ought to be inviolably preserved." For the most part, the state constitutions appeared to declare that freedom of the press was a natural right or fundamental value. "The liberty of the press is essential to the freedom in a State," according to the Massachusetts's 1780 Declaration of Rights, "it ought not, therefore, to be restricted in this commonwealth." Meanwhile, five state constitutions protected a right of assembly, and six states protected a right of petition. Pennsylvania, Massachusetts, New Hampshire, and Vermont combined their respective protections of assembly and petition in one provision and, significantly, tied these rights explicitly to the republican democratic pursuit of the common good. Massachusetts, for example, provided: "The people have a right, in an orderly and peaceable manner, to assemble to consult upon the common good; give instructions to their representatives, and to request of the legislative body, by the way of addresses, petitions, or remonstrances, redress of the wrongs done them, and of the grievances they suffer."[14]

Regardless of the state constitutional protections of free expression, and regardless of the tradition of dissent that sheltered patriotic Americans, Tories continued to go largely unprotected. In fact, again with the encouragement of the Continental Congress, every state enacted laws intended to oppress Tories in multiple ways, with many overtly restricting expression. Rhode Island passed a statute "to punish persons who shall acknowledge the King of Great Britain to be their sovereign." Virginia enacted a law that imposed a fine and imprisonment for, among other things, wishing that the king enjoy "health, prosperity, or success." Every state denied Tories the rights to vote and hold office and forced individuals to swear to a loyalty or test oath. The purpose of the oaths was to unmask Tories because, in the words of Thomas Jefferson, a Tory might "be a traitor in thought, but not in deed."[15]

WITH THE REVOLUTIONARY WAR ending in the early 1780s, the Americans set forth in a time of peace to struggle through the growing pains of republican democratic government. During the next decade, the question of seditious libel, in particular, arose in two states, Pennsylvania and Massachusetts. Americans began to contemplate, however tentatively, whether their conception of republican democracy, grounded on the sovereignty of the people, might affect the legal prohibition of seditious libel. In Philadelphia, the state arrested and charged Eleazar Oswald, publisher of the *Independent Gazetteer,* with "seditious, scandalous, and infamous LIBEL" because he had criticized the state supreme court as biased. When released on bail, Oswald published additional inflammatory articles, calling one of the judges, "that excrescence." When the state again arrested Oswald, in 1782, the *Gazetteer* published a number of attacks on the concept of seditious libel. "Candid" declared that all criminal prosecutions for libel should be eradicated because they infringed a free press, which supplied information to voters. "Junius Wilkes" argued "that governmental officials, as servants of the people, could not be libeled by criticism of their performance, even by false statements." A prosecution for seditious libel was just as harmful as a prior restraint. "The danger is precisely the same to liberty," wrote "Junius Wilkes," "in punishing a person after the performance appears to the world, as in preventing publication in the first instance." "Candid" and "Junius Wilkes," in other words, at least suggested tensions between the punishment of seditious libel and aspects of republican democracy, including voting and representation. Oswald himself subsequently wrote an essay similarly hinting at such a tension: "The doctrine of libels [is] a doctrine incompatible with law and liberty, and at once destructive of the privileges of free country, in the communication of our thoughts."[16]

While Oswald and his cohorts advocated for a broad freedom of the press, Oswald's primary nemesis, Chief Justice Thomas McKean, sought to indict him. McKean's efforts came to naught, though, thwarted by a resistant grand jury. Unfortunately for Oswald, McKean was not easily discouraged. In 1788, Oswald criticized a court's action against him in a civil suit and was promptly charged with contempt, which in this case resembled a charge of seditious libel except that McKean could now try and convict Oswald without a jury. Significantly, McKean's opinion confronted the relations between, on the one hand, Pennsylvania's two constitutional provisions protecting freedom of the press and, on the other hand, the law of seditious libel. "The true liberty of the press," McKean explained, consists of a prohibition on prior restraints. Criminal punishment after publication is permissible if the writer intended to "delude and defame" rather than to advance the "public good." McKean concluded that the "tendency" of Oswald's writing was "of prejudicing the public," and therefore, Oswald's "object" or purpose must have been "to dishonor the administration of justice." In sum, McKean's approach seemed entirely consistent with the emerging notions of republican democracy: the government could not criminally punish a writer who furthered the common good but could punish one whose expression had a bad tendency (and thus contravened the common good).[17]

The patent tensions between McKean's views and those of Oswald's supporters riddled discussions when Pennsylvania sought to frame a new state Constitution in 1790. Eventually, the delegates, including McKean and James Wilson, agreed on a new free press provision that tied free expression to free government but also followed Blackstone: prior restraints are impermissible, but an individual can be subsequently held "responsible" in a criminal prosecution for an "abuse" of the liberty of the press. The provision then incorporated modified Zengerian reforms for the prosecution of seditious libel. First, following *Zenger* unequivocally, juries could decide not only the fact of publication but also the legal question of whether the writing was libelous. Second, instead of following *Zenger* by making truth a defense in all circumstances, the constitution limited the truth-defense to publications that were, in effect, intended for the public good — "investigating the official conduct of officers, or men in a public capacity, or where the matter published is proper for public information." Pennsylvania thus became the first state to constitutionalize *Zenger*, if only in part.[18]

In 1790 and 1791, shortly after the adoption of Pennsylvania's new constitution — and while the states debated ratification of the proposed national Bill of Rights — James Wilson delivered the seminal lectures on American constitutional law to an audience at the College of Philadelphia that included George Washington, among other luminaries. Wilson, ranging widely, explored the relations between republican democracy and seditious libel. He stressed that republican government depends on virtue, particularly in governmental officials. All citizens, then, have a responsibility to show due respect for those holding governmental office. "Under a republican government," Wilson explained, "it is prudent as well as proper — it is the interest as well as the duty of the citizens, to show a political respect for office. In the government they have an interest: this interest requires, that every department and every office should be well filled." Moreover, Wilson continued, virtue goes hand-in-hand with honor, character, and reputation, and "[v]iewed in this light, the honor of character is a property, which is, indeed precious." Given this, the defamation of a public official is a crime of uncommon severity because it can undermine republican government. "[W]hat epithet shall we assign to that conduct, which plucks the wreath of honor from those temples, around which it has been meritoriously placed? Robbery itself flows not from a foundation so rankly poisoned as that, which throws out the waters of malicious defamation." Thus, republican democracy depended both on free expression and on the vigorous protection of virtuous officials from seditious libel. "The citizen under a free government has a right to think, to speak, to write, to print, and to publish freely, but with decency and truth, concerning public men, public bodies, and public measures." The law of seditious libel, consequently, is "wise and salutary when administered properly, and by the proper persons." But what, then, is the proper administration and understanding of seditious libel? Zengerian reforms, Wilson argued, should be followed in full: truth should always be a defense, and juries should always decide whether the disputed speech was libelous. Truth as a defense is especially important because, contrary to Blackstone's position, seditious libel chiefly protects the character of the governmental official rather than the public peace. If a citizen's written attack on a governmental official is true — and the official's character is, in fact, flawed — then the official does not deserve the protection of the law.[19]

Massachusetts was the only other state in which libel became an important issue during the mid- to late 1780s. Like Pennsylvania, Massachusetts had a free press clause in its state constitution: "The liberty of the press is essential to the freedom in a State; it ought not, therefore, to be restricted in this commonwealth." A future U.S. Supreme Court justice, William Cushing, and a future president, John Adams, exchanged letters discussing the meaning of this provision. Adams had initially drafted the clause, while Cushing, the state's chief justice, had served at the state's constitutional convention. Cushing sent the first letter, confessing that "I have had a difficulty about the construction of [the clause]," which Cushing hoped Adams could "clear up." Cushing's question was straightforward: was it consistent with the state constitution to punish a publication as seditious libel "when such charges are supportable by the truth of fact?" Cushing and Adams agreed, at a minimum, that under the republican democratic system of the Massachusetts Constitution, expression was protected more than under the British governmental system. Blackstone was not the final word. Even so, Cushing did not doubt that false publications should be punishable: "When the press is made the vehicle of falsehood and scandal, let the authors be punished with becoming rigour." But truth should be a defense, Cushing speculated, because the threat of subsequent punishment, as much as a prior restraint, will often effectively deter a would-be writer from publishing. A free press should be protected because it "tends to the security of freedom in a State." That is, "[t]his liberty of publishing truth can never effectually injure a good government, or honest administrators;

but it may save a state from the necessity of a revolution, as well as bring one about, when it is necessary." In sum, with admitted uncertainty, Cushing believed that the best reading of the state free press clause maintained the law of seditious libel as modified by Zengerian reforms. Adams's response was less equivocal: "I . . . am very clear that under the Articles of our Constitution . . . it would be safest to admit evidence to the jury of the Truth of accusations, and if the jury found them true and that they were published for the Public good, they would readily acquit." To Adams, then, not only was punishment of seditious libel consistent with the free press clause, but no more than diluted Zengerian reforms were appropriate. Adams agreed with Pennsylvania's McKean: truth was a defense only if the defendant intended to publish for the public good.[20]

In sum, by the late 1780s and early 1790s, only one conclusion regarding free expression is possible: it was unclear. Numerous Americans, including Bollan, Cushing, "Candid," "Junius Wilkes," and several Anti-Federalists, had followed "Cato's Letters" by linking free government with free expression, particularly freedom of the press. Most often, these Americans asserted that a free press protected other liberties as well as free government itself. Freedom of the press was the grand palladium, the bulwark of liberties. Nonetheless, the law of seditious libel was still in effect, though many advocated for Zengerian reforms to greater or lesser degrees. There remained the American tradition of dissent, but there also remained the tradition of suppression. With so many competing extant views of free expression, an individual involved in a particular and concrete dispute could readily find support from tradition, law, or both to correspond with his or her political inclinations.

YET, THE ENTRENCHMENT in the states of republican democratic governments, grounded on the sovereignty of the people, opened the possibility for rethinking free expression. Probably no mere coincidence, Americans in the early 1780s for the first time began to suggest that governmental punishment of seditious libel contravened a free press. To be sure, in America, this idea was neither widespread, extensively developed, nor (at this time) explicitly derived from republican democracy and the sovereignty of the people. No prominent American writers seized the opportunity to elaborate expressly the links between seditious libel and a form of government now repudiated in America. The English law of seditious libel, after all, had originated within a monarchical system that sought to protect the dignity of royal officials as well as preserving the public peace and order. Indeed, in England during the American Revolutionary era, Radical (or Real) Whigs (or Commonwealthmen) like James Burgh, Joseph Priestly, and Richard Price emphasized the importance of popular sovereignty. Following in the footsteps of John Trenchard and Thomas Gordon, the early-eighteenth-century Opposition writers who authored "Cato's Letters," these Radical Whigs focused primarily on corruption at home in England itself, but they also argued that popular sovereignty undermined the law of seditious libel. "Punishing libels public or private is foolish," explained Burgh. "[A]ll history shews the necessity, in order to the preservation of liberty, of every subject's having a watchful eye on the conduct of Kings, Ministers, and Parliament, and of every subject's being not only secured, but encouraged in alarming his fellow-subjects on occasion of every attempt upon public liberty, and that private, independent subjects *only* are likely to give fair warning of such attempts." These Radical Whig writings were enormously popular in America, but Americans appropriated the ideas on popular sovereignty, in general, and British corruption, more specifically, rather than the implications for seditious libel. Even so, regardless of the stunted American development of these possibilities, the mere fact that, in the Oswald-McKean disputes, "Junius Wilkes," "Candid," and Oswald contended that seditious libel prosecutions should be eliminated and at least suggested that they clashed with the republican democratic form of government seems significant.[21]

But how significant? Once again, the answer is unclear. On September 12, 1789, as the First Congress debated the proposed first amendment, the now venerable but still sardonic Benjamin Franklin wrote of liberty of the press. "[F]ew of us, I believe, have distinct Ideas of its Nature and Extent," but anyone who can write reasonably well appears to have "the privilege of accusing and abusing" other citizens. Consequently, Franklin proposed, if we must have full liberty of the press, then we ought also to have "liberty of the cudgel." If an "impudent writer attacks your reputation," then "break his head," though you might exercise moderation by merely "tarring and feathering." Franklin concluded on a more serious note: "If by the Liberty of the Press were understood merely the Liberty of discussing the Propriety of Public Measures and political opinions, let us have as much of it as you please: But if it means the Liberty of affronting, calumniating, and defaming one another, I, for my part, own myself willing to part with my Share of it when our Legislators shall please." Franklin, in other words, believed that the government's power and willingness to punish printers provided a useful palliative for the press's occasional excesses.[22]

More important than Franklin's humorous musings were James Wilson's scholarly conclusions. The leading constitutional scholar of the framers' generation, Wilson linked free expression and free government, as did numerous other Americans. But more so than anyone else, Wilson explicitly explored the relations between republican democracy and the law of seditious libel. Yet, instead of following the English Radical Whigs and concluding that the American form of sovereignty and government destroyed the foundation for the law of seditious libel, he argued the opposite. Republican democracy and popular sovereignty supplied a whole new justification for the law of seditious libel, if properly modified and understood in accordance with Zengerian reforms. Libel injured the sovereign people themselves because it could cause them to lose faith in a virtuous elected official. Crucially, Wilson was not a reactionary conservative; to the contrary, he was one of the most populist and democratic of the framers.[23]

THE FRAMING AND THE BILL OF RIGHTS

The question: did the framing of the U.S. Constitution and the adoption of the Bill of Rights substantially change the law or traditions regarding free expression? The answer: not much.

The delegates to the Constitutional Convention devoted little energy to issues of free expression. Early in the proceedings, Thomas Pinckney of South Carolina presented a comprehensive plan for a constitution, which received little consideration; the delegates accepted an alternative, the Virginia Plan. Pinckney's plan included several limitations on the legislative powers of the national government, including the following: "The Legislature of the United States shall pass no Law . . . touching or abridging the Liberty of the Press." Pinckney did not forget about this concern even after the Convention bypassed his comprehensive plan. On August 20, 1787, he asked the delegates to consider a number of amendments, many of which might be found in a Bill of Rights, including a free press clause: "The liberty of the Press shall be inviolably preserved." Without debate or further consideration, the delegates referred these propositions to the Committee of Detail, charged with transforming the delegates' ideas into a workable draft constitution. Then on September 12, 1787, during the final week of the Convention, in the midst of discussing a right to a jury trial, George Mason of Virginia commented: "He wished the plan had been prefaced with a Bill of Rights, & would second a Motion if made for the purpose — It would give great quiet to the people; and with the aid of the State declarations, a bill might be prepared in a few hours." Consequently, Elbridge Gerry of

Massachusetts "moved for a Committee to prepare a Bill of Rights"; Mason seconded; but the state delegations unanimously defeated the motion. Two days later, Pinckney tried again, moving—with a second by Gerry— "to insert a declaration 'that the liberty of the Press should be inviolably observed.'" "It is unnecessary," Roger Sherman observed, "[t]he power of Congress does not extend to the Press." The motion failed, seven to four.[24]

The Convention proceedings strongly suggest that the overwhelming majority of delegates believed a Bill of Rights, including an express protection of either free speech or a free press, was unnecessary. Not a single delegate even mentioned a free speech clause, other than a speech and debate clause for Congress. Apart from Pinckney, nobody, including Mason and Gerry, considered a Bill of Rights overly important. If the delegates were to add a Bill of Rights to the Constitution, it would be, in effect, an afterthought, dashed off rather quickly. Of course, the final Constitution contained a provision protecting members of Congress "for any Speech or Debate in either House." This type of protection for legislative members had a long history going back to pre–Civil War England. The House of Commons' 1621 Protestation against James I asserted a legislative immunity for speech and debate, and the 1689 English Bill of Rights included an express protection for parliamentary speech and debate. Several of the early American state constitutions had included speech and debate clauses, as did the national Articles of Confederation.[25]

ONCE THE CONVENTION DELEGATES had completed their work, the national debate over ratification began. The Anti-Federalist opponents of the Constitution voiced numerous objections to the proposed document, but their overriding concern was the continuing viability of state sovereignty vis-à-vis the enhanced power of the national government. Even so, the Anti-Federalists quickly realized that their apprehensions might garner the most popular traction if they stressed the lack of a Bill of Rights (which, for many, was also a genuine worry). If the Constitution would vest enormous power in the national government, as the Anti-Federalists feared, then the government could trample many essential individual liberties. A Bill of Rights, the Anti-Federalists therefore argued, was essential to protect those liberties and to prevent governmental tyranny. Over and over again, the Anti-Federalists hammered on this supposed defect in the proposed Constitution and, in doing so, repeatedly stressed that freedom of the press, in particular, was unprotected. For instance, "Cincinnatus" wrote: "I have proved, sir, that not only some power is given in the constitution to restrain, and even to subject the press, but that it is a power totally unlimited; and may certainly annihilate the freedom of the press, and convert it from being the palladium of liberty to become an engine of imposition and tyranny."[26]

The chief Federalist counterargument, first asserted by James Wilson, emphasized the nature of congressional power as delineated in the proposed Constitution. A Bill of Rights was unnecessary, the Federalists maintained, because Congress would be limited to exercising its enumerated powers, such as the power to regulate interstate commerce. Congress would not be invested with a broad or open-ended police power to regulate for the general health and welfare of the people. Consequently, Congress would not be empowered to infringe on individual rights and liberties such as freedom of the press. The energetic and aggressive Alexander Hamilton, always eager to follow his convictions to their logical ends, pushed this argument even further. He audaciously insisted that not only would a Bill of Rights be superfluous but that it would endanger individual rights and liberties. By delineating "exceptions to powers which are not granted," a Bill of Rights "would afford a colorable pretext to claim more than were granted." Power-hungry "men disposed to usurp" would be given a "plausible pretense" for claiming that governmental powers extended over any rights and liberties not expressly protected.[27]

The Anti-Federalists responded by underscoring their primary issue: Congress would be invested with so much power that it would, in fact, be empowered to tyrannize the people. The Anti-Federalists especially feared that the congressional power to tax could be implemented to suppress the freedom of the press. "I am not clear," the "Federal Farmer" worried, "that congress is restrained from laying any duties whatever on printing, and from laying duties particularly heavy on certain pieces printed." Elaborating, he wrote: "Printing, like all other business, must cease when taxed beyond its profits; and it appears to me, that a power to tax the press at discretion, is a power to destroy or restrain the freedom of it."[28]

The Federalists replied: regardless of the details of Congress's enumerated powers, the nature of republican democratic government, combined with the nature of the American people, rendered a Bill of Rights irrelevant. A republican democratic government differs fundamentally from a monarchy. In a monarchy, the subjects need a Bill of Rights to demarcate limits on the monarch's powers, but when the people are sovereign and rule themselves, no such protection is necessary. In a republican democracy, the protection of individual rights and liberties arises primarily from the virtue of the people and their elected representatives. Roger Sherman, writing as a "Countryman," explained that "[t]he only real security that you can have for all your important rights must be in the nature of your government. If you suffer any man to govern you who is not strongly interested in supporting your privileges, you will certainly lose them." If the people and their elected representatives are not sufficiently virtuous, then the "mere paper protection" of a Bill of Rights would be useless. "For, guard such privileges by the strongest expressions, still if you leave the legislative and executive power in the hands of those who are or may be disposed to deprive you of them — you are but slaves."[29]

The Anti-Federalists, naturally, saw things differently. Yes, Americans had republican democratic government — a free government — but freedom of the press was necessary to keep it that way. "As long as the liberty of the press continues unviolated, and the people have the right of expressing and publishing their sentiments upon every public measure, it is next to impossible to enslave a free nation." As the Anti-Federalists repeatedly reminded other Americans, a free press was the "grand palladium of freedom." Besides, the Anti-Federalists asked, if Bill of Rights constraints on governmental power were truly unnecessary, then why did the proposed Constitution contain Article I, section 9, which expressly limited congressional power in numerous ways, such as by prohibiting bills of attainder and ex post facto laws? After all, the constitutional text did not appear to empower Congress to pass bills of attainder or ex post facto laws, so the framers' inclusion of the Article I, section 9, exceptions suggested that the Constitution would give Congress implied powers beyond those expressly enumerated. Given this, the Anti-Federalists asked, why not expressly protect freedom of the press and other fundamental liberties as well?[30]

Among their varied arguments, the Anti-Federalists invoked the lack of protection of free *speech* with striking *infrequency*, though they constantly fretted about freedom of the *press*. Since the Anti-Federalists generally did not use the terms "free speech" and "free press" interchangeably, they apparently considered free press the more important. In fact, when the "Federal Farmer" delineated an exhaustive list of rights and liberties that ought to be included in a Bill of Rights, he failed to include free speech (nowadays, of course, this omission would be considered a stupendous gaffe).[31]

ULTIMATELY, THE STATES ratified and adopted the Constitution, but only after Madison and other Federalist leaders committed to adding a Bill of Rights. Five states had included specific recommendations for a Bill of Rights when ratifying the Constitution. Two additional states, North

Carolina and Rhode Island, had ratified only after the new national government was already in operation, and they had done so also with recommendations for bills of rights. Madison, as a member of the first House of Representatives, therefore introduced to the First Congress, as promised, a draft of a Bill of Rights on June 8, 1789. Once the Federalists initiated the official amendment process, many Anti-Federalists quickly lost their enthusiasm for a Bill of Rights. Regardless, Madison's initial draft included the following provision (call it the national amendment or provision): "The people shall not be deprived or abridged of their right to speak, to write, or to publish their sentiments; and the freedom of the press, as one of the great bulwarks of liberty, shall be inviolable." Furthermore, Madison included an additional provision related to freedom of the press that focused on state governments (call it the state amendment or provision): "No State shall violate the equal rights of conscience, or the freedom of the press, or the trial by jury in criminal cases." The national provision was eventually adopted in modified form as the free speech and free press clauses of the first amendment, while the state provision fell by the wayside.[32]

Given that the ratification debates had stressed a free press and practically ignored free speech per se — and only two state constitutions (Pennsylvania and Vermont) had pure free speech clauses — one must wonder why Madison's proposed protection of free expression (in the national provision) referred to *both* press and speech. One clear answer is political inertia. Four of the seven states that had recommended bills of rights during ratification had included free speech provisions together with free press provisions. All four — Pennsylvania, North Carolina, Rhode Island, and Madison's home state of Virginia — closely modeled their free speech and press recommendations on the 1776 Pennsylvania Declaration of Rights (which Vermont had also followed in its 1777 Constitution): "That the people have a right to freedom of speech, and of writing, and publishing their sentiments; therefore the freedom of the press ought not to be restrained." Perhaps, more important, Madison himself had sat on the special committee created at the Virginia ratifying convention that had subsequently prepared the state's recommended Bill of Rights.[33]

Madison, fully aware of what not only Virginia but also the other states had requested, presented his first draft to the House primarily to pacify the Anti-Federalist opponents of the Constitution. After asserting, with faint praise, that the addition of a Bill of Rights would be "neither improper nor altogether useless," Madison stated "that if Congress will devote but one day to this subject, so far as to satisfy the public that we do not disregard their wishes, it will have a salutary influence on the public councils, and prepare the way for a favorable reception of our future measures." With this purpose, Madison had little to lose and much to gain by including in his draft any reasonable protection that the several state ratifying conventions had requested for a Bill of Rights. Indeed, three days after Madison presented his amendments to the House, Fisher Ames of Massachusetts complained in a letter about the proposed constitutional amendments: "They are the fruit of much labour and research. [Madison] has hunted up all the grievances and complaints of newspapers — all the articles of Conventions — and the small talk of their debates. It contains a Bill of Rights. . . . There is too much of it." Yet, Ames acerbically acknowledged the political advantage likely to be gained, both by the Federalists and by Madison himself: "Upon the whole, it may do good towards quieting men who attend to sounds only, and may get the mover some popularity — which he wishes." If Madison had omitted any significant requested guarantee, such as a right to jury trials, he would likely have sparked hostility and opposition. Gerry was adamant: "I must inform [my congressional colleagues] that I wish *all* the amendments, proposed by the respective states to be considered."[34]

If Madison's inclusion of both press *and* speech in his first draft of the national amendment was due partly to political inertia — he complied with the state recommendations — one must still ask: why had so many states followed the Pennsylvania constitutional model by recommending both free speech *and* free press together? Certainly, greater protection for free expression resonated with the general trend of the times. Recall that the constitutional framers sought to combine the civic republican principles of Revolutionary era Americans with a greater Lockean concern for individual rights and liberties. More consequential from a political standpoint, the first such state to request the addition of a Bill of Rights was Pennsylvania itself. Although Pennsylvania became the second state to ratify (Delaware had been first), the Pennsylvania Anti-Federalists offered strong opposition. Eventually, they moved that the Constitution not be ratified until it included a specifically proposed Bill of Rights, which the Anti-Federalists naturally based on Pennsylvania's own Declaration of Rights. The delegates defeated the Anti-Federalist motion and then ratified the Constitution as presented (forty-six yeas, twenty-three nays). Rather than meekly accepting the majority vote of the state convention, however, the Anti-Federalists issued an Address and Reasons of Dissent of the Minority of the Convention of the State of Pennsylvania to Their Constituents, which included the proposed Bill of Rights. The Pennsylvania Anti-Federalists then disseminated their Dissent in the other states, providing a model for those states (or their dissenters) to recommend the addition of a Bill of Rights. In sum,

Pennsylvania was the first state to recommend a Bill of Rights alongside its ratification of the Constitution; Pennsylvania's recommendation unsurprisingly followed its own state Constitution, which included express protection for both press and speech; and at least some other states followed Pennsylvania's model.[35]

The Pennsylvania constitutional prototype might have especially appealed to Anti-Federalist opponents of the Constitution in other states because it "was the most radical constitution of the Revolutionary era." A demand for a Bill of Rights modeled on the Pennsylvania Declaration of Rights would confront the Federalist supporters of the proposed Constitution with the greatest possible challenge. No slapdash protection of the few "great rights, trial by jury, freedom of the press, [and] liberty of conscience" would do; only the comprehensive protections of the Pennsylvania Constitution would suffice. Specifically, a demand for a typical Bill of Rights protection of a free press was inadequate; a more elaborate protection of free expression was needed. In Madison's home state, Virginia, the special state committee that recommended a Bill of Rights had followed the initial proposal of Patrick Henry, the most aggressive and eloquent Anti-Federalist leader at the Virginia ratifying convention. Vilifying the proposed Constitution, Henry brooded that it "goes to the utter annihilation of the most solemn engagements of the states." Inspired by his oppositional fervor, Henry sought the most comprehensive limits on the national government possible.[36]

In the end, Madison momentously followed those state ratifying conventions that had recommended explicit protection for both a free press and free speech when he presented to Congress his first draft of a Bill of Rights. That first draft became all important because Congress devoted little time and energy to the substance of the various provisions. Many members of Congress considered a Bill of Rights an unnecessary redundancy: it would reiterate what already was understood—that the national government lacked the power to infringe on individual rights and liberties, such as freedom of the press. For many Federalists, the Bill of Rights remained little more than a political bone that they were tossing to the Anti-Federalists, who would, it was hoped, quietly lie down. When Madison initially presented his first draft, numerous representatives, Federalists and Anti-Federalists alike, opined that Congress needed to remain focused on more important matters. "[T]he present time [was] premature [for considering a Bill of Rights]," Benjamin Goodhue of Massachusetts observed typically, "inasmuch as we have other business before us, which is incomplete, but essential to the public interest."[37]

EVENTUALLY, THOUGH, CONGRESS turned to Madison's proposed Bill of Rights. On July 21, 1789, six weeks after Madison had introduced his amendments, the House sent the matter to a Select Committee of eleven members, including Madison. Since numerous Federalists viewed the Bill of Rights as a political offering to the Anti-Federalists, to pacify their oppositional qualms, many Federalists preferred to avoid extensive discussions of substance. Predictably, the bulk of the ensuing congressional deliberations revolved around the form or felicity of phrasing in the various amendments. For instance, on August 15, 1789, when the full House first took up the proposed national amendment on free expression, Theodore Sedgwick of Massachusetts decried the redundant language. "Shall we secure the freedom of speech, and think it necessary, at the same time, to allow the right of assembling? If people freely converse together, they must assemble for that purpose; it is a self-evident, unalienable right which the people possess; it is certainly a thing that never would be called in question; it is derogatory to the dignity of the House to descend to such minutiae." Given such attitudes toward the amendments, the issue whether separate free speech and free press clauses should both be included in a Bill of Rights apparently never became a topic of discussion as the future first amendment moved through the House and Senate. One of the few substantive debates involving free expression — whether the provision for rights of assembly and petition should include a right of the people "to instruct their Representatives" — led to a sarcastic and testy exchange regarding whether Congress was wasting its time. This recommendation, incidentally, was one of the few from the state ratifying conventions that Madison had omitted from his initial proposals. The Anti-Federalist Gerry, wishing to discuss the matter at length, sneered: "Gentlemen say it is necessary to finish the subject, in order to reconcile a number of our fellow-citizens to the government. If this is their principle, they ought to consider the wishes and intentions which the conventions have expressed for them." John Vining responded: "If . . . there appears on one side too great an urgency to despatch this business, there appears on the other an unnecessary delay and procrastination equally improper and unpardonable." The politically shrewd Madison was blunt: simplicity would grease political wheels. "I venture to say," he declared during the congressional debates, "that if we confine ourselves to an enumeration of simple, acknowledged principles, the ratification will meet with but little difficulty."[38]

Congressional passage of the Bill of Rights was an exercise in sluggish politics partly because Congress was not, to a great degree, confronting live concrete issues related to the various protections in the proposed amendments. Current issues, such as import duties, seemed far more significant. Yet, one overarching substantive issue remained critical during the congressional deliberations, especially for the Anti-Federalists: namely, would the Constitution's centralization of power in the national government critically impair state sovereignty? This (federalism) issue, one might recall, had originally led the Anti-Federalists to focus during the ratification debates on the more politically viable question of a Bill of Rights. This overriding concern for state sovereign power helps explain two changes made to Madison's original proposals. Madison had initially proposed two constitutional amendments related to free expression. One (the national provision) referred to both freedom of speech and the press and would eventually become, in modified form, the first amendment, while the other (the state provision) focused explicitly on state governmental power and a free press. The House passed both the national and state provisions, with modifications. The Senate rejected the state amendment, however, and the Conference Committee did not try to resuscitate it. The Senate did not explain its action, but in the House, Thomas Tudor Tucker had worried that the state provision would "interfere" with state government. The second change relating to state sovereignty involved the national provision, which would become the first amendment. The House, Senate, and Conference Committee all modified Madison's initial proposal by juxtaposing different phrases, combining it with other proposed provisions, and smoothing out the language. Most important, the Senate changed the proposal from the passive to the active voice, thus clarifying that the guarantees would apply against only the national government. On September 24 and 25, 1789, both congressional houses concurred in an Agreed Resolution on the final language of a Bill of Rights consisting of twelve articles or amendments. The third article (the future first amendment) read: "Congress shall make no law respecting an establishment of religion, or prohibiting the free exercise thereof, or abridging the freedom of speech, or of the press, or the right of the people peaceably to assemble, and to petition the Government for a redress of grievances."[39]

The Bill of Rights, as resolved by Congress, still required ratification by at least three-fourths of the states (totaling eleven because Vermont had officially joined the Union). In six months, nine states had ratified. Vermont became the tenth, but one more state's approval was needed. In the end, Virginia became the eleventh, but only after a prolonged battle between Federalists and Anti-Federalists. When Virginia finally ratified on December 15, 1791, the Bill of Rights officially became part of the Constitution.

Unfortunately, scant evidence documents the course of the ratification debates in the various states, even Virginia. We do know, of course, that the states rejected the first two proposed articles or amendments, related to the number of representatives and the compensation of senators and representatives. Consequently, the third article moved up ordinally to become the first amendment.[40]

How significant was the framing and ratification of the first amendment, with its express protections for free expression? The lack of extensive discussion about either the meaning of freedom of the press, the meaning of free speech, or the propriety of including protections of either speech, press, or both in the Bill of Rights suggests that the first-amendment adoption did little to clarify or to elaborate the law or the traditions related to free expression. The first-amendment protections of speech and press certainly did not have a determinative meaning. The same ambivalent mix of attitudes toward seditious libel and the freedom to speak one's mind continued unabated. Yet, three important consequences flowed from the framing and ratification processes. First, as Madison and other Federalists had hoped, the Anti-Federalists' popularity shriveled, so opposition to the Constitution, in Jefferson's words, "almost totally disappeared." Second, as some Anti-Federalists had hoped, the debate over the Constitution and a Bill of Rights, as well as the eventual passage of the Bill of Rights, enhanced American sensibilities regarding individual rights and liberties. As the "Federal Farmer" had commented in 1787: "[T]he discussion of [a Bill of Rights] has had a happy effect — it has called forth the able advocates of liberty, and tends to renew, in the minds of the people, their true republican jealousy and vigilance, the strongest guard against the abuses of power." While the "Federal Farmer" feared that this vigilance would quickly diminish in intensity, it still cast light over the next decade, when issues related to free expression came to the forefront. Finally, and perhaps most important, the mere existence of the first amendment, with its protections of speech and press, gave Americans another basis for protesting against governmental efforts at suppression. Madison himself eventually acknowledged that a Bill of Rights provided "additional guards in favour of liberty" by putting, as Jefferson explained to Madison, a "legal check . . . into the hands of the judiciary." Zengerian reforms had already weakened the law of seditious libel and the American tradition of dissent remained vigorous, but now the first amendment placed another arrow, a strong legal one, in the American quiver of liberty, to be used if and when live issues of suppression loomed.[41]

CHAPTER 4

The Sedition Act Controversy

As President George Washington and his administration tackled the problems confronting the young nation, they began implementing and testing the structures of the new constitutional system. The Constitution, they learned, was not a smooth-running machine. The framers had hoped that a qualified elite would be elected and appointed to national offices and would coalesce around a common good. True, the framers had expected factionalism, but they had not foreseen the imbroglios of the 1790s. These disputes became so ferocious that the Federalists, so recently united in support of constitutional ratification, were rent apart into two opposed "proto-parties," the Republicans and the Federalists. Divergent visions of national power, citizenship, and commercial development emerged. Most notably, James Madison and Thomas Jefferson articulated the Republican vision, based on Virginia's agrarianism, while Alexander Hamilton enunciated the Federalist vision, based on the Northeast's mercantilism and incipient industrialism. Both sides believed they represented the common good, but instead of consensus, there was competition and conflict.[1] Eventually, this political turmoil generated battles over free expression, but the overarching struggle of the 1790s was about the operation of republican democracy under the new Constitution. Were the sovereign people, for instance, to deliberate actively and frequently about governmental policies even after electing officials, as Republicans argued, or were the people to concentrate on, first, electing virtuous officials and, then subsequently, pursuing commercial endeavors, as Federalists insisted? At the time, the outcome of this struggle was unclear; more than once, the nation seemed to teeter on the edge of dissolution through either secession or civil war.[2]

POLITICS, EXPRESSION, AND REPUBLICAN DEMOCRACY IN THE 1790S

Political consensus under the new Constitution ruptured in the early 1790s as Congress and the president contemplated the nation's economic straits, partly engendered by national and state debts going back to the Revolutionary War. Hamilton, in his position as secretary of the treasury, devised a "grand design" for a "utopian financial system" that would spur mercantile and industrial development and thus, in Hamilton's opinion, remedy the economic problems. Many Southerners, however, reasonably viewed the plan as favoring the Northeast; this resentment helped to fuse the political interests of wealthy Southern planters and the multitude of small farmers. Madison stepped forward to lead a fight in Congress against the creation of a national bank, a major building block in Hamilton's multifaceted financial plan. Madison opposed the bank for political and practical reasons, including a belief that the nation would benefit more from having numerous state banks rather than a single national bank. Equally important, though, Madison argued against the bank on constitutional grounds by reasoning that Congress lacked the power to incorporate a bank. Despite Madison's arguments, Congress approved the bank measure by voting along sectional lines. Contemplating a veto of the congressional act, the uncertain Washington asked his secretary of state, Jefferson, for his opinion on the bank. Jefferson followed Madison's strict-constructionist reading of the Constitution: Congress must be limited to exercising only those powers expressly enumerated. Congress had not been granted the "power to do whatever would be for the good of the United States." Rather, the Constitution "was intended to lace [Congress] up straitly within the enumerated powers." A power to incorporate a national bank, quite simply, was not within the compass of congressional power.[3]

Washington requested Hamilton to reply. Hamilton articulated a compelling argument for the recognition of implied powers in Congress. He began by reasoning that, as a general matter, a sovereign nation such as the United States has an inherent power to charter corporations. Yet, Hamilton admitted, one must still ask whether the Constitution, which would take precedence over general notions of sovereignty, either granted or refused the national government this power. "It is not denied," Hamilton then insisted, "that there are implied as well as express [constitutional] powers, and that the former are as effectually delegated as the latter." But once one recognizes the existence of implied congressional powers, then one must specify what precise powers are implied. Hamilton articulated a test: "If the end be clearly comprehended within any of the specified [enumerated] powers, and if the measure have an obvious relation to that end, and is not forbidden by any particular provision of the Constitution, it may safely be deemed to come within the compass of the national authority." Hamilton therefore concluded by identifying numerous express congressional ends (or, in other words, powers), including taxing and providing for the common defense, that were closely related to the proposed national bank.[4]

Washington's ultimate decision, not to veto Congress's incorporation of the bank, failed to diminish the strains between Jefferson and Madison, on the one side, and Hamilton, on the other. To the contrary, Republicans and Federalists viewed each other with ever-greater suspicion, each fearing that their respective opponents constituted a factional party bent on destroying the republic. Another plank in Hamilton's financial program, an excise tax on distilled liquor, exacerbated the tensions. After initially rejecting it in 1790, Congress enacted the tax law in 1791, with votes again following sectional lines. Many whiskey distillers, especially in western Pennsylvania, refused to pay the tax, thus leading Hamilton to recommend that the national government forcefully execute the law. Washington declined and instead issued a proclamation in September 1792 condemning opposition to the tax. Two years later, though, as opposition continued, Washington agreed to enforce the law "more energetically." When a federal official joined a local Pennsylvanian to serve writs ordering approximately sixty distillers to appear in court in far-off Philadelphia, the insurgents responded by breaking into and burning the local official's house. The Whiskey Rebellion had taken a violent turn. Hoping to seize military equipment and ammunition, the insurgents planned an attack on Pittsburgh. More negotiations followed, with Washington again deflecting the possible use of troops. Eventually, however, Washington felt compelled to repress the insurrection and ordered the assembly of a fifteen-thousand-man militia. Hamilton enthusiastically led the army, which Washington himself briefly joined. In the face of this show of force, the insurgents scattered.[5]

Even before the Whiskey Rebellion, the political turmoil of the 1790s had forced Americans, governmental officials and ordinary citizens alike, to contemplate how republican democracy could work under the new constitutional system. True, the government should pursue the common good, but what if the elite governmental leaders could not agree about which specific policies represented the common good? Could some leaders legitimately oppose a governmental policy even after Congress and the administration had chosen to follow it? If the people were sovereign, what was the role of ordinary citizens once they had chosen their representatives through elections? Were citizens merely to defer to the decisions of elected officials, or were citizens to adopt a more vigorous and active role in government? The Whiskey Rebellion helped bring these questions to the forefront of the national stage. Soon after the government quashed the insurrection, many of the insurgents "repented" and promised to uphold the law. Nonetheless, Washington committed a strategic error by condemning the local Democratic-Republican societies. These voluntary associations, which had begun springing up around the country, were grassroots organizations that provided forums for ordinary people to discuss governmental policies. Citizen-participants viewed their societies as leagues of "the virtuous"—a new type of government watchdog that implicitly revealed a growing distrust of elite leaders. To the chagrin of Madison and Jefferson, Washington followed the Federalist view: the societies were factional party-like organizations forming, as one newspaper essayist phrased it, "secret cabals and intrigues" bent on derogating "the equal rights of others." Given this, Washington denounced "these self created societies" for supposedly encouraging the Whiskey Rebellion.[6]

The Whiskey Rebellion became the crucible in which the nation's political turmoil began to generate free-expression issues under the developing republican democratic constitutional system. From the Republican standpoint, the people were sovereign, so they should be able to debate the advantages and disadvantages of their government's actions. From the Federalist side, however, the sovereign people elected representatives, and a subsequent lack of support for the representatives' decisions contravened the people's own republican democratic government. To oppose "legitimate government," one Federalist newspaper would declare, "is treason against the People." Washington himself tended to group all opponents of his programs grossly together; any dissent appeared, to him, close to insurrectional. During the months preceding the Whiskey Rebellion, Hamilton had argued that the federal government should criminally punish criticisms of the excise tax as seditious, while the attorney general, Edmund Randolph, insisted that the published attacks did not constitute indictable sedition. In the wake of the Rebellion, Pennsylvania prosecuted a justice of the peace for misdemeanor in office because he had not attempted to prevent the erection of a liberty pole, a symbol of the insurrection. "Though freedom of speech is secured to us by the [state] constitution, yet we are responsible for an abuse of that liberty," the court observed. "The people may meet and discourse on public measures, and the public mind may thus be illustrated and informed; but if they meet for seditious purposes, or when met, go into seditious resolutions, they are amenable to the law."[7]

Many newspapers denounced the Federalists and their implementation of republican democratic government throughout the early to mid-1790s. In essays published in numerous papers, "Gracchus" insisted that "an examination of the conduct of public men is necessary for the preservation of liberty, and should be encouraged and promoted." Yet, Federalists unfairly stigmatized their critics "as foes of tranquility, of union and virtue." According to "Gracchus," Federalists condemned every critic of the Washington "administration" as "an enemy to the Federal Constitution." Republicans especially targeted Hamilton, "the most contemptible secretary of one of the departments," comparing him to "a toad or a cock-roach" and describing his "ruling passion" as an "inordinate desire to aggrandize himself." "Atticus" not only asserted the people's "right . . . to express disapprobation of an iniquitous law" but also argued that if the people were dissatisfied with the Constitution itself, then "who would dispute their right to make another?" Despite such attacks, Federalists continued to disagree about the wisdom of instituting criminal prosecutions for sedition. At the time, most Americans, Federalists and Republicans alike, would have agreed that the state governments retained the power to punish seditious libel, but a national power to act similarly was unclear. Regardless, among Federalists themselves, the disputes over sedition usually focused on the political costs and benefits of prosecutions, not on the legality or constitutionality of such actions. In effect, Federalists recognized the strength of the American tradition of dissent. While the law might permit federal prosecutions, Federalists realized, the tradition of dissent augured caution before taking such action.[8]

Matters only worsened when John Adams succeeded Washington as president. France presented the Adams administration with one of its greatest problems. For most Americans, the beginning of the French Revolution in 1789 had provoked sympathy for the French people. Their revolution and the establishment of a republic appeared to confirm the righteousness of the American Revolution. But when the French Revolution turned violent in 1792 and Great Britain became enmeshed in war against France, many Americans swung against the revolutionaries. Most important, Federalists feared that the French Revolution represented democracy gone mad, exactly the type of populist chaos that Federalists believed Republicans were fomenting in the United States. Republicans, meanwhile, worried that the Federalists' repudiation of France combined with their desire for British trade portended an aristocratic counterrevolution in America. From the Republican perspective, Federalists seemed thinly disguised monarchists. Until the end of the Washington administration, one event after another seemed to suck the nation ever further into the maelstrom of the French and British dispute. Washington officially declared the nation's neutrality, but to be neutral in practice proved difficult. In 1793, France sent to the United States a new minister, Edmond-Charles (Citizen) Genet, who alternately charmed the Americans and outraged them with startling acts of indiscretion, such as deploying "American ports as virtual French naval bases." Britain started in the meantime to detain American ships intent on trading in the French West Indies. Washington, attempting to avoid war, sent Chief Justice John Jay to England to negotiate a compromise of the nations' differences. The resultant Jay Treaty, however, thoroughly polarized the American people because, according to many, it favored the British so much as to subvert American independence. "Gracchus" charged Federalists with attempting "to assimilate our government to the aristocracies of Europe." Jefferson accused Federalists of the baldest party-inspired factionalism, using their control of the presidency and the Senate to push through the treaty despite strong opposition from the Republicans, who had gained a majority in the House. Even the iconic Washington wore down under the ever-increasing political sniping.[9]

Adams, taking office in March 1797, stepped into this foreign and domestic snarl. Often undone by his own contrarian candor, the Federalist Adams nonetheless relished opportunities to strike a virtuous pose above partisan battles. He viewed his election with a Republican vice president, Jefferson, as just such an opportunity, at least initially. And remarkably, for a brief period, the nation appeared to unite behind Adams's bipartisan administration. The terms of the Jay Treaty, favoring Britain, had irked French officials, and in response, they threatened to start seizing American ships (which France already had been doing intermittently for several years). Trying to avoid war, Adams decided to send a three-person negotiating commission to France, but various political machinations over the makeup of the commission quickly drove a new wedge between Adams and Jefferson; national unity ended all too quickly. By the time the commission of Charles Cotesworth Pinckney, John Marshall, and Elbridge Gerry arrived in France in October 1797, war seemed imminent. Increasingly arrogant because of its recent military successes, France had begun consistently seizing American ships — within a year, French privateers had seized more than three hundred American ships — and moreover, France seemed poised to invade England. Even so, relations between France and the United States then took a turn for the worse.[10]

When Pinckney, Marshall, and Gerry reached France, the French foreign minister, Charles-Maurice de Talleyrand-Périgord, rebuffed their efforts to negotiate with him directly and officially. Instead, he sent a series of underlings, later dubbed by the Americans as X, Y, and Z, to issue demands: that the Americans apologize for a speech by Adams, that the Americans extend an exorbitant loan to France, and that the Americans pay a bribe (around $250,000) to French officials. When the administration divulged news of the XYZ affair in the United States — partly in response to misplaced Republican demands — it unloosed a wave of anti-French sentiment. Consequently, Adams's popularity soared uncharacteristically to "dizzying" heights, albeit for a brief few months, and the Federalists recaptured Congress in the next elections. Even many previously pro-French Republicans could not abide France's contemptuous treatment of the American emissaries. During the spring and summer of 1798, Adams would have welcomed an official declaration of war, though he did not openly seek one. He decided, however, to press for an enhanced navy, and by the summer, the United States and France were engaged in an undeclared naval quasi war that would last almost to the end of Adams's presidency.[11]

Adams's popularity declined precipitously because of two actions strongly supported by many Federalists. Hamilton led a group of hawkishly aggressive Federalists, wanting a declared war, who successfully encouraged Congress to create and strengthen a new standing army. Adams readily accepted Washington himself — coming out of retirement — as the commander of the army, but Adams resisted Hamilton's desire to be installed as second-in-command. Nonetheless, Adams's cabinet and Washington pressured him until he relented and appointed Hamilton. Adams then watched moodily as Hamilton, with his typical energy, embraced his new job so enthusiastically that many worried he was building a permanent and unrepublican army. Adams confided to Elbridge Gerry "that he thought Hamilton and a Party were endeavoring to get an army on foot to give Hamilton the command of it & then to proclaim a Regal Government, place Hamilton at the Head of it & prepare the way for a Province of Great Britain." Given such concerns about Hamilton, Adams's desire for an official declaration of war ebbed, so on February 18, 1799, Adams announced to Congress that he would appoint a new minister to France for the purpose of negotiating the two nations' differences. Even though Hamilton had already encountered administrative and financial difficulties in augmenting the army, Adams's announcement and, after much further temporizing, his final decision to send a three-person mission to France fatally defeated Hamilton's military ambitions (whatever precisely they might have been). Regardless, by this time, the buildup of the army and the taxes imposed for that purpose had become exceedingly unpopular.[12]

The second Federalist action that would politically doom Adams was the enactment of four statutes known as the Alien and Sedition Laws.

THE ALIEN AND SEDITION ACTS

By 1797, the law related to free expression had not changed since earlier in the decade, when the Bill of Rights had been adopted. During a state trial, Thomas McKean, now a Republican judge, charged a grand jury as follows: "The liberty of the press is, indeed, essential to the nature of a free State, but this consists in laying no previous restraints upon public actions, and not in freedom from censure for criminal matter, when published. [If one] publishes what is improper, mischievous or illegal, he must take the consequences of his temerity. . . . Thus the will of individuals is still left free; the abuse only of that free will is the object of punishment. Our presses in Pennsylvania are thus free. The common law, with respect to this, is confirmed and established by the Constitution." In short, just before the Alien and Sedition disputes erupted, the Republican McKean followed something akin to the Blackstonian view—the government cannot impose prior restraints but can punish seditious libel. The criminal punishment of writings of a bad or "pernicious tendency" was, McKean explained, "the only solid foundation of civil liberty."[13]

Before 1798, when Federalists had considered the possibility of punishing Republican criticisms of Federalist actions, the discussions had revolved largely around the political advantages and disadvantages. The debates surrounding the Alien and Sedition Laws were no different, at least initially. The issue was politics, not legality. But in 1798, developments in France led Federalists to see a political situation radically unlike that of earlier in the decade. For years, Federalists had associated Republicans with the violent Jacobin excesses of the French Revolution. If Republicans could have their way, Federalists had feared, the United States would spiral uncontrollably into the democratic excesses of French factional insanity. Then, in the wake of the XYZ affair, the Federalists' long-standing distrust of France finally seemed vindicated. And if their views of France were correct, then so were their condemnations of those American Jacobins, the Republicans. Thus, partly due to their commitment to republican democratic principles and partly due to political opportunism, Federalists recognized that the current widespread American disgust with the French presented them with a chance to crush their Republican opposition, once and for all—for the common good of the nation. Republican Senator Theodore Sedgwick excitedly proclaimed that the XYZ affair afforded "a glorious opportunity to destroy faction." Federalists thundered their denunciations of the Republicans. "It is the overthrow of your government and constitution," exclaimed Federalist lawyer Joseph Hopkinson, "it is the disorder and ruin of your country, it is your annihilation as a nation, they seek." On the Fourth of July, the president of Yale, Timothy Dwight, condemned Jefferson himself for seeking to have "the bible cast into a bonfire . . . our wives and daughters the victims of legal prostitution . . . our sons become the disciples of Voltaire, and the dragoons of Marat." As the likelihood of war with France grew and war fever spread across the country, a Boston newspaper exemplified how conceptions of republican democracy, fears of French artifices, and desires for suppression swirled together in the Federalist mind: "Whatever American is a friend to the present administration of the American government, is undoubtedly a true republican, a true patriot. . . . Whatever American opposes the administration is an anarchist, a jacobin and a traitor. . . . It is Patriotism to write in favor of our government — it is Sedition to write against it."[14]

In the summer of 1798, as the House debated the proposed Alien and Sedition bills, South Carolina Federalist Robert Goodloe Harper accused Republican opponents of attempting "to completely stop the wheels of Government, and to lay it prostrate at the feet of its external and internal foes." Counseling caution, Hamilton warned his Federalist compatriots that an unduly harsh sedition law might "endanger civil War." While not opposing enactment, he urged Congress not to "establish a tyranny." He explained that "if we make no false steps we shall be essentially united; but if we push things to an extreme we shall give to faction body and solidarity." Soon after the Alien and Sedition Laws had passed, John Marshall admitted that, if he had been in Congress, "I should have opposed them because I think them useless; and because they are calculated to create unnecessary discontents and jealousies at a time when our very existence, as a nation, may depend on our union." Marshall, though, was the exception — perhaps the only Federalist to advise against the Sedition Act, and that on only political rather than constitutional grounds. Most Federalists echoed Harper's sentiments: Republicans and their supporters constituted a dangerous faction, twisted by a passion for the French, and intent on destroying the American republic.[15]

THE THREE ALIEN LAWS enacted in the summer of 1798 manifested the propensity of republican democracy for facilitating exclusion from the polity. Ominously, moreover, this propensity now combined with a relatively new phenomenon, American nativism, which seemed to blossom with American nationhood. With war imminent, Federalists worried that immigrants threatened American security and civil order. Harrison Gray Otis, a Federalist representative from Massachusetts, unabashedly pronounced the xenophobic character of the Alien Laws. He admitted that "[i]n the infancy of the country it was necessary to encourage emigration, and foreigners of all countries had been wisely invited and allowed to settle in our country." But now, he warned, he did "not wish to invite hordes of wild Irishmen, nor the turbulent and disorderly of all parts of the world, to come here with a view to disturb our tranquility, after having succeeded in the overthrow of their own Governments." In less than one month, Congress passed three laws imposing restrictions on aliens and naturalization.[16]

A fourth statute, the Sedition Act, enacted on July 14, appeared moderate from the Federalists' perspective. The second section of the Act provided for the criminal punishment of any criticisms of the national government or its officials, though supposedly only if the defendant had acted with criminal intent. "[A]ny person [who] shall write, print, utter or publish . . . any false, scandalous and malicious writing or writings against the government of the United States, or either house of the Congress of the United States, or the President of the United States, with intent to defame . . . or to bring them, or either of them, into contempt or disrepute" shall be guilty of sedition and subject to punishment. The third section significantly qualified this definition of seditious libel by fully adopting Zengerian reforms. First, "it shall be lawful for the defendant, upon the trial of the cause, to give in evidence in his defence, the truth of the matter contained in the publication charged as a libel." Second, "the jury who shall try the cause, shall have a right to determine the law and the fact, under the direction of the court, as in other cases." The final section created a time limit for the Act: it would "continue and be in force" only until March 3, 1801, the last day of Adams's presidency unless he was reelected.[17]

The Sedition Act was like the Big Bang. All the ambiguities that had, for decades, swirled around American conceptions of free expression now exploded in the fires of Federalist-Republican political turmoil. Federalists undoubtedly sought to exploit their political advantage by squelching Republican criticisms of the Adams's administration and the Federalist-controlled Congress. By doing so, Federalists hoped to retain their hold on the executive and legislative branches through the next elections. Yet, Federalists were mindful of the American tradition of dissent — of speaking one's mind — and therefore, by including the Zengerian reforms, enacted the most liberal seditious libel statute then imaginable. Even so, Federalists also seemed cognizant of that other American tradition: the tradition of suppression. After all, many Federalists could remember how, during the American Revolution, Patriots harassed and banished Tories for speaking their minds. And now, Federalist mobs repeatedly threatened and attacked Republicans, including congressmen and newspaper editors. So, whereas earlier in the decade, Federalists had hesitated to suppress the Republican opposition, the Federalists of 1798 warmed to the heat of suppression, especially as that tradition now seemed to combust with the exclusionary component of republican democracy. The spark that ignited it all was the political crisis of war. From the Federalist vantage, war against France justified suppression, particularly because Republicans, it appeared, were acting in concert with the French to destroy American republican government.[18]

IN THE MIDST OF THIS political explosion, Republicans and Federalists finally began to formulate an elaborated definition of free expression. The discussions about free speech and free press that one might have expected when the nation adopted the first amendment — but that never took place — now crystallized, within the forge of partisan politics. Congressmen voted along straight party lines: every Federalist voted for the Sedition Act, and every Republican voted against it. The Act attempted to insulate the president and members of Congress from the ravages of criticism, but the Act tellingly failed to encompass within its protections the vice president — the Republican Thomas Jefferson. President Adams himself did not actively seek enactment of the Sedition Act or the Alien Laws, but neither did he affirmatively oppose them. He believed sincerely "that falsehoods or wrong opinions of a bad tendency warranted [punishment]," and he happily anticipated reaping the political benefits that ostensibly would accrue when the government prosecuted his Republican enemies.[19]

In Congress, Connecticut Representative "Long John" Allen, typified the Federalist attitude toward sedition and free expression. "If ever there was a nation which required a [Sedition] law of this kind, it is this. Let gentlemen look at certain papers printed in this city and elsewhere, and ask themselves whether an unwarrantable and dangerous combination does not exist to overturn and ruin the Government by publishing the most shameless falsehoods against the Representatives of the people [and by encouraging the people] to raise an insurrection against the Government." From the Federalist perspective, the national government possessed the power to punish seditious libel in order to protect the common good. Republicans spread lies that encouraged the people to rebel against the legitimate republican democratic government, so Congress acted virtuously by proscribing such harmful speech and writing. The Sedition Act did not violate the Constitution.[20]

While Republicans stood politically unified against the Sedition Law, their views about the interrelationships of the statute, seditious libel, and free expression significantly and rapidly evolved during the crisis. They moved from cautious patience, to jurisdictional attacks on the Law as beyond national governmental power, to expansive declarations of free expression, unprecedented in their depictions of individual freedom from governmental interference with speech or writing.

Little more than a month before the Sedition Law would pass, Jefferson anticipated some such Federalist-inspired antisedition action. Jefferson recommended prudence to his fellow Republicans and particularly discouraged secession from the Union. "A little patience," Jefferson wrote, "and we shall see the reign of witches pass over, their spells dissolve, and the people, recovering their true sight, restore their government to it's true principles." He remained optimistic that the people would recognize the Republicans' virtue and the Federalists' corruption. "[O]ur present situation is not a natural one. The body of our countrymen is substantially republican through every part of the Union. It was the irresistable influence & popularity of Gen'l Washington, played off by the cunning of Hamilton, which turned the government over to anti-republican hands, or turned the republican members, chosen by the people, into anti-republicans." Soon after Jefferson had penned this letter, Congress was openly debating a Sedition Law, and Jefferson's patience had worn thin. "[T]his bill and the alien bill," Jefferson wrote to Madison, "are so palpably in the teeth of the Constitution as to show [the Federalists] mean to pay no respect to it." During the House debates, Republican Albert Gallatin of Pennsylvania asked "how [according to the Federalists] has that seditious spirit been exhibited?" He impatiently denounced the Federalists' factional self-protection. Their antisedition bill deemed "that whoever dislikes the measures of Administration and of a temporary majority in Congress, and shall, either by speaking or writing, express his disapprobation and his want of confidence in the men now in power, is seditious, is an enemy, not of Administration, but of the Constitution."[21]

But Gallatin, like Jefferson and apparently all their contemporaries, failed to recognize how their image of the Federalists mirrored the Federalist image of the Republicans. From both sides of the dispute, the other side appeared to be an illegitimate faction plotting to undermine the nation's republican government. With hindsight, we can see that one reason for the intensity of mutual distrust was the lack of a two-party (or multiparty) system, which would not become an accepted component of republican democratic government for another three decades. In a two-party system, vigorous opposition to those controlling the government is expected (though rarely welcomed); opposition is legitimated. Without such a system, party equaled faction—corruption, self-interest, and danger. Gallatin thus accused the Federalists of being a "party" who aimed to subvert the constitutional government by corruptly securing their own power. "If you put the press under any restraint in respect to the measures of members of Government; if you thus deprive the people of the means of obtaining information of their conduct," Gallatin explained, "you in fact render their right of electing nugatory; and this bill must be considered only as a weapon used by a party now in power, in order to perpetuate their authority and preserve their present places."[22]

Very quickly, Republicans settled upon a jurisdictional attack as their primary grievance against the Sedition Law. Just as Madison and Jefferson, when arguing against the chartering of the national bank, had insisted that Congress must be limited to its expressly enumerated powers, Republicans now argued similarly against the Sedition Act. Moreover, the first amendment had been adopted, in the words of the Virginian John Nicholas, "to quiet the alarms of the people," to reassure and reiterate that Congress did not have power to restrict speech and writing. The potential significance of the first amendment now became apparent: the express constitutional protection of free speech and a free press did not create a unique rationale for protesting against governmental suppression but rather bolstered a legal argument that Republicans would have asserted regardless (with or without the first amendment). In the House debates, Nicholas proclaimed that he "looked in vain amongst the enumerated powers given to Congress in the Constitution, for an authority to pass a law like the present; but he found [only] what he considered as an express prohibition against passing it." If Congress claimed the power to punish speech or writing, Edward Livingston of New York insisted, it would create "a principle which goes to the destruction of State authorities, and makes [the Constitution] mean anything or nothing." Yet, Livingston declared that the Republican position did not imply that libels would go unpunished. "But, it is said, will you suffer a printer to abuse his fellow-citizens with impunity, ascribing his conduct to the very worst of motives? Is no punishment to be inflicted on such a person? Yes," Livingston answered his own rhetorical questions. "There is a remedy for offences of this kind in the laws of every State in the Union.

Every man's character is protected by law, and every man who shall publish a libel on any part of the Government, is liable to punishment."[23]

This jurisdictional (or federalism) argument — that the states but not the national government had the power to punish seditious libel — emerged to become the Republicans' main critique of the Sedition Act because it reverberated with a broader Republican agenda: national power must be circumscribed to ensure the continued vitality of state sovereignty. No less so than the Federalists, the Republicans believed that the punishment of seditious libel remained consistent with the tenets of republican democracy. The constitutional disagreement was about which government, state or national, possessed the sovereign power — the jurisdiction — to punish sedition, not whether sedition could be punished in the first place. Even so, the jurisdictional grievance was not the Republicans' only one. For instance, Gallatin noted that the Zengerian reform allowing truth as a defense, which was incorporated in the proposed Sedition Law, could save a defendant only if the alleged libelous statement was a matter of fact. In the likely event that the statement was more a matter of opinion, then it would be difficult to prove either true or false. More important, some Republicans alluded to an argument that had roots in "Cato's Letters," had been reiterated recently by the Anti-Federalists, and that resonated with the American tradition of dissent. Generally, the people have a right to speak their minds, and more specifically, free government requires free expression. The press, in particular, must be free to supply the people with information, both praiseworthy and critical, about the government and its officials, if the people are to be able to participate intelligently in their own governance. Nicholas declared that the press provides "the only means by which the people can examine and become acquainted with the conduct of persons employed in their Government." In a republican democracy, in other words, the press functions as a Fourth Estate, as an unofficial fourth branch of government scrutinizing the three official branches (the executive, legislative, and judicial)—a function that some American newspapers had been claiming for themselves since the early 1790s. The press, as such, served the sovereign people by alerting them to the virtues and vices of their elected officials. Gallatin, arguing similarly, asserted that tyrants sought "to prevent the diffusion of knowledge [so as] to throw a veil on their folly or their crimes." But governmental leaders "of elevated minds [and] pure motives . . . listened to animadversions made on their conduct." Such rulers "knew that the proper weapon to combat error was truth, and that to resort to coercion and punishments in order to suppress writings attacking their measures, was to confess that these could not be defended by any other means." Gallatin here echoed John Milton: as a response to malicious falsehoods, truthful counterspeech in the marketplace of ideas, as it would eventually be called, was far more effective than governmental coercion.[24]

Once Congress passed the Sedition Act, Republicans followed their own jurisdictional argument by, in effect, seeking refuge beneath the ostensible protections of state sovereign power. Some Southerners muttered about secession, and Virginia even began military preparations, with Hamilton threatening to send federal troops to test Virginia's resolve. As a formal matter, Kentucky and Virginia soon issued legislative resolutions to protest the Alien and Sedition Laws. Jefferson secretly wrote a first draft of the Kentucky Resolutions (he actually wrote it initially for North Carolina), which Kentucky adopted on November 10, 1798, though only after the legislative sponsor had softened Jefferson's radical assertion of state supremacy. Even so, Kentucky still followed Jefferson's strong avowal of state sovereignty: "[B]y compact, under the style and title of a Constitution . . . and of amendments thereto, [the several states] constituted a general government for special purposes, delegated to that government certain definite powers, reserving, each state to itself, the residuary mass of right to their own self-government." Whenever the national government attempted to act beyond its enumerated powers, its actions were "unauthoritative, void, and of no force." Focusing on free expression, Kentucky then resolved that "no power over the . . . freedom of speech, or freedom of the press, being delegated to the United States by the Constitution, nor prohibited by it to the states, all lawful powers respecting the same did of right remain, and were reserved to the states, or to the people." Consequently, it followed, the Sedition Act was illegal and void. Yet, the states retained "to themselves the right of judging how far the licentiousness of speech, and of the press, may be abridged without lessening their useful freedom." In sum, the Kentucky legislature concluded that the Alien and Sedition Laws attacked "republican governments" and provided a dangerous pretext "for those who wish it to be believed that man cannot be governed but by a rod of iron."[25]

The Virginia Resolutions, drafted by Madison, began conservatively, emphasizing that Virginia supported the Constitution and government of the United States. But then, like the Kentucky Resolutions, Madison described the national government "as resulting from [a] compact to which the states are parties." The national government's "powers" were therefore "limited . . . by the grants enumerated in that compact." If the national government attempted to act beyond its enumerated powers, then the states "have the right, and are in duty bound, to interpose, for arresting the progress of the evil." Congress, of late, had illegitimately attempted to expand its power so as "to transform the present republican system of the United States into an absolute, or, at best, a mixed monarchy." Members of Congress were self-interestedly corrupting the republican democratic system rather than virtuously pursuing the common good. Most specifically, Congress violated the Constitution when it enacted the Sedition Act. Congress had claimed "a power not delegated by the Constitution, but, on the contrary, expressly and positively forbidden by one of the amendments thereto, — a power which, more than any other, ought to produce universal alarm, because it is levelled against the right of freely examining public characters and measures, and of free communication among the people thereon, which has ever been justly deemed the only effectual guardian of every other right."[26]

Predictably, the Republican-inspired Kentucky and Virginia Resolutions sparked angry Federalist responses. The most moderate Federalist statement came in the form of a minority report from the Virginia legislature, written probably by John Marshall. Marshall (assuming he was the author) reasoned that not only was the Sedition Act constitutional, but protection of the government from calumny and slander promoted the common good. First, Marshall dismissed the Miltonian view that truth would overcome falsehood in a marketplace of ideas. "It is vain to urge that truth will prevail, and that slander, when detected, recoils on the calumniator. [Experience proves] that a continued course of defamation will at length sully the fairest reputation, and will throw suspicion on the purest conduct." Second, and more important, Marshall reprised James Wilson's argument — initially articulated before ratification of the first amendment — regarding republican democracy and freedom of the press. "To publish malicious calumnies against government itself," Marshall wrote, "is a wrong on the part of the calumniator, and an injury to all those who have an interest in the government." Thus, precisely because the people provided the sovereign foundation for republican democratic government in the United States, sedition injured the people themselves. "The people of the United States have a common interest in their government, and sustain in common the injury which affects that government. The people of the United States therefore have a right to the remedy for that injury, and are substantially the party seeking redress." The Sedition Act did not violate the first amendment, Marshall explained, if one had a proper understanding of freedom of the press. He then proffered, for that era, a perfectly reasonable definition — one that differed little from that given by the Republican Thomas McKean less than two years earlier. According to Marshall, freedom of the press "signifies a liberty to publish, free from previous restraint, any thing and every thing at the discretion of the printer only, but not the liberty of spreading with impunity false and scandalous slanders which may destroy the peace and mangle the reputation of an individual or of a community."[27]

Every Northern state rebuked Kentucky and Virginia with resolutions of their own. The Rhode Island Resolution typified these harsh responses. The Rhode Island legislature speared Virginia, in particular, on the horns of a dilemma: by assuming a power to interpose and to condemn Congress's Alien and Sedition Acts as unconstitutional and therefore void, the Virginia legislature itself violated the Constitution. The federal courts, not the state legislatures, possessed the constitutional power to judge the constitutionality of congressional acts. To underscore its point and to demonstrate appropriate state behavior, the Rhode Island legislators then declared "that, in their *private* opinions, [the Alien and Sedition Laws] are within the powers delegated to Congress, and promotive of the welfare of the United States."[28]

REGARDLESS OF WHETHER the Federalists or the Republicans had the best arguments, Federalists enthusiastically implemented the Sedition Act in an effort to stamp out Republican opposition. In all, the government brought at least fourteen prosecutions under the Act, thirteen of which produced convictions. Despite this high percentage of successful prosecutions, the Federalist actions ultimately proved politically disastrous. Whether it was the overbearing Federalist handling of the prosecutions or the mere enactment of the Alien and Sedition Laws in the first place, Federalists managed to alienate voters sufficiently to sweep the Republicans into control of the presidency and Congress.[29]

The first Sedition Act prosecution to be litigated was against a Republican member of Congress, Matthew Lyon of Vermont. An Irish immigrant and a Republican in Federalist-dominated New England, the bombastic and uncouth Lyon provided an attractive target. Elected to the House in 1797, Lyon immediately became embroiled in controversy. Roger Griswold, a Federalist representative, overheard Lyon maligning the people and politicians of Connecticut, Griswold's home state. When Griswold retaliated by accusing Lyon of cowardice during the Revolutionary War, Lyon spat in his tormentor's face. The infuriated Griswold stormed out, bought a cane, and returned to the House to beat Lyon, who seized a pair of fire tongs and returned the blows. Based on this incident, Federalists attempted but failed to expel from Congress "the Spitting Lyon of Vermont" (Griswold went undisciplined). Lyon, however, exposed himself to further Federalist harassment by writing a letter to a newspaper with passages that fit neatly within the strictures of the Sedition Act (Lyon's letter was written before but published after the Act's passage). In reference to Adams's preparations for war, Lyon wrote that "when I see every consideration of the public welfare swallowed up in a continual grasp for power, in an unbounded thirst for ridiculous pomp, foolish adulation, or selfish avarice . . . I shall not be their humble advocate." Then, after the enactment of the Sedition Act, Lyon worsened matters by quoting from an American living in Europe who had written that Adams's dealings with France suggested Congress should have sent the president "to a mad house." Lyon was indicted under the Sedition Act on October 5, 1798. The trial started only three days later, with Lyon representing himself.[30]

The presiding judge, U.S. Supreme Court Justice William Paterson, brushed aside Lyon's argument that the Sedition Act was unconstitutional, and the jury returned a guilty verdict. Lyon had expected a light sentence, but Paterson imposed a $1,000 fine and four months imprisonment. A federal marshal immediately dragged Lyon to a jail far from his home. He was dumped into a freezing cell, to be shared with vagrants and felons, that was without heat or glass windows. It contained a latrine that emitted "a stench about equal to the Philadelphia docks in the month of August." While Federalists celebrated their victory and the seeming destruction of Lyon's career, they unwittingly transformed him into a martyr. Despite his shortcomings, Lyon was a well-respected and wealthy Vermonter, married to the governor's daughter. His case became a *cause célèbre* around the nation, with Virginia's Republican Senator Stevens Mason helping to raise the money to pay Lyon's fine. While still in prison, Lyon was reelected to Congress, polling nearly twice as many votes as his Federalist challenger.[31]

SINCE FEDERALISTS VIEWED the Sedition Law as a legitimate mechanism for battling the corrupt schemes of a factional party, they shamelessly sought to silence the opposition press at the most opportune political moment. To that purpose, Adams's secretary of state, Thomas Pickering, initiated Sedition Act prosecutions against the leading Republican newspapers during the summer of 1799, as the next electoral season approached. On June 29, 1799, Republican editor and lawyer Thomas Cooper targeted himself for Federalist scorn by publishing an editorial that criticized the president. On July 12, he republished it in one of the Republicans' preeminent papers, the *Philadelphia Aurora*. While Adams and Pickering debated the propitiousness of a prosecution, Cooper continued to antagonize. Philadelphia and Boston newspapers had carried Federalist responses alleging that Cooper had written his editorial because the president had refused to appoint him to an official position. In reply, Cooper wrote a handbill in early November 1799. He admitted applying to Adams for a position but explained that "[a]t that time [Adams] had just entered into office. He was hardly in the infancy of political mistake. Even those who doubted his capacity thought well of his intentions." But now, Cooper continued (in the handbill), the nation was "saddled with the expense of a permanent navy, [and threatened] with the existence of a standing army." Moreover, Cooper claimed that Adams had improperly interfered "to influence the decisions of a court of justice," to the detriment of an American who had been "forcibly impressed by the British."[32]

On April 9, 1800, Federalist District Attorney William Rawle initiated a Sedition Act prosecution based on the handbill. Justice Chase and Judge Richard Peters presided at Cooper's trial, attended by numerous Federalist luminaries, including two senators, the secretaries of war and the navy, and Representative Harper, who had drafted part of the Sedition Act. In fact, the secretary of state, Pickering, joined the judges on the bench! Cooper represented himself, and in his address to the jury, he initially seemed to accept the power of the national government to punish seditious libel, though he proclaimed his innocence under the Sedition Act. "I shall . . . prove to your satisfaction," he argued, "that I have published nothing which truth will not justify. That the assertions for which I am indicted are free from malicious imputation, and that my motives have been honest and fair." Regardless, Cooper soon questioned the propriety of governmental efforts to restrict expression. First, he reiterated the Miltonian argument that truth is the best response to falsehoods: "whether my opinions are right or wrong, . . . I cannot help thinking they would have been better confuted by evidence and argument then by indictment." Second, and more important, he suggested that republican democracy requires free expression, though in doing so, Cooper followed the fashion of his times by accusing his Federalist opponents of being guilty of "the grossest misconduct"—that is, corrupt and bereft of virtue. "Nor do I see how the people can exercise on rational grounds their elective franchise, if perfect freedom of discussion of public characters be not allowed," Cooper stated. "Electors are bound in conscience to reflect and decide who best deserves their suffrage; but how can they do it, if these prosecutions in *terrorem* close all the avenues of information, and throw a veil over the grossest misconduct of our periodical rulers?" The prosecuting attorney, Rawle, responded by painting a different picture of republican democracy. Whereas Cooper had argued that free expression provides a necessary conduit between the sovereign people and their elected representatives, Rawle suggested instead that the people must show greater deference to their elected virtuous officials. Contrary to Cooper, Rawle emphasized that "the president of the United States, to whom this country has thought proper to confide its most important interests, is best qualified to judge whether the measures adopted by our government are calculated to preserve the peace and promote the happiness of America."[33]

When Chase charged the jury, he favored Rawle's position and unmistakably wanted a conviction. Like John Marshall in the Virginia minority report, Chase agreed with James Wilson's view that the structures of republican democracy did not diminish but rather strengthened the justification for punishing seditious libel. "[O]urs is a government founded on the opinions and confidence of the people. The representatives and the president are chosen by the people. It is a government made by themselves; and their officers are chosen by themselves," Chase explained. "Our government, therefore, is really republican; the people are truly represented, since all power is derived from them. It is a government of representation and responsibility. All officers of the government are liable to be displaced or removed, or their duration in office limited by elections at fixed periods." Because republican democratic government rests on popular sovereignty and public opinion, Congress had wisely chosen to punish seditious statements that might warp public perceptions and undermine the people's elected representatives. "If a man attempts to destroy the confidence of the people in their officers, their supreme magistrate, and their legislature, he effectually saps the foundation of the government. A republican government can only be destroyed in two ways; the introduction of luxury, or the licentiousness of the press. This latter is the more slow, but most sure and certain, means of bringing about the destruction of the government." In short, a libelous attack on elected officials equaled an attack on the people themselves. The jury returned a guilty verdict, and Chase sentenced Cooper to a $400 fine, six months imprisonment, and payment of a $2,000 bond to assure his "good behaviour" after his release.[34]

CONSEQUENCES OF THE
SEDITION ACT PROSECUTIONS

The numerous successful prosecutions against Republicans produced two effects that Federalists failed to anticipate. First, Republicans articulated new and far more expansive views of free expression that further undermined the Sedition Act and the concomitant prosecutions. Second, Republicans rode a political backlash against the Federalists into control of the national executive and legislative branches.

The Republicans' movement from a primary reliance on the jurisdictional argument against the Sedition Act to a more expansive vision of free expression crystallized in Madison's writings. On January 23, 1799, Madison issued an address to the Virginia state legislature to accompany the recently passed Virginia Resolutions. Madison argued against the Sedition Act, but like other Republicans at the time, he did so primarily on jurisdictional grounds. When the nation adopted the Constitution, Madison explained, "the State sovereignties were only diminished by [national] powers specifically enumerated, or necessary to carry the specified powers into effect." But Federalists wrongly claimed that national power can be "deduced from implication." Thus, "[t]he sedition act is the offspring of these tremendous pretensions," which inflict a death-wound on the sovereignty of the States." Madison, at this point, at least suggested the possibility of a more expansive protection of freedom of the press. Judges and scholars, over the years, had often harmonized the punishment of seditious libel with a free press by a simple argument: seditious libel punished the licentiousness but not the liberty of the press. But Madison now denounced "[t]he sophistry of a distinction," articulated only by those with an "insatiable . . . love of power." Madison's critique of the liberty-licentiousness dichotomy, it would seem, undermined the foundation for punishing seditious libel, but Madison apparently did not intend as much. While he argued that the national government could not punish seditious libel, he did not hesitate to maintain that states retained jurisdictional power over this crime: "Every libellous writing or expression might receive its punishment in the State courts."[35]

Just under a year later, in response to the Northern states' criticisms of the Virginia Resolutions, Madison wrote a Report on the Alien and Sedition Acts, which the Virginia legislature adopted on January 7, 1800. Madison began by reiterating some familiar themes. The Constitution, as originally adopted, did not grant Congress the power to enact the Sedition Act, and the first amendment reaffirmed that limitation. If Federalists were nonetheless allowed to expand Congress's powers, Madison feared, "the obvious tendency and inevitable result . . . would be, to transform the republican system of the United States into a monarchy." When Madison delved further into the meaning of liberty of the press, however, he started to explore new ground. True, the common law proscribed prior restraints while allowing the criminal punishment of seditious libel, but this "can never be admitted to be the American idea" of a free press. "[A] law inflicting penalties on printed publications," Madison elaborated, "would have a similar effect with a law authorizing a previous restraint on them. It would seem a mockery to say, that no law should be passed, preventing publications from being made, but that laws might be passed for punishing them in case they should be made." The common law, in other words, did not conclusively define liberty of the press, at least in America. Madison now realized that the different forms of government in Great Britain and the United States might engender different conceptions of a free press. Under the British parliamentary monarchy, where Parliament is "omnipotent," freedom of the press is justifiably understood to limit the monarch's prerogative. The monarch cannot impose a licensing requirement or prior restraint on printers, but Parliament's power is unlimited. Therefore, Parliament, if it wishes, can impose criminal punishment for seditious libel. But in the United States, "[t]he people . . . possess the absolute sovereignty." Consequently, Madison reasoned, "[t]he legislature, no less than the executive, is under limitations of power. Encroachments are regarded as possible from the one, as well as from the other." To be sure, then, in the United States, the executive cannot prescribe prior restraints, but just as surely, the legislature can neither impose prior restraints nor criminally punish libel after publication. The "security of the freedom of the press," Madison explained, "must be an exemption not only from the previous inspection of licensers, but from the subsequent penalty of laws." In America, executives and legislatures, "both being elective, are both responsible [to the people]." Republican democratic government, Madison now suggested, required free expression. The "essence" of free government is the right to elect officials. But the merits and faults of incumbents and candidates for office "can only be determined by a free examination thereof, and a free communication among the people thereon." The Sedition Act, Madison worried, would provide "those in power . . . an undue advantage" in the upcoming elections. "[B]y impairing the right of election," the Sedition Act "endangers the blessings of [republican democratic] government."[36]

Madison's argument might mean that republican democracy is always inconsistent with the punishment of seditious libel, whether the national government or the *state governments* sought to exercise criminal jurisdiction. Such a limitation on state power would be in tension with the Republicans' general concern for protecting state sovereignty. Did Madison, then, intend to maintain that even the state governments could not legally proscribe seditious libel? While much of his text suggested as much, he never explicitly reached this conclusion. Madison stressed, in particular, the practices rather than the laws in the states. "In every state, probably, in the Union,"

Madison wrote, "the press has exerted a freedom in canvassing the merits and measures of public men, of every description, which has not been confined to the strict limits of the common law. On this footing, the freedom of the press has stood; on this footing it yet stands." In other words, the American tradition of dissent, of speaking one's mind, was at least as, if not more, important as the law itself. Moreover, this tradition, when applied specifically to the press, accounted for the press's function as the Fourth Estate; the press alerted the people to the virtues and vices of their elected officials. Regardless of the law, the tradition or practice in the states had been to suffer the occasional libel so that the press could continue to fulfill its crucial function in republican democratic government. "Some degree of abuse is inseparable from the proper use of every thing, and in no instance is this more true than in that of the press." Finally, Madison added, governmental officials, whether at the national or state level, could always seek a civil remedy "for their injured reputations . . . in the same [state] tribunals, which protect their lives, their liberties, and their properties." A civil action for defamation was clearly permissible even if a criminal prosecution for seditious libel was not.[37]

What factors led Republicans like Madison to move so quickly from a jurisdictional argument against the Sedition Act to an expansive view of free expression grounded on republican democracy? Most significantly, Federalists had written the Sedition Act to encompass the most liberal protections imaginable in a statutory proscription of seditious libel. The Act not only appeared to require the prosecutor to prove the defendant's criminal intent but also incorporated the Zengerian reforms — truth was a defense, and juries were to decide whether the disputed speech was libelous. Given that the Federalists had written such a liberal statute, the Republicans scrambled to discover new arguments attacking the Federalist efforts at suppression. Republicans could not indignantly demand the inclusion of Zengerian reforms — when Federalists had already given them. The Republicans' struggle immediately led them to use the convenient jurisdictional argument — that the states but not the national government had the power to punish seditious libel — but given more time and motivation, Republicans began to develop a broader definition of free expression.[38]

The Zengerian reforms in the Sedition Act failed in practice to protect targeted Republicans; Federalists successfully prosecuted one after another. The statutory clause allowing the defendant to prove truth as a defense provided no refuge in many cases because the allegedly libelous statements seemed more a matter of opinion than a matter of fact. Recall, Matthew Lyon had been prosecuted for calling Adams pompous and foolish — assertions that he could not readily prove either true or false. Furthermore, the Sedition Act clause providing for jury decisions extended far less protection to defendants than recent history might have suggested. During the late-colonial and Revolutionary eras, American juries typically shielded sedition defendants who had criticized the British; jurors refused either to indict or to convict, regardless of the apparent strength of the case based on the law and the facts. During the late 1790s, however, Federalist prosecutors, judges, and marshals could easily find sufficient numbers of loyal Federalist citizens to stock grand and petit juries to secure convictions in Sedition Act cases. Moreover, regardless of the language in the Sedition Act, Federalist judges often drew upon the common law in their trial rulings and jury instructions. Judges could shape jury instructions, in particular, to influence sympathetic juries to convict Republican defendants. While the Act appeared to place the burden on the government to prove that a defendant's allegedly libelous writing was "false, scandalous and malicious," jury instructions often provided otherwise. In the trial of Thomas Cooper, for example, Chase charged the jury as follows: "the traverser in his defence must prove every charge he has made to be true; he must prove it to the marrow." In the end, the Federalists' attacks forced many Republican newspapers to shut down.[39]

When confronted with the seeming Federalist successes under the Sedition Act, Republicans regrouped to develop more imaginative and forceful views of free expression. Madison was neither the first nor the only Republican to do so. In February 1799, when Congress debated whether to repeal the Sedition Act, Nicholas issued a minority report for the Republicans. Written nearly a year before Madison would write his Report on the Alien and Sedition Acts, this minority report anticipated many of Madison's arguments. Like Madison, Nicholas stopped short of expressly denying states the sovereign power to punish seditious libel, but other Republicans took that step. In January 1799, almost simultaneously with Nicholas's issuance of his House minority report, George Hay published his brief (thirty-page) tract, "An Essay on the Liberty of the Press," the first theoretical exposition by an American of an expansive, even libertarian, concept of free expression. Hay argued that the traditional distinction between licentiousness and liberty was too nebulous to delineate the boundaries for freedom of the press. He then explained the concept of liberty: "The absolute freedom . . . is the power uncontrouled by law, of doing what he pleases, provided he does no injury to any other individual. If this definition of freedom be applied to the press, as surely it ought to be, the press . . . may do whatever it pleases to do, uncontrouled by any law, taking care however to do no injury to any individual." While Nicholas and Madison would also articulate expansive conceptions of free expression, Hay's was qualitatively different. Partly because both Nicholas and Madison derived their expansive notions of free expression primarily from the nature of republican democracy, they described a freedom oriented toward government and politics. The press was protected because of its function as the Fourth Estate, scrutinizing the conduct of governmental officials, while ordinary citizens' liberties revolved around their need for information enabling them to evaluate officials and candidates. Hay, meanwhile, seemed to describe a more libertarian conception of free expression — a liberty grounded on an inherent right of the autonomous individual to do as he or she pleases, free of governmental constraints. Hay's concept of freedom is rooted more in Lockean liberalism than in civic republicanism. "A man may say every thing which his passion can suggest; he may employ all his time, and all his talents, if he is wicked enough to do so, in speaking against the government matters that are false, scandalous, and malicious."[40]

But Hay repeatedly asserted that, despite his libertarian concept of freedom, one should take care "to do no injury to any individual." What did he mean with this qualification? "This injury," he explained, "can only be by slander or defamation, and reparation should be made for it in a state of nature as well as in society." Reparation? Was this a backdoor to allowing the criminal punishment of seditious libel? No. Hay introduced two distinctions that clarified his meaning. First, he distinguished the common law from legislation. Common law restrictions on expression might sometimes be permissible, but legislative restrictions never were. Freedom of the press, for example, means "total exemption of the press from legislative controul." Second, under the common law, Hay distinguished civil actions for defamation of private character, which are permissible, from criminal prosecutions for seditious libel, which are never legal or acceptable. For Hay, then, even state governments lacked the power to punish libels through criminal prosecutions.[41]

SHORTLY AFTER MADISON wrote his Report on the Alien and Sedition Acts, Tunis Wortman published *A Treatise Concerning Political Enquiry, and the Liberty of the Press*. Unlike Hay, with his brief thirty-page essay, Wortman developed his ideas in a comprehensive book-length tract. Crucially, Wortman elaborated the connection between republican democracy and an expansive free expression. He thus did not base free expression on a libertarian concept of the autonomous and unconstrained individual, as Hay had done, though Wortman nonetheless stressed the individual as a source of energy and ideas. "Society does not constitute an intellectual unity . . . [E]ach of its members necessarily retains his personal identity and his individual understanding." On issues of public concern, "it is the individual who is to reflect and decide." Moreover, characteristic of Republican tendencies in general, Wortman placed an antielitist spin on his individualism. Society should trust in the judgment of the common person, not just in the elite intellectuals. "Knowledge is not a rare and uncommon gem which a few are destined to monopolize: on the contrary, its treasures are susceptible of universal communication." Given Wortman's emphasis on an antielitist individualism, his theory of free expression resonated with Hay's libertarianism. For instance, Wortman explained: "Of all the rights which can be attributed to man, that of communicating his sentiments is the most sacred and inestimable. It is impossible that the imagination should conceive a more horrible and pernicious tyranny than that which would restrain the Intercourse of Thought."[42]

Wortman linked his individualism to the Miltonian idea that truth will overcome falsehoods in the marketplace of ideas. One cannot "combat Falsehood with Force," Wortman explained. "Coercion may, indeed, be adequate to the purposes of punishment: but it never can be rendered the instructor of mankind." Yet, "[r]eason and [a]rgument, whenever they are properly applied, possess the power of penetrating into every understanding." To Wortman, the marketplace of ideas allowed the unimpeded individual to advance personally, to the greater good of society:

The formation of general opinion upon correct and salutary principles, requires the unbiassed exercise of individual intellect; neither prejudice, authority, or terror, should be suffered to impede the liberty of discussion; no undue influence should tyrannize over mind; every man should be left to the independent exercise of his reflection; all should be permitted to communicate their ideas with the energy and ingenuousness of truth. In such a state of intellectual freedom and activity, the progress of mind would infallibly become accelerated; we would derive improvement from the knowledge and experience of our neighbour; and the wisdom of society would be rendered a general capital, in which all must participate. Exposed to the incessant attack of Argument, the existence of Error would be fleeting and transitory; while Truth would be seated upon a basis of adamant, and receive a perpetual accession to the number of her votaries.[43]

Yet, Wortman's theory of free expression ultimately arose from his ideas about republican democratic government. Thus, Wortman was not merely concerned with truth in general, he focused on truth in the political realm. "Public Good must constitute the exclusive object to the attainment of which our enquiries should ultimately be directed," he explained. "If it is the province of Investigation to enlighten the public mind, and destroy the abuses of Political Institution, it should be assiduously cherished, and esteemed as the most powerful benefactor of mankind." A government that seeks to achieve the common good, that pursues the truth, should encourage free and open discussion. "The government which is founded upon the adamant of truth, has nothing to fear from the progress of political discussion. It is the interest of such government to solicit, instead of eluding observation." The corollary of this theoretical position was that governmental interference with the free exchange of ideas can lead only to mischief and abuse. "The history of prosecutions for libel will constantly furnish us with the lesson, That Governments are impatient of contradiction; that they are not so zealous to punish Falsehood from an enlightened and disinterested attachment to Justice, as they are ready to smother opinions that are unfavorable to their designs." Wortman therefore concluded that the criminal punishment of libel is never permissible, even for state governments. In all situations, "[p]ublic prosecutions for libels are . . . more dangerous to Society than the misrepresentation which they are intended to punish." To be sure, the government retains the power to punish "every act of open disorder," to prosecute criminal conduct. But if an individual, instead of taking action, malevolently spreads falsehoods, governmental officials can do no more than attempt to provide information to the people so that the truth will become evident. As was true with Hay, though, Wortman allowed that a government official could institute a civil action in state court for defamation of his private character.[44]

All in all, Wortman presented a comprehensive and expansive theory of free expression, grounded on republican democracy yet linked closely to an antielitist individualism. The criminal punishment of seditious libel was "the offspring of a Monarchy," Wortman emphasized. Such punishment could "never be reconciled to the genius and constitution of a Representative Commonwealth." In a republican democracy, the government must respond to "Public Opinion," and public opinion arises from individual "personal judgments." Each citizen must be given full freedom to investigate public issues, particularly the qualifications of incumbent governmental officials and other candidates for office. Otherwise, the citizens will not be able to exercise their suffrage intelligently and reasonably. Moreover,

Wortman added, each citizen in a republican democracy is a potential officeholder. "It is for that reason absolutely indispensible to the existence of such system that each individual should be furnished with all the means of obtaining political information, and be permitted to exercise his faculties in the pursuit of such knowledge without interruption or restraint."[45]

A FINAL REPUBLICAN THEORIST worth discussing is John Thomson because, in justifying an expansive conception of free expression in his tract, *An Enquiry Concerning the Liberty and Licentiousness of the Press,* published in 1801, Thomson relied equally on republican democracy and a libertarian idea of the individual. With regard to republican democracy, Thomson stressed that the speech-or-debate clause of the Constitution clearly protects the expression of congressional members. "If then those men are at liberty to say what they please in Congress, why should they abridge this right in the people?" After all, Thomson reasoned, in the United States, the people are sovereign. "Why should they who are the servants or agents of the people; who are paid by the people for their services, why ought they to impose restrictions upon the thoughts, words, or writings of their sovereign?" Because republican democratic government is grounded on the people, it would be "absurd" for the government to tell the people what to think or to say. Without a right of free discussion protecting both legislators and citizens, "ignorance and despotism would soon be the inevitable consequence." Thus, Thomson concluded that "virtue and republicanism must rise or fall together." Both the people and their legislators should be virtuous, so sedition laws, which undermine virtue by discouraging people from speaking honestly and openly, must be barred.[46]

Thomson did not rest his expansive definition of free expression solely on this argument. Like Hay, Thomson relied on a libertarian theory, though Thomson's libertarianism differed strikingly from Hay's. Hay emphasized that the autonomous individual should remain beyond governmental control, while Thomson stressed that the individual cannot even control himself. And if the individual cannot control himself, then certainly, the individual cannot be controlled by others. "All men are endowed, by nature, with the power of thinking; yet have they no controul over their thoughts. As no individual can prevent the operation of this principle within himself, much less can he direct those of any other person. If this is the case with one individual, it must be so with all; therefore, no association of men, however numerous or respectable, can ever have a right to say you shall not think this, or you shall think that: this being a power which does not exist among mankind. Consequently it must follow, that men should be allowed to express those thoughts, with the same freedom that they arise. In other words — speak, or publish, whatever you believe to be truth."[47]

Both of Thomson's arguments, based on republican democracy and based on libertarianism, had far-reaching implications. Even though Thomson focused on the national government, his expansive concept of free expression, it would seem, would apply with equal vigor to state governments. Thus, Thomson concluded with a ringing endorsement of the Miltonian marketplace of ideas. "[L]et misrepresentation be exposed by the force of truth," he declared. "In *no case whatever* use coercive measures. Truth is at all times sufficiently powerful. Coercion may silence, but it never can convince." Indeed, Thomson maintained that even errors and falsehoods can contribute to the pursuit of truth. "When detected by accurate reasoning, the truth will appear with increased lustre. The only danger to be apprehended, is from investigation being fettered, and error allowed to become rooted in the mind." Governmental officials should never be entrusted with the power to regulate the people's speech and writing because officials, like other people, cannot control their own minds. During sedition trials, in fact, judges are likely to be prejudiced for the simple fact that they too are governmental officials. Even so, like Wortman, Thomson recognized that the government retains the power to punish criminal conduct.[48]

THE FEDERALISTS' SUCCESSFUL prosecutions against the Republicans not only influenced Republicans like Hay, Wortman, and Thomson to articulate more expansive notions of free expression but also sparked an eventual transfer of political power from the Federalists to the Republicans. While Federalists initially viewed the enactment of the Sedition Act as providing an opportunity to snuff out the Republicans' factional and corrupt opposition, the very opposite ensued. Republicans surged into dominance, and Federalists were pushed to the background. Why?

Earlier in the 1790s, Federalists had hesitated to suppress Republican opposition. Federalists had recognized the political danger of interfering with the exercise of the American tradition of dissent; Republicans must be allowed to speak their minds. Toward the end of the decade, however, Federalists believed that suppression was appropriate, even necessary. War with France seemed imminent, so Federalists could justify suppression as a means to protect American security. From the Federalist perspective, the Republicans now seemed, more than ever, to be a factional party bent on destroying the republic in collaboration with the French. The result was the Sedition Act and the subsequent prosecutions. But Federalists were guilty of two serious misjudgments, which led to their downfall.

First, the declared war with France never materialized. True, an undeclared naval quasi war lasted through much of Adams's term. During this quasi war, however, the United States aimed not to defeat France but to insure the safety of American commercial ships. Only three battle-like encounters between American and French public naval vessels occurred throughout this period. Consequently, the patriotic fervor that had swept across the country and had briefly united the people, when an all-out war seemed imminent, quickly dissipated. As such, the Sedition Act appeared more as a vindictive act of suppression, contrary to the American tradition of speaking one's mind, than as an expedient of war.[49]

Second, Federalists were moved to invoke the tradition of suppression against the Republicans. Just as the Tories, residing on American soil, had seemed to threaten the nation's security during the Revolution, Federalists saw the Republicans in the late 1790s as threatening the still young republic, particularly given the likelihood of war against France. If the Revolutionaries had justifiably suppressed the Tories' expression during the War, could not the Federalists justifiably suppress the Republicans? Moreover, while the Tories had often been harassed and banished by mobs, Federalists viewed their Sedition Act as a model of liberality — and reasonably so, given the contemporary law of free expression. But because they looked through the lens of republican democracy, Federalists necessarily saw the political world as conforming to distinctive categories. Civic virtue, the common good, and the sovereign people were good, while factions and partial or private interests were bad. Federalists could not recognize the Republicans as constituting a legitimate party of opposition — because such an entity was, at the time, unrecognizable. The Republicans, exactly because they were oppositional, were necessarily a corrupt faction motivated by selfish interests rather than civic virtue. This view of the political world helps explain the personal animosities that had developed among some of the leaders of the two protoparties —animosities that then only exacerbated the political tensions. Jefferson detested Hamilton who now disliked Madison who distrusted Adams. Thus, the Federalist claims that Republicans were wild-eyed Jacobin democrats were no more pretextual than were the Republican fears that Federalists were monarchists and aristocrats. Federalists, quite simply, failed to recognize the legitimacy and popularity of Republicans because they did not have the conceptual tools for doing so. Federalist District Attorney Rawle, prosecutor in the Cooper case, lamented that "[n]o conduct of the President however wise, no motives however pure, could

screen him from the attacks of party spirit." The implication, which followed from republican democracy, was that criticism of the president was
inherently a matter of factional or party spirit and could not be an expression of reasonable and legitimate disagreement about public policies.[50]

If the Republicans had been an ostracized group of outsiders, like the
Tories, or a marginalized minority, like the African American slaves, then
Federalists could have successfully suppressed Republican opposition, or
excluded them from the polity, or both. But Republicans were not like Tories or slaves. Hence, the Federalists' crucial mistake: they treated Repub-
licans as if they were outsiders who could be safely brushed aside, but the
Republicans enjoyed roughly as much support among the people as did the
Federalists. Republicans, it might be said, were substantially insiders who
stood, in some respects, temporarily on the outside. Men like Jefferson,
Madison, McKean, Gallatin, and Nicholas were not outsiders who could
be permanently suppressed or excluded or who would accept as much.
From the outset, they had too much popular support. The corollary of this
point — that Republicans were not truly outsiders — was that the Federalists were not ensconced insiders. They might have held the allegiance of
a slight majority of the people before the enactment of the Sedition Act,
but such favored status quickly dissipated. When Federalists concluded
that they could reasonably invoke the tradition of suppression by enacting
the Sedition Act, they sorely miscalculated. Then Federalists compounded
their mistake with their politically inept mishandling of so many prosecutions, like that of Matthew Lyon. The majority of American people did not
long acquiesce, but instead rose up indignantly, producing the Republican
electoral victories of 1800.[51]

CHAPTER **5**

Free Expression in the Nineteenth Century to 1865

The Sedition Act crisis arose within an overarching and decade-long dispute about the nature of republican democracy. What was the role of the people, for instance, once they had elected their officials? Could the people criticize official decisions and policies? In that context, the Sedition Act controversy swirled together the tradition of dissent, the tradition of suppression, and the strands of law radiating from the Constitution and the common law. Republicans invoked the tradition of dissent as they asserted a right to speak their minds, to criticize the government. Federalists relied upon the tradition of suppression as they sought to silence the voices of (temporary) outsiders, whom the Federalists viewed as a factional and corrupt party. And Republicans and Federalists both seized upon different aspects of the extant law: the doctrine of seditious libel, the Zengerian reforms, the constitutional limits on congressional power, and the implications of the first amendment.[1]

Given such a variety of inconsistent resources to draw upon — competing traditions and ambiguous legal directives — each side in the dispute articulated reasonable conceptions of free expression. In fact, partly because of the uncertain nature of republican democracy, the Sedition Act crisis demonstrated that two countervailing arguments could link democracy and free expression. First (on the Republican side), because the people are sovereign in a republican democratic government, the people must have the power to speak their minds on public issues. The people participate more than by occasionally voting and then deferring to the elected officials.

The people must continually deliberate about public officers and issues, and in doing so, they guard against corruption. If the people are to deliberate intelligently, they must be supplied with information (for instance, by the press) about governmental policies, elected officials, and candidates for office. Free government, in other words, requires unfettered free expression so that the people can ensure the virtuous pursuit of the common good. Second (on the Federalist side), a republican democracy depends upon the civic virtue of its citizens and governmental officials. Citizens exercise their virtue by voting for the candidates of the highest merit, of the greatest virtue, and then citizens ought to trust in the wisdom of their own choices by relying on their elected officials. The government, under this model of republican democracy, must attract the most virtuous leaders. If this is to happen, individuals must rest assured that, if elected to office, they will be protected from the calumnies of self-interested groups and individuals. When virtuous governmental officials are defamed, the sovereign people themselves are injured — because the officials are their chosen representatives. Therefore, it follows, while the government cannot impose prior restraints to prevent individuals from speaking or writing, the government must be able to punish seditious libel, within reasonable constraints (read: Zengerian reforms), if republican democracy is to be preserved.[2]

Both these arguments — for and against unfettered free expression under republican democracy — are reasonable, even persuasive. Yet, significantly, the second argument, favoring a narrower conception of free expression, might be the stronger of the two. To be sure, republican democracy presumed the existence of a protected private realm of individual liberties, including free expression. Even so, a preeminent principle of republican democracy was that the government could always act to advance the common good. Individual liberties remained subordinate to the community's good. Thus, the government ought to have the power to punish speech or writing if such punishment would further the common good. And criminal punishment would presumably be for the common good if the speech or writing had a bad tendency or likely pernicious consequences. Speech or writing that illegitimately criticizes the government and its officials, it would seem, has a bad tendency because it is likely to mislead the people. Because of deception, the people might reject an official who, in truth, had acted virtuously. Moreover, even if the people were not merely to defer to their elected officials but instead were to deliberate continually about public issues, the people should still be protected from calumnies and duplicity. How can the people deliberate intelligently if lies delude them? Federalist Representative James Bayard made the point: "The Government of the United States is immediately bottomed on public opinion. It originates with the people and depends on their will for its existence, and on their arms for its protection. Poison the fountain of its being and the whole frame is palsied, and must sink into lethargy or die in convulsions. The Government is bound not to deceive the people, and it is equally bound not to suffer them to be deceived. . . . This they cannot prevent unless they have a power to punish those who with wicked designs attempt to mislead the people."[3]

IN THE WAKE OF THE
SEDITION ACT CONTROVERSY

Regardless of the forcefulness of the respective arguments for and against an unfettered freedom of expression, the climax of the Sedition Act controversy was still to be played out in the elections of 1800. During the Sixth Congress, Federalists had held a forty-four to thirty-eight majority over Republicans in the House of Representatives, but after 1800, Republicans were in the majority, forty-four to twenty-four. Meanwhile, in the race for the presidency, Republicans defeated Adams and the Federalists, but the election was not yet over. The nation still needed to confront one final crisis. The Republican presidential candidate, Thomas Jefferson, ended with precisely the same number of electoral votes as his running mate, Aaron Burr, and pursuant to constitutional provision, the House of Representatives would vote to break the deadlock and determine the next president. Of no small significance, though, the House would decide before the new Seventh Congress was seated; the Sixth Congress, with its majority of Federalist representatives, would choose between the two Republicans, Jefferson and Burr.[4]

To win the presidency, either Jefferson or Burr would need to receive a majority in the House. With each of the sixteen states accorded a single vote, a minimum of nine votes would be necessary. Political machinations immediately were set into motion as many Federalists threw their support to Burr, who derived from New York rather than the Republican stronghold of Virginia. Regardless, Federalists did not relish their options. The House Speaker, Theodore Sedgwick, a Massachusetts Federalist, preferred the New Yorker. "[Burr] is ambitious — selfish — profligate. His ambition is of the worst kind — it is a mere love of power," Sedgwick explained. "[But even so] Burr must depend on good men for his support & that support he cannot receive but by a conformity to their views." Burr's fellow New Yorker, Alexander Hamilton, disliked Jefferson yet despised Burr. "I admit that [Jefferson's] politics are tinctured with fanaticism," wrote Hamilton, "that he is crafty & persevering in his objects, that he is not scrupulous about the means of success, not very mindful of truth, and that he is a contemptible hypocrite. . . . [But he] is as likely as any man I know to temporize — to calculate what will be likely to promote his own reputation and advantage; and the probable result of such a temper is the preservation of systems, though originally opposed, which . . . could not be overturned without danger to the person who did it." Balloting began on February 11, 1801, and would continue for a week. Burr, in a typically enigmatic act of evasion, neither actively sought the victory nor affirmatively withdrew; he clearly hoped to emerge as the president. Rumors of political deals flew, and many feared possible violence. The Republican governors of Pennsylvania and Virginia, Thomas McKean and James Monroe, began preparations for armed conflict. Finally, on the thirty-sixth ballot, Jefferson gained a majority and was designated the next president.[5]

Republicans now held national power, and Federalists had suddenly become the political outsiders. This very point — that after all the crises, power peacefully transferred from the Federalists to the Republicans — was crucial. The theoretical contours of republican democracy did not change, but for the first time, and after much uncertainty, the people had learned they could transfer power from one group of leaders to another (from one protoparty to another). No civil war; no secession. The controversies of the past decade, including the Sedition Act controversy, provided a vital lesson about republican democracy in the United States: the boundary between the inside and outside of American political power was permeable. Indeed, the insiders themselves — white Protestant men of some wealth — could fall into sharp disagreement, generating opposed groups of temporary insiders and temporary outsiders. Although such outsiders, like the Republicans of the 1790s, might not currently hold political power, they nonetheless remained part of "the people"; they were not permanently excluded. In a sense, they stood on the periphery rather than truly on the outside. While this lesson of permeability would not be fully comprehended for years, not until a two-party system became acceptable within the parameters of republican democracy, national confidence in the resiliency of the republic increased after the election of Jefferson. Fewer and fewer Americans overtly worried that the American republic, like previous republics, would necessarily fracture, decay, and die (at least until the mid-nineteenth century, when the slavery dispute would threaten national unity). The Republicans' dominance of national politics for more than two decades after 1800 contributed to this increasing national confidence. James Monroe, the last of three consecutive two-term Republican presidents from Virginia, declared in his second inaugural address: "In our whole system, national and State, we have shunned all the defects which unceasingly preyed on the vitals and destroyed the ancient Republics." Yet, of great significance, despite the Republican victories in the elections of 1800, despite the peaceful transfer of power, despite the now apparent permeability of political power, true (or effectively permanent) outsiders still existed in America. Groups such as African Americans and Native Americans did not confront a permeable membrane of political power that would allow them to pass through to the inside with just a bit of effort. To the contrary, republican democracy facilitated long-term exclusion, and the tradition of suppression bolstered such exclusion.[6]

THE REPUBLICANS' STATUS as merely temporary rather than true outsiders magnified the importance of their pronouncements about free expression. When Federalists enacted the Sedition Law and began to prosecute, Republicans were pressured to articulate broad rights of expression in their own defense. Madison, Hay, Wortman, Thomson, and other Republicans naturally and readily drew upon the tradition of dissent, of speaking one's mind, and combined it with republican democracy, emphasizing especially the sovereignty of the people, to develop their new and expansive conceptions of free expression. They developed theories, including libertarian theories, that justified unprecedented protections of expression, and they advocated for legal doctrines that would supposedly accord these broad protections to all speakers and writers. But Republicans would not long remain on the outside. They were instead soon dominating American politics. Partly for that reason, their pronouncements on free expression would carry special resonance over the next decades, particularly for other outsiders, both temporary and true. As it turned out, the Republican theorist with the broadest jurisprudential influence during the first half of the nineteenth century would be St. George Tucker. Tucker's prominence arose not because his ideas on free expression were original but because he edited the first American edition of Blackstone's *Commentaries*. Published in 1803, Tucker's Blackstone became the standard reference source for American lawyers and jurists for at least a quarter century. Tucker's views on free expression, which he articulated in two appendices to his Blackstone, closely echoed the (later) views of James Madison, as expressed in his Report on the Alien and Sedition Acts. Tucker, in fact, overtly quoted and paraphrased long sections of Madison's Report.[7]

Like Madison, Tucker unequivocally denounced the Sedition Act of 1798 as being beyond Congress's constitutional powers. Tucker emphasized, still like Madison, the differences between the British parliamentary monarchy and republican democracy in the United States. The Blackstonian common law doctrine — that liberty of the press prohibits the government only from imposing prior restraints — might be sensible under the British system, Tucker reasoned, but it did not fit with American republican democratic government. As was true with Madison, then, Tucker's arguments could be construed to proscribe the criminal punishment of seditious libel by any republican democratic government, whether at the national *or* state level. Tucker, moreover, in several passages, expressed views that seemed consistent with those of Hay, Wortman, and Thomson — the Republicans who had argued for the most expansive notions of free expression. Tucker, for instance, repeatedly referred to free expression as an "absolute," and in a similar vein, he recommended that any governmental official who did not like being criticized should "resign" his office.[8]

Nonetheless, just as with Madison, Tucker never explicitly pronounced that the state governments lacked the power to punish seditious libel. Instead, he concluded his discussion with a maddeningly ambiguous passage. He began with a question: "is there no remedy in the United States for injuries done to the good fame and reputation of a man; injuries, which to a man of sensibility, and of conscious integrity, are the most grievous that can be inflicted?" His answer was trenchant: "Heaven forbid, that in a country which boasts of rational freedom, and of affording perfect security to the citizen for the complete enjoyment of all his rights, the most valuable of all should be exposed without remedy, or redress, to the vile arts of detraction and slander!" Well, where shall a citizen seek such a remedy for a damaged reputation? Tucker reiterated that under the Constitution, "no such power [over speech or writing] should be exercised, or claimed by the federal government." But then Tucker added that the Constitution left "it to the state governments to exercise such jurisdiction and control over the subject, as their several constitutions and laws permit." Given that the state governments, at that time, continued to claim the power to proscribe seditious libel, did Tucker therefore intend to approve of the criminal punishment of expression? He never determinately answered this basic question. He proceeded to disapprove explicitly of the "licentiousness" of the press, and he appeared to recommend that the press self-censor to avoid staining itself "with falsehood, imposture, detraction, and personal slander." He explained that when the press deviates from the truth, it "is *both* an imposition upon the *public,* and an injury to the *individual* whom it may respect." When a man accepts a governmental office, he does not forfeit his "sacred and invaluable right" of character. Rather, if the press knowingly defames an official, the press "is guilty of a crime against the *community*, as well as against the person injured." Tucker's references to "an imposition upon the public" and "a crime against the community" strongly suggested that he intended to justify state criminal prosecutions for seditious libel. Yet, he concluded that "for injuries done the reputation of any person, as *an individual*, the state-courts are always open, and may afford ample, and competent redress." Tucker's reference here to the reputation of the person "as an individual" rather than as an official suggested that he meant only to approve state civil actions for defamation but not state criminal prosecutions.[9]

Two points bear emphasis. First, by following Madison — including Madison's ambiguous stance on state power to punish seditious libel — Tucker retreated from the incontrovertibly expansive views of free expression articulated by Hay, Wortman, and Thomson. Second, Tucker's ambiguity might have been the most fitting statement of Republican views on free expression — a worthy exemplar for the future. After all, the Republicans unquestionably strengthened the American tradition of dissent. But this did not mean that the tradition of dissent would soon overcome the competing tradition of suppression or lead to the radical transformation of the law. Far from it.

ALL TOO PREDICTABLY, once Republicans grasped the reins of national political power, their attitudes toward free expression changed. John Thomson had published his *Enquiry Concerning the Liberty and Licentiousness of the Press*, justifying a broad freedom of expression, on March 4, 1801, the very day that Jefferson became president. At least at that point in time, Jefferson himself seemed to endorse a similarly expansive free expression. In his inaugural address, after first calling for all to "unite in common efforts for the common good," and then denouncing "political intolerance," Jefferson declared: "If there be any among us who would wish to dissolve this Union or to change its republican form, let them stand undisturbed as monuments of the safety with which error of opinion may be tolerated where reason is left free to combat it." Jefferson, too, would soon pardon those convicted under the Sedition Act. Yet, Jefferson's support for the broad protection of speech and writing would be short lived.[10]

Once in office, Jefferson showed no principled opposition to the criminal punishment of expression, particularly through seditious libel prosecutions. Like the Federalists before him, Jefferson believed that the Republicans should determine whether to prosecute seditious libel based on a political calculus. Jefferson, though, astutely calculated the pluses and minuses, accounting for variable complexities. He recognized, for instance, that Republicans, given their recent record of opposition to seditious libel prosecutions, would appear hypocritical if they immediately launched into a campaign of prosecutions against Federalists. Moreover, Jefferson realized that the Federalists' prosecutions of Republicans had helped usher him into the presidency. He would learn from the Federalists' mistakes. Thus, on March 24, 1802, he wrote to his attorney general, recommending caution. "To punish . . . is impractible until the body of the people, from whom juries are to be taken, get their minds to rights; and even then I doubt its expediency," Jefferson explained, with reference to publications that he viewed as clearly seditious. "I would wish much to see the experiment tried of getting along without public prosecutions for libels. I believe we can do it. Patience and well doing, instead of punishment, if it can be found sufficiently efficacious, would be a happy change in the instruments of government."[11]

Yet, Jefferson did not welcome criticism. As became apparent in his private correspondence, Jefferson had soon calculated that it would work to his political advantage to encourage, at least discreetly, prosecutions against his Federalist critics. Jefferson wrote a letter to Thomas McKean on February 19, 1803:

On the subject of prosecutions, what I say must be entirely confidential. . . . The federalists having failed in destroying the freedom of the press by their gag-law, seem to have attacked it in an opposite form, that is by pushing it's licentiousness & it's lying to such a degree of prostitution as to deprive it of all credit. And the fact is that so abandoned are the tory presses in this particular that even the least informed of the people have learnt that nothing in a newspaper is to be believed. This is a dangerous state of things, and the press ought to be restored to it's credibility if possible. The restraints provided by the laws of the states are sufficient for this if applied. And I have therefore long thought that a few prosecutions of the most prominent offenders would have a wholesome effect in restoring the integrity of the presses. Not a general prosecution, for that would look like persecution: but a selected one. The paper I now inclose appears to me to offer as good an instance in every respect to make an example of, as can be selected.

This letter revealed much about Jefferson's thought at the time. Unsurprisingly, he still viewed the political world through the lens of republican democracy, so the Federalist newspapers were the "tory presses." He clearly believed the states retained power to prosecute libels, plus he had carefully calculated the costs and benefits of prosecutions. He still discouraged widespread prosecutions, but now urged a limited number of selected ones — like precision strikes in a war. For this purpose, he had chosen a specific target, a paper that he sent to McKean. Finally, he did not want the public to learn that he now overtly favored prosecutions, apparently because of his previous public statements advocating tolerance.[12]

By Jefferson's second inaugural, on March 4, 1805, he was openly less sanguine about, in his words, the "experiment" with "freedom of discussion." He candidly resented how "the artillery of the press has been levelled against us, charged with whatsoever its licentiousness could devise or dare." He unequivocally declared that the state governments retained the power to punish seditious libel, that the press's attacks on his administration "might, indeed, have been corrected by the wholesome punishments reserved and provided by the laws of the several States against falsehood and defamation." Even further, Jefferson now brazenly encouraged state officials to punish "false and defamatory publications [with] the salutary coercions of the law." Yet, equally important, Jefferson's own reelection demonstrated, in his opinion, that truth could overcome falsehood, that the experiment in free expression had worked to a degree. Despite the "outrages" being published in the press, "truth and reason have maintained their ground against false opinions in league with false facts." As Jefferson retreated from an expansive view of free expression, he initially resettled upon the Republicans' jurisdictional position: the states but not the national government had the power to punish seditious libel. Of course, when Republicans first articulated this position during the Sedition Act controversy, they intended to *question* congressional power to pass the Act. Now, they reasserted this view to *justify* state prosecutions. "Nor does the opinion of the unconstitutionality, & consequence nullity of [the Sedition Act], remove all restraint from the overwhelming torrent of slander, which is confounding all vice and virtue, all truth & falsehood, in the U.S.," Jefferson explained to Abigail Adams. "The power to do that is fully possessed by the several State Legislatures. It was reserved to them, & was denied to the General Government." Before long, several states, including Pennsylvania, New York, and Massachusetts had initiated libel prosecutions against Federalists.[13]

In light of the threat and reality of Republican-inspired prosecutions, some Federalists surprisingly yet presciently argued for reenactment of the Sedition Act because of its codification of Zengerian reforms. Robert Goodloe Harper, for instance, insisted that the Act could serve "as a shield." He feared "the overbearing sway of that tyrannical spirit, by which a certain political party in this country, is actuated." Naturally, the Republicans were the feared factional political party, "which, arrogating to itself to speak in the name of the people, like fanaticism arrogating to itself to speak in the name of God, knows neither moderation, mercy, nor justice." Given such apprehensions, Harper explained that if "indicted myself, for calmly and candidly exposing the errors of Government and the incapacity of those who govern, I wish to be enabled, by this law, to go before a jury of my country, and say that what I have written is true."[14]

In one of the most significant prosecutions, urged by both Jefferson himself and Republican Governor George Clinton, New York in early 1803 indicted Harry Croswell, the Federalist editor of a New York newspaper. Croswell had written that Jefferson paid Republican publisher James Thomson Callender to defame George Washington and John Adams. For that published attack against Jefferson, Croswell was accused of committing the common law crime of seditious libel. Croswell sought to delay the trial so that he could call Callender as a witness for the purpose of proving the truth of Croswell's statements. The Republican judge denied the motion and instructed the jury to follow the Blackstonian, pre-*Zenger,* common law conception of seditious libel. The jury could neither consider truth as a defense nor determine anything more than the fact of publication. The judge would decide, as a matter of law, whether the published matter was seditious. Croswell was convicted.[15]

On appeal, New York's Republican prosecutor argued that the court should affirm the trial court's Blackstonian notion of common law libel: "A libel is punishable, not because it is false, but because of its evil tendency; its tendency to a breach of the peace. This tendency equally exists, whether the libel be true or false. The malicious publication of truth will often affect, to a most pernicious degree, the harmony and happiness of society. A libel is correctly said to be the more libellous for being true, for it has an increased tendency to a breach of the peace." Unmistakably, this Republican conception of free expression was a far cry from the broad protections so recently advocated by Hay, Wortman, Thomson, and Madison.[16]

Croswell managed to secure Alexander Hamilton to represent him on appeal. Thus, the famed Federalist Hamilton now argued for a more expansive free expression revolving around qualified Zengerian reforms. On the one hand, Hamilton maintained that republican democracy required a right to a free press. "There was no other way to preserve liberty, and bring down a tyrannical faction," he explained. "If this right was not permitted to exist in vigour and in exercise, good men would become silent; corruption and tyranny would go on, step by step, in usurpation, until, at last, nothing that was worth speaking, or writing, or acting for, would be left in our country." Yet, on the other hand, Hamilton insisted that the press could not go "unchecked." Such a "pestilential doctrine" would destroy republican democratic government. "It would encourage vice, compel the virtuous to retire, destroy confidence, and confound the innocent with the guilty." Hamilton therefore recommended a hybrid approach, built on Zengerian reforms, with one important qualification. He fully supported the Zengerian reliance on a jury for resolving both the facts and law of a seditious libel trial. But he tempered (or conditioned) the other Zengerian point, that truth was a defense: "liberty of the press," he said, "consisted in publishing with impunity, truth with good motives, and for justifiable ends." Hamilton, in effect, asked for less protection than would have been afforded under the Sedition Act. Under his truth-conditional approach, truth would be a defense only when the publication was for good motives and justifiable ends.[17]

Judge James Kent wrote the most important opinion for a divided court. Kent, a Federalist who sided with Hamilton, reasoned that "the intent and tendency of the publication is, in every instance, to be the substantial inquiry on the trial, and that the truth is admissible in evidence, to explain that intent." Kent gushed in his admiration for Hamilton: "I adopt . . . as perfectly correct, the comprehensive and accurate definition of one of the counsel at the bar." Consequently, Kent adopted almost word for word Hamilton's recommended standard for seditious libel, including the truth-conditional defense — truth, if accompanied by "good motives" and "justifiable ends," would deflect a charge of libel. This approach resembled the one recommended by McKean in the 1780s, and thus, like McKean's approach, it resonated with republican democratic principles, at least as understood from one perspective. The standard for determining the scope of free expression, within the context of seditious libel prosecutions, arose not merely from a concern for truth but also from a concern for the common good. A writer who furthered the common good by publishing truthful statements for good motives and justifiable ends was protected from criminal punishment. A writer whose expression instead was malicious or had a bad tendency acted contrary to the common good and was therefore subject to punishment. Of course, only four years earlier, Tunis Wortman had argued that republican democracy precludes the punishment of seditious libel. The government's criminal punishment of speech, according to Wortman, could never advance the common good. Hamilton and Kent, apparently, viewed the connections among republican democracy, free expression, and the common good very differently. The *Croswell* truth-conditional standard had strong historical roots reaching back to Blackstone and the common law of seditious libel. It took the Blackstonian *justification* for punishing seditious libel and transformed it into the *definition* of seditious libel. Under the common law, as described by Blackstone, criticism of governmental officials was subject to criminal punishment *because* of its bad or pernicious tendencies. Under the truth-conditional standard, criticism of public officials was subject to criminal punishment *if* it had bad or pernicious tendencies. That is, under *Croswell,* if a defendant's expression was true and for the common good, then it did not constitute seditious libel. But if the expression was either false, or true but with bad tendencies, then it was punishable as seditious libel.[18]

In Connecticut, meanwhile, Federalists thwarted Republican efforts to indict Jefferson's critics under state law. Undaunted, Jefferson in 1806 appointed a new federal district court judge, who considered seeking federal indictments under the common law (since the Sedition Act had expired years before). Such federal prosecutions required Republicans to retreat from the jurisdictional argument that they had so vigorously and insistently asserted against the Sedition Act. Fortified by the tradition of suppression, though, Republicans did not hesitate. They indicted for seditious libel six Federalists, including three printers, a state court judge, and two ministers charged with preaching seditious sermons. By letter, Jefferson explicitly approved of these prosecutions, reasoning that so long as the defendants could "appeal to [the] truth," the prosecutions "cannot lessen the useful freedom of the press." The press, Jefferson added, becomes "impotent when it abandons itself to falsehood," as had happened in Connecticut. Thus, he willingly left it "to others to restore [the press] to it's strength, by recalling it within the pale of truth." With the benefit of the prosecutions, Jefferson concluded, "I trust we shall soon see [Connecticut's] citizens rally to the republican principles of our Constitution." Two of these prosecutions eventually wound their way to the U.S. Supreme Court, which held in 1812 that the federal courts are not vested with jurisdictional power over common law crimes.[19]

While the Supreme Court aborted the possibility of subsequent federal common law seditious libel cases, the *Croswell* case would have lasting significance. The year after *Croswell,* Republicans and Federalists in the New York legislature joined together to codify the doctrine in a statute. Then, in

1821, New York explicitly included this approach to libel as part of its new Constitution. "In all prosecutions or indictments for libels, the truth may be given in evidence to the jury; and if it shall appear to the jury that the matter charged as libellous is true, and was published with good motives and for justifiable ends, the party shall be acquitted; and the jury shall have the right to determine the law and the fact." More important, New York's *Croswell* truth-conditional approach would serve as a model for other states for decades. States adopted the truth-conditional standard through legislation, constitutional amendment, and common law decision making. Some state statutes and constitutional provisions, such as the Ohio Constitution of 1851, explicitly followed the truth-conditional language. Others were less clear. For instance, the 1836 Arkansas Constitution allowed a defendant to introduce evidence of truth without specifying the precise extent to which the truth defense would be qualified. Regardless of the exact terms of the various state constitutions, the truth-conditional standard became the preponderant nineteenth-century approach.[20]

In 1805, the Supreme Court of Pennsylvania interpreted ambiguous state constitutional language harmoniously with *Croswell*. In 1824, in *Updegraph v. Commonwealth*, the same court elaborated the truth-conditional standard in relation to the bad tendency of seditious libel. Pennsylvania prosecuted Updegraph under a statute prohibiting blasphemy. The court explained that, when it comes to the criminal punishment of an author or printer, "a malicious and mischievous intention is . . . the broad boundary between right and wrong." The state could not criminally punish an author or printer who expressed the truth for good motives and justifiable ends, but it could punish one who had bad intentions. Yet, how might such bad intentions be proved? "[I]t is to be collected from the offensive levity, scurrilous and opprobrious language, and other circumstances, whether the act of the party was malicious; and since the law has no means of distinguishing between different degrees of evil tendency, if the matter published contains any such evil tendency, it is a public wrong. An offence against the public peace may consist either of an actual breach of the peace, or doing that which tends to provoke and excite others to do it." According to this reasoning — called the doctrine of constructive intent — if expression creates a bad tendency, then the speaker or writer must have uttered or published it with malicious and mischievous intent. The intent is inferred from the bad tendency or likely harmful consequences of the expression because such expression is a "public wrong" contravening the common good and republican democratic government.[21]

While the doctrine of constructive intent gained wide acceptance, some courts narrowed the reach of the truth-conditional standard in other ways. The Supreme Judicial Court of Massachusetts decided *Commonwealth v. Blanding* in 1825. Blanding had been convicted for publishing "a false, scandalous and libellous paragraph" concerning a local inn holder. The court hewed closer to the common law than the *Croswell* court had done. As the *Blanding* court detailed, on the one hand, the common law did no more than prohibit the government's imposition of prior restraints; truth was never a defense against a charge of criminal libel. Under the *Croswell* truth-conditional standard, on the other hand, a defendant could always present evidence of truth so as to prove to the jury his good motives and justifiable ends. The *Blanding* court, though, thought *Croswell* too liberal: proof of truth should be allowed only to promote "certain public interests, which are of more importance than the character or tranquillity of any individual." The judge, therefore, must make the initial decision: whether the defendant should even be allowed to present evidence of truth to the jury. Such evidence should be admitted, the court reasoned, only if the publication concerned a public issue and was communicated to an individual or institution that could address the issue. Thus, for example, if the defendant had communicated a "complaint to the executive against an officer holding his place at its pleasure," then the court should allow admission of evidence of truth. But if the defendant had instead disseminated the same complaint to the public at large, evidence of truth would be inappropriate. If the court were to decide that such evidence is admissible, then the truth-conditional standard would be effectively triggered: "the jury must determine the motives and the end [of the defendant]."[22]

Two noteworthy points follow from *Blanding*. First, while some state courts resisted implementing the *Croswell* standard, reasoning that it unjustifiably diluted the common law, popular opinion favored the truth-conditional approach. The Massachusetts legislature, for instance, responded to the *Blanding* decision by immediately enacting a statute that required the application of the truth-conditional standard in all cases. Second, whether a court willingly adopted the truth-conditional standard or something less liberal, the overarching consideration always remained the same: how to achieve the common good for the polity. To be sure, individual liberties, including free expression, were important, but such liberties were subject to the community's power to act for the common good. Thus, nineteenth-century state constitutional provisions that protected free speech and a free press in general — rather than focusing on criminal libel — typically declared, in one phrase, the importance of freedom and then, in the next phrase, the limits of freedom (individual responsibility for abuse). The 1821 New York constitutional language was typical: "Every citizen may freely speak, write, and publish his sentiments on all subjects, being responsible for the abuse of that right; and no law shall be passed to restrain or abridge the liberty of speech, or of the press." Constitutions from states as diverse as Arkansas, California, and New Jersey had practically identical language. Most often, moreover, these general provisions were immediately followed by a more specific constitutional provision adopting the truth-conditional approach for criminal libel. The *Croswell* standard was, in effect, a specific implementation of the more general guarantees of free expression: indictments for the abuse of free expression would be adjudicated in accordance with the truth-conditional defense.[23]

THE CLASSIC MID-NINETEENTH-CENTURY treatises of James Kent and Joseph Story elucidated free-expression doctrine. Declaring "that the liberty of speech, and of the press, should be duly preserved," Kent grounded free expression on free government. "The liberal communication of sentiment, and entire freedom of discussion, in respect to the character and conduct of public men, and of candidates for public favour," Kent wrote, "is deemed essential to the judicious exercise of the right of suffrage, and of that control over their rulers, which resides in the free people of these United States." Because of the connection between free expression and republican democracy, Kent maintained that the government can punish those who abuse this right. With regard to criminal libel, "[a] malicious intent towards government, magistrates, or individuals, and an injurious or offensive tendency, must concur to constitute the libel." Predictably, given that Kent had authored the *Croswell* opinion articulating the truth-conditional standard, he largely agreed with that approach. Surprisingly, though, Kent criticized state statutes and constitutions that allowed the defendant *always* to present evidence to the jury of the truth of the allegedly libelous statements. Kent reasoned that criminal libel prosecutions engender a "collision" between two rights: "the protection which is due to character, and the protection which ought to be afforded to liberty of speech, and of the press." By the time he wrote his *Commentaries*, in 1827, Kent believed that "the tendency of measures" in some states had "been to relax too far" the vigilant protection of character. Indeed, Kent criticized the New York constitution, which echoed *Croswell*, because it made "the facts in every possible case a necessary subject of open investigation . . . however improper or unfit those facts may be for public information." Somewhat similarly to *Blanding*, Kent reasoned that evidence of the truth should be admissible only if necessary "to explain [the defendant's] intent."[24]

Perhaps better than any of his contemporaries, Joseph Story explained the relationship between the individual right of free expression and the (republican democratic) governmental power to act for the common good. Story began his discussion of free expression by focusing on the first amendment of the national Constitution. He disparaged the idea that "every citizen [has] an absolute right to speak, or write, or print, whatever he might please [as] a supposition too wild to be indulged by any rational man." Moreover, he cited approvingly and extensively to Blackstone, yet Story ultimately concluded by endorsing the truth-conditional standard. The first amendment, Story explained, "is neither more nor less, than . . . that every man shall be at liberty to publish what is true, with good motives and for justifiable ends." Freedom of expression, as so limited, is the crux of republican democratic government, but both the freedom *and* the limits are equally important. "[W]ith this reasonable limitation [free expression] is an inestimable privilege in a free government," Story explained. "[But w]ithout such a limitation, it might become the scourge of the republic, first denouncing the principles of liberty, and then, by rendering the most virtuous patriots odious through the terrors of the press, introducing despotism in its worst form."[25]

When Story turned to an analysis of state constitutions, he continued to argue that republican democracy requires the government to have the power to punish seditious libel. Story denied "that the liberty of the press is so much more valuable, than all other rights in society, that the public safety, nay the existence of the government itself [should] yield to it." He thus explicated free expression within the broader parameters of governmental power and individual rights under republican democracy. On the one hand, "[n]o one can doubt the importance, in a free government, of a right to canvass the acts of public men, and the tendency of public measures, to censure boldly the conduct of rulers, and to scrutinize closely the policy, and plans of the government." That is, free expression is "the great security of a free government." On the other hand, government is instituted to protect "all personal liberty, all private peace, all enjoyment of property, and good reputation." Story then adverted to the maxim *sic utere tuo,* which nineteenth-century courts often invoked to help demarcate the boundary between the government's police power and individuals' rights and liberties. As Story explained, individual liberties, including free expression, must be exercised in accord with the doctrine "*sic utere tuo, ut non alienum laedas;* so exercise your own freedom, as not to infringe the rights of others, or the public peace and safety." Free expression, like other individual liberties, was important but always subordinate to the common good. Speech and writing therefore must be "free, but not licentious"; liberty of expression "is essentially different from an abuse of it." Republican democracy obligated each individual to exercise his or her free expression so as not to harm others or society at large, and the government possessed the power to punish any individual who breached this duty. In other words, a republican democratic government could punish expression that, because of its bad tendency — its likelihood of injuring others — would undermine the common good.[26]

WHILE THE TRUTH-CONDITIONAL (bad tendency) standard remained the predominant legal doctrine, states seldomly instituted prosecutions for libel during the nineteenth century. As early as 1835, Tocqueville observed that "nothing is more rare" in the United States than criminal prosecutions of the press. In an 1811 Virginia case, *Commonwealth v. Morris,* the court adopted the truth-conditional standard, but in 1912, another Virginia court observed: "Since [*Morris*] was decided, more than a century has elapsed, and, so far as we have been able to discover, it is the only reported case in our books of a criminal libel." Given the tradition of dissent, of speaking one's mind, the potential political fallout from criminal prosecutions often became too costly vis-à-vis the supposed benefits. Moreover, technological improvements in the printing press rendered newspapers and other publications far less expensive and more widely available. In a sense, as Tocqueville phrased it, printing had "accelerated the progress of equality." As a practical matter, critics of officials could spread their views quickly and widely, and just as practically, supporters of those same officials (as well as the officials themselves) could respond most effectively by rapidly spreading their views through the mass media. Finally, the emergence of the two-party system in the 1820s and 1830s meant that criticisms of governmental officials became rote, with one party criticizing the other, and vice versa. Such party-inspired criticisms, standing alone, were no longer grounds for accusing the other side of being factional maniacs bent on destroying the republic. Largely for these reasons, criminal prosecutions for libel became exceptional occurrences.[27]

Yet, even with prosecutions becoming problematic, governmental officials were not without recourse. During the nineteenth century, officials increasingly turned toward civil actions for private defamation if they were sufficiently aggrieved. Through a civil action, officials could gain retribution and quiet their critics, at least to a degree, without risking the appearance of impropriety. A civil action would neither obviously flout the tradition of dissent nor seemingly appropriate the criminal justice system for selfish purposes (insulating the official from public scrutiny). In the civil context, truth long had been a good defense, and given that limitation, the power of states to entertain such causes of action went unquestioned. Even in civil cases, however, courts would continue to pay homage to *Croswell* and the idea of a limited free press. For example, in an Ohio case, Charles Timberlake instituted a civil action for defamation against the *Cincinnati Gazette,* which had published a story falsely accusing him of petit larceny. The state Supreme Court rejected the newspaper's claim of privilege and, in doing so, commented on the nature of freedom of the press. "In a government like ours, characterized by free institutions, we are by no means disposed to underestimate the importance of a free press. It is, doubtless, one of the strongest bulwarks of liberty, and the people of this country have ever guarded it with jealous care." Yet, the court continued, every citizen is "responsible for the abuse of the right" of free expression. "The liberty of the press, properly understood, is not, therefore, inconsistent with the protection due to private character." The court then elaborated the parameters of liberty of the press by quoting from Kent's *Croswell* opinion: "It has been well defined as consisting in 'the right to publish, with impunity, the truth, with good motives, and for justifiable ends, whether it respects government, magistracy, or individuals.'"[28]

THE TRADITIONS OF DISSENT AND SUPPRESSION

Despite the widespread acceptance of the truth-conditional standard as legal doctrine, significant disputes regarding the appropriate scope of free expression occurred at various times during the mid-nineteenth century. But because these disputes frequently centered in forums other than the courts, invocations of the traditions of dissent and suppression could be more important than citations to legal authorities and doctrine.[29]

The Republicans' Sedition Act era declarations of expansive rights to free expression combined with the burgeoning individualism and anti-elitism of the nineteenth century to invigorate the tradition of dissent. In numerous realms of American life, including politics and religion, each individual seemed empowered to make important decisions, from casting one's vote to declaring one's faith in Christ. Deference to elites was no longer necessary or even admirable. The common people—at least the white, male, preferably Protestant, common people—now considered themselves as virtuous as any religious, political, or economic blue bloods. The individual was to think for himself, and thus, it would follow, the individual ought to be able to speak and write whatever he wants. Regardless of the legal doctrine of free expression, individual Americans tended to believe they could speak and write freely. In 1834, William Duane, a Republican editor whom the Federalists had hounded in the late 1790s, extolled the now widespread experience of press freedom. Publishers and editors, he wrote, "are not incarcerated, nor are the courts and lawyers arrayed against the press—they will not prosecute each other—'dog will not eat dog'—for they have all the slander to themselves, and enjoy a plenary indulgence." Newspaper editors freely criticized anyone, with undiluted vitriol. Here is one journalist's characterization of President Andrew Jackson: "[T]he language of Jackson has been that of a heartless despot, solely occupied with the preservation of his own authority. He governs by means of corruption, and his immoral practices will redound to his shame and confusion. His conduct in the political arena has been that of a shameless and lawless gamester."[30]

The tradition of dissent could be manifested through official as well as unofficial channels. An Ohio state court pronounced in dictum that the Alien and Sedition Laws "are now repudiated by the force of public sentiment as wholly unwarranted by the constitution." Those laws, the court declared, "vested arbitrary and despotic power in the President . . . and abridged the freedom of speech and of the press." Lawyers, meanwhile, sought to invoke the tradition of dissent to support their causes. In an 1845 Mississippi case, an attorney emphasized "the vast debt due to the press and unshackled popular inquiry and discussion." After all, the attorney explained, freedom of the press nurtured the American Revolution. "Are we to forget [Benjamin] Franklin's *Journal*—[Thomas Paine's] *Common Sense* . . . —and, not the least, the songs, composed, printed, and circulated, to be chanted by the patriot bands, whose naked, bleeding feet marked the march to liberty?" Any legislation checking the freedom of speech or press "would be flagrantly void." Yet, even such ringing declarations of free expression could be, in the end, qualified. "No one is to be molested for any opinion," the attorney grandly concluded, "and every citizen may freely speak, write, and publish his sentiments on all subjects, 'being responsible for the abuse of that liberty.'"[31]

Despite the vitality of the tradition of dissent, it did not overwhelm the competing tradition of suppression. An individual was free to speak or write so long as he remained roughly within the broad mainstream of culture and opinion, but social penalties were severe for those who ventured outside those borders. "In America the majority raises formidable barriers around the liberty of opinion," Tocqueville observed, "within these barriers an author may write what he pleases, but woe to him if he goes beyond them. Not that he is in danger of an auto-da-fé, but he is exposed to continued obloquy and persecution." Monarchs sought to coerce submission through physical punishments and threats; republican democracies induced conformity through more subtle means. "[D]emocratic republics of the present day have rendered [oppression] entirely an affair of the mind." In monarchies, "the body was attacked in order to subdue the soul; but the soul escaped the blows which were directed against it and rose proudly superior. Such is not the course adopted by tyranny in democratic republics; there the body is left free, and the soul is enslaved." The force of public opinion renders republican democracies far more effective than monarchies in controlling the people's thoughts and words. "I know of no country," he concluded, "in which there is so little independence of mind and real freedom of discussion as in America."[32]

The tradition of suppression, like the tradition of dissent, could be manifested through both official and unofficial channels. While the tradition of dissent was popularly invoked, so too was the tradition of suppression. In many states, the *Croswell* truth-conditional standard was adopted not by judicial fiat but by the more popular majoritarian processes of legislation or constitutional amendment. The people of Ohio, for example, ratified its 1851 Constitution, explicitly adopting the truth-conditional standard, by a vote of 126,663 to 109,699. Californians overwhelmingly ratified, 12,061 to 811, an 1849 Constitution that also adopted the truth-conditional standard. To be sure, the people in these states ratified entire constitutions, not solely the truth-conditional provisions, so these votes should not be understood as referenda on the *Croswell* standard. Nonetheless, such strong expressions of majoritarian support for state constitutions that included explicit truth-conditional provisions suggests that this conception of free expression did not contravene popular opinion.[33]

Most important, one should remember that, under republican democracy, large segments of the population were denied individual rights and liberties. The suppression of speech and writing, for individuals in these groups, was merely one aspect of their diminished participation in political and civil society. Even if an individual enjoyed an ostensible freedom of expression, it would mean little if he or she were denied suffrage, prohibited from holding public office, otherwise excluded from the polity, or coerced into subjugation. Significantly, then, African Americans, women, and Native Americans were denied basic rights, including suffrage, through the Civil War era and later. Moreover, given the nation's de facto Protestantism, religious minorities or outgroups, including Roman Catholics, Mormons, and Jews, often suffered under both official and unofficial acts of persecution. Expressions of religious beliefs or practices contrary to the mainstream could trigger either sudden and fierce reactions, long-term legal disabilities, or both. For instance, Maryland prohibited Jews from holding public office until 1826, when the state changed the law to allow them to hold office if they declared a "belief in a future state of rewards and punishments." In many states, religious minorities lived with the threat that overt repudiation of mainstream Protestantism might provoke a prosecution for blasphemy. A Delaware court, upholding a blasphemy conviction in 1837, explained that it had "been long perfectly settled by the common law, that blasphemy against the Deity in general, or a malicious and wanton attack against the christian religion individually, for the purpose of exposing its doctrines to contempt and ridicule, is indictable and punishable."[34]

During the nineteenth century, African Americans undoubtedly constituted the single societal group that endured the worst suppression, given the preservation of slavery as a legal institution. African Americans were the archetypical true (rather than temporary) outsiders. Even free blacks lacked the civil rights of white citizens, as the Supreme Court held in *Dred Scott v. Sandford*, decided in 1857. As Judge Joseph Lumpkin of Georgia explained in 1853, courts should never put "the thriftless African upon a footing of civil or political equality with a white population which are characterized by a degree of energy and skill, unknown to any other people or period. Such alone can be citizens in this great and growing Republic." Slaves, of course, were subjugated with the most sweeping legal disabilities. They could not, for instance, enter contracts, own property, or stand as witnesses; they were virtually devoid of any rights at all. Free expression, then, was a right inconsistent with the status of a slave, as the Alabama Supreme Court observed: "[A slave's] social relation to his master and mistress, and to the other white persons present, [forbids] the freedom of speech allowed among equals."[35]

ONCE ABOLITIONISM BEGAN to spread among whites in the 1830s, slavery and abolition became the flashpoints that sparked the greatest controversies involving free expression during the pre–Civil War period. The principles of the American Revolution, especially the declarations of natural rights to liberty, inspired some founding-generation Americans to protest against slavery. Partly for that reason, within the first twenty-five years of nationhood, all states north of Delaware either abolished slavery or began gradual emancipation. Furthermore, many Southerners of that time agreed that slavery was indefensible, though it had to be temporarily tolerated as a "necessary evil." Once the United States banned international slave trading in 1808, however, antislavery sentiments dissipated, even in the North, while the Southern economy became increasingly dependent on the cultivation of cotton, which relied heavily on plantation slavery. Yet, by the early 1830s, the Protestant revivalism of the Second Great Awakening had sparked a new abolitionist movement in the North led by William Lloyd Garrison and, subsequently, Wendell Phillips. According to the American Anti-Slavery Society's constitution of December 4, 1833, "Slaveholding is a heinous crime in the sight of God, and . . . the duty, safety, and best interests of all concerned, require its *immediate abandonment*." The Garrisonians thus uncompromisingly advocated for the immediate end of slavery and denounced the national Constitution as, in the words of Garrison, a proslavery "covenant with death and an agreement with hell." Overall, abolitionism spread slowly through the North, though it was countenanced most readily in areas running from upstate New York to northeastern Ohio, lands joined by a series of canals and lakes. The population there included many former New Englanders who were receptive to evangelical Protestantism and committed to the now increasingly intermingled concepts of republican self-sufficiency and capitalism. Family farms raising cash crops filled these areas, fast becoming "centers of rural capitalism," antithetical to Southern plantation life.[36]

Nonetheless, many Americans, including Northerners, condemned the Garrisonians' immediatism as wild-eyed fanaticism. In 1835, a New York newspaper sardonically denounced abolitionists for not being content despite already "having distracted the churches, destroyed the peace of families and communities, embarrassed the literary and religious institutions, menaced the property and even the existence of the union." Some Northerners reacted by arguing in support of slavery, though many others instead advocated for a more gradual end to slavery. White Southerners, seemingly with the most at stake, soon became more vigorous proslavery advocates, repudiating the earlier Southern view that slavery was a temporary evil. Tensions between North and South thus intensified not only because of the new aggressive abolitionism but also because of the enhanced militancy of slaveholders. The almost constant geographical spread of the nation further fanned the political controversy. Slave states and free states clashed over the status of new states and territories: would they be slave or free? The status of new states, in particular, could determine the balance of power in Congress.[37]

While many Northerners and Southerners argued the substantive and practical merits of abolition and slavery, many others sought to suppress discussion of these issues through both official and unofficial means. During the Jacksonian era, a common method for dealing with societal or cultural outsiders, in general, was through mob violence and vigilantism. Thus, as abolitionism began to gather supporters, violent efforts to suppress it began to increase. Many Northerners viewed slavery as evil, but other factors dissuaded them from supporting immediatism. Racist fears of African Americans, economic interests tied to Southern cotton production, and concerns for maintaining peace and order influenced these Northerners. Led often by prominent citizens, including congressmen, bankers, ministers, lawyers, and judges, Northern mobs sought to drive abolitionists from their midst or to scare them into silence. The first major Northern antiabolitionist riot took place in New York, on October 2, 1833, when abolitionists sought to organize a New York City Anti-Slavery Society. A mob of 1,500 antiabolitionists, bent on disruption, gathered at the appointed time and place of the organizational meeting, but the abolitionists, fearing trouble, wisely had switched to another location, the Chatham Street Chapel. The mob, undaunted, moved on to the chapel only to find that the abolitionists' meeting had already concluded. Many abolitionists would not be so lucky in the future. For example, in October 1835, a mob chased Garrison from the headquarters of the Boston Female Anti-Slavery Society. The mob found him hiding, tied a rope around his neck, and started to lead him to the Commons, where he was likely to be either tarred and feathered or lynched. Several men, however, helped Garrison escape after he agreed to be charged with a breach of the peace. On his way to jail, the mob attacked again, but Garrison eventually spent the night in jail.[38]

Mob violence was worse in border areas such as southern Illinois and southern Ohio. "When a body of men with such feelings and principles begins to distract the nation with their mad schemes, it is high time for a community to notice them," wrote an Ohioan, explaining his approval of antiabolitionist violence. "I am no advocate of Lynch law, but I must say that if Lynch law is to be practised, I know of no fitter subjects for its operation than such fanatics." The abolitionist newspaper publisher James Birney, after being chased from Kentucky, began operating in 1836 just outside of and then, after four months, directly in Cincinnati, Ohio. Public meetings produced resolutions warning Birney of likely violence if he continued publishing his paper, the *Philanthropist*. Other local newspapers failed to rally to Birney's defense and instead joined the call for his suppression. "Southern feeling is strong in this city," it was written in one paper. "[T]he interests of her merchants, her capitalists, and her tradesmen, are too deeply interwoven with the interests of the slave states" to contemplate the disruptions that abolition would cause. Little more than a week later, the same paper encouraged citizens to "put down abolition and abolitionists, peaceably if we can, and forcibly if we must." Birney nevertheless persisted, until July 12, 1836, when a small group broke into the *Philanthropist* offices and destroyed some printing equipment. This incident led to more meetings and warnings as Birney continued to publish. One resolution read as follows:

[A]lthough we deprecate the existence of slavery as a great evil, yet we hold it to be one for which the present generation is not responsible; and disclaiming all right to interfere with the regulations of our sister states on this subject, we regard the conduct of the abolitionists as justly calculated to excite unfriendly dispositions on their part, and thus to effect injuriously our own business and prosperity. . . . While we recognize the constitutional right of liberty of speech and of the press, in its utmost extent; yet, being anxious to preserve the peace and tranquility of our city, and continue those amicable relations which have hitherto existed between the States, we deem it our duty to utter a warning voice. . . . Be it therefore . . . *Resolved,* That in the opinion of this meeting nothing short of the absolute discontinuance of the publication of the said abolition paper in this city, can prevent a resort to violence, which may be as disastrous to its publisher and supporters, as it must be to the good order and fair fame of our city.

The resolution concluded with the citizens comparing themselves to the "Patriots" of the Boston Tea Party, who also acted illegally for "the best interests and happiness of our common country"—that is, for the public good.[39]

On July 29, 1836, Birney and other members of the Executive Committee of the Ohio Anti-Slavery Society replied, insisting that slavery "must cease to exist." In response to the attempted suppression of their calls for abolition, they invoked the tradition of dissent: they refused to stop publishing the *Philanthropist* because doing so would be "a tame surrender of the FREEDOM OF THE PRESS—THE RIGHT TO DISCUSS." Finally, in conclusion, Birney and his colleagues sounded a politically astute note: "We decline complying — because the attempt is now first made in our case, formally and deliberately to put down the freedom of speech and of the press. *We* are, to be sure, the object of the attack," they acknowledged. "But there is not a freeman in the State whose rights are not invaded, in any assault which may be made on us, for refusing to succumb to an imperious demand to surrender our rights."[40]

Birney and his colleagues had struck upon an effective strategy that many other abolitionists would reprise. Initially, abolitionists sought to persuade whites, including Southern slaveholders, to support abolition because it was right from a moral, religious, and legal standpoint. As abolitionists quickly discovered, though, the nobility of this approach matched only its ineffectiveness in generating a mass movement. But once anti-abolitionists began to suppress abolitionist messages violently, then abolitionists were able to chart a convergence of interests among themselves, other whites, and slaves. Abolitionists could now argue that slaveholders and their cohorts not only sought to deny liberty to black slaves but also to free whites. In this context, the reality of the law of free expression mattered little; what mattered was that an increasing percentage of Northern whites began to perceive that the "slave power" purposefully denied whites their rights and liberties so as to protect the slaveholders' interests. With this perception of the slave power, whites could be encouraged to support abolition not merely because it was right — a claim that abolitionists never wavered from — but also, and perhaps more importantly, because abolition was in the interest of free whites. Abolition was necessary to thwart the unquenchable thirst of Southern slaveholders who sucked at the juices of American liberties only to satisfy their own desires. Regardless of the long-run effectiveness of the abolitionists' interest-convergence strategy — appealing to the rights and liberties of free whites in general — it proved fruitless for Birney himself. On July 30, 1836, when Birney fortunately happened to be out of town, a mob broke into the *Philanthropist* newspaper office and, as subsequently described by Birney himself, "scattered the type into the streets, tore down the presses, and completely dismantled the office. . . . A portion of the press was then dragged down Main street, broken up and thrown into the river." The mob next attacked several African Americans in their homes and destroyed a saloon.[41]

Less than two years later, another abolitionist printer, Elijah Lovejoy, would also fall victim to mob violence in a border area, but Lovejoy would ultimately fare even worse than Birney. Lovejoy, a Presbyterian minister from Maine, moved to St. Louis, Missouri, to edit a religious newspaper, the *Observer*, in which Lovejoy voiced his antislavery and anti-Catholic views. Lovejoy's antislavery writings, in particular, offended a number of citizens, who issued a resolution: "Freedom of speech and press does not imply a moral right . . . to freely discuss the subject of slavery . . . , a question too nearly allied to the vital interests of the slaveholding States to admit of public disputation." Initially, Lovejoy refused to cease his writings, but he soon was physically coerced to leave, moving his newspaper to nearby Alton, in the free state of Illinois. When Lovejoy's printing press arrived in Alton, the shippers conveniently left it unattended at the wharf, and before long, St. Louis "ruffians" had dumped it in the river. Undaunted, Lovejoy purchased another press and continued his work. By the spring of 1837, he had become an immediatist, and the *Observer* was a full-fledged abolitionist paper. Various public officials, citizen groups, and even the state legislature repeatedly warned Lovejoy to stop publishing incendiary materials, but to no avail. On August 23, 1837, a mob "composed of 'gentlemen of property and standing,' including the postmaster and the Methodist minister" attacked Lovejoy's office and again destroyed his press. Lovejoy purchased yet another press, which was destroyed on September 21 while it still sat in a warehouse; Lovejoy, though, continued printing, using the press of another paper. Lovejoy's fourth and (what would be his) final press arrived on November 5 and was again placed in a warehouse. This time, Lovejoy asked the mayor for police protection. Refusing, the mayor nonetheless acknowledged that "Lovejoy could legally defend his own property." On November 7, 1837, a mob attacked the warehouse, defended by approximately fourteen men, including Lovejoy. Shots were fired; Lovejoy and one of the attackers fell dead. The mob, not yet satisfied, continued their rampage until they had destroyed the press. The owner of the warehouse and eleven of its defenders plus eleven of the attackers were indicted — nobody for murder. Everybody on both sides was acquitted.[42]

Lovejoy's murder transformed free expression into a political weapon in the national struggle over slavery. The abolitionists, recognizing their opportunity, however tragic the precipitating cause, launched into their interest-convergence strategy by depicting Lovejoy's death as an attack on the rights of all free white men. The Reverend Silas McKeen, delivering a eulogy for the Lovejoy family in Maine, epitomized this approach: "Those balls which pierced his heart were aimed at the heart of Liberty! Your liberty and mine." Northern newspaper publishers, in particular, readily sympathized with the plight of a fellow printer, abolitionist or not. The *New York Evening Post* explained: "Whether [Lovejoy and his abolitionist colleagues] erred or not in their opinion, they did not err in the conviction of their rights as citizens of a democratic government, to express them; nor did they err in defending their right with an obstinacy which yielded only to death." An editor in the *Elmira Republican* lamented: "Let one editor be shot for attempting to print a newspaper for a minority, and none are safe." Over the next years, abolitionist writings would constantly refer to Lovejoy as "the first MARTYR to American LIBERTY."[43]

The murder of Lovejoy, in other words, was more than the death of one abolitionist, more than an attack on abolitionism, more than even an attack on the free expression of abolitionists. It was an attack on republican democratic government and the tradition of dissent that undergirded it. Or at least, that is how abolitionists sought to portray the incident and how many Northerners grew to understand it. The *Hudson River Chronicle* declared that Lovejoy's blood had been "shed in the defence of the freedom of the press, and the right of every American citizen to think, speak and print his own honest opinions." If the murderers were not punished, then "our republican institutions, our boasted freedom, our vaunted safety of property and life will become . . . the scoff and derision of the world." And without doubt, after Lovejoy's murder, not only did violence against abolitionists in the North diminish, but the homages to Lovejoy's martyrdom and to liberty generated new Northern support for abolitionism. According to the American Anti-Slavery Society's New York newspaper, the *Emancipator,* "more than two hundred newspapers had 'fully and decidedly' condemned the 'Alton outrage.'" In perhaps the most important illustration of how the Lovejoy incident could influence Northerners, Wendell Phillips was moved to make his first abolitionist speech: to denounce Lovejoy's murder. Phillips, a Boston Brahmin who would soon become one of the most prominent abolitionist leaders, declared: "The gun which was aimed at the breast of Lovejoy . . . brought me to my feet."[44]

Many antiabolitionists fought back, resisting the characterization of Lovejoy as a martyr for individual liberties. At the trial of the Alton warehouse owner, the prosecutor declared increduously that the defendant, standing alongside Lovejoy, had "violated the laws of man and God . . . for . . . a printing press!" Lovejoy, the prosecutor said, was an outsider whom the community needed to suppress to protect peace and order. He had brought a printing press to Alton "to teach rebellion and insurrection to the slave; to excite servile war; to preach murder in the name of religion; to strike dismay to the hearts of the people, and spread desolation over the face of the land." Some Northern and border-state newspapers agreed. The *Boston Atlas,* in language that would be repeated in the *New York Journal of Commerce,* insisted that Lovejoy "was no martyr to the liberty of the press; but a martyr to his own folly, insubordination and independence of the laws." The *Cincinnati Whig* condemned "the indomitable abolitionism of the Rev. E. P. Lovejoy; who seems to have utterly disregarded the sentiments and feeling of a large majority of the people of that place and who, apparently, has taken no little pains to bring about the awful catastrophe." Many newspaper editors maintained that Lovejoy should be held responsible for his "imprudent" actions, for abusing freedom of the press: a publisher has a duty to conform to the dominant norms or values of his community, and if he cannot do so, he should leave. "We must remember that republicanism implies concession on all sides," explained the Reverend Hubbard Winslow of Boston, "that republican liberty is not the liberty of an isolated individual, or of a despot . . . but liberty to say and do what the prevailing voice and will of the brotherhood will allow and protect."[45]

The potential political use of the Lovejoy murder was itself an active topic of discussion. The *Barre Gazette,* published in Massachusetts, maintained that "[t]his outrage upon the liberty of the Press, and upon the right of Free Discussion . . . will create a feeling in our Country, the effect of which will be totally different from that intended by the Savages who committed this bloody deed!" Southern newspapers, in particular, worried about the abolitionists' manipulation of the Lovejoy incident for their political advantage. The *Louisville Herald* brooded that "[e]very drop [of Lovejoy's blood] will, as it were, spring up into a new Abolition Society, that will, hydra-like, lift its head in the land, and we fear no Hercules will be found who can vanquish it." The *Alexandria Gazette* was equally concerned about possible abolitionist uses of Lovejoy's death, but concluded by reassuring its readers that abolitionists "will never raise seed from the blood of such martyrs as Mr. Lovejoy, however freely it may be poured on the ground." Indeed, until the early 1830s, many Southern states had permitted a reasonable degree of debate about slavery and abolition. At that point, a number of slave revolts together with the increasing abolitionist agitation led Southern states to crack down on antislavery expression through official and unofficial means. For instance, Virginia already had a statute that imposed punishment for the incitement of a slave insurrection, but in 1836, the state broadened this law so as to punish the advocacy of abolitionism. The statute also directed postmasters to notify a justice of the peace if any abolitionist literature were received at a post office, and the justice of the peace was "to have such book, pamphlet, or other writing, burned in his presence." As if this were not enough, Virginia amended and strengthened this statute again in 1848. Southern states justified suppression pursuant to republican democracy: abolitionism, according to the *Richmond Enquirer,* was "inflammatory, dangerous, mischievous"—threatening the common good—so Southerners could choose "to suppress, to the uttermost of our power." Southern states, though, rarely resorted to prosecutions under these laws because public opinion in conjunction with the threat of mob violence adequately discouraged abolitionist expression. Many Southern communities granted mobs a "quasi-legal status," referring to them as "vigilance committees" or "committees of safety," similar to the Revolutionary War patriot Committees of Observation. Prominent citizens, including judges, lawyers, and planters, led these mob-committees. Their goals were clear: pursuant to "the laws of natural justice and self-preservation," one South Carolina committee explained, "we are deliberately and advisedly determined that the guilty [abolitionists] shall not escape." Southern governments, in effect, gave the mob-committees free rein to target supposed troublemakers and to run them out of town or to tar and feather them.[46]

WHILE SOUTHERNERS WIELDED their methods of suppression, Garrison and his abolitionist colleagues, after having founded the American Anti-Slavery Society in 1833, developed their own methods for spreading their message of immediate abolition. One chief method was to mail immense quantities of abolitionist literature to the South, where the abolitionists could not otherwise readily disseminate their ideas. A second method was to flood Congress with petitions demanding abolition. Each of these methods would spark national disputes involving free expression.

In May 1835, the Society initiated its mass mailings project, "the great postal campaign," taking advantage of the recently invented steam-driven printing press, which allowed the Society to print thousands upon thousands of inexpensive pamphlets and newspapers that "depicted the horrors of slavery in words and pictures." In July 1835 alone, the New York City post office dispatched over 175,000 abolitionist mailings, and within less than three years, the Society had mailed over one million items. While abolitionists initially reckoned that slaveholders could be persuaded to support emancipation, the mailings sparked a firestorm of protest and attempted suppression in the South, where whites believed abolitionists intended to generate slave rebellions. The first major conflagration was in Charleston, South Carolina. On the evening of July 29, 1835, a mob broke into the post office and stole several satchels containing hundreds of abolitionist publications. The next evening, the mob dumped the stolen abolitionist literature at a public square and burned it in a bonfire along with effigies of abolitionist leaders, including Garrison. Charleston Postmaster Alfred

Huger immediately wrote to U.S. Postmaster General Amos Kendall to ask how he should handle future shipments of abolitionist literature. Kendall responded by maintaining that he had "no legal authority to exclude newspapers from the mail," but he also would not direct Huger "to forward or deliver the papers of which you speak." Rather, as the local postmaster, Huger could exercise his discretion to act for the common good. "We owe an obligation to the laws, but a higher one to the communities in which we live," explained Kendall, "and if the former be perverted to destroy the latter, it is patriotism to disregard them."[47]

The Charleston postal incident together with Kendall's acquiescence seemed to exhort other Southern postmasters to censor abolitionist mailings while encouraging communities to create mob-committees to oversee the mails and other shipping. As William Leggett complained in the *New York Evening Post,* Kendall was "establishing a censorship of the press . . . by allowing every twopenny postmaster through the country to be the judge of what species of intelligence it is proper to circulate, and what to withhold from the people." Many in the South were nonetheless dissatisfied. They wanted legislation that could help control the abolitionist use of the Postal Service, though, as it turned out, not all Southerners agreed on what type of legislation would suffice. President Andrew Jackson, a Southerner born in the western farm country of North Carolina, had settled in Tennessee, made a fortune in land speculation, lived in an imposing mansion called the Hermitage, and owned more than a hundred slaves. The American Anti-Slavery Society's mass mailing campaign outraged him. Initially, Jackson suggested that postmasters identify and expose subscribers to abolitionist literature so that they would suffer social exclusion, or as Jackson put it, "coventry." But by December 7, 1835, when Jackson greeted the Twenty-fourth Congress with his seventh annual message, he was ready to call for the enactment of a federal law that would restrict the use of the mails. Echoing the typical Southern view of the abolitionist literature, Jackson condemned the mailings as "inflammatory appeals addressed to the passions of the slaves . . . calculated to stimulate them to insurrection and to produce all the horrors of a servile war." The mailings were "destructive of the harmony and peace of the country, and . . . repugnant to the principles of our national compact and to the dictates of humanity and religion." Given such concerns for the common good of the nation, Jackson thought it "proper for Congress to take [action]." He concluded with a specific recommendation: that Congress pass "such a law as will prohibit, under severe penalties, the circulation in the Southern States, through the mail, of incendiary publications intended to instigate the slaves to insurrection."[48]

Senator John C. Calhoun of South Carolina also wanted legislative action, but strongly opposed federal control. Calhoun had been vice president during Jackson's first term, but the two had a falling-out earlier in the decade partly because Calhoun had insisted South Carolina could nullify a federal tariff law he deemed unconstitutional. On December 21, 1835, in response to Jackson's call for a federal law restricting the mailing of abolitionist literature, Calhoun moved that the matter be sent to a specially appointed Select Committee. Calhoun worried that the Committee on the Post Office and Post Roads, which otherwise would consider such legislation, included "only a single gentleman from that section of the country [read: the South] which was most deeply interested in the proper disposition of this very important subject." The Senate approved Calhoun's motion, with the Select Committee consisting of one Northerner, from Massachusetts, and four Southerners, including Calhoun, designated the Committee chair.[49]

On February 4, 1836, the Select Committee issued its report, written by Calhoun himself, proposing a bill consistent with Calhoun's rather than Jackson's desires. Calhoun's overriding goal was to harmonize two concerns, both grounded on the protection of slavery: first, to suppress the distribution of abolitionist literature, yet second, to preserve state sovereignty vis-à-vis federal power. Many Southerners fretted that any expansion of federal power, for any purposes whatsoever, would eventually be twisted to justify congressional power over slavery. Calhoun thus began the report by agreeing with Jackson on a basic point: the abolitionist mailings were incendiary, contrary to the common good, and needed to be suppressed, by some means. But, Calhoun insisted, Congress did not have the power to pass the law requested by Jackson. Calhoun explicitly recalled the Sedition Act controversy and reiterated the Republicans' jurisdictional argument. Congress lacked the constitutional power to regulate speech and writing, but the states retained such power. The Constitution left the regulation of the free press "under the exclusive authority and control of the States." The states, Calhoun insisted, can "determine what is, or is not, calculated to disturb their peace and security, and of course, in the case under consideration, it belongs to the Slave holding States to determine what is incendiary and intended to incite insurrection." In fact, Calhoun added, not only did the states have the power to restrict expression, but the states could insist that Congress enact laws "to co-operate" in the execution of the state laws. The Select Committee's proposed bill provided that local postmasters — federal employees — were to enforce state laws. Section 1 of the bill proscribed deputy postmasters from knowingly receiving and putting "into the mail any pamphlet . . . or other paper . . . touching the subject of slavery, addressed to any person or post office in any State, Territory, or District, where, by the laws of the said State, Territory, or District, their circulation is prohibited."[50]

Not all Southerners agreed with Calhoun; some sided with Jackson. Partly for that reason, and partly because some senators opposed any federal action at all, Congress passed neither Calhoun's nor Jackson's proposed law. Even so, Southern states assumed that once mail arrived in a local post office, state law governed its handling. In effect, then, Southerners implemented Calhoun's approach de facto, without the benefit of a federal statute. Slave states, if they had not already done so, enacted laws imposing greater restrictions on the dissemination of abolitionist literature (complementing the unofficial means that already suppressed antislavery sentiments). Even further, Southern states, including Virginia, Georgia, Alabama, and North Carolina, expressly requested Northern states to help suppress the abolitionists. For instance, after expressing "every confidence in the justice and friendship of the non-slaveholding states," the South Carolina legislature "earnestly" requested the Northern states to "promptly and effectually suppress all those associations within their respective limits, purporting to be abolition societies [and to] make it highly penal to print, publish, and distribute [abolitionist literature]."[51]

Southern requests for Northern statutes backfired. Instead of engendering Northern compliance, the Southerners facilitated the abolitionists' interest-convergence strategy. Many Northerners disliked the abolitionists, condemned the mass mailings program, and suppressed abolitionist expression through unofficial means, including mob violence, but they resented Southern efforts to intrude into Northern political affairs. Here were Southerners practically insisting that Northern states enact laws to suppress the expression of white Protestant Northerners — albeit abolitionists. Anti-slavery advocates, like Alvan Stewart of New York, did not hesitate to stress this point: he repudiated the claim that abolitionism was a threat justifying "loss of liberty of the press, of conscience, discussion, and of the inviolability of the mail." All New York citizens, Stewart insisted, had a right to express "their sentiments on any moral problem, or any question of right and wrong, of liberty and slavery." Many Northerners responded favorably to these invocations of free expression, whether grounded on natural rights, constitutional guarantees, or the tradition of dissent. The Ohio legislature, for example, reported that "the states have no power to restrain the publication of private opinion on any subject whatever, and the principle, if admitted, involves much greater evils to the peace of the states, than the toleration of errors and the excitements they cause can ever produce."[52]

WHILE THE NEW TECHNOLOGY of the steam-driven printing press sparked the American Anti-Slavery Society's mass mailing campaign, the Society's second chief method of spreading its immediatist message arose from the members' lingering faith in a venerable means of political expression: the petition to a legislature. The right to petition arose, in part, from the republican democratic idea of the sovereign people; petitioning allowed citizens to communicate with their representatives. It had been important to the Northern emancipation efforts after the Revolutionary War, and antislavery advocates had continued to send occasional petitions to Congress over the years. But in December 1834, the Society initiated a concentrated drive, flooding Congress with abolitionist petitions, many demanding the end of slavery in the District of Columbia. The District, as a general matter, was under congressional control, though Southerners disputed Congress's power to emancipate slaves anywhere, in the District or not. The petitioners initially concentrated their efforts on the House of Representatives, supposedly more democratic than the Senate because the people directly elected the representatives. Individuals, often women who were otherwise excluded from participating in the democratic process, would carry the petitions door-to-door through their own neighborhoods and towns in a quest for more and more signatures. In 1836, abolitionists sent approximately three hundred petitions to Congress with between thirty and forty thousand signatures. By the middle of 1838, the number of signees had grown to over four hundred thousand.[53]

On December 16, 1835, early in the Twenty-fourth Congress's first session, Maine Representative John Fairfield presented a petition to the House from "one hundred and seventy-two ladies residing in his district, praying the abolition of slavery in the District of Columbia." He added, though, "that he did not desire to be understood as favoring the views of the petitioners." Following normal procedure, Fairfield moved that the petition be referred to the appropriate committee, here the Committee on the District of Columbia. Typically, the petition would be forwarded to the Committee where it would die for lack of attention, but this time, a New York representative intervened, moving "to lay the petition on the table," which under parliamentary rules of procedure would preclude any further discussion (unless the House later removed it from the table). Representatives voted to approve the motion to table. When Fairfield presented a second abolitionist petition, it met the same fate.[54]

Two days later, Massachusetts Representative William Jackson presented another petition for abolition in the District. This time, James Henry Hammond, an ambitious South Carolinian, was not satisfied with merely moving to table. Instead, he "moved that the petition be not received." He explained that he wanted the House "to put a more decided seal of reprobation on [such petitions], by peremptorily rejecting them." Hammond, in effect, proposed a gag rule that would prevent the House from receiving and discussing abolitionist petitions. He insisted that "[he] could not sit there and see the rights of the southern people assaulted day after day by the ignorant fanatics from whom these memorials proceed." Hammond's motion never passed. The House tangled itself in a series of motions and countermotions and debates over proper procedure. Basically, the representatives became hamstrung between their widespread condemnation of the abolitionists and their pervasive confusion about the appropriate processes for dealing with the abolitionists' petitions.[55]

The crisis over the abolitionist petitions moved next to the Senate. On January 7, 1836, Ohio Senator Thomas Morris presented two petitions and moved that they be referred to the Committee on the District of Columbia. Calhoun immediately "asked that the question should first be taken on receiving the petition." Calhoun, that is, raised the same issue in the Senate that Hammond had raised in the House. "[O]ne half of the Union was deeply slandered in these [abolitionist] petitions," Calhoun explained, by way of justification. "[T]hese memorials aimed at a violation of the Constitution. We have not the power . . . under the Constitution to interfere with the subject of slavery," whether in the states or in the District of Columbia. Many Northerners had suspected that Calhoun had helped his fellow Carolinian, Hammond, develop the gag-rule strategy in the first place. Such perceived plottings, whether true or not, were propitious for abolitionists seeking to forge a convergence of interests: Southern actions prompted Northerners, not just abolitionists, to worry that there was a "Great Slavepower Conspiracy" aiming to undermine republican democratic government and liberty. The efforts to impose gag rules provided concrete evidence of such a conspiracy. Not only were slaveholders specifically attacking the right to petition, but they were effectively attacking free expression in general. The right of petition had historically been understood as providing a channel for communication between legislative representatives and their constituents. A gag rule would close that essential channel of communication. Indeed, some Southerners opposed Calhoun's efforts exactly because they feared that a gag rule would stoke Northern suspicions of a slave-power conspiracy. John King of Georgia worried that Calhoun's tactic already "had produced tenfold agitation." Calhoun's efforts, King declared, would nurture abolitionists' hopes, as they thought: "'[Well], that is precisely what I wanted; . . . I wished to provoke the 'aristo-cratic slaveholder' to make extravagant demands on the North, which the North could not consistently surrender them. I wished them, under the pretext of securing their own rights, to encroach upon the rights of all the American people.'" Regardless of Calhoun's "nice constitutional distinc-tions and parliamentary rules," King concluded, "a refusal to receive peti-tions . . . would be looked upon as an arrogant attack upon a popular right, and would be so used by the enemies of the South." Calhoun responded to King's attack in kind. If anyone was making a strategic error, it was King, not Calhoun. King betrayed Southern interests; his arguments would have a "tendency to divide and distract the Southern delegation on this, to us, all-momentous question."[56]

In fact, the Senate voted to defeat Calhoun's gag-rule strategy. Sub-sequently, James Buchanan, a Pennsylvania senator and future president, moved to receive an abolitionist petition but to reject it summarily. This motion passed easily, thirty-four yeas to six nays, with Calhoun refusing to vote in protest. He insisted that the mere reception of abolitionist peti-tions "gave a fatal stab at our liberties." Before long, though, the Senate adopted an alternative means for disposing of abolitionist petitions: as soon as one senator presented a petition, another senator would question whether it should be received, and then the Senate would table that ques-tion. In other words, instead of tabling the petition itself, the Senate tabled the question whether the petition should be received. By following this torturous approach, the Senate avoided suggesting that the abolitionist petitions themselves were worthy of consideration.[57]

A final long episode in the petition crisis would take place in the House. On February 4, 1836, South Carolina Representative Henry Laurens Pinck-ney moved that all petitions "praying for the abolition of slavery . . . be referred to a select committee." The Committee should be instructed "to report that Congress possess no constitutional authority to interfere in any way with the institutions of slavery in any of the States." Then, in impor-tant words of apparent compromise, Pinckney added, "Congress ought not to interfere in any way with slavery in the District of Columbia, because it would be a violation of the public faith, unwise, impolitic, and dangerous to the Union." This approach, repudiating congressional power over slavery in the states but merely discouraging congressional action in the District, reflected the wishes of both President Jackson and the vice president and master politician, Martin Van Buren, a New Yorker. This seeming admission of congressional power over slavery in the District outraged many Southerners, including Calhoun. Regardless, Pinckney's motion passed, with Pinckney appointed chair of the Select Committee.[58]

On May 18, 1836, the Select Committee issued a report, which included three resolutions tracking Pinckney's initial recommendation. The first resolution declared unequivocally that Congress lacked the power "to interfere in any way with the institution of slavery in any of the States." The second contained the compromise that "Congress ought not to interfere in any way with slavery in the District of Columbia." The third resolution proposed a new gag rule: "all petitions . . . relating in any way . . . to the subject of slavery, or the abolition of slavery, shall, without being either printed or referred, be laid upon the table, and . . . no further action whatever shall be had thereon." This gag rule was not quite as extreme as the one Calhoun had sought in the Senate, but it was close. To Pinckney, the House needed this gag rule to quell further agitation for abolition. That same day, when the House began considering the Select Committee Report and its resolutions, the Southern representatives managed to focus not on the gag rule but on the second resolution, which seemed to admit congressional power over slavery in the District. South Carolinian Waddy Thompson declared that he "would not allow one moment to pass without his unmeasured denunciation of the report." Many Southerners condemned Pinckney as a "traitor" to their cause; Calhoun and Thompson even orchestrated his defeat in the next congressional election.[59]

In the midst of the debates over the Select Committee resolutions, John Quincy Adams, representative from Massachusetts and former president, entered the fray. Given Adams's advanced age, almost sixty-nine years old, he unsurprisingly understood the right to petition in the traditional sense, as a means for the people to communicate with their legislators. In 1832, years before the petition battle and shortly after Adams began serving in the House, he wrote in his journal: "Being Monday, the states were successively called for presentation of petitions; a most tedious operation in practice, though to a reflective mind a very striking exemplification of the magnificent grandeur of our nation and of the sublime principles upon which our government is founded." Moreover, during the first series of House debates on the right of petition, in December 1835, Adams briefly spoke against the proposed gag rule, characterizing the right to petition as a "sacred right." He maintained that the best course to follow with abolitionist petitions was the normal one: "to refer [them] to a committee, to receive their report, and unanimously to adopt that report." By doing so, the House would effectively send the petitions "to the tomb of the Capulets." At this time, then, Adams claimed to oppose abolitionism, but the perceived threat to free expression aroused him. "[W]hat will be the consequence?" he asked. "You suppress the right of petition; you suppress the freedom of the press; you suppress the freedom of religion; for in the sentiments of many respectable men, fanatics if you please to call them, they are found to act under a sense of duty to their God."[60]

When the House first began debating the Select Committee's report and its resolutions, Adams remained quiet. After a week, on May 25, 1836, he decided to address his colleagues, but the Speaker of the House, James Polk of Tennessee, instead recognized George Owens of Georgia, who immediately called the question. Adams asked for permission to speak, but Polk, following parliamentary procedure, ruled that once the question had been called, no further discussion of the merits of the underlying motion (the resolutions) should be allowed unless and until the House defeated the call to question. Adams, after noting that "a slaveholding Speaker occupied the Chair," asked Polk, "[A]m I gagged, or not?" The answer: he was. The House approved the call to question and then overwhelmingly adopted the first two resolutions. When Adams was called to vote on the third resolution, the gag rule, he declared, "I hold the resolution to be a direct violation of the Constitution of the United States, the rules of this House, and the rights of my constituents." But "loud cries of 'Order!' from all parts of the Hall" forced him to retake his seat. The House approved the gag rule, 117 yeas to sixty-eight nays.[61]

While other Northern representatives hesitated to challenge the gag rule, Adams persevered in presenting abolitionist petitions. He remained careful, however, not to violate House procedures. He would introduce a petition and, pretending innocence, ask whether it fell within the scope of the gag rule. The South responded by strengthening its resolve. On January 20, 1840, Waddy Thompson moved to make the gag rule permanent and successfully guided his motion to the House floor for debate. When Adams attempted to substitute an alternative motion, William Cost Johnson of Maryland parried by amending Adams's motion. Johnson proposed the most draconian gag rule yet: "That no petition . . . praying the abolition of slavery in the District of Columbia, or any State or Territory . . . shall be received by this House, or entertained in any way whatever." Johnson brazenly declared his intention to "kill the hydra, Abolition, in an instant, in such manner that it could not germinate its species again." The House adopted Johnson's permanent gag rule in a close vote.[62]

Adams continued to present abolitionist petitions despite the permanent gag rule. Southern representatives bided their time, looking for an excuse to censure Adams, despite his formal compliance with House procedures. On January 24, 1842, Southerners saw their chance. Adams presented a petition, signed by forty-six citizens of Haverhill, Massachusetts, which prayed "that you will immediately adopt measures peaceably to dissolve the Union" because the South's maintenance of slavery would eventually and "certainly overwhelm the whole nation in utter destruction." Isaac Holmes of South Carolina pretended incredulity: "This is a petition for the dissolution of the Union." Adams responded, with the seriousness he thought all petitions deserved: "I move its reference to a select committee, with instructions to report an answer to the petitioners, showing the reasons why the prayer of it ought not to be granted." George Washington Hopkins snapped: "Is it in order to move to burn the petition in the presence of the House?" After a motion to table, Virginia's Henry Wise asked the chair: "Is it in order to move to censure any member presenting such a petition?"[63]

The Southern gambit was now apparent. Southern representatives would attempt to have the House censure Adams for presenting an abolitionist petition, on the pretext that it prayed for the dissolution of the Union. Adams's response? "Good!" One can practically see the elderly Adams rubbing his wrinkled hands together in glee. The Southerners nonetheless pressed on, with Thomas Walker Gilmer of Virginia making the official motion: "That, in presenting to the consideration of this House a petition for the dissolution of the Union, the member from Massachusetts (Mr. Adams) has justly incurred the censure of the House." While other representatives sought to table the motion, Adams "welcomed and encouraged his 'trial.'" In fact, when a motion to table came to a vote, Adams voted nay. Adams won, so to speak; his trial would proceed.[64]

Adams initiated his defense by asking the clerk to read the Declaration of Independence. Adams's point, he explained, was that the people have a right to challenge an oppressive government and a right to petition facilitates such a challenge. The trial of Adams — that is, the debate on the censure motion — would last two weeks, with Adams gaining the floor to speak in his own defense on February 2, 1842. He talked, and talked, and talked some more; abolitionist leader Theodore Dwight Weld worked diligently to help Adams stay prepared. The Southerners had unwittingly granted Adams the right to expound about slavery and abolition on the

House floor. As Weld wrote to his wife, "[In] defending himself [Adams] will take up nearly all the relations of *slavery* to this government." As Adams continued day after day, Northern support for censure dissipated, and even Southern support started to weaken. Southerners sulked because they had adopted the gag rule to inhibit discussion of abolition and slavery, and here was Adams, supposedly defending himself from a House censure, talking incessantly about those very subjects. Gilmer, at one point, offered to withdraw his motion to censure if Adams would "withdraw the petition he had offered praying for a dissolution of the Union." Adams refused, claiming that "in presenting the petition, [he] had acted under a sense of duty." On February 7, however, having already consumed six days for his defense, Adams announced that he would acquiesce to a motion to table. By now, thoroughly outmaneuvered, Southerners wanted no more than to move on. Georgian James Meriwether lamented that the debate had been "a useless consumption of time. [The] whole matter played as a political game before the country, to the prejudice of one party and the benefit of another." The House voted to table the censure motion, and Adams celebrated his victory by immediately presenting a multitude of "Abolition petitions of every description."⁶⁵

REGARDLESS OF ADAMS'S VICTORY, the politics of slavery and abolition continued to engender suppression. In 1857, for instance, Hinton Rowan Helper, a North Carolinian, published his book *The Impending Crisis of the South: How to Meet It*. That rare breed, a Southern abolitionist, Helper was a virulent racist who appealed to the economic self-interest of poor white Southerners. He maintained that aristocratic slaveholders used slavery to depress the wages of free white laborers and to diminish the profits of white farmers. Many Southerners blamed Helper for spurring John Brown's 1859 raid on the federal armory at Harpers Ferry, Virginia — a raid intended to launch a slave rebellion. Southern suppression of Helper took a variety of forms. Helper initially had difficulty finding a publisher, and once he did so, those who sold the book were threatened with prosecution. In Helper's own North Carolina, the penalty for distributing the book (or any other abolitionist literature, for that matter) was a public whipping and one year of imprisonment; a second offense was punishable by death.⁶⁶

During the years leading up to the Civil War, Republicans tended to emphasize the importance of free expression and the tradition of dissent. But once the war started, the Republican commitment to free expression wavered. Northern Democrats who opposed the War, known as

Copperheads, and their newspapers, like the *Chicago Times,* constantly "denounced the war as a failure and the [Union] leaders as corrupt and demagogic." The *New York Daily News* called President Abraham Lincoln "that compound of cunning, heartlessness, and folly," and demanded that the North negotiate a peaceful end to the war. "[N]o man of ordinary perceptive faculties honestly believes today that further bloodshed will secure a political result more desirable than such, whatever it may be, than can be secured by negotiation. Why do we persist in dealing death-blows that vindicate no principle?" Such dissident views were sometimes tolerated and sometimes suppressed through either official or unofficial channels. Unofficial suppression typically took the form of mob violence. On August 8, 1861, a gang of soldiers attacked and "completely stripped" the office of the *Democratic Standard,* published in Concord, New Hampshire. Similar attacks on other newspaper offices were common. In Haverhill, Massachusetts, a Copperhead editor was dragged from his house, "covered with a coat of tar and feathers, and ridden on a rail through the town." The mob then forced him to proclaim that he would "never again write or publish articles against the North and in favor of secession."[67]

Meanwhile, General Ambrose Burnside engineered a controversial series of official acts of suppression. In March 1863, Lincoln appointed Burnside to command Ohio and the surrounding areas. Burnside discovered that, in his own words, "newspapers were full of treasonable expressions" and "large public meetings were held, at which our Government authorities and our gallant soldiers in the field were openly and loudly denounced for their efforts to suppress the rebellion." Distressed, he issued General Order No. 38: "The habit of declaring sympathies for the enemy will not be allowed in this department. Persons committing such offences will be at once arrested, with a view to being tried . . . or sent beyond our lines into the lines of their friends."[68] Clement Vallandigham, a former Democratic representative from Ohio, made a speech on May 1, 1863, intended to revive his fading campaign for the Democratic gubernatorial nomination in Ohio. He hoped to force Burnside to order his arrest and to spark public sentiment in his favor. As part of this campaign ploy, Vallandigham filled his speech with Copperhead vituperatives. He called the Civil War "'a war for the purpose of crushing out liberty and erecting a despotism;' [and] 'a war for the freedom of the blacks and the enslavement of the whites.'" On May 5, Vallandigham was arrested and charged with violating Order No. 38 for "declaring disloyal sentiments and opinions with the object and purpose of weakening the power of the government in its efforts to suppress an unlawful rebellion." After a two-day trial, a military commission found Vallandigham guilty. Vallandigham filed a petition for a writ of habeas corpus arguing, in effect, that having been tried before a military commission, he had been denied the ordinary protections of a criminal trial. District Judge Humphrey Leavitt denied the petition, deferring to the discretion of the executive and the military during a time of war. Leavitt reasoned that, for the sake of the nation's "[s]elf-preservation," a court "cannot shut its eyes to the grave fact that war exists, involving the most imminent public danger, and threatening the subversion and destruction of the constitution itself." Vallandigham's sentence, as directed by President Lincoln, was banishment to the Confederacy.[69]

Burnside was not yet finished. He turned his attention to the *Chicago Times,* a rabid Copperhead paper that had denounced Vallandigham's arrest as "the funeral of civil liberty." Less than one month after Vallandigham's conviction, Burnside issued General Order No. 84: "On account of the repeated expression of disloyal and incendiary sentiments, the publication of the newspaper known as the *Chicago Times* is hereby suppressed." A federal district court granted the editor of the *Times* a temporary restraining order that supposedly prohibited Burnside from implementing Order No. 84. Burnside, disregarding the court order, sent his troops to close the *Times.* After three days of intense political pressure, however, Lincoln ordered Burnside to allow the *Times* to reopen. Democrats howled that Burnside's policies and Vallandigham's arrest and conviction amounted to gross violations of free expression. Indiana Representative Daniel Voorhees complained that Lincoln and Burnside had, in effect, resurrected the Sedition Law of 1798, without even the benefit of congressional action. In Albany, New York, a Democratic meeting produced ten resolutions, called the "Albany Resolves," which protested that Vallandigham had been convicted "for no other reason than words addressed to a public meeting." Republicans, of course, reacted differently. They supported yet worried about Burnside's actions. The *Cincinnati Commercial* praised Order No. 38 for drawing a clear line "between traitors and patriots" and labeled Vallandigham an enemy of the government. Liberty was not the same as licentiousness. Yet, some Republicans fretted that Burnside had undermined the first amendment — after they had so long advocated for free expression. The *New York Evening Post* emphasized the importance of free expression to republican democratic government: "[N]o governments and no authorities are to be held as above criticism, or even denunciation. We know of no other way of correcting their faults, spurring on their sluggishness, or restraining their tyrannies, than by open and bold discussion."[70]

Other Republicans worried that Burnside had erred politically. In fact,

Vallandigham's campaign strategy would ultimately prove effective. While exiled, he received the Democratic gubernatorial nomination for Ohio! Burnside's suppression of Vallandigham sounded loudly through the halls at the nominating convention, as the delegates resolved "that the will of the people is the foundation of all free government: that to give effect to this will, free thought, free speech and a free press are absolutely indispensable." The Republican editor of *Harper's Weekly* grumbled: "Vallandigham was fast talking himself into the deepest political grave ever dug . . . when Burnside resurrected him." Political prudence therefore drove Lincoln to temper Burnside's zealotry. When Lincoln rescinded Order No. 84, which had closed the *Chicago Times,* he had the secretary of war, Edwin Stanton, communicate his directive to Burnside. Stanton's letter revealed Lincoln's concern that Burnside was a political bumbler: "The irritation produced by such acts is in [the president's] opinion likely to do more harm than the publication would do. . . . [U]pon administrative questions such as the arrest of civilians and the suppression of newspapers not requiring immediate action the President desires to be previously consulted." Even so, Lincoln believed that, during wartime, suppression sometimes was justifiable. He insisted that the government could punish an individual who intended "to prevent the raising of troops [or encouraged] desertions from the army." The first amendment did not protect expression that "was damaging [to] the Army, upon . . . which the life of the Nation depends." Thus, in 1864, Lincoln closed two New York newspapers that had published false and damaging information about the draft. "Must I shoot a simple-minded soldier boy who deserts," Lincoln asked rhetorically, "while I must not touch a hair of a wily agitator who induces him to desert?"[71]

ASSESSING THE STATUS OF FREE EXPRESSION

From the early 1830s through the Civil War, the suppression of speech and writing was commonplace, but no more so than were the calls for free expression. Yet, given this stretch of more than three decades, the theoretical exploration of free expression during these years was disappointingly shallow when compared with the discussions that took place during the relatively brief Sedition Act period. In a three-year period around the turn into the nineteenth century, Madison, Hay, Wortman, Thomson, and even Nicholas in a congressional report, all produced enlightening theoretical writings that justified an expansive concept of free expression (and in 1803, Tucker reiterated Madison's views in his influential American edition of

Blackstone's *Commentaries*). In contrast, the mid-nineteenth-century discussions of free expression were in many ways "familiar renditions" of the earlier Sedition Act debates. Americans constantly invoked free expression throughout these decades, but largely for instrumental purposes within the overarching slavery-abolition dispute. True, Sedition Act era advocates for free expression were also politically motivated. Yet, mid-nineteenth-century advocates for free speech and a free press typically seemed far less interested in the protection of free expression per se, as a principle or in the abstract, than in the use of free expression as a sword against slavery (and understandably so). The Republicans' 1856 campaign slogan epitomized the political use of free expression: "Free Speech, Free Press, Free Men, Free Labor, Free Territory, and Frémont."[72]

Thomas Cooper conspicuously illustrates the political malleability of the concept of free expression. In 1800, the Federalists had prosecuted and convicted Cooper under the Sedition Act. Cooper, representing himself, had suggested republican democracy required a broad conception of free expression. Over the next decades, Cooper continued to maintain that "no criminal action for libel ought to be permitted." During this time, Cooper, who was originally from England, settled in the South and became president of South Carolina College. Then, in 1835, disregarding his earlier views on free expression and following the political interests of his fellow Southerners, Cooper maintained that abolitionist literature should be barred from the mails. He now called individual rights "a great deal of nonsense." Cooper's transformation showed that Americans cared about free expression but that they understood and implemented it through the prism of politics. Deeply ingrained political desires and cultural outlooks necessarily shaped how Northerners and Southerners alike respectively understood free expression. During the mass mailings debates, for example, John C. Calhoun maintained that Congress should enact a statute to enforce repressive state laws. To generate opposition to Calhoun's bill, Massachusetts Senator John Davis paid homage to the importance of free expression. "The press is the great organ of a free people," Davis declared on the Senate floor. "It is the medium through which their thoughts are communicated, through which they act upon one another, and by which they reason with, instruct, and move each other. It rouses us to vigilance, warns us of danger, rebukes the aspiring, encourages the modest, and, like the sun in the heavens, radiates its influence over the whole country." Yet Davis ultimately did no more than endorse the jurisdictional argument: Congress could not regulate the press in any manner, but state governments retained the power to do so. Suppression did not violate the tenets of republican democracy.[73]

Perhaps more than anyone else of his time, John Quincy Adams appeared to champion free expression regardless of his political views. He began his stalwart defense of the right to petition even while he did not openly support the abolitionist cause, though he disliked slavery. Yet, Adams had political reasons of his own for defying the Southerners in Congress and for emphasizing democratic principles, above all else. In the 1828 presidential election, Jackson had defeated the incumbent Adams largely because the Jacksonian Democrats had portrayed Adams as corrupting republican democracy. During Adams's presidential term, Jackson's congressional supporters often appeared to aim merely at discrediting Adams. As Adams viewed his defeat, the unvirtuous Jacksonians "had undemocratically destroyed 'the great object of my life.'" Once Adams returned to public life as a congressman, he unequivocally was not a disinterested apolitical defender of individual rights and liberties. The petition battles presented Adams with an opportunity to vindicate himself and his own democratic credentials while simultaneously thwarting Southern designs.[74]

The fulcrum for the mid-nineteenth-century free-expression debates, as well as most other debates of the time, was of course slavery. Every issue, it seemed, revolved around slavery and abolition. Thus, when William Cost Johnson advocated for a permanent gag rule on petitions in the House, he elaborated not the parameters of a right to petition but the rights of slaveholders. He insisted upon "the impropriety and unconstitutionality of the people of the North attempting to deprive the people of the South of their slave property, which was valued at twelve hundred millions of dollars." Indeed, the theoretical explorations of free expression of this period seem skeletally thin when compared with the expansive, complex, and contemporaneous arguments both for and against slavery. Northerners and Southerners published numerous multifaceted essays and books on both sides of this overriding question. Like William Cost Johnson, when Calhoun advocated for suppressing abolitionist petitions, he devoted his energies more to the defense of slavery than to delineating the parameters of free expression, however limited. Calhoun became renowned as one of the foremost advocates for the positive-good defense of slavery. "I take higher ground," he proclaimed. "[I]n the present state of civilization, where two races of different origin, and distinguished by color, and other physical differences, as well as intellectual, are brought together, the relation now existing in the slaveholding States between the two, is, instead of an evil, a good — a positive good." Calhoun continued by exploring the role of slavery in a capitalist economic system. He maintained that "there never has yet existed a wealthy and civilized society in which one portion of the community did not, in point of fact, live on the labor of the other." In any advanced civilization, that is, "a conflict between labor and capital" necessarily arises, and given this inherent conflict, slavery provides for the most "stable and quiet" societal organization.[75]

Calhoun elaborated his arguments in his subsequently published book-length *Disquisition on Government*. He began by maintaining that people are social rather than isolated creatures and that they therefore need government. In effect, he rejected the philosophical (and Lockean) construct of a state of nature where individuals are free, equal, and independent. The primary end of government, it followed, was "the protection of the community," not the protection of individual liberty. Calhoun thus justified slavery as a common good, or in other words, as a positive good for the community as a whole as well as for the slaves themselves. Equal liberty for all would be a "curse" instead of a blessing. Liberty "is a reward to be earned, not a blessing to be gratuitously lavished on all alike," he explained. It is "a reward reserved for the intelligent, the patriotic, the virtuous and deserving; — and not a boon to be bestowed on a people too ignorant, degraded and vicious, to be capable either of appreciating or of enjoying it." Calhoun, that is, took the long-standing argument for excluding certain groups from the republican democratic polity — group members lacked the requisite civic virtue — and extended the argument so as to justify slavery.[76]

On the abolitionist side, many of the immediatists merely declared that an inalienable right to liberty necessitated immediate emancipation. Immediatists would ground this right on a variety of sources, including religion, the Declaration of Independence, and natural law or natural rights in general. But some immediatists justified abolition and criticized the proslavery positions with more complex arguments. Weld criticized the proslavery positive-good position. "Are slaveholders dunces, or do they take all the rest of the world to be, that they think to bandage our eyes with such thin gauzes? Protecting their kind regard for those whom they hourly plunder of all they have and all they get! What! when they have seized their victims, and annihilated all their rights, still claim to be the special guardians of their happiness!" Weld bolstered his position with empirical evidence, particularly eyewitness accounts of the brutal mistreatment of slaves. But, Weld wondered, how can slaveholders see their treatment of slaves so differently? How can slaveholders believe they treat their slaves beneficently rather than barbarically? Weld's answer: a category error. Slaveholders mistakenly categorized slaves as property rather than as true humans. If free whites were treated as slaves, then slaveholders would immediately recognize the conduct "as a monstrous outrage and horrible cruelty." But when black slaves were subjected to such mistreatment, the slaveholders shrugged indifferently, thinking it for the slaves' own good. But why did slaveholders consistently make this category error? Again, Weld had an answer: acculturation. "Accustomed all his life to regard [slaves] as domestic animals," Weld explained, "to hear them stormed at, and to see them cuffed and caned; and being himself in the constant habit of treating them thus, such practices have become to [the slaveholder] a mere matter of course, and make no impression on his mind."[77]

The depth of the intellectual debates over slavery and abolition accentuates the shallowness of the contemporaneous debates over free expression. Americans of the mid-nineteenth century were perfectly capable of devoting vast intellectual resources to abstract theoretical defenses of their interests and values. Slavery and abolition were politically significant enough to engender such intellectual exercises. Free expression generally was not. But why? Why did Americans invoke free expression so often during these decades, yet so rarely elaborate or justify it in a theoretical manner? For one thing, the disputes of the 1830s and thereafter, quite simply and obviously, followed the Sedition Act controversy as a matter of chronology. The disputants in the Sedition Act era did some intellectual heavy lifting, developing innovative theories of free expression, while also elaborating older ones. When the disputes of the 1830s arose, the proponents could draw upon the previously developed theories and arguments, which were ready and waiting to be used. More important, the political alignments of the mid-nineteenth century diminished the likelihood of exploring free expression in depth. Americans found the gravitational force of slavery and abolition too powerful to withstand. Its push and pull shaped all other issues. The likely proponents of suppression—the proslavery Southerners who wanted to stamp out abolition—brooded about national power and congressional claims of control over slavery or its spread. Consequently, these Southerners, while wanting to suppress abolitionists, would not accept federal suppression. During the mass mailings dispute, many Southerners adamantly opposed President Jackson's proposal for a federal law because they feared its enactment would implicitly acknowledge excessive congressional power.

At the state level, in the South, the motivation to suppress was strong enough to produce numerous instances of restrictive legislation and occasional prosecutions. Such governmental actions might be thought likely to produce in reaction not only invocations of the tradition of dissent but also theoretical elaborations of free expression. As a general matter, official rather than unofficial suppression is most likely to trigger formal responses. When the government officially suppresses expression through statutory enactments or criminal prosecutions, then the government itself sparks responses manifested in legal arguments for or theoretical justifications of free expression. If concretely and officially suppressed, individuals will divert their energies to articulating the tradition of dissent, of speaking one's mind, in more formal terms. At the turn into the nineteenth century, the congressional enactment of the Sedition Act and the concomitant prosecutions prompted, to a great degree, more sophisticated discussions of free expression. Nonetheless, during the mid-nineteenth century in the Southern states, near-hegemonic social and cultural pressure compelled individuals to conform with proslavery views. Notwithstanding Hinton Helper, few individuals were likely even to contemplate abolition, and of those few who might do so, even fewer would be willing to voice their views openly. The probable penalties, whether social ostracism, prosecution, tar and feathering, or death, were too obvious and too frightening to risk. In the North, meanwhile, unofficial suppression of abolitionism through mob violence was common in the 1830s, but it diminished considerably after Lovejoy's murder in 1837. While many Northerners opposed immediate abolition, they did not have enough at stake to support legal restrictions on abolitionist speech. Such legal restrictions, if they had been enacted into state statutes, would have appeared too solicitous to the Southern slave power. Suppression was fine, in other words, so long as it was informal, but the countervailing political interests combined with the tradition of dissent to prevent official suppression.

TO BE SURE, during the antebellum period, there were exceptions to the general observation that most invocations of free expression were largely rhetorical and went unelaborated. In 1835, the Unitarian minister William Ellery Channing elucidated the relationship between republican democracy and unofficial suppression through mob violence. Channing unequivocally endorsed the republican democratic principle of the sovereign people, but he carefully distinguished a mob from the people. "Mobs call themselves, and are called, the People, when in truth they assail immediately the sovereignty of the People," Channing explained. The people is constituted by "the Community formed into a body politic, and expressing and executing its will through regularly appointed organs. There is but one expression of the will or sovereignty of the people, and this is Law." The people, it might be said, cannot possibly act (as the people) unofficially. The people can only act through the official and legal mechanisms of constitutional government.[78]

The next year, Channing sent a long letter to James Birney after having read Birney's account of the Cincinnati riots and the suppression of Birney's abolitionist newspaper. Channing began by recognizing the importance of the abolitionists' interest-convergence strategy. While he had originally opposed slavery, he had nonetheless disapproved of the abolitionists' aggressive techniques. Yet, Channing had watched while "[d]eliberate, systematic efforts have been made, not here or there, but far and wide, to wrest from [abolitionists] that liberty of speech and the press, which our fathers asserted unto blood, and which our national and state governments are pledged to protect as our most sacred right." Consequently, abolitionists were no longer "champions" of only black slaves. Instead, in the persons of the abolitionists, "the most sacred rights of the white man and the free man have been assailed." Abolitionists "are sufferers for the liberty of thought, speech, and the press." Thus, Channing reasoned, through the abolitionists' perseverance, through their disregard for their own suffering, they had demonstrated for all the futility of suppression, "the folly as well as crime of attempting to crush opinion by force." To appreciate the proper scope of free expression, Channing articulated the Miltonian theory of a marketplace of ideas:

The greatest truths are often the most unpopular and exasperating; and were they to be denied discussion, till the many should be ready to accept them, they would never establish themselves in the general mind. The progress of society depends on nothing more than on the exposure of time-sanctioned abuses, which cannot be touched without offending multitudes, than on the promulgation of principles which are in advance of public sentiment and practice, and which are consequently at war with the habits, prejudices, and immediate interests of large classes of the community. Of consequence, the multitude, if once allowed to dictate or proscribe subjects of discussion, would strike society with spiritual blindness and death. The world is to be carried forward by truth, which at first offends, which wins its way by degrees, which the many hate and would rejoice to crush.[79]

Given this theoretical foundation — and writing from the dissident viewpoint of an abolitionist — Channing worried about the majority's suppression of the minority. He thus repudiated the notion that the government could punish expression because of supposedly bad tendencies.

Channing admitted that "[i]t is said that abolitionism tends to stir up insurrection at the South, and to dissolve the Union." He nonetheless maintained that "[a]lmost all men see ruinous tendencies in whatever opposes their particular interests or views." Given this—that most individuals naturally view their opponents' ideas as inherently bad—the supposed bad tendencies of speech or writing should not determine the scope of free expression. "All the political parties, which have convulsed our country have seen tendencies to national destruction in the principles of their opponents." Those very ideas that currently seem to have a bad tendency, even to a majority of the people, might eventually generate truth through the marketplace of ideas. Abolitionist expression, Channing concluded, should be restricted only if its tendency was "so palpable and resistless as to require the immediate application of force for its suppression." Although Channing did not further generalize, this approach to abolitionism resonated with an overt-acts test, an approach suggested during the Sedition Act era by Wortman and Thomson. According to this approach, the government could restrict only that expression likely to produce imminent unlawful or similarly harmful action.[80]

Frederick Grimke, who had been a lawyer in South Carolina and a judge in Ohio, also advocated for a marketplace of ideas. He developed this concept in *The Nature and Tendency of Free Institutions*. One of the earliest American-written books to focus on American democracy, this tome attracted little attention when published in 1848. Unlike Channing and Grimke's own prominent sisters, Sarah and Angelina, Grimke himself was no abolitionist. His ideas on government instead reflected mainstream Jacksonian era developments: the reality of political parties and the rhetoric of egalitarianism. To Grimke, free government required a free press. The press "is the organ of public opinion, and the great office which it performs is to effect a distribution of power throughout the community." The popular press provides the mechanism for generating a marketplace of ideas, where the people develop and disseminate knowledge and truth. The "extent to which an opinion prevails indicates the number of persons whom it interests and the degree of concert which is established among them." Grimke unabashedly reiterated the Jacksonian rhetoric of the virtuous common man. In the marketplace of ideas, a free press gave "voice to an immensely numerous class of the population who before composed a mere lifeless and inert body." A great egalitarian ethos infused America. "The great mass of mankind acquire knowledge with surprising facility when it is communicated in detail," Grimke explained. "The sagacious and inquisitive spirit of very obscure men in the inferior walks of life frequently stirs the public mind on questions of the greatest interest to society." Even advocates of diverse ideas that appear to conflict can influence each other. Thus, "[h]owever irreconcilable the views of [political] parties may appear to be, a free communication cannot be established between them without producing a visible influence of each upon all." Political parties were not factions corrupting republican democracy but rather were worthy contributors to free government and the search for truth.[81]

SO, IN CONCLUSION, what was the status of free expression through the middle decades of the nineteenth century? Legal doctrine established free speech and a free press as crucial rights, yet individuals were responsible for their abuses. Like other liberties within the republican democratic regime, free expression was subordinate to the community's power to act for the common good. When implemented in the context of criminal libel, this concern for the common good engendered the *Croswell* truth-conditional standard: truth was a defense to a charge of criminal libel but only if the defendant published for good motives and justifiable ends. If the published material was false, or true but with bad tendencies, then the government could punish it as criminal. When interpreted in accordance with the doctrine of constructive intent, the truth-conditional standard became, in effect, a bad tendency test. Proof that expression had bad tendencies — was likely to produce harmful consequences — rendered the expression unprotected and punishable.

Regardless, much of the action involving free expression during the nineteenth century did not occur in the courts, so the *Croswell* doctrine often was beside the point. And the law in action — in Congress, in the state legislatures, and in the streets — was sometimes more repressive and sometimes more liberating than the law in the books.[82] Both the traditions of dissent and suppression were vibrant, regardless of the niceties of legal doctrine. The Sedition Act controversy had already provided political fodder engendering extensive legal and theoretical arguments about the scope of free expression. The results were the truth-conditional standard and a wealth of theoretical positions supporting both narrow and expansive views of free expression. Significantly, while the culmination of the Sedition Act controversy had not weakened the tradition of suppression, it had strengthened the countervailing tradition of dissent by generating the first American theoretical justifications for a broad concept of free expression.

During the middle decades of the nineteenth century, the traditions of dissent and suppression repeatedly clashed within the crucible of the slavery-abolition struggle. Slavery was the political issue that drove nineteenth-century actors, that forced one confrontation after another, until the final confrontation of the Civil War. Hence, while Americans cared about free expression, it was largely a rhetorical tool to be used for political advantage throughout most of these conflicts. At the level of free-expression theory, nineteenth-century Americans did not progress far beyond their compatriots from the turn of the century. Free expression was a concept to be invoked, not explained. There were exceptions: Channing's and Grimke's theoretical excursions were noteworthy, yet even these deeper examinations of free expression tended to reiterate much of what had already been articulated during the Sedition Act era. An argument that was not made underscores the paucity of theoretical development during this era. Even before the Sedition Act controversy, some Americans had maintained that republican democracy justified restrictions on expression. Typically, this argument presumed that governmental officials were especially virtuous and therefore, for the common good, should be protected from the calumnies of partisan factions and individuals. But the transformation of republican democracy during the Jacksonian era might, it would seem, weaken this argument. First, Jacksonians reconceived the common good so that the partisanship of party politics became an acceptable component of republican democracy rather than a source of corruption. Partisan criticism of elected officials therefore became a normal manifestation of party politics. Second, the situs of virtue appeared to shift from the elites to the common people. Consequently, with regard to individual merit for governmental office, Americans supposedly became fungible. As Andrew Jackson put it, "no one man has any more intrinsic right to official station than another." But if the people were, in this sense, fungible, then anyone could, in theory, step into governmental office. The justification for restricting expression so as to protect virtuous officials would no longer hold. Elected officials were supposedly no more virtuous, no more knowledgeable, no more capable, than any other average American — or at least, any white, male, Protestant American. But tellingly, nobody articulated this theoretical defense of an expansive free expression. Grimke came closest, as his explanation of free expression relied in part on the idea of the virtuous common people, yet he failed to recognize the full theoretical potential of the changing conception of republican democracy. Instead, through the middle decades of the nineteenth century, Americans continued invoking republican democracy to justify either broad *or* narrow conceptions of free expression — with one's view of free expression typically turning on whose political ox was being gored.[83]

Unsurprisingly, then, perhaps the most significant nineteenth-century development concerning free expression related to its instrumental use rather than its theoretical development. Many Americans began to hang the tradition of dissent from their tool belts rather than storing it in the toolshed. Free expression was ready at hand. It became an instrument of political rhetoric and legal argument that many Americans would quickly pull from their belts and put to good use, at the slightest hint of suppression — so long as the suppression was either directed at themselves or appeared to threaten their own liberties. So many Americans invoked free expression so often and for so many decades that it became ingrained in the legal and popular cultures. The invocation of the tradition of dissent became commonplace. Nonetheless, the tradition of dissent, even with its enhanced popularity, never effaced the tradition of suppression. Suppression remained a prominent component of American culture. The free-expression disputes of the mid-nineteenth century as well as of the Sedition Act era reveal that while the traditions of dissent and suppression compete against each other, they are also mutually reinvigorating. When a group, like the abolitionists, expresses ideas that challenge the social and cultural mainstream, then suppression — whether official, unofficial, or both — is likely to follow. Yet, from the fires of suppression, the tradition of dissent tends to rise again like a phoenix. Dissent begets suppression, which begets dissent. And the spark that starts a cycle of dissent and suppression is politics. Intense political desires drive Americans to speak their minds, and then to trample others who do the same.

CHAPTER **6**

————•◀

Republican *Democracy from* Reconstruction through 1920

The Civil War sundered America along multiple jagged lines. A cataclys-mic event by any account, the mortality figures alone were staggering. Between the Union and the Confederacy, 665,000 American soldiers died, 50 percent more than during World War II.[1] After the war, during Reconstruction, the North sought to solidify its victory over the South, yet Northerners themselves divided among radical Republicans, moder-ate Republicans, and (Northern) Democrats, many of whom had been wartime Copperheads. Moderate and radical Republicans disagreed, for instance, about the degree to which national governmental power should be expanded. Moderates preferred that national power remain within tra-ditional federalism limits, while radicals pushed for broader national pow-ers. Among Democrats, Northerners and Southerners had split before the war on the question of popular sovereignty. While Southern Democrats had sought federal protection of slavery within the territories, Northern Democrats had insisted that the people within local communities should always reign supreme. The Northern Democratic antebellum leader, Ste-phen Douglas, insisted "that the people of every separate political com-munity (dependent colonies, Provinces, and Territories as well as sovereign states) have an inalienable right to govern themselves in respect to their internal polity." After the war, Northern Democrats maintained their emphasis on popular sovereignty within local communities, apparently justifying a more forgiving attitude toward the supposedly contrite white

Southerners (both before and after the war, Northern Democratic conceptions of the sovereign "people" did not include blacks).[2]

Partly because of these political divisions, Northerners never precisely
agreed on the meanings of the Reconstruction amendments: the thirteenth,
fourteenth, and fifteenth. The thirteenth amendment declared that slavery
shall no longer "exist within the United States," but the various proponents
of this change did not delineate its implications. Would former slaves become the *social equals* of whites? Would African Americans have the same
political rights as whites enjoyed? These and other questions initially went
unanswered. The Republican framers of the amendments purposefully left
many issues unsettled for political reasons. They sought to broaden the
political consensus in support of the amendments by avoiding clear stances
on controversial issues. To attain widespread agreement on an ambiguous
general principle of equality was far easier than achieving consensus on,
let's say, whether government-sanctioned racial segregation should be allowed in streetcars or public schools.[3]

Given such a political strategy, Republicans of different ilks recognized
that they shared certain important overlapping views — views that coincided with even some Northern Democratic positions. The crux of these
corresponding outlooks was republican democracy: most Republicans and
Northern Democrats agreed that state governments, particularly those in
the South, should be compelled to follow republican democratic principles.
Especially for Republicans, the political wellspring of this stance was their
prewar free labor, free soil ideology. Free labor intertwined the private virtue
of economic independence with the public virtue of republican citizenship;
private and public virtue each redounded on the other. With the conclusion
of the war, Republicans aspired to enforce their free labor ideology across
the nation — to reaffirm republican democratic principles. The Union victory, Horace Greeley proclaimed, signified "the triumph of republicanism
and free labor." Republicans recognized that white Southerners, if left to
their own devices, would violate the free labor ethos by enacting Black
Codes to force the freedmen into alternative forms of servitude. Republicans consequently sought, through legislation and constitutional amendments, to protect African Americans' civil rights as a means for upholding
free labor ideals. Civil rights included, in the words of the 1866 Civil Rights
Act, protections "to make and enforce contracts, to sue, be parties, and give
evidence, to inherit, purchase, lease, sell, hold, and convey real and personal
property." Generally, these rights encompassed guarantees to the "full and
equal benefit of all laws and proceedings for the security of person and

property." Such rights were, for the most part, integral to the pursuit of "an economic livelihood" and central to the free labor ideology.[4]

In other words, Reconstruction amendments and statutes proscribed state governmental actions for partial or private interests. This republican democratic proscription, always understood as a mandate for equality under the law, now extended to African Americans. A state governmental action, such as the enactment of a statute that favored one race over another — whites over blacks — constituted illegitimate class legislation contrary to the common good. While Congress struggled to craft the language of the fourteenth amendment, New York attorney general, J. H. Martindale, sent a letter to Senator John Sherman. "[W]here is the Constitutional power to classify American citizens, giving to one class and their posterity, exclusive & perpetual political rights & government, and denying them utterly to the other class & their posterity?" Martindale asked rhetorically. "The entire absence of the power to make this classification of our people & citizens is the peculiar and distinguishing feature of the systems of Govt in the United States." The Republican members of Congress agreed. Senator Jacob Howard, who introduced the fourteenth amendment for congressional debate, explained that the first section, particularly the equal protection and due process clauses, "abolishes all class legislation in the States and does away with the injustice of subjecting one caste of persons to a code not applicable to another." This prohibition against class legislation, against legislation for partial or private interests rather than for the common good, was a mandate for "equality before the law." This "principle of equal justice to all men and equal protection under the shield of the law" was a prerequisite for "republican government." Even President Andrew Johnson, a Democrat who would soon clash with the Republicans, concurred. "Monopolies, perpetuities, and class legislation are contrary to the genius of free government, and ought not to be allowed," Johnson declared in his 1865 State of the Union address. "We shall but fulfill our duties as legislators by according 'equal and exact justice to all men,' special privileges to none."[5]

In short, republican democracy simultaneously empowered and constrained a free government of the people. State governments retained their police powers but could not pass laws that were, as it was sometimes phrased, either arbitrary or unreasonable. Of course, this republican democratic conception of government was not new. As Thomas Cooley would write: the three Reconstruction amendments "required of the States the surrender of no power which any free government should ever employ." The transition from the antebellum world lay in the national insistence on republican democracy at the state level and in the definition of "the people." But Reconstruction era legal changes were ambiguous and could provoke disagreement. Republicans undoubtedly intended to broaden the scope of republican democratic principles by including African Americans within the mandate for equality, yet the Reconstruction amendments and statutes had severe limits.[6]

EXCLUSION

As in the past, republican democracy allowed for and even facilitated exclusion. The Republicans' free labor ideology always revolved around economic independence: free labor on free soil supposedly assured that each individual possessed the autonomy to contract freely and to own property. The postwar emphasis on contract and property rights, however, not only provided a goal for but also imposed a limit on Republican political pursuits.[7]

The thirteenth amendment officially ended slavery, but what did this mean for African Americans, especially in the Southern states? The Civil Rights Act of 1866 and the fourteenth amendment, ratified on July 9, 1868, partially answered this question. Integral to the enforcement of the free labor ideology, the fourteenth amendment's first section protected the civil rights of African Americans as follows: "No state shall make or enforce any law which shall abridge the privileges or immunities of citizens of the United States; nor shall any State deprive any person of life, liberty, or property, without due process of law; nor deny to any person within its jurisdiction the equal protection of the laws." Even so, the law left other rights unprotected; the Republicans differentiated various types of rights, including civil and political rights most explicitly. When debating the Civil Rights Bill, moderate Republican Senator Lyman Trumbull elucidated: "[T]he granting of civil rights does not, and never did in this country, carry with it . . . political privileges. A man may be a citizen in this country without a right to vote or without a right to hold office." Many moderate Republicans did not support the congressional expansion of African Americans' political rights, at least initially. To be sure, Republicans occasionally questioned the distinctions among types of rights and their protections under proposed federal laws. Senator Richard Yates insisted that "the people do not understand that argument which says that Congress may confer upon a man his civil rights and not his political rights. It is the pleading of a lawyer; it is too narrow for statesmanship." He incredulously asked: "What is liberty, what is emancipation without enfranchisement?" Less assured, John Bingham, the author of the first House draft of the fourteenth amendment, section 1, equivocated over whether Congress could regulate political participation in the states.[8]

Generally, though, Republicans agreed that civil rights revolved around the economic liberties of the free labor ideology (Republicans, overall, were ambivalent about free expression, as discussed in the next chapter). The 1866 Civil Rights Act would, in the words of Representative Martin Thayer, prevent states from enacting "laws which declare, for example, that [freedmen] shall not have the privilege of purchasing a home for themselves and their families; laws which impair their ability to make contracts for labor . . . and which then declare them vagrants because they have no homes and because they have no employment." Despite such protection of economic liberties, nearly all Republicans refused to support the enforcement of social equality for blacks. Even a radical, like Thaddeus Stevens, declared that equality "does not mean that a negro shall sit on the same seat or eat at the same table as a white man. That is a matter of taste which every man must decide for himself." Moreover, whereas the Reconstruction amendments and statutes protected black civil rights — and civil rights revolved around economic liberties (not social equality) — Reconstruction ultimately failed to generate widespread economic change. Stevens and some other radical Republicans suggested that Southern plantations ought to be carved up and the freedmen given homesteads — a policy of "forty acres and a mule" — an unsurprising idea given the apparent importance of property and labor to republican democracy (and a program that General William Tecumseh Sherman had unilaterally begun implementing after his devastating march through Georgia). Equally unsurprising, though, was the cold reaction congressmen gave this idea, which found few supporters. While property ownership would be significant for blacks, many Republicans resisted the seemingly bald taking of private property, even from Southern plantation owners. Yet without such a transfer of property, the economic class structure of the South remained largely intact; indeed, by the 1870s, many blacks had become sharecroppers. Initially, sharecropping appeared to invest blacks with a significant degree of freedom — sharecroppers supposedly worked for themselves and owned part of the produced crops — but sharecropping combined with an insidious credit system to become "synonymous with economic oppression and, in some cases, debt peonage."[9]

Many Northerners were happy to see blacks stay in the South and work the cotton fields. True, the burgeoning factories of the postbellum North needed more workers, so one might have expected manufacturers

to welcome the four million emancipated slaves as potential wage laborers. Manufacturers, however, looked elsewhere, particularly to immigrant
workers. Why? Economic self-interest and racism. Economically, Northern
manufacturers needed the South to produce the cotton that supplied the
Northern textile industries. If Southern blacks had left en masse for Northern factories, the South would have lost its laborers. European immigrants
readily came to the American North, but they were wary of the agrarian
South, where working conditions too closely resembled European serfdom.
Meanwhile, Senator Willard Saulsbury of Delaware, a border state, exemplified the contemporary racial attitudes common among white Northerners and Southerners alike: "[I]t is impossible that [the white people of
Delaware] and their descendants can ever so degenerate as to feel pride
and honor in association, politically or socially, with an inferior race [read:
African Americans]." Such racism of course undergirded the Republican
acceptance of segregation and disregard for black social equality. In the
South, legally sanctioned segregation remained the norm throughout the
postbellum era. *Plessy v. Ferguson,* which upheld the constitutionality of
"separate but equal" public facilities in 1896, reaffirmed already-prevalent
Southern practices. When Justice Henry Brown wrote that "[t]he object
of the [fourteenth] amendment was undoubtedly to enforce the absolute
equality of the two races before the law, but, in the nature of things, it
could not have been intended to abolish distinctions based upon color, or
to enforce social . . . equality," he reiterated sentiments many Republicans
had voiced during Reconstruction.[10]

LIKE THE PURSUIT of black civil (or economic) rights, a postbellum political movement to institute black suffrage also met with uneven support
and eventual frustration. During the early stages of Reconstruction, radical
leaders like Stevens advocated for suffrage, but moderate Republicans opposed it — thus the repeated distinctions between civil and political rights.
The Republican position, however, evolved rapidly in the late 1860s, partly
in reaction against President Johnson's antagonism to Republican Reconstruction. By the time Congress enacted the first Reconstruction Act in
March 1867, setting conditions for the readmission of Southern states,
Johnson and the Republicans were locked in struggle. More Republicans
supported black enfranchisement in Southern states so as to bolster Republican political power. Hence, the 1867 Act required Southern states not
only to approve the proposed fourteenth amendment but also to adopt new
constitutions providing for universal manhood suffrage, except for those

"disfranchised for participation in the rebellion." Then, in February 1869, mere months after the fourteenth amendment had been ratified, Congress approved the fifteenth amendment: "The right of citizens of the United States to vote shall not be denied or abridged by the United States or by any State on account of race, color, or previous condition of servitude."[11]

While some Republicans believed the fifteenth amendment culminated the struggle for black liberation and equality, the amendment embodied numerous limitations. On its face, the fifteenth amendment protected only an equal right to suffrage, not an equal right to hold public office. Both the House and Senate had approved a provision that would have protected office holding, but the ensuing Conference Committee deleted it. This change provoked a howl of protests, particularly from radical Republicans. Vermont Senator George Edmunds insisted that the Conference Committee had exceeded its "authority": the Committee members, Edmunds charged, possessed power only to reconcile differences between the House and Senate versions, none of which related to office holding. No mere procedural technicality, this Committee maneuver altered a point of substance, a matter of "real republicanism and . . . real democracy." The change was "deadly to a republic" because it established class distinctions, with only those of an "aristocratic class" eligible for public office. Senator Henry Wilson, a radical Republican leader, grudgingly supported the "half-way proposition" of the fifteenth amendment only because it was "the best I can get." In fact, Congress pared down the fifteenth amendment's protection of political rights to the bare minimum. Congress not only deleted the protection for office holding but also considered and rejected a prohibition against state-imposed property and education requirements for voting. The fifteenth amendment, as ratified, did not even guarantee a right to vote, as radical Republican Senator Jacob Howard unhappily admitted; it merely proscribed states from racially discriminating with regard to suffrage. States still had portentous power. The fifteenth amendment, Republican Senator Frederick Frelinghuysen underscored, "does not take away from the States the right to regulate. It leaves the States to declare in favor of or against female suffrage; to declare that a man shall vote when he is eighteen or when he is thirty-five; to declare that he shall not vote unless possessed of a freehold, or that he shall not vote unless he has an education and can read the Constitution."[12]

Why did the Republican-controlled Congress limit the scope of the fifteenth amendment? As a matter of political strategy, many Republicans feared that if they pushed too strongly to protect black office holding, they risked losing white Northern support. More generally, Northern states wanted to retain for themselves the power to regulate suffrage. Several Northern states, including Massachusetts and Pennsylvania, continued to restrict voting based on literacy requirements, the payment of taxes, or race. State power over suffrage enabled white Republicans to manipulate democratic participation to manifest their prejudices against blacks and immigrants as well as to garner pure "partisan advantage." Northerners, moreover, wanted the power to restrict voting by white Southerners who had supported the Confederacy. Regardless of Northern purposes, Southern practices during the latter-nineteenth century led to the de facto disfranchisement of African Americans. Starting in 1868, after the enactment of the first Reconstruction Act, Southern whites unleashed a relentless campaign of vigilante violence against blacks, partly to discourage and prevent political participation. Of the blacks who had participated in Southern state constitutional conventions during Reconstruction, at least one-tenth were attacked, with seven being murdered. During this period, the Ku Klux Klan first emerged as a powerful force — brutalizing and murdering hundreds of blacks each year. An Alabama freedman, in 1869, described how Klansmen had beaten him at his home and had "ravished a young girl who was visiting my wife." He recalled: "The cause of this treatment, they said, was that we voted the radical ticket."[13]

At first, the Republican-led national government responded vigorously to these attacks against black political participation. Congress approved the fifteenth amendment in February 1869; the states ratified it the following February. The Ku Klux Klan Act, enacted on April 20, 1871 (eventually codified as 42 U.S.C. § 1983), created a federal cause of action for state violations of federal constitutional and statutory rights. In fact, Southern violence briefly diminished in the face of these and other federal actions. Before long, however, Republican enthusiasm for the enforcement of black rights waned. For the most part, the economic panic of 1873 and the ensuing depression provoked this turn of events. The panic started when a major bank collapsed after failing to market several million dollars of the Northern Pacific Railroad's bonds. Involving two central economic institutions, the railroads and the banks, the collapse reverberated across the nation. Within two years, eighteen thousand businesses failed; eighty-nine of the nation's 364 railroads went bankrupt; and almost half of the iron furnaces shut down. Moreover, the depression dragged on and on; in 1878, another ten thousand businesses failed. The panic and the depression profoundly altered national politics; many people naturally blamed the party in power. Thus, in the 1874 midterm elections, the Republicans lost control of the House of Representatives; 1875 would be the first year since the war that Republicans had not dominated both the House and the Senate (plus, since the end of Andrew Johnson's partial term, the Republicans had held the presidency, in the person of Ulysses S. Grant). The shift in the House was stark: the Forty-third Congress had 86 Democrats and 201 Republicans, while the Forty-fourth Congress had 174 Democrats and 111 Republicans.[14]

When the Republicans lost the 1874 elections, they did not drift idly away. Instead, the party shifted its political emphasis to shore up its diminishing popularity. As the battles of the war receded into the past, increasing numbers of Northern whites lost interest in the protection of African American rights, even while the national government defended blacks in the South during the early 1870s. This diminishing Northern enthusiasm for Reconstruction coalesced with the economic depression to snap the Republican party's attention toward "economic nationalism." With improved communication and transportation technologies, particularly the extensive railroads, manufacturers sought to fuse together a national marketplace. The Northern industrial powers that had supported the Republican party now willingly downplayed or outright sacrificed black civil rights so as to pursue their own economic concerns. A typical state Republican platform emphasized the "promotion of national industry" and the "development of national power, wealth, and independence." The Republicans had always been willing, to a degree, to enlist national power to advance their causes, whether preserving the Union, protecting civil rights, or promoting industry and commerce. Now, Republican leaders sought to have the federal government "sweep aside regional and local barriers to the development of a national capitalist market and directly assist in the construction of the physical and financial infrastructure necessary for that market."[15]

As Republican interest shifted to economic matters, Southern vigilantism against blacks escalated. While in 1873, 1,271 federal prosecutions supported the enforcement of black rights, only two years later a Republican newspaper called the fourteenth and fifteenth amendments "dead letters." President Grant rued the adoption of the fifteenth amendment: "It had done the Negro no good, and had been a hindrance to the South, and by no means a political advantage to the North." In 1878, the federal government prosecuted only twenty-five criminal cases in support of black rights, and over the next dozen years, the government averaged less than a hundred prosecutions per year. Southern Democrats aggressively minimized black political power by any means possible. Fraud and violence supplemented literacy tests, poll taxes, and gerrymandering. In South Carolina in 1876, the Democrats developed a "Plan of Campaign": each Democrat was to "control the vote of at least one negro by intimidation, purchase, keeping him away or as each individual may determine." The Plan reminded whites that "argument has no effect on [blacks]: They can only be influenced by their fears." These techniques successfully diminished, practically eliminated, Republican and especially black political power in the South. One African American Republican feared that "[we are] drifting back under the leadership of the slaveholders." A Georgia black declared that "you may vote till your eyes drop out [but] there's a hole gets in the bottom of the [ballot] boxes some way and lets out our votes."[16]

THE PRESIDENTIAL ELECTION of 1876, to a great extent, concluded Reconstruction. Ohio Governor Rutherford B. Hayes ran for the Republicans, while New York Governor Samuel J. Tilden ran for the Democrats. On election night, Tilden seemed headed for victory, and in the end, he carried the popular vote and undisputed electoral college votes totaling one less than the majority required for victory. But the electoral votes from several states, including Florida, Louisiana, and South Carolina, were disputed. The twelfth amendment had established a process that supposedly would resolve elections when no candidate received a majority of electoral votes, but in this case of disputed votes, the amendment was inadequate. Tensions climbed to a point where another civil war seemed possible. Hayes's supporters claimed that many of Tilden's electoral votes were due to the intimidation of and fraud against blacks and Southern Republicans. Meanwhile, Tilden's supporters emphasized his victory in the popular vote. A headline in one Democratic newspaper screamed, "Tilden or War." In actuality, neither side wanted another armed conflict. A series of negotiations followed, with the parties reaching an agreement only days before the scheduled inauguration on March 4, 1877. The compromise awarded the Republicans the presidency (in the person of Hayes) and the Democrats the effective end of Reconstruction. Hayes appointed to the Cabinet a Democrat from Tennessee who advocated for the "economic modernization" of the South. Plus, Hayes withdrew federal troops from the South Carolina and Louisiana statehouses, thus allowing Democrats to claim victories in still-disputed gubernatorial elections. Even while some federal troops remained in the South, white Southerners gained de facto power to rule once again in their respective states. The South supposedly had been redeemed.[17]

The Hayes-Tilden compromise did not *force* Republicans to relinquish their pursuit of Reconstruction. Rather, the contested presidential election and the ensuing compromise arose only because Northern Republicans had already lost interest in black rights and Southern Reconstruction. Hayes and the Republicans thus turned their attention squarely to economic advantage, with Hayes filling his cabinet with "corporate attorneys and railroad directors." By early 1882, the *Philadelphia Evening Bulletin* readily acknowledged that white America mistreated blacks yet nonetheless opined that the "time has passed when the federal government can interfere for the protection of these people." The next year, the Supreme Court struck down the Civil Rights Act of 1875, which the lame-duck Republicans had enacted after losing the 1874 midterm elections. The Court reasoned, in part, that Congress had exceeded its powers by prohibiting racial discrimination in privately operated places of public accommodation, such as inns and theaters. The Court elaborated: "When a man has emerged from slavery, and by the aid of beneficent legislation has shaken off the inseparable concomitants of that state, there must be some stage in the progress of his elevation when he takes the rank of a mere citizen, and ceases to be the special favorite of the laws, and when his rights as a citizen, or a man, are to be protected in the ordinary modes by which other men's rights are protected." The Court's message was unequivocal: blacks were on their own and should not expect assistance from the federal government, even though slavery had ended less than two decades earlier. Who authored the Court's majority opinion? Justice Joseph P. Bradley — a Republican.[18]

In sum, despite the Civil War, the end of slavery, and the constitutional and statutory changes wrought by Reconstruction, whites largely excluded blacks from participating in republican democracy, especially in the South. A variety of moves and methods achieved such exclusion. First, Republicans focused initially on the protection of civil rights to the exclusion of political and social rights. Second, as understood at the time, civil rights revolved around economic liberties, but racism, white self-interest, and free labor ideology all minimized the extent of black economic gains. Third, when the Republicans turned their attention to black political rights, they protected the bare minimum, an equal right to vote. Finally, Republicans allowed the violent and legally sanctioned destruction of even that minimal political protection when their own economic and political interests were at stake. Subsequently, white Southerners felt little compunction about the open exclusion of blacks. At the Virginia constitutional convention of 1901–2, one delegate exclaimed: "Discrimination! Why, that is precisely what we propose." Throughout the South, black political participation became negligible. From 1888 to 1902, black voting turnout in Alabama, Louisiana, North Carolina, and Virginia fell by over 90 percent. In 1904 Louisiana, only 1,342 blacks were registered to vote. Black disfranchisement had profound political ramifications. In the South, the large black population counted when apportioning the states' respective congressional representatives and electoral votes (the fourteenth amendment, section 2, ended the three-fifths constitutional compromise). But since most blacks could not vote, Southern white Democrats enjoyed disproportionate political power at the national level for decades, all the way into the 1950s. Even so, white Republicans usually controlled two and sometimes all three branches of the national government until the Great Depression hit in the 1930s. The Republican party learned, over the years, that it could prosper without African American voters, and hence it lacked political incentive to challenge Southern black disfranchisement. Finally, it should be noted, African Americans enjoyed free-expression rights no more so than other rights.[19]

BLACKS WERE NOT the only societal group whose participation in republican democracy was either diminished or denied during the postbellum era. The women's suffrage movement traced back to the late 1840s, so when Congress debated the fifteenth amendment, suffragists sought to add the protection of women to the agenda. They failed miserably. To many men, women still seemed incapable of intelligently participating in the republican democratic debates of the public realm. In fact, the fourteenth amendment, section 2, introduced an explicit distinction between males and females with regard to voting and state representation. In the ensuing years, women gained some small successes in western territories and states, most notably gaining the vote in Wyoming, Utah, Idaho, and Colorado. Yet even in these territories and states, the government granted the franchise largely as an incentive, to induce settlement and population growth, not because of a principled commitment to political equality.[20]

The postbellum years also saw efforts to disfranchise large numbers of immigrants, especially non-Protestants. Many Protestant elites lamented the effects of expanded or universal manhood suffrage. For instance, in 1869, Charles Francis Adams, Jr., wrote: "Working upon such a mass as must result from the blending of all these incongruous elements, Universal Suffrage can only mean in plain English the government of ignorance and vice." Critics of immigrant suffrage often cast their attacks in the language of republican democracy, disparaging immigrants as insufficiently virtuous for the American polity. Historian Francis Parkham complained: "A New England village of the olden time . . . has grown into a populous city, with its factories and workshops, its acres of tenement-houses, and thousands and ten thousands of restless workmen, foreigners for the most part, to whom liberty means license and politics means plunder, to whom the public good is nothing and their own most trivial interests everything." The point of republican democratic government was to attain the common good, not merely to participate. "Good government is the end," Parkham insisted, "and the ballot is worthless except so far as it helps to reach this end." Despite these concerns about immigrants, especially in the large Northern cities, efforts to deny suffrage were far more successful in the South than in the North. New York reformer Thomas Shearman explained: "For strictly practical purposes, . . . the debate is scarcely more likely to have any effect than an argument in favor of abolishing railroads and going back to stagecoaches. Universal suffrage is established." Unlike in the South, where disfranchisement efforts primarily targeted blacks, Northern proponents of suffrage restrictions could not as readily draw on the wellspring of entrenched racism to sustain their reform efforts. Yet, even when Northern reformers realized they could not deny the vote, they did not surrender politics and government to the immigrant. They instead developed alternative means to limit immigrant participation.[21]

During the mid-nineteenth century, political parties developed to become effective institutions for engendering mass political participation. In 1824, before the acceptance of the two-party system, voter turnout for the presidential election was only 16.2 percent. By 1840, with the party system established, voter turnout jumped to 77.5 percent. In 1876, it was a remarkable 82.4 percent. Partly because of this political-party success in getting the average person to the polls, postbellum Protestant elite reformers (the Mugwumps) began to attack the party system. Henry Adams explained that the nation must "go back to the early practice of the government and . . . restore to constitutional organs those powers which have been torn from them by the party organizations for purposes of party aggrandizement." To be sure, reformers did not envision an end to the two-party system but rather sought to reduce, in Adams's words, "[t]he fabric of party . . . to a size that corresponds with its proper functions." Hence, reformers encouraged citizens to minimize party loyalties and to vote based on "the character of the candidate." Republican virtue, these reformers emphasized, must manifest Protestant old-stock values; the "best men" should be allowed to govern.[22]

Reformers, though, did not rely merely on ideology to weaken mass popular politics; they developed more tangible mechanisms. Some reformers pushed to lengthen the time of residence needed for naturalization — to as much as twenty-one years — and when that failed, they more successfully persuaded state governments to require naturalized citizens to show their papers as a prerequisite to voting. Equally important, reformers managed to modify civil service processes in the late-nineteenth and early-twentieth centuries. Instead of allowing elected officials to reward party loyalists with patronage jobs — thus encouraging voting — many governmental positions would now be awarded based on merit as measured through supposedly objective tests. Moreover, as the immigrant population grew, material forces created obstacles to immigrant political participation and thus aided the reformers' cause. Twenty percent of immigrants, as of 1910, spoke no English, while many worked exhaustively long days in hazardous factories. These immigrants often had neither the energy nor the wherewithal to get out and vote or otherwise participate politically. To a great extent, then, the reformers' efforts to diminish mass political participation proved successful. Voter turnout gradually declined in the late-nineteenth and early-twentieth centuries. By 1924, voter turnout in the presidential election had plunged to 48.8 percent, a far cry from the 82.4 percent of 1876.[23]

STRAINS ON REPUBLICAN DEMOCRACY

In the late-nineteenth and early-twentieth centuries, numerous forces placed republican democracy under intense pressure. Republican democratic principles withstood these pressures because of their flexibility, their dynamism. But for precisely that same reason, the meanings of virtue and the common good were subject to contestation and change. When Lincoln invoked the free labor ideology in support of republican democracy, he appealed to a preindustrial economy and way of life. The ideal of work was agricultural: the farmer decided when to rise, when to work, when to rest, and when to eat. The farmer's production belonged to him, to share with his family. If a farmer brought goods to market, it was a local market. Artisan workshops, rather than factories, produced most manufactured goods. To be sure, some individuals labored for others, but at least in theory, they could always look forward to the day when they would work for themselves. In the years after the Civil War, this way of life faded rapidly from the American picture.[24]

Industrialization, more than any other single factor, caused this transition. Even before the war, the North had industrialized considerably more than had the South. In 1860, 84 percent of the Southern labor force worked in agriculture, compared with 40 percent in the North. According to the 1860 census, Virginia stood as the most industrialized Southern state, with

5,385 manufacturing establishments producing just over $50 million worth of products. North Carolina was second with 3,689 establishments producing almost $17 million. These figures paled next to those of the Northern states. New York and Pennsylvania combined to have 44,987 manufacturing establishments that produced a whopping $669 million in value. Then, the war itself spurred Northern cities to become even more focused on manufacturing, on producing the supplies of an army—iron, firearms, leather, and the like—and the North's advantage in manufacturing capacity eventually facilitated its victory. By the mid-1860s, despite the war, the United States stood "second in the world in manufacturing output."[25]

After the war, the Republicans' entrenchment in positions of political power enabled them to craft policies consonant with their interests and values. From an economic standpoint, Northern Republicans stood to benefit by further developing industry and commerce. They accomplished this goal primarily through three interrelated policies: the enactment of tariffs protective of American industries, the adherence to an international gold standard, and the development of a national economic marketplace. Protective tariffs bolstered American industries by engendering higher prices and profits despite competition from foreign enterprises. Simultaneously, the tariffs solidified political support for the Republicans by funding various types of economic assistance for their constituencies, including pensions for Civil War veterans (on the Union side, of course). In a similar vein, the Republicans granted enormous tracts of public land, most importantly to the railroads, both to nurture political fidelity and to encourage development. In one decade, from 1862 to 1871, the national government granted 128 million acres to the railroads. Meanwhile, partially to offset potential repercussions from the protective tariffs, the Republicans adhered to the international gold standard, thus providing comfort and certainty for foreign investors, who responded by plunging their capital into American enterprises. Finally, the Republicans sought to cultivate a national marketplace so as to aid and encourage the expansion of businesses, now able to transcend the limits of local markets and to reach vast numbers of new consumers.[26]

While these Republican policies helped construct a "physical and financial infrastructure" that constantly added fuel to the fire of industrialization, other forces were at work. The corporation, for instance, evolved into a bureaucratic organization oriented toward the efficient running of large businesses. In the past, businesses had tended to be small, intimate operations that relied on capital from family or friends. The emerging postbellum business corporation facilitated the raising of capital "from myriad private investors in impersonal credit markets" and the ordered management of hundreds or even thousands of workers. A corporate bureaucracy, most typically, divided labor among specialized positions, with a sharp distinction between management and worker. Pioneered in the railroad industry from the 1850s to the 1870s, the modern corporation "spread by 1900 first to other transport and communications firms, then to the iron and steel industry, meatpacking, agricultural implements, and other key sectors of the economy." Technological advances also sparked the development of old and new industries. Electricity, electric lighting, canned goods, and improved methods for refining petroleum appeared. Before the war, smelters produced steel from iron but only with great difficulty. In the 1860s, they put into widespread use the recently invented Bessemer process, and the steel industry exploded, leaping from 19,643 tons produced in 1867, to 198,796 tons in 1873, to over 10 million tons in 1900, and to over 20 million in 1905. The improved production techniques for steel radiated throughout the American economy. Skyscrapers climbed upward, subways tunneled under cities, and railroads replaced their old iron rails with steel, improving speed and reliability.[27]

Advances in transportation and communication keyed the developing infrastructure, which engendered a national marketplace and produced near-frenzied economic activity. The total miles of telegraph wire and number of messages handled grew astronomically. From 1867 to 1890, the number of miles of wire stretched from 85,000 to 679,000, while the number of messages grew nearly tenfold, from 5,879,000 to more than 55 million. By 1910, there were 1,429,000 miles and over 75 million messages handled. In 1876, Alexander Graham Bell introduced the telephone; within twenty years, over 400,000 phones were in use. These networks of telegraphs and telephones allowed corporate managers to communicate rapidly with their market operatives and customers across the nation. The railroads, meanwhile, enabled corporations to ship their goods rapidly to any nook or cranny that the ever-growing web of tracks reached. In 1830, railroads laid only 40 miles of track. By 1860, that number had climbed to 1,500, though production tailed off during the Civil War. In 1866, production returned near to prewar levels, with 1,404 miles laid. At that point, production took off: in 1871 alone, railroads added 6,660 miles of track, and they continued laying thousands of miles of track every year until the 1910s. The railroads stimulated the economy in numerous ways. Besides fusing discrete geographical regions into a national marketplace, the railroad corporations themselves employed thousands upon thousands of individuals and consumed enormous quantities of iron, steel, lumber, and coal. Equally important, as the enhanced network of railroads tied the nation together, economies of scale encouraged the growth of ever-larger corporations. In 1895, for example, corporations merged 43 times, while by 1899 (the peak year until the late 1920s), 1,208 mergers occurred in "a virtual orgy of horizontal consolidation." In 1901, 158 companies merged into a single corporation, U.S. Steel. Even though the nation battled through long periods of depression, GNP rocketed upward, increasing sixfold from 1869 to 1911.[28]

In a matter of decades, the lifeblood of the nation had flowed from agriculture to manufacturing. In 1870, those engaged in agriculture numbered close to 7 million, while approximately 4 million worked in manufacturing, construction, transportation, and related jobs. By 1900, agricultural workers were in the minority, 10,710,000 to 13,990,000. In 1859, the value added from manufacturing (equaling the value of shipments minus the cost of materials and the like) for the entire nation totaled less than $9 million. By 1899, that total had jumped to nearly $5.5 billion, and by 1919, the figure had catapulted to almost $24 billion. From a geographical standpoint, though, economic development was strikingly uneven. After the Civil War, the North's manufacturing capacity grew exponentially, leaving the South far behind. In 1870, New York and Pennsylvania combined to have 73,406 manufacturing establishments that produced nearly $1.5 billion worth of products. Virginia and North Carolina, meanwhile, had not yet even returned to their prewar production levels; together they had 9,575 establishments producing less than $58 million in value. By 1900, Virginia and North Carolina together still had just over 15,000 manufacturing establishments, while New York alone had more than 78,000.[29]

The startling changes in the economic and social structures of postbellum America prompted the economist David Wells to observe in 1889: "An almost total revolution has taken place, and is yet in progress." As the economy shifted from agriculture to manufacturing, the population moved from rural to urban, with ever-increasing numbers in the cities of the Northeast and Midwest. In 1850, only 3,543,716 Americans lived in urban areas, while 19,648,160 lived in rural regions. Ten years later, just before the war, the proportions remained similar, with only a slight shift toward the urban. By 1870, a perceptible shift toward urban living had occurred, even though the rural population remained nearly three times as large as the urban. But spurred partly by the late-nineteenth-century closing of the American frontier, the trend toward the urban continued. By 1910, the population divided almost evenly: 49,973,334 rural, and 41,998,932 urban. By 1920, urbanites had overtaken the rural, and from thereon, the margin of urban residents continued to increase. Overall, the population exploded from just under 40 million in 1870, to over 76 million in 1900, to over 100 million by 1915.[30]

Traced back to Jeffersonian rhetoric and earlier, republican democracy supposedly rested on agricultural work, rural living, and a relatively homogenous society. Rural agrarianism assured the liberty needed to promote civic virtue and to discourage the likely corruption of economically dependent individuals. A relatively homogenous society engendered the shared values and overlapping interests that nurtured a pursuit of the common good and discouraged factionalism. Now, though, urban industrialism had supplanted agrarianism as the primary form of American life, leaching the republican democratic soils. Even further, industrialism contributed to the diversification of American society. The need for factory workers motivated urban industrialists to facilitate and encourage immigration. If a pool of surplus workers existed, then the industrialists could more readily depress wages; any worker who expressed dissatisfaction, with wages or otherwise, could be quickly replaced. Partly for this reason, many new immigrant Americans streamed into the burgeoning cities. As of 1910, for example, 76 percent of clothing-factory workers were immigrants. In steel mills, the foreign-born constituted 51 percent.[31]

Thus, not only did the American population grow dramatically, but the demographic makeup of the population radically transformed. During the antebellum years, most immigrants had come from Ireland, Germany, Scandinavia, and Britain, but after the war, most came from Italy, Russia, and the Balkans. Indeed, already during the mid- to late-nineteenth century, American Catholics — mostly of Irish descent — had become the largest Christian group in the nation; the total number of Protestants still far outnumbered Catholics, but Catholics nonetheless exceeded the largest Protestant denomination. Partly for this reason, Protestant anti-Catholicism became especially intense in large cities, like New York and Boston, where Catholic populations had surged and often helped stock the local Democratic political machines. In 1882, 87 percent of immigrants still arrived from western Europe (including Ireland), and 13 percent came from southern and eastern Europe. By 1902, however, only 22 percent of immigrants were from western Europe, while 78 percent were from southern and eastern Europe. And the total number of immigrants swelled. In 1860, total immigration equaled 153,640. By 1873, the number jumped to 459,803, and in the 1890s, immigration hovered typically around a half million per year. In the decade from 1905 to 1914, total immigration topped one million six times![32]

Of course, white Protestant males had always preserved the homogeneity of the American polity partly by excluding various societal groups from political participation; groups like African Americans, Native Americans, and women were deemed insufficiently virtuous. Predictably, then, in the late-nineteenth century, many old-stock Americans regarded immigration as a threat to republican democratic government. These old-stock Americans frequently responded with nativist denunciations of the immigrants. Immigrants could be blamed for whatever ailed America, whether it was an economic depression, labor unrest, or radicalism. Although the United States had, from its inception, maintained a largely open immigration policy, pressure mounted after the war to introduce restrictions. The very first federal statute to restrict immigration passed in 1875. It focused primarily on preventing the immigration of criminals, but subsequent enactments revolved around the exclusion of groups adjudged racially inferior and incapable of participating in the American polity. In 1882, for instance, Congress enacted legislation to restrict Chinese immigration, and in future decades, various mechanisms limited the entrance of other Asians. As total immigration nonetheless continued to grow, efforts to restrict European immigration on racial grounds began to emerge. Many Americans deemed eastern and southern Europeans racially inferior to the Nordic and Anglo-Saxon peoples who previously had come to the country. The Supreme Court, upholding a deportation in 1904, explained that Congress could promote the "public weal" by protecting "the country from the advent of aliens whose race or habits render them undesirable as citizens."[33]

From 1907 to 1910, the U.S. Immigration Commission (the Dillingham Commission) conducted a massive study of immigration that culminated in a forty-two-volume report recommending numerous restrictions on immigration. One volume in the report, the *Dictionary of Races or Peoples,* was unapologetically racist. But after all, that was the very point: race established an individual's fitness (or unfitness) for participation in American free government, and therefore race should be the determinative criterion for immigrant admissibility. The Dillingham Commission's *Dictionary* expressly set forth its purpose: "[to promote] a better understanding of the many different racial elements that are being added to the population of the United States through immigration." As such, the *Dictionary* brimmed with gross generalizations about different peoples. "The 'Jewish nose,' and to a less degree other facial characteristics," the *Dictionary* stated, "are found well-nigh everywhere throughout the race, although the form of the head seems to have become quite the reverse of the Semitic type." Serbo-Croatians were described as "now exalted, now depressed, melancholy, and fatalistic. Much goes with this: Fanaticism in religion, carelessness as to the business virtues of punctuality and often honesty, periods of besotted drunkenness among the peasantry, unexpected cruelty and ferocity in a generally placed and kind-hearted individual." The *Dictionary* excruciatingly detailed Italians, who supposedly displayed a high degree of criminality, illiteracy, and poverty. The South and North Italians "differ as radically in psychic characters as they do in physical. [The] South Italian [is] excitable, impulsive, highly imaginative, impracticable; as an individualist having little adaptability to highly organized society. The North Italian, on the other hand, is . . . cool, deliberate, patient, practical, and as capable of great progress in the political and social organization of modern civilization. Both North and South Italians are devoted to their families, are benevolent, religious, artistic, and industrious. . . . In America [Italians] have not attained distinguished success as farmers, although as fruit and wine growers, especially in California, they rank among the foremost." The Dillingham Commission's views on race were not unique; they were widespread and respected. Harry Laughlin of the Carnegie Foundation applauded the Dillingham Commission Report and its implications for "democracy." Calvin Coolidge, when vice president, wrote an article for a popular magazine asserting that "biological laws show us that Nordics deteriorate when mixed with other races." In 1917, after years of pressure, the federal government finally imposed a literacy requirement on immigrants.[34]

While immigrants diminished the homogeneity of American society, not all native-born Americans denounced them as unfit for free government. Some educators claimed that the common or public schools could Americanize them. "Education will solve every problem of our national life," one New York principal declared, "even that of assimilating our foreign element." As the rate of immigration rose, Americanization not only became an increasingly important issue but also became associated with a melting pot ideology that demanded the dissolution of immigrants' native cultures. President Woodrow Wilson epitomized this outlook when he described Americanization as "a process of purification." In 1915, the U.S. Commissioner of Education initiated an "America First" program that emphasized adopting English as one's language and becoming a virtuous citizen with an American consciousness. The immigrant, it was explained, must achieve "active cooperation with fellow citizens in furthering the common welfare through government, [and] a universal consciousness of our national and social organization and the impelling forcefulness of its evolution."[35]

Some Americans even advocated for a type of "cultural pluralism," a term coined by Horace Kallen in 1915. Kallen, a German-born Jew who came to the United States when he was five, anticipated the development of pluralist democracy with his article, "Democracy versus the Melting Pot." He argued that immigration had already destroyed the homogenous America of the nineteenth century: "the older America, whose voice and whose spirit was New England, is gone beyond recall." America had not become a melting pot, but rather had spurred immigrant groups to develop "cultural pride." Consequently, America could become "a great republic consisting of a federation or commonwealth of nationalities." Yet, Kallen concluded, the future of America was uncertain: "What do we *will* to make of the United States — a unison, singing the old Anglo-Saxon theme 'America,' the America of the New England school, or a harmony, in which that theme shall be dominant, perhaps, among others, but one among many, not the only one?" Despite the prescience of Kallen's views, when he published this article in 1915 his voice represented a lonely minority. Old-stock Americans, particularly national leaders, believed mainly that either immigrants must be forcefully assimilated into mainstream American culture, immigration must be severely restricted (because most immigrants were unfit for republican democratic government), or both. Wilson, once again, reflected the prevailing view, including opposition to any form of pluralism: "[Y]ou can not dedicate yourself to America unless you become in every respect and with every purpose of your will thorough Americans. . . . America does not consist of groups. A man who thinks of himself as belonging to a particular national group in America has not yet become an American."[36]

WHILE INDUSTRIALIZATION PROMPTED ever-more immigration, the societal divisions between old-stock Americans and swelling numbers of immigrants shattered the illusion of American homogeneity. Industrialization, moreover, engendered other interrelated chasms in American society. As the rich grew richer, the gap between rich and poor expanded. The 1890 census reported that 9 percent of American families possessed 71 percent of the nation's wealth, leaving only 29 percent of the wealth for the remaining families (91 percent). Indeed, the top 1 percent of families possessed over half the wealth, while the bottom 44 percent, many of whom were immigrants, possessed a meager 1.2 percent. As the economist Richard Ely observed in 1903, "[industrial] development has brought with it widely separated classes, the common laborer marking one extreme, the railway magnate the other, the one living in a shanty, the other in a palace, and both presumably never knowing each other."[37]

Related to this wealth gap, another division, between laborers and capitalists, cracked the American landscape. The antebellum free labor ideology presumed that the independent farmer or artisan exemplified the ideal republican democratic citizen. Any laborer who had not yet achieved the freedom commensurate with such work could aspire to achieving it in the future, or so it was believed. Thus, before the war and still in the years immediately afterward, most Republicans as well as many Northern Democrats viewed labor and capital as a unified whole. Ohio Representative Henry Banning, supporting a bill for the incorporation of the National Iron-molders' Union, declared: "I am among those who believe that a true knowledge of capital and labor finds harmony in both. [In] this free land of ours the laborer of to-day is the capitalist of to-morrow, while the capitalist in turn may become the laborer." Labor and capital were not opposed, but rather shared in one common good — a common good that, not incidentally, strongly reflected the needs of capitalists. "The interests of the capitalist and the laborer," explained an economist, "are . . . in perfect harmony with each other, as each derives advantage from every measure that tends to facilitate the growth of capital."[38]

Given the rapid rate of postbellum industrialization, Northern factory workers soon began to question the relevance of the free labor ideology. Few workers lived the idyllic existence of the artisan or farmer; few could even aspire to such a life. By the 1870s, many workers were locked into lives of wage labor, with little hope of gaining the capital to escape their dreary days. The 1873 Declaration of Principles of the International Labor Union of America labeled the "wage-system" a "despotism," and concluded that "there can be no government of the people, by the people, and for the people, where the many are dependent upon the few for an existence." The desire for labor organizing grew within this crucible, in the recognition that the interests of labor and capital might not, after all, be in harmony. Workers realized that their republican independence could not be grounded on agrarian ideals, that the republican common good was sometimes a disguise for the interests of capital, and that they needed to organize to assure their own independence. Otherwise, workers would remain buried on the bottom of corporate bureaucracies, with capitalists reaping the profits of industrialized production. Workers suggested different ways of reinvigorating their republican citizenship, such as the "republicanization of industry" through the transformation of factories into cooperatives. The *New York Times* even reported that "cooperative shops and manufactures" had recently been "all the rage."[39]

Before long, a vigorous union movement emerged. Just as businesses had perceived the benefits of organizing as corporate bureaucracies, workers began to appreciate the need for organizing national unions. Local organizations could not protect workers subject to the vagaries of national markets, business cycles, depressions, unemployment, the introduction of machines, the influx of immigrants, and so on. The Knights of Labor formed in 1869, and by the 1880s, it had leapfrogged to a membership of nearly one million. Reaching out to a wide array of workers, skilled and un-skilled, men and women, blacks and whites, immigrant and native born, the Knights advocated for worker co-ops, workplace democracy, and "wise, ju-dicious legislation" that would "prevent the unjust accumulation of wealth." The Knights' 1878 constitution evinced these goals and this unionizing ecu-menism, while emphasizing the growing gulf between capital and labor and its implications for republican democracy. The Knights aimed "to secure to the toilers a proper share of the wealth that they create." They demanded "those rights and privileges necessary to make them capable of enjoying, appreciating, defending and perpetuating the blessings of *good government.*" Indeed, in this early stage of the American labor movement, the Knights stressed equal treatment under the law — the republican democratic prohi-bition against laws that benefited partial or private interests. They sought "[t]he abrogation of all laws that do not bear equally upon capital and labor, [and] the removal of unjust technicalities, delays and discriminations in the administration of justice." As their leader, Terence Powderly, phrased it in 1882: "[The people must judge] whether a law be passed in the interests of a class or for the public good. Labor, all its rights — capital, all its rights — no special laws or privileges for either, but 'equal and exact justice for all.'" Ar-ticulating a "working-class version" of republican democracy, the Knights looked "to the day when cooperation shall supersede the wage system, and the castes and classes that now divide men shall be forever abolished." But the Knights encountered numerous obstacles. Worker co-ops, for instance, needed to profit like any other business. And of course, capitalists mar-shaled their wealth and political power to oppose the Knights' agenda, while the Knights themselves often divided between the leaders and the rank and file.[40]

Equally important, these early labor hopes and demands generated one bitter strike after another. The Knights and workers in general might have aspired to republican harmony between capital and labor, but strikes viv-idly illustrated the fractious divisions within American society. During the first half of the 1880s, approximately 500 work stoppages occurred each year, but from 1885 to 1886, the number nearly tripled, from 695 to 1,572. In subsequent years, to the early-twentieth century, the annual number of strikes fell below 1,000 only once (946 in 1888) and climbed over 3,000 by 1901. Major strikes hit the railroads in 1877, 1886, and 1894, while coal min-ers struck in 1887–88 and 1897. Many of these strikes took on the nature of "industrial warfare." In 1877 alone, artillery was turned on strikers in Chicago; the federal government sent troops to Pittsburgh and West Virginia; and state militia killed more than fifty strikers in Baltimore.[41]

In early May 1886, the Knights supported a general strike to advocate for eight-hour workdays. The strike began peacefully, but violence erupted again in Chicago, where the greatest number of workers had gathered. On May 4, the police sought to break up a large public rally at Haymarket Square. A bomb exploded, and the police opened fire. Nearly seventy police officers were injured, with seven dying; two hundred demonstrators were wounded, and an undetermined number died. In the wake of this violence, antilabor sentiment spread across the country. The city arrested and convicted eight immigrant anarchists, even though only one of them was at the scene of the violence. Regardless, the Haymarket Affair contributed to a public perception that many labor organizers were not only immigrants, but socialists, communists, or anarchists. Nativism and antiradicalism surged across the nation. Justice David J. Brewer, speaking to the New York State Bar Association, denounced unions for waving both "the black flag of anarchism, flaunting destruction to property, [and] the red flag of socialism, inviting a redistribution of property . . . in order to secure the vaunted equality."[42]

Given these forces, the balloon of the Knights deflated as quickly as it had risen. The American Federation of Labor (AFL), founded in 1886, quickly replaced the Knights as the preeminent national labor organization. Whereas the Knights had challenged the factional division between laborers and capitalists, the AFL acquiesced to, even embraced, this class-based division. According to the preamble of the AFL's 1886 constitution, "A struggle is going on in the nations of the civilized world between the oppressors and the oppressed of all countries, a struggle between capital and labor, which must grow in intensity from year to year and work disastrous results to the toiling millions of all nations if not combined for mutual protection and benefit." In 1893, AFL President Samuel Gompers stressed "the separation of the capitalistic class from the great laboring mass." Capitalists had their "origins in force and fraud," he explained, while workers deserved "the earth and the fullness thereof." While this acceptance of a radical division between capital and labor sat uneasily with republican democratic principles, it eventually led the AFL to adopt a moderate form of unionism. The AFL acceded to the basic structures of industrialism and the capitalist marketplace, but then pushed for economic reward. The AFL thus differed significantly from the Knights. The Knights had sought to remake the industrialized economy to correspond better with republican democracy, while the AFL more readily accepted factional division and set forth to pursue its own interests. Simultaneously, the AFL's concentration on the private or nongovernmental sphere tempered potential implications of their strategy for democratic government. The AFL accepted that their members would remain wage laborers within a corporate bureaucratic structure and, at least initially, focused on collective bargaining with management to capture a larger share of the profits for the workers. Compared with the Knights, the AFL sought to benefit less from forms of overt governmental intervention, including legislation. Moreover, the AFL less stridently encouraged strikes and more exclusively limited membership, accepting only skilled workers organized into specific craft unions. To Gompers, this approach to labor organizing would lead to the "common good." All types of unionizing, however, generated issues related to free expression (as discussed in the next chapter). Employers would rely on the tradition of suppression, laborers would invoke the tradition of dissent, and courts would intervene by applying legal doctrines.[43]

INDUSTRIALIZATION HELPED GENERATE numerous interrelated divisions within American society—unions versus management, workers versus capitalists, immigrants versus native borns, rich versus poor, urban versus rural—which strained the fabric of republican democracy. Yet even more pressure came from other diverse sources. During the antebellum era, most Americans had believed science and religion were harmonious, but during the 1870s, a dispute over Darwin's theory of evolution provoked calls to secularize science. Science and religion increasingly seemed separate and irrelevant to each other. At least initially, many scientists remained pious, though their religiosity became extraneous to their scientific work. Then, in reaction against this growing secularism, some Protestants turned to a more fundamentalist biblicism. Over time, this chasm between science and religion deepened. Many intellectuals eventually began to see science and religion as antithetical, while some Protestants turned away from the public realm and politics altogether and concentrated instead on private salvation. Although secularization certainly did not sweep across the entire nation, the potential conflict between secularization and piety became more visible.[44]

This division between religion and science, with the latter's emphasis on objectivity, reverberated through intellectual circles. A new type of American university developed, emphasizing research and service rather than "mental discipline, . . . piety and strength of character." The universities

became the training grounds for scientific and social scientific professionals. These trained experts, including economists, psychologists, sociologists, and political scientists, aimed "to identify social problems and to formulate policies for solving them." From this perspective, the government
and the American people were to follow the recommended policies because they were "scientifically formulated." Legal academics, too, claimed
a place in the new universities. These professional teachers and scholars,
led by the first Harvard Law School dean, Christopher C. Langdell, sought
to describe a science of law, a discipline of "pure law" worthy of university
study. And just as other scientists distanced their disciplines from religion,
so too legal scientists. In doing so, they repudiated natural law, which in
America had been grounded on Protestant Christianity, and instead embraced positivism.[45]

The repudiation of natural law intertwined with the emergence of a
"historicist sensibility" and a burgeoning modernist conception of progress. With industrialization following on the heels of the Civil War, many
Americans experienced a "radical discontinuity between past and present."
For most Americans, the goals of their childhoods, lives as self-sustaining
farmers or artisans, now lay beyond their grasps. For intellectuals, meanwhile, Darwinian theory suggested that the nation's radical changes represented a type of advance that transcended the timeless principles of premodern natural law. The theory of evolution, explained Richard Ely, was
an "idea which has made the world different [and was] giving direction to
human history." Evolution helped unleash the idea of progress from religious convictions; modern secular progress entailed potentially endless
improvement, springing forth from human ingenuity. This idea of progress
resonated with industrialization: the technological wonders of the Gilded
Age provided, for many, incontrovertible evidence of human inventiveness
and social progress.[46]

This movement toward modernism placed yet further stress on republican democracy, which had roots winding back to premodern natural-law
philosophies. Not only could republican theory be traced to classical
thinkers like Aristotle, but the constitutional framers synthesized classical republican principles with Lockean natural rights. When postbellum
legal thinkers rejected premodern natural-law concepts, including natural
rights, they implicitly questioned the wellsprings of republican democratic
government. Even so, while professional legal academics led the transition
from natural law to positivism, many politicians and judges continued to
invoke natural rights. Reconstruction era Republicans, for instance, did not

hesitate to invoke natural rights to liberty and property as they sought to enforce their free labor ideology after the war. Intellectual developments might have imposed additional strains on the republican democratic regime, but the system remained intact.[47]

THE SAME, YET DIFFERENT

The preeminent constitutional law treatise of the postbellum period, Thomas Cooley's *Constitutional Limitations,* first published in 1868 and by 1903 in a seventh edition, illustrates the resiliency of republican democracy. Cooley began by declaring that "[t]he theory of our political system is that the ultimate sovereignty is in the people, from whom springs all legitimate authority." Equally important, Cooley retained the republican democratic notion that individual liberties were always subordinate to the legislative power to enact laws for the common good. When discussing the definition of due process or the law of the land, Cooley quoted approvingly from Daniel Webster: "'The meaning is, that every citizen shall hold his life, liberty, property, and immunities under the protection of general rules which govern society.'" Cooley observed that under the state police power "persons and property are subjected to all kinds of restraints and burdens, in order to secure the general comfort, health, and prosperity of the State." Thus, Cooley reasoned, judicial review over legislative acts should be exercised only "with reluctance and hesitation."[48]

Even so, Cooley continued by explaining how the requirement that legislation be for the common good not only empowered but also limited the government. After all, the title of Cooley's treatise was *Constitutional Limitations.* It is "the very nature of free government," he wrote, for the legislature "to make laws for the public good, and *not* for the benefit of individuals." Consequently, "[t]he bills of rights in the American constitutions forbid that parties shall be deprived of property except by the law of the land; but if the prohibition had been omitted, a legislative enactment to pass one man's property over to another would nevertheless be void." More generally, Cooley explained, republican democratic principles restrained legislatures from enacting laws for partial or private interests. "[E]very one has a right to demand that he be governed by general rules, and a special statute that singles his case out as one to be regulated by a different law from that which is applied in all similar cases would not be legitimate legislation, but an arbitrary mandate, unrecognized in free government." This limit on legislative power translated into a demand for equality under the law: "Special privileges are obnoxious, and discriminations against persons or classes are still more so."[49]

Cooley's *Constitutional Limitations* emblematized the lasting importance of republican democratic principles. Yet, the enormous pressures placed on republican democracy during the late-nineteenth and early-twentieth centuries engendered an extended period of contestation, when Americans disputed the meanings of virtue and the common good. Republican democratic virtue had always been invested with a strong dose of individualism: from the time of the framing, a private realm of individual liberty and property supposedly stood protected from governmental action unless in furtherance of the common good. During the early-nineteenth century, a private-sphere virtue evolved, celebrating independence and the pursuit of self-interest, tempered by a Protestant civility. This individualist ethos intertwined with the sense of equality integral to republican democratic government, as captured in the Jacksonian rhetoric, "Equal rights for all; special privileges for none." During the postbellum period, though, the meaning of virtuous individualism splintered as capital and labor increasingly came to loggerheads. Capitalists tended to understand virtue in terms of "acquisitive individualism," justifying the pursuit of profits. Laborers emphasized independent self-reliance, which could in turn justify governmental intervention to nurture substantive justice. From the laborers' standpoint, capitalists lacked virtue and corrupted the governmental and economic systems.[50]

Such disputes, however, more often played out on the fields of the common good. Ever since the framing, factionalism seemed an unavoidable consequence of republican democracy, but particular factions had been considered temporary, arising during moments when the nonvirtuous pursuit of private interests predominated (with the intransigent division between abolitionists and slaveholders being the exception that proved the rule, given the fact of the Civil War). Constitutional structures supposedly checked and balanced such factions until government adjusted, resuming its rightful pursuit of the common good. But during the postbellum period, divisions in American society—between capitalists and laborers, rich and poor, immigrants and native born, and on and on—had deepened and become increasingly intractable. Too often, these societal groups seemed as if they might become permanent factions, with distinct interests pursued in a systematic fashion, such as through a labor union, a professional organization, a business monopoly, or even a political machine, particularly in the large cities. The societal homogeneity that had previously grounded the republican democratic common good, while always in part a pretense, became increasingly difficult to maintain — even as a myth.[51]

Yet, the rhetoric of republican democracy had become so deeply ingrained in the national psyche that many Americans could not readily accept the legitimacy or permanence of class-based conflicts. The assumption that the people of the nation could harmoniously pursue a common good could not be swept aside, as if it were no more than the dust of days gone by. Hence, a legal encyclopedia condemned lobbying on behalf of an interest group as a corrupt pursuit of partial or private interests contrary to the common good. "[A]ll legislators should act solely . . . with an eye single to the public interest. [The] courts universally hold illegal all contracts for services which involve . . . the exercise of sinister or personal influences upon the legislators to secure their votes in favor of a legislative act." In the midst of an 1886 congressional discussion about labor unrest, Pennsylvania Representative Andrew Curtin insisted: "We have no classes here; and the great prizes of life are open to [laborers] as to other citizens." The welfare of laborers was "linked [with] the welfare of all the citizens of this country." Yet, while Americans remained committed to the republican democratic principle of the common good, they vigorously debated its meaning in concrete situations. The central disputes revolved around the regulation of the industrial economy, including the employment relationship.[52]

Numerous Americans, not solely labor leaders, believed that the common good demanded restrictions on corporate activities, whether through union demands or legislation. In 1888, the Democratic president, Grover Cleveland, explained that "the fortunes realized by our manufacturers are no longer solely the reward of sturdy industry and enlightened foresight. [They] are largely built upon undue exactions from the masses of our people. [Corporations] are fast becoming the people's masters." Cleveland therefore proposed legislative remedies, including a reduction in tariffs protective of industry, a revision of federal pension laws, and a change in the distribution of public lands. The very next year, the new Republican president, Benjamin Harrison, acknowledged that "[when trusts are] organized, as they often are, to crush out all healthy competition and to monopolize the production or sale of an article of commerce and general necessity, they are dangerous conspiracies against the public good, and should be made the subject of prohibitory and even penal legislation." Meanwhile, labor leaders, such as George McNeill, insisted that "legislative bodies are bound . . . to protect the sovereign citizen against the insidious inroads of the usurping power [of corporate capitalism]."[53]

First, state legislatures and, then, Congress began to respond to these calls for action in the name of the common good. In the late-nineteenth century, numerous states enacted laws restricting the employment of children, while New York, Pennsylvania, Illinois, California, Connecticut, and New Mexico statutorily mandated eight-hour workdays. Many states, including Ohio and Illinois, enacted safety laws protecting factory employees; other states, like Colorado and New Mexico, passed safety regulations for mines. States passed legislation proscribing discrimination against union members, requiring the regular (weekly or monthly) payment of wages, and regulating the corporate payment of wages in company-store scrip. Several states passed laws restricting the doctrine of criminal conspiracy, which had been used to thwart strikes in the 1870s and 1880s. In the first two decades of the new century, state legislatures enacted more than fifty laws restricting labor injunctions, another antistrike device.[54]

While many state legislatures were convinced of the need to regulate industry for the common good, the development of a national economic marketplace generated calls for national regulations. State regulation of industries lacking localized boundaries no longer seemed workable. In a transportation industry like railroading, for example, commerce now wound its way from one state to another. Congress, after haggling for a number of years, made the railroads the first nationally regulated industry, partly because railroad patrons were disgruntled, partly because the railroad industry itself sought unified regulation, and partly because the Supreme Court ruled in 1886 that states could not regulate interstate commerce. The Interstate Commerce Act (ICA), enacted in February 1887, mandated that railroad rates be "reasonable and just," that railroads not discriminate among patrons by charging differential rates, and that railroads not enter into "pooling" or cartel agreements. The ICA also empowered an Interstate Commerce Commission to investigate alleged violations of the Act's substantive provisions. When debating the ICA, congressmen naturally invoked the common good. "[W]hat benefits the public must control against private interests," observed Illinois Representative Ransom Dunham. Congress followed the ICA with the Sherman Anti-Trust Act, passed on July 2, 1890, which imposed criminal penalties on contracts, conspiracies, and attempts to form monopolies or trusts that would restrain trade or commerce. "It is the right of every man to work, labor, and produce in any lawful vocation and to transport his production on equal terms and conditions and under like circumstances," said the bill's sponsor, Ohio Senator John Sherman, harking back to the free labor ideology of Reconstruction. "This is industrial liberty and lies at the foundation of the equality of all rights and privileges." The statute, most importantly, would warn Americans "that all trade and commerce, all agreements and arrangements, all struggles for money or property, must be governed by the universal law that the public good must be the test."[55]

NOT ALL AMERICANS believed the regulation of the industrial economy promoted the common good. Already before the Civil War, a growing number of Americans had begun to conceive of the common good as harmonious with a private-sphere virtue oriented toward economic profits. After the war, partly in response to the rising profits flowing from industrialization, more and more Americans infused the common good with increasingly strong tinges of laissez-faire coloring. In 1866, when Congress debated a graduated income tax, Representative Justin Morrill insisted that "in a republican form of government we cannot justify this inequality of taxation"; differential taxation could "only be defended on the same ground as the highwayman defends his acts." To the end of the century, the graduated tax consistently provoked similar condemnations. David Wells called it "simply confiscation," and the *New York Tribune* denounced it as "class legislation on a tremendous scale." In 1886, the House debated proposed legislation to deal with labor unrest. "I protest against any legislation," exclaimed Benjamin Butterworth of Ohio, "that shall segregate [any people and set] them apart as belonging to a peculiar portion of the great constituency that we represent; as belonging to a class possessing under the laws of our country less or fewer rights and privileges and fewer opportunities than their fellows." Such class legislation "can have no proper place in the free soil of America."[56]

From the perspective of laissez-faire ideology, any governmental regulation that shifted money or property from A to B or otherwise interfered with the operation of the economic marketplace necessarily transgressed the common good. Unregulated competition in the economic marketplace supposedly led to the survival of the fittest, which ultimately advanced the public good; the rich deserved their riches, while the poor deserved their poverty. In the words of John D. Rockefeller, "The American Beauty rose can be produced in the splendor and fragrance which bring cheer to its beholder only by sacrificing the early buds which grow up around it. This is not an evil tendency in business. It is merely the working-out of a law of nature and a law of God." Thus, as the nineteenth century wore on, laissez-faire ideology shifted the border between the public and private realms, as manifested in the distinctions between governmental actions for the common good (properly within the public realm) and governmental actions for partial or private interests (class legislation improperly interfering with the private realm).[57]

What caused this turn toward laissez-faire? Raw economic greed certainly played a major role, as the wealthy had a vested interest in protecting their riches from governmental redistribution. Nativism and racism played roles as well, since many poor laborers were immigrants from southern and eastern Europe. Intellectual trends also contributed. Herbert Spencer's social Darwinism inspired some Americans, perhaps most prominently Yale professor William Graham Sumner. In his 1883 book, *What the Social Classes Owe to Each Other,* Sumner explained that the "aggregation of large fortunes is not at all a thing to be regretted." He condemned as "social quackery" all types of social reform and welfare legislation. "Society needs first of all to be freed from these meddlers-that is, to be let alone," he concluded. "Here we are, then, once more back at the old doctrine — Laissez faire. Let us translate it into blunt English, and it will read, Mind your own business. It is nothing but the doctrine of liberty." More so than social Darwinism, the tenets of political economy shaped American outlooks. Like many other intellectuals, political economists sought scientific objectivity, a hallmark of professionalization in the new universities. As the Harvard professor Charles Dunbar phrased it, economists quested after "the laws which govern all economic progress." Sharing some views with the social Darwinists, late-nineteenth-century political economists generally resisted the governmental redistribution of wealth. But while social Darwinists tended to celebrate unrestrained competition, many political economists supported governmental regulation if beneficial to the common good, particularly the maximization of wealth. Amasa Walker asked incredulously: "If . . . capital, then, from first to last, was honestly and honorably acquired, has anyone occasion to complain that large wealth has been realized by those who used it?" Yet laborers, he added, are entitled to seek legislation, so long as it is in the "general welfare," which is consistent with the "interests of capital." F. W. Taussig emphasized the accumulation of wealth, yet argued that "every [legislative] measure that aids in maintaining 'fair' or normal competition is good."[58]

Regardless of the precise intellectual antecedents, many Americans in the late-nineteenth century, certainly more than previously, understood the common good from the vantage of laissez-faire. The well-regulated society had become more libertarian; the American ethos of individualism had intensified. Economic liberalism, emphasizing the individual pursuit of self-interest, bore ever deeper into republican democracy. The leading constitutional law treatises of the era illustrate this transformed common good. Cooley warily guarded against governmental interference with private-sphere economic activities. Although never countenancing judicial activism in the name of individual rights, he nonetheless worried about "the rights of personal liberty and private property." Judges should be especially sensitive to the likelihood that economic regulations were for partial or private interests, Cooley cautioned. "[I]f the legislature should undertake to provide that persons following some specified lawful trade or employment should not have capacity to make contracts, . . . or in any other way to make such use of their property as was permissible to others, it can scarcely be doubted that the act would transcend the due bounds of legislative power. . . . The man or class forbidden the acquisition or enjoyment of property in the manner permitted to the community at large would be deprived of *liberty* in particulars of primary importance to his or their 'pursuit of happiness.'" Even so, Cooley did not advocate for a social Darwinist type of laissez-faire, an economic marketplace totally free of governmental regulation. Instead, Cooley remained consistent with the principles of republican democracy, which entailed both the empowering and limiting of government. He opposed class legislation, but not legislation in general.[59]

Christopher G. Tiedeman, who published *A Treatise on the Limitations of Police Power in the United States* in 1886, argued to imbue the common good with a far stronger dose of laissez-faire ideology. Tiedeman immediately and expressly stated his purpose: to support "laissez-faire doctrine, which denies to government the power to do more than to provide for the public order and personal security by the prevention and punishment of crimes and trespasses." He lamented how the spread of "universal suffrage" had allowed "the great army of discontents" to oppress the rights of the minority through social welfare legislation. For Tiedeman, the courts primarily functioned, whether in the name of due process or otherwise, to limit the exercise of governmental power. "Wherever by reasonable construction [a] constitutional limitation can be made to avoid an unrighteous exercise of police power, that construction will be upheld." Even so, Tiedeman never abandoned republican democratic principles, but rather interpreted them from his laissez-faire perspective. "[T]he police power of the government . . . is simply the power of the government to establish provisions for the enforcement of the common as well as civil-law maxim, *sic utere tuo, ut alienum non laedas*, . . . 'it being of universal application, it must of course be within the range of legislative action to define the mode and manner in which every one may so use his own as not to injure others.'" After invoking this familiar nineteenth-century principle of republican democracy,

Tiedeman elaborated: "Any law which goes beyond that principle, . . . to limit the exercise of rights beyond what is necessary to provide for the public welfare and the general security, cannot be included in the police power of the government."[60]

Thus, at the height of laissez-faire ideology in the late-nineteenth century, Americans still understood their governments to be republican democracies. To be sure, political and economic interests and cultural values shaped various Americans' respective conceptions of the common good. Most Americans conceptualized the common good harmoniously with their own interests and values. Corporate capitalists tended to dismiss economic and employment regulations as illegitimate class legislation, while laborers tended to view the same regulations far more favorably. But still, political preferences filtered through the ideological prism of republican democracy. As if to prove the point, some steadfast laissez-faire devotees would occasionally protest against governmental actions, like protective tariffs and corporate subsidies, that favored corporate interests. Ultimately, then, even a laissez-faire constitutionalist such as Tiedeman admitted that government possessed power to regulate for the common good. Of course, Tiedeman and his ilk condemned most such purported regulations as being for partial or private interests; after all, nothing advanced the common good (supposedly) like an unregulated economic marketplace.[61]

Given the persistence of the principle that government could regulate for the common good — and despite the disagreements about the definition of the common good — the nation never adopted a true laissez-faire system. At the national level, the postbellum government always remained heavily involved in the economy. Often, this involvement took the form of assistance to corporations and capitalists, such as the grants of public lands to railroads and the tariffs protecting American industries from foreign competition. In the early-twentieth century, moreover, the national government still sent payments to Civil War veterans and widows (analogous to old-age social security). And of course, by this time, the government had moved into the business of overtly regulating the economy with the ICA and the Sherman Anti-Trust Act. True, the government did not always enthusiastically enforce legislated regulations; in the decade immediately after the enactment of the Sherman Act, corporate America went through a frenzy of mergers. Even so, in the many areas that the national government either did not legislate or did not enforce legislation, the economy still was not free of governmental structure. Besides the many state regulatory statutes, state common law always provided a government-sanctioned framework for economic interactions and relations. For instance, the fellow-servant rule and other common law doctrines insulated employers from liability for employee injuries attributable to the negligence of another employee. In fact, the common law rules of employer-employee relations ordered the industrial workplace with a feudal-like hierarchy, as the U.S. Commission on Industrial Relations observed in 1912. Thus, laissez-faire never achieved hegemony, even as its older cousin, economic liberalism, burrowed snugly into republican democracy.[62]

In any event, during the late-nineteenth-century, political calls for greater control over corporate industrialism always countered the push toward a laissez-faire flavored common good. As the century drew to a close, an increasing number of Americans recognized and questioned the inequities of the capitalist economy. Industrial capitalism effectively produced wealth and consumer goods, but it also produced gross disparities of wealth, frequent severe depressions, and social dislocations. Indeed, political economists and social Darwinists rarely denied these problems. They instead justified or explained them: for example, disparities of wealth supposedly arose because of merit — the corporate rich deserved their wealth supposedly because of their intelligence, strength, moral fiber, and work ethic. Taussig emphasized the "inborn capacity" of businessmen and explained that "a process very like natural selection is at work." The successful businessman "must have imagination . . . judgment . . . courage . . . administrative capacity [and] sagacity." Despite such encomiums to the businessman, industrialization and the concomitant divisions within American society blew heavy winds of change that bent and swayed republican democracy. These winds of change eventually brought two mass political movements: Populism and Progressivism.[63]

POPULISM AND PROGRESSIVISM

During the postbellum era, as the nation transformed, southern, midwestern, and western farmers began to view themselves as "victims." Industrialization, urbanization, and immigration challenged their status in America as ideal republican citizens, as the economic backbone of the nation. They anxiously confronted obstacles like steep railroad-shipping rates, aggressive banking interests, and a bewildering array of middlemen in the increasingly complex national economy. Fused together by Protestant evangelical fundamentalism and an agrarian way of life, they finally coalesced in the early 1890s into the People's party, the Populists.[64]

The Populists found ready targets for their wrath. From the Populist vantage, a "natural harmony" existed among producing peoples—like themselves—but avaricious corporate capitalists and bankers lacked the virtue necessary for republican democratic government. "Wealth belongs to him who creates it, and every dollar taken from industry without an equivalent is robbery. 'If any will not work, neither shall he eat.'" The corporate plutocrats corrupted the American government and economy because they never sated their thirst for wealth. For their own advantage, they supposedly limited the flow of currency, causing depression and poverty. On top of this, immigrants flooded the cities and brought religious heresy and moral depravity with them. Thus, while the Populists attempted to broaden their appeal—by endorsing, for example, the eight-hour workday to attract wage laborers—they drew their sustenance largely from the social and cultural divisions that fissured the American landscape: rural versus urban, agriculture versus industry, native versus immigrant, and Protestant versus Catholic and Jew. Intellectuals might be talking about political economy and social Darwinism, but the people were talking simple, agrarian, evangelical Protestantism.[65]

The preamble to the 1892 People's party platform highlighted the foundations of Populism. "Corruption dominates the ballot-box, the Legislatures, the Congress, and touches even the ermine of the bench." Economic inequity related to republican democracy. "The fruits of the toil of millions are boldly stolen to build up colossal fortunes for a few, unprecedented in the history of mankind; and the possessors of those, in turn, despise the Republic and endanger liberty." The "plain people" of "the Republic" needed a third political party because the Democrats and Republicans "propose to sacrifice our homes, lives, and children on the altar of mammon; to destroy the multitude in order to secure corruption funds from the millionaires." The Populists ostentatiously invoked the icons and traditions of republican democratic government. They traced their message back to Washington— calling on "the spirit of the grand general and chief who established our independence"—and through Jefferson, Jackson, and Lincoln. Partly for this reason, the Populists' agenda revolved around a "bad apple" conception of republican politics. The people, for the most part, were hardworking, imbued with common sense, and grounded on solid Protestant values; in a word, the people were virtuous. Thus, they just needed to dump the bad apples who had seized control of the government—to throw the rascals out of office—and to elect instead men like Jefferson and Jackson. They did not repudiate republican democracy; they dreamed of resuscitating it as if it were a "lost agrarian Eden." In the words of the preamble, they sought "to *restore* the government" to the people.[66]

When it came to concrete policy proposals, Populists moved uncertainly. They supported a number of measures that would increase governmental power so as to combat the strength of corporate America, including a graduated income tax and governmental ownership of railroads. Yet, overall, they tended toward moderation. Their most important policy proposal was free silver: this issue anchored their nomination of the Democrats' free-silver candidate, William Jennings Bryan, for the 1896 presidential election. Free-silver advocates insisted that plutocratic control of the monetary supply impoverished the producing peoples. "[O]ur annual agricultural productions amount to billions of dollars in value, which must, within a few weeks or months, be exchanged for billions of dollars' worth of commodities consumed in their production," explained the 1892 preamble. But "the existing currency supply is wholly inadequate to make this exchange; the results are falling prices, the formation of combines and rings, the impoverishment of the producing class." The solution, it seemed, was to switch from a gold standard to a silver-based currency, which supposedly would increase the flow of money and boost prices.[67]

When Bryan lost the 1896 election, however, the Populist movement quickly dissipated. Republicans and Democrats already had learned they could co-opt Populist rhetoric, and once the Populists tied their future to the single issue of free silver and the Democrat's Bryan — and then lost — the Populists' mass appeal evaporated. In fact, the implications of free silver — the key to the Populist-Democratic alliance — were never too clear; free silver certainly would not have been the panacea that some Populists had claimed. Moreover, the Populists' Protestant-laced rhetoric and moralizing tended to alienate the urban laborers — including Catholic and Jewish workers — who could have broadened the party's base. Bryan's famous "Cross of Gold" speech, given at the 1896 Democratic National Convention, bristled with religious indignation: "The humblest citizen in all the land, when clad in the armor of a righteous cause, is stronger than all the hosts of error. I come to speak to you in defense of a cause as holy as the cause of liberty — the cause of humanity." Bryan masterfully wove Protestant imagery with populism: "With a zeal approaching the zeal which inspired the crusaders who followed Peter the Hermit, our silver Democrats went forth from victory unto victory, until they are now assembled, not to discuss, not to debate, but to enter up the judgment already rendered by the plain people of this country." Such Populist sermonizing often edged over into nativist denunciations of immigrants, urbanites, and non-Protestants. Thomas Watson, the Populists' 1896 vice presidential nominee, exploded: "Some of our principal cities are more foreign than American. The most dangerous and corrupting hordes of the Old World have invaded us. The vice and crime which they have planted in our midst are sickening and terrifying." Despite such self-destructive pronouncements, and the Populists' eventual downfall, the movement had significant ramifications for the future. Most important, the Populists engendered greater concerns for economic equality and reform, which helped clear a path for Progressivism and eventually pluralist democracy.[68]

LESS THAN A DECADE after the disastrous 1896 election, a new and distinct reform movement arose. Like Populism, Progressivism responded to problems arising from industrialization, urbanization, and immigration, but Progressives viewed these problems differently and thus often (though not always) sought different solutions. While Populists looked backward to an idyllic past — bereft, for instance, of giant corporations — the Progressives tended to accept as given the modern institutions of turn-of-the-century America: corporations, banks, and unions. Similarly, Progressives generally acceded to the entrenchment of strident social and economic classes in the United States. According to Herbert Croly, "[t]he vast incoherent mass of the American people is falling into definite social groups, which restrict and define the mental outlook and social experience of their members." These social and economic realities generated well-publicized problems. Muckraking journalists published numerous revelations of corruption in both business and government, often linking the two together. With gritty realism, muckrakers chronicled the avaricious graspings of self-interested though seemingly successful businessmen and politicians. The famed Lincoln Steffens denounced "the big business man" as "a self-righteous fraud [and] the chief source of corruption [in politics]." Partly because of growing newspaper circulations, muckrakers' exposés enraged millions of middle-class Americans. In 1870, 574 daily newspapers had a total circulation of 2,602,000; by 1900, circulation (of 2,226 papers) had leaped nearly sixfold; and by 1909, 2,600 dailies had a circulation over 24 million.[69]

Progressives were, in important ways, modernists. The Populists had looked backward to an Edenic past, but the Progressives looked forward to a better future. They had fully absorbed the modern historicist attitude: society could endlessly progress because of human will power and creativity. "The only possible cohesion now is a loyalty that looks forward. . . . To do this men have to substitute purpose for tradition," Walter Lippmann declared. "We can no longer treat life as something that has trickled down to us. We have to deal with it deliberately, devise its social organization, alter its tools, formulate its method, educate and control it." To fulfill the "promise of American life," according to Croly, Americans had to be proactive, creating a far more activist government than in the past, particularly at the national level. With such commitments to purposive action, Progressives unsurprisingly relied on modernist methods for implementation. In Lippmann's terse prose, "there is a new world demanding new methods." Science was the key to democratic government. Science could help Americans redirect their impulses to civilized objectives by engendering "growing self-consciousness." Ultimately, Lippmann and other Progressives advocated for a pragmatic instrumentalism. Lippmann celebrated the "type of statesman . . . who regards all social organization as an instrument. Systems, institutions and mechanical contrivances . . . are valuable only when they serve the purposes of men."[70]

Progressives, in other words, wanted the government to pursue the common good instrumentally through legislation and judicial decision making. Legal scholars like Roscoe Pound, who would be dean of Harvard Law School for two decades, denigrated the postbellum academic focus on pure or "mechanical" law because of its arid and abstract formalism. He developed instead a sociological jurisprudence that encouraged judges to engage in "social engineering," making law for the good of society. Institutional economists like Richard Ely repudiated classical political economy and insisted that America needed "a vast body of legislation in and through which society seeks liberty." Progressives stressed that unmediated conflicting interests rarely produced the common good, either in government or the marketplace, at least in modern American society. So-called freedom of contract, in reality, facilitated social "degradation," wrote Ely. "The coercion of economic forces is largely due to the unequal strength of those who make a contract. . . . Contract does not change existing inequalities and forces, but is simply the medium through which they find expression." Such problems led Progressives to recommend numerous forms of corrective social legislation. The Progressive party platform of 1912 specified legislation, "looking to the prevention of industrial accidents, occupational diseases, overwork, involuntary unemployment, and other injurious effects incident to modern industry; [t]he fixing of minimum safety and health standards for the various occupations . . . ; [t]he prohibition of child labor; [m]inimum wage standards for working women . . . ; [o]ne day's rest in seven for all wage workers; [t]he eight hour day in continuous twenty-four hour industries [and so on]."[71]

Who was to design and implement the precise social-legislative measures — the instrumental governmental actions seeking social justice? Progressives had a ready answer: an elite constituted of the "best men" and (social) scientific experts. (Of course, the "best men" and the experts frequently seemed to be one and the same.) Often the sons of Mugwumps, Progressive leaders ranged from the Republican Theodore Roosevelt to the Democrat Woodrow Wilson, from the muckraking Steffens to the intellectual Lippmann. They were the virtuous elite, mostly old-stock Protestants from old wealth, who could lead the nation between the Scylla and Charybdis of confused laborers and greedy nouveau riche industrialists. In the words of one of their own, the reform lawyer and eventual Supreme Court justice Louis Brandeis, they could maintain "a position of independence between the wealthy and the people, [and thus were] prepared to curb the excesses of either." They could harness the forces of social change and direct it into "'constructive' channels." The nation could rely on these "experienced, educated, and well-trained men" to pursue the common good. Hence, while Progressives both acknowledged the growing fixedness of class divisions and accepted political support from the "common people," they acknowledged neither that a competition among class-based interest groups should determine governmental policies nor that the "democratic mass" should lead the nation. Instead, Progressive elites and trained experts, drawn from the growing ranks of educated professionals, were to lead the democratic masses to the common good despite the class divisions of American society.[72]

The principles of republican democratic government presented Progressives with a potential difficulty. Republican democracy proscribed the government from enacting class legislation for partial or private interests. Given that Progressives tended to accept the class divisions of contemporary America, would not legislation favoring any social or economic class, even a degraded class of laborers, violate the tenets of republican democracy? Faced with this potential difficulty, Progressives refused to repudiate republican democracy and instead reasserted its principles. Progressives argued that so-called private actions in the economic marketplace were corrupting republican democratic government. Gross disparities of wealth and power were not merely private-sphere matters but rather engendered government for partial or private interests. The institutional economist Thorstein Veblen objected that businessmen's excessive desire for "pecuniary gain" leads them to disregard how their enterprises bear "upon the welfare of the community." One Progressive after another found that corporate capitalists twisted republican democracy to their own purposes. Wilson lamented that "[t]he great Government we loved has too often been made use of for private and selfish purposes." Consequently, Progressives began to insist that capitalists exercise civic virtue even in economic interactions, so as to promote the common good. More important, Progressives suggested that a proper concern for the common good *demanded* social legislation; Progressive elites and experts *must* control the vested interests. The gist of the Progressive position was that a failure to enact social legislation constituted governmental action favoring partial or private interests — namely, the interests of corporate capitalists. Over the years, the national government had affirmatively promoted business in a variety ways, such as by imposing protective tariffs. Wilson now wanted Progressives "to drive all beneficiaries of governmental policy into the open and demand of them by what principle of national advantage, as contrasted with selfish privilege, they enjoy the extraordinary assistance extended to them." But even when the government had not overtly favored business interests, it had still facilitated the aggregation of corporate wealth — or so Progressives maintained. Progressive (sociological) jurisprudents like Pound criticized the "deep-seated conviction of the American lawyer that the doctrines of the common law are part of the universal jural order." To the contrary, the common law of contract and property amounted to affirmative governmental action, far from neutral. In the words of Freund, the common law was "a system of public policy." Moreover, as Pound explained, economists and sociologists readily saw "the deficiencies" of the common law, even if lawyers and judges sometimes did not. Ely argued, for example, that contract law "gives expression to inequalities, and allows existing social forces to flow on." Laissez-faire (or approximations of it) had cultivated such gross disparities of wealth and power that it could no longer be tolerated. A failure to enact social legislation effectively contravened the common good.[73]

Progressives advocated for social legislation at all levels of government, but they especially emphasized the need for *national* governmental action because society had become so complicated and economic institutions so large. The romantic American ideal of the Horatio Alger hero who pulls himself up by the bootstraps no longer matched social realities. "The economic ties uniting men in society were relatively few and simple in 1776," observed Ely. "[But today, it] is a mere truism to say that our well-being in industrial matters depends on others, as well as on ourselves." In light of such societal complexity, the average individual rarely could succeed if standing alone. The playing field slanted too much to allow fair competition, especially when one acknowledged that burgeoning behemoths of economic power, corporations, banks, and unions, towered over the field. State and local governmental actions could help in some realms, such as education, but national control was crucial if the gargantuan economic institutions were to be bent to the common good. Croly stressed that "[t]he problem belongs to the American *national* democracy, and its solution *must* be attempted chiefly by means of official *national* action." And, in fact, during the Progressive era, Congress enacted numerous statutes, including the Pure Food and Drug Act (protecting consumers), the Federal Trade Commission Act (restricting unfair methods of commercial competition), the Clayton Act (declaring a right of laborers to organize), the Federal Reserve Act (coordinating banking and business), the Keating-Owen Child Labor Act (restricting the employment of children), and the Adamson Act (imposing an eight-hour workday for railroad employees).[74]

From the Progressives' standpoint, all such social legislation aspired to, in a word, *progress.* In the early-twentieth century, like in the 1790s, the very nature, the very future, of republican democracy seemed to be at stake. Progressivism represented a final effort at retaining republican democratic government within an urban, industrial, and increasingly diverse America. And if republican democracy was to survive, it required modification; it must move forward with purposive action based on clear thinking. The "common good," Roosevelt proclaimed, must "become a vital force for progress." Hence, Progressives called their leading periodical, founded in 1914, "The *New* Republic." In its first issue, the editors, including Croly, Lippmann, and Walter Weyl, encapsulated their modernist optimism in the declaration that "aggressive thinking is necessary to fruitful action, and criticism can be made constructive."[75]

Progressives not only advocated for social legislation but also sought to refine the operation of republican democracy. They continued to consider virtue a precondition for full participation in republican democracy. Ely stressed that "there are certain mental and moral characteristics that are of importance . . . , such as foresight, industry, honesty, and capacity for social cooperation." Thus, for the immigrant, Croly insisted, the promise of American life becomes "a responsibility, which requires for its fulfillment a certain kind of behavior on the part of himself." Numerous Progressives still understood virtue in traditional American Protestant terms, yet many impoverished workers mashed under the capitalist industrial juggernaut were non-Protestants, including large numbers of immigrants and their children. To the extent that these workers participated at all in governmental processes, corrupt political machines often held them in vicelike grips, especially in the cities, with political support being exchanged for citizenship, governmental services, jobs, and other favors. Given this, many of the Progressives' sought-after reforms revolved around the quelling of non-Protestant influences on American culture and government. These reforms came in two basic types. The first aimed to inculcate or to impose Protestant values. To nurture republican democracy, government needed to promote virtue by encouraging Protestant morality — or so many Progressives believed. Roosevelt declared that public life was "a fundamental fight for morality," while Wilson called "to correct the evil" that had arisen because of American heedlessness about "our morals." At the Progressives' 1912 presidential convention, the delegates sang "Onward, Christian Soldiers," and the nominee, Roosevelt, proclaimed, "We stand at Armageddon and we battle for the Lord." The second type of reform sought to adjust the procedures of republican democratic government. In doing so, Progressives aimed to diminish the potential political strength of immigrants and other non-Protestants, to weaken political machines, and ultimately to facilitate government by the "best men" (read: virtuous old-stock Protestant Progressives).[76]

The Protestant social gospel leader Josiah Strong struck the keynote for the first type of reform: "Christianize the immigrant and he will be easily Americanized." This Progressive attitude crystallized in the temperance and prohibition movement. Temperance long had been a Protestant cause, yet the massive immigration of the late-nineteenth and early-twentieth centuries magnified its importance. Temperance or abstinence became more than an important Protestant value; for some, it now seemed necessary to preserve the character of America in the face of an alien invasion. The Anti-Saloon League, formed in 1895, sought to generate support for the enactment and enforcement of prohibition legislation, first locally and then nationally. By 1915, the League was cooperating with forty thousand churches, including many Methodist and Baptist ones, especially in the South, and by 1917, two-thirds of the states were dry. When World War I arrived, Prohibitionists relied on nativist and patriotic sentiments to boost their cause. By emphasizing the Germanic names of major brewers, like Busch and Pabst, the temperance crusade culminated with the 1919 constitutional amendment imposing national Prohibition.[77]

When it came to the second type of reform — adjusting republican democratic processes — Progressives took aim at government corruption. The 1912 Progressive party platform identified numerous such measures, including "the direct election of United States Senators" and the introduction of "the initiative, referendum and recall." Yet, purification from corruption frequently equated with reducing the political power of immigrants and other non-Protestant outsiders while facilitating the rule of the "best men." In many cities, political machines relied on single-district elections. A local boss would control each electoral district, precinct, or ward, through a combination of favors to and close ties with the populace, usually heavy with immigrants and their children. Local ward bosses then would support the city boss. Progressives maintained that a switch to at-large (or multimember) elections would cripple the machines. In an at-large election, citizens vote for representatives from throughout the city — let's say, for a multimember city council — and thus a ward boss could not get elected merely by supplying favors to his local constituents. Indeed, with a switch to at-large elections, many poor immigrant workers likely would no longer vote because the candidates were too distant; they lacked a presence in the neighborhood or ward and could not, it appeared, provide tangible benefits. All the better, then, from the Progressive vantage. After all, those individuals who refused to endorse and pursue traditional, mainstream, American Protestant values supposedly lacked the virtue needed for free government. If such individuals did not participate, only the "best men," the most virtuous, would be elected. Did Progressive reforms to republican democratic procedures successfully diminish corruption in government? Often so. But simultaneously such reforms disadvantaged non-Protestant outsiders, whose tenuous ties to American political processes severed easily.[78]

Clearly, Progressives were not radicals declaring all Americans equally entitled to lead and to participate in government. Progressivism tended toward moderation, and purposefully so. Progressive legislation typically either shrank from extremes, fizzled in implementation, or failed in the courts. Even so, many Americans found Progressivism too drastic. The *New York Times* brooded that "the initiative, the referendum, and the recall" would amount to "a frank adoption of the principle and practice of government by mob." Women's suffrage epitomized the complexities of many Progressive era reforms. Without doubt, the ratification of the nineteenth amendment in 1920, extending the right to vote to women, further democratized the nation, and dramatically so. Even so, numerous proponents of the nineteenth amendment hoped that it would help maintain Protestant domination despite the increasingly diverse American population. Many American Protestants had long opposed women's suffrage as contravening the traditional role of women in the family. Yet, Progressive leaders eventually realized that women's enfranchisement would add millions of white Protestant voters to the rolls and could help offset the threat of non-Protestant political power. As one suffragist put it in the late-nineteenth century: "There are in the United States three times as many American-born women as the whole foreign population, men and women together, so that the votes of women will eventually be the only means of overcoming this foreign influence and maintaining our free institutions." Like Prohibition, then, the women's suffrage movement finally triumphed during the Progressive era partly because anti-immigrant sentiments broadened the movement's support base. The nineteenth amendment granted (white Protestant) women suffrage, even while many African Americans remained effectively disenfranchised and immigrants saw their political influence questioned and diminished.[79]

JUDICIAL REVIEW IN A TIME OF STRESS

At the outset of Reconstruction, most Republicans believed that if they were to expand national power appreciably, the governmental institution to exercise this new power should be Congress rather than the federal courts. Congressional Republicans still smarted from Taney's 1857 Supreme Court opinion in *Dred Scott v. Sandford,* which had declared that Congress lacked the power to restrict slavery as well as holding that African Americans were not citizens. Moreover, the postwar Supreme Court had immediately displayed hostility toward Reconstruction. In these circumstances, congressional Republicans assumed that successful implementation of the Reconstruction amendments would depend primarily on legislative, not judicial, power. Thus, the most important provisions in the respective Reconstruction amendments appeared to be the clauses explicitly empowering Congress, such as section 2 of the thirteenth amendment: "Congress shall have power to enforce this article by appropriate legislation." Despite this general consensus, that congressional rather than judicial power would predominate, Republicans disagreed about the extent of congressional power vis-à-vis state sovereignty. All accepted the fundamental republican democratic principles. The national government should still be limited to acting for the common good, so national governmental actions for partial or private interests would constitute illegitimate class legislation. As had long been true, disagreements revolved around the implementation rather than the importance of these principles. In each instance, one had to ask whether the particular (national) governmental action was for the common good.[80]

This overarching question engendered a more specific one: what degree of federal governmental control over state and local governments constituted the common good? Many radical Republicans, like Senator Charles Sumner, insisted on the need for broad national power to crush the "demon of Caste." For Sumner, "[t]he same national authority that destroyed slavery must see that this other pretension is not permitted to survive." Sumner therefore would exercise federal power to prohibit racially segregated accommodations in hotels and on railroads. Yet, moderate Republican Senator Edgar Cowan contended that "[t]his world," as it currently stood, "is pretty well arranged." After all, Cowan added, someone has to "black boots and curry the horses, [and] do the menial offices of the world." Meanwhile, as might be expected, Northern Democrats were far more alarmed about the changing constitutional system. They brooded about the destruction of the basic federalist framework due to the centralization of power. New Jersey Representative Andrew Rogers exclaimed that the proposed fourteenth amendment "destroys the elementary principles of the States; it consolidates everything into one imperial despotism."[81]

Even though congressional Republicans anticipated that they would determine which governmental actions promoted the common good — for example, through the enactment of statutes defining federal crimes and civil causes of action — the national judiciary soon became a central institution in such determinations. Why? The Reconstruction amendments themselves established substantive constitutional guarantees judicially enforceable against state and local governments. During the antebellum period, state governments might have professed to be republican democracies, but such professions could not be enforced pursuant to federal law. Now, though, the Reconstruction amendments provided substantive mandates for the imposition of republican democratic principles on state and local governments. Thomas Cooley explained in the third edition of his *Constitutional Limitations,* published in 1874, that principles of state constitutional law had "now been made a part of the Constitution of the United States" and could be invoked in the federal courts, particularly in the Supreme Court. Moreover, the development of national economic markets generated legal problems that transcended local boundaries. A corporation operating across the country, for instance, would raise legal questions that had ramifications beyond any single state. These legal issues eventually wound their way into federal courts. Finally, when circumstances seemed propitious, the Reconstruction Congresses began to expand federal court jurisdiction, albeit in a piecemeal fashion. Congress augmented federal court jurisdiction for habeas corpus petitions in 1866 and 1867, and the Civil Rights Acts of 1866 and 1871 both extended jurisdiction to the federal judiciary for violations of the respective Acts. Before long, subsequent events led to a substantial increase in the power and importance of the federal judiciary.[82]

When the Democrats won the 1874 midterm elections (because of the

1873 economic panic), the lame-duck Republicans quickly passed the Judiciary and Removal Act of 1875. This statute significantly expanded federal jurisdiction by, for the first time, extending general federal question jurisdiction to the judiciary. The federal courts now had jurisdiction over cases "arising under the Constitution or laws of the United States, or treaties made, or which shall be made, under their authority." Claimants could institute in the lower federal courts civil actions to enforce federal rights, including but not limited to those protected under the Reconstruction amendments and statutes; moreover, litigants could remove state civil actions involving issues of federal law to the federal courts. Consequently, the case load of the federal judiciary increased dramatically. From 1873 to 1890, the number of pending cases in the lower federal courts grew from 29,013 to 54,194. In the U.S. Supreme Court, the October 1870 term opened with 636 cases on the docket. By 1884, this number had almost doubled, and by 1890, it had nearly tripled. And despite the 1874 Democratic advances in the House, Republicans still held the White House and Senate. Under the constitutional provisions for the appointment of federal judges, the Republicans thus could fill the federal judiciary, including any new positions, with their supporters. Not incidentally, then, the Republicans would continue to control the White House and Senate for most of the nineteenth century: the only Democratic president between 1870 and 1913 was Grover Cleveland (1885–89 and 1893–97), while the only Democratic-controlled late-nineteenth-century Senates were the forty-sixth (1879–81) and the fifty-third (1893–95). Given this control, Republicans continued stocking the federal bench with their own and thwarted Democratic efforts to curtail federal judicial power. Partly because of new federal judgeships engendered by the 1875 Judiciary and Removal Act, Grant appointed forty-one judges (while all the presidents before Grant together appointed fewer than two hundred). By the end of Grant's second term, in 1877, the lower federal judiciary was 85 percent Republican, and by the end of Rutherford B. Hayes's presidency, in 1881, it was 91 percent. Although the Republicans could not hegemonically control legislative processes — from 1875 through 1895, the Democrats usually controlled the House — the Republicans could still protect their interests and values through judicial processes.[83]

Innumerable late-nineteenth and early-twentieth legal disputes turned on the distinction between the common good and partial or private interests, or as it was sometimes phrased, the difference between reasonable and arbitrary (or class) legislation. Some judges, seeking precision, would equate reasonableness with a means-ends nexus: the governmental action must be a reasonable means for achieving the government's purpose, which must constitute the common good. Regardless, for most judges, the crucial division between the categories of the common good, on the one hand, and partial or private interests, on the other, seemed formalistic. Although the line between the opposed categories might initially be obscure in any concrete dispute, the judge could discern it through careful analysis. This analysis did not involve a balancing of the government's interests against countervailing ones; the judicial conclusion ostensibly rested on the proper understanding of preexisting category-boundaries. Thus, judges continued to perform the function of "boundary pricking," tracing the border between public goods and partial or private interests, point by point, or case by case. Nonetheless, through this supposedly formalistic judicial decision making, Republican-appointed federal judges helped integrate and reinforce national marketplaces, consistent with Republican political goals. When state and national legislatures began to enact more social legislation, including labor laws, federal judges often resolved whether disputed statutes constituted impermissible class legislation. In doing so, judges expanded the private realm of protected economic interests. To be clear, judges did not need to pursue the Republican political agenda self-consciously to facilitate economic nationalism. Rather, judges could decide according to the rule of law — demarcating the common good — but as with any judge, they always interpreted the relevant doctrine from their own perspective, from their own horizon of political interests and cultural values. Therefore, these federal judges often favored capital over labor; they tended to understand the common good as embodying a strong dose of free-labor-cum-laissez-faire ideology. Around the turn into the twentieth century, for example, four states enacted statutes that protected unions from antitrust and restraint-of-trade lawsuits. Federal courts struck down all of these prolabor statutes. In one case, the federal district judge celebrated the free marketplace. "[I]f such legislation is valid, is not the boasted right of liberty of contract entirely subject to legislative control? And there is no more sacred right, under our government, than the right of contract." Can a law protecting "organized labor" accord with equal protection? "I do not believe it."[84]

THE SEMINAL SUPREME COURT decision confronting this categorization problem under the umbrella of the Reconstruction amendments was *The Slaughterhouse Cases,* decided in 1873. The Louisiana state legislature granted a monopoly to one slaughterhouse (the Crescent City Stock Landing and Slaughter-House Company) for the butchering of cattle within an area including New Orleans. A group of local butchers challenged the legislation as violating the thirteenth and fourteenth amendments, including the equal protection, due process, and privileges or immunities clauses. Justice Samuel Miller wrote the majority opinion in a five-to-four decision upholding the statute. Miller, an Iowa Republican who had left his home state of Kentucky before the war, followed a roughly Northern Democratic vision of Reconstruction. The North, according to this view, supposedly fought to free the slaves and to provide them with civil rights but not to restructure the federalist system, which should continue to emphasize popular sovereignty within local communities. To Miller, the fact that the monopoly statute did not specifically discriminate against former slaves suggested that the thirteenth and fourteenth amendments were inapposite. When construing the new privileges or immunities clause, Miller reasoned that any rights attaching to state citizenship "must rest for their security and protection where they have heretofore rested," with the states themselves. When determining whether the statute was an appropriate exercise of the state's "police power," Miller quoted James Kent in underscoring that the common good takes precedence over individual rights. Not only was the regulation of animal butchering a typical police power exercise, this particular statute isolated the slaughtering businesses "where the convenience, health, and comfort of the people require they shall be located." The statute thus was a reasonable regulation of a "noxious" business. It also mandated the equal treatment of all butchers; the Crescent City Slaughter-House Company was "required, under a heavy penalty, to permit any person who wishes to do so, to slaughter in their houses."[85]

Justice Stephen J. Field dissented in an opinion joined by Chief Justice Salmon P. Chase and Justices Bradley and Noah Swayne. Field agreed with the majority that the case presented issues related to an exercise of the state's "police power," which "undoubtedly extends to all regulations affecting the health, good order, morals, peace, and safety of society." But Field stressed that, unlike during the antebellum period, the fourteenth amendment now protected every U.S. citizen "under the guardianship of the *National* authority." As a matter of *federal* law, republican democracy mandated that state legislation could infringe individual liberties only for the common good. The fourteenth amendment demanded that all citizens be treated equally under state law, including laws related to work and jobs. "This equality of right, with exemption from all disparaging and partial enactments, in the lawful pursuits of life, throughout the whole country, is the distinguishing privilege of citizens of the United States." Therefore, the Louisiana statute, creating a monopoly for the Crescent City

Slaughter-House Company, ought to be struck down because it favored partial or private interests; it was impermissible class legislation. The act, Field reasoned, "is a mere grant to a corporation created by it of special and exclusive privileges by which the health of the city is in no way promoted."[86]

While Field was a California Democrat, his political roots reached back, somewhat ambivalently, to the Jacksonian hostility toward privilege for the few. Consequently, for the most part, Field brought a Republican sympathy to the Reconstruction amendments and their intended shift of power to the national government. He readily acknowledged that states now had to satisfy republican democratic principles pursuant to federal constitutional law. Equally important, he tended to interpret the police power and the distinction between the common good and partial and private interests in accordance with the Republicans' free labor ideology. "[I]t is to me," Field explained, "a matter of profound regret that [the statute's] validity is recognized by a majority of this court, for by it the right of free labor, one of the most sacred and imprescriptible rights of man, is violated." Significantly, though, Field elaborated the concept of free labor with a footnote quoting Adam Smith. "'The property which every man has in his own labor,' says Adam Smith, 'as it is the original foundation of all other property, so it is the most sacred and inviolable. The patrimony of the poor man lies in the strength and dexterity of his own hands; and to hinder him from employing this strength and dexterity in what manner he thinks proper, without injury to his neighbor, is a plain violation of this most sacred property. It is a manifest encroachment upon the just liberty both of the workman and of those who might be disposed to employ him.'" Whereas the antebellum Republicans had linked free labor with free soil, with the potential for each man to achieve economic independence by owning and farming his own land, Field now drew on the great British economist of the Industrial Revolution to elucidate free labor. Given that America had embarked on its own Industrial Revolution, Field's reference to Smith marked a pivotal turn toward classical political economy: Field had begun to incorporate touches of laissez-faire into his conception of free labor. Free labor, to Field, was becoming the freedom "of an employee contracting with his employer, . . . something more like 'free contract.'"[87]

Besides joining Field's dissent, Bradley and Swayne each wrote separate opinions, both of which resonated with Field's. Bradley, for example, wrote that "the rights of life, liberty, and property . . . are the fundamental rights which can only be taken away by due process of law, and which can only be interfered with, or the enjoyment of which can only be modified, by lawful regulations necessary or proper for the mutual good of all." Consequently, when it comes to employment, each individual "must be left free to adopt such calling, profession, or trade as may seem to him most conducive to that end." Bradley then added a flourish, echoing free labor ideology: "Without this right [the individual] cannot be a freeman."[88]

After *Slaughterhouse,* the Supreme Court justices continued to follow and to apply the fundamental principles of republican democracy. Moreover, the justices continued to disagree about whether specific exercises of governmental power constituted the common good. Gradually, though, the justices as well as other judges began to understand the distinction between the common good and partial or private interests more consistently with Field's dissent than with the majority opinion. In the 1883 *Butchers' Union Company v. Crescent City Company,* the Crescent City Slaughter-House Company, whose monopoly had been upheld in *Slaughterhouse,* challenged a subsequent state law that had terminated its monopoly. Sustaining the new statute, a unanimous Court reasoned that the legislature would contravene the common good if it "sold [or] bargained away" its power to promote "the health of its citizens" by granting an irrevocable monopoly. Field, now concurring instead of dissenting, seized the opportunity to elucidate the interplay between states' police powers and the republican democratic mandates of the fourteenth amendment. States can still "legislate to promote health, good order, and peace, to develop their resources, enlarge their industries, and advance their prosperity"; the fourteenth amendment "only inhibits discriminating and partial enactments." As such, it proscribes "any arbitrary invasion by state authority of the rights of person and property, and [secures] to every one the right to pursue his happiness unrestrained, except by just, equal, and impartial laws." Once again quoting Adam Smith to support his conception of the common good, Field gave vent to his laissez-faire flavored notion of liberty. Each individual has "the right to pursue any lawful business or vocation, in any manner not inconsistent with the equal rights of others. . . . The common business and callings of life, the ordinary trades and pursuits, which are innocuous in themselves, and have been followed in all communities from time immemorial, must therefore be free in this country to all alike upon the same conditions." Joined by Justices John Marshall Harlan and William B. Woods, Bradley also concurred, reiterating Field's position as well as his own *Slaughterhouse* opinion. "[O]ne of the inalienable rights of freemen [is the] right to follow any of the common occupations of life," Bradley explained. "To deny it to all but a few favored individuals, by investing the latter with a monopoly, is to invade one of the fundamental privileges of the citizen, contrary not only to common right, but, as I think, to the express words of the Constitution."[89]

At this point, in the late-nineteenth century, judicial sentiment swung strongly in Field's (and Bradley's) direction. State court judges, in case after case, endorsed laissez-faire versions of the common good. In *In re Jacobs,* decided in 1885, New York's highest court invalidated a law prohibiting the manufacture of cigars in tenement houses, "an urban cottage industry of the era." After quoting Field's *Butchers' Union* concurrence, the court warned that it would closely scrutinize whether legislative actions infringing individual rights and liberties, especially property rights, were truly for the common good. And in construing the common good, the court underscored "the fierce competition of trade and the inexorable laws of supply and demand." The individual's "freedom of choice" was crucial in "the unceasing struggle for success and existence which pervades all societies of men." The next year, the Pennsylvania Supreme Court invalidated a law proscribing iron companies from underpaying workers based on the weight of processed iron. A legislature cannot "prevent persons who are *sui juris* [or competent] from making their own contracts," the court emphasized. This statute "is an infringement alike of the rights of the employer and the employé." The law puts "the laborer under a legislative tutelage, which is not only degrading to his manhood, but subversive of his rights as a citizen of the United States."[90]

The Court was still to decide two cases that would, for future generations, epitomize this era of Supreme Court decision making: *Allgeyer v. Louisiana,* decided in 1897, and *Lochner v. New York,* decided in 1905. In holding that a state restriction on insurance contracts violated due process, the *Allgeyer* Court solidified the laissez-faire–flavored transformation of free labor into "liberty to contract." Justice Rufus Peckham's unanimous opinion acknowledged the "right of the state to enact . . . legislation in the legitimate exercise of its police or other powers." But such exercises of the police power, Peckham stressed, must be consistent with the individual liberties protected by a republican democratic form of government. The fourteenth amendment guarantees the citizen's liberty "to live and work where he will; to earn his livelihood by any lawful calling; to pursue any livelihood or avocation; and for that purpose to enter into all contracts which may be proper, necessary, and essential to his carrying out to a successful conclusion the purposes above mentioned." To elaborate this liberty to contract, Peckham cited and quoted from Bradley's *Butchers' Union* concurrence. He then explicitly linked liberty to contract with republican democratic equality: the individual should enjoy "'upon terms of equality with all others in similar circumstances . . . the privilege of pursuing an ordinary calling or trade, and of acquiring, holding, and selling property.'"[91]

Lochner perfectly exemplifies the nature and difficulty of judicial review under republican democracy in this time of political strain (while the Court decided *Lochner* in 1905, many constitutional historians designate the period from 1887 to 1937 as the *Lochner* era). The case arose from a due process challenge to a state law that restricted the number of hours employees could work in bakeries (ten per day and sixty per week). In a five-to-four decision, the Court invalidated the law. Peckham's majority opinion acknowledged that the state could exercise its police power to regulate for "the safety, health, morals, and general welfare of the public." Moreover, "[b]oth property and liberty are held on such reasonable conditions as may be imposed." Yet, simultaneously, the fourteenth amendment prescribed "a limit to the valid exercise of the police power by the state." The state cannot infringe on individual rights and liberties under the "mere pretext" of pursuing the common good. To determine whether the state had, in this case, appropriately exercised its police power, the Court considered two alternative justifications for the statute: as a regulation of labor relations and as a regulation for health purposes. Given that bakers were equal "in intelligence and capacity to men in other trades or manual occupations," Peckham readily concluded that the statute, if viewed as "a purely labor law," did not benefit the common good. "[A] law like the one before us involves neither the safety, the morals, nor the welfare, of the public." Hence, if the law were to be upheld, it must be as a health regulation. But, Peckham reasoned, "there can be no fair doubt that the trade of a baker, in and of itself, is not an unhealthy one to that degree which would authorize the legislature to interfere with the right to labor." Indeed, Peckham suspected that the New York legislature, similar to other state legislatures passing social welfare laws, had disingenuously expressed its purpose. "It seems to us that the real object and purpose were simply to regulate the hours of labor between the master and his employees (all being men, *sui juris*), in a private business, not dangerous in any degree to morals, or in any real and substantial degree to the health of the employees." Given this, the Court condemned the law as impermissible class legislation. The dissenters, like in previous cases, agreed with the majority on the fundamental principles of republican democracy but disagreed on their application. After reviewing the evidence concerning the health of bakers, Harlan concluded that "there is room for debate and for an honest difference of opinion." Unlike the majority, however, Harlan refused to presume that the legislature had "acted in bad faith"; instead, given the uncertain connection between bakers' hours and their health, Harlan deferred to the legislative judgment. "We are not to presume that the [legislature] did not determine this question upon the fullest attainable information and for the common good." Dissenting similarly, Justice Oliver Wendell Holmes, Jr., argued that the Court should have deferred to the legislative judgment because "[a] reasonable man might think [the disputed statute] a proper measure on the score of health." Moreover, Holmes added, social Darwinist or laissez-faire ideology unduly influenced the majority's demarcation between the common good and private or partial interests. "The Fourteenth Amendment does not enact Mr. Herbert Spencer's Social Statics."[92]

During subsequent years, the justices struggled in numerous cases to distinguish the common good from partial or private interests, with individual justices changing sides depending on the facts in the respective disputes. In *Chicago, Burlington, and Quincy Railway Company v. Illinois,* for instance, Harlan wrote for a majority upholding a state law that forced the railway to improve a bridge and culvert. Harlan concluded that the law was a "reasonable" exercise of the police power because it advanced the "common good." In *Adair v. United States,* Harlan again delivered the majority opinion, but this one invalidated a federal law proscribing yellow dog contracts—employment contracts that prohibited employees from belonging to labor unions. Harlan reasoned that Congress had impermissibly favored one side in the contractual relation of employment. "In all such particulars the employer and the employee have equality of right, and any legislation that disturbs that equality is an arbitrary interference with the liberty of contract which no government can legally justify in a free land." When the nation entered World War I, the Court continued confronting such disputes about republican democratic government and continued to resolve them in the traditional fashion, distinguishing the common good from partial or private interests—which would soon become especially significant in the realm of free expression.[93]

While prediction of case outcomes could prove difficult, the Supreme Court during the period from Reconstruction to 1920 upheld far more statutes, both state and national, than it invalidated. Yet, critics frequently berated the Court for its specific decisions as well as for its generally activist approach toward judicial review—for its willingness to scrutinize and strike down legislative actions. Why? First, regardless of the overall statistics, the Court invalidated laws at a rate far exceeding that of the antebellum period. Until 1864, the Court had invalidated forty-one state laws, "at a rate of less than one a year," but from 1864 to 1895, the rate increased to "about three laws a year." In reaction, Harvard law professor James Bradley

Thayer presented a paper at the Chicago World's Fair in 1893 urging the courts to defer to legislative determinations of the common good so long as they were "rational." Apparently, many justices disregarded this plea for judicial restraint. In the generation after 1898, the Court invalidated more than three times as many federal and state laws as in all prior Court history.[94]

Second, the justices and other judges treated certain types of laws more harshly than others. Especially hostile to statutes favoring labor unions, courts struck down approximately three hundred such laws by 1920. Judges repeatedly concluded that legislative regulations correcting for inequalities of bargaining power between management and worker did not promote the common good. Once such labor statutes were stricken, then courts could govern in accordance with common law doctrines, which judges consistently interpreted to the disadvantage of unions. Given such judicial actions, workers, unions, and their supporters understandably denounced judges, including Supreme Court justices, for imposing their political biases under the guise of law.[95]

Third, as Progressivism emerged in the early-twentieth century and successfully sought the passage of at least some social legislation, many Progressives became increasingly disgruntled with judicial decision making. True, courts did not stymie all Progressive actions, but they invalidated enough of them to spur an angry backlash. Progressive leaders emphasized the need for trained experts, including educated professionals, to lead the democratic masses to the common good. Legislatures could readily turn for guidance to such experts, through hearings for instance, as the legislators sought to draft effective reform statutes. Judges, though, tended to rely on case precedents, arid legal doctrines, and their own intuitive grasps of social reality, even as they evaluated novel social welfare enactments. Lacking in expertise and disregarding experts with relevant knowledge, judges all too often decided cases involving social issues in ignorance — from the Progressives' perspective. Progressives responded in two ways to the invalidation of legislation and the general judicial disregard for scientific (or social scientific) expertise. Some Progressives advocated for direct popular intrusion into judicial processes by granting citizens a right of recall — a right to overturn specific judicial decisions through referenda or, at a minimum, to subject judges themselves to reelection votes. Other Progressives, particularly those lawyers, judges, and law professors, like Roscoe Pound and Louis Brandeis, who fit into the school of sociological jurisprudence, encouraged judges to change, to become more sensitive to the realities depicted by social scientists. Judges should determine whether governmental action benefited the public health or safety, and hence the common good, by attending to empirical evidence. Rather than reasoning, as the *Lochner* majority did, that the job of a baker was not "unhealthy" to "the common understanding," judges should carefully consult expert knowledge in the disputed area. This desire to encourage judges to consider social realities led sociological jurisprudents to file so-called Brandeis briefs, named after Brandeis's argument in *Muller v. Oregon*. Brandeis filled more than a hundred pages with references to empirical evidence showing a public need for the challenged state law, which prescribed maximum hours for female employees; the evidence suggested that excessive hours endangered the health of women. And as the result in *Muller* illustrated — the Court upheld the law — the justices occasionally accepted such sociological arguments.[96]

CHAPTER 7

Free Expression, American Society, and the Supreme Court

Despite the changes that swept across the nation after the Civil War, the law and traditions of free expression remained largely the same.[1] Of course, Northerners disagreed about Reconstruction's implications for free expression just as they disagreed about many other issues. Republicans in the Reconstruction congresses remembered Southern efforts to restrict antislavery expression before the Civil War. As one representative recalled, "if a citizen of a free State visiting a slave State expressed his opinion in reference to slavery he was treated without much ceremony to a coat of tar and feathers and a ride upon a rail." Many Republicans thus believed that the fourteenth amendment extended first-amendment protections to apply against state governments. In *The Slaughterhouse Cases,* the Republican-appointed Justice Bradley insisted that the fourteenth amendment remedied "not merely slavery and its incidents and consequences [but also] that intolerance of free speech and free discussion which often rendered life and property insecure." Bradley, though, was dissenting. Only three years later, in 1876, *United States v. Cruikshank* emphasized state sovereignty in invalidating indictments of Klansmen who had murdered two African Americans. The case raised free-expression questions, and in the lower court opinion, Bradley himself had suggested the fourteenth amendment applied or incorporated first-amendment protections so that they now pertained to state governments. But the Supreme Court disregarded Bradley's opinion and this possibility. Writing for the majority, Chief Justice Morrison Waite explained that neither the first nor the fourteenth amendment created a general right to assemble (or petition) that Congress could enforce.[2]

Apparently, many Republicans (and other Northerners) understood the concept of free expression to be no different after than before the war. During Reconstruction, the Republican-controlled congresses approved the new constitutions adopted by Southern states. Mirroring antebellum law, the free-expression provisions not only explicitly stated that individuals were responsible for any abuse of the liberty of expression but, in most instances, also included language implicating the *Croswell* truth-conditional standard. And as before the war, postbellum state courts interpreted such constitutional language to subsume a bad tendency standard. Moreover, consistent with the tradition of suppression, Republicans were not above punishing expression inconsistent with their own views. Mississippi newspaper editor William McCardle drew Republican wrath by publishing articles harshly critical of Reconstruction. The Union army prosecuted him for libel, among other charges, after he condemned Northern generals for being "each and all infamous, cowardly, and abandoned villains, who, instead of wearing shoulder straps and ruling millions of people, should have their heads shaved, their ears cropped, their foreheads branded, and their persons lodged in a penitentiary." After the lower federal courts denied McCardle's petition for habeas corpus, he appealed to the Supreme Court pursuant to a jurisdictional statute enacted in 1867. Fearing that the Court's decision might weaken Reconstruction, the Republican-controlled Congress quickly repealed the 1867 statute. In *Ex parte McCardle,* decided in 1869, the justices upheld the congressional repeal and concluded that the Court lacked the jurisdictional power to decide the merits of McCardle's petition. McCardle would remain imprisoned for his anti-Reconstruction writings.[3]

IMMORALITY, EXPRESSION, AND LIBERTARIAN THEORY

Over the next decades, in the midst of concrete political disputes, the traditions of suppression and dissent emerged strongly in opposition to each other. One major stage for this confrontation was the regulation of vice, particularly obscenity. During the antebellum period, morals regulations had primarily been a matter for state and local governments; local restrictions on obscenity and other moral vices seemed integral to the common good of a well-regulated society. Twenty states had laws restricting obscenity by the end of the Civil War. During the postbellum period, however, the national government became increasingly involved in such issues. This transition manifested a general shift toward national regulation and control rather than a specific reliance on Reconstruction era constitutional amendments. Many morals issues encompassed economic components — the distribution and sale of liquor, the distribution and sale of obscene materials, and so on — so the development of national economic marketplaces rendered such issues national in scope. As time went on, the national movement to restrict obscenity gathered strength partly in reaction to immigration. The elite leaders played on middle-class anxieties about the increasingly diverse urban populations of poor immigrant workers. Whether the antiobscenity advocates primarily hoped either to impose on the immigrants traditional American Protestant values or to prevent immigrants from spreading seemingly un-American values to the innocent children of true Americans, the restriction of sex-related expression provided a means of control that intertwined with the republican democratic propensity toward exclusion. The very same societal groups — say, Italian immigrants — who had their republican democratic virtue doubted were also most likely to find their expressive activities questioned and suppressed.[4]

The unquestioned leader of the national suppression movement was Anthony Comstock, round-faced, mutton-chopped, potbellied, and humorless but with a keen sense for publicity. Raised in a devout Connecticut Congregationalist household, Comstock lived by his religious beliefs and fears, especially condemnation to hell. After serving during the Civil War, Comstock moved to New York City and began working in the dry goods business, but his religious zealotry sparked worry about his coworkers' possession of bawdy written materials. In response, he arranged not only for police to arrest several purveyors of such materials but also for newspaper coverage of the arrests. These early political successes prompted the wealthy president of the Young Men's Christian Association (YMCA) and his colleagues, including J. P. Morgan, to throw their substantial financial support behind Comstock. With this backing, Comstock helped create the New York Society for the Suppression of Vice (NYSSV). Thanks to favorable state laws, NYSSV members could be deputized to arrest violators of state or federal antivice laws, and as if in gratitude for its efforts, the NYSSV could retain half the fines collected for convictions that it helped secure. In a virtual celebration of the popular tradition of suppression, similar antivice societies sprang up in close to twenty other cities, including many with large immigrant populations such as Boston, Chicago, St. Louis, and San Francisco.[5]

Not satisfied with the creation of the NYSSV, Comstock began pushing for national antiobscenity legislation to facilitate his morals crusade. In March 1873, with little opposition, Congress passed An Act for the Suppression of Trade in, and Circulation of, Obscene Literature and Articles of Immoral Use, better known as the Comstock Act. This statute, expanding previous federal restrictions, included proscriptions against contraceptives and abortions as well as obscenity. The exclusion of women from direct participation in republican democracy undoubtedly eased passage of the reproductive restrictions, though many middle- and upper-class women supported the antivice crusade as a means for controlling immigrant immorality. The second section of the Act focused on the use of the mails: "no obscene, lewd, or lascivious book, pamphlet, picture, paper, print, or other publication of an indecent character, or any article or thing designed or intended for the prevention of conception or procuring of abortion, nor any article or thing intended or adapted for any indecent or immoral use or nature . . . shall be carried in the mail." Violation of this section would subject an individual to criminal punishment, including "hard labor not less than one year nor more than ten years."[6]

The postmaster general quickly appointed Comstock special agent responsible for enforcement of the statute, and for the next forty-two years, Comstock vigorously fought his campaign against immorality. Writing with an evangelical's fervor, Comstock feared that "Satan is permitted to place his traps where they will do him most good." And Satan baited his traps with lust, "the boon companion of all other crimes." Lust, Comstock warned, "breeds unhallowed living, and sinks man, made in the image of God, below the level of the beasts." Comstock's crusade succeeded remarkably. He aimed, for certain, to purge America of books with titles like *The Lascivious London Beauty,* but partly because of the breadth of the Comstock Act, he also initiated many prosecutions attacking materials unrelated to "commercial pornography." A person could be (and was in fact) arrested for publishing an article that advised pregnant women to avoid sexual relations. A person could be (and was in fact) arrested for distributing a pamphlet that explained birth control in terms understandable to relatively uneducated women. Within one year of the statute's enactment, "the YMCA boasted that Comstock had been responsible for seizing 130,000 pounds of books, 194,000 pictures and photographs, and 60,300 'articles made of rubber for immoral purposes, and used by both sexes.'" In 1882, Comstock reported that statistical evidence showed "[t]he danger is not so great as it was ten years ago, as there is not so much of this grossest business done." By 1913, two years before he would die, Comstock had been responsible for, by his count, the conviction of approximately four thousand people and the destruction of nearly 160 tons of obscene literature.[7]

The legal doctrine of free expression was but a small obstacle to Comstock's campaign. In the antebellum period, state and local governments routinely regulated morals by proscribing vices like prostitution. With regard to obscenity, state case-law developments during the early-nineteenth century harmonized with other free-expression issues adjudicated under republican democratic principles. In an 1815 prosecution under the common law, a Pennsylvania judge reasoned that courts "are guardians of the public morals," and thus a display of pictures "may be punishable, if in its nature, and by its example, it tends to the corruption of morals." As a general matter, throughout the nineteenth century, judges adjudicating obscenity cases would find that the government could punish expression contrary to the common good—expression likely to be harmful or to produce bad tendencies. During the postbellum era in particular, any material that a jury might find outside the mainstream of predominant Victorian values could be condemned as immoral and obscene. In an 1870 decision, for instance, a Pennsylvania court upheld a conviction for obscene libel. The judge reasoned that the validity of the published material was irrelevant; if the materials "were unfit to be published, and tended to inflame improper and lewd passions, it was an obscene libel." Even medical books, if "exposed in the open markets . . . and not to promote the good of society by placing them in proper hands for useful purposes, would, if tending to excite lewd desires, be held to be obscene libels." Moreover, the defendant's intent to benefit society would not preclude a conviction if the book had a harmful "character or tendency." In 1884, New York convicted a defendant under a state statute for displaying pictures of "nude females [that] were photographic copies of paintings . . . exhibited in the Salon in Paris, and . . . at the centennial exhibition in Philadelphia." In upholding the conviction, the judge explained that the test of obscenity, as stated in the frequently cited English case of *Queen v. Hicklin*, was "whether the tendency of the matter . . . is to deprave or corrupt those whose minds are open to such immoral influences, and who might come into contact with it."[8]

The federal courts treated prosecutions under the Comstock Act similarly. In one typical case, *Knowles v. United States*, the court upheld the conviction of a newspaper publisher. Summarizing an allegedly obscene article, the judge explained that it "glorifies fornication, and places it under the blessing of God. It designates the offspring of such intercourse as 'love children,' and declares that the 'army of genius has been largely recruited from the ranks of illegitimates.'" The judge then made three important points.

First, the statutory restriction on obscenity was unconnected to freedom of the press: the first amendment, the judge explained, "cannot be made a shield for violation of criminal laws which are not designed to restrict . . . a free press, but to protect society against practices that are clearly immoral and corrupting." Second, without expressly citing *Queen v. Hicklin*, the judge drew on its articulation of the bad tendency test to elaborate the meaning of obscenity. "The true test to determine whether a writing comes within the meaning of the statute is whether its language has a tendency to deprave and corrupt the morals of those whose minds are open to such influences, and into whose hands it may fall, by arousing or implanting in such minds obscene, lewd, or lascivious thoughts or desires." Finally, the question whether the article in the instant case was obscene — whether it "would have a tendency to arouse impure and lascivious thoughts and desires" — was "a question of fact for the determination of a jury."[9]

To be sure, judges occasionally blocked antiobscenity prosecutions, whether under the Comstock Act or state law. In such cases, the judge typically would reason that the indictment insufficiently specified the obscene content of the published materials, but far more frequently, courts would uphold indictments. In fact, Comstock maintained a conviction rate between 75 and 90 percent. Many judges would explain that the public record should not describe or reproduce the obscene materials with specificity because doing so would offend the court as well as public sensibilities. Regardless of judicial attitudes, though, Comstock encountered opposition from other quarters. A fair number of relatively well-educated and wealthy individuals fought against Comstock partly because they found his crusade contrary to their interests and values. True, Comstock rarely sought to suppress literary classics — though he did so occasionally — but he consistently sought to suppress nonfiction works, including medical books, related to human sexuality. Perhaps even more important, many of Comstock's opponents had forged a drive to political activism in the crucible of the abolition movement. They were not quick to cower in the face of Comstock's tactics; the tradition of dissent hung ready at hand from their tool belts. For these individuals, the laissez-faire–tinged conception of the common good developing in economic affairs — but rooted in the abolitionists' own antebellum free labor ideology — seemed to have implications beyond the marketplace. The burgeoning postbellum libertarianism, impinging the well-regulated society, suggested that each individual should enjoy the greatest possible liberty and autonomy in all realms of life, including sexual as well as economic activities. The moral realm was, from this perspective, a place for individual self-governance, not one for institutionalized governmental control. Needless to say, Comstock and his cohorts impugned this libertarian (and individualist) ethos through their actions and words.[10]

AS HAD BEEN TRUE in the past, the outburst of official or legal suppression sparked more formal enunciations of the tradition of dissent. The postbellum development of the new universities, with their emphasis on research, enhanced this renewed drive to elaborate the doctrine and theoretical justifications of free expression. Working within universities like Chicago, Columbia, Michigan, Missouri, and Northwestern, law professors and political scientists devoted new attention to the conceptualization of free speech and a free press. Several legal treatise writers advocated for more expansive conceptions of free expression, though the degree of expansiveness varied with the particular writer. The leading constitutional-law treatise writer, Thomas Cooley—both a professor at the University of Michigan and a justice on the Michigan Supreme Court—argued for a definition of free expression beyond common law protections, though he was unwilling to push libertarian views to an extreme. To be sure, Cooley's outlook on free expression sometimes resonated with his views on liberty in general. While wary of governmental interference with individual liberties, particularly in the realm of economic activities, Cooley always remained cognizant of the governmental power to regulate for the common good. He also realized that the law did not match the tradition of dissent. When explicating civil defamation in New York, for example, Cooley noted that "it is perhaps safe to say that the general public sentiment and the prevailing customs allow a greater freedom of discussion" than does the state law. Perhaps partly for that reason, ambiguities riddled Cooley's lengthy treatise-chapter *Liberty of Speech and of the Press.*[11]

At some points, Cooley suggested that individuals should be completely free to discuss "public measures," without any fear of criminal prosecution, even "if they exceed all the proper bounds of moderation." Cooley explained in his well-known *Atkinson v. Detroit Free Press* dissenting opinion that "the public interest" in allowing discussions of public affairs "is paramount." To promote the common good, "a person whose character and actions are impugned may suffer without remedy." Despite such ringing declarations of libertarianism, Cooley also articulated narrower views of free expression. Toward the end of his treatise-discussion of libels upon government, he wrote that "where the matter is proper for the public information, the truth justifies its publication." Thus, rather than following the *Croswell* truth-conditional standard, which required truth plus good faith to protect expression critical of government, Cooley apparently believed that truth standing alone should be an adequate defense. Yet, Cooley concluded his chapter on free expression with a straightforward rendition of the predominant and less speech-protective *Croswell* standard. In familiar language, he explained that state constitutional provisions "generally make the truth a defence if published with good motives and for justifiable ends." Moreover, he applauded the *Croswell* standard for giving more protection than the common law maxim, "The greater the truth the greater the libel." Indeed, many of Cooley's judicial opinions subsequent to *Atkinson* delineated more conservative conceptions of free expression consistent with traditional nineteenth-century doctrine.[12]

Cooley's ambiguities are emblematic of the divergent positions that emerged among other treatise writers. Christopher Tiedeman was, recall, more committed than Cooley to a laissez-faire libertarianism, yet Tiedeman did not translate his libertarianism into an expansive free expression. True, Tiedeman quoted approvingly from Cooley and wrote that "popular government . . . is only possible when the people enjoy the freedom of speech, and the liberty of the press." Nevertheless, Tiedeman reasserted the traditional distinction between licentiousness and liberty and stressed that the law did not protect abuses of liberty. While the Constitution proscribes prior restraints, "the slanderer or libeler may still be punished." Furthermore, "[a]ll obscene or blasphemous publications may be prohibited, as tending to do harm to the public morals." In short, Tiedeman limited free expression within his otherwise libertarian scheme. Consequently, not only could "anarchists and nihilists" be punished for their expression, but their "right to . . . continued publication may be forfeited." Tiedeman, though, did not articulate the narrowest conception of free expression. Francis Wharton went so far as to assert the constitutionality of the 1798 Sedition Act: both the national and state governments possessed the power to punish seditious libel. "[P]rivate interests [including free expression] must be subordinated to the public good."[13]

Regardless of Tiedeman's and Wharton's narrow conceptions of free expression, other commentators pushed beyond Cooley's guarded libertarianism in the opposite direction, toward broader protections for speech and writing. John Burgess, equating individual liberty with the absence of governmental action, argued that liberty should be maximized in all realms, including the expressive as well as the economic (though he was primarily concerned with economic pursuits). Henry Schofield, focusing more on free expression, particularly freedom of the press, argued in 1915 that the

Croswell truth-conditional standard was inadequate for factual propositions. Instead, truth alone should be "the dividing line between lawful and
unlawful publications on matters of public concern." For opinions, Schofield added, free expression should protect those that "any fair-minded average man could or might form from the facts." Ernst Freund, in his 1904
treatise on the police power, acknowledged that the law on the books in
most states allowed the government to punish abuses of free expression in
accordance with the truth-conditional standard. Yet, Freund insisted that,
in practice, prosecutions for seditious libel had become so infrequent that
"the offense may be said to be practically obsolete." Instead, "[c]ustom and
public sentiment have come to sanction the widest latitude of criticism of
the government." According to Freund, the tradition of dissent had become
constitutionalized: "The most ample freedom of discussion of public affairs
is now generally understood to be guaranteed by the freedom of speech and
of the press." Under this new constitutional definition of free expression,
an overt-acts test delineated the border of protected speech and writing: "a
statute may validly forbid all speaking and writing the object of which is to
incite directly to the commission of violence and crime." Even the punishment of anarchism, "the doctrine or belief that all established government
is wrongful and pernicious," would contravene the constitutional guarantee
"unless carefully confined to cases of solicitation of crime."[14]

Theodore Schroeder propelled the libertarian expansion of free expression even further than did Freund. In a series of essays and books mostly
written in the early-twentieth century, Schroeder merged a radical libertarianism with the tradition of dissent and sought to embed this combination in the law. Schroeder argued that each individual should enjoy the
maximum liberty consistent with an equal liberty for others. In the realm
of free expression, this libertarianism translated into an "absolute liberty
of thought." Such absolute liberty, in turn, generated a Miltonian marketplace of ideas. To Schroeder, "the greatest freedom of discussion and experimentation . . . are the only avenues to the correction of any opinions,
even upon the subject of sexual physiology, psychology, hygiene, or ethics." This marketplace approach to expression necessitated the rejection
of the bad tendency test, which Schroeder condemned as "infamous" for
making "the world a vale of tears [drenched] with the blood of martyrs."
Like Freund, then, Schroeder recommended an overt-acts test, of a sort.
Whereas Freund argued that expression likely to incite unlawful conduct
could be punished, Schroeder would instead permit punishment only of
expression that had actually caused unlawful conduct. "[N]ever punish any

opinion, until it had resulted in an overt act of invasion, and then punish the holder of the 'dangerous' opinion only for his real participation in that act, as a proven accessory, and not otherwise."[15]

As a general matter, a moderate libertarian approach to free expression remained consistent with republican democratic principles. The government could still restrict individual liberties, including free expression, if doing so furthered the common good. But as was true with the laissez-faire–tinged (libertarian) common good in the economic realm, the conception of the common good in the expressive realm of print and speech had shrunk. From the libertarian vantage, as Freund explained it, expression that merely had bad tendencies no longer contravened the common good and therefore could not be justifiably punished; the government could proscribe only that speech likely to cause unlawful conduct directly. The protected private realm of expression had expanded. Schroeder's more radical libertarianism, however, implicitly challenged the logic of republican democracy. To Schroeder, the common good could never justify the punishment of expression; only conduct could be proscribed. "No matter upon what subject, nor how injurious to the public welfare any particular idea thereon may be deemed to be, the constitutional right is violated whenever anyone is not legally free to express any such or other sentiments." Moreover, Schroeder subscribed to an ethical relativism that further subverted republican democracy. Neither a priori judgments nor empirical evidence could determine the truth or correctness of values. "In the realm of morals no age has ever shown an agreement, even among its wisest and best men, either as to what is morally poisonous, or by what test it is to be judged as morally deadly," Schroeder wrote. "Moral concepts are a matter of geography and evolution." In short, "all morality is relative." But republican democracy was premised on the discernment of supposedly preexisting category-boundaries separating the common good from partial or private interests, as was most evident in adjudicative disputes. Judicial analyses were, in theory, formalistic and led to objective conclusions. Schroeder's value relativism, it appeared, did not correspond with the premises of republican democratic politics and adjudication.[16]

Schroeder's relativism facilitated his pitched battle against Comstock's antivice crusaders. Schroeder insisted that "to-day there is no organized force in American life which is more pernicious or more productive of moral evil in the domain of sex, than the very work which has come to be known as Comstockery." Since moral values are relative, Schroeder reasoned, no one could objectively determine whether a particular item was obscene. "'[O]bscenity' is not a quality inherent in a book or picture, but wholly and exclusively a contribution of the contemplating mind, and hence cannot be defined in terms of the qualities of a book or picture, but is read into them." Obscenity, in other words, manifested a subjective state of mind that the observer imposed on an object. Moreover, the observation or reading of materials deemed to be obscene was inconsequential. To Schroeder, Comstock himself revealed the insignificance of obscenity vis-à-vis sexual mores. As Schroeder explained, Comstock "informs us that for thirty years he had 'stood at the mouth of a sewer,' searching for and devouring 'obscenity' for a salary." By his own admission, Comstock "has seen more 'obscene' pictures and read more 'obscene' books, and retained a larger collection of these, than any other living man." Yet, Comstock insisted that his own morality remained "unimpaired." Given such apparent insignificance of obscenity, and given Schroeder's commitment to absolute liberty, he concluded that access to obscene materials should be a matter of "sexual self-government."[17]

Schroeder presented, perhaps, the most expansive theoretical conception of free expression since the Sedition Act era Republicans: Hay, Thomson, and Wortman. Indeed, Schroeder could have bolstered his position by drawing on Hay's and Thomson's libertarian arguments. Hay, recall, argued that the autonomous individual should remain beyond governmental control. Thomson, meanwhile, articulated an argument that Schroeder would echo more than a century later. Focusing on individual psychology, Thomson argued that the individual cannot control his or her own thoughts, and consequently, the individual's thoughts cannot possibly be subject to the control of others. Schroeder similarly linked his libertarian view to psychology: "No man can help believing that which he believes. Belief is not a matter of volition." Because the individual cannot control his or her own beliefs, Schroeder continued, one should not "be held morally responsible" for those beliefs. Consequently, "no man should be punished for holding or expressing unpopular or unconventional or miscalled 'immoral' opinions." Although Schroeder did not fortify this psychological argument with reference to Thomson, Schroeder at least knew of Thomson and had read Wortman's writings.[18]

Schroeder's radical libertarianism departed far from the American mainstream, but he did not stand alone. Before the turn into the new century, Schroeder had aligned with other freethinkers, radical individuals who avidly opposed the Protestant religious orthodoxy of the Victorian era. Then, in 1902, Schroeder helped create the Free Speech League. While Schroeder might be labeled a "maverick radical," at least some of the other League founders and directors, such as the lawyer Gilbert E. Roe and the muckraker Lincoln Steffens, had close ties to the Progressive movement. Schroeder and his League cohorts hoped that recent celebrated instances of national governmental suppression might generate broader support for their cause. For example, in the wake of President William McKinley's 1901 assassination by an avowed anarchist, several states enacted criminal laws proscribing anarchy, and Congress passed immigration legislation in 1903 providing for the exclusion and deportation of alien anarchists (the assassination spurred a wave of xenophobia partly because the killer, though native born, had a foreign-sounding surname, Czolgosz). The League attempted to use such instances of governmental suppression to cultivate new supporters for its pronounced goal, "to maintain the right of free speech against all encroachments." Consistent with this goal, the League would defend anyone with a stake in free expression. The League often assisted the anarchist Emma Goldman and the birth-control advocate Margaret Sanger, both of whom were frequently arrested. The League helped pay Clarence Darrow and Edgar Lee Masters to defend a British journalist being deported under the 1903 immigration statute for discussing anarchy (the Supreme Court, upholding the deportation, reasoned in part that aliens do not have first-amendment rights). Through such activities, the League sought, in Schroeder's words, to establish judicial precedents "favorable to free speech as a constitutional principle or avoiding a precedent which is adverse." The popular Steffens mustered support for the League by explaining that, while Americans might be free to express their thoughts, they had not "thought very freely." They had been "too busy with facts and acts and things to pay much heed to ideas and theories and ideals." When Americans started thinking more widely, stretching outside the mainstream, Steffens warned, they would find that their expression was not so free. Steffens personally opposed obscenity, but he insisted that censorship could not successfully combat such immorality. Censorship destroyed only liberty. Knowledge and the "suggestion of reason," through free thought and free expression, were fitting means for nurturing a moral citizenry.[19]

A dispute over a book called *Cupid's Yokes* illustrated the dynamic interrelations among suppression, dissent, and legal doctrine. Ezra Heywood, who had cut his political teeth as an abolitionist, turned to labor and sexual reforms after the Civil War. In 1877, he published *Cupid's Yokes, or, The Binding Forces of Conjugal Life*, a widely distributed albeit short (twenty-three-page) book. He argued that the institution of marriage enslaved women and demeaned love. Marriage also injured men by turning them into savages and furnishing "food for his savage nature; and we have but to lift the roofs of 'respectable' houses to find the skeletons of its feminine victims." Comstock used his favorite tactic to secure "evidence" against Heywood. Under an assumed name, Comstock sent a letter requesting a copy of *Cupid's Yokes.* When Heywood mailed it, Comstock secured an arrest warrant. Wanting to execute the warrant immediately, Comstock found Heywood speaking at a "free-love convention." Given the danger of arresting Heywood amid his supporters, Comstock sought guidance through prayer, then "the devil's trapper was trapped," as Comstock pridefully described the scene. By himself, Comstock seized Heywood from an anteroom "by the nape of the neck" and hustled him out to a waiting carriage before the audience, a "horde of lusters," 250 strong, could interfere. During the prosecution, the trial judge severely limited Heywood's ability to argue in his defense; the only issue, was whether Heywood had mailed *Cupid's Yokes.* The judge precluded Heywood from explaining his philosophy of radical libertarianism. In *Cupid's Yokes,* after denouncing the Comstock Act as "the National Gag-Law," Heywood had exclaimed: "The belief that our sexual relations can be better governed by statute, than by individual reason, is a rude species of conventional impertinence, as barbarous and shocking as it is senseless."[20]

After Heywood's conviction, another freethinker, D. M. Bennett, advertised *Cupid's Yokes* in his paper, and he too was arrested for violating the Comstock Act. As had been true in Heywood's case, the trial judge would not allow the publication to be entered into evidence because it was "so lewd, obscene and lascivious, that the same would be offensive to the court here, and improper to be placed upon the records thereof." The judge, though, allowed Bennett to discuss the relation between obscenity and free expression. Bennett maintained that a defendant's intention to distribute materials for a useful purpose should preclude a conviction: "where words which might otherwise be obscene or indecent, are used in good faith, in social polemics, philosophical writings, serious arguments, or for any scientific purpose, and are not thrust forward wantonly, or for the purpose of exciting lust or disgust, they are justified by the object of their use, and are not obscene or indecent." Such arguments were to no avail, as the judicially interpreted legal doctrine supported Comstock. The appellate court upheld a jury charge that set forth the bad tendency test: "the matter must be regarded as obscene, if it would have a tendency to suggest impure and libidinous thoughts in the minds of those open to the influence of such thoughts, and thus deprave and corrupt their morals, if they should read such matter." In typical fashion, the court quoted from the case of *Queen v. Hicklin* and relied on the doctrine of constructive intent to deflect

Bennett's argument that good faith shielded him from prosecution. If the publication had bad tendencies, then "'the intention to break the law must be inferred, and the criminal character of the publication is not affected or qualified by there being some ulterior object in view, . . . of a different and an honest character.'"[21]

PROTECTING THE GOVERNMENT: LIBEL AND CONTEMPT

In the *Cupid's Yokes* cases, as in many cases during this era, some Americans brought to bear the forces of suppression, and in reaction, others invoked the tradition of dissent, of speaking one's mind. But the legal doctrine, to a great degree, supported suppression. With regard to obscenity, in particular, judges and juries readily condemned any materials inconsistent with mainstream morality as having bad tendencies and being contrary to the common good. Occasionally, though, in various contexts (beyond obscenity), a judge would be receptive to the theoretical arguments for broader protections of expression and would interpret the law accordingly. What about cases where governmental officials sought to insulate themselves from criticism?

Coleman v. MacLennan, a Kansas case decided in 1908, arose when a public official, running for reelection, brought a civil action for defamation against a newspaper publisher. The predominant rule in civil libel actions was that the press enjoyed no special privileges, even when publishing on a matter of public concern. In this instance, then, one might have expected a judgment for the plaintiff. The state constitution had familiar language: "The liberty of the press shall be inviolate; and all persons may freely speak, write or publish their sentiments on all subjects, being responsible for the abuse of such right; and in all civil or criminal actions for libel the truth may be given in evidence to the jury, and if it shall appear that the alleged libelous matter was published for justifiable ends, the accused party shall be acquitted." The judge, moreover, recited approvingly some of the common justifications for suppression, such as the distinction between licentiousness and liberty. Nonetheless, the judge struck off in a surprising direction. Partly because of technological developments, newspapers had transformed into a form of popular media; inexpensive evening newspapers oriented toward mass audiences had become the norm in large cities. "The press as we know it today is almost as modern as the telephone and the phonograph," the judge observed. "The functions which it performs at the present stage of our social development, if not substantially different in kind from what they have been, are magnified many fold, and the opportunities for its influence are multiplied many times." The judge believed that contemporary muckraking journalists provided important information to the public about governmental corruption. Consequently, freedom of the press needed to be reconceptualized with a more "liberal indulgence." Cooley's *Constitutional Limitations* provided guidance, as the court quoted passages suggestive of broad protections: "'the mere exemption from previous restraint cannot be all that is secured by the [state] constitutional provisions . . . [Otherwise] the liberty of the press might be rendered a mockery and a delusion, and the phrase itself a byword. . . .'" Following this lead, the court granted a qualified privilege to the publisher: "Any one claiming to be defamed by the communication must show actual malice, or go remediless. This privilege extends to a great variety of subjects and includes matters of public concern, public men, and candidates for office." What justified this actual-malice standard so highly protective of expression? Ultimately, it was the common good, the same rationale that most courts relied upon to justify the suppression of speech and writing, as the *Coleman* court realized. Despite the consensus favoring suppression, newspaper discussions of candidates for public office provided, according to this judge, a tremendous benefit to "the state and to society." In a republican democracy, public discussions of governmental officials, candidates, and affairs helped guard against corruption and deceit and thus promoted the appropriate pursuit of the common good itself. Given this, "occasional injury to the reputations of individuals must yield to the public welfare, although at times such injury may be great."[22]

Such expansive judicial interpretations of free expression were rare. Even though many late-nineteenth- and early-twentieth-century judges swung legal doctrine in a libertarian direction for economic liberties, they generally did not do the same for expressive liberties. Regardless of the precise type of case, the crux of most disputes involving speech or writing remained the tendency of the expression: was it pernicious or beneficial? And unlike in the economic realm (and unlike in *Coleman*), judges tended not to shift the category-boundaries separating the common good from partial or private interests to favor more libertarian or individualist conceptions — to broaden the protection of free expression. For instance, pursuant to a state statute, Massachusetts convicted John Karvonen for parading with a red flag that represented his local branch of the Socialist party. In upholding the conviction, the state's highest court wrote: "Constitutional freedom means liberty regulated by law. Personal rights may be curbed in a rational way for the common good. Liberty is immunity from arbitrary commands and capricious prohibitions, but not the absence of reasonable rules for the protection of the community." In this instance, because red flags often symbolized revolution and terror, the court found the statutory proscription to constitute a reasonable restriction on "the liberty of the citizens." Overall, while criminal prosecutions for libel remained relatively uncommon, they steadily increased in quantity during the late-nineteenth century. The number of civil defamation suits grew even more significantly, spurred partly by the development of newspapers into an inexpensive mass medium that often aimed for sensationalism. Public officials and figures frequently sued for large sums; one railroad promoter sued the *New York Times* for $1 million and the *New York Tribune* for $100,000. Thus, even as the entrenchment of political parties had routinized the harsh criticism of one's political adversaries — the party system, after all, legitimated opposition — legal doctrine still implicitly encouraged governmental officials and candidates to seek retribution. As an Alabama court suggested in an 1892 prosecution, the government can punish in criminal or civil libel cases any publication that "has such a tendency" as to harm society.[23]

In fact, threats of civil or criminal libel actions helped demarcate the borders of acceptable political disputation. Reformist and radical political statements were especially vulnerable to sanction exactly because they departed from the mainstream. In an 1891 libel prosecution, a Texas court convicted William Lamb, a leader of the Populist party, after he published a newspaper advertisement criticizing a local politician. That same year, a New York court upheld the conviction of an editor, Johann Most, for a speech given to a gathering of anarchists. The court rejected an overt-acts test because the government must be allowed to protect "the public peace." Whether the defendant sought to incite violence to be performed immediately or "at some future time" was, from this perspective, irrelevant. Judicial analysis should focus on the harmful tendency of the speech, not the time when the harm might reach fruition. Just over a decade later, Most was back in the New York courts, this time convicted under a breach of the peace statute. Most, in this instance, had published a newspaper article arguing that government relied on violence, that government "is nothing more than murder dominion." The court, explaining that licentiousness is not the same as liberty, focused on the tendency of the publication and even quoted the truth-conditional standard directly from the *Croswell* case, decided nearly a century earlier. No commentators, state courts, or state constitutions, the court explained, protect publications that might "destroy the reputation of the citizen, the peace of society or the existence of the government."[24]

Whether reformist, radical, or elsewhere on the political spectrum, newspaper publishers needed to be concerned about the law of libel. This concern did not necessarily translate into meek submission, however. Unlike small publishers, some major publishers classified the defense of libel suits as merely another cost of doing business. Wilbur Storey of the *Chicago Times* once juggled twenty-four separate libel cases in a year, while Joseph Pulitzer of the *New York World* handled twenty-one during a single presidential campaign. No one knew more about invoking the tradition of dissent than publishers, editors, and writers. For example, several newspapers denounced the 1903 treaty that gave the United States the right to build and control the Panama Canal; the papers alleged corruption that could be traced to private individuals, including President Theodore Roosevelt's brother-in-law. These reports so outraged Roosevelt that, in an address to Congress, he condemned the newspapers not only for their "infamous libels" against individuals but also for "a libel upon the United States Government." Because of "the great injury done . . . in blackening the good name of the American people," Roosevelt proclaimed, the responsible editors and publishers "should be prosecuted for libel by the governmental authorities." Soon, the attorney general instituted two criminal libel prosecutions, which sparked predictable declarations about the importance of free expression. Pulitzer, one of the charged publishers, wrote: "So far as the [*New York*] *World* is concerned, its proprietor may go to jail, if Mr. Roosevelt succeeds, as he threatens; but even in jail the *World* will not cease to be a fearless champion of free speech, a free press and a free people. It cannot be muzzled." Eventually, courts dismissed both prosecutions, albeit primarily on jurisdictional grounds, but one judge took the opportunity to comment on the function of the press: "Here was a matter of great public interest, public concern. I was interested in it. You were interested in it. We were all interested in it. Here was a newspaper printing the news, or trying to."[25]

Regardless, libel law was but one legal obstacle facing the press. Alternatively, the government could suppress expression through contempt of court. In a typical case, a Connecticut court charged the defendant with contempt based on the content of two articles he had published about a pending case. The articles allegedly "tended to unduly interfere with the administration of justice, to obstruct the court in the discharge of its duties, and to prejudice the public and the jury as to the merits of said cause."

Upholding the defendant's conviction, in *State v. Howell*, the state Supreme Court reasoned that neither the defendant's intentions nor the articles' actual effects determined the validity of the conviction. A contempt conviction could be sustained merely because the defendant had published the articles in circumstances where they might have influenced a pending case, though not "read by the court or jurors." Naturally, courts often interpreted the contempt power broadly so as to protect the prerogatives of their own dominion. Courts could convict writers, publishers, and editors for contempt not merely for actions taken in the courtroom but, as the *Howell* case illustrates, for publishing criticisms of judges and judicial proceedings. As newspapers became an inexpensive mass medium in the late-nineteenth century, courts increasingly turned to contempt charges in their efforts to control the press and to discourage criticism. After libel, contempt became "the second greatest threat" to newspapers. In theory, though, courts exercised the contempt power only to promote the "public good" in the "administration of justice." Consequently, once a case had reached a final disposition, then the press could criticize the decision mercilessly. Yet, so long as a party might seek a rehearing in an already-decided case, the court could still categorize the case as pending and thus wield its contempt power.[26]

LIBERTY AND LABOR

While judges and others generally interpreted free-expression rights more narrowly than economic rights, expressive and economic liberties were nonetheless linked during this era in an important manner. Those commentators and jurists who were strongly influenced by the libertarian-individualist ethos conceptualized rights to free speech and a free press as aspects of liberty, akin to property and contract rights. In his *Atkinson* dissent, for instance, Cooley analogized free speech to property: "Every man must exercise his rights with due regard to the corresponding and coincident rights of others, and he is responsible if he causes injury through malice or negligence, but not otherwise. This is as true of the right to speech as it is of the right to the free enjoyment of one's property." Free speech and a free press were expressive rights, of course, while property and contract were economic rights. But expressive and economic rights alike were components of "the same general principle of equal liberty," and as such, protected within the compass of due process.[27]

Different libertarian writers adverted in a variety of ways to this entwinement of expressive rights of speech and writing, economic rights of property and contract, and the republican democratic principle of equal liberty. Schroeder not only emphasized that each individual should enjoy the maximum liberty, including free expression, consistent with an equal liberty for others, but he also explicitly tied free expression to due process. He argued that any statutory proscription of obscenity necessarily violated due process because expression could never be found objectively obscene. Ethical values were relative, so obscenity was no more than an observer's subjective labeling of expressive materials. Hence, an antiobscenity statute "furnishes no standard or test by which to differentiate the book that is obscene from that which is not, because of which fact the definition of the crime is uncertain."[28]

The political scientist John Burgess more closely tied expression with economic rights. He maintained that liberty is one ultimate end of the state. Liberty, Burgess elaborated, "consists in freedom of the person, equality before the courts, security of private property, freedom of opinion and its expression, and freedom of conscience." But expressive and economic freedoms did not merely fit under the same umbrella, called liberty; they also interlaced. While liberty consisted of various specific freedoms, it was more generally, as defined by Burgess, the "absence of government in a given sphere of individual or social action." Therefore, Burgess insisted that "[m]odern political science favors the greatest possible limitation of governmental power." To achieve such a maximization of liberty (or minimization of government), political science "favors keeping open to private enterprise the widest possible domain of business." According to Burgess, then, private corporations like railroads and banks increased individual liberty. Finally, free expression was needed because it enabled such business enterprises to flourish and to advance. Political science, Burgess wrote, "absolutely demands that all institutions, through which new truth is discovered and the ideals of advancing civilization are brought to light . . . shall be so far free from governmental action as to secure and preserve . . . perfect freedom of scientific thought and expression." The state, in short, could not maximize individual liberty without protecting both economic and expressive freedoms.[29]

These theorists showed how expressive and economic liberties could be linked in arguments for expansive free expression rights, but the link could also be turned in the other direction. Frequently, in concrete disputes, due process liberty questions subsumed free expression issues. Two decisions from the Massachusetts Supreme Judicial Court, with opinions by Oliver Wendell Holmes, Jr., illustrate the submergence of free expression issues.

In the first, *McAuliffe v. New Bedford,* decided in 1892, a city dismissed a police officer for violating a department rule: "No member of the department shall be allowed to solicit money or any aid, on any pretense, for any political purpose whatever." The officer argued that the rule violated his "right to express his political opinions." Holmes, upholding the dismissal, deflected this free-expression claim. "The petitioner may have a constitutional right to talk politics, but he has no constitutional right to be a policeman." The sanctity of the employment contract eclipsed any free-expression issues. In the second case, *Commonwealth v. Davis,* decided three years later, the defendant was convicted for public speaking on Boston Common without a permit. The case turned on the construction of a city ordinance, but Holmes's opinion also addressed the relation between rights to free expression and to property. "For the legislature absolutely or conditionally to forbid public speaking in a highway or public park is no more an infringement of the rights of a member of the public than for the owner of a private house to forbid it in his house." The government's ownership interest was analogous to that of a private property owner. As such, the government's power to regulate the use of its property effaced any governmental obligations to respect a citizen's free-expression rights.[30]

As these cases demonstrate, the intertwinement of expressive and economic rights often translated into a disregard for or diminution of free-expression liberties. This potential vitiation of free expression was most evident in labor disputes. As workers and unions realized, labor protests entailed expressive or communicative activities: union organizers speaking to workers, union members carrying picket signs, and so on. The moderate AFL insisted that members ought to be able to use "moral suasion and argument" to advance its claims in a labor dispute. "Has not a man a right to induce another to violate an [employment] agreement ignorantly and foolishly made?" To be sure, like the abolitionists before them, union organizers and members invoked free expression, whether in the form of supposed legal rights or the tradition of dissent, largely as a tool to help achieve other, more primary goals, such as higher wages. When Eugene Debs complained in 1897 that labor had been "bound and gagged for the perpetual exploitation of corporate capital," he was not concerned with civil liberties in the abstract but rather with the effects of suppression on union activities. Regardless of labor's specific purposes for invoking free expression, the courts consistently emphasized the contract and property rights of employers and management to the neglect of any potential free-expression rights. Courts issued thousands of injunctions preventing all forms of expressive labor activities including "peaceable persuasion, meetings, publications, parades, and picketing." In the Chicago, Burlington, and Quincy (CB&Q) Railroad strike of the late 1880s, for instance, a federal judge enjoined workers on other railways from supporting the strike through a boycott (by refusing to interchange CB&Q railcars). Frequently, an employer would obtain a preliminary injunction before a strike had even begun, thus diffusing any momentum in favor of the union. Of course, the government had other ways to hinder labor activities. In January 1914, the octogenarian labor organizer Mother Mary Jones tried to speak in Trinidad, Colorado, only to be repeatedly arrested and finally imprisoned for twenty-six days. If Jones had been allowed to speak, the state governor explained, she might have "incited to violence."[31]

Such arrests, as well as the frequent injunctions issued against labor activities, could readily be categorized as prior restraints. The government did not prosecute and punish speakers after they had disseminated their ideas; rather, the government prevented them from participating in expressive labor activities before the fact. Even under the most restrictive common law doctrine of free expression, traced back to Blackstone, the government could not impose prior restraints on expression. Yet, in these hundreds upon thousands of labor incidents, courts blinked at the arguable violations of even such minimal free-expression protections by deeming the labor activities "coercive interferences with employers' property rights and with non-union workers' liberty of contract." Even a judge generally sympathetic to unions, like Justice Harlan, could stress the importance of protecting property rights in a labor dispute. Sitting on a three-judge circuit court panel in 1894, Harlan examined the validity of an injunction preventing strike-related actions. Upholding the injunction in part, Harlan reasoned that courts sometimes have a "plain duty" to exercise their equity powers to enjoin labor activities. If such activities, related to a strike or otherwise, would cause "irreparable injury to and destruction of property for all the purposes for which that property was adapted, as well as continuous acts of trespass, to say nothing of the rights of the public," then an injunction would be imperative. Given the regularity with which courts enjoined labor activities, judges apparently found the prerequisites for granting an injunction to be satisfied with surprising regularity, even though such equitable remedies were, in theory, extraordinary. Indeed, former federal judge and future Supreme Court justice William Howard Taft, in his presidential inaugural address, equated any denial of the federal courts' equitable "power to issue injunctions in industrial disputes" with impermissible class legislation. If courts could not issue injunctions, "it would create a privileged class among the laborers and save the lawless among their numbers from a most needful remedy available to all men for the protection of their business against lawless invasion." With such judicial sentiments toward the communicative activities of unions, labor lawyers sometimes decided not to raise potential free-expression claims, preferring to construe issues more in economic terms.[32]

In 1905, radical labor leaders, frustrated with the AFL's moderation, joined to form the Industrial Workers of the World (the IWW or Wobblies), led by Big Bill Haywood. While the AFL cooperated with management for mutual economic advantage, the IWW's goals were openly revolutionary: "the emancipation of the working-class from the slave bondage of capitalism," as Haywood declared. "The aims and objects of this organization shall be to put the working-class in possession of the economic power, the means of life, in control of the machinery of production and distribution, without regard to the capitalist masters." Initially aligned with Debs's Socialist party (though the two groups would eventually split), the IWW viewed the labor struggle as a class struggle: the workers versus the capitalists. Economics and politics were conjoined. Elite capitalists oppressed the same societal groups in both employment and in republican democratic government, as currently practiced. According to Debs, "[t]he trades-union expresses the economic power and the socialist party expresses the political power of the Labor movement." Thus, "[t]he fully developed labor-unionist uses both his economic and political power in the interest of his class." Because of this orientation toward class struggle, Haywood aimed to have "One Big Union," open to all workers, in all industries, regardless of race, sex, nationality, or skills. The IWW welcomed workers who were excluded from the craft-based AFL (and likely also excluded from direct participation in republican democracy as well). The Wobblies, for instance, sought to organize migratory workers, numbering in the millions, roaming mostly through the West in search of seasonal jobs. As Haywood said, "We are going down in the gutter to get at the mass of workers and bring them up to a decent plane of living."[33]

The IWW sought to achieve its goals through "direct action," which encompassed any activity advantageous to workers including strikes, general strikes, slowdowns, demonstrations, and public speeches. One provocative type of direct action was the "free speech fight." The Wobblies first tried this tactic in 1906, and between 1909 and 1913, they used it at least twenty-one times. In a free speech fight, the IWW attempted to take advantage of the tension between, on the one hand, the tradition of suppression, the narrow legal doctrine of free expression, and general judicial hostility toward labor activities, and on the other hand, the tradition of dissent — the deeply entrenched popular sense that, as Americans, we are free to speak our minds. In the typical free speech fight, one Wobbly would begin speaking on a street corner. Given the revolutionary nature of the message, the speaker would soon be arrested for vagrancy, breach of the peace, or some similar crime. Yet, as soon as the police carted away the first speaker, a second Wobbly would start speaking at the same spot. Once again, the speaker would soon be arrested, only to be replaced by yet another speaker, and so on. Before long, the jail would be overflowing with Wobblies. In the 1909 Spokane, Washington, fight, police arrested 1,200 Wobblies, twenty-eight of them crammed into a single seven-by-eight-foot jail cell. And in any free speech fight, both before and after arrest, the Wobblies would loudly claim that the police wanted to deny their right to speak. "'Have you ever read the Constitution?'" they might yell. "'Don't you believe in free speech?'" If police demanded to see a permit for public speaking, Wobblies would say they "'had none save the First Amendment.'"[34]

The Wobblies' free speech fights periodically provoked other individuals and groups to decry narrow interpretations of free-expression rights, even though these individuals and groups might not even remotely support the Wobblies' goal of economic revolution. The *Portland Journal* editorialized: "Unless a man can freely speak his thoughts on any subject whatever, there is no free speech." The Free Speech League often provided money, advice, and legal representation to the Wobblies during free speech fights. During the San Diego fight, the League president, Leonard Abbott, sent personal messages to the California governor and San Diego mayor and police chief protesting the "unconstitutional suppression of free speech." Theodore Schroeder lamented that "[t]he most remarkable feature of the [San Diego free speech fight was] the general indifference toward such usual, violent and lawless suppressions of free speech." University of Wisconsin professor Edward Ross, in his 1914 presidential address to the American Sociological Society, declared that in the free speech fights "the constitutional rights of free communication have been denied to socially insignificant persons." To Ross, no "apostasy to principle [could] be more contemptible." Even governmental officials occasionally maintained that Wobblies had a right to speak. The police commissioner of Denver, in his own words, "gave the wobblies the right to talk their heads off."[35]

Despite such sporadic successes in influencing others to support or to advocate for broader free-expression rights, the Wobblies invoked the first amendment mostly at a rhetorical level, as an effort to gain political advantage. After all, they never truly believed the courts would listen to their pleas. Such a belief — that the courts might respond positively to Wobbly arguments for free expression — would contravene the most basic Wobbly views of American capitalist society: the courts were "but the mirrors reflecting the prevailing mode of ownership in the means of production." Free expression could not exist "for workers who want more or all of the product of their toil." Ultimately, through the free speech fights, the Wobblies sought to generate additional support for their economic goals by demonstrating the seeming hypocrisy of the American legal system. Indeed, the Wobblies "practically demanded that they be incarcerated," according to one governmental investigator. According to a Wobbly journal, they staged free speech fights "to appeal not to the 'Supreme Court,' but to their fellow workers against the common enemy." Stop seeking equity through the system, the Wobblies suggested to other workers; take direct action to change the system.[36]

Regardless of the Wobblies' purposes in invoking rights to free expression, and regardless of their occasional successes in provoking more widespread support for enhancing free expression, the Wobblies' free speech fights tended overall to spark strong opposition and hostility. Numerous cities sought to discourage the Wobblies by passing ordinances to restrict street speaking (which ironically made the cities, in Wobbly eyes, inviting targets for free speech fights). The AFL could be especially vituperative in its opposition to the IWW. An AFL report on the Spokane free speech fight discouraged members from supporting the Wobblies, "an unAmerican organization [seeking to] carry on their unholy work of breaking the laws and defying the constituted authority of the various communities." From the AFL's perspective, the IWW was "an organization whose every act is that of falsehood, whose every utterance is that of infamy, destructive of all that is good, with the only purpose to destroy." Meanwhile, in 1912, the Socialist party officially repudiated Wobbly methods and, the next year, removed Haywood from its executive committee. Debs, who had sat on the speakers' platform at the Wobblies' founding convention, now denounced the IWW as "an anarchist organization."[37]

Newspapers frequently condemned the Wobblies' free speech fights by reiterating the traditional distinction between liberty and licentiousness. After a free speech strike in Paterson, New Jersey, the *New York Times* labeled free speech "a noble and an indispensable right." But "[s]peech that is meant and calculated to foment disorder, to incite to violence and crime, should not be free." For this reason, the "I.W.W. ranters [who] rush like vultures to carrion" should not be allowed to speak, the *Times* explained, and the Paterson officials who sought to crush the strike should be praised for driving "the breeders of anarchy out." After a bitter free speech fight, the *San Diego Tribune* denounced the Wobblies as "the waste material of creation [who] should be drained off into the sewer of oblivion there to rot in cold obstruction like any other excrement." The *Tribune* wrapped an open threat in the popular tradition of suppression: "If the sword of our own law is turned against us, we claim the right, under the unwritten law, to resort to the law of nature." These types of threats were not idle chatter. One Wobbly described his release from prison in San Diego. "We were taken out of the city. . . . [A] man in the rear struck me with a blackjack several times on the head and shoulder; the other man then struck me on the mouth with his fist. The man in the rear then sprung around and kicked me in the stomach. I then started to run away; and heard a bullet go past me. I stopped at about 100 feet distance and turned around. I saw them take out of the second car [another Wobbly] Joseph Marko, whom they proceeded to beat up. . . . I saw him knocked to the ground several times, and he gave several loud screams. . . . In the morning I examined Joe Marko's condition, and found that the back of his head had been split open."[38]

In the end, the sum total of the Wobblies' direct actions was to garner "nationwide opprobrium." While membership in the AFL soared well over a million, membership in the IWW hovered at between only five and twenty-five thousand. Given that the Wobblies' aggressive tactics and revolutionary goals generally alienated the middle class and that the Wobblies appealed to those who were otherwise disempowered and disenfranchised, the fate of the organization was predictable. By the early 1920s, the IWW was impotent. True, their free speech fights temporarily attracted attention to questions of free speech. They starkly illustrated the contemporary interrelations of the tradition of dissent, the tradition of suppression, and the legal doctrine of free expression. Yet, the Wobblies had little effect on the future development of free expression. Even at the time, the Wobblies' struggles did not significantly affect the doctrine of free expression. The Wobblies themselves rarely pushed their free speech claims into the upper echelons of the judicial system. The economic costs were too high and the likelihood of success seemed too remote. Their primary goal was revolutionary economic change, not reforms to legal doctrine.[39]

IN THE LATE-NINETEENTH and early-twentieth centuries, the legal doctrine of free expression remained relatively stable and narrow — despite the vitality of the tradition of dissent (manifested by the Wobblies' free speech fights), despite theorists' libertarian arguments favoring the expansion of free expression, and despite broader judicial protections for economic liberties. Whether conceptualized under the first amendment (or an analogous state constitutional provision) or subsumed under a due process (or economic) liberty umbrella, free expression remained subservient to the republican democratic common good. The basic question was whether the expression had bad tendencies, and typically, judges and other governmental actors would conclude as such. The succinct statement of legal doctrine in a 1901 legal encyclopedia makes the point. The *entire* entry on liberty of speech read: "The right to speak facts and express opinions." The entry on liberty of the press, while not extensive, was longer. Its first part presented the *Croswell* truth-conditional standard: "The liberty of the press consists in the right to publish, with impunity, the truth, with good motives and for justifiable ends, whether it respects governments or individuals." The second part specified certain recurrent types of expression deemed categorically contrary to the common good. Liberty of press did not protect publications that, "from their blasphemy, obscenity, or scandalous character, may be a public offense, or as by their falsehood and malice . . . may injuriously affect the standing, reputation, or pecuniary interests of individuals."[40]

THE SUPREME COURT AND FREE EXPRESSION: THE EARLY CASES

The Supreme Court was no more protective of free expression than were other courts during this era. The Court effaced potential free-expression problems by, for instance, subsuming free-expression issues within a due process or economic liberty analysis. *Davis v. Massachusetts,* decided in 1897, affirmed Holmes's state court decision validating a conviction for public speaking on Boston Common without a permit. The Supreme Court adopted Holmes's rationale — that state and local governments are empowered to control their property completely — adding only that the fourteenth amendment did not diminish such governmental power. Boston had no obligation to recognize or respect any liberty of expression on publicly owned property. Property rights trumped any potential rights to speak. Early in the twentieth century, attempts to regulate the new technology of motion pictures raised novel free-expression questions. The state of Ohio required that a censorship board preapprove any movies before they could be shown to the public. In a case decided in 1915, Mutual Film Corporation argued that this licensing requirement amounted to a prior restraint contravening the state constitution. The Court rejected this claim, reasoning "that the exhibition of moving pictures is a business, pure and simple, originated and conducted for profit." As such, the censorship statute constituted a reasonable regulation on personal liberty — that is, economic liberty — because it was "in the interest of the public morals and welfare." While many films might be "educational or entertaining," some might be "used for evil" by insidiously corrupting adults and children.[41]

In a series of three labor cases, the Court approved the frequent practice of issuing injunctions against unions. In the first two cases, the Court upheld injunctions that ostensibly protected the economic rights of the employers, but in so doing, implicitly proscribed expressive activities by union leaders and members. As was often true in the lower courts, the justices did not even acknowledge that these judicial actions implicated free expression. In the third case, *Gompers v. Bucks Stove and Range Company,* the majority opinion explicitly addressed the free-expression issue in dicta. Because injunctions often rendered strikes unsuccessful, unions sometimes resorted instead to boycotts, calling on all union members to stop patronizing "unfair" employers. The AFL, in fact, published "Unfair" and "We Don't Patronize" lists to facilitate support for these boycotts. The *Gompers* Court explained that when the enjoinment of a boycott was otherwise appropriate, "the strong current of authority is that the publication and use of letters, circulars, and printed matter may constitute a means whereby a boycott is unlawfully continued, and their use for such purpose may amount to a violation of the order of injunction." In other words, an injunction against union activities encompassing speech and writing — or what the Court called "verbal acts" — did not "abridge the liberty of speech or freedom of the press." The judicial focus should be the protection of economic liberties: "The court's protective and restraining powers extend to every device whereby property is irreparably damaged or commerce is illegally restrained."[42]

As *Gompers* suggests, even when the Supreme Court justices directly addressed free-expression issues, they tended to interpret the liberties of speech and writing narrowly. *Roberston v. Baldwin,* decided in 1897, held that a statute authorizing the apprehension of deserting seamen did not violate the thirteenth-amendment prohibition against involuntary servitude. In the course of the majority opinion, the Court explicated the meaning of the Bill of Rights, particularly the first amendment. "The law is perfectly well settled that the first ten amendments to the constitution, commonly known as the 'Bill of Rights,' were not intended to lay down any novel principles of government, but simply to embody certain guaranties and immunities which we had inherited from our English ancestors, and which

had, from time immemorial, been subject to certain well-recognized exceptions, arising from the necessities of the case," explained Justice Brown.
"In incorporating these principles into the fundamental law, there was no
intention of disregarding the exceptions, which continued to be recognized
as if they had been formally expressed. Thus, the freedom of speech and
of the press . . . does not permit the publication of libels, blasphemous or
indecent articles, or other publications injurious to public morals or private
reputation." If taken seriously, this dicta meant that the first amendment
did no more than proscribe prior restraints. To determine whether certain types of expression could be criminally punished, the common law
would provide the answer. And, recall, the *Croswell* truth-conditional standard provided more protection than had the English common law, which
not only allowed the punishment of any licentious or harmful expression
but also, in theory, followed the maxim, the greater the truth the greater
the libel (though American juries, given the tradition of dissent, had long
balked at applying this rule). The first amendment, according to this reading, might then proffer less protection than did the many state constitutions that had been interpreted during the nineteenth century to embody
the truth-conditional standard.[43]

In fact, two 1907 Supreme Court decisions articulated a narrow understanding of free expression, though neither case relied explicitly on the
first amendment. The first, *Halter v. Nebraska,* wonderfully illustrates the
Court's exercise of its power of judicial review under republican democracy in a case explicitly raising a free-expression issue. In *Halter,* the Court
upheld the conviction under a state flag-desecration statute of defendants
who used the American flag on beer bottles. As noted in Harlan's majority
opinion, over one dissenter, many states had similar statutes protective of
the flag. Harlan discussed free expression at length but as an aspect of due
process liberty rather than as a first-amendment right per se. He began by
explicating the powers of a republican democratic government: "a state
possesses all legislative power consistent with a republican form of government; therefore each state . . . may, by legislation, provide not only for
the health, morals, and safety of its people, but for the common good, as
involved in the well-being, peace, happiness, and prosperity of the people."
Thus, as Harlan explained, "[i]t is familiar law that even the privileges of
citizenship and the rights inhering in personal liberty are subject, in their
enjoyment, to such reasonable restraints as may be required for the general good." More specifically, then, free expression, as an aspect of personal
liberty, was subordinate to any state actions promoting the common good.
In this particular case, the protection of the flag from desecration, includ-

ing its use "for purposes of trade and traffic," would promote the common good. A state, Harlan added, would "be wanting in care for the well-being of its people if it ignores the fact that they regard the flag as a symbol of their country's power and prestige."[44]

The second 1907 decision, *Patterson v. Colorado,* warrants special attention because Holmes wrote the majority opinion, his first in a free-expression case at the Supreme Court. The Colorado Supreme Court held Thomas Patterson in contempt for publishing a cartoon and articles that allegedly could embarrass the court and interfere with its "impartial administration of justice" in pending cases. Holmes assumed, without deciding, that the fourteenth amendment proscribed state governments from infringing on free expression. While unclear, Holmes seemed to discuss free expression as an aspect of liberty, as had the *Halter* Court, rather than suggesting that the fourteenth amendment applied or incorporated the first amendment per se against the states. At the same time, Holmes seemed to equate fourteenth-amendment free-expression-as-liberty with first-amendment free expression. Either way, then, Holmes interpreted free expression, whether primarily a fourteenth- or first-amendment liberty, harmoniously with the *Halter* Court's understanding. Holmes wrote that "the main purpose of such constitutional provisions [protecting free speech and a free press] is 'to prevent all such previous restraints upon publications as had been practised by other governments.'" Yet, consistent with republican democratic principles, constitutional protections of free expression "do not prevent the subsequent punishment of such as may be deemed contrary to the public welfare." Thus, while the proscription of prior restraints protects even false statements, the government's power to impose criminal punishment on expression to benefit the common good extends "as well to the true as to the false." In short, Holmes's understanding of free expression corresponded with the standard nineteenth and early-twentieth century renditions of legal doctrine. The government could not impose prior restraints but could punish speech with bad tendencies because doing so would promote the common good—even if the expression asserted the truth. Holmes, here, by reasoning that truth alone did not constitute an automatic defense, might have been obscurely referring to the truth-conditional standard.[45]

Harlan, meanwhile, wrote a perplexing dissent in *Patterson.* He maintained that the fourteenth amendment unequivocally incorporated the first amendment, so the national Constitution now mandated state governments to uphold free speech and a free press. He then disagreed with Holmes's majority opinion "if it . . . meant that the legislature may impair or abridge the rights of a free press and of free speech whenever it thinks that the public welfare requires that to be done." This passage is open to multiple interpretations. Harlan might have intended to argue against judicial deference to legislative decisions regarding the common good vis-à-vis individual liberties (the Court should not defer merely because the legislature "thinks" the common good would be advanced). Or Harlan might have intended, more radically, to repudiate fundamental republican democratic principles by declaring that the common good does not take priority over individual liberties, including free expression. Indeed, Harlan's next sentence supports this second reading. "The public welfare," Harlan explained, "cannot override constitutional privileges [including] the rights of free speech and of a free press." But this extreme anti-republican-democracy interpretation of Harlan's dissent contrasts sharply with many of his other judicial opinions. Most important, Harlan's majority opinion in *Halter* explicitly adhered to the standard republican democratic scheme: individual liberties were always subordinate to governmental actions for the common good.[46]

Putting Harlan's *Patterson* dissent in the context of his overall jurisprudence, the two passages can together be given a more nuanced interpretation, consistent with republican democracy. Rather than asserting that the common good can never overcome individual liberties, Harlan perhaps meant that the identification of the common good delineates the appropriate boundaries of individual liberties, including free expression. Individual liberties are of the utmost importance, but their precise bounds must be determined in accordance with public needs and values. Legislatures must constantly decide whether proposed actions would promote the common good, while courts too, though respecting such legislative decisions, must independently discern whether the governmental action would promote the common good in the particular context. From this perspective, if a court concludes that a governmental action is justified because it advances the common good, then individual rights, including free expression, are not infringed, by definition. The individual does not have any protected rights that contravene the common good — precisely because the common good marks the outer borders of such rights.

Holmes's wrote his second free-expression opinion, this time for a unanimous Court, in *Fox v. Washington,* decided in 1915. The state convicted Jay Fox for publishing an article, "The Nude and the Prudes," which violated a criminal libel statute proscribing expression that tended "to encourage or advocate disrespect for law." Fox edited a newspaper for the Home Colony, an anarchist group of radical libertarian freethinkers. As Fox explained in the article, "'Home is a community of free spirits, who came out into the woods to escape the polluted atmosphere of priest-ridden, conventional society;' [and] 'one of the liberties enjoyed by the Homeites was the privilege to bathe in evening dress, or with merely the clothes nature gave them, just as they chose.'" Gilbert E. Roe of the Free Speech League represented Fox in his appeal to the Supreme Court. In response to Roe's constitutional arguments, Holmes discussed free expression but, as in *Patterson,* never clarified whether he was focused on the first amendment per se or on fourteenth-amendment liberty. Regardless, Holmes partially sidestepped Roe's constitutional challenges by interpreting the statute consistently with the bad tendency standard. Construing the statute harmoniously with constitutional standards as he understood them at the time, Holmes obviated any need to discuss further whether the statute as applied violated free-expression protections. "It does not appear and is not likely that the statute will be construed to prevent publications merely because they tend to produce unfavorable opinions of a particular statute or of law in general." Instead, in the "present case the disrespect for law that was encouraged was disregard of it, — an overt breach and technically criminal act."[47]

Did Holmes, by this latter statement, intend to suggest that an overt-acts test was the appropriate standard for free expression? Apparently not. Washington convicted Fox for merely encouraging disrespect for the law; no evidence suggested that any overt criminal conduct had occurred or was likely to occur because of his article. Indeed, earlier in the opinion, Holmes's description of Fox's article spotlights the tenuous and hypothetical connection between the article and unlawful conduct: "by *indirection,* but unmistakably, the article encourages and incites a persistence in what we must *assume* would be a breach of the state laws against indecent exposure; and the jury so found." More specifically, the article had explained how "a few prudes" had orchestrated the arrest of four Home Colony members for indecent exposure. In response, the Colony had organized a boycott of "the prudes." The article thus, as elaborated by Holmes, "predicts and encourages the boycott of those who . . . interfere with the freedom of Home, concluding: 'The boycott will be pushed until these invaders will come to see the brutal mistake of their action and so inform the people.'" The article, that is, merely encouraged a boycott of the Home Colony's antagonists and did not directly incite indecent exposure (which is why Holmes wrote that Fox had only encouraged a "persistence" in indecent exposure "by indirection").[48]

Thus, well before the United States would enter World War I in April 1917, the Supreme Court had established a doctrinal stance on free expression, whether viewed as a first- or fourteenth-amendment issue. The Court's doctrinal approach was no different from that of the lower courts. As in police power and other due process liberty cases, the Court would focus on whether the governmental action promoted the common good. The liberty of expression, like other liberties, was subordinate to the public welfare. In any particular case, if the Court found that the government acted to suppress speech or writing with bad tendencies, then the Court, in turn, would necessarily find that the governmental action benefited the common good. Beyond this, the Constitution proscribed only prior restraints, as the Court reiterated repeatedly. Yet at times, even that proscription seemed more rhetorical than real. As was true in the lower courts, the Supreme Court consistently upheld labor injunctions without acknowledging that they might be categorized as impermissible prior restraints.[49]

CHAPTER 8

Free Expression during the World War I Era

In the summer of 1914, a half-year before the Court would decide *Fox v. Washington,* war erupted in Europe.[1] President Woodrow Wilson immediately issued a Proclamation of Neutrality. Two weeks later, in a message to the Senate, Wilson elaborated: "Every man who really loves America will act and speak in the true spirit of neutrality." He cautioned Americans of divergent sympathies to avoid "passionately taking sides"; otherwise, they "may be divided in camps of hostile opinion, hot against each other." With the war dragging on, though, the nation recoiled as the death toll approached an astonishing ten million. Still, in January 1917, the nation remained noncommittal. Wilson explained that if either side prevailed, then the "victor's terms [would be] imposed upon the vanquished," resentment would arise, and peace would be ephemeral. Yet, less than three months later, on April 2, 1917, Wilson asked Congress to declare war on Germany to make "[t]he world . . . safe for democracy." Four days later, Congress issued its declaration.[2]

WORLD WAR I AND SUPPRESSION

Once Congress had declared war, Wilson sought congressional action to suppress dissent. In his own words, "censorship . . . is absolutely necessary to the public safety." In "every country there are some persons in a position to do mischief and whose interests or desires [would be] highly dangerous to the Nation in the midst of a war." From the Department of Justice, Assistant Attorney General Charles Warren drafted a bill "for suppressing or punishing disloyal and hostile acts and utterances." Before long, Congress opened debates on this Espionage Bill—debates that generated remarkable deliberations about free expression during wartime. At one point, Mississippi Representative Thomas Sisson had the whole of John Milton's *Areopagitica,* protesting against prior restraints, printed into the *Congressional Record.* Three provisions of the Espionage Bill, however, deserve special attention. The first two, a press-censorship provision and a nonmailability provision, generated the most lengthy congressional discussions. In the end, Congress defeated press censorship but enacted the nonmailability provision. The third key provision allowed the government to punish anyone either obstructing the draft or causing or attempting to cause insubordination or disloyalty within the military. Ironically, this third provision, Title I, section 3, provoked little congressional debate, including with regard to free expression, yet the government indicted the "overwhelming majority" of Espionage Act defendants under this section.[3]

The press-censorship section would have allowed the president, during wartime, to "prohibit the publishing or communicating of, or the attempting to publish or communicate any information relating to the national defense which, in his judgment, is of such character that it is or might be useful to the enemy." The nation needed this provision, according to its proponents, to further the war effort, to protect the safety of American troops. Representative Andrew Volstead recognized that "when we begin to send our troops across the water [then] we shall be anxious about their safety." He asked rhetorically: "If they are sent to the bottom of the sea as a result of information obtained contrary to a provision like this, how shall we feel if we cut it out of this bill to-day?" Thus, to Volstead, as well as to many others, it was "utterly ridiculous for anybody to contend that this provision is unconstitutional." But opposition to the press-censorship provision was strong. Numerous congressmen (especially Republicans) feared the proposed language was so vague that it would effectively vest the (Democratic) president with "legislative authority," as he decided what materials should be censored. The provision would be, according to Representative William Wood, "an instrument of tyranny in the hands of tyrants." Representative Martin Madden proclaimed that press censorship "is un-American; it is against freedom; and it is against the liberty for which we are fighting." Yet, perhaps, the predominant reason the press-censorship provision went down to defeat was the political power of the major newspapers across the country. The *New York Times* typified the predictable journalistic response to such censorship. The *Times* condemned the provision as "a Prussian measure, consistently modeled upon those press laws and practices which have forbidden the German newspapers to tell the German people what the Government was about." The American Newspaper Publishers' Association addressed a resolution to the Senate Judiciary Committee: "the press-censorship provision [in the pending] espionage bill . . . strikes at the fundamental rights of the people, not only assailing their freedom of speech but also seeking to deprive them of the means of forming intelligent opinion." If anything, the newspapers provided an even greater public service during wartime because "the people must have confidence that they are getting the truth."[4]

No such powerful and well-organized group as the Publishers' Association opposed the nonmailability provision. Indeed, given that the Comstock Act and other statutes already proscribed the mailing of numerous items and publications, the proposed provision would do little more than expand contemporary restrictions on the content of the mails, as several congressmen recognized. Pursuant to this section of the Bill, "treasonable or anarchistic" materials as well as any other items "in violation of any of the provisions of this act" would be deemed "nonmailable matter." Yet, even though this nonmailability provision built on the judicially approved congressional power to regulate the mails, some congressmen worried that the Bill was ambiguous and would vest postmasters with excessive discretion. Representative William Venable brooded that administrators would be defining "anarchy," and Representative William Stafford believed the postmaster general would gain "autocratic power."[5] Ultimately, Congress revised the nonmailability provision to render it more precise. Instead of proscribing the mailing of "treasonable or anarchistic" materials, the statute, as amended, deemed unmailable "any matter advocating or urging treason, insurrection, or forcible resistance to any law of the United States." With this change, Congress purposefully refused to eliminate the provision.[6]

Multifaceted congressional deliberations cannot be reduced to a single and simple intention, and much evidence in this instance suggests a "lack of common understanding" among the congressmen. Yet, one particular incident revealed a widespread sentiment that the Espionage Bill, if enacted, would facilitate suppression. After Representative Meyer London (a Socialist) realized that Congress would defeat the press-censorship provision, he pleaded passionately for the House to bolster free expression by rejecting the nonmailability provision as well. The nonmailability provision "is an attack on the liberties of the little fellow, of the helpless man, of the defenseless man, and not on the powerful newspapers. The big newspapers will find plenty of champions here. They own the country. [Let] us not, while we talk of fighting for liberty abroad, sacrifice and crush our liberties here." But, of course, London's colleagues disappointed him because they acted exactly as he feared. They rejected the censorship provision that alarmed the mainstream publishers, yet they retained the provisions that could suppress the indigent, the alien, the radical. At one point, Oklahoman Dick Morgan insisted Congress should "assume" that "several thousand aliens" were among the "criminal classes [and] are unfriendly to the United States." Thus, major publishers, like the *New York Times,* would enjoy their usual latitude both to praise and to criticize the government, but speakers and writers who were societal outsiders — Socialists, Wobblies, pacifists, and the like — would endure governmental suppression. Representative Leonidas Dyer observed approvingly that "this bill would not permit you to hold meetings and have speeches criticizing the President." Dyer added that "people should go ahead and obey the law, keep their mouths shut, and let the Government run the war."[7]

Apparently, many congressional members intended the Espionage Bill deliberations to specify the definition of free expression during wartime — to set an "appropriate wartime boundary between protected and unprotected speech." Of course, opponents of the Bill proclaimed that, if enacted, the law would violate first-amendment rights to free expression. But among proponents of the Bill, nobody announced that he or she favored suppression of speech or writing. Nobody advocated for violation of the first amendment. To the contrary, many proclaimed their commitment to liberty, including liberty of expression. "The object is not to restrict an American citizen in any just right he has under the Constitution and laws of this Nation," proclaimed Representative Morgan. "[I]t is to guard and protect those rights . . . and to provide for the general welfare, to conserve and protect our American free institutions." During congressional deliberations, President Wilson sent a letter to Arthur Brisbane of the *New York Evening Journal.* "I can imagine no greater disservice to the country than to establish a system of censorship that would deny to the people of a free Republic like our own their indisputable right to criticize their own public officials." Yet when Wilson sent this letter, he had already expressed a strong desire for censorship, and he continued to support suppression throughout the war. The Department of Justice, moreover, had left no doubt concerning its interpretation of the pending Espionage Bill. In a letter to Representative Harold Knutson, Charles Warren explained that "no current statute 'provides penalties for treasonable utterances or writings,' but . . . the proposed legislation would cover them."[8] Many Americans believed they could simultaneously celebrate free expression while enforcing its limits.

Regardless of congressional intentions, the government would prosecute the vast majority of suppression cases under Title I, section 3. Congressional debates on this section were relatively brief, though the House Committee on the Judiciary refined one phrase, which would have proscribed attempts "to cause disaffection" in the armed forces. According to Committee Chair Edwin Webb, the original language was "too broad and too elastic and too indefinite." The House Committee thus replaced the word, "disaffection," with the more precise phrase, "insubordination, disloyalty, mutiny, or refusal of duty." Section 3, as enacted, read: "Whoever, when the United States is at war, shall willfully make or convey false reports or false statements with intent to interfere with the operation or success of the military or naval forces of the United States or to promote the success of its enemies and whoever, when the United States is at war, shall willfully cause or attempt to cause insubordination, disloyalty, mutiny, or refusal of duty, in the military or naval forces of the United States, or shall willfully obstruct the recruiting or enlistment service of the United States, to the injury of the service or of the United States, shall be punished by a fine of not more than \$10,000 or imprisonment for not more than twenty years, or both."[9]

WITH THE ESPIONAGE ACT in place, the Wilson administration fervidly promoted the war effort and attacked any perceived disloyalties. Once Congress declared war, the administration had to overcome its recent insistence that neutrality remained imperative to national security and world peace. Many Americans still believed the war unnecessary. As John Dewey phrased the problem, "How could wrong so suddenly become right?" To pass "from friendly neutrality to participation" required the nation to turn an "immense moral wrench." To this end, on April 13, 1917, Wilson created the Committee of Public Information (CPI) and appointed journalist George Creel as its chair. The Committee's job was "to excite America's martial spirit," whether by disseminating propaganda or by encouraging suppression. Constitutional scholar Edward S. Corwin published a *War Cyclopedia* under the auspices of the CPI. Corwin emphasized that once Congress had declared war, the time for "discussion" had passed. The nation should act aggressively on its decision and should not waste energy by further pondering the propriety of war. "Congress has the power to pass all laws that are 'necessary and proper' to prosecute successfully a war which it has declared; and the subjection of the press to the power given Congress by the Constitution can hardly be said to *abridge* the freedom there recognized." Thus, Corwin explained, "Congress may penalize publications which are calculated to stir up sedition, to obstruct the carrying out of the laws, or to 'give aid and comfort to the enemy.'" Courts, Corwin added, should defer to such legislative determinations.[10]

In response to such proclamations, many Americans rallied to the tradition of suppression. The Americanization movement, under the pressures of war, mutated into a nativist drive for "100 percent Americanism." Ostensibly patriotic organizations like the American Defense Society (ADS), the American Protective League (APL), and the National Security League (NSL) flourished. The APL, for instance, encompassed 1,200 separate units with 250,000 members. Probusiness, antiunion, antialien, and antiimmigrant, the ADS, APL, NSL, and similar organizations "belligerently demanded universal conformity organized through total national loyalty." Encouraged and supported by the government, these organizations sought to enforce their version of Americanism through programs of propaganda, suppression, and harassment. In the words of Theodore Roosevelt, leader of the ADS, "either a man is a good American, and therefore is against Germany . . . or he is not an American at all." Any people who questioned governmental policies were "traitors to America." The ADS's avowed aims included the internment of "[e]nemies within the United States," the suppression of German publications, the proscription of teaching German within schools, and the disclosing and punishment of sedition. The organization boasted that it had "unceasingly fought to prevent disloyal and seditious 'soap box' oratory in the streets of cities."[11]

As part of its propaganda campaign, the ADS published William Hornaday's *Awake! America,* which mixed a generous helping of xenophobia with wartime nativism. "Under the fatal spell of our perfectly idiotic eagerness for quantity in immigration, we have flung aside nearly all considerations making for quality! . . . America has become the dumping-ground for the ashes and cinders of all nations," Hornaday blustered. "Presently the Anglo-Saxon stock will disappear, by submergence, and the result will be a nation of indecipherables, mongrels, with the mental handicaps and the vices of all contributors sharply accentuated." Hornaday's primary current concern, of course, was the war, not immigration, though he feared that immigrants, aliens, and other outsiders impeded the war effort. "This is a war of all the American People — except the alien socialists, the I.W.W. miscreants, the slackers and the militant pacifists." Hornaday compiled a list of socialists teaching at American universities and declared that "[i]t is time to drive [them] out of America, and keep them out!" For Hornaday, free-expression rights were "fetiches of foolish Americans." The "decent citizen" never invoked a right to free expression: he "knows that as such he is quite at liberty to express his honest opinion of the government, of public measures, and of most men in the public eye." During this time of war, anyone who advocated for free expression, whether for himself or another, endangered the American cause. "All the red-blooded men of America . . . now hold strongly that . . . the man who for technical or timid reasons fears to suppress disloyal meetings and publications easily becomes himself a source of danger, because of his weakness. . . . For God's sake, Americans, awake."[12]

The ADS and similar organizations were not satisfied with merely spreading nativist propaganda. Reminiscent of the Orwellian Committees of Observation that monitored publishing during the Revolutionary War, the 100-percent-American organizations encouraged members to report their neighbors' "seditious and disloyal utterances." A newspaper editor who led the so-called Iowa Council of Defense urged citizens not only to join a patriotic society but also "to find out what his neighbor thinks." To facilitate such spying, the organizations engaged, usually "with tacit immunity," in "breaking and entering, bugging offices, tapping telephones, and examining bank accounts and medical records." The War Department and the Bureau of Investigation (forerunner of the Federal Bureau of Investigation or FBI) actually issued "investigative assignments" to APL "operatives." ADS leader Roosevelt declared that disloyal Germans should be shot or hanged. In fact, in hundreds of incidences, German aliens, German Americans, Socialists, pacifists, Wobblies, and other outsiders were flogged, tarred and feathered, forced to kiss the flag, and murdered. In one emblematic incident, the Nevada governor condoned a tar and feathering because "it all helped the cause," even if "some of the boys," including the local sheriff, "were pulling a little rough stuff." All in all, the public strongly supported the 100-percenters. The *Haverstraw Times,* from New York state, applauded: "The *American Defense Society,* an organization made up of citizens to aid the Department of Justice and Secret Service men in every community in locating disloyal, doubtful, unknown alien enemies, pro-German and anti-government residents, is being organized in all localities. Disloyal acts, and utterances are warned against, and it is to be hoped such an organization will be perfected in Haverstraw. We have need for it."[13]

Meanwhile, the Wilson administration began a campaign of official suppression pursuant to the Espionage Act. Attorney General Thomas W. Gregory epitomized the administration's attitude toward draft and war protesters when he warned: "May God have mercy on them, for they need expect none from an outraged people and an avenging government." Within one year from the Act's passage, more than 250 people had been convicted, most under section 3. In most of these cases, the judges interpreted the statutory language broadly and allowed juries to determine guilt, with acquittals uncommon. The courts only rarely considered the constitutionality of the convictions under the first amendment. In one typical case, Frank Shaffer was convicted for possessing and mailing a book that asserted patriotism was "in reality murder, the spirit of the very devil." Shaffer continued: "The war itself is wrong. Its prosecution will be a crime." On appeal, Shaffer argued that the book contained opinions, not assertions of fact, and as such, stood outside the statutory proscriptions. Upholding the conviction, the Ninth Circuit Court of Appeals interpreted the Espionage Act consistently with the bad tendency standard that other courts had been applying for many decades. "[T]he question here is not whether the publication contained expressions only of opinion, and not statements of fact, but it is whether the natural and probable tendency and effect of the words quoted therefrom are such as are calculated to produce the result condemned by the statute." Furthermore, according to the doctrine of constructive intent, the defendant "must be presumed to have intended the natural and probable consequences of what he knowingly did."[14]

WHILE *SHAFFER* TYPIFIED the approach and result of most lower courts, a few judges protected expression by interpreting the Espionage Act narrowly. Barely a month after Congress passed the statute, Judge Learned Hand of the Southern District of New York decided *Masses Publishing Company v. Patten*. Pursuant to the statute, the postmaster had refused the revolutionary journal, *The Masses,* access to the mails, so Masses Publishing, represented by Gilbert Roe, sought a preliminary injunction to prevent this denial of access. In granting the injunction, Hand explicitly stated that the case neither raised the issue of congressional power to restrict the mails during wartime nor the issue of freedom of the press. Rather, to Hand, the question was solely a matter of statutory construction and application. Did Congress intend to proscribe the mailing of publications, like *The Masses,* that criticized the war and the draft? Despite so limiting the case, Hand implicitly discussed the constitutional parameters of a free press by interpreting the relevant sections of the Act, the nonmailability provision and section 3, in accordance with his understanding of protected expression. Most important, Hand suggested that a bad tendency standard did not sufficiently protect freedom. The Act, therefore, could not authorize the postmaster to deny Masses Publishing access to the mails merely because the "general tenor and animus of the paper as a whole were subversive to authority and seditious in effect." Instead, Hand suggested that the appropriate constitutional standard allowed punishment only of expression directly advocating or inciting an overt act of unlawful conduct. "If one stops short of urging upon others that it is their duty or their interest to resist the law, . . . one should not be held to have attempted to cause its violation." Because Congress did not expressly state otherwise, Hand reasoned it must have followed this constitutionally mandated direct-incitement-of-overt-acts standard when enacting the Espionage Act. Political agitation, which *The Masses* aimed to foment, did not equate with "direct incitement to violent resistance" and thus fell outside the scope of the Act, as interpreted by Hand.[15]

Another atypical case was *United States v. Hall,* decided by District Judge George M. Bourquin of Montana on January 27, 1918. After a two-week trial, Bourquin granted a directed verdict to Ves Hall, indicted for violating section 3. Among other things, Hall had "declared that he would flee to avoid going to the war, that Germany would whip the United States, . . . that the President was a Wall Street tool, . . . and that the United States was only fighting for Wall Street millionaires and to protect [J. P.] Morgan's interests in England." Hall had spoken in a small Montana village, "60 miles from the railway, [with] none of the armies or navies within hundreds of miles." At the outset, Bourquin rejected the possibility that any of Hall's "beliefs, opinions, and hopes" fell within the statutory prohibitions. Yet, Bourquin acknowledged, Hall's "slanders of the President and nation are false reports and false statements," within the compass of the Act. But such false reports or statements, as offenses under the Act, "are of the nature of [criminal] attempts." To be convicted of an attempt, Bourquin reasoned, two elements must be satisfied — intent and proximity — yet the government could satisfy neither of these elements. With regard to intent, Bourquin acknowledged the common rule concerning constructive intent, often invoked in bad tendency free-expression as well as criminal attempt cases: "When facts and circumstances will justify a finding that the accused intended the natural and ordinary consequences of his acts, the intent may be inferred." Nonetheless, in this case, given "the facts and circumstances, times and places, oral kitchen gossip and saloon debate, the impossibility of far-distant military and naval forces hearing or being affected by the slanders, and all else," an inference of constructive intent was "unjustified, absurd, and without support in the evidence." The most likely result of

Hall's declarations, Bourquin noted, would be "a broken head" for Hall himself. With regard to proximity, Hall's statements could not possibly "create public fear and alarm that they would interfere with the operation and success of far-distant armies and navy." Bourquin analogized the case to an attempted killing. "It is as if A. shot with a .22 pistol with intent to kill B., two or three miles away. The impossibility would prevent public fear and alarm of homicide, and A. could not be convicted of attempted murder." Bourquin concluded Congress had proscribed espionage but had "not denounced as crimes any mere disloyal utterances, nor any slander or libel of the President or any other officer of the United States."[16]

BOTH *MASSES PUBLISHING* and *Hall* were ill-fated decisions. The Second Circuit overruled Hand's decision and repudiated his infusion of the Espionage Act with a direct-incitement standard. Instead, like most other courts, the Second Circuit interpreted the Act in accordance with the bad tendency approach. Meanwhile, after Bourquin decided *Hall,* the Montana state legislature rose up in "indignation," according to U.S. Senator Thomas Walsh (of Montana), and in special session, enacted within nine days a statute designed precisely to punish "disloyal, profane, scurrilous, contemptuous, or abusive" utterances about the nation's government, Constitution, and military. Soon afterward, with the help of the Justice Department, Walsh drafted an amendment to section 3 of the Espionage Act that incorporated the state legislative language. When introducing the amendment to the Senate on April 4, 1918, Walsh explained that it would counter "the strained construction which has been given to the espionage act" in the "startling [and] most notorious" *Hall* decision. Much of the congressional debate entailed declarations that the nation needed the amendment to avoid vigilante justice. North Carolina Senator Lee Overman chided his colleagues that "if we want mob law, just go on and delay this bill." On May 16, 1918, less than a year after the enactment of the original Espionage Act, Congress overwhelmingly passed the amended section 3 (also called the Sedition Act of 1918). With this legislative proscription of "any disloyal, profane, scurrilous, or abusive" words concerning the nation's government, Constitution, military, or flag, Congress erased any lingering doubts regarding its willingness to foster suppression. Indeed, Congress defeated an amendment that would have qualified the Sedition Act with the truth-conditional standard. And without compunction, congressmen identified outsiders as the Act's targets. Representative Patrick Norton proclaimed that the Act "will stop much of the loose, lying, soap-box socialist and I.W.W. language that has been too generously tolerated in this country for a long time."[17]

The administration proceeded to apply the amended Espionage Act as a broad-ranging prohibition of seditious libel. The Justice Department initiated more than two thousand prosecutions and secured convictions in more than one thousand cases. Sentences could be severe, with twenty-four individuals receiving twenty-year prison terms, six receiving fifteen-year terms, and eleven receiving ten-year terms. Individuals were convicted for arguing that the government should fund the war effort through heavier taxation rather than with bonds, that conscription violated the Constitution, that Christian teachings proscribed fighting in a war, and that profiteers orchestrated the war. The head of the War Emergency Division in the Justice Department, John Lord O'Brian, eventually admitted that "immense pressure" had been "brought to bear" during the war for "wholesale repression and restraint of public opinion." Even so, he insisted that the prosecutions did not violate free expression because, consistent with republican democratic principles, "liberty meant obedience to law, self-control, and self-restraint."[18]

WHY DID THE NATIONAL government suppress civil liberties, including expression, so severely during World War I? The legal doctrine at this time differed little from the doctrine tracing back for decades into the early-nineteenth century. The key to analyzing this period, then, is not so much legal doctrine, but rather the relationship between the traditions of suppression and dissent. Unlike most periods of U.S. history, the two traditions did not remain close to counterpoise, balanced against each other. Instead, the tradition of suppression nearly overwhelmed the tradition of dissent. True, the legal doctrine facilitated suppression, but no more so than in the past. Hence, one must still ask why, at this point in time and in this context, suppression overcame dissent? Why was there such widespread popular support for suppression, with relatively weak voicings of dissent?

Most fundamentally, the nation entered the war while all the strains that had been pressuring republican democracy for decades remained in force. The demographic makeup of the nation was far more diverse than during any previous war. Millions of aliens, immigrants, naturalized citizens, and their children populated the large cities. Plus, the tensions generated within the industrialized American society, including the conflicts between labor and capital, remained ever present. Once the Bolsheviks'

Russian Revolution occurred in 1917, the threat of socialism and communism infiltrating the American governmental and economic systems seemed far greater. Many Americans feared alien outsiders would import radical views that would spread and destroy the United States from within. Both Lenin and Trotsky, after all, had lived on the Lower East Side of Manhattan. In the context of the war, such radical alien outsiders might weaken American resolve to pursue the war to a successful conclusion, or so it was believed.[19]

Thus, nativism and xenophobia fueled suppression during World War I. Wilson declared in a Flag Day speech on June 14, 1917, that the "military masters of Germany [had] filled our unsuspecting communities with vicious spies and conspirators and sought to corrupt the opinion of our people." Duped by these "masters of Germany," "socialists [and] the leaders of labor" had been uttering "thinly disguised disloyalties." In one revealing incident, a juror who voted for acquittal in an Espionage Act case commented afterward, "you fellows were just lucky in not having a Jew or a foreigner among the defendants." Suppression manifested a sustained drive toward conformity with mainstream views, values, and interests. Once the major publishers had defeated the proposed press-censorship provision in the original Espionage Act, they looked the other way when more radical publications suffered suppression. In effect, any Wobbly, Socialist, pacifist, or other outsider who criticized the administration or its war-related policies invited prosecution and conviction. The Socialist party had several hundred thousand members in 1916, and grew even stronger in 1917, precisely because it was the only political party to oppose war. But during the war, the government used the Espionage Act to deny the mails to Socialist publications and to prosecute most of the party's antiwar leaders. Meanwhile, the government arrested, indicted, and convicted hundreds upon hundreds of Wobblies. In a single trial in Chicago, a jury convicted 101 IWW leaders, with the guilty verdicts returned in less than an hour. The presiding judge, Kenesaw Mountain Landis, brushed aside any potential free-expression issues: "When the country is at peace it is the legal right of free speech to oppose going to war and to oppose even preparation for war. But when once war is declared this right ceases." By the end of the war, the government had ravaged the IWW, with nearly all executive-board members in prison. Big Bill Haywood was convicted in the Chicago trial and sentenced to twenty years. He jumped bail and fled to the Soviet Union, where he lived for the remainder of his life.[20]

The fate of the union movement, as a whole, illustrates the government's discriminatory treatment of radical outsiders. During the war, any union threat to strike and to disrupt farming, logging, or manufacturing could be construed as "seditious interference in war production." As such, labor activities were subject to possible suppression. Yet, while the Wilson administration sought to destroy the radical Wobblies, it abided by the activities of the moderate AFL. Wilson even appointed Samuel Gompers, the AFL president, to the Council on National Defense. In fact, other than for the IWW, the war years proved to be a brief golden period for labor organizing. The administration realized that it needed to nurture patriotic and nationalist sentiments among the majority of American workers. Union membership grew by nearly 70 percent, surging above five million. Wages increased and eight-hour workdays became more common. The government tolerated strikes, so long as the issues could be resolved through "mediation, conciliation, and concession." And even beyond moderate labor activists, many other outsiders experienced a new "sense of participation and belonging" in American society, so long as they adequately complied with the "national purpose." For immigrants and their progeny (with the exception of German Americans), a willingness to conform to mainstream goals and values could engender a new degree of societal acceptance — the white Protestant mainstream sought, above all, unity in the war effort — but any evidence of doubting or dissenting from the avowed national aims could provoke violent subjugation.[21]

One final factor facilitated governmental suppression: the centralization of power. In the past, state and local governments had harshly suppressed civil liberties — consider, for instance, the enslavement of blacks and the systematic silencing of abolitionists — but now the national government spearheaded the assault on liberty. When the United States entered World War I, the national government mobilized the people through unprecedented assertions of authority. Such centralization arose, to a degree, from the demands of waging a war against industrialized European powers. Thus, a War Industries Board sought to increase industrial output by controlling prices and by prioritizing the distribution of raw materials needed for manufacturing military supplies. The government managed the nation's railroads and the telegraph and telephone systems as consolidated wholes. The government also instituted only the second national draft in American history; the Civil War had seen the first. These assertions of centralized power manifested a temporary victory for Progressivism. Progressives had long insisted that national governmental power was needed to combat capitalist inequities. Now, the government asserted its power to mobilize an army, to control the economy, and to regulate resistance to the war effort. The Progressive agenda had, in effect, been preparing the nation for the types of governmental actions that suddenly appeared requisite to victory in a world war.[22]

Of course, World War I was not the first time that national governmental power had been brought to bear as a mechanism of suppression. Both the 1798 Sedition Act and the post–Civil War Comstock Act could be viewed as precursors laying the groundwork for the Espionage Act prosecutions. Yet, World War I suppression manifested a unique degree of integrated cooperation among the national branches: Congress, the administration (especially the Justice Department), and the federal courts. The 1798 Sedition Act produced only fourteen prosecutions compared with the more than two thousand of World War I. And while the Comstock Act led to four times as many convictions as did the Espionage Act — four thousand compared with just over one thousand — Comstock needed four decades to reach that total. Moreover, while many official and unofficial institutions cooperated to produce the Comstock Act convictions, Comstock himself generated the main energy for the national legislation and its implementation. Without Comstock, governmental regulation of morals undoubtedly would have occurred, but it would not have been Comstockery. World War I suppression was not the offspring of any single individual; rather it manifested a sustained cooperative effort. Wilson was important, but so were numerous individuals within Justice, as were many congressmen, as were many federal judges, as were the thousands of members of the 100-percent-American organizations. World War I saw the birth of the "national security state," a government-controlled apparatus for gathering information on Americans. By mid-1919, the twenty-four-year-old J. Edgar Hoover had been appointed head of a new General Intelligence Division within the Bureau of Investigation. Trained as a clerk at the Library of Congress, Hoover used his classification skills to develop a card-catalogue type of index on "political heretics" and their organizations. Relentlessly gathering and sorting information, Hoover soon had clandestinely compiled two hundred thousand entries.[23]

Many Progressive intellectuals favored suppression at the outset of the war, and many continued to do so throughout the conflict. Not only had Progressives long been calling for greater centralization of governmental power in industrialized America, but they also had been seeking to Americanize immigrants — this desire spurred Progressive moralizing. Many Progressives therefore did not object to the governmental push for conformity. Furthermore, Progressives had long advocated for greater judicial deference to legislative determinations of the common good, particularly with regard to economic regulations. From this perspective, the willingness of the courts to defer to legislative and executive determinations about the potential dangers — or bad tendencies — of speech and writing seemed unproblematic. Progressives readily acceded to a narrow free expression because it corresponded with their desire for a narrow liberty of contract. Unsurprisingly, then, for several months after the declaration of war, the *New Republic* editors, led by Herbert Croly, supported suppression as a general principle, even while occasionally questioning its implementation. Croly, for example, criticized local postal officials who lacked the "training or qualifications for the delicate job of placing wholesome restrictions on the freedom of public utterance."[24]

Also writing in the *New Republic,* John Dewey addressed the issue of free expression, though only obliquely. In fact, that obliqueness best characterized his attitude toward free expression, at least early in the war. In one essay, published July 28, 1917, Dewey criticized pacifists who had continued opposing the war after it had become inevitable. These pacifists failed to recognize that the war presented opportunities for changing the world. While Dewey did not concur with "the idea that pacifists who do not support the war must be pro-German at heart," he also did not condemn "their suppression," which he attributed to "the untimely character of their moves." In late-summer essays, Dewey emphasized the pragmatic need to undertake the distasteful "job" of war "in a business-like way." Because of "the importance of social solidarity" in wartime, some "surrenders and abandonments of the liberties of peace time are inevitable." Many Americans, their "nerves on edge," had already displayed "a morbid sensitiveness at any exhibition of diversity of opinion." These Americans had therefore justified the resulting "suppressions on the rational ground that social cohesion is a necessity, and that we are simply taking measures to secure union." From Dewey's standpoint, however, this technique — the forceful suppression of dissent — was pragmatically ineffective: "What is denied is the efficacy of force to remove disunion of thought and feeling." Suppression tends to "manufacture importance" for otherwise "obnoxious beliefs." Such beliefs then "breed and fester" instead of dying of "inanition." Ultimately, Dewey admitted indifference toward free expression. "I am not . . . specially concerned lest liberty of thought and speech seriously suffer among us, certainly not in any lasting way." He thought it "rather funny" to see socialists invoking "the sanctity of individual rights and constitutional guaranties."[25]

While Dewey complacently dismissed the dangers of suppression, more conservative writers explicitly defended the government's restriction of speech and writing. William Vance, the Law School dean at the University of Minnesota, articulated a position on free expression during wartime that mirrored the traditional view of free speech and a free press in a republican democratic regime. While the first amendment "does not contain the statement that persons are responsible for the abuse of the right given, as do most of the state constitutions," Vance noted, "such a limitation upon the apparently unqualified language of the federal constitution is necessarily implied." Indeed, all constitutional liberties are subordinate to governmental actions that "protect the public welfare." The first amendment, according to Vance, proscribed prior restraints and otherwise allowed the punishment of expression in accordance with "the rules of common law" at the time of the constitutional framing. From this perspective, the Espionage Act was clearly constitutional: "Congress has power to punish as seditious all utterances, whether spoken or written which advise or tend to cause disobedience to the law, or resistance to its officers, or which tend to subvert the government by inducing or encouraging attempts to change or hinder governmental actions or policies by any other methods than those sanctioned by law, or tend to incite riot and disorder or to cause disturbances of the public peace."[26]

ALTHOUGH SUPPORT FOR wartime suppression was widespread throughout American society, a few intellectuals opposed it from the outset. Dewey's *New Republic* essays, pragmatically acquiescing to wartime suppression, spurred a response from the literary critic Randolph S. Bourne, a frequent contributor to the *New Republic* and a prewar proponent of both Progressivism and Dewey's pragmatism. In an essay published in October 1917, Bourne lamented "suddenly being left in the lurch, of suddenly finding that a philosophy upon which I had relied to carry us through no longer works." Dewey's essays revealed "the inadequacy of his pragmatism as a philosophy of life in this emergency." Bourne worried about the "mob-psychology" that led to attempted lynchings, while Dewey naively dismissed such "explosive hatred." Dewey spoke a language that Bourne no longer found intelligible. "A philosopher [like Dewey] who senses so little the sinister forces of war, who is so much more concerned over the excesses of the pacifists than over the excesses of military policy, who can feel only amusement at the idea that any one should try to conscript thought, who assumes that the war-technique can be used without trailing along with it the mob-fanaticisms, the injustices and hatreds, that are organically bound up with it, is speaking to another element of the younger intelligentsia than that to which I belong." Dewey, Bourne suggested, would do well to confront "grim" reality rather than maintaining his "optimism-haunted mood that continues unweariedly to suggest that all can yet be made to work for good in a mad and half-destroyed world."[27]

Another wartime opponent of suppression was Roger N. Baldwin, born into an upper-class Massachusetts family and graduated from Harvard in 1905. In 1916, Baldwin joined the American Union against Militarism (AUAM), dedicated to preventing the nation's entry into the war. In early 1917, he moved to the AUAM's New York branch, where he became associate director. After Congress declared war, the AUAM, at Baldwin's urging, formed the Civil Liberties Bureau (CLB) primarily to defend conscientious objectors. On October 1, 1917, after an internal battle over the aims of the AUAM during wartime, the CLB became an independent organization, the National Civil Liberties Bureau (NCLB), which aggressively fought against conscription and the government's Espionage Act prosecutions of Socialists and Wobblies. The government soon viewed the NCLB to be a "suspect organization" and contemplated possible prosecutions. Then, in late-summer 1918, Baldwin himself was drafted and refused induction. He resigned his NCLB position and stood trial. "The compelling motive for refusing to comply with the Draft Act, is my uncompromising opposition to the principle of conscription of life by the state, for any purpose whatsoever, in war-time or peace," he explained. Baldwin was convicted and sentenced to one year imprisonment. Numerous organizations, including the American Association for Organized Charities and the Liberal Club of Harvard, applauded Baldwin's principled stance, though they otherwise would not support the NCLB activities. Indeed, while the war continued, neither Baldwin nor the NCLB successfully transformed the violation of civil liberties into "a legitimate public policy question" of widespread concern.[28]

Nonetheless, as the war proceeded, a small group of intellectuals reacted against the government's truculent campaign of suppression by shifting toward more speech-protective stances. This change emerged distinctly among the *New Republic* editors and writers. On October 6, 1917, while still believing that some Espionage Act prosecutions were defensible, Croly complained that the "war propaganda" had become "exclusively vindictive and coercive in spirit and method." In early November, Dewey admitted that "what I wrote [in the *New Republic*] a few weeks ago" now seems "strangely remote and pallid." To Dewey, "intolerance of discussion" had increased so rapidly that it had reached "the point of religious bigotry." Americans deemed "every opinion and belief which irritates the majority of loyal citizens" to be treasonous. Despite Croly's and Dewey's more speech-protective essays, some of their *New Republic* colleagues wanted the magazine to stake out a stronger position against suppression. Frequent contributor and Harvard political science professor Harold Laski suggested that Croly contact a young Harvard law professor, Zechariah Chafee, Jr. When Chafee had begun teaching at Harvard in the fall of 1916, he taught a course in equity that covered injunctions against libels. Would such an injunction constitute a prior restraint? Preparation for the course — and resolution of this issue — led Chafee to research freedom of the press, including eventually some of the Espionage Act cases. When Croly invited Chafee to write an essay on free expression, Chafee leaped at the opportunity. His prior research served as the springboard for his essay "Freedom of Speech," published in the *New Republic* on November 16, 1918.[29]

Given the numerous convictions under the Act and its 1918 amendment, Chafee inquired: "Where shall we draw the line [between punishable offenses and constitutionally protected speech and writing]?" He immediately dismissed some common platitudes. "It is useless to make a distinction between liberty and license, since 'license' is too often liberty to the speaker and what happens to be anathema to the judge. Nor can we brush aside free speech by saying it is war-time and the Constitution gives Congress express power to raise armies." Chafee next articulated a philosophical foundation that he thought justified an expansive concept of free expression under the first amendment. "The true meaning of freedom of speech seems to be this. One of the most important purposes of society and government is the discovery and spread of truth on subjects of general concern. This is possible only through absolutely unlimited discussion. . . ." Thus, Chafee reiterated the Miltonian marketplace-of-ideas rationale to justify the broad protection of speech and writing: the free and open exchange of ideas helps society arrive at truth. Chafee acknowledged, however, that the recognition of the social interest in the search for truth did not, by itself, determinatively resolve free-expression issues. "[T]here are other purposes of government, such as order, the training of the young, protection against external aggression. Unlimited discussion sometimes interferes with these purposes, which must then be balanced against freedom of speech, but freedom of speech ought to weigh very heavily in the scale." In other words, the social interest in free expression — the search for truth — must sometimes be balanced against other social interests, such as safety and order. But in this balance, courts should give special weight to free expression. "The First Amendment gives binding force to this principle of political wisdom." Chafee concluded by quoting from Hand's *Masses* opinion and by articulating a direct-incitement or overt-acts test. "[S]peech should be free [in wartime] unless it is clearly liable to cause direct and dangerous interference with the conduct of the war."[30]

THE SUPREME COURT AND THE WAR

What would the Supreme Court decide? The first four Espionage Act cases to reach the Court were not argued until January 1919, after hostilities had ended. The first two cases to be argued and decided were *Schenck v. United States* and *Sugarman v. United States.* In *Schenck,* the government indicted Socialist party leaders Charles Schenck and Elizabeth Baer under both section 3 and the nonmailability provision of the 1917 Act. They had printed and mailed to draft-eligible men almost sixteen thousand copies of a leaflet advocating for the repeal of the draft law, which they claimed violated the thirteenth amendment's proscription of slavery. Predictably, given the nativist antiradicalism rampant at the time, a jury convicted both defendants. Holmes wrote a unanimous opinion upholding the convictions.

When Holmes turned to the defendants' argument that the first amendment protected their expression (the leaflet), his opinion became murky. "It well may be that the prohibition of laws abridging the freedom of speech is not confined to previous restraints, although to prevent them may have been the main purpose, as intimated in *Patterson v. Colorado.*" Did Holmes mean that first-amendment protections extended beyond the common law proscription of prior restraints? Holmes, of course, had written the majority opinion in *Patterson.* In that ambiguous case, he had seemingly discussed free expression as an aspect of fourteenth-amendment liberty, though he had also connoted that fourteenth-amendment free expression–liberty equated with first-amendment free expression. Holmes's *Schenck* opinion, consequently, might clarify *Patterson,* given that *Schenck* explicitly addressed free expression as a first-amendment issue. *Schenck* suggests that Holmes's discussion of free expression in *Patterson* should be understood as an exegesis on the first amendment per se. But in *Patterson,* Holmes had emphasized that the "main purpose" of the constitutional protection of expression was to proscribe prior restraints and that the government was otherwise empowered to punish expression. Thus, in *Schenck,* Holmes probably intended to reiterate his *Patterson* position, though he did so with inverted language. He wrote that the first amendment did more than proscribe prior restraints, though that proscription was the first amendment's "main purpose." What, then, did the first amendment proscribe beyond prior restraints? *Patterson* had already answered that question. The first amendment imposed in the realm of expression (speech and writing) the standard republican democratic requirement that governmental actions promote the common good; expression with bad tendencies could therefore be punished. Hence, Holmes proffered, in his view, a prototypical example of unprotected expression: "The most stringent protection of free speech would not protect a man in falsely shouting fire in a theatre and causing a panic." Why so? Because shouting fire in a crowded theater would likely cause harm to other people; the expression would have bad tendencies.[31]

Still focused on the first amendment, in the same paragraph, Holmes next articulated a doctrinal standard delineating the scope of free expression. "The question in every case is whether the words used are used in such circumstances and are of such a nature as to create a clear and present danger that they will bring about the substantive evils that Congress has a right to prevent." Apparently, in light of his invocation of *Patterson,* followed by his example of falsely shouting fire, Holmes did not intend this "clear and present danger" language to delineate a new standard for free expression. Rather, he meant merely to reformulate the customary bad tendency test, adhered to by the Court in the past and by most other courts for over one hundred years. If so, one might still wonder why Holmes did not state the bad tendency doctrine in its more typical language. Most likely, Holmes drew on his understanding of the law of criminal attempts to inform his construal of bad tendency. In *Schenck,* immediately after Holmes articulated the clear and present danger test, he clarified its application in the particular circumstances of wartime. "It is a question of proximity and degree. When a nation is at war many things that might be said in time of peace are such a hindrance to its effort that their utterance will not be endured so long as men fight and that no Court could regard them as protected by any constitutional right." In any particular case, he seemed to say, the discernment of a clear and present danger — or a bad tendency — depended on the circumstances, as guided by legal concepts central to criminal attempts, proximity and constructive intent. When discussing criminal attempts in his book *The Common Law,* Holmes wrote: "Acts should be judged by their tendency under the known circumstances, not by the actual intent which accompanies them." As was his wont, Holmes emphasized his preference for a supposedly objective standard, one that did not turn in its application on the subjective motivations or desires of the actor. "[A]n act is punishable as an attempt, if, supposing it to have produced its natural and probable effect, it would have amounted to a substantive crime." In a close case,

Holmes explained, a judge should consider "the nearness of the danger, the greatness of the harm, and the degree of apprehension felt." From this passage in *The Common Law,* Holmes well might have derived his reiteration of the bad tendency doctrine as a clear and present danger test. Years later, Chafee asked Holmes by letter about the source of his clear and present danger language. Holmes's "hurried answer" did not clearly respond, but he noted: "I did think hard on the matter of attempts in my *Common Law* and [in a couple of cases]."[32]

The same day the Court decided *Schenck,* March 3, 1919, it also handed down the decision in *Sugarman v. United States.* This time, Justice Louis D. Brandeis wrote the unanimous opinion for the Court. Abraham Sugarman had been convicted for violating the 1917 Espionage Act, section 3, for his speech at a Socialist meeting attended by many draft registrants. Sugarman had condemned the war as a "capitalist conspiracy." His appeal to the Court arose from the trial judge's refusal to give, in the precise words requested, two jury instructions related to the first amendment and free expression. The first jury instruction accentuated that first-amendment protections remain in force during wartime. The second was a precise and straightforward statement of the bad tendency standard. The judge combined these two requests into one jury charge and, in so doing, actually articulated a standard more favorable to the defendant than bad tendency. "'A man has a right to honestly discuss a measure or a law, and to honestly criticize it. But no man may advise another to disobey the law, or to obstruct its execution, without making himself liable to be called to account therefor.'" This jury instruction almost required direct incitement of unlawful conduct. Regardless, the Court found it permissible. In his brief opinion, Brandeis reasoned that the judge's "charge clearly embodied the substance of the two requests made by the defendant." Thus, Brandeis either did not acknowledge or did not recognize the difference between the bad tendency test and the judge's charge. Sugarman, meanwhile, had bypassed the Circuit Court of Appeals and had instead invoked a jurisdictional statute that allowed a direct appeal to the Supreme Court for constitutional claims. The Court, having concluded that the jury instruction did not raise a "substantial constitutional question," dismissed the case "for want of jurisdiction."[33]

One week later, March 10, 1919, the Court handed down decisions in *Frohwerk v. United States* and *Debs v. United States,* both with unanimous opinions written by Holmes. Jacob Frohwerk, a copy editor for a German-language newspaper, was convicted and sentenced to ten years imprisonment under the Espionage Act, section 3. He had helped publish articles that denounced the justifications for entering the war as pretenses, yet as Holmes acknowledged, Frohwerk had not made "any special effort to reach men who were subject to the draft." In this regard, the case factually diverged from *Schenck*, where the defendants had mailed leaflets to draft-eligible men. Nonetheless, in upholding Frohwerk's conviction, Holmes reasoned that *Schenck* controlled. "[W]e think it necessary to add to what has been said in *Schenck v. United States, only* that the First Amendment while prohibiting legislation against free speech as such cannot have been, and obviously was not, intended to give immunity for every possible use of language." In other words, the first amendment did not provide absolute protection for speech and writing — not a novel proposition. Even though the record contained no evidence showing that the newspaper had influenced anybody to oppose the war, Holmes concluded: "it is impossible to say that it might not have been found that the circulation of the paper was in quarters where a little breath would be enough to kindle a flame and that the fact was known and relied upon by those who sent the paper out." Holmes's use of this language — "a little breath would be enough to kindle a flame" — reinforces the conclusion that he had not intended his clear and present danger phrase in *Schenck* to articulate a new and more protective standard for free expression. To the contrary, Holmes's subsequent *Frohwerk* language not only disregarded his clear and present danger phrasing, but it also resonated closely with the bad tendency test. Given the facts of the case and the Court's ready willingness to find the writings unprotected, the "kindle a flame" language appeared to be just another way to say bad tendency.[34]

The Court's first decision under the amended Espionage Act (the 1918 Sedition Act) was *Debs v. United States*. Eugene Debs, national leader of the Socialist party, was convicted because of a public speech given at a party convention. His eloquent statement to the district court judge apparently did not help Debs's cause. Just before sentencing, Debs declared that "while there is a lower class, I am in it; and while there is a criminal element, I am of it; and while there is a soul in prison, I am not free." The judge sentenced Debs to ten years imprisonment. At the party convention, Debs had spoken mostly about Socialism, though he had also confided to the audience "that he had to be prudent and might not be able to say all that he thought." He had glorified minorities, according to the Court, and predicted "the success of the international Socialist crusade, with the interjection that 'you need to know that you are fit for something better than slavery and cannon fodder.'" Holmes's opinion, affirming the conviction, explicitly approved a jury instruction that presented the bad tendency test in conventional terms. The jurors, as charged, "could not find the defendant guilty for advocacy of any of his opinions unless the words used had as their natural tendency and reasonably probable effect to obstruct the recruiting service, &c., and unless the defendant had the specific intent to do so in his mind." Based on the doctrine of constructive intent, Holmes allowed that the jury could infer the defendant's intent to obstruct the draft from the likely harmful effects of his words. Any further potential first-amendment issues, Holmes noted, had been "disposed of in *Schenck v. United States*."[35]

At this stage, after the Supreme Court's first four free-expression cases of the World War I era, Holmes had left a distinct impression: he did not consider the free-expression claims to be especially important. Not thinking the claims too important, he wrote his opinions as expeditiously as possible, without as much thought or analysis as he might have accorded to some other cases (though Holmes tended to write many opinions quickly). To Holmes, the four cases were little more than "'routine'" criminal appeals. Previously, Holmes had analogized "constitutional rights of free speech" to "idleness" and insisted that "free speech stands no differently than freedom from vaccination." Thus, in *Schenck*, Holmes finished his discussion of free expression by referring to a recent case that had upheld convictions under the Selective Draft Law, which instituted conscription. "Indeed that case might be said to dispose of the present contention," Holmes explained, "[b]ut as the right to free speech was not referred to specially, we have thought fit to add a few words." This passage is most telling. The Court in *Schenck* for the first time directly and explicitly discussed and decided a free-expression claim under the first amendment, yet Holmes "thought fit" merely "to add a few words" to a prior case that did not even deal with the first amendment. Certainly, an important issue would merit more serious and sustained attention.[36]

To Holmes, the law of free expression seemed perspicuous. Less than a week after the Court decided *Frohwerk* and *Debs*, Holmes wrote to his British friend, Harold Laski, still teaching at Harvard, that "on the only questions before us I could not doubt about the law." Sure about the legal doctrine, Holmes cavalierly used or accepted (in jury charges) various phrases to articulate the ostensibly plain boundary between protected and punishable expression. To Holmes, no significant difference existed, it seemed, between standards that required proof of a clear and present danger (*Schenck*), proof that in the circumstances a little breath would kindle a flame (*Frohwerk*), or proof that the punished expression would generate bad tendencies (*Debs*). If one accounts as well for Brandeis's unanimous *Sugarman* opinion, then the justices, including Holmes, also seemed to disregard any potential discrepancies between a bad tendency and a direct incitement standard. In fact, Learned Hand, after having read *Debs* and *Frohwerk,* wrote to Holmes to accentuate the apparent differences between his direct incitement approach from *Masses Publishing* and Holmes's clear and present danger test. The defendant's "responsibility," Hand explained, should only begin "when the words were directly an incitement." To Hand, a direct incitement test protected expression far more than did a clear and present danger test. Holmes responded by writing that "I don't quite get your point." "[Y]ou say 'the responsibility only began when the words were directly an incitement'—. . . but I don't see how you differ from the test as stated by me [in *Schenck*]." Therefore, Holmes concluded: "So I don't know what the matter is, or how we differ so far as your letter goes." In sum, to the Supreme Court justices, the varieties of phrasing in the sundry cases were all the same. Holmes and the other justices accepted the bad tendency approach, which they had, after all, previously followed (recall, Holmes himself had written two of the prior opinions, in *Patterson* and *Fox*). Given that the Court still operated within a republican democratic regime, with its emphasis on the common good, this approach was thoroughly predictable. Moreover, Holmes apparently did not think the amended Act (the 1918 Sedition Act) raised any novel first-amendment issues; otherwise, in *Debs,* he would not have invoked *Schenck* to deflect potential first-amendment issues.[37]

Baltzer v. United States, an Espionage Act prosecution of German American Socialists that reached the Court even before *Schenck,* does not suggest any other conclusions. Although the justices initially reached a tentative outcome, they ultimately did not decide the case on the merits. Instead, they reversed and remanded on motion of the solicitor general. Of note, while the majority had planned to uphold the conviction, Holmes prepared a dissent, which Brandeis intended to join. This unpublished dissent did not explicitly discuss the scope of protection under the first amendment, but rather focused on statutory construction. The defendants had petitioned the governor of South Dakota to ask that he change the implementation of the Draft Law. Holmes emphasized that the petition was "not circulated publicly" and thus could not constitute an obstruction of the draft under the Espionage Act, section 3. To the contrary, the petition was "an appeal for political action through legal channels." While Holmes believed the case turned on statutory construction, he nonetheless twice alluded to the scope of free expression. Both times, however, he appeared to do no more than express his approval of the bad tendency test, albeit in a somewhat convoluted fashion (as was typical for Holmes). First, he reaffirmed the Court's earlier decisions, which had embraced the bad tendency standard.

"I agree that freedom of speech is not abridged unconstitutionally in those cases of subsequent punishment with which this court has had to deal from time to time." Second, he wrote: "I think that our intention to put out all our powers in aid of success in war should not hurry us into intolerance of opinions and speech that could not be imagined to do harm." At first blush, this language might be viewed as expressing a disdain for suppression during wartime, but a closer look reveals an implicit endorsement of the bad tendency approach rather than the articulation of a more speech-protective stance. Expression is unprotected, Holmes seemed to say, if it can "be imagined to do harm." Indeed, this language might be deemed to be yet another Holmesian reiteration of the bad tendency standard.[38]

In conclusion, the first set of World War I free-expression cases reveal that Holmes, as well as the other justices, viewed free expression as an individual liberty like any other individual liberty under republican democracy. It was important and should be protected, but it was also subordinate to any governmental actions furthering the common good. The government, consequently, could punish any speech or writing that impeded the national effort during wartime because such expression would be deemed harmful or with bad tendencies. The crux of these cases, just as in contemporary liberty of contract cases, was the justices' understanding of the common good. During this period, of course, the Court often concluded that asserted governmental justifications for limiting economic liberties did not constitute the common good but were instead pretexts for furthering private or partial interests, such as the interests of laborers. At the same time, the Court consistently found that governmental justifications for limiting free expression, such as promoting the war effort or implementing the draft, fit within traditional conceptions of the common good. Holmes, though, deferred somewhat consistently to legislative and executive determinations of the common good, whether vis-à-vis free expression or liberty of contract. Holmes even wrote to Frederick Pollock: "I am so skeptical as to our knowledge about the goodness or badness of laws that I have no practical criticism except what the crowd wants."[39]

Holmes admitted what most others failed to recognize: the judicial conception of the common good could never be neutral or objective. Rather, the determination of the common good served as a fulcrum for the turn of political, cultural, and social interests. All the initial World War I free-expression cases involved Socialists and other antiwar proponents, and the Court always found their speeches and writings punishable under the Act and unprotected under the Constitution. During the wartime era, the strong nativist and antiradical sentiments ensured that the salience of any free-expression claimant as an outsider — as a cultural and social alien — would be especially high. Supreme Court justices and other judges were not apt to find such an outsider's written or spoken ideas relevant to community goals. The Court then, and for most of its history, remained a homogenous institution, with the overwhelming number of justices coming from "upper-middle or upper class [old-stock] American social backgrounds." From 1889 to 1919, "[n]inety-four percent of the justices were of Western European origin, fully 83 percent were of English, Scotch-Irish, or Irish derivation, and about four-fifths were Protestant." In sum, "upper class Anglo-Saxon Protestant values" infused the Court. To be sure, the makeup of the war-time Court was more religiously diverse than at most other times — with one Jewish (Brandeis) and two Catholic (McKenna and White) justices — and the justices did not rampage around in a wartime frenzy. Regardless, they succumbed to the allure of patriotic nativism, albeit of a relatively polite nature. Of course, the justices, Holmes included, would never admit to such prejudices. Writing to Laski about the *Debs* decision, Holmes simultaneously denied any bias and proclaimed his disgust with radicals: "I know that donkeys and knaves would represent us as concurring in the condemnation of Debs because he was a dangerous agitator. Of course, too, so far as that is concerned, he might split his guts without my interfering with him or sanctioning interference." Learned Hand was not so sanguine about the neutrality of the justices. "Besides their Ineffabilities, the Nine Elder Statesmen, have not shown themselves wholly immune from the 'herd instinct,'" he wrote. "[W]hat seems 'immediate and direct' to-day may seem very remote next year even though the circumstances surrounding the utterance be unchanged."[40]

THE ESPIONAGE ACT authorized the national government to prosecute its critics only during wartime. Hostilities ceased on November 11, 1918, but Congress did not ratify a peace treaty until 1921. Thus, the government's power under the Act remained ambiguous, and whether authorized or not, the government continued to arrest and harass Socialists, union activists, and the like. In 1919, the cost-of-living index shot upward — by 1920, it was nearly twice the 1916 average — forcing workers to press for higher wages. The brief golden era for labor unions ended abruptly, and the nation immediately succumbed to a wave of violent strikes. Starting in early 1919, nationwide strikes disrupted the steel and coal industries. A shipyard workers' strike hit Seattle and spread into a general strike, immobilizing the city for five days. The Boston police went on strike, and looting broke out. Racial tensions led to riots in several cities, including Chicago and Omaha, where federal troops were summoned to restore order. On May 1, 1919, newspapers reported an assassination plot aimed against several cabinet members, plus Justice Holmes, John D. Rockefeller, and J. P. Morgan. On June 2, 1919, a bomb exploded at the Washington home of A. Mitchell Palmer, who had become attorney general three months earlier. When the Communist Third International formed, "to encourage worldwide proletarian revolutions," American fears intensified that Bolshevism was spreading and causing the societal disruptions. With nativism and xenophobia flaring up, the first Red Scare burst into a conflagration. The American Legion emerged to push forward the 100-percent-Americanism movement; with the war over, a need for unity no longer tempered the drive to conformity. The Ku Klux Klan resurrected itself and flourished. During the war, five states had passed laws proscribing criminal syndicalism; fourteen more states followed suit in 1919. In the summer of 1919, Palmer, with Hoover's assistance, started a campaign to rid the nation of radicals. In the so-called Palmer raids, the government captured Russian immigrants, labor leaders, Jews, blacks, and any other outsiders considered inherently suspect. Deportation or prosecution awaited. Universities such as Harvard and Columbia restricted the admission of Jews, while Henry Ford declared that "[i]nternational Jewish bankers arrange [wars] so they can make money out of them." The black press had existed for decades, but now, in response to growing urban audiences, it increasingly reported the details of racial discrimination. The government reacted by targeting black writers and editors for investigations as Bolshevik revolutionaries. As early as February 8, 1919, the *Nation* recognized that the wartime suppression of civil liberties would not soon end. "The process of turning the thoughtful working people of the country into dangerous radicals and extreme direct actionists goes merrily on." Even though wartime apologists for suppression had refused to admit as much, "[it] required no prophet . . . to foretell that the hatred and intolerance born of war would in due time be turned against unpopular minorities."[41]

This burst of postwar suppression ignited, in response, a resurgence of the tradition of dissent. The aftermath of the war had left Progressives sorely disappointed in two interrelated ways. First, Progressives had believed the United States had fought the war to make the world "safe for democracy." But when Congress had swung Republican in the 1918 elections, Wilson's political strength ebbed. On November 19, 1919, after extensive national debate, Congress defeated the proposed Versailles Treaty and, with it, Wilson's Covenant for a League of Nations. Many Progressives now wondered why America had gone to war in the first place. Second, before the war, Progressives had believed the nation needed centralized governmental power to combat the economic inequities inherent to an industrialized society. Consistent with these views, most Progressives during the war viewed the national government's suppression of draft and war protesters as beneficial to the war effort — as promoting the common good. But as suppression of radical outsiders and others continued after the war, some Progressives began to recognize the potential dangers of governmental power. The national government, they saw, did not necessarily act as an agent for positive social change, for the common good. Too often, nativist and xenophobic biases as well as partisan political interests motivated governmental actors. If the nation had gone to war to spread American democracy, was this irrational suppression of outsiders to be the nation's gift to the world? To counter these problems, some of these disheartened Progressives joined those few intellectuals who had opposed suppression during the war to form an incipient civil libertarian movement.[42]

Thus, voices rose to challenge suppression. And as had sometimes happened in the past — during the 1798 Sedition Act crisis, for instance — potent governmental suppression eventually led to the articulation of formal theories elaborating and emphasizing the tradition of dissent. Ernst Freund, recall, had argued in his 1904 treatise that the tradition of dissent had become de facto constitutionalized and that, therefore, a direct incitement test delineated the appropriate scope of free expression (an approach Judge Hand would subsequently suggest in his *Masses Publishing* opinion). By 1919, Freund's confident earlier assertions had been proven unequivocally false. Nonetheless, in the May 3, 1919, issue of the *New Republic*, Freund criticized Holmes's opinion in the *Debs* case. Since "the war is virtually over," Freund argued, the time had arrived to hear "the voice of reason," yet Holmes had taken "the very essentials of the entire problem for granted." Most important, Holmes's metaphorical analogy between, on the one hand, political agitation including resistance to the war, and on the other hand, shouting fire in a crowded theater was "manifestly inappropriate." Free speech became "a precarious gift" if limited in accordance with the bad tendency standard, which allowed "a jury's guessing at motive, tendency and possible effect." Chafee, too, wrote again to oppose suppression. In a summer issue of the *New Republic*, Chafee lamented how both the state and national governments continued to suppress Socialists and suspected Bolsheviks even though the war had ended. The nation had grown accustomed to "the pleasure of being able to silence" radicals and other outsiders.[43]

The new cadre of civil libertarians faced a difficult intellectual and political conundrum. Many of the new libertarians had for years supported Progressive legislation that opponents claimed violated economic liberties. Courts, these new libertarians had previously argued, ought to defer to the legislatures. For the most part, these civil libertarians retained these views of economic regulations, though they now questioned legislative actions that, from their vantage, violated the liberties of speech and writing. Courts, they suggested, should protect free expression rather than deferring to legislative and executive actions. Thus, the challenge for the new civil libertarians: how could they justify governmental regulations in the economic realm but oppose them in the expressive realm? Some prewar constitutional theorists such as John Burgess and Thomas Cooley, influenced by libertarian concepts, had linked economic and expressive liberties. These earlier and more conservative libertarians had argued that, whether in the economic or expressive realm, government should minimize regulations and thus maximize individual liberty. How, then, could the new libertarians differentiate between economic and expressive liberties? Why should courts be less concerned with protecting liberty of contract while more concerned with protecting liberty of expression?[44]

Chafee attempted to respond to this dilemma in an article published in the June 1919 issue of the *Harvard Law Review* and then in a book published the following year. The article, "Freedom of Speech in War Time," restated and elaborated the argument from his first *New Republic* essay, while the book, *Freedom of Speech,* in turn elaborated and extended the argument from his article. In the *Harvard* article, Chafee quickly arrived at the question that animated his earlier essay: "to determine where the line runs between utterance which is protected by the Constitution from governmental control and that which is not." Chafee reviewed the history of suppression and free expression to show one way *not* to draw the line: through the bad tendency doctrine. Instead, and again like in the *New Republic* essay, Chafee located the line by emphasizing the value of free and open expression in a societal search for truth. Yet, despite the importance of discovering and spreading truth, this social interest did not render free expression an absolute right. Rather, the interest in free expression must be balanced against other social interests, such as security and order. In wartime, specifically, "[t]he true boundary line of the First Amendment can be fixed only when Congress and the courts realize that the principle on which speech is classified as lawful or unlawful involves the balancing against each other of two very important social interests, in public safety and in the search for truth." But, as Chafee underscored, the first amendment mandated that "freedom of speech ought to weigh very heavily in the scale." Given this, what test might identify the border between protected and unprotected expression in any particular case? If the bad tendency doctrine is inappropriate, what test should courts apply? Chafee drew upon the *Schenck* case, decided subsequently to the publication of his *New Republic* essay but before the *Harvard* article. Chafee quoted (and italicized) Holmes's clear and present danger language: "*The question in every case is whether the words used are used in such circumstances and are of such a nature as to create a clear and present danger that they will bring about the substantive evils that Congress has a right to prevent.*" As Chafee rephrased the test in the context of wartime, "speech should be unrestricted by the censorship or by punishment, unless it is clearly liable to cause direct and dangerous interference with the conduct of war."[45]

To Chafee, the clear and present danger test marked the line between protected and unprotected expression. Yet, recall, Holmes had apparently intended his clear and present danger language in *Schenck* to reiterate the bad tendency standard. Chafee meant otherwise, as he unequivocally repudiated bad tendency. In appropriating Holmes's clear and present danger phrasing, Chafee intended to imbue it with greater vitality. Indeed, Chafee construed the clear and present danger standard as if it "substantially agrees" with Learned Hand's direct incitement standard from *Masses Publishing*. Chafee, however, did not equate the two tests. While, according to Chafee, a direct incitement approach focused on the spoken or written words in the abstract, the clear and present danger test required an assessment of their likely effects in the circumstances of the case. Thus, Mark Antony's funeral oration, which "counselled violence while it expressly discountenanced it," would be protected expression under a direct incitement approach but would be punishable under Chafee's iteration of the clear and present danger test. To Chafee, then, "our problem of locating the boundary line of free speech is solved. It is fixed close to the point where words will give rise to unlawful acts." By shaping the clear and present danger test to subsume a direct incitement approach, Chafee transformed clear and present danger from a bad tendency test to a near-overt-acts test. If Holmes's *Schenck* language were to be meaningful, Chafee concluded, then it must protect any speech or writing that falls short of creating "'a clear and present danger' of overt acts." Consequently, as Chafee added in his book, the government can "meet violence with violence, since there is no other method." But when an individual utters words that merely offend us, however seriously, the solution for Chafee is counterspeech rather than suppression. "[A]gainst opinions, agitation, bombastic threats, [the government] has another weapon,—language. Words as such should be fought with their own kind, and force called in against them only to head off violence when that is sure to follow the utterances before there is a chance for counter-argument."[46]

How did Chafee differentiate the emerging civil libertarian position from the earlier conservative libertarian view? How did Chafee justify the broad protection of liberty of expression without analogously justifying the broad protection of liberty of contract? First, he consistently characterized free expression as a first-amendment rather than a due process right. Expressive liberties were not akin to economic liberties. The first amendment extended special protection to free speech and a free press. Second, Chafee stressed that free expression serves a substantial social interest, the search for truth. Even when the government asserted that it had enacted legislation to pursue some other interest, such as public safety, the government would not necessarily have free reign to suppress speech and writing. Instead, a court would need to weigh the social interest in free expression (the search for truth) against the competing social interest. In striking this balance, a court should remember that the first amendment accorded free expression such ample weight that it usually outweighed other interests.

Chafee derived his balancing approach to free expression partly from the Progressive or sociological jurisprudence of his mentor, Roscoe Pound. In two articles published in 1915, Pound distinguished among three types of interests: individual, public ("interests of the state as a juristic person"), and social ("interests of the community at large"). But, Pound quickly added, "[s]trictly the concern of the law is with social interests." In fact, Pound repeatedly demonstrated how social interests took priority over individual interests. The legal system, to Pound, evolved through a balance of various social interests; an individual interest would be legally protected only if there arose a social interest in securing it. The problem, according to Pound, "ultimately is not to balance individual interests [or rights] and social interests, but to balance this social interest [in individual rights] with other social interests and to weigh how far securing this or that individual interest is a suitable means of achieving the result which such a balancing demands." In this regard, the individual interest "in free belief and opinion," or that is, in free expression, was not unique: the law would protect it when it furthered a social value or interest and when other social interests did not outweigh it. Pound and other Progressive jurisprudents did not repudiate republican democracy; they sought to determine the common good more accurately through the empirical evaluation of various social interests. Thus, when Pound advocated for ascertaining the balance among social interests and then pursuing that result, he merely reiterated traditional republican democratic principles, albeit in more sociological and less formalistic terms. Social interests were those values that were relevant to ascertaining the common good.[47]

Likewise, Chafee articulated an argument for an expansive concept of free expression that remained harmonious with traditional republican democratic principles. He did not argue that individual rights or liberties, particularly free expression, took priority over the common good. He did not argue that an individual right to free expression was inviolate. Rather, he argued that in most circumstances the broad protection of free expression was itself for the common good. Chafee acknowledged that there are individual interests, including an individual interest in free expression. But it is the social interest in free expression — the search for truth — that is "especially important," particularly during wartime. The "great trouble" with most Espionage Act decisions, Chafee explained, was that judges viewed free expression as solely an individual interest. And of course, under republican democracy, any individual interest or liberty, despite its importance, was subordinate to the common good, including public safety during wartime. Chafee's argument turned on his identification of free expression with a social interest that courts needed to account for when determining the common good.[48]

Four months would pass between the publication of Chafee's *Harvard* article and the argument of the next two Supreme Court Espionage Act cases, *Abrams v. United States* and *Schaefer v. United States*. During that time, Holmes himself went through a transformation, of a sort. Why? No precise answer can be given, but a number of factors seem relevant. By the time the World War I cases arose, Holmes was in his mid-seventies and had been sitting on the Court for more than fifteen years. He had been raised in a Boston Brahmin family, in the shadow of his father, a renowned writer and doctor (in fact, his father had coined the term "Boston Brahmin"). Despite his many accomplishments, Holmes believed for many decades that he unjustly toiled in obscurity. Sparked partly by his *Lochner* dissent, this seeming obscurity metamorphosed into celebrity during the early 1910s. Numerous luminaries in political journalism as well as in the legal profession, including many young Progressives, praised Holmes and sought his friendship. Croly, Hand, Laski, Lippmann, and Felix Frankfurter were within his circle of admirers. Holmes, quite reasonably, valued his stature among such a distinguished group of acolytes. He wrote to British diplomat Lewis Einstein: "Do you see the *New Republic?* It is rather solemn for my taste; but the young men who write in it are, some of them, friends of mine, which doesn't prevent an occasional, flattering reference to this old man, and I get great pleasure from our occasional talks. They put me on to books that they think will be good for me, and please me by their latent or expressed enthusiasm, and their talent." Holmes would not have wanted to risk his hard-earned and long-denied preeminence among the young intelligentsia. Indeed, a former clerk to Holmes observed that he was "driven by an unusual longing for recognition."[49]

Most probably, Holmes was surprised when his first three World War I free-expression opinions provoked protests from his friends. Less than two months after the Court had issued its *Debs* and *Frohwerk* decisions, the *New Republic* had published Freund's essay reproaching Holmes's opinion in *Debs*. Besides printed criticisms, Holmes's friends questioned his decisions in personal exchanges. On June 19, 1918, even before *Schenck* and *Sugarman* had been argued, Holmes and Hand accidentally met on a train going from New York City to Boston. They discussed suppression, tolerance, and Hand's *Masses Publishing* decision. This chance meeting led to an exchange of letters. Hand not only pressed the superiority of his direct-incitement test but, after *Debs* and *Frohwerk,* he also criticized Holmes's approach in those cases. From Hand's perspective, Holmes allowed juries, "especially clannish groups," too much power to determine guilt or innocence, particularly during times of societal crisis. Meanwhile, Laski often recommended books to Holmes, a voracious reader, and that summer and early fall Holmes read several volumes related to civil liberties, suppression, and the nature of truth. Laski also sent Holmes a copy of Chafee's *Harvard* article. The article had so impressed Laski that he invited Holmes to meet Chafee over tea in July 1919. Before the meeting, Laski wrote to Chafee: "we must fight on it. I've read it twice, and I'll go to the stake for every word." So, for Laski and Chafee, the purpose of the tea was to persuade Holmes to adopt a more speech-protective stance. Chafee, however, thought his teatime chat failed, at least initially. In September, he wrote to Judge Charles Amidon: "I have talked with Justice Holmes about the article but find that he is inclined to allow a very wide latitude to Congressional discretion in the carrying on of the war."[50]

How did Holmes react to these criticisms? At first, he seemed defensive and even peevish. When Holmes began hearing objections shortly after the *Debs* decision, he wrote to Frederick Pollock that "[t]here was a lot of jaw about free speech, which I dealt with somewhat summarily in . . . *Schenck v. U.S.* [and] also *Frohwerk v. U.S.*" Laski soon asked Holmes about Freund's *New Republic* article, which Holmes denounced as "poor stuff." Holmes explained in a letter to Croly, which Holmes never sent: "Freund's objection to a jury 'guessing at motive, tendency and possible effect' is an objection to pretty much the whole body of the law, which for thirty years

I have made my brethren smile by insisting to be everywhere a matter of degree." Chafee, while believing he had not convinced Holmes to change, also believed that his criticisms had stung. In preparation for writing his book, Chafee had jotted annotations in the margins of a copy of his *Harvard* article, including one comment that "Holmes was a bit hurt at this accusation." At some point, though, Holmes's bruised ego recovered enough so that he could contemplate the substance of the various criticisms. Early on, Holmes said he wished the government had not prosecuted so many individuals under the Espionage and Sedition Acts. On March 16, 1919, he wrote to Laski about his first three Espionage Act opinions: "I greatly regretted having to write them — and (between ourselves) that the Government pressed them to a hearing. . . . I should think the President when he gets through with his present amusements might do some pardoning." If true, then Holmes apparently did not believe these prosecutions too important. The government did not need to send Schenck, Frohwerk, or Debs to jail. "I could not see the wisdom of pressing the cases," Holmes explained, "especially when the fighting was over and I think it quite possible that if I had been on the jury I should have been for acquittal."[51]

Chafee's *Harvard* article, then, became crucial; it provided Holmes with a road map. First, recognize that free expression promoted an important social interest — a common good. The war effort and public safety were not the only social interests at stake in an Espionage Act case. Next, Holmes should follow his own clear and present danger test, as initially articulated in *Schenck,* but now with a different gloss. Finally, find that the first amendment protected the speech of a few defendants — insignificant defendants, from Holmes's perspective — whom the government did not need to prosecute in the first place. If Holmes followed this route, marked by Chafee, then Holmes would once again be in the good graces of his young admirers. Holmes may not have wanted to be one of the new civil libertarians, but he certainly hoped to continue being "a figure of authority and eminence" among them.[52]

The government indicted Jacob Abrams and six others for printing and distributing five thousand leaflets in violation of the amended Espionage Act, section 3. One leaflet declared: "'Our' President Wilson, with his beautiful phraseology, has hypnotized the people of America to such an extent that they do not see his hypocrisy. . . . His shameful, cowardly silence about the intervention in Russia reveals the hypocrisy of the plutocratic gang in Washington." Abrams and his colleagues had attempted to distribute the leaflets by throwing them from the roofs of several Manhattan buildings. From the time of the arrests, the result of the prosecutions seemed foreordained. During the postarrest interviews, the police beat and humiliated the prisoners. Subsequent police denials rang hollow given that one indicted defendant died in jail, apparently pummeled to death. Throughout the trial of the remaining six defendants, the judge, former U.S. Senator Henry Clayton, displayed antagonism and bias. Before the defendants began presenting evidence, Clayton explained to the jury: "Now the charge in this case is, in its very nature, that these defendants, by what they have done, conspired to go and incite a revolt; in fact, one of the very papers is signed 'Revolutionists,' and it was for the purpose of . . . raising a state of public opinion in this country of hostility to the Government. . . . Now, they cannot do that. No man can do that, and that is the theory that I have of this case, and we might as well have it out in the beginning." The jury convicted Abrams and four other defendants, with one acquittal. Before sentencing, Clayton complained how he had listened to the defendants' attorney discuss "rot . . . ad nauseam." Yet, Clayton claimed, he sat and listened "to it all because I did not wish by any act of mine to influence the jury." Clayton sentenced Abrams and two others to twenty years imprisonment; one defendant received fifteen years; and the last received three years.[53]

The Supreme Court affirmed the convictions, with Justice John H. Clarke writing the opinion for a seven-justice majority. While Clarke did not appear as biased as Clayton, Clarke's opinion nonetheless accentuated the foreignness and radicalness of the defendants. Brushing aside their argument that the first amendment protected their writings, Clarke reasoned that *Schenck* and *Frohwerk* controlled. Holmes and Brandeis dissented, with Brandeis joining Holmes's opinion. So, for the first time in a decided Supreme Court case, Holmes and Brandeis together voted to overturn an Espionage Act conviction. After asserting the correctness of the Court's previous decisions in *Schenck, Frohwerk,* and *Debs,* Holmes reiterated his clear and present danger language from *Schenck.* "[T]he United States constitutionally may punish speech that produces or is intended to produce a clear and imminent danger that it will bring about forthwith certain substantive evils that the United States constitutionally may seek to prevent." While Holmes acknowledged that during wartime Congress must protect against unique dangers, he insisted that "the principle of the right to free speech is always the same." Thus, Congress "cannot forbid all effort to change the mind of the country." In applying the clear and present danger test to the facts of the case, Holmes stressed that the defendants were "poor and puny anonymities." For Holmes, Abrams and his codefendants were unimportant, their writings were insignificant, and the government should not have bothered to prosecute. "[N]obody can suppose," Holmes wrote, "that the surreptitious publishing of a silly leaflet by an unknown man, without more, would present any immediate danger that its opinions would hinder the success of the government arms or have any appreciable tendency to do so." In short, the government had not proven clear and present danger because the defendants and their writings were so inconsequential. When it came to the twenty-year sentences, Holmes could find only one explanation: the defendants were "made to suffer not for what the indictment alleges but for the creed that they avow — a creed that I believe to be the creed of ignorance and immaturity."[54]

Holmes articulated a theory justifying an expansive concept of free expression under the first amendment. "[W]hen men have realized that time has upset many fighting faiths, they may come to believe even more than they believe the very foundations of their own conduct that the ultimate good desired is better reached by free trade in ideas — that the best test of truth is the power of the thought to get itself accepted in the competition of the market, and that truth is the only ground upon which their wishes safely can be carried out." Holmes then explicitly linked the societal search for truth with the clear and present danger test. "[W]e should be eternally vigilant against attempts to check the expression of opinions that we loathe and believe to be fraught with death," he warned, "unless they so imminently threaten immediate interference with the lawful and pressing purposes of the law that an immediate check is required to save the country." To Holmes, then, the government generally should allow speech and writing to flow into a marketplace of ideas. From this free exchange of ideas, truth will emerge. Harmful ideas must be met with better ideas rather than with force or suppression. The only ideas (speech and writing) that should be restricted are those that would inhibit the further exchange of ideas. Which ideas would inhibit further exchange? Those that would engender a clear and present (or imminent) danger of unlawful or harmful conduct.[55]

Holmes rarely acknowledged the influence of others, and in this instance, he followed to form. Without admitting as much, Holmes largely followed Chafee's road map. As suggested by Chafee, Holmes claimed that society's search for truth required the broad protection of free expression. As suggested by Chafee, Holmes appropriated his own clear and present danger language from *Schenck,* now with a new gloss. Instead of equating clear and present danger with bad tendency, he reinterpreted it as highly protective of expression. And as suggested by Chafee, Holmes found that the first amendment protected the speech of a few (insignificant) defendants. Eventually, in a letter to Laski on December 17, 1920, Holmes called Chafee's *Harvard* article "first rate," though he still did not openly admit that it had influenced him.[56]

Yet, Holmes did not follow Chafee's directions exactly. Holmes added a few turns of his own. Unlike Chafee, Holmes explicitly analogized the societal search for truth to the economic marketplace — "the best test of truth is the power of the thought to get itself accepted in the competition of the market." Holmes here more than turned a clever phrase. Of course, neither Holmes nor Chafee invented this basic rationale for free expression, that a free exchange of ideas would lead to truth; it traced back to Milton and had been reiterated in 1859 by the British philosopher John Stuart Mill (in fact, Holmes had recently reread Mill's *On Liberty*). Regardless, while Chafee, in invoking this rationale, might have been more interested in separating free expression from economic liberties, Holmes seized upon the current, if controversial, passion for the economic marketplace to bolster his argument. Chafee talked of the value of "unlimited discussion," but Holmes suggested that ideas (speech and writing) operated like products in a marketplace. Consumers should have the opportunity to choose, unburdened by governmental restrictions — whether choosing products or ideas. At the same time, Chafee's article might have implicitly suggested the marketplace metaphor to Holmes. When Chafee articulated his search-for-truth rationale, he mentioned the English journalist Walter Bagehot, who wrote extensively on economic and political issues. Thus, while Chafee did not expressly analogize the search for truth to an economic marketplace, he alluded to economics through his reference to Bagehot (and Bagehot himself, in his political writings, subscribed to the search-for-truth theory). The erudite Holmes, who occasionally referred to Bagehot in letters, most likely understood Chafee's allusion and rendered it more striking and precise. Even though Holmes had dissented in *Lochner v. New York,* partly because he believed the majority had overemphasized the importance of an unregulated economic marketplace, Holmes recognized in *Abrams* that a marketplace metaphor would vividly symbolize to his contemporaries a realm largely beyond governmental control.[57]

Holmes departed from Chafee in additional ways. Holmes explicitly linked the search-for-truth rationale to the clear and present danger test. Intertwined together, both the rationale and the test seemed stronger. The search for truth no longer was a mere academic theory; now it appeared to have specific and concrete doctrinal implications. And the clear and present danger test became more than a doctrinal framework that might help resolve cases. Shaped (or reshaped) by Holmes's hands, it became a solid doctrinal structure arising from a firm philosophical foundation. Finally, though unclear, Holmes's rendition of the clear and present danger test in *Abrams* may not have been as rigorous as Chafee would have wanted. In his *Harvard* article, Chafee sculpted clear and present danger to be a near-overt-acts test. Holmes's dissent, to be sure, invigorated clear and present danger by grounding it on the search for truth, but Holmes appeared unwilling to push the clear and present danger test to the same extreme as Chafee had done.

Regardless of the precise points at which Holmes either followed or departed from Chafee's analysis, Holmes undoubtedly had changed. Viewed from an external standpoint, Holmes's conception of free expression transformed. Recall, in previous cases, Holmes had consistently voted to uphold the criminal punishment of speech and writing. And in a long list of those cases—*Debs, Frohwerk, Schenck, Fox,* and *Patterson*—he had written the majority opinion. Thus, Holmes's dissenting vote in *Abrams,* together with his rationale for dissenting, that the first amendment protected the defendants' writings, demonstrated a significant change. True, Holmes's unpublished dissent in *Baltzer* had revealed a willingness to strike down an Espionage Act prosecution. Even so, his *Baltzer* dissent had focused on statutory construction, and where it alluded to free expression, it had reiterated the bad tendency standard (expression is unprotected if it can "be imagined to do harm"). Holmes's subsequent reiterations of the bad tendency approach in *Schenck, Frohwerk,* and *Debs* underscored that he had not intended to repudiate that standard in *Baltzer.* Thus, when Holmes applied the clear and present danger test rigorously in *Abrams* to argue that the convictions should be overturned, he was not applying the same test that he had applied in *Schenck,* where clear and present danger equated with bad tendency. The *Abrams* clear and present danger test was an innovative doctrinal standard for determining the scope of free expression, a standard far more protective than any before articulated by the Supreme Court. In sum, Holmes's vote to dissent in *Abrams* and his expressed rationale justifying his dissent appeared to suggest an unprecedented appreciation, on Holmes's part, for free expression and its contributions to society.

Yet, from an internal standpoint, Holmes never personally believed— and thus never publicly admitted—that he had changed. At most, Holmes eventually acknowledged to Chafee in June 1922 that he had "wrongly" accepted the Blackstonian view of free expression. Otherwise, Holmes consistently maintained both that the Court's prior free-expression decisions were all correct *and* that he had always believed strongly in free expression, even though neither he nor the Court had ever previously found any specific speech or writing constitutionally protected. At the outset of his *Abrams* dissent, when he turned to the first-amendment issue, he immediately reaffirmed the correctness of the Court's earlier decisions in *Schenck, Frohwerk,* and *Debs.* Then, in a letter to Pollock written just over a month after the Court decided *Abrams,* Holmes again defended his earlier decisions, arguing that his votes in the first cases were justified on the facts. Yet, in an October 26, 1919, letter to Laski, written after Holmes had decided to dissent in *Abrams* but before the Court handed down the decision, Holmes declared: "I hope I would die for [freedom of speech] and I go as far as anyone whom I regard as competent to form an opinion, in favor of it." He repeated that sentiment, his willingness to "die" for free expression, in a letter written to Pollock on the same day. As a general matter, Holmes rarely admitted that he had been wrong or had changed his mind on any issue. Thus, in his October 26 letter to Pollock, Holmes unsurprisingly added: "It is one of the ironies that I, who probably take the extremest view in favor of free speech, . . . have been selected for blowing up." That is, from Holmes's vantage, he did not deserve to be criticized; his friends had been mistaken. In Holmes's next letter to Pollock, only days before the Court handed down *Abrams,* he explained that he was "stirred" about a dissent he had sent to the other justices. He then wrote: "I feel sure that the majority will very highly disapprove of *my saying what I think,* but as yet it seems to me my duty." "Now!" with his *Abrams* dissent, he seemed to say to his friends, "I will show you how I really feel (or think) about free expression — in terms that you cannot misunderstand."[58]

How could Holmes change his position on free expression so significantly without admitting as much to himself or to others? Chafee's road map helped. It provided Holmes with the precise terms that, when adopted by Holmes, would plainly show his friends his true commitment to free expression. Plus, since Chafee himself had appropriated Holmes's clear and present danger language from *Schenck,* Holmes could follow Chafee while still insisting that he was consistently following his own position, as previously established in *Schenck.* Through the traditional judicial mechanism of analogical reasoning — reasoning from one case to another — Holmes could maintain in *Abrams* that he merely followed the principle of an earlier case, *Schenck*—even if, in reality, the application of the clear and present danger test in *Abrams* resembled that in *Schenck* only nominally. Moreover, Holmes *sincerely* proclaimed that he had always believed in free expression — *but* it was the free expression that the majority of jurists and legal scholars believed in at the time. It was free expression as a liberty within a regime of republican democracy, a liberty subordinate to governmental actions for the common good. When Holmes followed Chafee's road map, his conception of free expression remained unchanged — a liberty subordinate to governmental actions for the common good. But following Chafee, Holmes for the first time gave free expression itself significant value when determining the common good, even if Holmes neither recognized nor acknowledged any novel appreciation, on his part, for speech and writing.

Finally, Holmes could readily flip-flop his position on these free-expression cases, whether he admitted it or not, exactly because he did not consider them too important. To Holmes, even after *Abrams,* these cases were mundane criminal appeals. In the October 26 letter to Pollock, written after Holmes had prepared his *Abrams* dissent, Holmes expressed the "hope that we have heard the last . . . of the Espionage Act cases." Even after Holmes had written his *Abrams* dissent articulating a rigorous clear and present danger test, he still believed that free-expression cases were not worth much time or energy. In the entire series of Espionage Act cases, from Holmes's perspective, the government had acted no less silly than had the defendants. The defendants had spoken or written nonsense, Holmes believed, and the government had prosecuted them for it. Surely, the government should have attended to more important matters, especially during a war. As Holmes explained in a letter to Hand, people tended "to fight" about issues that they intensely cared about; on other issues, they would bend. With regard to the issue of free expression, Holmes did not care enough to fight. In a July 7, 1918, letter to Laski, Holmes wrote: "My thesis would be (1) if you are cocksure, and (2) if you want it very much, and (3) if you have no doubt of your power — you will do what you believe efficient to bring about what you want — by legislation or otherwise." But, Holmes added, "In most matters of belief we are not cocksure — we don't care very much — and we are not certain of our power." Holmes himself just did not "care very much" about free expression.[59]

Despite Holmes's indifference toward free expression, he succeeded wildly in regaining the good graces of his acolytes, who now showered him with fawning praise. Just two days after the Court decided *Abrams,* Laski wrote to Holmes: "amongst the many opinions of yours I have read, none seems to me superior either in nobility or outlook, in dignity or phrasing, and in that quality the French call *justesse,* as this dissent." Frankfurter expressed "the gratitude and . . . the pride I have in your dissent." Writing in the *Harvard Law Review,* Chafee extolled "Justice Holmes' magnificent exposition of the philosophic basis" of the first amendment. In a *New Republic* essay entitled "The Call to Toleration," the editors focused on "the remarkable dissenting opinion of Mr. Justice Holmes," whom they described as "conspicuous at once for his learning, his grasp of juristic principles and his political wisdom." In "memorable words," Holmes had "expressed with unusual breadth and vivacity the theory about the function of freedom of speech and assemblage in the American political system."[60]

SCHAEFER V. UNITED STATES was argued the same day as *Abrams* but decided more than three months later, on March 1, 1920. The government convicted Peter Schaefer and four other defendants under the Espionage Act for publishing a German-language newspaper that had allegedly denounced and falsely reported on the American war effort. Justice Joseph McKenna wrote the majority opinion affirming three convictions; two were reversed because insufficient evidence connected the defendants to the publications. McKenna, in explaining the affirmed convictions, emphasized that the Court would not allow anarchists and enemies of the United States to use the Constitution as a shield when they sought to destroy constitutional government. Once again, the Court applied the Act consistently with the bad tendency standard. *Schaefer* is noteworthy, however, because Brandeis wrote his first free-expression dissent, joined by Holmes. Arguing that the convictions of all defendants should have been reversed, Brandeis focused on the issue of free expression and quoted Holmes's clear and present danger language from *Schenck*. The bulk of Brandeis's opinion then reviewed the evidence and concluded that it was insufficient to prove a clear and present danger. Brandeis explicitly distinguished the bad tendency and clear and present danger approaches and, unlike Holmes, explicitly cited Chafee. Thus, even though Brandeis quoted the clear and present danger test from *Schenck,* he interpreted it as highly speech protective, in accordance with Holmes's *Abrams* dissent and Chafee's *Harvard* article.[61]

The Court upheld yet another group of Espionage Act convictions in *Pierce v. United States,* with Brandeis again writing a dissent joined by Holmes. Like in *Schaefer,* Brandeis focused on showing that the evidence was insufficient to prove a clear and present danger.[62] And in a subsequent case, *Milwaukee Social Democratic Publishing Company v. Burleson,* not decided until 1921, the Court again upheld an Espionage Act conviction. Brandeis dissented, again closely analyzing the facts and again citing Chafee. Holmes wrote a separate dissent, saying little more than that he agreed "in substance" with Brandeis.[63]

Between these two cases, though, the Court decided *Gilbert v. Minnesota,* arising from a state prosecution. Minnesota convicted Joseph Gilbert for making a public speech that violated a state statute proscribing the discouragement of military enlistment. "If this is such a good democracy, for Heaven's sake why should we not vote on conscription of men?" Gilbert had complained. "I tell you if they conscripted wealth like they have conscripted men, this war would not last over forty-eight hours." McKenna wrote the majority opinion upholding the conviction. Gilbert argued that the Constitution protected his speech, and in so doing, he implicitly raised the issue of whether first-amendment protections applied against state governments. The Court, however, bypassed this issue, assumed arguendo that the first amendment applied, and decided the case on the merits. Concluding that the speech fell outside the first-amendment compass, McKenna again, like in *Schaefer*, emphasized that the Court would not allow a defendant to invoke the Constitution as a shield for expression harmful to the nation's interests. Brandeis wrote a dissent that reached the issue of whether the constitutional protection of speech and writing applies against state governments. He located a right to free expression, enforceable against state governments, in the privileges and immunities clause of Article IV: "The Citizens of each State shall be entitled to all Privileges and Immunities of Citizens in the several States." Thus, unlike Holmes and Chafee, Brandeis more closely tied free expression to citizenship and free government, though he also alluded to the search-for-truth rationale. "The right of a citizen of the United States to take part, for his own or the country's benefit, in the making of federal laws and in the conduct of the government, necessarily includes the right to speak or write about them; to endeavor to make his own opinion concerning laws existing or contemplated prevail; and, to this end, to teach the truth as he sees it." Because Congress had "the exclusive power to legislate concerning the army and navy," Brandeis reasoned, citizens had a right to discuss the propriety of any congressional actions related to the military, unless the expression created a "clear and present danger." Regardless, Brandeis did not conclude that Minnesota had violated Gilbert's right to free expression. Instead, Brandeis reasoned that Congress, by passing the Espionage Act, had preempted the field. Congress had left no room for states to pass laws regulating speech or writing related to the war, the draft, and the military.[64]

Gilbert is remarkable in two ways. First, Brandeis took steps toward a theoretical grounding of free expression on free government, steps that neither Holmes nor Chafee had taken. As some of the Jeffersonian Republican theorists had done more than a century earlier, during the 1798 Sedition Act crisis, Brandeis suggested that citizens must be allowed to speak their minds on public issues. Indeed, Brandeis had even earlier, when concluding his *Pierce* dissent, hinted at this connection between free expression and democratic government. Second, Holmes neither joined Brandeis's dissent nor wrote his own. Instead, Holmes concurred in the judgment, though not in the majority's opinion. Why would Holmes have voted to uphold the conviction? Unfortunately, because Holmes did not write an opinion, one is left to conjecture. Several different explanations are possible.[65]

Holmes might have concurred in the majority's judgment because he believed the constitutional guarantee of free expression did not apply against state governments. State governments, according to this position, remained free to suppress expression as they saw fit, subject to other constitutional limitations. But then why would Holmes not write a concurring opinion expressing this important conclusion?

Holmes, in the alternative, might have agreed with the majority's conclusion because in applying the clear and present danger test, as Holmes then understood it, Gilbert's speech was unprotected. Indeed, Holmes wrote to Pollock in December 1919 admitting doubt even about his vote in *Abrams* because the record, after all, might have contained sufficient evidence to support convictions on one of the counts in the indictment. And Holmes might have viewed the evidence in *Gilbert* as being far stronger than in *Abrams,* not because of the content of the respective messages but because of the identities of the respective communicators. Unlike in *Abrams,* where Holmes had described the defendants as "poor and puny anonymities," Gilbert was a prominent Minnesota leader of the National Nonpartisan League, "one of the most successful third-party movements in United States history." Gilbert thus might have wielded real influence. His speech might have induced his audience to question whether the government had contravened free government in deciding to go to war and to institute a draft. To Holmes, then, Gilbert's speech might have constituted a clear and present danger. Again, though, why would Holmes not write a concurring opinion clarifying his interpretation of the clear and present danger test? Perhaps, he did not want to risk losing his friends' praises, still flowing from his *Abrams* dissent.[66]

Then again, Holmes might have concurred in *Gilbert* because he simply had not thought much about the case. Free speech remained a relatively unimportant issue to him. Indeed, he might not have discerned the ramifications of his own *Abrams* dissent (or Brandeis's *Schaefer* dissent, for that matter), not because the issues were too complex for Holmes to grasp — this certainly was not true — but because he did not care. For Holmes, all the talk about free speech was still just talk and not worth a whole lot of time or energy. The world turned because of power. In a letter to Laski written during the war, Holmes explained that the "only limit that I can see

to the power of the law-maker is the limit of power as a question of fact."
Legal doctrine and theory were unimportant if not backed by the threat of
force. "I understand by human rights what a given crowd will fight for (successfully)." He concluded, "when men differ in taste as to the kind of world
they want the only thing left to do is to go to work killing." But if Holmes
did not give the *Gilbert* case much thought — exactly because it was a free-
expression case — why did he concur rather than join Brandeis's dissent
(or dissent without opinion)? Perhaps because, while he willingly garnered
praise for his ostensibly speech-protective *Abrams* dissent, Holmes genu-
inely believed he had never changed his position on free expression. And,
to his mind, his unwavering position still closely resonated with his *Schenck,
Frohwerk,* and *Debs* majority opinions, not with his *Abrams* dissent.[67]

All three possible explanations of Holmes's concurrence in the judgment in *Gilbert* point to one overarching conclusion: even after *Abrams,*
Holmes still did not intend to become a strong proponent of a highly
speech-protective first amendment. He had followed Chafee's road map,
but he had neither adopted Chafee's civil libertarian position as his own
nor seriously contemplated the implications of an expansive concept of
free expression. Thus, when Holmes read a draft of Brandeis's *Gilbert* dissent, Holmes told him, "I think you go too far." In fact, Holmes admitted
that he originally planned to vote to uphold the conviction in *Milwaukee
Social Democratic;* Brandeis persuaded him to dissent. If anything, *Gilbert*
illustrated a persistent difference between Brandeis and Holmes: Brandeis
largely agreed with the emerging civil libertarian position, while Holmes
was, at most, indifferent. Even though Holmes and Brandeis managed
to agree frequently on free-expression issues, they held fundamentally
different views about the potential for individual liberty and societal progress. Not many years earlier, Holmes had written a letter to John Wigmore,
dean of the Northwestern University School of Law, that laid bare a chilling
cynicism. "[D]oesn't this squashy sentimentality of a big minority of our
people about human life make you puke?" Holmes wrote. He denigrated
people who condemn "the sensible doctor and parents who don't perform
an operation to keep a deformed and nearly idiot baby alive — also of pacifists — of people who believe there is an upward and onward — who talk of
uplift — who think that something particular has happened and that the
universe is no longer predatory. Oh bring in a basin."[68]

Brandeis, as a general matter, expressed far more concern about civil
liberties and social progress. He concluded his *Schaefer* dissent with a fore-
warning. "The jury which found men guilty for publishing news items or

editorials like those here in question must have supposed it to be within their province to condemn men, not merely for disloyal acts, but for a disloyal heart." Brandeis thus worried about the future. "Nor will this grave danger end with the passing of the war. . . . In peace, too, men may differ widely as to what loyalty to our country demands; and an intolerant majority, swayed by passion or by fear, may be prone in the future, as it has often been in the past to stamp as disloyal opinions with which it disagrees." One of Holmes's former clerks would observe that "Brandeis feels sympathy for the oppressed, Holmes contempt for the oppressor." Compared with Holmes, Brandeis committed to a broader concept of free expression and ruminated about the doctrine and theory more thoroughly. Unlike Holmes, Brandeis recognized and openly admitted that his understanding of free expression changed after the Court decided *Schenck, Sugarman, Frohwerk,* and *Debs.* Does Holmes, then, not deserve his reputation as one of the foremost Supreme Court defenders of free expression? Unclear. To be certain, Holmes's contributions to the transformation of free expression should not be gainsaid: he wrote the first Supreme Court opinion, his *Abrams* dissent, that suggested free-expression doctrine should harmonize with the tradition of dissent more closely than with the tradition of suppression. Thus, perhaps more so than Brandeis, Holmes changed the thrust of free-expression doctrine. Yet, ironically, Holmes may have turned first-amendment law toward more expansive protections exactly because he thought free expression a mere trifle, not worth fighting for, either to suppress or to defend.[69]

REGARDLESS OF WHO more strongly supported the civil libertarian movement, Brandeis or Holmes, the national government provided crucial sustenance for the developing movement, albeit unwittingly. During the time when the Supreme Court began handing down the second set of World War I free-expression cases, starting with *Abrams,* the Department of Justice, still led by Attorney General Palmer, intensified its campaign of suppression. The Palmer raids became dragnets capturing massive numbers of ostensible radicals. On November 7, 1919, one coordinated raid ranging across eleven cities netted hundreds of alleged members of the Union of Russian Workers; the government deported 249 of the arrestees including the well-known anarchist Emma Goldman in little more than a month. During the first week of January 1920, aided by local police forces, Palmer led raids across thirty-three cities resulting in arrests of between four and ten thousand alleged members of the Communist and Communist Labor parties. Federal and local officers burst into homes, union headquarters and halls, any types of meeting places, even pool rooms, often arresting everyone present. As might be expected in such circumstances, the police arrested many innocent people, held many incommunicado, and conducted illegal searches and seizures and interrogations by intimidation. In Detroit, the government detained eight hundred people for up to six days, herding them all into a single corridor with only one drinking fountain, one toilet, and a stone floor for sleeping. Mere days later, the Speaker of the New York state legislature's lower house refused to seat five recently elected Socialists.[70]

These antiradical paroxysms helped solidify the civil libertarian movement. Liberals and conservatives, both, criticized these acts of governmental suppression, particularly the New York legislature fiasco, which seemed to undermine the foundation of republican democratic government — the right of the sovereign people to elect their own representatives. Republican party leader Charles Evans Hughes, a former state governor, U.S. Supreme Court associate justice, and presidential candidate, as well as a future Supreme Court chief justice, led the New York City Bar Association in a protest of the Speaker's action. Ohio Republican Senator and soon-to-be president Warren G. Harding likewise condemned the action. The Inter-Church World Movement, comprised of twenty-six Protestant denominations, denounced the national government's raids. A committee of twelve prominent lawyers and law professors, including Chafee, Frankfurter, and Pound, did likewise. Working under the auspices of the National Popular Government League, their *Report upon the Illegal Practices of the United States Department of Justice* rebuked the government for "utterly illegal acts which have been committed by those charged with the highest duty of enforcing the laws."[71]

Public denunciations of some prominent citizens as un-American, because they protested against the government's Red Scare actions, fueled the civil libertarian movement even further. Harvard alumni, for instance, pressured both Frankfurter and Chafee to resign their positions on the Harvard faculty.[72] If these men could be persecuted for their beliefs, what had happened to the vaunted American tradition of dissent? Could respectful Americans no longer politely express their viewpoints? Frankfurter was Jewish, which marked him as an outsider, but he was nonetheless a well-regarded Harvard professor. Chafee was not only a Harvard professor, he was an old-stock American of unquestionable pedigree. His mother and father both came from wealthy industrialist families in Providence, Rhode

Island. He earned his undergraduate degree from Brown, worked for three years in the family ironworks business, then earned a law degree from Harvard. He practiced law with a respected Providence firm for three years before joining the Harvard faculty. Neither Chafee nor Frankfurter even hinted at anarchism, Socialism, Bolshevism, or any other radical position. Thus, the persecution of such men, sometimes for merely defending a right to speak one's mind, prompted an increasing number of politically mainstream individuals to wonder: who's next? University of Chicago Law School Dean James Parker Hall expressed this sentiment in a convocation address. Some had questioned and some had defended the wartime Espionage Act prosecutions, Hall said, but "[t]wo years after the cessation of armed conflict we can do better." And two years after the war, some politically mainstream individuals no longer were willing to wait and find out who might be persecuted next. Instead, they committed themselves to the protection of civil liberties. Released from prison in July 1919, Roger Baldwin, the former leader of the NCLB who had refused induction, moved to New York City hoping to lead a reconstituted civil liberties organization. While his wartime organizing efforts had been largely fruitless, by January 1920 Baldwin had persuaded enough former prowar Progressives and liberals to oppose suppression that he could organize the American Civil Liberties Union (ACLU).[73]

From a political standpoint, the ACLU enjoyed a far broader support base than either the Free Speech League or the NCLB before it. Initially avoiding controversial issues of morality, such as obscenity, the ACLU focused on the protection of speech and writing related to public affairs — that is, political expression — including labor relations. Then, within that broad umbrella of public affairs, the ACLU pragmatically accommodated its politically diverse supporters by supporting expression related to any and all political viewpoints. This marked the uniqueness of the ACLU: it did not seek to promote any single political agenda or the interests of any single political group. To be sure, Baldwin's ACLU colleagues included numerous labor leaders, as well as Crystal Eastman (former leader of the pacifist AUAM) and James Weldon Johnson (of the National Association for the Advancement of Colored People, or NAACP). But the ACLU also included several corporate attorneys from New York City. Chafee and Frankfurter played important roles with the organization, and both carefully separated their desire to promote civil liberties in general from the political positions of specific speakers or writers. In the early years of the ACLU, it generally avoided taking controversial stances in litigation, likely to be futile anyway. The organization instead concentrated on nurturing public opinion to support civil liberties. Consequently, the ACLU would track civil liberties violations — Baldwin began each weekly Executive Committee meeting with a report on the civil liberty situation for the week — and would concentrate on publishing pamphlets. Its first early success was in publishing the National Popular Government League's *Report upon the Illegal Practices of the United States Department of Justice*, which helped spark a Senate investigation of the Palmer raids. Finally, while the organization initially stressed education and publicity, some ACLU attorneys pushed from the outset to litigate certain cases, and they did so throughout the 1920s. All was not pamphlets and reports.[74]

WHILE THE ACLU helped generate political opposition to the infringement of civil liberties, public support for suppression remained strong and widespread. In the midst of the Palmer raids, many newspapers applauded the government's actions. On January 5, 1920, the *New York Times* praised "the alacrity, resolute will, and fruitful, intelligent vigor of the Department of Justice in hunting down . . . enemies of the United States. . . . The agents of the department have planned with shrewdness . . . and carried out with extraordinary success, the nabbing of nearly four thousand radicals." Even better, from the perspective of the *Times,* "this 'raid' is only a beginning." The *Washington Post* likewise applauded the Justice Department and added that it "is entitled to the earnest and vigilant assistance of every patriotic citizen in the United States in the task of apprehending the reds." The *Post* fretted that too much attention had been focused on the protection of free expression. "It is quite evident that Congress has not yet enacted satisfactory laws preventing abuse of the freedom of speech, of the press and of public assembly. . . . The time has come when foreign enemy propaganda must be prevented from utilizing freedom of speaking and printing in America for the purpose of destroying America itself."[75]

Later that year, 1920, scholarly articles praised the Supreme Court's *Abrams* decision and criticized both Holmes's dissent and Chafee's first *Harvard* article, "Freedom of Speech in War Time." Corwin reproved both Holmes and Chafee on multiple grounds. Most important, Corwin favored the bad tendency standard over the clear and present danger test and argued that a defendant's (constructive) intent could "be presumed from the reasonable consequences" of the spoken or written words. Moreover, Corwin reasoned that courts in free-expression cases should defer to both jury decisions and legislative enactments. Corwin found unconvincing Chafee's response to the civil libertarian dilemma: distinguishing the judicial treatment of expressive and economic liberties. Chafee had argued that free expression should be accorded extra weight in determining the common good because of its role in the societal search for truth. Corwin argued instead that free expression was the same as other liberties. Therefore, "the cause of freedom of speech and press is largely in the custody of legislative majorities and juries, which, so far as there is evidence to show, is just where the framers of the Constitution intended it to be."[76]

No scholarly article better captured the mood of the times than Wigmore's "Abrams v. United States: Freedom of Speech and Freedom of Thuggery in WarTime and PeaceTime." Wigmore detailed the horrors of the Bolshevik Revolution in Russia and then turned to the *Abrams* defendants. He described them and their activities in incendiary terms accentuating their foreignness. With "nothing American" about them, the defendants appealed to "thousands of alien-born and alien-parented of their own races." Consequently, they published their leaflets in "Yiddish," not in English. Once the American democratic majority decides to enter a war, Wigmore reasoned, it has the right to protect itself from "alien parasites," like Abrams, who might undermine the war effort. In peacetime the bad tendency test remained appropriate, but in wartime "all principles of normal internal order may be suspended." Wigmore found "shocking" Holmes's (and Brandeis's) "obtuse indifference to the vital issues at stake." Finally, Wigmore did not view himself as justifying suppression. To the contrary, he was demarcating, even celebrating, the contours of free expression, pure and simple, a principle that all true Americans fully enjoyed. "Has not the struggle for the establishment of that freedom [of speech] been won, and won permanently, a century ago?" Wigmore asked rhetorically. "Do we not really possess, in the fullest permanent safety, a freedom and a license for the discussion of the pros and cons of every subject under the sun?"[77]

DESPITE SUCH PERSISTENT SUPPORT for suppression, the wartime Espionage Act prosecutions and the postwar Red Scare triggered an important turn in the historical development of free expression. Through the efforts of individuals like Chafee and organizations like the ACLU, the suppression of civil liberties, particularly free expression, shifted closer to the public spotlight. Even though the Red Scare and the concomitant raids ended by mid-1920, the ACLU had been established and continued to pursue its goals. True, the tradition of dissent reached back to before the nation's founding, and free expression had periodically during American history become an issue of moment. But only after World War I and the ensuing Red Scare could one truly refer to a civil liberties "movement." The tradition of dissent now had institutional support. Still, and most significantly, despite this new political movement and despite the propensities of Holmes and Brandeis to protect expression, the overwhelming majority of Supreme Court justices remained committed to the bad tendency standard and a narrow free expression.[78]

CHAPTER 9

Transition to Pluralist Democracy

During World War I, the national government consolidated power to an unprecedented degree due to the needs of modern warfare and in accordance with prewar Progressive demands for centralization. But with the end of hostilities, the government retreated to a less imposing posture. Progressivism, as a political movement, lost its coherence and drive. Warren G. Harding's 1920 presidential campaign called for a "return to normalcy." As he explained in a campaign speech, "America's present need is not heroics, but healing; . . . not revolution, but restoration." The Republican Harding, with the support of many disenchanted Progressives, won the election in a landslide. Calling on Congress to repeal "unproductive and . . . artificial and burdensome" taxes, the Harding administration began slashing federal expenditures. Calvin Coolidge's administration continued the process, so the government's spending, which had climbed to $18.5 billion in 1919, plunged to less than $3 billion in 1927. "If the Federal Government should go out of existence," Coolidge boasted, "the common run of people would not detect the difference in the affairs of their daily life for a considerable time." Apparently, the "common run of people" embraced this state of affairs and exulted in the comforts of the roaring twenties. Certainly, the nation seemed in no mood to burst apart the seams of republican democracy.[1]

THE 1920S

Despite the return to normalcy and the persistence of republican democracy, the steaming pressures that had been building in the nation before the war did not dissipate. Rather, cultural, social, and economic divisions continued to simmer, though mostly out of sight, covered under an apparently secure lid of economic prosperity. After a brief depression at the outset of the 1920s, the nation enjoyed an economic boom. From 1919 to 1929, GNP increased more than 33 percent. Personal income increased almost as momentously. Manufacturing production nearly doubled during the decade. Although unemployment rose for the first two years after the war, it then declined to a low of only 1.9 percent in 1926, far below the prewar percentage of 1916. Many Americans were not just making more money; they were spending it. In fact, they increasingly spent money before they earned it. First introduced in the automobile industry in 1915, consumer-credit buying took off in the 1920s. Besides issuing mortgages for houses, banks and sellers granted loans for cars, vacuum cleaners, furniture, phonographs, washing machines, even kitchen sinks. In 1926, 15 percent of all retail sales were on credit. Given Americans' increased income and their new-found aptitude for buying on installment, total personal consumption expenditures jumped from approximately $55 million in 1921 to over $80 million in 1929. Spending on cars alone zoomed upward nearly 2.5 times from 1921 to 1929.[2]

This economic boom did not happen serendipitously. The three Republican administrations of the 1920s, those of Harding, Coolidge, and Herbert Hoover, all sought to use governmental power to promote business. Despite cutting expenditures, the government managed to provide financial support to businesses through a variety of mechanisms, such as high tariffs that protected American corporations from foreign competition. Coolidge appointed a chair to the Federal Trade Commission who had previously been hostile to the idea of having a Commission in the first place. Hoover, serving as secretary of commerce under both Harding and Coolidge, helped businesses form trade associations that established industry standards in production, accounting, and even wages and prices, all the while skirting antitrust laws. The *Wall Street Journal* proclaimed that "[n]ever before, here or anywhere else, has a government been so completely fused with business." The 1920s was a time when politics effaced societal divisions, when all Americans supposedly shared in one overriding interest, the profitability of business enterprises, deemed in republican democratic parlance the common good. Harding said he "meant to have less of government in business as well as more business in government," while Coolidge declared succinctly that "[t]he chief business of the American people is business."[3]

Despite such proclamations of the common good, the affluence of the

1920s did not spread equally through American society. For most years of the decade, the wealthiest 5 percent of Americans received more than 25 percent of the total annual income. The wealthiest 1 percent usually received around 14 percent of the income and never less than 12.28 percent. Within the working class, profit (or lack thereof) varied. The average hourly earnings for factory workers increased by only five cents from 1921 to 1929. But as little as factory workers gained in this age of prosperity, they did far better than coal miners, who suffered a loss of more than fifteen cents per hour from the beginning to the end of the decade. The difference in wages between skilled and unskilled workers reached record proportions by 1929. Furthermore, not all Americans shared equally in the purchasing power of consumer credit. While many middle-class Americans now bought consumer products on installment plans — including big-ticket items, like automobiles — few low-income workers did so. And when they did "buy now, pay later," they typically limited themselves to small-item purchases, such as phonographs or, maybe, a piece of furniture. One reason for the unequal prosperity was the continued desuetude of the union movement, which fell into disarray after World War I. Union membership sank from 5 million, attained during labor's brief wartime golden era, to less than 3.5 million in 1929. The causes of labor's decline were many, including mismanagement by union leaders, continued resistance by employers, and perhaps most important, governmental antagonism, emanating particularly from the federal judiciary. In Chief Justice William Howard Taft's view, "organized labor was a faction 'we have to hit every little while.'"[4]

TO A DEGREE, the nation's overall prosperity obscured the underlying tensions within American society — including the divisions between management and labor — but mainstream Americans remained anxious about the country's diversity, as the postwar Red Scare and its spasm of suppression had suggested. World War I had severely dampened immigration — in 1918, only 110,618 immigrants arrived — but this downturn proved temporary. Immigration approximately tripled from 1919 to 1920 (with 430,001 immigrants) and then nearly doubled the next year. With this resurgence in immigration, many old-stock Americans found themselves yearning nostalgically for a "homogeneous society," one that would theoretically be "harmonious, held together by shared values and assumptions." Given the long-running strains on republican democracy, virtue seemed to be invoked only in its supposed absence, as a justification for exclusion. The white Protestant mainstream often blamed Catholics, southern and eastern European ethnics, or African Americans for whatever seemed wrong in America. Coolidge declared that the "ability for self-government is arrived at only through an extensive training and education. In our own case it required many generations." Many old-stock Americans did not wish to wait the several generations supposedly needed for racial, ethnic, and religious outsiders to achieve a level of virtue sufficient for republican democratic government.[5]

In this atmosphere, the Ku Klux Klan reemerged, and membership surged. Open only to "native born, white, gentile Americans," the Klan aimed to be a "militant wing of Protestantism," enforcing "100 percent Americanism," particularly "the Protestant moral code." As one Klansman explained, ethnic and religious outsiders threatened American government. "Everybody knows that politicians nowadays cater to all kinds of 'elements' mostly selfish, some corrupt, and some definitely anti-American. They cater to the German vote, the Catholic vote, the Jewish vote, the Italian vote, the bootleg vote, the vice vote, and sometimes even to the violently criminal vote." Despite the Klan's frequent vigilante actions targeting Catholics, Jews, and blacks, many Americans ignored the violence and accepted the Klan as merely another fraternal order, one especially concerned with the political integrity of the nation. In some sections of the country, membership could further political aspirations or promote business. Stores would display TWK (Trade with Klan) signs to generate patronage, while members organized boycotts against Catholic- and Jewish-owned businesses. The Klan, moreover, was not concentrated solely in the South. At one point, approximately 15 percent of Chicago's "eligible population" belonged. From around 1920 through 1925, the Klan exercised considerable political sway, partly because its views resonated with so many Americans. Membership climbed as high as five million — far exceeding contemporary union participation. In Oklahoma, the Klan-controlled legislature impeached and convicted the governor after he publicly opposed their activities. In Oregon, the Klan helped elect a new governor — a Democrat in a strong Republican state — and pushed the passage of an initiative that required all children to attend public schools, effectively precluding parochial education.[6]

The Klan's prominent role at the 1924 Democratic convention emblematized the nation's cultural tensions. The party divided between, on the one side, white Protestant Klan supporters primarily from the South and the West and, on the other side, white ethnic and Catholic voters primarily from the North. The Klan side of the party backed William Gibbs McAdoo, a supporter of Prohibition, while the anti-Klan side endorsed Al Smith, a New Yorker, an Irish Catholic, a child of an immigrant, and an opponent of Prohibition. Smith, quite simply, personified everything that the Klan abhorred. The convention could not settle on a candidate — it was "deadlocked as no other party convention before or since"—until after 102 ballots, they compromised on John W. Davis, a Wall Street lawyer whom Coolidge defeated easily.[7]

Although old-stock Protestant Americans did not unequivocally triumph at the Democratic convention, they nonetheless asserted their preeminence under republican democracy in numerous other ways, suppressing or excluding racial, ethnic, and religious outsiders. Prohibition was but one example, albeit an important one. It not only symbolized old-stock cultural dominance but also implicitly authorized the official infliction of indignities at the street level. Police would daily break into working class homes on the pretense of searching for bootleg liquor. Meanwhile, the postwar increase in immigration combined with xenophobia lingering from the Red Scare to provoke demands for potent immigration restrictions, directed especially at southern and eastern Europeans, particularly Jews and Catholics. Not only Klansmen and their ilk wanted to limit immigration. The far "more respectable" Masons, for instance, complained that "'[t]he Protestant has been practically ousted from political life, the city is Catholic-governed, and schools as well as municipal departments reflect the influence of the Church of Rome.'" During the first half of the 1920s, Henry Ford published a newspaper, the *Dearborn Independent,* that incessantly attacked Jews with traditional anti-Semitic diatribes, claiming Jews controlled American banking, American agriculture, and American journalism. With this tactic, Ford increased circulation almost tenfold within four years to seven hundred thousand copies per week, only fifty thousand less than the nation's best-selling paper. Such xenophobic sentiments readily translated into denunciations of immigrants for a lack of civic virtue and unwillingness to pursue the common good. "The chief argument against the wholesale admission of unassimilable aliens," wrote the editor of *World's Work,* "is that it creates nationalistic and racial blocs which are constantly bringing pressure to bear upon law-making bodies in the interests of their particular nationalities, which do not think like Americans, but which retain indefinitely their European and Asiatic consciousness."[8]

Such nativist and xenophobic sentiments had long been part of the American scene. Yet, the nation had mostly refrained from limiting immigration because industrialists supported open immigration as a source of cheap labor. In the 1920s, industrialists changed their general position. Technological advances had automated many factories and diminished the need for immigrant workers. Plus, in the wake of the Russian Revolution, industrialists feared more intensely the communist tendencies of radical immigrants. Given that many Americans associated Jews with radicalism, a 1920 Congressional House Committee Report on Immigration predictably lamented the large number of recent Jewish immigrants and called for a two-year suspension. A leader of this movement to ban Jewish immigration was the committee chair, Albert Johnson, who relied on a report from Wilbur Carr, head of the U.S. Consular Service (in the State Department): "[The Jews hoping to come to America were] of the usual ghetto type. Most of them are. . . . filthy, un-American and often dangerous in their habits." Potential Jewish immigrants are "[p]hysically deficient. . . . [m]entally deficient. . . . [e]conomically undesirable [and] [s]ocially undesirable: Eighty-five to ninety per cent lack any conception of patriotic or national spirit. And the majority of this percentage is mentally incapable of acquiring it." In 1921, a new immigration law imposed a quota system indisputably favoring potential immigrants from northwestern Europe, and in 1924, Congress tightened the quota. The country would limit immigration to only 2 percent of the number of the foreign born of each nationality present in the United States as of 1890, when few southern and eastern Europeans lived in the United States. The nation now would admit each year a total of less than ten thousand individuals from Poland, Russia, and Romania all combined—countries with large numbers of Jews desperate to escape pogroms—while over a hundred thousand individuals from Great Britain, Ireland, and Germany could still immigrate. Regardless, reliance on the 1890 census was "not discriminatory," claimed a House Committee Report. "It is used in an effort to preserve, as nearly as possible, the racial status quo in the United States. It is hoped to guarantee, as best we can at this late date, racial homogeneity in the United States."[9]

Despite such efforts to exclude immigrants and otherwise to force outsiders to assimilate culturally into the white Protestant mainstream, many ethnic groups resisted the pressure to Americanize. With the statutory stranglehold on immigration, many neighborhood leaders in big cities, like Chicago, realized they no longer could rely on newcomers to sustain cultural ties to ethnic homelands; they needed to fight to preserve their distinctive cultures, especially among the young. Within the respective ethnic enclaves, the communities would provide for their own unemployed and unfit. Ethnic banking institutions formed, making close ties to the community economically profitable. Individuals might buy new-fangled products like phonographs—even purchasing in the American way of "buying now and paying later"—but these individuals would then listen to recordings in their native languages. Rather than shopping in the burgeoning chain stores, which catered to the middle and upper classes, these same individuals would shop with local merchants out of "cultural loyalty." As one Chicago grocer explained, "People go to a place where they can order in their own language, be understood without repetition, and then exchange a few words of gossip or news." People might listen to radio programs, but they often did so in communal groups tuned to local stations. Moreover, few people in ethnic urban neighborhoods felt connected to the national government. If they participated at all in electoral politics, they did so locally, dealing with the dominant political machine's ward boss, who might control the provision of services (like fire fighting) or other benefits (like a street-vendor's license). The national government "seemed of another world, having little significance for or interest in their survival." In short, people in ethnic urban communities remained focused on day-to-day living, not on how they might conform to the mainstream culture. They were being Americanized, but only to a limited degree: the still strong cultural nettings of their respective ethnic communities filtered their absorption of American ways.[10]

ULTIMATELY, THE 1920S was a decade of incongruities. Anxious old-stock Americans appeared to achieve tremendous victories in their quest to maintain their traditional values and government. Prohibition was in place; outsider political participation was minimal, especially at the national level; and most important, immigration had finally been reduced to a trickle. But with these triumphs, old-stock Americans became complacent. They had hammered planks of wood across the door where they had seen ethnic, racial, and religious outsiders pressing for changes. Now the old-stock Americans relaxed in their homes, comfortable in their "enervating satisfaction"; after all, they had shut the door tight, and it couldn't be opened. Yet, in the meantime, other forces of change seeped unnoticed through the windows. By the end of the decade, the regime of American democracy stood poised on the cusp of change.[11]

In 1920, the nation's urban population for the first time surpassed its rural population, but the difference remained minimal, less than three million. But the trend toward urban living continued unabated through the 1920s. By 1930, the marginal difference had increased approximately five-fold; urbanites numbered over fifteen million more than rural residents. Why was this rise of the cities so significant? Because the cities became the nesting grounds for cultural and political pluralism. The cities — from Boston to New York to Philadelphia to Detroit to Chicago to St. Louis to

San Francisco — were where immigrants and their children lived, where the respective ethnic groups competed and compromised, where Americans of different stripes began to develop "a pluralistic vision of American identity that would accord them cultural influence and political power." Southern blacks, too, started an exodus to the northern and midwestern cities and, once there, began to challenge the racial status quo: this was the time of the Harlem Renaissance in art and Marcus Garvey's black nationalism movement, emphasizing commercial success within African American communities (as well as black separatism and a return to Africa). As early as 1915, Horace Kallen had suggested that the growing cities might serve as models for a new type of democracy: "Politics and education in our cities . . . present the phenomenon of ethnic compromises . . . ; concessions and appeals to 'the Irish vote,' 'the Jewish vote,' 'the German vote'; compromise school committees where members represent each ethnic faction." Of course, the nativists had been battling against precisely this type of pluralist democracy, which would recognize the legitimacy of ethnic interests.[12]

Despite the nativists' efforts, the urban upsurge continued, intertwined with another development, the rise of a mass-consumer culture. Not only were many Americans making more money, which could then be spent on consumer products, but industrialists began to focus increasingly on the encouragement of consumption. Searching to find new markets for their products, industrialists eventually realized they needed to look no further than their shop floors. Henry Ford had already introduced methods of assembly-line mass production in his Model T automobile factories. Now, he recognized that he could increase sales for his rapidly produced cars if he could transform his workers into car-buying consumers. To do so, he followed Frederick W. Taylor's ideas on the scientific management of factories: workers would willingly acquiesce in management's severe control of the workplace if they received higher wages and shorter hours. Ford, rabidly antiunion, saw that this approach not only could ease labor-management strains but could increase his sales. He introduced the $5 eight-hour workday even before World War I, and he continued to support his workers' efforts to increase both their earnings and their leisure time (so long as they did not advocate unionizing). With more money and freedom, and with affordable Model T's rolling off the production line, Ford's factory workers became customers. Other industrialists followed the same approach, even welcoming immigrants — typically relegated (with some African Americans) to the least desirable factory jobs — to spend their money just like other Americans on mass-produced items. According to Edward Filene, the Boston department-store magnate, "large-scale production . . . demands increased buying. [The] greatest total profits can be obtained only if the masses can and do enjoy [an] ever higher standard of living. . . . Mass production is . . . production for the masses."[13]

With workers converted into potential customers, industrialists turned their attention toward fulfilling that potential. To accomplish that goal — indeed, to convert any and all potential consumers into active buyers — industrialists relied on advertising, on speech and writing encouraging commerce. Since the industrial revolution of the late-nineteenth century, manufacturers had depended on advertising, but ads had mostly provided consumers with information about the products. These "reason-why" advertisements explained to consumers the utility of the product. The decision to buy, in theory, arose from rational need. In the 1920s, however, advertising strategy changed. Instead of providing useful information, advertisements associated products with an image or lifestyle. In the auto industry, General Motors (GM) pioneered this new advertising; one ad showed "a lushly colored scene of the countryside," with the caption reading, "You find a *Road of Happiness* the day you buy a Buick." Even further, advertisers would attempt to generate desires or anxieties within consumers — desires or anxieties that the consumer could satisfy or resolve by purchasing the product. Thus, unlike in the past, advertisements for toiletries like mouthwash and deodorant became common. As Charles Revson of Revlon, Inc., explained, "In the factory we make cosmetics, in the store we sell hope."[14]

What were the results of these new types of advertisements? First and foremost, they increased sales. One advertising campaign catapulted sales of Lucky Strike cigarettes 47 percent in one year. GM's ad campaigns were so potent that Ford's market share fell from 55 percent in 1921 to 25 percent in 1927. Such success led industrialists to invest ever-increasing amounts of money in their advertisements. Advertising revenues jumped nearly $0.5 billion between 1920 and 1929. Much of that revenue funneled into the emerging mass media. Newspapers, magazines, and especially radio enabled industrialists and their advertisers to reach the largest possible audiences. The first commercial radio broadcast occurred in Pittsburgh in 1920. Within two years, three million Americans spent $60 million purchasing radios. In 1927, approximately one-fourth of American homes already had radios, while three years later, nearly one-half of the households had one. Initially, local radio stations broadcast to their respective insular communities, but before long, networks linked together the stations as affiliates. By 1924, American Telephone and Telegraph operated a network with tentacles reaching into approximately 65 percent of the homes with radios. At the end of 1927, forty-eight affiliated stations participated in the National Broadcasting Company's (NBC) network. Network broadcasting changed the content of radio shows. Instead of having numerous independent stations catering to local community interests, networks standardized programming. They broadcasted shows that appealed broadly to their diverse national audiences. Radio stars like the singer and bandleader Rudy Vallee became celebrities. A mass-media culture developed hand in hand with the developing consumer culture. Network radio provided advertisers with ready entrée into the homes of Americans across the country. Indeed, by 1929, advertising agencies were themselves producing 33 percent of the network radio programs, while corporate sponsors produced another 20 percent.[15]

The rise of this mass-consumer culture had far-reaching ramifications for American society and government. The mass-consumer culture intensified the American ethos of individualism. Mass consumerism depicted the individual as a bundle of desires, then legitimated the individual's focus on fulfilling those desires. And of course consumer culture imbued individuals with the belief that fulfillment was no farther away than the nearest store, where they could purchase mass-produced objects. Besides enhancing individualism, the mass-consumer culture also nurtured a populist egalitarianism. As the decade wore on, the power of the mass-consumer culture encompassed many ethnic and religious outsiders; they were included as part of the buying public along with white Protestant Americans. Even as some ethnic leaders struggled to resist cultural assimilation in their urban neighborhoods, the mass-consumer culture insidiously spread its web through the communities, transforming outsiders into American consumers. Just as network affiliates replaced independent radio stations, chain food stores and movie palaces invaded and conquered neighborhoods by driving independent merchants and theaters out of business. By the late 1920s, ethnic outsiders were subject to "a vast Americanization program," sharing "the same symbolic world" with other Americans through "advertising, radio, and movies — media that painted goods with meaning." Old-stock Americans and ethnic and religious outsiders alike shared a common currency of culture, generated by the mass media and by a craving for consumption. As Dewey observed in 1930, "The radio, the movies, the motor car, all make for a common and aggregate mental and emotional life." A new type of participatory equality spread through the society as advertisers created homogenized individual desires that could be satisfied through the consumption of brand-name products. All Americans (or All-Americans) knew, enjoyed, and purchased Coca-Cola to quench their insatiable thirsts.[16]

Yet, outsiders were assimilating into an American culture that differed markedly from the white Anglo-Saxon Protestant culture of turn-of-the-century America. The new American culture was the mass-consumer culture, shaped overwhelmingly by the corporate quest for profit. Significantly, the mass media—with their corporate centers in the cities—also spread bits and pieces of urban cultures throughout the rest of American society. Dance halls, amusement parks, and vaudeville became respectable forms of entertainment, "'mass' commodities," so to speak. White Protestant America began accepting, whether consciously or not, elements of minority cultures. The legislative restrictions on immigration accelerated this process, as far fewer greenhorns now stepped off the boats and irritated old-stock Americans with their alien ways. Second-generation Americans—the children of immigrants—were often more interested in rebelling against their parents and acting "American" than in preserving their parents' traditional cultures. With the salience of ethnic and religious minorities as outsiders thus diminishing, nativism ebbed. Mass-media heroes included the Italian-immigrant actor Rudolph Valentino and the iconic baseball player Babe Ruth, raised in a "poor Catholic immigrant family." The KKK quickly shrunk in size and influence, while the American Jewish Committee (AJCommittee) secured an apology and retreat from Henry Ford in 1927 for his earlier anti-Semitic vendettas. European immigrant groups were less and less demarcated as belonging to separate races. Now, they were often designated as Caucasians, and as such, they could still retain subcultural remnants—their ethnicities. An individual could "participate in a common material culture without necessarily giving up 'who you really are.'"[17]

This "racial alchemy" also underscored that the populist egalitarianism of the mass-consumer culture had its limits. Even while the so-called Caucasian race gradually absorbed ethnic outsiders, the white Protestant mainstream pressured the erstwhile outsiders to discriminate against non-Caucasians. Numerous immigrant families included restrictive covenants in house-sale contracts, thus precluding black families from moving into immigrant neighborhoods. In one telling instance, the secretary of labor expressed incredulity when ethnics refused to acquiesce: "[A]re the American people to understand that the Union of American Hebrew Congregations does not believe in the exclusion of Orientals? Your Resolution clearly indicates that you would throw down the bars and admit the Chinese and other Eastern races indiscriminately. [T]o truly American peoples . . . [these Orientals] will never become assimilated into a united American Republic. They are not of us." Most distinctly, though, African Americans did not become Caucasians. Instead, they were segregated in places of public accommodation, like theaters, and in public activities, like professional baseball, in the North as well as in the South. While movies, theater, and radio facilitated the cultural absorption of European ethnics, the mass media parodied blacks and banned black performers.[18]

With such racialized exceptions, then, many outsiders became at least marginal insiders. As such, they forged new bonds among themselves. Employers unwittingly accelerated this process. Aiming to break the workers' loyalties to their ethnic communities, the employers purposefully mixed together workers from different ethnic and religious backgrounds. Plus, the employers sought to isolate the workers by offering them incentives for increased individual production. Employers believed that, once they had individuated the workers and snapped their traditional communal ties, the workers would become enthusiastically committed to their companies and occupations. In fact, the employers' strategies worked effectively—they altered the cultural orientations of many workers—but not in the direction that the employers had planned. Assisted by their shared participation in the mass-consumer culture, the workers realized new communal and political ties among themselves, as workers qua workers, while retaining their original ethnic identities (albeit in diluted form). By the late 1920s, far more so than immediately after World War I, workers from different ethnic communities could talk together—in English—while they worked side by side. They could discuss the same movies, they could laugh about the same radio shows, and they could pine for the same mass-produced objects. They realized that they shared certain work-related problems, and that by joining together, they might resolve their mutual problems satisfactorily. Employers ironically had equipped workers with the tools needed to press for unions and to challenge the employers' hegemony. In hard times, like during a strike, workers still shared their "common cultural life"; they could still debate about which baseball player would hit the most home runs or what popular song was best. Workers enjoyed an enhanced political solidarity, seeing themselves as more of a coalition. To be sure, their previous experiences with politics tended to be limited. City dwellers, including immigrants, had dealt with local machine politicians who could satisfy basic needs, yet some of these urbanites gradually expanded their political awareness during the 1920s, even to the national level. Compared with their immigrant parents, second-generation children were more comfortable with American ways, as well as with speaking English, and thus were more apt to be conscious of and to participate in politics. Moreover, national governmental actions like Prohibition and the restriction on immigration often struck directly at immigrant families, provoking greater attention to national politics.[19]

The presidential election of 1928 revealed the potential ramifications of this political shift. The Republican candidate was the former Secretary of Commerce Herbert Hoover. The Democratic candidate was none other than Al Smith, the unsuccessful anti-Klan candidate from the deadlocked 1924 convention. Now, in 1928, he became the first Catholic nominated by a major party. He was the first presidential candidate to favor the repeal of Prohibition. And he was a four-time governor of New York who reveled in his Lower East Side (Manhattan) identity: "The derby hat set at a slightly rakish angle, the flashy suits, the big cigar, the slight swagger, the striking pronunciations all bespoke New York." Smith represented what William Jennings Bryan had called "the enemy's country." The Smith-Hoover confrontation symbolized the nation's multiple interrelated divisions: "Catholics versus Protestants, wets versus drys, immigrants versus natives, and city versus country." Smith's nomination therefore partly resulted from the urban ethnic outsiders' already-enhanced political consciousness, but he also struck a spark that further inflamed their future active political participation. He successfully mobilized many such citizens to vote for the first time in a national election. The percentage of eligible citizens who voted jumped nearly 10 percent from 1924, as Smith won the nation's twelve largest cities, all of which had gone Republican in the previous two elections. Moreover, even though the North had been solidly Republican since the Civil War, he carried 120 northern counties, 77 of which were predominantly Catholic. Smith's candidacy showed that the nativists' strikes against outsiders, particularly the 1924 cut in immigration, came too late to preserve white Protestant hegemony. By 1928, immigrants and their children constituted approximately one-third of the American population. When this demographic transformation combined with, in particular, the force of the mass-consumer culture, the salience of ethnic, immigrant, and religious minorities as outsiders diminished to the point that they could participate politically far more than ever before.[20]

The citizenry had become more diverse, and politics became more pluralistic. If individuals could express their desires in the economic marketplace, then why not in politics? Numerous voluntary organizations formed as mechanisms for individuals to voice their interests and values, and while many such organizations had long existed, they now openly advocated to achieve political goals, institutionalizing a "new lobbying." Racial, religious, and ethnic minorities joined organizations like the NAACP, the National Catholic Welfare Council (NCWC), and the AJCommittee. Many organizations represented professional groups, including doctors, lawyers, and educators. Small businessmen formed chambers of commerce. By the mid-1920s, more than 150 lobbying groups had established offices in Washington, D.C. World War I had contributed to the legitimation of this new lobbying. When President Wilson and Congress had worked to centralize power to strengthen the war effort, they had enlisted the aid of various private associations — even the AFL — to help coordinate the work of war. While national governmental power receded after the war, the precedent had been set for cooperation between voluntary associations and the government. Moreover, the wartime government itself, through its Committee on Public Information, demonstrated how organized propaganda efforts could shape public opinion. Many of the emerging lobbying groups in the 1920s sought to do exactly that, to shape public opinion in favor of their respective memberships.[21]

While politics became more pluralistic, the republican democratic regime did not yet collapse. Much of the nation might have been ready for a transformation of democratic practices, but resistance remained strong. Smith lost the election, and decisively so, garnering only 15 million popular and 87 electoral votes to Hoover's 21 million popular and 444 electoral votes. Smith ran poorly in most areas with large native-born populations, including the traditionally strong Democratic South, where he lost almost all major cities, including Birmingham, Dallas, and Atlanta. Most distinctly, Smith lost votes because of his Catholicism. "Protestant opposition to Smith's religion was remarkably widespread, extending to all regions of the nation, to city and country, to church members and unaffiliated Protestants." Anti-Catholicism was a traditional mode of American nativism, but it's salience intensified in the 1928 presidential election exactly because of Smith's candidacy. The *Christian Century*, a liberal Protestant publication, encouraged its readers to resist "the seating of a representative of an alien culture, of a mediaeval Latin mentality, of an undemocratic hierarchy and of a foreign potentate in the great office of President of the United States." The denunciations of Smith as an outsider were as pointed as a bloody dagger. "I'd rather see a saloon on every corner in the South than see the foreigners elect Al Smith President!" proclaimed an Alabama reverend.[22]

Hence, while religious, racial, and ethnic minorities may have begun participating in national politics, they certainly were not yet welcome participants. Smith recognized that his ties to the national populace were tenuous. He ran as an economic conservative and, like Hoover, invoked the republican democratic principles of virtue and the common good. Whereas Protestant nativists castigated Smith for his Catholicism, Smith and other

Democrats realized they should not attempt to attract Catholic voters qua Catholics. Democratic supporters did not "launch a sectarian campaign on behalf of Al Smith," but rather called for religious freedom. This hesitancy of outsiders, gingerly stepping into the political arena, also appeared in the new lobbying. Through the 1920s, many Americans were still ambivalent "about the expansion of pressure groups," even as lobbying efforts grew. Numerous commentators allowed for lobbying but only if supposedly for the common good rather than for private interests. A 1929 article in the *North American Review* argued that lobbyists benefited public purposes when they provided legislators with needed expert knowledge: lobbying organizations served as a "clearing house for the views of the 'best minds' in the particular group concerned." Partly for that reason, the organizations representing racial, religious, and ethnic minorities — like the NAACP, the NCWC, and the AJCommittee — remained cautious about overtly lobbying for their members' interests. Put in different words, these organizations responded to forces of suppression discouraging political expression that might swerve too far from the mainstream.[23]

THE MODERN INTELLECT, THE GREAT DEPRESSION, AND THE DOUBTING OF DEMOCRACY

During the late-nineteenth and early-twentieth centuries, the emergence of the interrelated attitudes of historicism and secularism had marked an intellectual transition from premodernism to modernism. Intellectuals reasoned that, unleashed from religious constraints, human ingenuity could engender potentially endless societal improvement. Driven by human inventiveness, history could be a tale of progress, not a repetitive and cyclical story of the rise and fall of one civilization after another. Yet, many Americans clung to the certainties of a premodern worldview; certainties that, they believed, supported the American way of life. The Scopes monkey trial, more than any other single event from the 1920s, epitomized this confrontation between modernism and premodernism. Protestant fundamentalism first emerged in the late-nineteenth century in reaction against the increasing secularism of science, though it gained its name only after the publication of a series of articles, "The Fundamentals," from 1909 to 1915. After World War I, the movement grew stronger, especially when Woodrow Wilson's former secretary of state, the great populist William Jennings Bryan, joined the fight. Fundamentalists saw themselves in pitched battle against the forces of modernity. One fundamentalist blazoned: "The Modernist juggles the Scripture statements of His deity and denies His virgin birth, making Him a Jewish bastard, born out of wedlock, and stained forever with the shame of His Mother's immorality." Fundamentalists stressed the Darwinian theory of evolution as symbolizing the modernist challenge to scripture, and in this battle, the state of Tennessee became a fundamentalist stronghold. The state constitution prohibited the establishment of religion, but it also proclaimed that "[n]o person who denies the being of God, or a future state of rewards and punishments, shall hold any office." Not only were school prayers common, but a state statute mandated all public school teachers to read verses from the Protestant Bible each day. Then, in early 1925, the state legislature enacted a law proscribing public school teachers from teaching "any theory that denies the story of the divine creation of man as taught in the Bible and teaches instead that man has descended from a lower order of animals." Within months, a high school biology teacher, John Scopes, agreed to violate the law, invite prosecution, and serve as a test case. Bryan volunteered to prosecute the case for the state, while the famed Clarence Darrow, an avowed agnostic, assumed Scopes's defense.[24]

The case pitted the modernists' reliance on scientific expertise against the fundamentalists' faith in the plain meaning of the Protestant Bible. According to Bryan, "It is better to trust in the Rock of Ages than to know the age of rocks; it is better for one to know that he is close to the Heavenly Father than to know how far the stars in the heavens are apart." As was often true throughout the decade, the reactionary forces appeared to win the battle. Tennessee convicted Scopes and fined him $100. Yet, the modernist forces of change churned onward. During the trial, the judge ruled that Darrow could not present expert evidence probative of the theory of evolution. Momentarily stymied, Darrow cleverly decided to call Bryan himself as an expert witness on the Bible. Bryan and other fundamentalists insisted that any common person could understand the Bible because it was to be read literally; interpretation was unnecessary. But in response to Darrow's questioning, Bryan admitted the biblical depiction of the six-day creation might not mean, literally, that God had made the world in 144 hours. The biblical day might be equivalent to years. Bryan, in other words, imposed an interpretive gloss on the biblical text that implicitly undercut the fundamentalist tenet of literalism. The trial had become a mass-media circus — hundreds of reporters attended — and the clear contemporary public verdict was that Darrow had shown Bryan to be a fool. The nation would change — modernism would march forward — even if many might prefer otherwise.[25]

HOOVER WON THE 1928 election by a landslide, but he would only briefly enjoy his victory. Inaugurated on March 4, 1929, Hoover faced an economic slowdown by the fall of that year. Despite the development of consumer credit, many workers could not afford to buy the mass of products they helped manufacture. Consequently, overproduction and underconsumption threatened the nation's economic stability, particularly that of the overinflated stock market. Partly because of, in Hoover's words, an "orgy of mad speculation," some stock market prices had skyrocketed to the point where they "had no discernible relation to values." Radio Corporation of America, for instance, soared from $94.5 per share in March 1928 to $505 per share in September 1929! Much stock buying was on margin; the buyer would put up a minimal amount of cash and borrow the rest. So long as the stock prices continued their climb, all was fine. But if prices fell, the broker would need to call in the loan. The stockholder then would be forced either to sell or to invest more cash. Thus, a drop in prices could lead to a cascade of sales, which would cause another drop in prices, and another cascade of sales, and so on. In early September 1929, it began; prices started to drop. On Wednesday, October 23, the selling of shares accelerated so quickly that the market's telegraphic ticker could not keep pace. The next day, Black Thursday, losses at one point reached $9 million. The worst was yet to come. Black Tuesday, October 29, started a steady three-week spiral downward that left stocks at one-third their value from two months earlier. Whether the crash caused the Great Depression or merely marked its beginning, the age of prosperity had ended.[26]

With the Depression following on the heels of the 1920s affluence, the plunge for many to economic deprivation was jarringly quick. The ranks of the unemployed leaped nearly fivefold in two years, from 3.2 percent of the labor force in 1929 to 15.9 percent in 1931. Two years later, unemployment had climbed to nearly 25 percent, a staggering figure, even higher among nonagricultural workers. Between 1929 and 1933, nearly one-third of the nation's factories closed. In that same time, GNP fell 29 percent. Many of the large industrial cities were hit the hardest; the unemployed sometimes constituted a voting majority. In 1931 Chicago, 57.2 percent of unskilled and 40.4 percent of skilled workers were unemployed. In Detroit, unemployment hovered around 50 percent. For those lucky enough to work, wages tumbled precipitously. In Chicago, the payroll index plummeted nearly 75 percent in four years. In Detroit, average weekly earnings fell by 67 percent in two years. Rural agricultural workers suffered as well. Annual average worker income fell by 42 percent between 1929 and 1933, while the total value of farm property dropped 36 percent. Employers usually fired African Americans first, whether in factories or on farms, so black unemployment, nearly 50 percent nationwide by 1932, was almost always higher than the norm. As one elderly observer noted, "The Negro was born in depression. . . . It only became official when it hit the white man."[27]

In many ethnic urban communities, the unemployed and unfit did not initially seek assistance from the government. Rather, consistent with prior practices, they depended on their local communities for support. Neighborhood institutions could help the needy tide over until their fortunes turned, or so it seemed at first. Of course, few fortunes turned, at least not for the better. The depth and length of the crisis drained these traditional neighborhood institutions, often to destruction. The Depression, consequently, accelerated the decay of ethnic cultures and communities. Individuals lost their faith in their "benefit societies, churches, banks, building and loan associations, and neighborhood stores." When these people finally sought governmental assistance, they mostly were rebuked. One unemployed worker, after spending another futile day at a state employment office, grumbled, "God, I'm disgusted with this place, and everybody else is that I know. Some fine day a mob's going to drop down on this place and tear it apart." Before long, people were organizing massive protest demonstrations that sometimes ended with looting, especially in quests for food. Poor people would band together in rent riots to fight evictions. Desperate people would take desperate actions, sometimes leading to tragedy, as when Detroit police fired on marching unemployed workers, killing four and wounding others.[28]

When the Depression first began, many Americans blamed the unemployed and destitute for their problems; if they were poor, they must have purposefully chosen not to work hard or not to work at all. When unemployment continued to increase, however, these attitudes softened. Then, as local institutions proved incapable of dealing with the mounting crisis, a growing number of Americans called for national governmental action. Hoover's earlier success as secretary of commerce, contributing to the 1920s prosperity, had earned him the nickname the "Great Engineer." He now came under pressure to construct some type of relief and recovery for the nation. Hoover, in fact, took action, but he generally opposed governmental regulation of business and was ill disposed to expanding national power. He believed the Depression was due more to "unsound institutions of Europe" than to American economic mistakes or deficiencies. Ironically, and tragically, the Great Engineer's attempted remedies proved far "too cautious" for the exigencies at hand. Whereas the interrelated rises of the cities and the mass-consumer culture had laid the foundation for a transformation of democracy, the Depression motivated Americans to crave a transition. More so than any other factor, the deepening Depression altered Americans' attitudes about the relation between government and economy and charged their desire for aggressive national governmental actions. Losing one's job and house can do that to a person.[29]

MEANWHILE, DESPITE THE persistent premodern challenges epitomized by the Scopes trial, modernist intellectual trends of the 1920s and 1930s introduced the conceptual tools — the methods and attitudes — that could facilitate a new practice and ideology of democracy. In the first stages of modernism, during the late-nineteenth and early-twentieth centuries, university researchers sought to discover objective truths through the use of formalist methods, identifying axiomatic principles and building logically coherent systems upon those principles. In jurisprudence, Langdell's disciples studied judicial decisions in an effort to discover, through inductive reasoning, axiomatic principles of law. The Langdellians then deduced from the principles, through abstract reasoning, more specific legal rules and the correct resolutions of legal issues. Ultimately, the Langdellians would logically arrange the small number of principles and the more multitudinous rules and decisions into a formal and conceptually ordered system.[30]

By the 1920s and 1930s, the modernist components of historicism, secularism, and progress had become deeply entrenched in the intellectual culture and were being manifested in new ways. More so than in the early stages of the American modernist era, intellectuals perceived a distinct separation between past and present. Similar to premodernists, the early modernists, like Langdell, had studied history because the past revealed certain underlying principles, including republican democratic principles, which structured and limited the present and future. With the deepening of the modern historicist attitude emphasizing the inventive power of humans, people seemed free to remake the present and to determine the future. Rather than being controlled by historical principles, modernist Americans now controlled "historical change." But if the rational analysis of history no longer seemed to yield knowledge of underlying principles, how would the new wave of modernists uncover objective truths? The answer lay in experience. Empiricism replaced abstract formalism as the primary method of research.[31]

Professor Charles Edward Merriam was "the guiding light" of the nation's "most influential" political science department, at the University of Chicago. In 1924, Merriam and Harold Gosnell published *Non-Voting*, an empirical study of nonvoters in the April 1923 Chicago mayoral election. After interviewing six thousand nonvoters, Merriam and Gosnell ascertained the causes of nonvoting and recommended how to increase turnout. In Merriam's next book, published in 1925, he sketched an agenda for empirical research in political science. His explicit goal — in which he succeeded — was to lead others to "take up the task and through reflection and experiment eventually introduce more intelligent and scientific technique into the study and practice of government." In jurisprudence, a 1922 lecture by Dewey inspired law professors Walter Wheeler Cook and Underhill Moore to direct their research toward a more "experimental" or realist method. As others followed, Cook, Moore, and their legal realist cohorts denounced the Langdellians' abstract formalism; the Langdellians' axiomatic principles and logically deduced rules were often no more than "transcendental nonsense" — concepts with no basis in social reality. "[G]eneral propositions are empty," Karl Llewellyn proclaimed, "rules alone . . . are worthless." But many realist scholars insisted that empirical studies carefully attending to the observable behavior of legal actors could reveal the stimuli that caused predictable judicial responses. As Cook explained, "[o]nly empirical observation can give one postulates useful in any particular science, including legal science." Realists conducted empirical studies where they observed legal actors, gathered data based on their observations, and inductively described repetitive patterns of behavior. Moore, for instance, studied Connecticut banking practices with regard to maturing time notes. Instead of analyzing this issue by examining doctrine and cases, as a Langdellian might do, Moore sent questionnaires consisting of twenty-seven inquiries to all commercial banks in Connecticut, gathered the answers, and sought to identify the actual banking practices. In economics, the predominant empiricists, the institutionalists, had been waging a battle against neoclassicists since around the turn of the century. Ironically, the neoclassicists largely defeated the institutionalists in the 1920s and 1930s, just when the social sciences in general turned toward empiricism. Even so, the victorious neoclassicists retained the institutionalists' concern for quantitative analysis while replacing their orientation toward Progressive politics with a renewed emphasis on moderate-conservative principles of marginal utility, supply, and demand. One component of the neoclassical victory was a growing stress on horizontal competition. Classical economics had mostly conceptualized competition vertically, between levels within a hierarchy, so the buyer competes with the seller and the employer competes with the employee. Neoclassical economics focused on competition among "people operating at the same level in the same market, such as two sellers of shoes in the same city or two prospective employees seeking the same job." By the early 1930s, neoclassical economists were dwelling on the differences between perfect and imperfect horizontal competition.[32]

The modernist turn toward empiricism intertwined with a concomitant appearance and entrenchment of ethical relativism. Writing in 1929, Walter Lippmann recognized that the "acids of modernity" were dissolving the threads that had previously held American society together. Ethical values no longer appeared to rest on firm ground. Individuals "are likely to say that they know of no compelling reason which certifies the moral code they adhere to, and that therefore, their own preferences, when tested . . . seem to have no sure foundation of any kind." At a phenomenological (or experiential) level, some individuals might have worried about the certainty of their values because of advancing secularism, which weakened religious commitments and foundations. But at an intellectual level, ethical relativism seemed to be a corollary of empiricism. If knowledge and (scientific) research must be based on experience and empirical methods, then ethical values seemingly could not be verified. Individuals could assert values, but the scientific researcher could not empirically test the validity of particular values. In philosophy, the logical positivists of the Vienna Circle accentuated this problem in the 1920s and 1930s. A. J. Ayer and Rudolf Carnap argued that only empirical and analytic propositions are meaningful. Empirical propositions can be verified directly or indirectly from experience, while analytic or logical propositions, such as those of mathematics, "explicate the meanings of terms" without asserting "how things are in the world." But ethical propositions, Ayer and Carnap reasoned, are meaningless because they are neither empirical nor analytic. As Ayer phrased it, ethical assertions are "mere pseudo-concepts."[33]

Empiricism contributed not only to ethical relativism but also to an increased intellectual focus on individual behavior. Lippmann observed that modern American civilization dissolved "psychological bonds" by weakening "clannishness and personal dependence." Individuals tended "to become more or less independent persons rather than to remain members of a social organism." When Merriam advocated that political scientists adopt the empirical methods of science, he especially emphasized psychology. Experimental psychology could provide "a much clearer view of the human 'personality'" and thus could facilitate "the understanding of the process and the modes of control over social and political behavior." In 1929 and 1930, Dewey published in the *New Republic* a series of essays entitled "Individualism, Old and New." He specified "the crucial issue" for the age: "How shall the individual refind himself in an unprecedentedly new social situation, and what qualities will the new individualism exhibit?" Worrying about the relationship between the individual and mass-consumer culture, he rued "the irony of the gospel of 'individualism' in business conjoined with suppression of individuality in thought and speech." Mass-consumer culture and its advertising appeared to cater to the individual while simultaneously molding individuals to conform to norms oriented to product consumption. "One cannot imagine a bitterer comment on any professed individualism," Dewey concluded, "than that it subordinates the only creative individuality — that of mind — to the maintenance of [an economic] regime."[34]

In fact, the mass-consumer culture aimed in part to capitalize on the irrationality of individuals. Advertising sought to persuade individuals to buy a product not because doing so accorded with their rational assessment of its costs and benefits, but rather because purchasing the product seemed requisite to satisfy personal desires induced by the advertising itself. Unsurprisingly, the two opposed conceptions of psychology that had risen to prominence in the early-twentieth century — Freudianism and behaviorism — both stressed the irrationality of human behavior. Freudians posited that individual behavior could be understood partly as the product of unconscious drives or mental processes, while behaviorists insisted that individuals acted in response to identifiable and measurable external stimuli. Neither of these psychological orientations suggested that individuals acted rationally in accordance with their professed principles and values. Other causes, whether internal or external, shaped behavior. In the words of the political scientist Harold Lasswell: "The findings of personality research show that the individual is a poor judge of his own interest."[35]

The research into individual irrationalities provoked intellectuals to worry about republican democracy: could it withstand these psychological insights and other "acids of modernity"? For many Progressives, their prewar efforts had represented a last-ditch struggle to save republican democracy. They had emerged from the war disillusioned, and now modernity relentlessly burned away at their remaining faith in republican democratic principles. Dewey admitted "democracy is today under a cloud," and

Lippmann proclaimed a "disenchantment" with democracy. While Dewey still held hope for the future, Lippmann was more dispirited. "[T]he number of mice and monkeys known to have been deceived in laboratories is surpassed only by the hopeful citizens of a democracy," Lippmann sneered. "Man's reflexes are, as the psychologists say, conditioned. And, therefore, he responds quite readily to a glass egg, a decoy duck, a stuff shirt or a political platform." Lippmann dismissed as "mythical" the republican democratic notion that virtuous citizens come together as "the People" and pursue the common good. Merriam, too, lost much of his optimism during the 1920s and early 1930s. "My purpose is to set forth what role political power plays in the process of social control," he wrote in 1934. Merriam now analyzed government not as the virtuous pursuit of the common good but as a mechanism for the management of power. In law, legal realists questioned the coherence of the rule of law in a democratic system. In 1930, Llewellyn suggested that individual conduct constituted the very substance of the law. "[The] doing of something about disputes . . . is the business of law. And the people who have the doing in charge, whether they be judges or sheriffs or clerks or jailers or lawyers, are officials of the law. What these officials do about disputes is, to my mind, the law itself." But what, then, produced these individual actions? Jerome Frank, attempting to apply psychological insights to judges, concluded that stimuli as arbitrary as the hair color of a witness or the nasal twang of an attorney typically swayed judicial determinations of fact and law. Legal principles and doctrines were beside the point.[36]

WHILE NUMEROUS INTELLECTUALS in the late 1920s and early 1930s doubted the coherence of republican democracy and the rule of law, they did not yet envision a clear future. In a prescient book published in 1908, Arthur Bentley had conceptualized politics as the processes of interest-group conflicts. Bentley, however, was an "academic outcast" whose book had little immediate effect. Progressive historians like Charles Beard had far more influence. Similar to Bentley, Progressive historians understood politics as conflict among groups with competing economic interests, yet like other Progressives, these historians generally held to the tenets of republican democracy. They condemned the vested interests, powerful conspiratorial groups who corrupted democratic government by defeating the common good. As Progressivism waned in the 1920s, some political thinkers still worried that universal suffrage, more than anything else, was undermining (republican) democracy. In 1928, William Munro, former president of the American Political Science Association (APSA), wrote that "about twenty percent of those who get on the voters' list have no business to be there." Munro believed that universal suffrage was too entrenched to be outright repudiated, but he nonetheless hoped that various mechanisms could effectively limit suffrage (rendering it universal only in name). The *New York Times* repeatedly praised an examination, "scientifically devised" in 1923 by the New York State Department of Education, to screen new voter registrants for intelligence and literacy. The test, given only in English, thwarted thousands of would-be voters. A surprising number of Americans suggested that Europe might offer possible remedies for the ostensible failures of a republican democracy devolving into mobocracy because of universal suffrage. Some Americans praised Russian communism or Italian fascism as reasonable experiments in coping with the problems of modern industrial societies. In 1928, Dewey complimented the Russian communists for releasing "human powers on such an unprecedented scale that it is of incalculable significance not only for that country, but for the world." Then, when the Depression came crashing down on Americans, many feared that democratic government was too "unintelligent and inefficient" to respond. Walter Shepard's presidential address to the APSA in late 1934 admitted that democracy was failing both as an idea and as an institutional practice. Sketching a "beginning" for a "new ideology" of democracy, Shepard ambiguously combined the protection of certain rights with "a large element of fascist doctrine." Still, most Americans remained critical of fascism and communism even though workable alternative forms of government were elusive.[37]

THE NEW DEAL AND PLURALIST DEMOCRACY

By March 4, 1933, when Franklin Delano Roosevelt was inaugurated as president and initiated the New Deal, the traditional governmental principles of civic virtue and the common good hung in tatters. Built on agrarian economics, widespread landownership, and Protestant values, republican democratic government no longer even remotely fit the urban, industrial, and demographically diverse America that had plunged into Depression. The forces of industrialization, immigration, and urbanization had been pulling at republican democracy since long before World War I; then during the 1920s, social and cultural changes had begun tearing at its seams. The Great Depression finally had shredded republican democracy, leaving contemporary intellectuals to ponder the future vitality of democratic government.

When Roosevelt ran for the first time, he did not anticipate the radical transformation of democracy that he would lead. To be sure, he hinted at significant change; steps would be taken to fight the Depression. Politics demanded as much. But to a degree, FDR's role was a matter of happenstance. He did not consciously set forth to create a new democratic regime, yet he was the right person at the right time. A "patrician politician" from rural upstate New York, he appealed simultaneously to urbanites because he was a New Yorker and to many others because he was a "gentleman farmer." He had a background in Progressivism but did not strongly oppose machine politics. Most important, he recognized the latent shift of direction in American constitutional government and then willingly sought to build momentum for the new democracy. Instead of fighting change, he embraced and then directed it.[38]

Although some of FDR's campaign speeches reflected his advisors' sentiments as much as his own, these early speeches hinted at his willingness to spearhead change. In his "Forgotten Man" radio address, given in April 1932, he explained: "These unhappy times call for the building of plans that rest upon the forgotten, the unorganized but the indispensable units of economic power." He would "build from the bottom up and not from the top down, [putting] faith once more in the forgotten man at the bottom of the economic pyramid." Roosevelt castigated Hoover for catering only to "the top of the social and economic structure."[39] Al Smith himself condemned the "Forgotten Man" speech as a "demagogic appeal to the masses of the working people of this country." Smith was at least partly correct. Roosevelt would not ignore poor or unemployed laborers. The republican democratic concept of civic virtue no longer justified protecting old-stock Protestant values and interests while disregarding those of workers, indigents, and immigrants. Roosevelt's speech to the Commonwealth Club in September 1932 went even further. He declared that "the central and ambitious [corporation] is no longer a servant of national desire, but a danger." He did not wish the government to destroy corporations, although "their power is susceptible of easy abuse," yet the government must control them. Roosevelt sought to lead the government into action — action that would involve it deeply in the affairs of the economy. The government would no longer merely facilitate private economic ordering but would instead affirmatively shape the order itself. Moralizing about the content of virtue and the common good was now beside the point. FDR's first inaugural address emphasized that restoration of the nation did not depend on "changes in ethics" but on "action, and action now."[40]

But what actions would be taken? While religious fundamentalists insisted that the average person could immediately grasp the most important truths — and that education therefore counted for little — Roosevelt accepted the modernist orientation toward knowledge, empirical experimentation, and expertise. Firmly committed to using scientists, social scientists, and lawyers in government, he sought to benefit from expertise in two primary ways. First, even before being elected, he gathered together a "Brain Trust" for the purpose of advising him on policy questions, such as how to stimulate the economy. The Brain Trust consisted of FDR's close confidants and elite academic experts, including Raymond Moley, a Barnard College government professor; Rexford Guy Tugwell, a Columbia University economist; Adolf Berle, Jr., a Columbia law professor; and Felix Frankfurter, a Harvard law professor. Second, given his modernist outlook, FDR favored the centralization of governmental power in the national government and the creation of administrative agencies to implement that power. The agencies would be staffed with experts in the respective regulated areas. The national government would no longer allow either local governmental officials who were only dimly aware of broader problems, private participants who sought their own profits, or political cronies who held their jobs because of patronage to set haphazard policies regarding overarching issues related to farm crops, railroad rates, the stock market, and so on.[41]

Hence, FDR's election and his development and implementation of the New Deal helped crystallize a new practice of democracy — a pluralist democracy. Under republican democracy, the individual's overarching political goal was to act virtuously in contributing to the government's pursuit of the common good. Under the new democracy, the individual's goal, it appeared, was to participate in politics: to express one's values and interests, to have governmental officials listen to those expressions of values and interests, and to have the government, acting through experts, fulfill one's desires in a reasonable number of instances. Roosevelt set the tone for this new democracy by welcoming many different types of people to participate in government in a variety of ways. Consistent with his campaign speeches and inaugural address, FDR led a national government that largely refrained from actively imposing moral values. The New Dealers undid the Progressive-inspired eighteenth amendment: the twenty-first amendment, ratified during Roosevelt's first year in office, repealed Prohibition. As Tugwell of the Brain Trust explained, "the New Deal is attempting to do nothing to people, and does not seek at all to alter their way of life, their wants and desires." Freed from the moralizing so common under republican democracy, numerous Americans were inspired by the government's recognition that they, too, belonged to the polity. Merely listening to FDR's Fireside Chats on the radio imbued many Americans with a newfound sense of participation; their president, after all, took the time to come into their living rooms to talk to them. And the people responded in turn. Whereas Hoover received an average of 800 letters each day, Roosevelt received 8,000, and sometimes as many as 150,000.[42]

At the outset of his first term, Roosevelt attempted "to hold together a coalition of all interests," including bankers and corporate business leaders. He told Frances Perkins, his secretary of labor and the first female cabinet member, that "[w]e are going to make a country in which no one is left out." To vote in elections for governmental officials was merely the most obvious but not the only means of participating, of being included, in the new democratic government. In the first "100 days" of the New Deal, FDR signed fifteen bills into law, creating hosts of new programs that provided jobs and assistance to grateful people around the country. The Agricultural Adjustment Act (AAA) aided farmers; the Emergency Banking Act helped save failing banks; the Civilian Conservation Corps and the Federal Emergency Relief Administration provided jobs and relief for the unemployed; the National Industrial Recovery Act (NIRA) benefited manufacturers and also industrial workers; the Tennessee Valley Authority was to control flooding, to generate hydroelectric power, and to resuscitate the economy throughout the rural and "chronically depressed upper South." In this burst of governmental action, the New Dealers created new administrative agencies that would, in turn, develop procedures enabling multitudes of individuals and interest groups to express their views and influence agency decisions. Meanwhile, the Roosevelt administration implemented a meritocratic system when hiring governmental employees to fill both old and new positions: educational accomplishments became more important than family lineage. At a time when many law firms refused to hire Jewish attorneys, regardless of the job applicants' qualifications, Roosevelt welcomed them into governmental positions. Both the president and the attorneys benefited. FDR needed talented lawyers to staff his New Deal agencies, while most of these young unemployed or underemployed Jewish attorneys were thrilled to secure governmental jobs. To a great degree, Roosevelt forged a coalition that encompassed many societal outsiders simply because he refused to act on traditional American nativist sentiments. When appointing federal judges, for example, FDR named Catholics more than 25 percent of the time. Under the three previous presidents, only 4 percent of judicial appointees were Catholic. Before 1932, only four Catholics had served in cabinet positions; Roosevelt named two to his first cabinet.[43]

Roosevelt did not always successfully incorporate societal groups into his New Deal coalition. Most important, he lost big business early in his first term. Many corporate leaders and bankers resented FDR's repudiation of single-interest politics, where corporate interests equated with the common good. Roosevelt's willingness to balance multiple interests and to regulate the economy seemed to many conservatives a betrayal of traditional American principles of government. And while "betrayal" might have been unfairly pejorative, he was in fact now leading a fundamental transition in American democracy—a transition that the nation had been edging toward for decades, that Roosevelt had not intentionally initiated, but that he was now aggressively moving forward. When business leaders grumbled about his policies, FDR retorted that "[g]overnment by the necessity of things must be . . . the judge of the conflicting interests of all groups in the community, including bankers." Business leaders, Roosevelt lamented, consistently disregarded "the human side, the old-age side, the unemployment side." A sharp break with business came in early February 1934 when Roosevelt asked Congress to introduce legislation that would regulate the stock market. Financiers were outraged; the president of the New York Stock Exchange (who apparently had forgotten the 1929 crash) exclaimed, "The Exchange is a perfect institution." Meanwhile, the U.S. Chamber of Commerce, at its convention, officially "denounced" the New Deal. Roosevelt's closest advisors, including Frankfurter, urged him to recognize an "irrepressible conflict" with business and to act accordingly.[44]

When Roosevelt broke with business, he developed a more aggressive strategy "to gather into the Democratic Party many minorities, including the labor unions," explained Brain Truster Raymond Moley. This strategy of inclusiveness ranged from allowing millions of farmers to vote for referenda related to crop management under the AAA, to the production of a twenty-six-part radio series, *Americans All, Immigrants All.* Each week, the series would focus on a different ethnic group, including African Americans, Jews, and Slavs, explaining the group's history and "positive contributions" to the nation. By his 1936 campaign, FDR was invoking overt class-based language even more strongly than in the past, as he attempted to appeal to the lower and middle classes. He described a "roll of honor" that included "men at starvation wages, women in sweatshops, children at looms . . . farmers whose acres yielded only bitterness, business men whose books were portents of disaster, home owners who were faced with eviction, frugal citizens whose savings were insecure. [The roll of honor included] Americans of all parties and all faiths." Roosevelt unequivocally targeted corporate interests as the enemy. "They are unanimous in their hate for me — and I welcome their hatred."[45]

The key to the strategy of inclusiveness was unionizing. Once FDR relinquished the idea of holding business interests within his New Deal coalition, he vigorously pushed to bring workers into the fold. In 1932, he had not run especially well in northeastern industrial cities; journalist Heywood Broun, first president of the American Newspaper Guild, had even called Roosevelt "[l]abor's public enemy Number One." During the early months of Roosevelt's first term, he had generally supported workers and unionizing, but recoiled when pressured to become the "midwife of industrial unionism." In the context of the Depression, FDR did not find potentially divisive labor-policy questions especially compelling vis-à-vis other economic and social issues. Several senators, including New York's Robert Wagner (Democrat) and Wisconsin's Robert La Follette, Jr. (Republican), were known to be far stronger supporters of labor. Even with Roosevelt's only lukewarm support, though, workers became increasingly assertive in their demands, partly because the government no longer strongly favored management. From 1932 to 1933, the number of industrial disputes doubled, while the number of striking workers tripled. In 1933 and 1934, massive strikes erupted across the nation. In Toledo, Ohio, 10,000 workers joined a violent strike that led to higher wages and partial union recognition. Similar strikes broke out in San Francisco and Minneapolis, where 100,000 people marched in a funeral procession for a slain striker. In September 1934, 375,000 textile workers struck, mostly in the southern states. In the midst of this labor militancy, Roosevelt supported enactment of the NIRA and establishment of a National Labor Board (NLB), partly to calm worker unrest. Section 7(a) of the NIRA guaranteed workers "the right to organize and bargain collectively through representatives of their own choosing," but management easily evaded this paper mandate. Fiery labor-management confrontations continued, leading Roosevelt to create by executive order the first National Labor Relations Board (NLRB), which similar to the NLB, proved impotent to quell the disputes.[46]

On February 21, 1935, Senator Wagner introduced a new bill that would provide stronger protection for unionizing and would create a permanent NLRB empowered to enforce the Act's provisions. Even though FDR temporized about its merits, the bill sailed through the Senate on May 16. While the House debated the companion bill, Roosevelt finally relented.

On May 24, 1935, he declared that the proposed National Labor Relations (or Wagner) Act — the NLRA — was "'must' legislation." Three days later, the Supreme Court helped cement Roosevelt's new supportive stance by holding the NIRA unconstitutional, leaving "the administration without a labor policy." On July 5, 1935, with Roosevelt's blessing, the NLRA became law. A central piece of the so-called second New Deal (or second "100 days") — a renewed burst of legislative activity that also included the Social Security Act — the NLRA radically reoriented labor-management relations for years to come. It explicitly aimed to correct for the "inequality of bargaining power" between employees and employers. In indubitable terms, it stated: "Employees shall have the right of self-organization, to form, join, or assist labor organizations, to bargain collectively through representatives of their own choosing, and to engage in concerted activities, for the purpose of collective bargaining or other mutual aid or protection." The Act then specified how *employers* might commit unfair labor practices by, for instance, interfering with the formation of a union. The Act established a new NLRB and expressly empowered it to prevent unfair labor practices and to investigate suspected statutory violations. Labor leaders gushed; the president of the United Mine Workers, John L. Lewis, exclaimed that the Wagner Act was labor's Magna Carta and Emancipation Proclamation.[47]

During the debates and hearings, opponents of the proposed NLRA repeatedly condemned it as class legislation inconsistent with republican democratic principles. The Pittsburgh Chamber of Commerce deplored the proposed Act because it would be for "the selfish advantage of [a] particular class . . . and the detriment of the people as a whole." Senator Millard Tydings complained that the bill distinguished "employers of a class and employees of a class" and treated the two classes differently; it condemned unfair labor practices of employers but not of employees. These objections could have been raised ten, twenty, or fifty years earlier, and similar ones had often derailed previous legislative attempts to protect labor. When legislatures had, in fact, passed prolabor statutes, courts frequently invalidated them as contravening republican democratic principles. Given this history, the debates over the NLRA revealed a stunning disregard for these standard criticisms. The bill passed by an overwhelming majority, 63 to 12 in the Senate and 132 to 42 in the House. The enactment of the NLRA epitomized the changing practice of democracy, from a regime of republican to pluralist democracy. Labor, to be sure, was an interest group: a labor union aimed, quite simply, to promote the interests of its members. But management was no different. Management, corporate leaders, and bankers aimed to further their own interests. The NLRA might have favored labor, but that fact alone no longer rendered the legislation impermissible — or so it seemed to members of Congress. Negotiation and compromise between competing interest groups now appeared to be the essence of the democratic process — not its corruption. The national government became more of a "broker state," mediating among various interests. No longer would the government condemn labor's interests as partial and private while condoning corporate interests as the common good.[48]

In the 1920s and early Depression, union membership decreased, including in the predominant AFL, built around affiliated craft unions. Despite shrinking rolls, AFL leadership continued to fight inclusion of unskilled industrial workers until, in fall 1935, Lewis mustered sufficient support to establish the Committee for Industrial Organization (CIO), ostensibly as a component of the AFL but, in reality, as an independent entity. In October 1938, the new union officially split from the AFL and renamed itself the Congress of Industrial Organizations. As soon the CIO formed in 1935, it benefited from an explosion in union membership, due partly to the passage of the NLRA. Total union membership had dropped under three million in 1933. In 1934, it inched to just over three million, while major industries including auto manufacturing and steel production remained open shop (free to hire nonunion employees). By 1936, though, total membership climbed over four million, and in 1937, membership rolls leaped over seven million and continued to climb in subsequent years. The percentage of nonagricultural workers in unions nearly doubled from 1934 to 1937, then rose over 27 percent in 1938. CIO membership increased so rapidly that, in 1937, it passed the AFL as the largest confederated union.[49]

That same year, 1937, the CIO won two astounding victories. On December 30, 1936, workers in GM's Fisher body plant in Flint, Michigan, initiated a sit-down strike. Knowing that GM, "the world's largest manufacturing corporation," relied on the Flint plant to produce the majority of its auto bodies, the workers strategically chose to strike there so as to inflict the greatest injury. By using a sit-down strike, moreover, the workers literally seized "the means of production" and "shut down" the factory. The workers' primary demand was simple yet momentous: they sought recognition of the United Auto Workers (UAW) as the exclusive representative of GM employees. As the sit-down strike spread to other GM factories, the corporation sought governmental assistance, but neither the federal nor state governments would help. Lewis unabashedly parlayed labor's newfound political clout within FDR's New Deal coalition to strengthen the workers' position. He reminded Roosevelt that "[t]he time has passed in America when the workers can be either clubbed, gassed or shot down with impunity. . . . Labor will . . . expect the protection of the Federal Government in the pursuit of its lawful objectives." Lewis more brazenly threatened Michigan Governor Frank Murphy: "If you break this strike, that washes us up and washes you up. General Motors fought you in the election and when we are gone you are gone. If you stand firm you will aggrandize your political position enormously and there will be talk of Governor Murphy in 1940." After forty-four days, GM capitulated, recognizing the UAW. The workers' victory was due more to their organization, persistence, and raw political power than to the NLRA, but the Act emboldened workers. When the strike started, many legal commentators predicted that the Supreme Court would soon hold the NLRA unconstitutional. Yet, even with the Act's precise ramifications murky, Congress's passage of the NLRA had signified to workers that the government would no longer actively suppress labor activities. And when push came to shove, the national government refused to put its shoulder alongside that of GM. Instead, FDR encouraged GM "behind the scenes" to settle and to recognize the union. Then, less than one month after the GM strike ended, U.S. Steel Corporation saw that the political winds blew so strongly for workers that it surrendered without a fight, recognizing the Steel Workers Organizing Committee. Forcing a strike could only compound the corporation's losses. A year later, *Fortune* magazine bemoaned the NLRA and its "G — — D — — Labor Board."[50]

The acceptance of labor and management as competing interest groups, equally entitled to press for favorable governmental action, underscored the legitimation of lobbying. In the 1920s, mass-consumer culture had encouraged individuals to seek to satisfy their personal desires. Insofar as a private-sphere virtue existed, it had become the mere satisfaction of self-interest — the acquisition of desired products. The Depression did not quell this culture of consumption. To be sure, many Americans became frustrated consumers, frequently unable to purchase desired products. But at the same time, they retained their desire to consume, to purchase. And despite the dire economic straits, many Americans managed to continue buying. From 1930 to 1940, the number of families with radios increased every year, more than doubling during that time. Sales of refrigerators increased sevenfold from 1929 to 1935. This self-focused acquisitiveness had oozed into the public sphere during the 1920s; lobbying had developed into a relatively common practice, though in many instances it remained hesitant, as if it had to be tied to a common good. By the 1930s, though, the culture of mass consumerism had pervaded politics. The pursuit of one's self-interest became legitimate in all realms of life, private and public. Democratic participation became another path to self-fulfillment. Invocations of civic virtue and the common good became rhetorical tactics bereft of substantive content. Only private interests seemed to exist; no longer could one distinguish between a common good and private or partial interests. And as the centralized power of the national government grew, the apparent need to influence governmental actions to coincide with one's own interests increased proportionately. Lewis's efforts to pressure Roosevelt and Murphy during the GM sit-down strike now seemed to be acceptable political maneuvers within a pluralist democratic regime, not attempts to undermine or corrupt it. Labor was not alone; numerous other voluntary groups and associations purposefully sought to shape governmental decisions. Lobbying became open, aggressive, institutionalized, and widespread, as emblematized by the list of groups advocating for or against passage of the NLRA. Even a small sample could include the American Petroleum Institute, the Associated General Contractors of America, the Manufacturing Chemists of the United States, the Brotherhood of Railroad Shop Crafts of America, and the International Union of Operating Engineers. As the legal scholar Louis Jaffe observed in 1937, citizens and governmental officials in the past were supposed "to promote the public interest," but many recognize today that "all legislation . . . is an immediate response, in a greater or less degree, to some group pressure." Consequently, "Congress and the state legislatures pass laws for the farmer, laws for labor, laws for business."[51]

The emergence of labor as a powerful political force further solidified the practices of pluralist democracy (the importance of labor to free-expression developments is discussed in chapter 11). Many of the workers who joined unions in the mid- and late 1930s were first- and second-generation Americans who had rarely participated in politics, particularly at a national level. Belonging to a union, though, educated many of these individuals in the ways of democracy. The unions provided institutional procedures where members could express their views and register their preferences through voting. The unions taught their members that, by joining together, they could accomplish their desired goals through systematic processes. The CIO purposefully sought "to create a culture of unity" among its diverse members, regardless of ethnic background. One worker explained: "Once in the Ford plant, they called me 'dumb Polack,' but now with UAW they call me brother." These democratized workers — these union members — then became participants in the new pluralist democratic regime. They not only could vote in union elections, they also could vote in local, state, and national elections. And when they voted en bloc, they could determine the outcome. At a personal level, many workers were moved to vote for the first time because FDR seemed to recognize their existence, their importance.

They believed he was "their friend." As one worker put it, "Mr. Roosevelt is the only man we ever had in the White House who would understand that my boss is a sonofabitch." At a broader level, once Roosevelt broke with big business, he and labor developed a symbiotic relationship. The unions would mobilize their members as voters bolstering the New Deal, and FDR would amplify governmental support of unions. In 1936, the CIO's Lewis organized Labor's Non-Partisan League to muster electoral support for Roosevelt among laborers, while Roosevelt invited Lewis to the White House and pledged his continued backing. With labor and the New Deal so closely linked, people who had never before voted now did so. In the presidential elections of 1936 and 1940, voter turnout moved above 60 percent, unheard of since 1916. In 1936, because many of the first-time voters were urbanites, FDR won 104 of the cities with populations of one hundred thousand or more; his Republican opponent, Alf Landon, won two.[52]

Myriad old-stock Protestants also supported FDR. Many of them still lived across rural America, and Roosevelt had not ignored their needs. In the early 1930s, only one in ten farms had electricity. Numerous farmers toiled like their nineteenth-century ancestors, while the modern cities glittered. In 1935, Roosevelt created the Rural Electrification Administration to build electric power plants and to string power lines through the farm country. "By 1941, four out of ten American farms had electricity; by 1950, nine out of ten." Practically all types of people, except for the super rich, would vote for FDR. In 1936, he garnered 523 electoral college votes to Landon's eight! But in terms of the transition from republican to pluralist democracy, the central importance of Roosevelt's 1936 victory (as well as his 1940 victory) was not his total number of votes. Rather, the key was that Roosevelt accepted those outsiders whom mainstream Protestants had for so long fought to keep at bay. Roosevelt neither feared these people nor plotted to yoke them under Protestant morality. Unskilled ethnic workers, previously alienated from national politics, metamorphosed into voters, primarily through the avenue of the labor movement. Unions added members by the millions and, in turn, activated those new members as democratic participants (swelling support for the New Deal). With Roosevelt's help, massive numbers of immigrants and their children became part of a new and more inclusive democratic system.[53]

BY THE END of the 1930s, many ethnic, religious, and racial outsiders had gained vested interests in two now powerful institutions: the national government and the unions. Many believed they "had made the New Deal and the CIO possible." This institutionalized inclusion of erstwhile outsiders reveals how the transition to pluralist democracy was simultaneously radical and conservative. On the radical side, the government had stopped, at least overtly, trying to force Protestant morality onto these relatively new Americans and instead accepted them into the polity. Thus, an individual could now identify himself simultaneously as Polish, Catholic, union member, and Democrat. Equally important, governmental power expanded and became centralized at the national level. No longer ostensibly constrained by the limits of the common good, the government could now reach, it seemed, into any facet of economy and society. The boundary between the public and the private, which had been demarcated by the albeit nebulous line separating the common good from partial or private interests, faded to nothingness. While the Supreme Court would soon begin to draw new lines limiting the government, public power to regulate the economy seemed boundless. The Depression, of course, immediately precipitated this transition. Economic suffering compelled many Americans — old-stock, immigrants, and second-generation ethnics alike — to seek governmental actions that would generate relief. Enhanced centralized power, often implemented through legislatively created administrative agencies, provided a needed counterbalance to that of big business, blamed by many for the Depression, as well as providing a venue for the application of expert knowledge to economic (and other social) problems. From 1930 to 1936, the percentage of GNP consumed by the national government more than doubled, from 4 to 9 percent. By the end of the 1930s, "few questioned the right of the government to pay the farmer millions in subsidies not to grow crops, to enter plants to conduct union elections, to regulate business enterprises from utility companies to air lines, or even to compete directly with business by generating and distributing hydroelectric power."[54]

While the transition to pluralist democracy was radical — institutionalizing a far more inclusive polity and dramatically expanding the national government's role in the economy — this transition also had conservative elements. Many former outsiders now belonged to the incipient pluralist democracy, but with the centralization of power at the national level, these individuals participated in a distant and hierarchical government. The extent of individual participation typically was limited to an occasional vote and, perhaps, to belonging to an association or organization, maybe a labor union, that lobbied the national government. Some individuals or organizations might participate in various administrative agency proceedings. Moreover, for members of ethnic and religious minorities, participation came at a cost. Previously, immigrants had learned that to gain economic success they would "have to shed at least the more obvious marks of their immigrant background." Now, second- and third-generation individuals realized that, to move up governmental or professional hierarchies into positions of greater influence, they had to wash away vestigial signs of ethnic or religious difference in a "kind of cultural bleaching." Thus, when a law partner boasted that his large firm had just hired a Jewish attorney, the partner emphasized that the new lawyer was "devoid of every known quality which we in New York mean when we call a man 'Jewy.'" To the extent that language is linked to culture, the diminishing number of native-language speakers starkly revealed the compass of cultural bleaching. Among ethnic Italians, for instance, the second generation had 2,300,000 native-language speakers; the third had 147,000.[55]

In addition, partly because of the persistent appeal of the mass-consumer culture, most workers never wanted to jettison the basic structures of capitalism, even at the depths of the Depression. The number and severity of labor strikes during the early 1930s demonstrated that the Depression engendered a potential for politically disruptive economic actions, and these economic-political pressures accelerated the transition to pluralist democracy. Yet, no more so than most workers, Roosevelt and the New Dealers did not want to destroy capitalism. Rather, they sought to restructure the economy so as to resuscitate and then sustain capitalism in an industrial society. In doing so, the New Deal normalized the unemployed, the indigent, and other outsiders. They were incorporated into the political and economic systems, and consequently, no longer presented an external source of danger. The New Deal and pluralist democracy muted rebelliousness. The unemployed would be less likely to start a rent riot and more likely to wait in line at a government office to speak to a case worker or relief administrator. Workers became union members, and unions became intertwined with the pluralist democratic New Deal government. Workers' frustrations would channel through the union and through established governmental procedures for resolving labor-management issues. As the NLRB evolved, it aimed increasingly "to promote productivity, economic growth, and above all industrial peace." Union leaders gained a vested interest in keeping workers within the bounds of the established bureaucratic processes.[56]

Even as former outsiders gained political power and economic protection, the preservation of capitalism conjoined with the transition to pluralist democracy to protect the wealth and power of old-stock elites. Just when the political process absorbed ethnic and religious outsiders — when they gained access to official political deliberations so that they might, in theory, influence governmental goals — the purpose of democratic government changed. Instead of aiming to achieve a common good, government now aimed to mediate among competing interests. Pluralist democracy supplanted republican democracy. All individuals and groups became free to pursue their respective interests, without regard for any supposed public good. Given that capitalism remained intact, wealthy old-stock elites could draw on their accumulated economic resources to sway governmental decision making either directly, by contributing money to election campaigns, or indirectly, by funding lobbying organizations. Pluralist democracy, in conjunction with capitalism, contained a built-in conservative brake, likely to slow any democratic urges to restructure the society (beyond the transition to pluralist democracy).

Other forces contributed to the conservative maintenance of cultural, economic, and political traditions (including the tradition of suppression, discussed in chapters 11 and 12). While many ethnic and religious outsiders Americanized and melded into the new pluralist democratic regime, many old-stock Americans resented these changes and sought to retain remnants of their cultural hegemony. Attacks might appear in overtly racist or anti-Semitic diatribes or in more veiled denunciations. Many critics of the New Deal called it the "Jew Deal." Other critics could be more discreet. The 1940 Republican presidential nominee Wendell Wilkie castigated the New Deal by implicitly contrasting traditional American Protestant values with those of eastern urban ethnic intellectuals who had supposedly hijacked the country. "They are all cynics who scoff at our simple virtues, particularly those simple virtues that you and I learned here in the Midwest. They think that the people and most of us are too dumb to understand. Their idea is that they, the intelligentsia, can govern us. . . . Give our country back to us. It belongs to us. We want it." Moreover, while the New Deal government hired numerous members of peripheral groups, discrimination in the private economic marketplace remained rampant. In the spring of 1936, for example, only eight *Harvard Law Review* editors had been unable to secure postgraduation jobs; all eight were Jews.[57]

Unquestionably, though, the most conservative strain of the New Deal and the initial transition to pluralist democracy surfaced in the government's treatment of African Americans. On the one hand, the New Deal government supported black Americans more than any national administration since Reconstruction. Many blacks secured jobs through federal programs; a few were appointed to governmental positions; Roosevelt met occasionally with an informal "black cabinet"; and he nominated the first black federal judge, William Hastie. African Americans had traditionally supported the Republican party, going back to Lincoln and the Civil War, but by the late 1930s, 84.7 percent supported FDR. On the other hand, the New Deal coalition included southern whites, and Roosevelt often acquiesced to their insistence on preserving the South's "way of life." As a result, numerous New Deal legislative programs facilitated discrimination in three major ways: by excluding groups of beneficiaries who were disproportionately black, by allowing state and local officials to administer the federally funded programs, and by not proscribing racial discrimination in the implementation of federal programs. The NLRA, for instance, excluded from its coverage agricultural and domestic service workers, "constituting more than 60 percent of the black labor forces in the 1930s and nearly 75 percent of those who were employed in the South." The Social Security Act contained similar exclusions, even though Roosevelt had expressly recommended otherwise. Consequently, Social Security did not cover 65 percent of African Americans nationally and between 70 and 80 percent in the South. As the famed NAACP lawyer and Howard University Law School Dean Charles Hamilton Houston testified to the Senate Finance Committee: "[The Social Security bill] looks like a sieve with the holes just big enough for the majority of Negroes to fall through." Because Social Security benefits varied in accordance with prior earned wages, private employers' wage discrimination meant that even statutorily covered blacks generally received lower benefits than did whites. And because local officials administered Social Security Act sections providing aid to families with dependent children, African Americans received a disproportionately low percentage of the benefits, especially in southern states. In Georgia in one year, only 1.5 percent of eligible blacks received payments. Partly because of such congressional actions, blacks participated in pluralist democracy only minimally. Wealth facilitated power in the pluralist democratic pursuit of self-interest, so the continued economic oppression of African Americans engendered diminished political influence. And just as New Deal programs allowed state and local officials to determine precise beneficiaries and benefits, the national government continued to allow states to determine eligibility for voting. Because of the fifteenth amendment, states could no longer overtly deny suffrage on the basis of race, but southern states continued to use long-effective mechanisms including literacy tests, poll taxes, gerrymandering, and whites-only primaries to restrict black voting.[58]

THE WORLD IN CRISIS AND THE DEVELOPMENT
OF PLURALIST DEMOCRATIC THEORY

With limitations, such as the restrictions on black participation, the practice of pluralist democracy was well established by the end of the second "100 days." Regardless, Roosevelt's administration still encountered domestic and international problems. During the summer of 1937, the economy fell back into a recession. Treasury Secretary Henry Morgenthau warned FDR that "[w]e are headed right into another Depression." This looming "depression within a depression" generated puzzlement within the administration: how to attack it? Ultimately, a reluctant Roosevelt accepted John Maynard Keynes's argument, at least to a degree, that deficit spending would help refuel the economy. Even so, the nation seemed sluggish, and Republicans gained 7 Senate and 79 House seats in the 1938 midterm elections. To be sure, the 1938 results did not repudiate the New Deal. The Republicans still held only 24 of 96 Senate and 168 of 435 House seats. FDR nonetheless had to face sometimes stronger congressional resistance to his programs, and at this stage, he appeared unlikely to run for a third term.[59]

Yet, managing the domestic economy was not the administration's largest problem. The greatest difficulty, the most portentous threat — not just to the Roosevelt administration but to American democratic government itself — came from outside the country: confronting the world-wide rise and strengthening of totalitarian governments. As Adolf Hitler's Nazis transformed Germany from a republic into an authoritarian power preparing for war, some Americans questioned how democratic governments could simultaneously develop the tools needed for defense, protect individual liberty, and allow their people to flourish. The Nazis unleashed their modern war machine on Europe beginning in 1938. In March, Germany annexed Austria; in September, it took the Sudetenland area of Czechoslovakia, with British Prime Minister Neville Chamberlain's acquiescence (he hoped that appeasement would assure peace); in November, with a burst of brutality on *Kristallnacht* (the night of the broken glass), the Nazis began murdering and arresting German Jews by the thousands and then seizing their assets; in March 1939, in one day, the Nazis overran the rest of Czechoslovakia; in September, they took Poland in a three-week *Blitzkrieg*. The Germans' merciless destruction of opponents and subjugation of individuals erased any doubts for most Americans: the affirmation of democracy became paramount. An October 1939 Gallup poll reported that only 2 percent of Americans wanted Germany to win the European war, while 84 percent wanted the Allies to win. In a presidential address to the

APSA, Robert Brooks condemned Germany's "concentration camps, its torturers and sadists," and described its plundering of other nations as "the most vicious and sordid" in history. While early in the 1930s, intellectuals could speculate about the advantages of fascism or communism, equivocation about the merits of democracy now became largely unacceptable. John Mulder, University of Pennsylvania law professor and editor of the *Bill of Rights Review,* tersely phrased the problem: American intellectuals must "prove democracy the master of totalitarianism."[60]

Although the intellectual challenge was clear — democracy must be defended — the solution was not. Political and legal thinkers confronted a crisis, partly of their own making. The problem arose from the correlative rises of empiricism and ethical relativism during the 1920s and 1930s. The academic-intellectual community had increasingly emphasized empirical research as the only source of knowledge, but this trend had rendered ethical values seemingly unverifiable. Initially, this value relativism had been little more than a scholarly puzzle, but with the aggressive rise of totalitarian governments, relativism became a more practical problem. American intellectuals needed to assert and demonstrate the superiority of democracy, not admit that from an ethical standpoint one governmental system was as good as another (because all values were relative). But how could empirical research prove the superiority of American democracy and the rule of law? In fact, some prominent Americans such as Charles Lindbergh and Robert McCormick (publisher of the *Chicago Tribune*) advocated for isolationism while invoking various degrees of relativism. Americans, they insisted, should be wary about assigning responsibility and taking sides in another chiefly European conflict. Some isolationists even argued that the European "war was not a contest between right and wrong, but a struggle between different conceptions of what is right."[61]

For many intellectuals, such isolationist arguments only intensified their determination to assert the superiority of democracy. Early in the 1930s, Charles Merriam had realistically assessed the importance of power, but later in the decade, he affirmed his faith in democracy. In the first sentence of his 1939 book, Merriam wrote: "This is a statement of the assumptions of democracy and the validation of its program."

> I affirm the possibility of vast gains in social production, in the light of modern science, and of speedy advance in standards of human living, within the forms of free society. . . . I affirm the relative advantages of rational discussion and of general consent and cooperation as against force and violence as a means of social reorganization and

human progress. . . . I affirm that democratic social planning wisely conceived may be directed toward the release of human capacities and the opening of opportunities for human liberty and personality through agencies of common consent and cooperation. . . . I repudiate the doctrine of despotism in government, either (1) in the form of the totalitarian state, right or left wing, or (2) of the centralization of irresponsible authority in the hands of One or of the Few.

While such affirmations of democratic conviction became increasingly common, most political and legal commentators understood that they now believed in a "new democracy," as Merriam phrased it, rather than in a republican democracy. Lippmann astutely described a "polity of pressure groups" who, through their "leaders and lobbyists," sought to "persuade, cajole, coerce, and occasionally corrupt the electorate or the parliament."[62]

But still, the problem remained: to develop a theory explaining and justifying democracy in a modern, diverse, and industrial society. Ironically, the key to developing a new democratic theory became the intellectual embrace of ethical relativism. From the mid-1930s onward, relativism had obstructed the theoretical justification of democracy: if all values were relative, then was not one governmental system as good as another? But in the late 1930s and early to mid-1940s, American political theorists began to argue that relativism itself accorded democracy a normative superiority over fascist, Nazi, and communist governments. Totalitarian governments claimed access to known objective values and goals, then claimed that this ostensible knowledge justified the authoritative enforcement of such values and goals on their respective peoples. Democratic governments did not arrogate such prerogatives. Lippmann argued that governmental officials had "no criterion" for determining the "best" public policy. The official must not fancy "himself the contriver of the human destiny and its master." Carl Friedrich unequivocally celebrated "the absence of . . . absolute standards": "Whether there be an ultimate right or wrong, good or bad, no man knows what it is."[63]

Joseph Schumpeter acknowledged that such relativism undermined *republican democracy* or, in his terminology, the "classical doctrine of democracy." The concept of the republican democratic "common good implies definite answers to all questions so that every social fact and every measure taken or to be taken can unequivocally be classed as 'good' or 'bad.'" The insurmountable problem, Schumpeter explained, was that "a uniquely determined common good" did not exist; rather, "to different individuals and groups the common good is bound to mean different things." But if democracy could no longer be described in substantive terms, as the pursuit of the common good, then what defined democracy? The answer: process. Dewey argued, for instance, that the crux of democracy was the following of "democratic methods"—including consultation, persuasion, negotiation, and communication. At the communal level, no higher standard existed for determining the public rightness or legitimacy of a normative (governmental) decision than acceptance through the democratic process itself. As individuals and organized pressure groups sought to satisfy their respective interests and fulfill their values and desires, institutionalized democratic processes structured the "competitive struggle for political power," in Schumpeter's words. And for most theorists, the opportunity for widespread participation, consistent with the relative inclusiveness of New Deal politics, assumed a central role in the democratic process. Friedrich emphasized "the common man's political capacity" to contribute to "collective" political judgments, while Lippmann explained that the "fairest" policies emerged when all interests were "represented and properly heard."[64]

But what could prevent democracy from deteriorating into totalitarianism, as it had in Germany? What could sustain democratic processes, particularly in a society as heterogeneous as America? Dewey believed that American culture provided the solution. A democratic culture could generate "a basic consensus and community of beliefs" about the worthiness of democratic methods. Attorney General Robert Jackson described "democratic culture" as encompassing "[r]espect for civil rights, tolerance, the will to live and let live, [and] the determination to see fair play." How could America nurture its culture of democracy? Education was key, thought Jackson, John Mulder, and others. "It must be taught endlessly," Jackson wrote, "until it is as much a daily habit of thought with laymen as with lawyers." Lippmann evoked the difference between democratic and totalitarian governments with an analogy to automobile driving. In a democracy, the government provides rules of the road that enable each driver to choose a destination, a route, and a time of travel. Under a totalitarian system, "the officials seek to prescribe the destination of each driver, telling him when he must start, by what route he must go, and when he must arrive." Dewey, Jackson, and Mulder might have added that the democratic system would continue to function only if drivers were educated to respect and follow the rules of the road—to participate in the culture of democratic driving, so to speak. This theoretical reliance on democratic culture, it should be noted, manifested a lingering vestige of republican democracy. Whereas republican democracy had assumed that a homogeneous people share a common good, pluralist democracy assumed that a heterogeneous people share a cultural commitment to govern themselves through democratic processes.[65]

POLITICAL SCIENTISTS AND other intellectuals elaborated these ideas after World War II when they fully developed a theory of pluralist democracy. Just as neoclassical economists in the 1930s had explored the implications of horizontal competition in the marketplace, postwar political theorists analyzed a democratic politics conceptualized as a contest among equally empowered self-interested actors. As early as 1948, C. Herman Pritchett argued that even Supreme Court justices acted pursuant to their "individual predilections"; they cast their votes to decide cases in accordance with their political values. The justices, like other political actors, participated "in the power struggles of American politics." To be sure, pluralist democratic theory did not go unchallenged. Émigrés like Leo Strauss and Eric Voegelin, who had fled Nazi-controlled Europe, feared the implications of relativism and shied away from American pragmatism. Although the émigrés disputed many specific issues among themselves, they generally agreed that democracy could not rest on the swirling plurality of interests and values evident in American society. They demanded some firmer ground, some indubitable substantive truth that could prevent a slide to nihilism.[66]

Nonetheless, pluralist democratic theory, based on ethical relativism, achieved near-hegemonic status within the American academy. Political theorists stripped away any remaining pretense that individuals achieved fulfillment through the virtuous pursuit of the common good. If a politician (or academic) invoked a public interest (or common good) at all, he or she used it either as an instrument of propaganda or to refer merely to an aggregation of private interests. Self-fulfillment, whether in the economic or political sphere, arose solely from the pursuit of self-interest. Theorists thus began to flesh out the details of pluralist democracy. Some political scientists focused on the likelihood that individuals would pursue their interests and values by forming into pressure or interest groups. Wilfred Binkley and Malcolm Moos wrote in 1949 that "[t]he basic concept needed for an understanding of the dynamics of government is the multi-group nature of modern society." The only means for determining governmental policies, they explained, was "through the free competition of interest groups." David Truman, writing in 1951, examined how individuals become associated with multiple groups and how those groups seek "effective access to the institutions of government"—the "centers of interest-based power."[67]

Legal scholars, meanwhile, explored the implications of pluralist democratic theory for the rule of law. The combination of empiricism and relativism had presented a distinct problem: could law be objective if substantive
values and goals were relative? Was law no more than the idiosyncratic be-
haviors of various governmental officials? In fact, since the early 1930s, critics had castigated the legal realists for undermining the American commitment to following legal rules. Postwar legal scholars, repudiating realism,
attempted to accept pluralist democratic theory, including the underlying
ethical relativism, while simultaneously explaining the vitality of the rule of
law. As was true for theorizing in political science, the crux of this postwar
legal scholarship was its focus on process. Henry Hart and Albert Sacks
explained: "[governmental] decisions which are the duly arrived at result
of duly established procedures . . . ought to be accepted as binding upon
the whole society unless and until they are duly changed." For instance,
these "legal process" scholars maintained that a court's decision should
be deemed legitimate if the judge or judges followed the appropriate processes or procedures for judicial decision making. These processes, called
"reasoned elaboration," required a judge to give reasons for a decision, to
articulate those reasons in a detailed and coherent manner, and to relate the
decision to a relevant rule of law applied in a manner logically consistent
with precedent. Reasoned elaboration, as such, specified the preconditions
for resolving disputes in accordance with the rule of law. Judicial decision
making was not arbitrary, even if democracy was based on relativism.[68]

Starting in the 1950s, political scientist Robert Dahl published several
books comprehensively articulating the theory of pluralist democracy.
"If unrestrained by external checks," he asserted, "any given individual
or group of individuals will tyrannize over others." Given this primacy of
self-interest, democracy — or "rule by the people" — requires "some way of
ruling, a *process* for ruling." Thus, Dahl asked: "What are the distinctive
characteristics of a democratic process of government?" A "perfect democratic government," he reasoned, follows five criteria or conditions, with
the first and foremost being "effective participation." During government
decision making, citizens "must have adequate and equal opportunities for
placing questions on the agenda and for expressing reasons for endorsing
one outcome rather than another." The five conditions cannot be satisfied, Dahl added, unless citizens possess certain enforceable rights, such
as freedom of speech and press. If such rights are unprotected, "the democratic process does not exist." Well, then, Dahl asked, what happens "if
a majority acting by perfectly democratic procedures deprives a minority
of its freedom of speech?" Dahl's answer: it's impossible. "[I]n such a case

the majority would not — could not — be acting by 'perfectly democratic procedures' [because rights such as free speech] are integral to the democratic process." Although pluralist democratic theory focuses on process, the process requires the protection of certain substantive rights. Democracy has limits "built into the very nature of the process itself." Otherwise, individuals would be unable "to participate fully, as equal citizens, in the making of all the collective decisions by which they are bound." Finally, Dahl maintained that American culture nurtured a needed consensus regarding democratic processes. Individuals and interest groups might clash in political struggles, but they shared certain elementary cultural norms that prevented the society from splintering into embittered fragments. "To assume that this country has remained democratic because of its Constitution seems to me an obvious reversal of the relation," Dahl wrote, "it is much more plausible to suppose that the Constitution has remained because our society is essentially democratic." And our democratic culture encouraged self-interested individuals to bargain and compromise.[69]

STRUGGLES TO FULFILL THE PROMISE OF PLURALIST DEMOCRATIC THEORY

As Dahl and other political thinkers developed a theory of pluralist democracy, they helped solidify its entrenchment in American society. First, they proffered a theory that appeared to correspond ineluctably "with the realities of power." Second, while intellectuals like Merriam and Lippmann had already begun in the mid-1930s to describe democracy as a structuring of power, the postwar theorists proved instrumental in establishing the normative legitimacy of pluralist democratic government. Widespread participation, the pursuit of self-interest, and the organization of pressure groups were not regrettable social realities; rather, they exemplified how democracy *ought* to operate. Hence, with the normative blessings of political theorists, the roots of pluralist democracy penetrated deeper into the American soil. But this growth was often painful. During the 1930s, when the practice of pluralist democracy had taken hold, an underlying conservatism had limited the extent of social transformation. Soon, however, World War II initiated a fresh burst of change. The war finally catapulted the American economy far out of depression. Many war-related products became scarce, yet with regulation of the economy already well established, the government could move quickly to ration commodities like gasoline, automobiles, rubber, meat, milk, and sugar. Even so, the economy flourished. From 1938 to 1942, GNP nearly doubled, from \$85.2 to \$159.1 billion; by 1945, it was \$213.6 billion. The federal budget increased more than tenfold from 1939 to 1945, while personal consumption nearly doubled during that time. Many Americans believed the nation was fighting for a democracy that encompassed consumer capitalism. A Nash-Kelvinator advertisement depicted a paratrooper saying, "We have so many things, here in America, that belong only to a free people . . . warm, comfortable homes, automobiles and radios by the million." A 1943 book explicitly linked democracy and consumption: "The concept of representative government," wrote Leland Gordon in *Consumers in Wartime*, "includes your freedom as a consumer to choose whatever you wish in the way of economic goods or services to satisfy your wants."[70]

Wartime Americans achieved an unprecedented national unity as they together confronted aggressive and brutal external enemies. Unlike in World War I, once the United States entered the war, draft and war resistance was relatively minor. Mulder wrote that even before the attack on Pearl Harbor, "we were entering upon the task of becoming the 'arsenal of democracy,'" a nickname often applied particularly to the city of Detroit during the wartime era. Then, Mulder added, "[s]ince December 7, 1941, we have been a united nation." Americans of all types joined to sacrifice and to fight the common menace. Totalitarian governments threatened, it seemed, all Americans, mainstream and minority alike. Seeing the Nazis' and fascists' manifest attacks against societal outsiders, many Americans became more receptive to religious and ethnic minorities, who urged that the nation's strength lay in tolerance and diversity. By the end of the war, more than 120 national organizations worked "for better intergroup relations."[71]

The widespread unity of purpose combined with the economic boom to open new opportunities for women and African Americans. With so many men in the military and demand for products high, industries were forced to turn to untapped sources of labor; female and black employees filled positions previously denied to them. Moreover, under pressure, Roosevelt issued an executive order proscribing racial discrimination in war industries and creating the Fair Employment Practices Commission to enforce the antidiscrimination mandate. Unions, meanwhile, both facilitated and retarded these advances in employment fairness. On the one hand, the leaders of the UAW and other industrial unions pushed for inclusion of black workers despite opposition from many whites in the rank and file. Union leaders recognized that inclusiveness would in the long run undermine employer efforts to divide and conquer the work force. On the other hand, many unions cooperated with employers to maintain "segregated seniority lists" that often impeded black workers from progressing beyond low-paying menial jobs.[72]

Unions and employers were not alone in continuing to manifest traditional prejudices against minorities, despite the unifying inclusiveness of the war era. Social and economic discrimination against blacks remained widespread. In some towns, German prisoners of war could eat at lunch counters closed to African American soldiers. In a sixth-grade all-white Detroit classroom, the teacher assigned the students to write essays discussing "Why I like or don't like Negroes." The answers reflected customary biases: "they are mean"; "they are not very clean"; and with unintended irony, "[s]ome of them don't like white people." Partly in response to black advances — as African Americans moved into new jobs and new neighborhoods — racial tensions erupted into wartime riots in cities including Detroit, Los Angeles, New York, Chicago, and Mobile. Anti-Semiticism, too, remained strong. A 1945 poll focusing on a standard indicium of anti-Semiticism revealed that 58 percent of Americans believed Jews possessed too much power — a percentage higher than during the prewar years. Yet, perhaps the most egregious wartime example of racial or religious discrimination was the national government's internment of more than a hundred thousand individuals of Japanese descent, two-thirds of whom were American citizens. The War Department encouraged Roosevelt to issue the executive order that initiated the relocation process, which Congress then reinforced with a criminal statute.[73]

AFTER WORLD WAR II ended in 1945, the storyline of pluralist democracy becomes twofold. One narrative follows the development of the mass-consumer culture. The other emphasizes political and social struggles that aimed to bring the practices, the reality, of pluralist democracy into alignment with the emerging theory. Insofar as the professed aim of pluralist democracy was to achieve full and equal participation in democratic processes, these struggles sometimes produced advances. But they also sometimes failed, sparking retaliation and setbacks. Either way, the two narrative threads intertwined in the further evolution of pluralist democracy.

During the postwar era, the mass-consumer culture became even more richly embedded in the American ethos. The nation emerged from the war as the most powerful economic and military force in the world. GNP leaped from $213.6 billion in 1945 to nearly $300 billion in 1950 and then to $440.3 billion in 1957. American pluralist democracy was a consumers' democracy. The mass-media culture taught Americans "how to spend and enjoy." Spurred by the baby boom, spend they did. From 1945 to 1955, the total personal expenditures for various products, including clothing, jewelry, and furniture, more than doubled. Americans bought self-fulfillment, through consumption, while political participation aimed only at further self-fulfillment. The satisfaction of self-interest, either in the economic marketplace or the democratic arena, became the hallmark of a "good citizen." The "purchaser" was an ideal "citizen who simultaneously fulfilled personal desire and civic obligation by consuming." *Brides* magazine explicitly proclaimed that "when you buy 'the dozens of things you never bought or even thought of before . . . you are helping to build greater security for the industries of this country. . . . [W]hat you buy and how you buy it is very vital in your new life — and to our whole American way of living.'" Freedom and consumption were one and the same. And no product seemed to enhance freedom more than the automobile. In 1945, Americans spent $357 million to purchase cars; by 1950, the amount was $10,729 million, and by 1955, it was $15,800 million.[74]

The national government itself fueled this frenzy of consumption. Most important, in 1944, Congress enacted the Servicemen's Readjustment Act, commonly called the GI Bill of Rights, which encompassed "the most wide-ranging set of social benefits ever offered by the federal government in a single, comprehensive initiative." With other statutes, the GI Bill initiated four key programs, three of which would have enormous long-term consequences. First, and least important for the long term, the Bill provided that returning veterans would receive payment of $20 per week for fifty-two weeks to facilitate readjustment to civilian life. Second, the government would pay the tuition and fees for veterans who wanted to continue their educations. Third, the government would guarantee low-interest home loans for veterans. Finally, the government would assist veterans in seeking employment and would encourage employers to favor veterans when choosing among job applicants. With this springboard of governmental assistance, many veterans who had faced bleak futures before the war were now empowered to jump into a burgeoning middle class. The government helped them go to school, get a good job, and buy their first houses. These prosperous veterans and their families then became avid consumers during the booming 1950s.[75]

The government's support for home buying, in particular, rippled through the economy. In 1945, Americans spent $720 million building new dwelling units. In two years, that figure had increased more than seven times over. By 1955, nearly $15 billion went to new construction. By 1960, one-quarter of all homes had been built during the previous decade. And these new homes needed to be stocked with household products large and small — refrigerators, washers, dryers, televisions, vacuum cleaners, radios, kitchen tables, easy chairs, and on and on. The introduction of general credit cards rendered the extension of consumer credit practically instantaneous. President Harry Truman had declared that home building was "a job for private enterprise," but governmental subsidization encouraged developers to continue building and convinced "millions of Americans . . . it was cheaper to own than to rent." Much of the new building occurred in suburbs; from 1946 to 1953, suburban home building increased by 43 percent. Facilitating this shift of population away from cities, the 1956 Interstate Highway Act created a network of roads that allowed suburbanites to drive to jobs and to newly built shopping centers. By 1970, more people resided in the suburbs than in the cities.[76]

The postwar mass-consumer culture thus infused American society with an economic, cultural, and political glue that held diverse elements together. Many lower-class uneducated ethnic city dwellers metamorphosed into satisfied sedate educated middle-class suburban consumers. In 1956, *Fortune* magazine exclaimed: "Never has a whole people spent so much money on so many expensive things in such an easy way as Americans are doing today." During the 1950s, more than one million new families joined the middle class each year; one-half of the families in America would be middle class by the end of the decade. By 1960, less than one-fifth of white Americans would live in poverty, while in 1940, two-thirds had done so. National prosperity meant that (nearly) everyone could share in a larger pie; more people could flourish economically without threatening their neighbors. In 1955, Will Herberg asked what is the "'common religion' of American society, the 'common set of ideas, rituals, and symbols' that give it its 'overarching sense of unity'?" His answer: the "American Way of Life." It unified American society "amid conflict [and] provides the framework [in which] the crucial values of American existence are couched." The American Way of Life manifested a cultural consensus arising from consumer capitalism and sustaining the political negotiations and compromises of pluralist democracy. The American Way of Life "synthesizes all that commends itself to the American as the right, the good, and the true in actual life. It embraces such seemingly incongruous elements as sanitary plumbing and freedom of opportunity, Coca-Cola and an intense faith in education — all felt as moral questions relating to the proper way of life." Herberg concluded that diverse Americans — "Catholics, Protestants, and

Jews"—lived "in harmonious coexistence . . . under the benevolent aegis of American democracy."[77]

The mass media molded Americans to conform, to express homogeneous tastes and desires. Although the technology for television had developed by the late 1920s, the industry did not take hold of the American imagination (and economy) until after World War II. The number of families with television sets then increased tenfold from 1950 to 1957. In 1960, almost 90 percent of American households had at least one television and "watched an average of five hours per day." Much of this TV time was spent watching commercials; in 1957, the average viewer watched 420 advertisements each week. Both the TV shows and commercials depicted and shaped an America joined in harmonious consensus. Television encouraged families not only to purchase all the same goods but also to aspire to live like Donna Reed's TV family. "There were no Greeks, no Italians, or no Jews in this world, only Americans, with names that were obviously Anglo-Saxon and Protestant; it was a world of Andersons and Nelsons and Cleavers." The only exception was Lucille Ball's family, and only because she insisted that her real-life husband, Desi Arnaz, a Cuban bandleader, be given the role of her TV husband. Television families did not worry about money; they did not divorce; and they rarely got sick. "Families liked each other, and they tolerated each other's idiosyncrasies."[78]

As the twentieth century wore on, pluralist democracy and the mass-consumer culture completely intertwined. In the midst of the Cold War, Vice President Richard Nixon distinguished American from Communist government by explicitly linking pluralist democracy with consumption. "The United States comes closest to the ideal of prosperity for all in a classless society," he declared. The variety and availability of consumer goods in the United States symbolized "our right to choose. We do not wish to have decisions made at the top by governmental officials [regarding our] kind of house [or our] kind of ideas." Before long, politics and commercial consumption became barely distinguishable. A citizen's function, it seemed, was to consume, to pursue self-interest, whether in the economic or political marketplace. The prototypical public space became the shopping mall, a forum devoted to consumption and self-gratification. A voter was a consumer, and a political candidate was a product. In the 1950s, the Republican party chairman insisted that you must "sell your candidates and your programs the way a business sells its products," and Dwight Eisenhower listened. His two presidential campaigns relied on major New York advertising agencies to market "Ike." Afterward, candidate and product marketing would only grow more similar.[79]

WHEN COMPARED WITH republican democracy, pluralist democracy had its distinct advantages. The common good of republican democracy often seemed a veneer for the imposition of dominant cultural values and societal interests. Civic virtue (or the lack thereof) often appeared to be a pretext for excluding massive segments of the population from participating in free government. Pluralist democracy instead provided mechanisms for widespread participation, generated economic opportunities for many, and recognized the legitimacy of diverse interests and values. When compared with the 1928 Al Smith–Herbert Hoover presidential election, the successful 1960 presidential candidacy of John F. Kennedy epitomized the differences between the two democratic regimes. A Catholic could be elected president.

But in both practice and theory, pluralist democracy had (and has) its drawbacks and limitations. At the level of theory, a political approach that urges no more than the pursuit of self-interest seems ethically inadequate. Unsurprisingly, some theorists have argued for alternative approaches that encourage attention to more altruistic goals. At the level of practice, many Americans recognized the obvious: that the promises of pluralist democracy remained unfulfilled for many peripheral groups. Theorists like Charles Black, Jr., demanded that African Americans "be allowed . . . to participate fully in the public life of the society." But the practice of pluralist democracy also encountered more subtle problems. Organizations might claim to speak for broad interest groups yet actually give voice to only a small number of individuals. Pluralist democracy might guarantee an opportunity to participate in politics, yet discourage activities, like voting, that do not seem to gratify self-interest in a sufficiently tangible manner. In the 1970s and 1980s, voter participation in even presidential elections hovered around only 50 percent. The mass-media culture might have been glue for a diverse American society under a pluralist democratic regime, but it also appeared to generate a dulling of sensibilities, a discouragement of creativity, a demand for conformity masquerading as individuality. Then, in the 1960s, the ostensible consensus of the 1950s splintered into hundreds of shards. Encouraged by pluralist democracy itself, numerous groups emerged to assert their interests, values, and rights. One could find a women's movement, a consumers' movement, an environmental movement, a black power movement, and of course, a protest movement against the Vietnam War. In the 1970s and 1980s, conservative Christians became a predominant interest group seeking to satisfy its values and desires in the democratic marketplace. These and other interest groups rarely sought to deliberate about public issues; they typically sought to press their preexisting interests and values in the most forceful manner possible.[80]

During the sixties, the antiwar movement, in particular, engendered a counterculture that claimed to reject the provincial values nurtured by the profit-driven mass-consumer culture. Regardless, while the fifties homogeneity now looked like a shattered facade, the mass-consumer culture adjusted rapidly. Nonconformity became a product to market. Drink Pepsi and be part of a new generation. Mass-marketing analysts realized they could sell ever-more goods by targeting distinct segments of the population — a single producer might market, let's say, one beer for lower-economic class consumers, another for the middle class, another for the wealthy, another for white females, another for black males, and yet another for the weight conscious. Following the cue, political campaigns likewise began to target population segments. If anything, these segmented advertising and political campaigns encouraged individuals to focus even more on the satisfaction of self-interest, on self-fulfillment. A Cadillac advertisement "featured a young black male doctor saying, 'I don't drive the car for the prestige. I drive it for my own feelings of satisfaction.'" In politics, campaigns did not encourage voters to contemplate and to deliberate about possible resolutions of controversial issues. Campaigns sold voters prepackaged candidates or resolutions that fit their predetermined interests.[81]

The integration of pluralist democracy with consumer capitalism engendered other problems. As political campaigns became commercial-advertising campaigns, the costs of running for office increased dramatically. Vast independent wealth became a near prerequisite for anyone interested in running for a major governmental office, and corporate donations to political campaigns shaped discussions of issues and policies. Equally important, while corporate interests had retained significant political power even during the New Deal, the government's post–World War II focus on economic expansion rather than equity enhanced corporate political power. When the Republicans regained control of the Senate and the House in 1947, for the first time since 1931, they flexed their muscles to modify the legislative framework governing labor-management relations. The watershed NLRA had concentrated on controlling management during labor disputes, but the Republican-controlled Congress countered with the Taft-Hartley Act of 1947, which focused instead on controlling unions. The new Act "banned the closed shop, permitted employers to sue unions for breaking contracts, forbade union contributions to political campaigns, and required unions to give 60 days' notice before inaugurating strikes." Congress overrode President Truman's veto of the Act when southern Democrats voted with their Republican congressional colleagues. Unions remained strong through the 1950s, but since that time, union membership and power has declined. By "the end of the 1980s, the United States had a smaller proportion of its labor force unionized than any other advanced industrial nation." President Ronald Reagan's appointment of Donald Dotson as chair of the NLRB epitomized the decline of union power. Dotson denounced collective bargaining as equivalent to "labor monopoly, the destruction of individual freedom, and the destruction of the marketplace as the mechanism for determining the value of labor."[82]

Union members did not like the Taft-Hartley Act, yet they accepted it in exchange for higher wages and contributions to pensions and health insurance. The wages and benefits combined with the governmental assistance manifested especially in the GI Bill of Rights to help usher many blue collar workers into the middle class. The trouble was that neither the labor-management tradeoff nor the governmental programs provided equal benefits or opportunities for all Americans. To the contrary, these pathways to middle-class comforts were either strewn with obstacles or completely closed to many, especially racial minorities. Governmental programs tilted strongly against African Americans. The most important postwar legislation, the GI Bill, extended its bounty to veterans only, of course. Yet, during the war, the military forces had turned away a disproportionate number of black men, who consequently could not benefit from the various GI Bill programs (also, only a small percentage of women could benefit). Even so, many blacks had served in the military and should have qualified for GI benefits, but they faced additional impediments. Numerous veterans' programs consisted of a statutory framework, supported with national funding, that delegated administration to state and local officials as well as to private (nongovernmental) actors. The GI Bill provided funds for veterans to attend college, but the colleges themselves still determined whom to admit. The veterans' homeowners' mortgage insurance program required the would-be buyer to secure a loan from a bank or other private lending institution, but these institutions continued to discriminate on the basis of race. Lenders typically "redlined" predominantly black neighborhoods as "high risk" and denied loans as a matter of course to hopeful borrowers. The government encouraged employers to favor veteran job applicants but did not proscribe racial discrimination. In the South, the postwar introduction of a mechanical cotton picker eliminated agricultural jobs and led whites to support black emigration. Many African Americans, hoping to secure factory employment, moved to northern cities, only to be met with closed doors. Numerous companies overtly discriminated on the basis of race when deciding whom to hire and for what positions. In Detroit, Michigan, employers' job advertisements routinely distinguished between races, until the state enacted a fair employment statute in 1955. When employers hired blacks, they typically placed them in menial positions. The good blue collar jobs, the jobs that facilitated a transition from lower- to middle-economic status, were overwhelmingly open only to whites. Over the past century, "the black poor [had] progressed from slave labor to cheap labor to (for many) no labor at all."[83]

Such enormous racial loopholes in facially neutral postwar national governmental programs were not accidental. To secure southern Democratic support, these laws were "deliberately designed to accommodate Jim Crow." An openly racist and anti-SemiticMississippi Democrat, John Rankin, chaired the House Committee on World War Legislation and controlled much of the initial drafting of bills related to veterans' benefits. The GI Bill had been written, one 1947 report concluded, "as though the [benefits] had been earmarked 'For White Veterans Only.'" This postwar discrimination would help sustain the structural patterns of American society through the end of the century. For instance, the "absolute median income gap between black and white men actually widened in the 1950s, rising from $5,000 to almost $8,000 by 1960." But in the long term, discrimination in housing benefits had the deepest societal implications. A 1947 study reported that in thirteen Mississippi cities, the Veterans' Administration (VA) had guaranteed 3,229 loans; only two had gone to African Americans. In the North, black veterans did not fare much better despite their efforts to garner benefits. As of 1950, blacks in the New York metropolitan area had received only one-tenth of the VA mortgages even though such mortgages accounted for more than 15 percent of home loans. Discrepancies in lending naturally led to discrepancies in home ownership. The exploding suburbs became de facto white havens. The prototype, Levittown, Long Island, offered inexpensive starter homes, especially for veterans. To induce buyers, the builders even offered gifts, including free televisions and washing machines. By 1953, Levittown's population numbered 70,000 —with not a single African American. In 1960, the 65,276 Levittown residents included only 57 blacks. Such discrepancies in home ownership in turn engendered subsequent inequalities in the accrual of equity and wealth. By 1984, largely because of differences in homeownership, the median net worth of black families stood at $3,397, only 9 percent of the white-family median of $39,135.[84]

In a pluralist democracy completely intertwined with consumer capitalism, this racially skewed distribution of wealth has nurtured other inequalities. Regardless of race, wealth facilitates political participation and influence. Given that blacks and other racial minorities constitute a high percentage of the poor, they are less likely to control, or even touch, the levers of power in our democratic system. In short, the reality of pluralist democracy has never matched the theory, particularly the theory's ideal of near-universal participation. Nonetheless, for a variety of reasons, including sustained struggles by peripheral groups, especially African Americans, the reality has approached the theory in at least some ways. While the national government acceded to white southern demands to facilitate racial discrimination in the administration of postwar federal programs, the national ethos simultaneously turned against overt racism. Before the war, overt racism and anti-Semitism had been commonplace and socially acceptable among many Americans, but awareness of the Holocaust forced Americans to reconsider their attitudes. Adolf Hitler gave racism and anti-Semitism a "bad name." In late 1946, Truman appointed a Committee on Civil Rights, and its report condemning racial discrimination led Truman to issue an executive order in 1948 mandating the desegregation of the armed forces. Meanwhile, one survey conducted immediately after the war concluded that 56 percent of Americans believed Jews had too much power, but the percentage dropped to 13 by 1964, and then dropped again to 10 percent in 1981. Many Americans had internalized a new ethos of racial and religious equality: Nazis had been racist monsters, but Americans were different.[85]

Laying claim to that American difference remained problematic in the 1950s, however, while the South continued to enforce Jim Crow laws that racially segregated all sorts of public accommodations and facilities, including schools, restaurants, buses, water fountains, and swimming pools. Black men who had fought in the war — fought supposedly to secure liberty and equality — found the indignities of Jim Crow increasingly difficult to accept. Resistance became more common, with Rosa Park's refusal to give her bus seat to a white passenger in December 1955 sparking the spread of the civil rights movement (the importance of free expression to civil rights protests is discussed in chapter 11). Yet, black resistance alone might not have spurred social change if not for other factors that generated more widespread white support for black civil rights, for greater inclusion of African Americans within pluralist democratic processes. Despite the reaction against the Holocaust, despite black demands for "simple justice," the white South's intransigent resistance to change continued to harm the nation in two ways perceptible to many Americans. First, while the rest of the country enjoyed an economic boom, the South remained in an economic mire. Many corporations viewed the social stratification mandated by Jim Crow as an impediment to prosperity and therefore refused to invest in southern states. Black southerners, after all, were potential consumers largely precluded from purchasing goods because discrimination relegated them to poverty. Second, the United States became locked in the Cold War with the Soviet Union. Both nations sought to solicit support from emerging third-world nations, yet people of color populated many of these emerging nations. With southern states still enforcing a type of apartheid, the United States struggled to champion the advantages of democracy over communism. Thus, partly as a matter of economic development, and partly as a matter of Cold War imperatives, white political support (outside the South) shifted to support the civil rights movement.[86]

The mass media played a key role here, too. Throughout the 1950s, many white southerners had resisted social change, thwarting civil rights protesters with force, intimidation, and legal sanctions. But by the early 1960s, television had become the primary source of news for most Americans. Each night, then, white Americans recoiled in horror as they watched southern governmental officials beset black (and white) protesters with billy clubs, fire hoses, and attack dogs. By the mid-1960s, unprecedented national support for legal and social changes existed, leading to legislative actions that significantly expanded democratic participation. In early 1964, 71 percent of nonsouthern whites favored passage of a law prohibiting racial discrimination in places of public accommodation. Speaking before a television audience seventy million strong, President Lyndon B. Johnson, himself a southerner (from Texas), urged Congress to respond to the "outraged conscience of a nation." He declared it "deadly wrong . . . to deny any of your fellow Americans the right to vote." Black leaders as different as the nonviolent Martin Luther King, Jr., and the more aggressive Malcolm X agreed on the benefits of suffrage.[87]

Legislative-type changes first emerged in the late 1950s and early 1960s. Ratified in 1961, the twenty-third amendment extended a right to vote in presidential elections to citizens in the heavily black District of Columbia. Yet, this measure was qualified. The amendment granted the District no more (electoral college) electors "than the least populous State" rather than electors commensurate to its population. Nonetheless, additional action soon followed. Just as the national government had asserted unprecedented power over the economy during the New Deal, it now exercised power over suffrage, traditionally (under republican democracy) left largely to state and local prerogatives. At a constitutional level, the twenty-fourth amendment, ratified in 1964, proscribed poll taxes in federal elections, while the twenty-sixth amendment, ratified in 1971, guaranteed the right to vote for anyone eighteen years of age or older. In terms of statutory law, the Voting Rights Act of 1965 (VRA) and parts of the Civil Rights Act of 1964 eradicated literacy, educational, and character tests that had been used to deny or discourage minority voting. The VRA proved especially effective in expanding suffrage. In Mississippi, for example, the percentage of blacks registered to vote leaped from 6.7 to 66.5 percent by 1969. By 1975, the national electorate had grown "in excess of twenty million." The VRA led to the election of black mayors, county executives, and state legislators. By the end of the century, the VRA had also engendered a greater number of black congressional members. In the late 1980s, only three blacks represented southern states in the House, even though nearly one-half of the black population still resided in the South. But the 1990 census in conjunction with earlier (1982) amendments to the VRA led to the creation of new minority-majority districts — congressional districts where a racial minority constituted a voting majority — which facilitated the election of African Americans. Consequently, with thirteen blacks being elected from new southern districts, the total number of African American representatives jumped to forty-one.[88]

Additional legislation proscribed other manifestations of overt discrimination. Most important, the Civil Rights Act of 1964 prohibited discrimination "on the ground of race, color, religion, or national origin" in employment and in places of public accommodation, such as hotels and restaurants. This and other antidiscrimination statutes generated economic opportunities for some African Americans and other racial minorities — with breakthroughs even into white-collar jobs. And in the pluralist democratic regime, greater wealth generally translated into greater political influence. Yet, for many African Americans, these social changes often proved hollow, more form than substance. Indeed, the widespread support for legislation in the early to mid-1960s might have arisen partly for that very reason: that the proposed social changes were formal, creating a right to vote (not a right to have proportional representation or political power), creating a right against overt racial discrimination (not a right to a job or to a reasonable income). In truth, by the time the Civil Rights Act proscribed employment discrimination, many of the good blue collar factory jobs — the jobs in midwestern and eastern cities that had catapulted numerous whites to middle-class status after World War II — had disappeared. The quest for corporate profits had induced auto manufacturers and other industries to begin an exodus to greener pastures overseas. Moreover, in the late 1960s, as increasing numbers of African Americans began to find Stokely Carmichael's demand for "Black Power" more appealing than King's integrationist plea of "We Shall Overcome," as more blacks sought substantive change, widespread white support for the transforming civil rights movement dissipated. King himself acknowledged, "Jobs are harder and costlier to create than voting rolls. The eradication of slums housing millions is complex far beyond integrating buses and lunch counters."[89]

Consequently, more than three-quarters of a century after the initial transition to pluralist democracy and nearly one-half century after the civil rights movement burst onto the national scene, the economic disparities that became entrenched after World War II — the unequal accruals of wealth for white and black families — remain intact to a great degree. And economic disparities still translate into political inequalities in our consumers' democracy. Percentage-wise, far more blacks than whites remain today explicitly disenfranchised — now partly because of disparities within the American criminal justice system. A disproportionate percentage of African Americans spend time in prison; at the end of the twentieth century, the imprisonment rate for black men was 8.5 times that for whites. Approximately 45 percent of prisoners were African American. "Twenty-three percent of all black males in their twenties were either in prison, on parole, on probation, or awaiting trial." In any society, unemployment and poverty are likely to generate crime, but this empirical link is likely to be exacerbated in a society that equates self-fulfillment with consumption. Because many states prohibit convicted felons from voting, nearly 13 percent of African American men are disfranchised, a rate "seven times the national average." Some states disfranchise one in four black males; three states disenfranchise African Americans at a rate "more than 17 times higher" than that for nonblacks. Compared with other democratic nations, the United States is unique for its high felon conviction rate and its disfranchisement of nonincarcerated felons. In the fourteen states that disfranchise some or all nonincarcerated felons, approximately "40 percent of the next generation of black men is likely to lose permanently the right to vote." Remarkably, felony disfranchisement might have recently altered the outcomes in seven Senate races and one presidential election (Bush versus Gore). The theory of pluralist democracy mandates universal participation, but the reality still falls far short of this ideal.[90]

———————•◄

Pluralist Democracy and Judicial Review

As the nation emerged from World War I, the Supreme Court as well as the rest of the federal judiciary still exercised the power of judicial review in accordance with republican democracy. Courts determined whether governmental actions were either for the common good—and therefore permissible—or for partial or private interests—and therefore impermissible. For example, in *Adkins v. Children's Hospital,* decided in 1923, the Court held that a District of Columbia law setting minimum wages for women and children violated due process liberty to contract. The statute amounted to impermissible class legislation, "a naked, arbitrary exercise of power," because it accounted for "the necessities of only one party to the contract." Such judicial applications of republican democratic principles continued into the mid-1930s for three reasons. First, while the practice of pluralist democracy began to emerge during the early 1930s, the theory did not crystallize until later in the decade. Living through the transformation of democracy, many observers did not immediately recognize or grasp the ramifications of the transition. Second, the institutional practice of adjudication, with its emphasis on stare decisis, has a natural reliance on the past, on precedents, on tradition. As such, one would expect the judiciary often to lag behind other institutions when change is afoot. Third, and related to the previous point, federal judges (including Supreme Court justices) receive lifetime appointments. In a time of critical transition, such as the 1930s, many judges would have matured, learned their professional norms, and been appointed to the federal bench during the prior regime. Such judges would be apt to continue applying the principles and doctrines they had become accustomed to earlier in their careers.[1]

CRISIS AND CHANGE

During the early and mid-1930s, the national and state governments' efforts to boost the country out of the Depression by comprehensively regulating the economy clashed with the Court's traditional methods of judicial review. Yet, the Court still upheld legislation it found to promote the common good, and more important, the Court even hinted it might respond favorably to the pull of pluralist democracy. As early as 1931, the Court upheld a first-amendment free speech claim by reasoning that free expression intertwined with democratic government — a position that would eventually become axiomatic under pluralist democracy. Then, in 1934, in *Home Building and Loan Association v. Blaisdell,* Chief Justice Charles E. Hughes's majority opinion explained that the societal changes engendered by industrialization had produced "a growing appreciation of public needs." Similarly, that same year, Justice Owen J. Roberts's majority opinion in *Nebbia v. New York,* upholding state regulations of milk prices, reasoned that the "category of businesses affected with a public interest" was flexible and expandable. Both these cases suggested that the Court might be ready to enlarge the republican democratic common good to such a degree that the concept would become meaningless; any interests or values could, in theory, be deemed equivalent to the common good.[2]

Nonetheless, in 1935, the Court's hinted readiness to embrace pluralist democracy vanished like a will-o'-the-wisp. Both *Blaisdell* and *Nebbia* were close five-to-four decisions, with the same four conservative dissenters, sometimes disparaged as the "Four Horsemen": James C. McReynolds, Willis Van Devanter, George Sutherland, and Pierce Butler. Moreover, despite Roberts's *Nebbia* opinion, he generally adhered to republican democratic principles and often voted with the Four Horsemen, though he occasionally joined the more progressive-liberal justices, Harlan F. Stone, Benjamin Cardozo, and Brandeis — and quite often, Hughes, who was more of a centrist, like Roberts. In a spate of 1935 and 1936 cases invalidating key New Deal and state social welfare statutes, Roberts repeatedly joined the conservatives. *Railroad Retirement Board v. Alton Railroad Company* struck down the Railroad Retirement Act of 1934 as being beyond Congress's power under the commerce clause. Reasoning that the statute contravened the common good, the Court categorized it as an effort "to impose by sheer fiat noncontractual incidents upon the relation of employer and employee . . . as a means of assuring a particular class of employees against old age dependency." In short order, the Court invalidated the NIRA, the Bituminous Coal Conservation Act, and provisions of the AAA. In *Carter v. Carter Coal Company,* the Court clarified that acting for the common good was a necessary but not sufficient condition for establishing the constitutionality of congressional legislation. Not only must a statute be for the common good, but Congress must also act pursuant to one of its specifically enumerated powers. And the Court consistently resolved such congressional power issues in accordance with a formal conceptualism similar to that used to determine whether a governmental action furthered only partial or private interests. For instance, in *Carter Coal,* the Court distinguished national and local activities as if they were preexisting a priori categories. Reasoning that mining, like manufacturing, growing crops, and other types of production, was "a purely local activity," the Court concluded that Congress's attempt to regulate bituminous coal mining exceeded its constitutional powers.[3]

Even the progressive-liberal justices analyzed cases in accord with the traditional structures of republican democratic judicial review. They did not subscribe to the new legal realist jurisprudence, which hewed closely to the emerging pluralist democracy. Instead, Stone had joined longtime adherents Brandeis and Cardozo in following sociological jurisprudence, which encouraged courts to determine the common good by focusing on empirical evidence, rather than a priori formal categories. In particular cases, the progressive justices would vote based on whether, given the evidence, they assessed the common good consistently with the conservatives' analysis. Thus, in *A.L.A. Schechter Poultry Corporation v. United States,* Stone, Brandeis, and Cardozo joined the other justices in unanimously invalidating the NIRA, but in *United States v. Butler,* they dissented, determining that the disputed AAA provisions promoted the "general welfare" and fulfilled a "public purpose."[4]

The Court's adherence to republican democratic principles provoked the ire of many intellectuals. Robert Hale, a political scientist associated with the legal realist movement, published an article in 1935 exemplifying three interrelated criticisms. First, Hale questioned the justices' republican democratic assumption that a private sphere of individual freedom existed distinct from a public sphere of governmental action, with the common good demarcating the border between the spheres. Duties and obligations in the so-called private realm exist only because of governmental support; property and contract rights arise and are enforceable only if the courts recognize and sanction them. In Hale's words, governmental officials, including judges, effectively carry "out the mandates of property owners." Second, one party to a contract typically lacks true freedom, especially in the employment context. While the Supreme Court rhapsodized about liberty to contract, most employees either accepted the employer's offer or starved. As Hale elaborated, private entities (individuals or corporations) often exert coercive power over other individuals who, lacking reasonable alternatives, are forced to accept inequitable contracts. The justices' laissez-faire–inspired interpretation of the common good, in which the absence of governmental regulation supposedly maximized individual liberty, disregarded social reality. Third, Hale suggested the Court should modify its approach to judicial review in accordance with the realities of democracy—that is, in accordance with the emergent pluralist democracy. When Congress enacted economic or social welfare legislation, it did not infringe liberty. Instead, Congress chose among the competing interests of different individuals and groups.[5]

Other realists denounced the *Lochner* era justices for their ostensible reliance on formal doctrinal categories. The justices wrote opinions suggesting that these doctrinal categories, including the distinction between the common good and partial or private interests, mandated case outcomes. The sociological jurisprudents had long rejected the a priori formalism that predominated among the Langdellians and the (non-Progressive) justices, but they then sought to ascertain the common good by assessing social interests. The realists went further, questioning the meaningfulness of abstract categories and the accessibility of firm values (a victim of ethical relativism). Felix Cohen argued that judges should decide cases by attending closely to the factual details and the specific interests at stake in each case. In any particular dispute, there were likely to be numerous competing interests or values. Judges should balance any and all interests germane to the dispute, not only those that supposedly qualified as social interests relevant to a so-called common good. The realists, consequently, favored ad hoc judicial decision making. Cohen argued that a judge, when confronted with the legal issue, "Is there a contract?" should not focus on abstract principles like consideration and mutual assent. The judge should instead weigh the competing interests and determine what real-world consequences would follow from the respective possible decisions.[6]

While intellectuals like Hale and Cohen constructed complex theoretical arguments, other critics were more decidedly political. And once the Court began bulldozing the New Deal in 1935 and 1936, such critics intensified their harangues of the justices. After *Butler* invalidated AAA provisions, the *New York Times* reported that Iowa State students hung the six majority justices in effigy. A standard critique became that the justices were a group of crotchety old men out of step with modern times. Among the Four Horsemen, in particular, Van Devanter had been appointed in 1910, McReynolds in 1914, and Sutherland and Butler in 1922. Only McReynolds had not been a Republican appointee; Wilson had nominated him. In a best-selling 1936 book, Drew Pearson and Robert Allen denounced the justices as "Nine Old Men" who refused "to take cognizance of the speed of modern civilization in industrial and economic development, and [denied] posterity the right to express itself in regard to social and economic reform in its own way." The problem was not that the justices acted politically but rather that their politics contravened the desires of many Americans — or more to the point, their politics clashed with the New Deal. And the 1936 election seemed to prove the continuing popularity of Roosevelt and the New Deal in general. FDR received close to twenty-eight million popular votes compared with Alf Landon's total of less than seventeen million.[7]

In the wake of his landslide victory, Roosevelt pressed for change. If the Court, as an institution, insisted on politically opposing the New Deal, Roosevelt would change its politics. He could not force the Four Horsemen to retire and open spots for new appointees, so he decided to ask Congress to add new positions to the Court. Roosevelt would then be able to appoint New Deal supporters to counterbalance the Four Horsemen. FDR did not hatch this court-packing plan on his own. Congress had previously enacted legislation to restrict federal court jurisdiction in response to judicial decisions interfering with congressional objectives. FDR himself knew of a politically successful 1911 court-packing threat in Great Britain, and his attorney general, Homer Cummings, had raised the idea that a statute, rather than a constitutional amendment, might be the best way to alter the makeup and politics of the Court. In fact, a book published in 1935 explored the possibility of "packing the bench," by means of a statute, so as to limit the Court's power. Regardless of the origins of court packing, Roosevelt revealed his proposal in a message to the Senate on February 5, 1937. Early the next month, on March 9, Roosevelt pleaded his case for reform to the American people during one of his radio-broadcasted Fireside Chats. He lamented that "chance and the disinclination of individuals to leave the Supreme bench have now given us a Court in which five Justices will be over seventy-five years of age before next June and one over seventy." These justices had created a "crisis" by casting "doubts on the ability of the elected Congress to protect us against catastrophe by meeting squarely our modern social and economic conditions." Roosevelt thus sketched the following proposal: "Whenever a Judge or Justice of any Federal Court has reached the age of seventy and does not avail himself of the opportunity to retire on a pension, a new member shall be appointed by the President then in office, with the approval, as required by the Constitution, of the Senate of the United States." The Court, under this proposed legislation, could have anywhere between a minimum of nine and a maximum of fifteen justices. If implemented, this plan would render judicial decision making "speedier and therefore less costly" and would "bring to the decision of social and economic problems younger men who have had personal experience and contact with modern facts and circumstances."[8]

FDR's court-packing plan sparked immediate controversy. Even many of Roosevelt's congressional supporters questioned its wisdom; they claimed it would unduly skew the balance of power among the three national branches, endanger individual liberties, and diminish state sovereignty. While Congress debated the proposal, its fate still uncertain, the Supreme Court announced two decisions — *West Coast Hotel Company v. Parrish,* and *NLRB v. Jones and Laughlin Steel Corporation* — that revealed a new willingness to uphold economic and social welfare statutes and ultimately doomed the court-packing plan. To a great degree, Roberts was responsible for the so-called switch in time that saved nine because he abandoned the Four Horsemen and began to vote more consistently with the progressive-liberal justices. These two 1937 decisions not only had enormous political ramifications — because of Roberts's apparent transition — but, equally important, also marked a Court turn toward accepting the new regime of pluralist democracy.[9]

West Coast Hotel, decided March 29, involved a state law setting minimum wages for women. The Four Horsemen, dissenting, accepted the employer's argument; *Adkins* had already held that such a statute violated freedom of contract as protected by due process. In an opinion written by Sutherland, the dissenters reasoned that this minimum wage law, applicable only to women, constituted "arbitrary" class legislation. The five-justice majority, with an opinion written by Hughes, overruled *Adkins* and upheld the law. Much of the opinion invoked concepts familiar from earlier cases, concepts echoing republican democratic government. The Court referred to the common good with various iterations, explaining that liberty can be restrained to promote "the health, safety, morals, and welfare of the people" and that, more specifically, freedom of contract could be infringed "in the public interest." Yet, near the end of the opinion, Hughes appeared to accept the realist-inspired criticisms of the formalist distinction between public and private spheres. The unregulated economic marketplace did not maximize employees' liberty. To the contrary, employers coerced employees to work for unreasonable wages; the workers "are in an unequal position with respect to bargaining power and are thus relatively defenseless against the denial of a living wage." If the government did not act to correct these inequities, it would "provide what is in effect a subsidy for unconscionable employers." When employers failed to pay a living wage, the government needed to provide relief; the government would no longer allow indigents to starve. By questioning the separatedness of the public and private spheres, Hughes implicitly doubted the conceptual distinction between a common good and partial or private interests, so central to republican democracy. The Court might still be using terms resonant with earlier cases decided under republican democracy, but such terms, such as "the public interest," now apparently meant something different. Thus, the majority refused to invalidate the law as class legislation, even though it extended protection only to women and not to men. Instead, the justices emphasized that the legislature can choose the manner and the degree to which it responds to social problems.[10]

NLRB v. Jones and Laughlin Steel Corporation, decided two weeks later, erased doubts about whether the Court in *West Coast Hotel* had turned toward pluralist democracy. Again, in a five-to-four decision, with the same majority and dissenters (and with Hughes again writing for the majority), the Court upheld legislation that it could have readily invalidated under the strictures of republican democratic judicial review. Significantly, this legislation was not only federal, it was the NLRA, the statute that ushered in an era of dramatically expanding union rolls and nurtured the transformation of ethnic outsiders into politically active voting citizens. The NLRB had found that Jones and Laughlin had engaged in statutorily proscribed unfair labor practices, while Jones and Laughlin insisted that Congress had exceeded its power in passing the NLRA. In sustaining the law, the Court articulated two points crucial to the transition to pluralist democratic judicial review. First, the Court refused to restrict Congress's commerce power by reference to formal doctrinal categories. Jones and Laughlin argued that manufacturing was, by definition, a form of production rather than a type of interstate commerce and, consequently, beyond congressional control. In the past, such ostensibly noncommercial activities could be regulated only if they could be categorized as an "essential part" of "a 'stream' or 'flow' of commerce." In this case, though, the justices repudiated such categorical limits on congressional power. Likewise, when Jones and Laughlin argued that the regulated activities had only an indirect rather than direct effect on interstate commerce — a categorization that previously would have judicially doomed legislation — the Court declared: "We are asked to shut our eyes to the plainest facts of our national life and to deal with the question of direct and indirect effects in an intellectual vacuum." Instead of resolving the case in such a vacuum, pursuant to formal categories, the justices insisted that they must understand interstate commerce as a "practical conception." And whether particular activities bore a sufficiently "close and substantial relation to interstate commerce" to justify legislative regulation was now, according to the Court, "primarily for Congress to consider and decide."[11]

Second, the Court refused to classify employees or labor unions as illegitimate factions who could not pursue their interests in the political process. In the past, the Court had frequently deemed statutes that benefited unions to be impermissible class legislation furthering partial or private interests rather than the common good. Labor relations therefore had largely been governed by the common law, which judges ordinarily had interpreted favorably to employers. Meanwhile, courts had consistently concluded that statutes promoting commerce or business advanced the common good. Now, the justices abjured such a distinction between employees and employers. "Employees have as clear a right to organize and select their representatives for lawful purposes as the [manufacturer-employer] has to organize its business and select its own officers and agents." Employees and employers stood on equal footing: each group had its respective interests and values. True, a manufacturer has a "right to conduct its business in an orderly manner," but employees also have a "correlative right to organize for the purpose of securing the redress of grievances and to promote agreements with employers relating to rates of pay and conditions of work." Indeed, the Court explained that even if the legislation were "one-sided" — subjecting "the employer to supervision and restraint" while leaving "untouched the abuses for which employees may be responsible" — the statute would still be constitutional. As a matter of policy, Congress could choose which "evils" to remedy and in what manner to do so.[12]

This case left the traditional republican democratic structure of judicial review in shambles. If competing interests, pressed by opposed groups, produced all legislation, then the courts could no longer invalidate a statute as class legislation favoring partial or private interests. The Court might still explain that a particular statute promoted the general welfare, the public interest, or the common good, but these terms had different connotations under the new pluralist democratic regime. Insofar as a common good existed under pluralist democracy, it was no more than an aggregation of private interests and values; the common good no longer signified the virtuous transcendence of self-interest. Congress, at its discretion, could legitimately and openly act in response to the entreaties of the most powerful or persuasive interest groups.[13]

In 1937, commentators debated the significance of the Court's shift, but it was conspicuous enough that a *New York Times* banner headline "hailed [the] bench change." The *Washington Post* called *Jones and Laughlin* "a historic opinion which may well be a turning point in American political and economic life." The *Post* added that "[n]oncombatant Senators said [the decision] definitely gave Congress a free field for action under the commerce clause." Yet, the turn toward a form of judicial review consistent with pluralist democracy was not precisely revolutionary, nor for that matter, evolutionary. It was not sudden and unanticipated—that is, revolutionary—because the constitutional system had been undergoing a gradual transition from republican to pluralist democracy. This transition started with demographic, economic, and cultural pressures that traced back to before the 1920s. These pressures built over the years until a transition in democracy became a fait accompli; a reversal of direction became near impossible. Hence, with hindsight, one might reasonably conclude that, at some point, the Court's acceptance of the new system of pluralist democracy became foreordained, a corollary to systemic changes already in place. From this perspective, the *Blaisdell* and *Nebbia* decisions might be characterized not as mere will-o'-the-wisps but rather as early manifestations of a gradual transition. Yet, the 1937 Court turn should still not be depicted as an inevitable moment in a long process of evolutionary change. The democratic practices presaging the shift had developed over the prior few years, but Roberts might not have altered his posture. Not only had he previously resisted doing so, but in 1936, in one of the cases invalidating New Deal legislation, he articulated a quintessential statement of mechanistic formalism: "When an act of Congress is appropriately challenged in the courts as not conforming to the constitutional mandate, the judicial branch of the government has only one duty; to lay the article of the Constitution which is invoked beside the statute which is challenged and to decide whether the latter squares with the former." To be sure, Robert's receptiveness to New Deal legislation might have been temporary or circumstantial, but "Roberts' Switch," as it was trumpeted in the *Post*, was crucial to the "turn of events," as he "cast his vote on the side of Chief Justice Charles Evans Hughes and the so-called liberal trio of Justices [Brandeis, Stone, and Cardozo]." Although at the time, one could of course not predict the future—would FDR ever have an opportunity to replace the Four Horsemen with new justices more sympathetic to the New Deal and pluralist democracy? — *West Coast Hotel* and *Jones and Laughlin* would ultimately mark a distinct change in judicial orientation. Pressures may have been building for years, but during the two weeks in 1937, the earth finally quaked and a new terrain emerged.[14]

Regardless of how the 1937 turn is characterized, the question arises: why did the Court and particularly Roberts change at that point? No single clear answer is apparent, though several factors seem pertinent. First, political pressure undoubtedly played a role. The Four Horsemen remained too intransigent to respond to pressure, but Roberts and the progressive justices were flexible enough to care that widespread opprobrium greeted many of the Court's decisions. True, Roberts had already cast his vote in *West Coast Hotel* before Roosevelt publicly revealed his court-packing plan (though the Court did not announce its decision until afterward). Even so, in response to the Court's series of anti–New Deal decisions, political commentators and administration insiders had long been discussing several possible solutions, including a constitutional amendment. Nearly three weeks before the justices would cast their *West Coast Hotel* votes during a December 19, 1936, conference, the *Times* reported that the administration and Congress were examining arrows "in the Congressional quiver" for dealing with the Court. For example, "Congress can enlarge the Supreme Court, increasing the number of justices from nine to twelve or fifteen." In fact, still before the *West Coast Hotel* conference, the *Post* reported an Institute of Public Opinion poll concluding that 41 percent of Americans favored "a constitutional amendment to curtail the power of the Supreme Court."[15]

Second, by this time, not only was the practice of pluralist democracy well established, but intellectuals had been questioning the theoretical underpinnings of republican democracy for more than a decade. In fact, the first threads of a pluralist democratic theory were already being spun. While the justices may not have read, let's say, Charles Merriam's latest political science tome, they would not have been oblivious to such intellectual rumblings. The Court was still applying principles of democracy that had for years been under intellectual (as well as political) attack; the Court's concept of judicial review was an anachronism.[16]

Finally, whatever factors prompted the Court's turn in early 1937, personnel changes on the Court would soon ensure its continuing embrace of pluralist democracy. In May 1937, during the heated congressional debates over the court-packing plan, which eventually would be defeated, Justice Van Devanter resigned. Roosevelt finally had his first opportunity to name a new justice. In August, after more than two months of procrastinating, FDR nominated Senator Hugo Black of Alabama, a die-hard New Dealer.

This first opening on the Court broke the dam, and Supreme Court vacancies came rushing at Roosevelt. In 1938, he appointed Stanley F. Reed, his solicitor general, to replace Sutherland, another of the Four Horsemen. The next year, FDR appointed both his confidant, Felix Frankfurter, and the then chair of the Securities and Exchange Commission, William O. Douglas, to the Court. In 1940, it was attorney general Frank Murphy's turn. In 1941, Roosevelt promoted Stone to chief justice and appointed Robert H. Jackson, who had been Murphy's successor as attorney general, and South Carolina Senator James F. Byrnes, who filled the seat of the last of the Four Horsemen, McReynolds. FDR made his final appointment in 1943, naming Wiley B. Rutledge, whom Roosevelt had previously appointed to the District of Columbia Court of Appeals. Hence, although FDR had been locked in a constitutional confrontation with the Supreme Court from 1935 to 1937, by the end of his presidency, he had created the "Roosevelt Court," as political scientist C. Herman Pritchett would call it in 1948.[17]

Thus, regardless of Roberts's (and Hughes's) lingering ambivalences, the Roosevelt appointees repeatedly reiterated their commitment to a judicial power consistent with pluralist democracy. This attitude was nowhere clearer than in *Wickard v. Filburn,* decided in 1942. Roscoe Filburn challenged the constitutionality of the AAA of 1938, which subjected his production of wheat to regulation even if raised "wholly for consumption on [his] farm." In upholding the congressional action, a unanimous Court emphasized three points. First, it would not rely on formalist categories to restrict congressional power. "[Q]uestions of the power of Congress are not to be decided by reference to any formula which would give controlling force to nomenclature such as 'production' and 'indirect' and foreclose consideration of the actual effects of the activity in question upon interstate commerce." Second, the Court would not invalidate legislation merely because Congress had apparently favored one class or interest group over another; such class-based legislation typified (pluralist) democratic processes. "It is of the essence of regulation that it lays a restraining hand on the self-interest of the regulated and that advantages from the regulation commonly fall to others. The conflicts of economic interest between the regulated and those who advantage by it are wisely left under our system to resolution by the Congress." Third, and related to the prior point, the justices reasoned that while Congress did not possess unbounded power, the "effective restraints" on congressional power arose "from political rather than from judicial processes." If the people did not like congressional enactments, then they could vote for new legislators.[18]

THE PUZZLE OF PLURALIST
DEMOCRATIC JUDICIAL REVIEW

Once the Court had accepted the structures of pluralist democracy, then judicial review itself became problematic. Under republican democracy, courts had determined whether governmental actions promoted either the common good or partial and private interests. Through this judicial process, courts demarcated a conceptual boundary between the public and private realms. But when the Court stopped distinguishing between the common good and partial or private interests — when the Court repudiated republican democracy — then the purpose of judicial review blurred. The judicial function of limiting the government to acting within the public sphere and therefore (supposedly) maximizing individual liberty within the private sphere no longer seemed sensible. Moreover, if the structures of pluralist democracy logically implied a new framework for exercising the power of judicial review, it was not readily apparent. How were pluralist democratic courts to review the legitimacy — the constitutionality — of governmental actions? From an intellectual standpoint, the justices confronted a typical modernist dilemma. Under republican democracy, with its roots tracing back to a premodern worldview, the foundation for objective judicial decision making was, in theory, indubitable: it was the categorical specification of the common good. But now with the Court's movement into the world of modernity, with the Court accepting pluralist democracy, the firm republican foundation for decision making had crumbled. The justices, it seemed, needed to find a new foundation to ground their decisions.[19]

With the Court confronting the uncertainties of pluralist democracy and the puzzle of judicial review, scholars and justices began worrying about, in Alexander Bickel's words, the "counter-majoritarian difficulty" — that judicial review itself was inconsistent with democratic government. Soon after Congress rejected FDR's court-packing plan, the then assistant attorney general, Robert Jackson, acknowledged the significance of the Court's turn: it "cleared the way toward improving the functioning of the United States." Yet, he brooded that potential "friction" between the Supreme Court, on the one hand, and Congress and the executive, on the other hand, still "presents the most vexing problem." Because the justices (and other federal judges) received lifetime appointments and thus were insulated from political-democratic pressures — they could not be voted out of office — he insisted that "[e]ither democracy must surrender to the judges or the judges must yield to democracy." As Thomas Reed Powell would explain, the "primary requisite of a democratic society is a fairly wide popular participation," so the Court, "not democratically organized and . . . least subject to democratic pressure," is inherently not "a democratic agency."[20]

If Jackson presented the choice — the countermajoritarian dilemma, where either elected legislative representatives or unelected judges rule — then Judge Learned Hand became one of the most articulate advocates for the legislative representatives — for democracy, as he saw it. In a 1942 speech published by the Massachusetts Bar Association, Hand described "enacted law" from a distinctly pluralist democratic vantage: legislation is enacted in response "to the pressure of the interests affected" and "ordinarily [manifests] a compromise of conflicts." The success of such a law "depends upon how far mutual concessions result in an adjustment which brings in its train the most satisfaction and leaves the least acrimony." What about judicial review of such laws? Hand insisted that judges must restrain their own powers with a "self-denying ordinance." Courts "should not have the last word in those basic conflicts of 'right and wrong,'" even in cases involving Bill of Rights guarantees. Such constitutional rights must "serve merely as counsels of moderation." They are precatory, and their specific implementation and effect must depend on the people and their elected representatives. Hand realized that many critics would fume that civil liberties could not survive without judicial protection. He responded: "[A] society so riven that the spirit of moderation is gone, no court can save; . . . a society where that spirit flourishes, no court need save; . . . in a society which evades its responsibility by thrusting upon the courts the nurture of that spirit, that spirit in the end will perish."[21]

Yet, other scholars were not as quick to abandon the Court's power of judicial review on the shoals of pluralist democracy, even if the Court acted in a counterdemocratic fashion. Indeed, some scholars denied that judicial review contravened democracy in the first place. Eugene Rostow, for one, argued that judicial review constituted an important part of pluralist democracy, properly understood. "The task of democracy is not to have the people vote directly on every issue, but to assure their ultimate responsibility for the acts of their representatives, elected *or appointed*." To Rostow, federal judges might be politically insulated, but they are not politically isolated. The electorate bears "responsibility for the quality of the judges and for the substance of their instructions, never a responsibility for [judicial] decisions in particular cases." Explicitly criticizing Hand's position,

Rostow attributed the desire to straitjacket the Court's power of judicial review to the lingering "dark shadows thrown upon the judiciary by the Court-packing fight of 1937."[22]

Why did the countermajoritarian difficulty become so central to judicial and scholarly thinking in the pluralist democratic regime? Under republican democracy, the judicial categorization of governmental actions as promoting either the common good or partial or private interests sometimes provoked detractors to charge that judges exercised too much discretion. Moreover, critics could easily denounce judges for thwarting legislative desires, as was most evident during the New Deal. Yet, the potential for countermajoritarian judicial decision making rarely seemed as distinct or momentous in the old (republican) democratic regime as it would in the new (pluralist) one. Unsurprisingly, the respective characteristics of the two types of democracy structured the problems (or difficulties) that seemed to inhere within judicial review. Unlike pluralist democracy, republican democracy did not stress widespread participation and the pursuit of self-interest. The fact that judicial decisions might not accord with the sentiments of the majority, thus, did not seem too problematic. Indeed, under republican democracy, politics supposedly demanded the virtuous pursuit of the common good. A judge, then, could in theory be political without being partisan and arousing indignation. Judges, it seemed, were unlikely to equate the common good with their own private interests because, lacking the power of the purse, they could not readily profit from the potential "spoils of legislative office." If a judge were to decide in a *partisan* fashion, however—in pursuit of self-interest (or a faction's interests)—then the judge's decision would be corrupt. But under the new pluralist democratic regime, politics equaled partisanship; the pursuit of self-interest had become legitimate and normal. Consequently, a judge who appeared to be political was necessarily partisan, or so it seemed.[23]

Many observers began to view the Court through the prism of pluralist democratic interest group struggles. The realist-inspired critiques of the rule of law, so predominant during the 1930s, had led many to fear that adjudication was rudderless. Then after the 1937 turn, the justices themselves added fuel to this fear. Starting in the early 1940s, they began writing an increasing number of dissents and concurrences. By the 1946–47 term, the percentage of unanimous opinions had fallen to a then record low of 36 percent. While the explanation for this development remained obscure, one implication—suggested by Pritchett—was that the justices used their opinions to assert their respective interests and values. And even if the justices did not crassly pursue their own political preferences, they appeared at best merely to referee among contesting interest groups. Indeed, led by Pritchett, postwar political scientists largely accepted the realist critique of the rule of law and argued that the Supreme Court was "a political institution performing a political function." If true, if the Court functioned to adjudicate among competing interests and values — if the Court, in fact, made law that would gratify certain societal groups and disappoint others — then interest groups, it seemed, ought to begin pressing their claims to the Court. Predictably, then, aided by changes in Supreme Court rules, the number of amicus curiae briefs began to increase dramatically. By 1953, more than 10 percent of the cases had at least one amicus. That year, Fowler Harper and Edwin Etherington wrote that "[m]ore and more the Court was being treated as if it were a political-legislative body, amenable and responsive to mass pressures from any source." And while Harper and Etherington rued this development, the number of amici continued to grow; by 1993, more than 90 percent of the cases had at least one.[24]

While scholars buzzed about the Court's countermajoritarian difficulty in a pluralist democratic system, the justices themselves confronted the puzzle of judicial review in the most practical of contexts: deciding cases. In the shadow of the *Lochner* era Court's aggressive review of New Deal statutes, which had engendered the court-packing crisis, the Roosevelt Court justices' solved this conundrum clearly in at least one realm. They were to presume the constitutionality of any economic or social welfare legislation. In fact, for the next several decades, courts would in effect rubber-stamp all economic and social welfare regulations, rather than questioning whether the action was for the common good. The quintessence of the Court's 1937 turn, this judicial deference was integral to the New Deal expansion of governmental power. Without the Court's extreme respect for such legislative actions, the government's wide-reaching regulations of the economy and society would constantly be called into doubt (as they had been during the *Lochner* era). In 1938, the Court explained: "[T]he existence of facts supporting the legislative judgment is to be presumed, for regulatory legislation affecting ordinary commercial transactions is not to be pronounced unconstitutional unless in the light of the facts made known or generally assumed it is of such a character as to preclude the assumption that it rests upon some rational basis within the knowledge and experience of the legislators."[25]

But was the Court ever to review any governmental actions more closely, or had judicial review transformed into one long series of rubber stamps? If the Court was to defer to economic and social welfare statutes, should the Court defer as well to other legislative actions, which after all were now understood to be the product of interest group competitions and compromises? While the justices would disagree among themselves about the degree of deference owed noneconomic legislative actions, and while scholars might recommend deference regardless of context, neither the Supreme Court justices nor the lower federal court judges were likely to abrogate their power over other governmental actors. The power of judicial review, particularly at the Supreme Court level, was too strongly established in the institutions of American government to atrophy and disappear. Moreover, the sanctity of individual rights and liberties had become part of the American creed. In the realm of free expression, the deeply entrenched tradition of dissent had long manifested an American ethos of liberty. Then, if anything, the desire to protect individual liberties in general had intensified between the two World Wars. The ACLU, forged in the crucible of the post–World War I Red Scare, had actively sought to stiffen Americans' resolve to protect civil liberties, including free expression, through an integrated campaign of education and litigation. Plus, an enhanced protection of individual liberty harmonized with the 1920s rise of mass consumerism, which intensified the American individualist ethos by portraying the person as a bundle of desires. Civil rights then became especially beneficial, it seemed, to protect the individual's legitimate quest for self-fulfillment. Congressional developments from the 1930s illustrate how important the cause of civil liberties had become in national politics. After Congress had passed the NLRA in July 1935, many employers fought compliance and thwarted unionization through an assortment of strategies, such as industrial espionage. Frustrated with such concerted efforts to neutralize the Act, Wisconsin Senator La Follette spearheaded the formation of a subcommittee, the La Follette Civil Liberties Committee, which conducted over a four-year period "the most extensive investigation of civil liberties infractions ever undertaken by a congressional committee." Focusing on the connection between civil liberties and labor organizing, the Committee reported startling transgressions of freedom. The "principal private purchasers" of munitions and tear gas were employers anticipating or resisting a strike. The Committee found, for example, that the Youngstown Sheet and Tube Company had bought in one month "$8,500 worth of [tear] gas equipment, 424 police clubs, six 12-gage repeating shotguns, 11,500 rounds of .38 caliber pistol ammunition and 300 shotgun shells."[26]

Given the political significance of civil liberties — in 1939, the American Bar Association (ABA) formed a Bill of Rights Committee, *and* the Department of Justice created a Civil Liberties Unit — the Court would not likely relinquish its power of judicial review, especially in the World War II and Cold War eras, as the nation confronted the external menace of totalitarian governments. Nazis and Communists authoritatively dictated to their populaces, arbitrarily imposed punishments, and suppressed religious, racial, and other minorities. In opposition, Americans stressed democracy, the rule of law, including constitutional rights, and the protection of minorities — or so Americans now wanted to believe. These ostensible components of American life and government separated *us* from *them*. In *Martin v. City of Struthers*, decided during World War II, the Court struck down the conviction of a Jehovah's Witness under an ordinance proscribing door-to-door distributions of written materials. Black's majority opinion reasoned that "[f]reedom to distribute information . . . is so clearly vital to the preservation of a free society that . . . it must be fully preserved." Murphy's concurrence accentuated the difference between American and totalitarian governments. "Repression has no place in this country. It is our proud achievement to have demonstrated that unity and strength are best accomplished, not by enforced orthodoxy of views, but by diversity of opinion through the fullest possible measure of freedom of conscience and thought."[27]

Finally, two more intertwined factors, both central to the emergence of pluralist democracy itself, ensured that the Court would not cede its power of judicial review. First, the expansion of governmental power, especially at the national level, prompted some Americans, conservatives and liberals alike, to worry about potential tyranny. The ACLU's 1933–34 annual report warned that the increased "power of the federal government" could engender "inroads" against civil liberties, while New York corporate lawyer Grenville Clark cautioned the Chicago Bar Association in 1938 that "the existence of a vast centralized power is a danger to civil liberty." Second, in many instances, dominant elite conservatives were particularly motivated to encourage and support the judicial protection of civil liberties. Pluralist democracy had emerged partly because of the actual expanding political power of outsider or peripheral groups, such as Irish Catholics, eastern European Jews, and laborers in general — a burgeoning power that undergirded the New Deal. Thus, from the conservative perspective, not only had national governmental power increased, but perhaps even worse, a congeries of outsiders — the most tenuous of Americans — wielded this enhanced power. The flowering of outsider political power, within the framework of the pluralist democratic regime, threatened the status and influence of old-stock Americans. Under compulsion, they retreated from their former hegemonic position, where Protestant-elite interests and values were translated into the republican democratic common good. Yet, even as they necessarily acquiesced to the emergent pluralist democracy, the dominant elites refused to abandon their long-held prerogatives of power and wealth. Rather, they sought to retrench: forced to retreat, they searched for positions where they could fortify and thus protect their dominant (though no longer hegemonic) interests and values. One such position of fortification was in the courts.[28]

Especially after the 1937 turn, dominant elites recognized that the judicial enforcement of constitutional rights could provide a potential bulwark against the majoritarian threat posed by the (pluralist) democratic empowerment of peripheral groups. Frank Hogan, the president-elect of the ABA, urged lawyers in 1938 to remember that civil liberties protected not only the "downtrodden" but also the "wealthy and privileged." That same year, Clark specifically urged "conservatives," partly out of "self-interest," to act "as the intelligent, enlightened guardians of . . . civil rights." As if heeding the call, old-stock Americans sought "the constitutionalization" of their own interests and values — the designation of their interests and values as constitutional rights enforceable through the courts. When constitutionalized, their interests and values were effectively protected from the vagaries of the democratic processes — democratic processes that now included peripheral groups and that therefore dangerously encompassed the interests and values of previously excluded outsiders. Of course, dominant elites had long understood the potential benefits of judicial power. Throughout the *Lochner* era, they had protected their economic interests through the mechanisms of the courts by seeking labor injunctions, the invalidation of labor laws as contrary to the common good, and similar favorable judicial rulings. But even when the Court forced dominant elites to retreat — when economic regulation became subject to mere (rubber-stamp) rational basis review — they still sought to protect their interests and values through the judicial enforcement of noneconomic rights, including free expression and religious freedom.[29]

This strategy contributed especially to the judicial invigoration of first-amendment freedoms. For instance, in a 1941 labor case, the Court reviewed whether an employer had engaged in proscribed unfair labor practices under the NLRA. The employer, in response, pressed a first-amendment free-expression claim. Concluding that the NLRB had made insufficient findings, the Court remanded for additional proceedings. The Court could not ascertain whether the Board had found that either the employer's utterances alone or the utterances combined with other actions had constituted coercion, and hence an unfair labor practice. The former possibility would be problematic. The first amendment, the Court explained, protected the employer, who remained free to express "its view on labor policies or problems." Because of first-amendment protections, "the utterances of an employer, in themselves, may not constitutionally be considered to constitute an unfair labor practice."[30]

Meanwhile, in the 1940s, a Protestant-controlled Supreme Court incorporated the religion clauses to apply against state and local governments through the due process clause. American Catholics had long constituted the largest Christian group in the nation; the total number of Protestants far outnumbered Catholics, but Catholics nonetheless outnumbered the largest Protestant denomination. While Catholics had traditionally wielded minimal national political power, they became increasingly active in national as well as local politics during the 1920s and 1930s. Thus, judicially invigorated establishment and free exercise clauses, now applicable against state and local governments (through the incorporation doctrine), provided Protestant refuge from the potential reach of Catholic political power within the pluralist democratic regime. In other words, when Catholic and Protestant interests and values diverged, the religion clauses offered a judicially enforceable mechanism that Protestants could invoke to prevent or retard the imposition of Catholic views through democratic processes. And the Protestant justices not only were cognizant of the Protestant-Catholic division, they seemed especially sympathetic to Protestant interests. To take one instance, during a post–oral argument conference for a case involving a released time school program, Justice Jackson commented that "[t]his cuts the Protestants out of the schools at the same time that we are paying for Catholic schools' buses. Protestants don't have a good means of standing out." Unsurprisingly, in cases challenging governmental aid to nonpublic (predominantly Catholic) schools, the Court nearly twice as often invalidated as upheld the governmental action. In this way, the Court's post-1937 protection of civil liberties was partly a conservative defense against pluralist democracy, with its inclusion of former outsiders and its expansive governmental power.[31]

FOR NUMEROUS REASONS, then, the Court would continue to exercise its power of judicial review, most significantly in cases involving civil liberties. But a doctrinal framework for resolving such cases remained elusive, for the justices as well as for others. As Jackson would understatedly lament: "[T]he task of translating the majestic generalities of the Bill of Rights, conceived as part of the pattern of liberal government in the eighteenth century, into concrete restraints on officials dealing with the problems of the twentieth century, is one to disturb self-confidence." Consequently, the justices experimented, in a sense, developing over the years three primary approaches to pluralist democratic judicial review.[32]

The first approach began to emerge almost immediately after the Court's 1937 turn. In *United States v. Carolene Products Company,* decided in 1938 after two of the Four Horsemen had resigned, the Court upheld an economic regulation that restricted the interstate shipment of milk. Stone's majority opinion showed great deference to Congress, as typified pluralist democratic judicial review of economic and social welfare laws, but he added a footnote explaining that such deference might sometimes be inappropriate. His footnote 4, initially drafted by one of his clerks, suggested that a "presumption of constitutionality" would be improper if legislation either would likely cause or had resulted from defective democratic processes. Pluralist democracy, as the justices were just coming to understand, required an open and free-wheeling legislative process. A legislative outcome was legitimate not because it promoted the common good but because it arose from interest-group competition and compromise. Thus, if legislation would subsequently prevent some groups from voting or organizing politically, then Stone suggested it should "be subjected to more exacting judicial scrutiny." If allowed to stand, the enactment would impinge in the future "those political processes which can ordinarily be expected to bring about repeal of undesirable legislation." Likewise, if the pluralist democratic processes of competition and compromise had been closed to certain groups or had been otherwise defective, then the legitimacy of any resultant legislative actions would be doubtful. For this reason, if the government had intentionally discriminated against a "discrete and insular" minority, like African Americans, then judicial deference would be inappropriate. In a pluralist democratic regime, societal groups supposedly could press their interests and values in a fair competition with other groups. But when the government intentionally discriminated against a group — against a discrete and insular minority — then "the operation of those political processes ordinarily to be relied upon to protect minorities" would be undermined.[33]

Consistent with Stone's footnote, almost all post-1937 appointees agreed that the Court should bolster pluralist democratic processes. Even so, the justices often disagreed about how to do so: how precisely could the Court best nurture democracy? One group of justices, led by Frankfurter and Jackson, placed extraordinary trust in the self-corrective powers of pluralist processes. From their perspective, the Court generally ought to allow pluralist democracy to rectify its own problems. The other group of justices, including Stone, Douglas, and Black, insisted that courts must be more vigilant in monitoring pluralist democracy, which otherwise could too easily deteriorate into tyranny. The tension between these two judicial camps animated the 1946 case of *Colegrove v. Green,* in which a plurality held that the drawing of congressional district lines in Illinois presented a nonjusticiable political question. Writing for a plurality, Frankfurter emphasized that the point of pluralist democracy, including congressional districting, was to assure widespread participation in political processes. Yet, Frankfurter added, pluralist democracy was inherently partisan, and the drawing of district lines reflected "party contests and party interests." The Court, Frankfurter concluded, should avoid entering "this political thicket." If a state legislature drew unfair district lines, the proper remedy lay not in the courts but in the partisan democratic process itself: "to secure State legislatures that will apportion properly, or to invoke the ample powers of Congress."[34]

Black, joined by Douglas and Murphy, dissented. Black agreed with Frankfurter that a pluralist democratic system should promote widespread participation. He disagreed, however, with Frankfurter's reasoning that the best way to promote participation was to allow the further operation of legislative processes, particularly in the midst of a districting dispute. Instead, Black underscored that the current district lines in Illinois engendered grossly disparate representation. Some districts had fewer than two hundred thousand people, while one district had more than nine hundred thousand, yet each district, regardless of population, could elect one representative. Consequently, each vote was not accorded "equal weight"; a vote in a high-population district was worth less than a vote in a low-population district. According to Black, "[a]ll groups, classes, and individuals shall to the extent that it is practically feasible be given equal representation in the House of Representatives, which, in conjunction with the Senate, writes the laws affecting the life, liberty, and property of all the people." The Court could not trust the pluralist democratic process to self-correct in this instance precisely because the challenged legislation prevented certain groups from fully participating, from having adequate opportunity to influence future legislative actions.[35]

Despite such disagreements among the justices, John Hart Ely would eventually develop Stone's footnote 4 approach into a full-fledged theory of judicial review: representation reinforcement. Other approaches to pluralist democratic judicial review might founder on the countermajoritarian difficulty, but Ely explained why representation reinforcement (or Stone's footnote 4 approach) was different—and why it would persistently appeal to the Court and scholars. Properly understood, representation reinforcement theory dissolved the countermajoritarian difficulty because it promoted rather than undermined democracy. The Court, Ely argued, should generally presume the constitutionality of legislative decisions. Regardless of the outcome of the legislative process, the Court should not disapprove legislation as contravening some substantive criterion, like the common good, because no such criterion existed (or, at least, the justices could not reliably identify such a criterion). Legislative goals supposedly manifested no more than the interests and values of the democratic winners. As the Court explained in 1955, "[t]he day is gone when this Court [strikes down] laws, regulatory of business and industrial conditions, because they may be unwise, improvident, or out of harmony with a particular school of thought." Yet, Ely reasoned, the Court could review the *processes* that had led the legislature to take aim at one substantive goal rather than another. If those processes were fair and open, then the Court must defer to the legislative choice. But if the processes appeared skewed, then the Court should scrutinize the legislation more closely. Judicial invalidation of legislation that had arisen from a defective or malfunctioning democratic process would not be countermajoritarian. It would be the very opposite: it would foster fair and open pluralist democracy. The Court's role, in short, was to "police" the democratic process.[36]

A second approach to judicial review in the pluralist democratic regime required the justices to balance competing interests. Throughout the 1930s, legal realists had criticized the a priori formalism characteristic of *Lochner* era judicial decisions. Judges could not resolve cases, the realists argued, by mechanically applying abstract doctrinal categories, like the common good, to clear and certain facts. In any particular dispute, opposed parties asserted competing interests and values that courts should balance or weigh against each other. Starting in the late 1930s, even as the realists' broadside critique of the rule of law fell into disfavor, the Court followed this cue and resolved an increasing number of constitutional issues by balancing interests. In the balancing calculus, constitutional rights were political interests to be weighed against other interests, particularly governmental or state interests. For instance, in 1939, Roberts wrote for an eight-justice majority in a free-expression case: "[T]he delicate and difficult task falls upon the courts to weigh the circumstances and to appraise the substantiality of the reasons advanced in support of the regulation of [constitutional] rights." Such balancing tests soon became commonplace in numerous contexts, not only in individual-rights cases. In *Pike v. Bruce Church, Inc.*, the Court held that a state law regulating the shipment of fresh fruit violated the negative implications of the commerce clause (or, in other words, the dormant commerce clause). "Where the statute regulates even-handedly to effectuate a legitimate local public interest, and its effects on interstate commerce are only incidental, it will be upheld unless the burden imposed on such commerce is clearly excessive in relation to the putative local benefits." The balance, the Court elaborated, is "one of degree."[37]

The Court's third approach to pluralist democratic judicial review had been suggested by Stone in his *Carolene Products* footnote 4. Besides emphasizing the protection of democracy, he wrote: "[t]here may be narrower scope for operation of the presumption of constitutionality when legislation appears on its face to be within a specific prohibition of the Constitution, such as those of the first ten Amendments." For a brief period afterward, the Court called these protected liberties "preferred freedoms"—freedoms or rights that deserved special judicial protection. Thus, in *Murdock v. Pennsylvania,* decided in 1943, the Court stated that "[f]reedom of press, freedom of speech, freedom of religion are in a preferred position." Although suggested by Stone in footnote 4, the preferred-freedoms doctrine had historical roots winding back to the incorporation doctrine. Early in the twentieth century, the Court had begun to hold that the fourteenth-amendment due process clause incorporated or implicitly included various Bill of Rights guarantees, which then applied against state and local governments just as they applied against the national government. As recently as 1937, in *Palko v. Connecticut,* Cardozo had reasoned that due process encompassed Bill of Rights protections integral to "the very essence of a scheme of ordered liberty." Such rights rested within "a 'principle of justice so rooted in the traditions and conscience of our people as to be ranked as fundamental.'" During the 1940s, the justices denominated some of these incorporated (fundamental) rights as preferred freedoms, distinguishing them from economic liberties. The government could regulate economic relations whenever reasonable, but it could not so readily restrict the preferred liberties. Hence, the *Murdock* Court invalidated a regulation on the sale of religious literature by emphasizing that the government sought to restrict a preferred freedom (religious freedom) rather than a commercial transaction (the sale of literature). After the 1940s, however, the justices rarely invoked the preferred-freedoms doctrine.[38]

While the preferred-freedoms doctrine per se fell into desuetude, the underlying principle did not. The point was to protect certain liberty-interests (or rights) from the pluralist democratic process itself, regardless of whether the liberties were called preferred freedoms. Thus, justices and scholars would occasionally assert that the Constitution carved certain areas out of the pluralist democratic process, placing them beyond the majoritarian reach. During World War II, Jackson wrote: "One's right to life, liberty, and property, to free speech, a free press, freedom of worship and assembly, and other fundamental rights may not be submitted to vote; they depend on the outcome of no elections." Subsequently, Black and Douglas argued that the Constitution warranted absolute protection of free expression. According to Black, when the first amendment declares that "Congress shall make no law," it means that "Congress shall make no law." This judicial approach rested on a key assumption: that certain liberties or rights are so important they should not be exposed to "the vicissitudes of political controversy." Given that pluralist democracy encourages individuals and groups to pursue their own interests to the disregard of others, it engenders possibilities too dangerous to abide. To take an obvious example, a democratic majority might decide to satisfy its interests by forcing a particular minority into slavery. To be sure, one might argue that such a slavery law would necessarily undermine pluralist democratic processes by excluding the would-be slaves from political participation (thus triggering heightened judicial scrutiny under representation reinforcement). Yet, what if the courts were to disagree? What if a defect in the process of enacting the slavery law could not be proven in court? The crux of the third judicial approach — the protection from pluralist democracy — is that some liberty-interests simply should not depend on such uncertainties.[39]

Even so, a majority of justices rarely agreed that any liberty, free speech or otherwise, should be absolutely protected, regardless of context. Instead, they allowed the government to argue that infringement of the liberty was, in the circumstances, appropriate. This flexibility typically led back to a balancing test. The justices weighed the constitutional liberty-interests against competing interests. The Court, though, would often put its collective thumb on one side of the scale: the justices generally accorded individual liberties (or rights), especially those expressly enumerated in the constitutional text, like free speech and equal protection, extra weight in the balance. The Court, in a sense, created no-fly zones (where pluralist majorities could not go), but simultaneously acknowledged that the zones could be infringed for sufficiently important or compelling reasons. If the government proved that its action was closely enough related to achieving a sufficiently weighty goal, then the Court would allow the government to infringe the individual liberty. Thus, in any particular case, the individual liberty-interest became, in effect, an enforceable constitutional right only if it outweighed the government's interests. During World War II, for instance, the Court upheld the national government's internment of Japanese

Americans in the face of an equal protection challenge. The Court found that equal protection effectively created a no-fly zone, but the Court allowed the government to justify infringement pursuant to a balancing test, albeit one supposedly skewed strongly toward the protection of individual liberties. "[A]ll legal restrictions which curtail the civil rights of a single racial group are immediately suspect. That is not to say that all such restrictions are unconstitutional," the Court explained. "It is to say that courts must subject them to the most rigid scrutiny. Pressing public necessity may sometimes justify the existence of such restrictions; racial antagonism never can." Thus, the so-called strict scrutiny test, a refined balancing test, originated in the Court's post-1937 struggle to solve the riddle of pluralist democratic judicial review. The Court has used strict scrutiny in a variety of circumstances, ranging from equal protection to religious freedom to free expression. For example, the Court for years required the government to grant exemptions from generally applicable laws that burdened the free exercise of religion unless the government could show that the law was necessary to achieve a compelling state interest.[40]

TWO OF THE COURT'S approaches to judicial review—balancing of interests and removal from pluralist democracy (creating no-fly zones)— exacerbated the hand-wringing over the countermajoritarian difficulty. Critics condemned balancing as judicial decision making without principles, without law. What, for instance, qualifies as an interest (and thus becomes part of the balancing calculus)? What weight should be accorded to different interests? How should different kinds of interests be weighed or compared? How, for example, should one weigh an interest in economic prosperity against an interest in speaking freely? They are the proverbial apples and oranges (though it would be easier to balance apples and oranges). Constitutional issues often "demand the appraisal and balancing of human values which there are no scales to weigh," Hand observed. "Who can say whether the contributions of one group may not justify allowing it a preference? How far should the capable, the shrewd or the strong be allowed to exploit their powers?" As Hand elucidated, the problem "does not come from ignorance, but from the absence of any standard, for values are incommensurable." Even more important, given the omnipresent worries about the countermajoritarian difficulty, if legislatures enacted laws in response to competing interests, and the Court resolved disputes by balancing countervailing interests, then what distinguished legislative from judicial decision making? Legislatures and courts, the critics charged, should do more than provide different forums for competing interest groups to do battle. If the Court lacked some better justification for invalidating legislative actions, other than that the Court's assessment of the parties' interests differed from the legislature's assessment, then the Court should defer to the people's elected legislative representatives.[41]

The justices themselves appeared concerned that balancing provided only a makeshift solution to the problem of pluralist democratic judicial review, but it was a solution that persisted, perhaps because of the lack of adequate alternatives. After the 1937 turn, it seemed, the justices realized the mechanism of judicial review needed repair, but they were uncertain how to fix it. So they dug down into the bottom of the toolbox, pulled out the electrical tape, started wrapping it around, and tried to fix the problem as best as possible. The sociological (Progressive) jurisprudents had recommended that the Court assess social interests, but for the purpose of more accurately discerning the republican democratic common good. The realists had advocated for balancing interests, but they were renowned for a broad-based skepticism toward the rule of law—which the justices could not abide, given their position on the Supreme Court. But then, for what purpose, under the new democratic regime, was the Court to weigh competing interests—other than to repeat the pluralist legislative process? Regardless, the tape-job kept the judicial mechanism together, though the justices fretted over their flimsy patchwork. At times, they seemed defensive, attempting to justify balancing as truly principled. "[S]triking the balance implies the exercise of judgment," Frankfurter wrote. "It must be an overriding judgment founded on something much deeper and more justifiable than personal preference. As far as it lies within human limitations, it must be an impersonal judgment. It must rest on fundamental presuppositions rooted in history to which widespread acceptance may fairly be attributed."[42]

As problematic as balancing seemed, the judicial removal of certain liberty-interests from the reach of pluralist democratic majorities proved even more so. This approach to judicial review had to confront the countermajoritarian whammy twice: first, in the creation of the no-fly zones; and second, in the application of balancing tests to determine, in any particular case, whether the government could justifiably infringe the protected zone. The Roosevelt Court justices, in particular, struggled through no-fly-zone cases as they confronted the uncertain nature of pluralist democracy and the conundrum of judicial review. Even Roberts, the ambivalent but key justice in the 1937 turn, chided his colleagues when they held that a governmental action violated the first amendment. "We may deem the statutory provision under review unnecessary or unwise," he wrote in 1945, "but it is not our function as judges to read our views of policy into a Constitutional guarantee, in order to overthrow a state policy we do not personally approve."[43]

MEANWHILE, FRANKFURTER, STONE, and other justices shaped and smoothed the contours of pluralist democracy. Showing his trust in the self-corrective powers of pluralist democracy, Frankfurter wrote the 1940 majority opinion in *Minersville School District v. Gobitis,* upholding compulsory flag salutes. The local school board in Minersville, Pennsylvania, required teachers and students to salute the flag and to recite the pledge of allegiance every day. Raised as Jehovah's Witnesses, the Gobitis children "had been brought up conscientiously to believe that such a gesture of respect for the flag was forbidden by command of scripture." When the school board expelled the children, aged ten and twelve, for refusing to salute the flag, the Gobitis family went to court, arguing that the penalty violated the children's rights to free exercise of religion and free expression. Rejecting both constitutional claims, Frankfurter reasoned that the best means for maintaining democracy was to nurture a democratic culture: democracy must be "ingrained in a people's habits and not enforced against popular policy by the coercion of adjudicated law." The Court therefore should generally defer to the results of the legislative process—regardless of the substance of those results—"so long as the remedial channels of the democratic process remain open and unobstructed." Frankfurter, in other words, followed a representation-reinforcement approach but refrained from recognizing no-fly zones. Even if legislation impinged on first-amendment freedoms, the Court was to defer to the legislature unless the justices identified some defect in the democratic process. Indeed, from Frankfurter's viewpoint, the Court's deference to controversial democratic decisions would not only harmonize with its post-1937 economic-rights decisions but would also provoke political debates generative of democratic culture. Dissenting, Stone agreed with Frankfurter that the Court should not defer when the democratic process was obstructed; this viewpoint echoed his footnote 4 representation-reinforcement position. Yet, Stone believed the Court must do more. The Court must not presume the constitutionality of legislative actions that infringed designated no-fly zones. Otherwise, the Court would "surrender . . . the constitutional protection of the liberty of small minorities to the popular will." Consequently, "freedom of mind and spirit," encompassing expressive and religious freedoms, must be judicially protected, regardless of the consequences for pluralist democracy. "The Constitution expresses more than the conviction of the people that democratic processes must be preserved at all costs." Even so, Stone explained, these freedoms were prerequisite to "free government" itself. No-fly-zone judicial review was not antithetical to democracy.[44]

Spurred partly by the Court's *Gobitis* decision and partly by fears of the nation's impending entry into World War II, school boards across the nation quickly imposed flag-salute requirements. Vigilantes then attacked Jehovah's Witnesses in retribution for their supposed disloyalty, demonstrated by their refusal to salute the flag. Less than three weeks after the Court announced *Gobitis,* the Department of Justice already had reports of hundreds of such attacks. Under this cloud, the Court reconsidered the flag-salute issue in 1943. *West Virginia State Board of Education v. Barnette* overruled *Gobitis* and held that a compulsory flag salute violated the first amendment. This time, the kindred spirits of judicial restraint, Frankfurter and Jackson, split. Jackson, writing the majority opinion, applied a no-fly-zone approach. He reasoned that the first amendment categorically withdrew free expression and religious freedom from the vagaries of pluralist democracy. Because democracy is grounded on consent of the governed, the Bill of Rights precludes the government from coercing such consent; self-government cannot exist without first-amendment freedoms. Frankfurter, now dissenting, stressed again that the promotion of democratic culture would best preserve democracy. The judicial enforcement of individual rights was likely, in the end, to undermine democracy. "Particularly in legislation affecting freedom of thought and freedom of speech much which should offend a free-spirited society is constitutional," Frankfurter wrote. "Reliance for the most precious interests of civilization, therefore, must be found outside of their vindication in courts of law. Only a persistent positive translation of the faith of a free society into the convictions and habits and actions of a community is the ultimate reliance against unabated temptations to fetter the human spirit."[45]

LEGAL INTERPRETATION AND THUS judicial decision making might always be partly political, but under both republican and pluralist democracy, certain overarching issues spotlight the politics of adjudication. In republican democracy, it was the judicial determination of the common good. In pluralist democracy, it was (and is) the identification of no-fly zones and the application of balancing tests. Under pluralist democracy, anxieties over judicial-political discretion ordinarily translate into the language of the countermajoritarian difficulty. When the emphasis of political theory is on widespread participation and a full and fair opportunity to sway a majority — rather than on the virtuous pursuit of the common good — then judicial discretion necessarily appears contrary to democracy. The cloud of the countermajoritarian difficulty, casting a persistent gray pall over pluralist democratic judicial review, provoked the Court to expand its representation-reinforcement (footnote 4) function and to construe cases as raising issues concerning the democratic process. Chief Justice Earl Warren wrote his most important opinion, *Brown v. Board of Education,* to underscore the process-based underpinnings of the unanimous Court's conclusion. Decided in 1954, *Brown* held that racial segregation of public school children violated the fourteenth amendment's guarantee of equal protection. Warren's brief opinion stressed, more than anything, the integral connection between education and democratic government. "Compulsory school attendance laws and the great expenditures for education . . . demonstrate our recognition of the importance of education to our democratic society," Warren explained. Education "is required in the performance of our most basic public responsibilities, [and] is the very foundation of good citizenship." After *Brown,* two developments pushed the Court to emphasize pluralist democratic processes even more strongly. First, a national political coalition formed during the 1950s and early 1960s in support of legal protections for civil rights and democratic participation. This broad-based coalition, which would engender legislation like the Civil Rights Act of 1964, also signaled the Court that active judicial policing of the pluralist democratic process would be publicly approved. Second, Felix Frankfurter, the Court's leading proponent of judicial restraint — or in less generous terms, the predominant countermajoritarian worrywart — resigned in 1962. With Arthur J. Goldberg replacing Frankfurter, and Byron White replacing Charles E. Whittaker the same year, the Warren Court entered a second and more liberal stage.[46]

Even before Frankfurter's resignation, the post-*Brown* Court had become more assertive in questioning racially tinged defects in the political process. In *Gomillion v. Lightfoot,* decided in 1960, the Court reviewed the constitutionality of a state law that had transformed the city of Tuskegee, Alabama, "from a square to an uncouth twenty-eight-sided figure." With an opinion by the redoubtable Frankfurter himself, a unanimous Court held this claim justiciable. Writing for eight justices, Frankfurter distinguished the case from *Colegrove v. Green,* which had held the drawing of congressional district lines a nonjusticiable political question. Unlike in *Colegrove,* where Frankfurter had written the plurality opinion, the claim in *Gomillion* alleged an intentional deprivation of the right to vote on the basis of race, in violation of the fifteenth amendment. The new Tuskegee boundaries removed "from the city all save four or five of its 400 Negro voters while not removing a single white voter." To Frankfurter, then, *Colegrove* remained good law, but *Gomillion* presented a clear case of racial gerrymandering that denied African Americans "the municipal franchise and consequent rights." Despite Frankfurter's reaffirmance of *Colegrove,* the Court reconsidered its holding only two years later, in *Baker v. Carr,* mere months before Frankfurter's resignation. The *Baker* claimants argued that a law establishing state legislative district lines, drawn decades earlier, violated equal protection because of disproportional representation. *Baker* and *Colegrove* could be distinguished: *Colegrove* had focused on congressional district lines, while *Baker* involved state lines. Nonetheless, in a six-to-two decision, Justice William J. Brennan's majority opinion overruled *Colegrove* and held that an allegation of disproportional representation and concomitant vote dilution constituted a justiciable claim (whether for a state legislature or for the House of Representatives). In dissenting, Frankfurter continued to insist that the precise parameters of pluralist democracy should be determined through the democratic process itself.[47]

The *Baker* decision, coupled with Frankfurter's resignation (and the continuing political support for expanding civil rights and political participation), sparked the Court to police the pluralist democratic processes with alacrity. Most important, in 1964, the court held in two cases that, "as nearly as is practicable," one person's vote "is to be worth as much as another's." Thus, *Wesberry v. Sanders,* focusing on congressional districts, and *Reynolds v. Sims,* focusing on state legislative districts, established the doctrine: one person, one vote. To use John Ely's phrasing, malapportionment cases — "where one person's vote counts only a fraction (and sometimes it was a very small fraction) of another's"—presented a "quintessential stoppage" of the pluralist democratic process. The justices' embrace of pluralist democracy and their representation-reinforcement decisions generally received a warm welcome. The day after the Court handed down *Baker,* the *New York Times* reported that the New York City mayor "was pleased by the . . . decision" and looked forward to reapportionment. As Ely put it, "most people could sympathize" with the idea that all votes should be equally weighted. Indeed, by 2001, few would question another constitutional scholar's assertion that "the goal of our constitutional polity is preservation and adaptation of a peaceable pluralism." The "polity consists of numerous and often competing groups, including not just economic groups but also social groups; the goal of politics," he elaborated, "is moderation and accommodation of the interests of as many salient groups as possible." In "a pluralist system, the role of the judiciary is not to ensure the triumph of any particular group or norm, but is instead to assure that all groups pursue their interests and normative goals through the regular organs for change and debate."[48]

While the Court's decisions focusing on pluralist democratic processes tended to be relatively uncontroversial, the same was not true for many of its other decisions. Whenever the Court invalidated legislation — other than pursuant to representation reinforcement — someone stood poised to decry the justices' countermajoritarian pretensions. No cases would prove more contentious than those protecting no-fly zones over so-called unenumerated rights, rights not explicit in the constitutional text. *Griswold v. Connecticut,* decided in 1965, invalidated a Connecticut statute proscribing the use of contraceptives by married couples, while *Roe v. Wade,* decided in 1973, invalidated Texas laws that prohibited most abortions. Both cases relied on the right of privacy — a right nowhere expressly enumerated in the Constitution. While the dissenting justices and Court critics almost unanimously attacked the decisions for undermining democracy, the majority opinions had warily attempted to bolster the Court's ostensible reliance on an objective rule of law. In *Griswold,* Douglas asserted: "We do not sit as a super-legislature to determine the wisdom, need, and propriety of laws that touch economic problems, business affairs, or social conditions." In *Roe,* Justice Harry Blackmun insisted that the justices decided "by constitutional measurement, free of emotion and of predilection." Such efforts could not deflect the critics. None was more vitriolic than Robert Bork. He demanded that no-fly zones be limited to expressly enumerated rights, like free speech. "When the Constitution has not spoken," Bork wrote, "the Court will be able to find no scale, other than its own value preferences, upon which to weigh the respective claims." From Bork's vantage, *Griswold* was "an unprincipled decision" that "fails every test of neutrality." In *Roe,* the Court had "legislated the rules [it] considered appropriate for abortions by balancing the interests of the woman and those of the state," and in so doing, the Court had usurped "the democratic authority of the American people." Whatever one might think of "the right to abort," Bork fumed, "[it] is not to be found in the Constitution."[49]

PLURALIST DEMOCRATIC JUDICIAL REVIEW differs radically from republican democratic judicial review, yet similarities exist. At the most general level, the Supreme Court's institutional role is identical under both democratic regimes: the Court reviews (or passes judgment on) the constitutionality of actions taken by other governmental institutions or officials. As the post-1937 Court struggled to elucidate its precise functions under pluralist democracy, it naturally drew upon familiar legal concepts and practices, even if rooted in the republican democratic past. For instance, under republican democracy, the Court questioned whether legislation substantively favored a particular class (or a partial or private interest). Under pluralist democracy, the Court questions whether a particular class (a discrete and insular minority) had insufficient opportunity to participate in the lawmaking processes. Even the balancing test — an archetypal manifestation of the pluralist democratic competition of interests — echoes republican democracy. Under republican democracy, the government could interfere with individual liberties if in furtherance of the common good, while now, under pluralist democracy, the government can overcome liberty-interests if state interests are weighty enough. Indeed, the commonly invoked concept of the "state interest" also resonates with the republican democratic concept of the common good. Under pluralist democracy, the legislature supposedly acts in response to the push and pull of diverse and conflicting interests. But when the Court reviews the constitutionality of a legislative action, the Court often asks whether the state (or governmental) interest outweighs the individual interests. Such judicial invocations of a state interest reconceptualize the polity as a unity: the government supposedly represents a unified interest (similar to the republican democratic common good) rather than a mélange of competing interests.[50]

Most important, the republican democratic Court generally interpreted the common good to correspond with mainstream and dominant values and interests, while the pluralist democratic Court usually interprets constitutional rights similarly. As discussed, one reason for the post-1937 Court's enhanced focus on civil liberties was that dominant elites realized the judicial enforcement of constitutional rights could provide a bulwark against the majoritarian threat posed by the (pluralist) democratic empowerment of peripheral groups. So, for instance, Protestant claimants have invoked the first-amendment separation of church and state to block Roman Catholics from using their political power within the democratic process to funnel tax revenues to parochial schools. Once the Court recognizes a constitutional right, however, then members of peripheral groups can attempt to invoke such rights to their advantage. Indeed, the judiciary provides a forum relatively conducive to peripheral groups because they can readily articulate their positions in the rhetoric of legal rights and principles. If a peripheral group bluntly announces its interests and values, in either the legislatures or the courts, more powerful groups are likely to respond with indifference or hostility. Under pluralist democracy, why should a dominant group sacrifice its interests for those of another group? Judicially enforceable principles and rights offer an alternative language for the expression of a peripheral group's position. True, a constitutional right might be no more than a "specialized mandate"—an interest that governmental officials (including judges) have deemed a trump over other interests—but such an alternative language nonetheless is likely to be more palatable to dominant groups. After the Court held in the 1940s that the fourteenth amendment incorporated the religion clauses to apply against state and local governments—consistent with Protestant interests—then Jehovah's Witnesses, Jews, and other religious minorities could also press first-amendment religious-freedom claims. In such cases, though, the Court usually upheld the minority's claims only if they were consistent with (or at least not contrary to) prevailing interests and values. During the post–World War II era, Jewish organizations sometimes won cases when they advocated for positions explicitly overlapping with Protestant interests and values. In *Engel v. Vitale,* where the Court held that the recitation of nondenominational prayers in public schools violated the establishment clause, the Synagogue Council of America had argued in an amicus brief that "[m]any Christian groups and publications have similarly expressed opposition to the Regents' Prayer." Meanwhile, the same organizations consistently lost cases that accentuated Jewish-Christian differences. When Orthodox Jews, who strictly follow a Saturday Sabbath, sought free exercise exemptions from Sunday closing laws, one brief admitted that "there is no real relationship between the Jews' Sabbath and the Christians' Sunday." The two Sabbaths "are not the same either in conception or in manner of observance." The Court rejected the free exercise claims even though many Sunday laws already contained long lists of statutory exceptions, including for amusement parks, beach resorts, and businesses selling tobacco, bread, frozen desserts, and works of art.[51]

Overall, then, while the post-1937 Court became more receptive to civil liberties claims, the Court's record in such cases has been spotty. The decades since the turn have not witnessed a steady march toward the enhanced judicial protection of minorities' rights. Although justices and scholars have anguished over the countermajoritarian difficulty, judicial review might contravene pluralist democracy more in theory than actuality. Even as the countermajoritarian difficulty ripened into a scholarly obsession during the 1950s, a handful of political scientists and legal scholars questioned its accuracy. Empirical research suggests that the Court, in the words of Robert Dahl, "is inevitably a part of the dominant national alliance." For this reason, the justices rarely interpret the Constitution and other laws to contravene predominant political views. "[I]t would appear to be somewhat naive to assume that the Supreme Court either would or could play the role of Galahad." Whereas at a microlevel the Court always acts, by definition, contrary to the legislative will when it invalidates a statute, at a macrolevel the Court is unlikely to diverge from the mainstream. Even in *Brown,* the prototypical judicial protection of minority rights, the Court acted consistently with the desires of a national majority (while contravening the desires of local white southern majorities). Despite such empirical research, fears of the countermajoritarian difficulty remain prominent among legal scholars, politicians, and the general public.[52]

CHAPTER 11

Free Expression, Pluralist Democracy, and the Supreme Court

The World War I era Supreme Court decisions, running from *Schenck v. United States,* decided in 1919, to *Milwaukee Social Democratic Publishing Company v. Burleson,* decided in 1921, left no doubt about the Court's approach to free-expression claims. Regardless of Holmes's and Brandeis's dissents, a solid majority of justices interpreted the first amendment consistently with traditional republican democratic principles. Free expression constituted an important individual liberty, but the government could restrict it in pursuit of the common good. Consequently, as the justices persistently reasoned, the government could punish expression with bad tendencies.[1]

Through the 1920s, then, the Court continued to interpret free expression in accord with republican democracy. During the war and the postwar Red Scare, numerous states had passed criminal syndicalism statutes, and challenges to convictions under these laws began to reach the Court in mid-decade. *Gitlow v. New York,* decided in 1925, was first. Benjamin Gitlow had been convicted under the New York statute, which proscribed advocating the overthrow of the government, after he published *The Left Wing Manifesto* and a paper called the *Revolutionary Age.* Writing for a seven-justice majority, Justice Edward T. Sanford began with a point that would support the future expansion of free-expression protections. The fourteenth amendment's due process clause incorporated the free speech and free press clauses to apply against state and local governments. This holding assured a steady flow of first-amendment cases into the federal courts, including the Supreme Court. Nonetheless, Sanford continued by distinguishing two types of statutes: those that explicitly proscribed expression and those that proscribed conduct but were applied to punish expression. In the latter case, Sanford suggested the appropriate standard would be clear and present danger, which he equated with the bad tendency test. Citing *Schenck* and *Debs v. United States,* he explained that such a "statute may be constitutionally applied to the specific utterance of [a] defendant if its natural tendency and probable effect was to bring about the substantive evil which the legislative body might prevent." Because the New York statute explicitly proscribed certain types of expression, however, Sanford reasoned that the bad tendency–clear and present danger test did not apply. Instead, the Court must defer to the legislative determination that the punished language was "inimical to the public welfare," so long as this determination was not arbitrary or unreasonable. As Sanford explained, in language reminiscent of Holmes's *Frohwerk* opinion, the legislature reasonably protects "the public peace and safety" when it proscribes revolutionary speech or writing that "may kindle a fire that, smouldering for a time, may burst into a sweeping and destructive conflagration."[2]

Holmes, joined by Brandeis, wrote a brief dissent. Holmes agreed with the majority that the due process clause incorporated the free speech and free press clauses. But, unlike the majority, he maintained that the appropriate standard for determining the scope of constitutional protection was clear and present danger, as he had articulated it in *Schenck* and interpreted it in *Abrams v. United States.* Holmes now explained that the crux of the test was imminence. "If the publication of this document had been laid as an attempt to induce an uprising against government *at once* and not at *some indefinite time in the future* it would have presented a different question." Holmes even went so far as to declare that if Americans were to accept revolutionary Marxist ideas in the marketplace of ideas, so be it. "If in the long run the beliefs expressed in proletarian dictatorship are destined to be accepted by the dominant forces of the community, the only meaning of free speech is that they should be given their chance and have their way."[3]

Two years later, the Court upheld another conviction in *Whitney v. California.* Sanford wrote the opinion for a seven-justice majority, while Brandeis, joined by Holmes, wrote a separate opinion concurring in the judgment. California prosecuted Charlotte Whitney under its criminal syndicalism statute, which proscribed "advocating, teaching or aiding and abetting the commission of crime, sabotage . . . or unlawful acts of force and violence or unlawful methods of terrorism as a means of accomplishing a change in industrial ownership or control or effecting any political change." At the Communist Labor party convention in California, Whitney had advocated for a resolution that would have opposed violence and sought peaceful political change. The party defeated her resolution and instead adopted a more radical position. Nonetheless, the state convicted Whitney for organizing and belonging to an organization advocating criminal syndicalism. Following the *Gitlow* holding—the fourteenth-amendment due process clause incorporated the first amendment—the Court acknowledged that the conviction implicated free-expression issues. Sanford thus reiterated the traditional parameters of free expression under republican democracy. A "State in the exercise of its police power may punish those who abuse [freedom of expression] by utterances inimical to the public welfare." Finally, as in *Gitlow,* Sanford emphasized that the Court must give "great weight" to the state legislative judgment that certain language creates "danger to the public peace and the security of the State."[4]

Brandeis concurred only because, from his perspective, Whitney had not adequately raised the free-expression issues in the lower courts. Even so, Brandeis wrote an opinion, more in the nature of a dissent than a concurrence, that stands as one of the most eloquent defenses of free expression in Supreme Court history. Like Holmes in his *Gitlow* dissent, Brandeis refused to defer to the legislative judgment. The proper standard to determine the scope of first-amendment protection was clear and present danger. Given this, the defendant should have the opportunity to show that, based on the specific facts of the case, the statute was unconstitutionally applied because no clear and present danger existed. Brandeis acknowledged, however, that the parameters of the clear and present danger test remained murky. To clarify this standard, he alluded to three justifications for broadly protecting free speech and press—justifications that theorists would develop over the next decades into the primary rationales for an expansive interpretation of the first amendment. While Holmes had largely followed Chafee in arguing that society searches for truth through a marketplace of ideas, Brandeis went further. First, he reiterated the search-for-truth rationale, emphasizing that counterspeech "affords ordinarily adequate protection against the dissemination of noxious doctrine." Second, Brandeis linked free expression to democratic government, though he did not argue that freedom to express one's opinion on political issues is prerequisite to full democratic participation. Rather, he maintained "that public discussion is a political duty" and that free discussion of "supposed grievances and proposed remedies" nurtures stable government. Thus, consistent with Brandeis's roots in Progressive politics, he continued to understand free expression in accordance with republican democratic principles. Political discussion manifested civic virtue for the republican citizen and engendered the common good. Like in Brandeis's dissent in *Gilbert v. Minnesota*, he intertwined free government with the search for truth: the nation's founders "believed that freedom to think as you will and to speak as you think are means indispensable to the discovery and spread of political truth." Through public discussion of political issues, Brandeis implied, the citizenry discerns the public good. Finally, Brandeis alluded to the inherent value of individual liberty: the founders "valued liberty both as an end and as a means." Free expression not only was a means to truth or free government; it was valuable in and of itself. This rationale for protecting speech and writing could be traced historically back to the libertarianism of the Sedition Act era Republicans, especially Hay and Thomson. It also anticipated a Kantian emphasis on the dignity and autonomy of the individual that first-amendment theorists would develop in the decades after World War II.[5]

Brandeis explicated the contours of the clear and present danger test by linking it to these justifications for protecting expression, particularly the intertwined search-for-truth and free-governance rationales. "[N]o danger flowing from speech can be deemed clear and present, unless the incidence of the evil apprehended is so imminent that it may befall before there is opportunity for full discussion," Brandeis wrote. "If there be time to expose through discussion the falsehood and fallacies, to avert the evil by the processes of education, the remedy to be applied is more speech, not enforced silence." Thus, similar to Holmes in his *Abrams* dissent, Brandeis stressed imminence by grounding it on the marketplace of ideas. The only expression that should be punished is that which would likely engender an imminent (or "present") danger of unlawful or harmful conduct and would therefore preclude any further discussion or exchange of ideas. "Only an emergency can justify repression." Meanwhile, for expression to constitute a "clear" danger, Brandeis explained that it must generate a probability of "serious evil" or injury. Because free expression is so significant to republican democratic government, punishment "would be inappropriate as the means for averting a relatively trivial harm to society."[6]

DESPITE THE RESULTS in *Gitlow* and *Whitney*, a handful of other cases from the 1920s reveal a growing ambivalence on the part of the justices toward free expression. These cases might be categorized as "remote" free-expression cases: they implicated free-expression values, but the

Court decided without explicitly discussing free speech or a free press. For instance, in *Fiske v. Kansas*, decided the same day as *Whitney*, the Court focused exclusively on due process under the fourteenth amendment; Sanford's opinion for a unanimous Court did not even mention the first amendment, though it did cite *Gitlow* and *Whitney*. Kansas had convicted Harold Fiske of violating the state criminal syndicalism statute after he encouraged workers to join the IWW. The Court concluded that insufficient evidence supported the conviction and that, as applied to Fiske, the statute was "an arbitrary and unreasonable exercise of the police power of the State, unwarrantably infringing [his] liberty." *Fiske* illustrates that the justices were not intransigently opposed to validating claims which implicated free expression. Nonetheless, the justices' willingness to respond positively to such remote free-expression cases should not be overstated. In *Schwimmer v. United States*, decided in 1929, the Court upheld the denial of naturalization to a well-educated "linguist, lecturer, and writer," born in Hungary but resident in the United States since 1921. Previously, the Court had held that aliens do not have first-amendment rights, so the case did not raise a free-expression issue per se. Yet, it did implicate free-expression concerns: the sole reason for denying naturalization was Schwimmer's declaration that, for reasons of conscience, she was an "uncompromising pacifist" who would be unwilling to "take up arms personally." Pierce Butler's majority opinion emphasized that naturalization determinations could turn upon the applicant's ideas or opinions; Schwimmer might "exert her power to influence others" to become pacifists.[7]

Holmes's *Schwimmer* dissent, joined by Brandeis, arguably manifested a changed attitude. Albeit unclear, Holmes suggested that he now personally ascribed an enhanced importance to free expression. Instead of demeaning the claimant and her beliefs, as he had done in his *Abrams* dissent, Holmes expressed respect for her position, though he disagreed with her optimistic belief that warfare could be eradicated. To maintain that the Constitution could be improved, Holmes reasoned, signified intelligence, not a "lack of attachment" to American principles. Holmes offered an arresting example: "only a judge mad with partisanship would exclude [from naturalization] because the applicant thought that the Eighteenth Amendment [and Prohibition] should be repealed." Indeed, Holmes appeared to accord a special value to free expression. "[I]f there is any principle of the Constitution that more imperatively calls for attachment than any other it is the principle of free thought — not free thought for those who agree with us but freedom for the thought that we hate." To Holmes, "we should adhere to that principle with regard to admission into, as well as to life within this country."[8]

AT THE END OF the 1920s, the Court's approach to free expression still resembled that of a decade earlier. Regardless of Holmes's and Brandeis's views of free speech and press, the majority of justices did not imbue first-amendment freedoms with special importance — some justices seemed to value economic liberties more highly. The Court continued to adjudicate free-expression issues in accord with republican democratic principles — showing great deference to legislative determinations of the common good — or to subsume such issues within due process liberty analyses. Yet, the remote free-expression cases suggested that some justices seriously considered free-expression values when determining the common good and the reasonableness of governmental actions. Then, in 1930, Hughes replaced Taft as chief justice, and Roberts replaced Sanford as an associate justice. In 1931, both of the new justices voted to protect expression in the first two Supreme Court cases to validate free-expression claims. Hughes wrote the majority opinion in both cases.

In the first case, *Stromberg v. California,* the state convicted Yetta Stromberg for displaying a red (Communist) flag as a sign of "opposition to organized government." After reiterating that the right of free speech applied against state governments through the fourteenth amendment's due process clause, Hughes emphasized the "indefiniteness and ambiguity" of the state law. The statute, as interpreted by the state courts, "'might be construed to include the peaceful and orderly opposition to a government as organized and controlled by one political party by those of another political party." A seven-to-two majority held that this statutory proscription on expression was "so vague" on "its face" that it was unconstitutional. Hughes justified this conclusion by linking free expression to democratic government: "The maintenance of the opportunity for free political discussion to the end that government may be responsive to the will of the people and that changes may be obtained by lawful means . . . is a fundamental principle of our constitutional system." Given that the year was 1931, when the first stirrings of pluralist democracy were swirling about, one must wonder whether Hughes, in tying free expression to government, contemplated republican or pluralist democracy. Apparently, at this point, he still conceptualized democracy in republican terms. Earlier in the opinion, he had described free speech with standard republican democratic rhetoric: "[t]he right [of free speech] is not an absolute one, and the State in the exercise of its police power may punish the abuse of this freedom." Moreover, even though suppression could be readily justified under republican democratic principles, many jurists and theorists had previously linked free expression with republican democracy. Most recently, Brandeis in *Whitney* had argued that free government required free expression.[9]

Stromberg, to be sure, marks a significant turn by the Court as an institution. Subsequently categorized as the first "explicit victory for free speech" in the Supreme Court, *Stromberg* demonstrated that an emerging majority of justices would be receptive to free-expression claims. The result thus bolstered the civil libertarian movement by suggesting the judiciary might become a haven of protection. Yet, simultaneously, the Court's holding was limited. Most important, the Court did not explicitly hold that the Constitution protected Stromberg's expression, the display of a red flag. The Court held the statute unconstitutional on its face, not in its application to Stromberg. Hence, even though the case arose a decade after the Red Scare — during a period when, because of the Great Depression, the American willingness to discuss Communism as an alternative to capitalism would reach a peak — the Court did not declare that the advocacy of Communism was constitutionally protected. Furthermore, one might even question whether *Stromberg* is accurately categorized as an "explicit" free speech case. The Court specifically held that the statute was void for vagueness, but vagueness is usually characterized as a due process rather than a first-amendment doctrine. And Hughes's opinion was, if anything, ambiguous: it could be construed as either relying on free speech, due process, or both.[10]

The second 1931 free-expression case, *Near v. Minnesota,* was a close five-to-four decision. Holmes, Brandeis, Roberts, and Harlan F. Stone, who had been appointed in 1925 (and had been in the *Stromberg* majority), joined Hughes's majority opinion, while the Four Horsemen dissented. J. M. Near's weekly newspaper consistently published anti-Semitic articles accusing Minneapolis public officials of corruption. Pursuant to a state statute providing "for the abatement, as a public nuisance, of a 'malicious,' scandalous and defamatory newspaper, magazine or other periodical,'" a county attorney sought to enjoin further publications. The state courts granted the injunction, but with the support of the ACLU, Near appealed to the Supreme Court. Reversing, the Court held that the injunction constituted a prior restraint violating freedom of the press. Both Hughes's majority opinion and Butler's dissent conceptualized free expression from within the parameters of a republican democratic system. Hughes explained that, despite the constitutional protection of individual liberties, "the authority of the state to enact laws to promote the health, safety, morals, and general welfare of its people is necessarily admitted." The state, specifically, may "punish [an] abuse" of the freedom of the press. The majority and the dissent disagreed, however, about whether the injunction, granted under the state statute, constituted a prior restraint. Butler distinguished the statutory scheme from a prototypical prior restraint — when an official must grant a license before publication — because it required a court, before granting an injunction, to find that a publication amounted to a nuisance. Hughes, meanwhile, reasoned that the statute allowed "public authorities" to initiate injunctive proceedings against a publisher. If the statutory requirements were satisfied, then the "newspaper or periodical is suppressed and further publication is made punishable as a contempt." As Hughes concluded: "This is of the essence of censorship."[11]

The Court decided two more free-expression cases on the merits before the 1937 turn. In *Grosjean v. American Press Company*, decided in 1936, a unanimous Court invalidated a state's special gross receipts (or "license") tax imposed only on periodicals with a certain minimum circulation. After emphasizing the importance of a free press for republican democratic government, Sutherland's opinion cited *Near* and observed that prior restraints might take many forms, not merely licensing schemes. This state tax, in fact, constituted an impermissible prior restraint because it imposed a special burden not only on the press but on certain publishers (those with large enough circulations). Why must the press be constitutionally protected from this type of tax? "The predominant purpose of the grant of immunity [from special taxes] was to preserve an untrammeled press as a vital source of public information," Sutherland wrote. "[S]ince informed public opinion is the most potent of all restraints upon misgovernment, the suppression or abridgement of the publicity afforded by a free press cannot be regarded otherwise than with grave concern." The Court, in effect, reiterated the republican democratic maxim that free government requires a free press: "A free press stands as one of the great interpreters between the government and the people. To allow it to be fettered is to fetter ourselves."[12]

The justices heard oral arguments for *De Jonge v. Oregon* on December 9, 1936, one week before the *West Coast Hotel* oral argument. The Court issued the *De Jonge* decision on January 4, 1937, approximately one month before Roosevelt publicly announced his court-packing plan and almost three months before the *West Coast Hotel* decision. With an opinion by Hughes, the *De Jonge* Court unanimously invalidated a conviction under the Oregon criminal syndicalism law. Hughes stressed that the only criminal charge under the statute, as applied, was that Dirk De Jonge "had assisted in the conduct of a public meeting . . . held under the auspices of the Communist Party." *De Jonge* therefore implicated the first-amendment freedom of "peaceable assembly," rather than free speech or press. Partly for that reason, Hughes distinguished *De Jonge* from earlier criminal syndicalism cases, like *Gitlow* and *Whitney*. De Jonge himself could not be held personally responsible for either advocating or forming an organization that advocated the violent overthrow of the government. Hughes acknowledged that the legislature could enact laws to punish the "abuse" of free expression, yet he intertwined this governmental power with the admonition that free government requires free expression. "The greater the importance of safeguarding the community from incitements to the overthrow of our institutions by force and violence," Hughes explained, "the more imperative is the need to preserve inviolate the constitutional rights of free speech, free press and free assembly in order to maintain the opportunity for free political discussion, to the end that government may be responsive to the will of the people and that changes, if desired, may be obtained by peaceful means." Regardless of the Communist party's goals, De Jonge enjoyed a personal right "to discuss the public issues of the day . . . in a lawful manner."[13]

On the cusp of the Court's 1937 turn, the Court's recent free-expression jurisprudence could be reduced to three main points. First, the justices had developed, over the prior decade, a new-found concern for the importance of free speech and a free press, a concern more attune to the tradition of dissent than the tradition of suppression. Even the Four Horsemen sometimes voted to invalidate laws as violating expressive liberties — a position at once consistent with their elsewhere-voiced concerns for individual liberties (particularly in economic transactions), yet generally in tension with their conservative political stances. The Court's invigoration of first-amendment freedoms largely harmonized with the earlier dissenting views of Holmes and Brandeis, though the justices never invoked Holmes and Brandeis's clear and present danger language. Second, to support the Court's invigoration of first-amendment freedoms, the justices had begun to emphasize that free government required free expression. They had raised this maxim in three of the four cases validating free expression claims: *Stromberg, Grosjean,* and *De Jonge* (*Near* was the exception). Third, this link between free government and free expression had roots deep in republican democracy, and the justices, albeit often ambiguously, continued to consider free-expression claims within republican democratic structures. Even so, in cases earlier in the twentieth century, the Supreme Court justices had rarely invoked the free government–free-expression maxim — Brandeis's 1927 *Whitney* concurrence and, less clearly, his 1920 *Gilbert* dissent being the exceptions. Indeed, given how frequently the justices would mention this maxim in the 1930s, one might conjecture that Brandeis effectively reminded the other justices of a forgotten connection — between expression and democracy — a connection that had seemed paramount in the late-eighteenth century. Perhaps more important, though, the justices' repeated invocations of the free government–free-expression maxim in the 1930s underscores that the 1937 turn was truly neither revolutionary nor evolutionary. In the late 1920s and early to mid-1930s, republican democracy was crumbling and the practices of pluralist democracy were developing. While many of these changes in democratic government would not become apparent until later in the 1930s, many scholars had already begun talking about the workings of democracy by the middle of the decade. In this political and intellectual atmosphere, the justices' renewed interest in the free government–free-expression maxim hardly seems coincidental. Rather, the free-expression cases seemed to augur the coming of the 1937 turn and the Court's acceptance of pluralist democracy.

FREE-EXPRESSION DOCTRINE AND THEORY AFTER THE 1937 TURN

On April 12, 1937, the same day the Court decided *Jones and Laughlin*, the Court decided a case involving the first amendment. In *Associated Press v. NLRB*, the Court reviewed the NLRB's finding that the Associated Press (AP) had committed an unfair labor practice by dismissing an employee because of union organizing. In defense, the AP claimed that, because it was part of the press, the application of the NLRA restrictions to its activities violated freedom of the press. According to the AP, the NLRA would interfere with its ability to employ impartial reporters and editors. The Court rejected this argument on two grounds. First, it was unrelated to the facts of the case. The AP had dismissed the employee because he had agitated for collective bargaining, not because of editorial bias. Second, the first amendment did not immunize the AP from a general law, the NLRA, that proscribed unfair labor practices. The statute left intact the AP's discretion to hire and fire employees based on their job performances, so the first amendment was beside the point. The Court did not need to decide the scope of constitutional protection.[14]

Thus, the first true free-expression case decided after the 1937 turn was *Herndon v. Lowry*. The justices heard oral arguments on February 8, 1937, three days after the court-packing plan had been revealed but still before the Court announced the *West Coast Hotel* decision. The Court, however, did not issue its *Herndon* decision until April 26, 1937, nearly a month after

West Coast Hotel and two weeks after *Jones and Laughlin*. By the time *Herndon* came down, the Court had undermined the structures of republican democratic judicial review and had turned toward pluralist democracy. Yet, none of the Four Horsemen had yet resigned, and they all dissented in a five-to-four decision. The state of Georgia had convicted Angelo Herndon, a black Communist party organizer, for attempting to persuade other individuals, mostly African Americans, to join the party. The state invoked "an old Georgia slave insurrection statute," which provided that "[a]ny attempt, by persuasion or otherwise, to induce others to join in any combined resistance to the lawful authority of the State shall constitute an attempt to incite insurrection." The Court reversed Herndon's conviction. Roberts's majority opinion appeared to rest on two alternative grounds: the statute as applied to Herndon violated free expression, and the statute was vague on its face. Yet, Roberts mixed these two grounds together, invoked a multitude of previous decisions, and issued an opinion redolent of confusion. Roberts's opinion suggests a Court in the throes of change, floundering about, and uncertain how to proceed.[15]

Roberts initially reiterated the *Gitlow* majority's distinction between statutes that explicitly proscribe expression and those that proscribe conduct but are applied to expression. Regardless, while the Georgia statute proscribed expression, Roberts refused to follow the *Gitlow* admonition to defer to the legislative determination. He instead found the statutory language so general as to invite the jury to convict for the bad or "dangerous tendency" of the defendant's words, which the majority deemed impermissible. Even though Roberts had already quoted the clear and present danger test, he did not apply it; rather, he talked of a "reasonable apprehension of danger." In language still resonating with republican democratic principles, Roberts cited *De Jonge* for the proposition that the state "goes beyond the power to restrict abuses of freedom of speech" if it punishes "innocent participation in a meeting held with an innocent purpose." Roberts then cited *Stromberg* for the proposition that a statute is void on its face because of vagueness if it might "make criminal an utterance or an act which may be innocently said or done with no intent to induce resort to violence." Temporarily abandoning the vagueness issue, Roberts reviewed the evidence and concluded that "the requisite proof is lacking" to show that Herndon had incited or attempted to incite insurrection. "[A]s applied to him, the statute unreasonably limits freedom of speech and freedom of assembly." Returning to the issue of vagueness, Roberts treated it as a matter of free expression as well as due process. Vagueness was demonstrated partly by the statutory failure to specify when a "defendant's utterances or activities [would beget] a clear and present danger of forcible obstruction of a particular state function." Roberts thus concluded: "So vague and indeterminate are the boundaries thus set to the freedom of speech and assembly that the law necessarily violates the guarantees of liberty embodied in the Fourteenth Amendment."[16]

Despite this mishmash of doctrinal starts and stops, *Herndon* proved significant in three ways. First, it continued the Court's trend toward a more expansive concept of free expression. Second, in terms of doctrine, the Court majority invoked the clear and present danger standard, even if they did not unequivocally apply it. Moreover, the majority appeared to repudiate the bad tendency test, at least implicitly. Third, and most important, the Court appeared to create a presumption in favor of protecting expression. Roberts wrote: "The power of a state to abridge freedom of speech and of assembly is the exception rather than the rule." Under republican democracy, the broad governmental power to regulate for the common good always limited free expression. This approach engendered the bad tendency test and the typical conclusion that a challenged governmental action did not infringe freedom of speech or press. But now, Roberts suggested, the Court would presume that the Constitution protected speech and writing. Liberty would demarcate the reach of governmental power, not vice versa — at least when the liberty was that of expression. Two years later, the Court confirmed this reversal from republican democratic principles. In *Schneider v. State,* an eight-to-one decision, the Court wrote: "Although a municipality may enact regulations in the interest of the public safety, health, welfare or convenience, these may not abridge the individual liberties secured by the Constitution to those who wish to speak, write, print or circulate information or opinion." In other words, the government might still pass laws for purposes that would have constituted the common good under republican democracy, but within the new pluralist democratic regime, such purposes would not justify restrictions on free expression.[17]

Consequently, in a phenomenal string of cases from 1938 to 1940, the Court upheld one free-expression claim after another. *Lovell v. Griffin* held that an ordinance requiring a permit for the distribution of literature constituted a prior restraint violating the first amendment. *Hague v. C.I.O.* upheld the right of labor unions to organize and distribute literature in the streets and parks. More than forty years earlier, *Davis v. Massachusetts* had emphasized the power of a government to control its property, but the *Hague* plurality opinion recognized a first-amendment easement in the streets and parks — creating a public forum — because these government-owned properties "have immemorially been held in trust for the use of the public and, time out of mind, have been used for purposes of assembly, communicating thoughts between citizens, and discussing public questions." In *Schneider*, the Court emphasized this first-amendment easement to invalidate convictions for distributing literature in the streets, parks, and sidewalks. *Thornhill v. Alabama* and *Carlson v. California* relied on the first amendment to uphold a right of unions to picket businesses during labor disputes. *Cantwell v. Connecticut* held that a conviction for breach of the peace violated free expression even though the defendant had "incensed" passersby by playing a phonograph record attacking their religion.[18]

REGARDLESS OF THE RESULTS in these cases, the presumption favoring speech and writing was problematic. The Court's 1937 turn manifested not only an acceptance of pluralist democracy but also a willingness to defer to economic and social welfare regulations. Thus, the Court seemed to have presumptions running in opposite directions: presuming legislation infringing economic liberties to be constitutional, while presuming legislation infringing free expression to be unconstitutional. In the eyes of many, free expression became a constitutional "lodestar," the preeminent constitutional right among the increasingly important civil liberties. In a case decided toward the end of 1937, Cardozo explained that "freedom of thought and speech . . . is the matrix, the indispensable condition, of nearly every other form of freedom." Stone wrote in 1939 that "[n]o more grave and important issue can be brought to this Court than that of freedom of speech and assembly." But why did free expression rise to such prominence? Why did the Court invest free speech and writing with such importance under pluralist democracy when it had so readily permitted suppression under republican democracy?[19]

From the standpoint of theory, the search-for-truth (marketplace-of-ideas) rationale remained vital. In 1941, Zechariah Chafee published a new version of his 1920 book. While the new book, *Free Speech in the United States*, substantially revised and expanded the earlier one, Chafee steadfastly emphasized the search-for-truth rationale. And the Court, too, would invoke this rationale. The next year, 1942, the Court reasoned that certain types of speech, particularly so-called fighting words — "those which by their very utterance inflict injury or tend to incite an immediate breach of the peace" — do not deserve constitutional protection because "such utterances are no essential part of any exposition of ideas" and thus do not contribute to the discovery of "truth." The justices have continued to invoke the search-for-truth rationale ever since.[20]

Despite the persistent vigor of the search-for-truth rationale, justices and scholars increasingly relied on a self-governance rationale that harmonized with pluralist democracy. To be sure, the new self-governance rationale echoed the republican democratic maxim that free government requires free expression. Under republican democracy, however, theorists typically conceptualized free expression as contributing to government in two interrelated ways. First, a free press and public discussion checked the tendencies of elected officials toward corruption. Free expression encouraged the exercise of civic virtue. Second, free expression nurtured dialogue among virtuous citizens who quested after the common good. Under pluralist democracy, justices and scholars who articulated the self-governance rationale usually did so for other reasons. Most often, pluralist democratic theorists emphasized the importance of following certain governmental processes (rather than the importance of arriving at certain substantive outcomes in accord with the common good). No liberty seemed more central to those governmental processes than free expression.

Free expression allowed diverse groups and individuals to contribute their views in the pluralist political arena. This process of contribution, of political participation, grounded interrelated tenets of pluralist democratic government. The process established the legitimacy of the outcome. Pluralist democracy assumed that ethical values were relative: no criterion other than acceptance in the democratic arena could determine governmental goals. And the government could legitimately choose goals and values in the democratic arena only if everybody could participate by contributing their views. As one constitutional scholar would explain, "a democratic society must commit itself to a principle of epistemological humility: no governmental body may impose restrictions on expression on the basis of predetermined moral values." Also, the process established the consent of the governed. All citizens could be deemed to have consented to governmental actions and decisions only if all citizens had been given a full and fair opportunity to participate in the governmental processes. In short, pluralist democracy did not exist without free expression. If governmental officials interfered with the pluralist political process by controlling or restricting public debates, then they would skew the democratic outcomes and undermine the consent of the governed. No less so than voting, free expression was a sine qua non of pluralist democratic processes.[21]

Throughout the 1940s (and afterward), the justices avowed that free expression was integral to the process of pluralist democracy. Discussing "[a]bridgment of freedom of speech and of the press," Murphy wrote in 1940 that government cannot be allowed to "diminish the effective exercise of rights so necessary to the maintenance of democratic institutions." In 1943, Jackson emphasized the role of free expression to consent: "We set up government by consent of the governed, and the Bill of Rights denies those in power any legal opportunity to coerce that consent. Authority here is to be controlled by public opinion, not public opinion by authority." Jackson underscored that free expression is necessary to foster diverse ideas. "If there is any fixed star in our constitutional constellation, it is that no official, high or petty, can prescribe what shall be orthodox in politics, nationalism, religion, or other matters of opinion or force citizens to confess by word or act their faith therein." And "diversity of opinion," nurtured by free expression, generates national "unity and strength." In sum, as the Court stated at the end of the decade, "[t]he vitality of civil and political institutions in our society depends on free discussion."[22]

The Court's emphasis on protecting free expression intertwined with the Court's self-proclaimed role as guardian of pluralist democratic processes; the protection of free expression, that is, went hand-in-hand with representation reinforcement. Sometimes, however, the justices disagreed about how to safeguard the crucial role of free expression in pluralist democracy. In *Terminiello v. Chicago,* decided in 1949, the police arrested a speaker whose inflammatory pronouncements were provoking a hostile audience. Finding the expression constitutionally protected, the Court emphasized the freewheeling give-and-take of pluralist democracy. "[A] function of free speech under our system of government is to invite dispute," wrote Douglas. "It may indeed best serve its high purpose when it induces a condition of unrest, creates dissatisfaction with conditions as they are, or even stirs people to anger. Speech is often provocative and challenging. It may strike at prejudices and preconceptions and have profound unsettling effects as it presses for acceptance of an idea." Jackson, joined by Harold Burton, dissented. Agreeing that free expression must be protected to insure democratic processes, he nonetheless argued that provocation of mob violence undermines those precise processes. "Violent and noisy shows of strength discourage participation of moderates in discussions so fraught with violence and real discussion dries up and disappears."[23]

PARTLY BECAUSE THE judicial protection of free expression could be so closely tied to representation reinforcement, many scholars were drawn to the emerging self-governance rationale. As early as 1939, the prominent lawyer and occasional author, Grenville Clark, emphasized that "all government should rest on 'the consent of the governed.'" Such consent cannot be "coerced" and must be "reasonably well-informed." Consent therefore requires free expression: "any substantial limitation on frank discussion of matters of public concern is flatly inconsistent with the acceptance of the underlying philosophy on which the American system is based."[24] In 1948, a philosophy professor and college administrator, Alexander Meiklejohn, presented what would become the most renowned articulation of the self-governance rationale. Meiklejohn premised his brief book, *Free Speech and Its Relation to Self-Government,* on a sharp distinction between two types of expression: on the one hand, political expression — speech and writing related to political issues or governmental matters — and on the other hand, all other expression. The first amendment, Meiklejohn argued, absolutely protected political expression. The due process clauses of the fifth and fourteenth amendments conditionally protected other expression as a type of liberty. From a constitutional standpoint, the government could always restrict nonpolitical expression and other types of liberty if in furtherance of the common good, but the government could never restrict political expression.[25]

According to Meiklejohn, the absolute protection of political expression arose from "the structure and functioning of our political system" — "from the necessities of the program of self-government." The unconditional protection of free expression "is a deduction from the basic American agreement that public issues shall be decided by universal suffrage." More than anything, then, Meiklejohn stressed that "men can, by processes of free public discussion, govern themselves." Through unfettered discussion of political issues, citizens discerned the "general welfare" or "common good." To elaborate this political process, Meiklejohn turned to "the traditional American town meeting," an institution that "is commonly, and rightly, regarded as a model by which free political procedures may be measured." In a town meeting "the people of a community assemble to discuss and to act upon matters of public interest — roads, schools, poorhouses, health, external defense, and the like," Meiklejohn explained. "Every man is free to come. They meet as political equals. Each has a right and a duty to think his own thoughts, to express them, and to listen to the arguments of others." Nonetheless, the absolute protection did not guarantee "unregulated talkativeness." Virtual expression — the articulation of one's viewpoint by oneself or by another citizen — ensured the legitimacy of the "self-governing process" epitomized by the town meeting. "What is essential is not that everyone shall speak, but that everything worth saying shall be said."[26]

Meiklejohn's defense of free expression dripped with unwitting irony.

Subsequent theorists would cite his book as the definitive statement of the self-governance rationale, yet in actuality, Meiklejohn defended the importance of the first amendment within a form of government, republican democracy, that had already collapsed. Two explanations are possible. Either Meiklejohn, disregarding the work of political scientists and legal scholars, remained ignorant of the transition to pluralist democracy, or Meiklejohn, all too aware of the transition, purposefully attempted to resuscitate republican democracy through philosophical analysis. Given Meiklejohn's erudition, the latter seems more likely. If only he could explain the importance of free expression, Meiklejohn seemed to suggest, then republican democratic government could spring again to life. Hence, he gamely elucidated republican democratic principles and their relation to free government. Somewhat as Jürgen Habermas, decades later, would seek to specify the conditions of an "ideal speech situation" purified of corrupting influences, Meiklejohn sought to describe a realm of political discussion that would produce the best public decisions — the common good. According to Meiklejohn, the common good consisted of "our individual desires and intentions," yet was not made "by simply adding them together." The raw pursuit of self-interest — "competitive individualism" — might be appropriate for the economic marketplace, but it would corrupt the political process of self-government. The "public interest" is "an organization of [private interests], a selection and arrangement, based upon judgment of relative values and mutual implications."[27]

But Meiklejohn could not resurrect republican democracy. The United States had changed too much. A small traditional New England community, governed through town meetings, no longer represented a microcosm of American society, if it ever had. The homogeneous rural, white, and Protestant New England town might have served as a model for republican democratic government in early-nineteenth century America, but in the mid-twentieth century, it grossly distorted the social and cultural reality. Even at a philosophical level, Meiklejohn depicted a republican democracy that differed radically from the traditional theory of republican democracy. A fundamental principle of republican democracy had always been the commitment to the common good, as Meiklejohn himself acknowledged. The government could overcome any individual interest or liberty, including free expression, in order to promote the common good. But with regard to free expression (that is, political expression) — and free expression only — Meiklejohn sought to change this basic premise of republican democracy. The first amendment sheltered political expression with an impenetrable shield, according to Meiklejohn. The government's pursuit of the common good could justify the restriction of any liberty, pursuant to due process, except for free expression.[28]

In short, Meiklejohn did not truly defend free expression in a republican democratic regime. To justify the absolute protection of free expression, he needed to alter the most fundamental republican democratic principle. For this reason, theorists of pluralist democracy would readily appropriate Meiklejohn's defense of free expression, which resonated in numerous ways with pluralist democracy. Whereas traditional republican democratic theorists had understood the common good to equate with particular substantive outcomes, Meiklejohn defined the common good in accord with the proper *processes* of self-government (especially the process of free expression). What was the common good in any particular situation? The outcome reached by following the proper processes. Whereas earlier republican democratic theorists usually emphasized the importance of free expression to *free* government, Meiklejohn stressed *self*-government. Hence, while republican democracy, through American history, had been readily harmonized with the exclusion of societal groups, Meiklejohn posited "universal suffrage" as a component of self-government. True, Meiklejohn deemed the virtual expression of diverse viewpoints as satisfying the need for full participation in the process of self-government. Thus, later constitutional theorists would push Meiklejohn's desideratum even further, emphasizing that the unfettered actual opportunity to express political ideas was necessary both to assure full participation in self-government and to establish consent to governmental decisions. Ultimately, Meiklejohn's attempt to shelter political expression from the reach of democratic majorities — free expression, and solely free expression, could not be restricted to promote the common good — not only contravened republican democracy but mirrored the specification of no-fly zones, characteristic of the emerging pluralist democratic practices. Despite his efforts to follow republican democracy, Meiklejohn justified the pluralist democratic establishment of free expression as a constitutional lodestar. The first amendment's protection of free expression, in Meiklejohn's words, was the Constitution's "most vital assertion, its most significant contribution to political wisdom."[29]

Subsequent to Meiklejohn, a legion of constitutional and political theorists justified strong first-amendment protections by emphasizing the integral role of free expression in pluralist democratic processes. For example, in 1964, Harry Kalven described the "'central meaning'" of the first amendment: "a core of protection of speech without which democracy cannot function." In 1983, Frederick Schauer explained that, quite simply, "[g]overnments are called 'democracies' when they permit freedom of speech and press." Meanwhile, like Meiklejohn, Robert Dahl, the pre-eminent theorist of pluralist democracy, defined democracy as the "right to self-government." And if "people are entitled to govern themselves," Dahl reasoned, "then citizens are also entitled to all the rights that are necessary in order for them to govern themselves, that is, all the rights that are essential to the democratic process." Foremost among those rights is free expression. Indeed, Dahl defined democratic participation in terms of free expression. "Freedom of speech . . . is necessary both for effective participation and for enlightened understanding; so too are freedom of the press and freedom of assembly." Throughout the pluralist democratic process, all citizens must have an "adequate" and "equal" opportunity "for expressing their preferences" toward possible substantive goals and values. "They must have adequate and equal opportunities for placing questions on the agenda and for expressing reasons for endorsing one outcome rather than another."[30]

WHILE THEORY ALONE did not determine the Court's direction in free-expression cases, it did provide an intellectual linchpin for a strong reading of the first amendment. Equally important, other factors pushed the Court in that direction — in the direction of presuming that the Constitution protected expression. The tradition of dissent was, in a sense, ready and waiting. Regardless of theoretical arguments, the justices could legitimate the constitutional protection of expression by invoking the tradition of dissent while ignoring or downplaying the tradition of suppression. In *Bridges v. California,* decided in 1941, lower courts had issued contempt orders because of editorials criticizing the state judiciary's treatment of labor disputes. The Court reversed. "[T]he First Amendment does not speak equivocally," wrote Black for the majority. "It prohibits any law 'abridging the freedom of speech, or of the press.' It must be taken as a command of the broadest scope that explicit language, read in the context of a liberty-loving society, will allow." Black explicitly grounded his strong reading of the first amendment on an intermingling of the process of self-government with the American tradition of speaking one's mind, whether about governmental officials (including judges) or other public matters. The Court was especially concerned that the contempt orders attempted to "remove from the arena of public discussion" labor controversies that otherwise would "command [the] most interest." The people must be allowed to voice their opinions, come what may. "[I]t is a prized American privilege to speak one's mind, although not always with perfect good taste, on all public institutions. . . .

[A]n enforced silence, however limited, solely in the name of preserving the dignity of the bench, would probably engender resentment, suspicion, and contempt much more than it would enhance respect."[31]

Given the Court's developing doctrinal approaches to pluralist democratic judicial review, the location of the free speech and free press guarantees in the textual provisions of the first amendment also proved significant. The presumption in favor of protecting expression created a no-fly zone — which would always be controversial — but at least it was a no-fly zone marked by the text of the first amendment. Hence, the justices could distinguish free-expression cases, presuming the unconstitutionality of governmental actions, from economic liberty cases, presuming the opposite. Free speech and a free press were expressly enumerated rights, while economic liberties, particularly liberty to contract, were not. The 1940s, recall, was the decade when the justices referred to free expression as a preferred freedom. Conscious of the tension between this doctrine and the Court's deference to economic legislation, the justices recognized the forcefulness of linking such preferred freedoms both to the constitutional text and to self-government. In another case involving free expression in a labor dispute, the Court stressed that it needed "to say where the individual's freedom ends and the State's power begins." The Court would not defer to the legislative determination. The separation of individual liberty from state power, "now as always delicate, is perhaps more so where the usual presumption supporting legislation is balanced by the preferred place given in our scheme to the great, the indispensable democratic freedoms secured by the First Amendment."[32]

NONETHELESS, EVEN DURING the 1940s, most of the justices refused to deem the first amendment an absolute. Sometimes, the government should be able to overcome the presumption favoring the protection of speech and writing. Consequently, in specific cases, the Court needed to draw a line between protected and unprotected expression. This need often led the justices to balance competing interests — a judicial approach that became commonplace in numerous realms of constitutional law, including free expression. In *Martin v. City of Struthers,* the Court reviewed a municipal ordinance restricting the time, place, and manner (rather than the content) of expression. The Court held that Thelma Martin's conviction for distributing leaflets door-to-door violated free expression. "We are faced in the instant case with the necessity of weighing the conflicting interests of the appellant in the civil rights she claims," explained the majority opinion, "as well as the right of the individual householder to determine whether he is willing to receive her message, against the interest of the community which by this ordinance offers to protect the interests of all of its citizens, whether particular citizens want that protection or not." While the *Martin* Court suggested that it weighed the various interests evenhandedly, the Court often skewed the balance against the government to account for the presumption favoring the protection of speech and writing. In *Schneider v. State,* the Court distinguished free-expression balancing cases from others. "Mere legislative preferences or beliefs respecting matters of public convenience may well support regulation directed at other personal activities, but be insufficient to justify such as diminishes the exercise of rights so vital to the maintenance of democratic institutions," wrote Roberts for an eight-justice majority. Applying a skewed balancing test, the Court invalidated convictions under an ordinance that proscribed the distribution of handbills to pedestrians on the streets and sidewalks.[33]

In numerous free-expression contexts, the Court translated the skewed balancing test into the clear and present danger standard. Two points bear emphasis. First, the Court explicitly repudiated the republican democratic bad tendency test because it did not sufficiently protect expression. Second, in its stead, the Court invoked the clear and present danger test because it struck the proper (skewed) balance between free expression and other interests. In *Thornhill v. Alabama,* yet another free-expression case involving a labor dispute, the Court reasoned that it "should 'weigh the circumstances' and 'appraise the substantiality of the reasons advanced' in support of the challenged regulations." Yet, in weighing the interests, Murphy's opinion for an eight-justice majority focused on whether the statutorily proscribed behavior created a "clear and present danger of destruction of life or property." As then interpreted, the clear and present danger test strongly protected speech and writing. "What finally emerges from the 'clear and present danger' cases is a working principle that the substantive evil must be extremely serious and the degree of imminence extremely high before utterances can be punished." By 1943, the Court had called the clear and present danger test "a commonplace."[34]

The two leading twentieth-century theorists of free expression, Chafee and Meiklejohn, sharply diverged over the suitability of the clear and present danger test. Chafee, of course, had championed the clear and present danger test during the World War I era and had perhaps influenced Holmes to interpret it more rigorously. Meiklejohn, in his 1948 book, criticized the clear and present danger test exactly because it allowed courts to balance free expression against other interests, particularly the government's interest in preventing danger. From Meiklejohn's perspective, the first-amendment protection of political expression should be absolute; balancing, even if skewed to favor protection, should never be permissible. The following year, Chafee published a review of Meiklejohn's book. Chafee argued that Meiklejohn's thesis, that the first amendment protected only political expression, was too narrow. The first amendment, Chafee insisted, also shielded other types of expression, which should not be relegated to mere due process protection. Simultaneously, Chafee argued that Meiklejohn's demand for absolute protection of political expression was too extreme. Because of his absolutism, Meiklejohn did not even attempt to argue that, for example, "the dangers of Communism" were either serious or trivial. Instead, to Meiklejohn, such dangers were constitutionally "irrelevant." Exasperated with Meiklejohn's impracticality, Chafee grumbled: "No matter how terrible and immediate the dangers may be, he keeps saying, the First Amendment will not let Congress or anybody else in the Government try to deal with [them]." According to Chafee, adjudication of constitutional issues must be more pragmatic: "Balancing among interests must go on."[35]

Chafee, of course, was not the only advocate for balancing, a standard method of pluralist democratic adjudication. Likewise, Meiklejohn was not the only critic of balancing, especially in first-amendment cases. One did not have to be an absolutist like Meiklejohn or Justice Black to believe the first amendment created a principle of free expression that should not (and perhaps could not) be weighed against ordinary political interests. Unsurprisingly, then, the Court's need to distinguish between protected and unprotected expression under pluralist democracy led not only to balancing but also to an alternative: a two-level approach to free expression. The Court would often rely on this alternative when the government sought to restrict expression based on its content (rather than on the time, place, or manner of the expression). Under the two-level approach — one level of expression was fully protected, while the other was unprotected — the Court established that the first amendment protected speech and writing *unless* the expression fell into a low-value category, in accordance with the presumption favoring the protection of expression. Thus, consistent with Chafee's counterargument against Meiklejohn and consistent with the tradition of dissent, the Court held that first-amendment protections extended well-beyond political expression (though, pursuant to the self-governance rationale, the Court often would emphasize the importance of protecting political discussion). But when the justices deemed particular expression to be low value, it was outside the refuge of the first amendment.

In 1942, the Court identified several low-value categories: "There are certain well-defined and narrowly limited classes of speech, the prevention and punishment of which has never been thought to raise any Constitutional problem. These include the lewd and obscene, the profane, the libelous, and the insulting or 'fighting' words." If the Court designated disputed speech to be, let's say, obscene, then the government could punish the speaker; the first amendment did not shield the expression. While the Court sometimes justified its categorization of expression as low value by relying on theories (search for truth and self-governance), the categories also were remnants of the republican democratic past. Under pluralist democracy, the Court might reason that the government could restrict obscenity because it was low-value expression beyond the reach of the first amendment, while under republican democracy, the Court would have reasoned that the government could restrict obscenity because it had bad tendencies contravening the common good. The justification for governmental suppression of obscenity might have changed, but obscenity remained unprotected.[36]

Given the Court's two-level approach to free expression, the justices sometimes disagreed about the criteria that should identify expression as falling within a specific low-value category. Even if the first amendment clearly did not protect obscenity, for example, the Court would still need to decide whether certain materials were obscene. In 1957, in *Roth v. United States,* a Comstock Act prosecution, Brennan defined obscenity for a five-justice majority. Brennan rejected the *Hicklin* standard, which had originated in England and had long been applied in many lower courts, and instead categorized materials as obscene if, "to the average person, applying contemporary community standards, the dominant theme of the material taken as a whole appeals to prurient interest." Even so, the *Roth* majority relied on the republican democratic past, which troubled the other justices. Warren, concurring in the result, emphasized that "[t]he history of the application of laws designed to suppress the obscene demonstrates convincingly that the power of government can be invoked under them against great art or literature, scientific treatises, or works exciting social controversy." Too readily in the past, judges and juries had condemned materials for having bad tendencies.[37]

A majority of justices did not long remain committed to the *Roth* standard. Justice Potter Stewart, concurring in a 1964 case, lamented that *Roth* may have tried "to define what [is] indefinable." Refusing to offer an alternative doctrinal definition of obscenity, Stewart declared: "I know it when I see it." Three years later, in *Redrup v. New York,* the Court began issuing *per curiam* reversals of convictions under antiobscenity statutes. As

Brennan would explain several years later, the Court decided "[n]o fewer than 31 cases" in this fashion — without full opinion — whenever "at least five members of the Court, applying their separate tests, deemed [the challenged material] not to be obscene." In 1973, a majority of five justices finally coalesced around one standard for identifying obscenity. In *Miller v. California*, Chief Justice Warren Burger wrote that "[t]he basic guidelines for the trier of fact must be: (a) whether 'the average person, applying contemporary community standards' would find that the work, taken as a whole, appeals to the prurient interest; (b) whether the work depicts or describes, in a patently offensive way, sexual conduct specifically defined by the applicable state law; and (c) whether the work, taken as a whole, lacks serious literary, artistic, political, or scientific value." Of course, this doctrinal statement did not end controversy. As Douglas complained in his *Miller* dissent, obscenity law was a "hodge-podge," and the Court has repeatedly been called upon to clarify the parameters of the *Miller* test.[38]

The series of obscenity cases illustrates two points about the Court's two-level approach to free expression. First, it can be contentious. The Court's initial designation (or failure to designate) a category of expression as low value can provoke vigorous disagreement. And once the Court identifies a low-value category, the characterization of specific materials as falling within that category can generate disputes. Second, the Court's two-level and balancing approaches to free expression can intertwine with each other. *Roth* and *Miller* exemplify one type of intertwining, called "definitional balancing," where the Court weighs competing interests not to resolve a particular dispute but to formulate a general rule, which then is applied to resolve subsequent cases. In the obscenity cases, the Court balanced interests to determine the proper boundaries of obscenity as a low-value category. "All ideas having even the slightest redeeming social importance — unorthodox ideas, controversial ideas, even ideas hateful to the prevailing climate of opinion — have the full protection of the [first-amendment] guaranties," explained the *Roth* Court, "unless excludable because they encroach upon the limited area of more important interests." Obscenity, therefore, fell outside constitutional protections because it was "utterly without redeeming social importance." Another intertwining between the two-level and balancing approaches can arise within the doctrines for identifying certain types of low-value expression. Often, the Court creates a standard that, when applied, requires the weighing of interests. For instance, when the Court reasoned that incitement of unlawful conduct was unprotected if it created a clear and present danger, the justices were identifying low-value expression through a form of balancing.

During the 1950s, Chief Justice Frederick M. Vinson explicitly reformulated the clear and present danger test to accentuate balancing: "'In each case (courts) must ask whether the gravity of the 'evil,' discounted by its improbability, justifies such invasion of free speech as is necessary to avoid the danger.'"[39]

THE POLITICS OF FREE EXPRESSION

The Court never adopted an absolutist approach to the first amendment — recognizing exceptions under the balancing and two-level approaches — but free expression nonetheless became a constitutional lodestar for many justices and scholars. While multiple factors supported the Court's invigoration of the first amendment, no force for change was more important than politics. Politics, of course, engendered the transition from republican to pluralist democracy during the 1930s and contributed to the Court's eventual acceptance of a pluralist democratic form of judicial review. Even beyond this, though, politics contributed to the development of free expression in unique ways.

Justices and scholars obscured or denied many of the political realities of free expression. For instance, Meiklejohn's depiction of American democracy as a New England town meeting exemplified such a blinking of reality. Free expression about political issues did not truly occur in a pristine forum where a homogeneous citizenry deliberated politely about the common good. Rather, political debate was wrung out of the hurly-burly give-and-take of a democratic marketplace skewed by poverty, racism, sexism, and other inequities of power and wealth. More often, scholars and justices effaced the republican democratic past. After the Court's 1937 turn, many acted as if the suppression of speech and writing to promote the republican democratic common good had never occurred. In a remarkable disregard for history, Douglas would write that "[t]he idea that the First Amendment permits punishment for ideas that are 'offensive' to the particular judge or jury sitting in judgment is astounding." Of course, the bad tendency test had allowed precisely such punishment under republican democracy for well over a century. From a political standpoint, the post-1937 justices' erasure of history facilitated their endorsement of free expression as the "fixed star in our constitutional constellation." The Court could portray its first-amendment decisions as enforcing well-established American principles rather than as responses to political and democratic changes.[40]

Politics further fueled the emphasis on free expression as constitutional lodestar. The coalition that had crystallized between the two world wars to advocate for the protection of civil liberties emphasized free expression, in particular. This broad-based coalition included intellectuals, drawn together by the ACLU, and blue collar workers, gravitating toward the labor unions. The ACLU pushed especially for the protection of political rather than sexually related expression — in harmony with the emerging self-governance rationale. Then, within the realm of political expression, the ACLU civil libertarians declared that there should be "'free speech for everyone.'" By the late 1930s, free expression was the ACLU's "holy writ." John Dewey had acquiesced in the suppression of antiwar and antidraft protesters at the outset of World War I, unsurprising given that he had allocated only one paragraph to the freedoms of speech and press in his 1908 book *Ethics*. Yet, Dewey helped form the ACLU after the war and devoted more than ten pages to free expression in revised editions of *Ethics* published in 1932 and 1936. "Liberty to think, inquire, discuss, is central in the whole group of rights which are secured in theory to individuals in a democratic social organization," Dewey wrote. "It is central because the essence of the democratic principle is appeal to voluntary disposition instead of to force, to persuasion instead of coercion." Even politically conservative lawyers joined the fight for free expression by enlisting in the ABA's Bill of Rights Committee. The ACLU had already begun filing amicus briefs in prominent free-expression cases, like *Stromberg* (1931), and the Bill of Rights Committee, once formed, began doing so as well. In cases like *Gobitis* (1940), and *Barnette* (1943), both organizations filed briefs. Free expression had become such a politically salient issue that in FDR's January 6, 1941, speech rallying Americans to prepare for likely war, the president invoked "four essential human freedoms," with "[t]he first [being] freedom of speech and expression." After that, many Americans would echo Roosevelt and call free expression the first freedom.[41]

Labor constituted a key component not only of the New Deal but also of the "free-expression" political coalition. Management had impeded unions for so long that, in the 1930s and early 1940s, an advance in free-expression protections often equaled a victory for labor. When the NLRA created a statutory right to organize, it cleared the way for the recognition of workers' and union leaders' first-amendment rights. And workers and unions were motivated to seek the judicial enforcement of free-expression rights to facilitate labor activities. Labor naturally worked together with the ACLU because of their mutual interest in the first amendment. Realizing as early as 1923 that workers and unions must be enlisted in the fight for free expression, the ACLU declared that "its chief task was to 'champion the rights of labor to organize, strike, meet and picket.'" By the early thirties, the ACLU was publishing pamphlets like *Legal Tactics for Labor's Rights*. And, as might be expected after 1937, especially once FDR began appointing New Deal justices, the Supreme Court tended to favor the free-expression coalition in first-amendment cases arising from labor disputes. In *Hague, Thornhill,* and *Bridges,* the Court concluded that the first amendment protected a right to distribute literature in the streets and parks, to picket businesses (despite the effects on property and economic revenue), and to comment on public and legal controversies without fear of the judiciary's contempt powers. Unionizing epitomized democratic self-government, from the justices' perspective, so the process of labor organizing required free expression just as did the process of pluralist democracy.[42]

EVEN THOUGH MANY Court observers celebrated the first amendment as a constitutional lodestar, the justices did not validate every free-expression claim. As (most of) the justices repeatedly declared, the first amendment was not an absolute. In 1940, the Court broke the post-1937 string of free-expression victories in *Gobitis,* which upheld compulsory flag salutes. While the Court would soon overrule *Gobitis,* the justices also rejected the next free-expression claim they saw, in *Milk Wagon Drivers Union v. Meadowmoor Dairies, Inc.*, decided in 1941. Upholding an injunction of labor picketing, the six-justice majority, with a Frankfurter opinion, deferred to the lower court's finding that the union's peaceful picketing was so entwined with violent conduct as to be inseparable. Later that same year, *Cox v. New Hampshire* reviewed a statute that required groups to obtain and to pay for parade permits. Treating the requirement as a time, place, and manner restriction on the public forum (the streets), the Court balanced the competing interests and concluded that the statutory application to Jehovah's Witnesses was constitutional. One year later, in *Chaplinsky v. New Hampshire,* the Court unanimously upheld the conviction of a Jehovah's Witness for breach of the peace by reasoning that his expression fell into the low-value category of fighting words.[43]

Indeed, if one focuses on the politics underlying specific first-amendment cases, instead of examining the doctrinal surfaces of the Court's opinions, then one might question the designation of free expression as constitutional lodestar. Predictably, given that the transition to pluralist democracy nurtured the constitutionalization of dominant interests and values, the Court rarely resolved free-expression issues contrary to elite or mainstream views. Correlatively, "the outliers in American politics were more often than not the victims than the beneficiaries" of the Court's decisions. Many cases upholding first-amendment rights involved situations where the protected expression attacked or injured outsiders or peripheral groups. In *Cantwell,* decided in 1940, the Court held that the first amendment protected the expression of the defendant — himself a religious outsider, a Jehovah's Witness. The state could not convict Cantwell for breach of the peace, though he had offended passing pedestrians. But the pedestrians were Roman Catholics, and Cantwell's speech specifically assailed the Catholic Church. Three years later, *Murdock v. Pennsylvania* held unconstitutional an ordinance requiring individuals to pay a license fee before they could distribute literature and solicit contributions. Once again, though, as Jackson emphasized in dissent, the protected expression attacked Catholicism. The defendants had knocked on doors, "including those of devout Catholics on Palm Sunday morning," and declared that the Church was a "whore" and that "the paying over of money to a priest" was a "great racket."[44]

Two decisions involving the prosecution of a speaker for provoking a hostile audience further suggest that the status or identity of the purported target of barbed speech might influence case outcomes. *Terminiello v. Chicago,* decided in 1949, concluded that the defendant's conviction under a disorderly conduct ordinance violated the first amendment. The defendant, this time, was a Catholic priest, but his speech was an anti-Semitic diatribe. He condemned "atheistic, communistic Jewish or Zionist Jews." He claimed that Jewish doctors performed atrocities on Germans, and asked, "Do you wonder they were persecuted in other countries?" Then he proclaimed that "we want them to go back where they came from." The American Jewish Congress's amicus brief emphasized the frightening threat posed to Jews by such anti-Semitic hate speech, especially coming so soon after the Nazi Holocaust, yet the justices deemed the expression protected. Two years later, however, the Court upheld a disorderly conduct conviction in another hostile audience scenario. In *Feiner v. New York,* a college student spoke to a racially mixed crowd of seventy-five to eighty whites and blacks gathered together on a sidewalk in Syracuse, New York. Irving Feiner encouraged the audience to attend a meeting of the Young Progressives of America, protested the city's cancellation of a permit for an earlier Young Progressives meeting, and made "derogatory but not profane" remarks about "President Truman, the American Legion, the Mayor of Syracuse, and other local political officials." Vinson's majority opinion upheld the lower court's conclusion that Feiner's speech created a clear and present danger of violence even though the evidence showed only that "[t]he crowd was restless and there was some pushing, shoving and milling around." Vinson seemed especially concerned that Feiner had urged African Americans to "rise up in arms and fight for equal rights." But witnesses swore that Feiner had instead encouraged his listeners to "rise up and fight for their rights by going arm in arm to the [Young Progressives meeting], black and white alike." If true, then in one hostile audience case, *Terminiello,* the Court protected inflammatory anti-Semitic speech, while in another, *Feiner,* the Court allowed the punishment of speech criticizing mostly public officials and encouraging blacks to take political action.[45]

In 1969, the Court decided a case that has been described as a "landmark decision," establishing "the most speech-protective standard yet evolved by the Supreme Court." *Brandenburg v. Ohio* revisited the issue that had first confronted the Court during the World War I era: when, if ever, did the Constitution protect expression encouraging unlawful conduct, particularly subversive advocacy? The state convicted a KKK leader "under the Ohio Criminal Syndicalism statute for 'advocat(ing) . . . the duty, necessity, or propriety of crime, sabotage, violence, or unlawful methods of terrorism as a means of accomplishing industrial or political reform.'" This statute closely resembled the one upheld in *Whitney,* decided in 1927. But now, in a *per curiam* opinion, the Court repudiated its earlier standards (bad tendency and clear and present danger) for determining when expression that encouraged unlawful conduct should be deemed low value and beyond the scope of the first amendment. The Court expanded free-expression doctrine to an unprecedented degree. Under the *Brandenburg* test, the first amendment protects expression unless the speaker specifically intends to incite imminent unlawful action, and such unlawful action is likely to occur imminently.[46]

What expression did the *Brandenburg* justices protect with their expansive interpretation of the first amendment? A film of the Klan "rally" showed hooded figures gathered around a burning cross, Clarence Brandenburg repeatedly denouncing blacks and Jews, and then Brandenburg warning that "if our President, our Congress, our Supreme Court, continues to suppress the white, Caucasian race, it's possible that there might have to be some revengeance taken." In short, the Court constructed its most speech-protective first-amendment standard in response to primarily malicious hate speech directed against racial and religious minorities. Cases like *Brandenburg, Terminiello,* and *Murdock* do not prove that the justices purposefully discriminate against peripheral groups. Yet, the results in these cases suggest that the Court is most likely to emphasize the principled protection of free expression when the speech or writing attacks or harms outsiders rather than the American mainstream or elites. Other cases, moreover, suggest that the Court tends to protect the expression of outsiders when doing so corresponds with predominant interests, values, or practices. For instance, *Martin v. City of Struthers* invalidated an ordinance proscribing door-to-door distributions of written materials as applied to a Jehovah's Witness. Black's majority opinion emphasized how the Witnesses' method, the door-to-door distribution of literature, resonated with mainstream practices. "The widespread use of this method of communication by many groups espousing various causes attests its major importance. . . . Many of our most widely established religious organizations have used this method of disseminating their doctrines."[47]

Another case often labeled a "landmark" epitomizes how the convergence of mainstream and outsider interests can influence first-amendment decisions. In *New York Times v. Sullivan,* decided in 1964, the Court confronted the issue whether the first amendment protected the press from civil libel actions brought by governmental officials. In 1960, the *Times* had published a full-page advertisement soliciting support for the civil rights movement, including "'the struggle for the right-to-vote,' and the legal defense of Dr. Martin Luther King, Jr." The advertisement contained several minor factual errors. For instance, it stated that students in Montgomery, Alabama, had sung "'My Country, 'Tis of Thee' on the State Capitol steps," but they had, in fact, sung the national anthem. Because the advertisement also criticized police reactions to civil rights protests, L. B. Sullivan, a Montgomery city commissioner (in effect, the police commissioner) brought a civil action in the state courts for defamation against the *Times* and four black clergy whose signatures appeared at the bottom of the advertisement. The state Supreme Court upheld a jury award of $500,000.[48]

The U.S. Supreme Court had never before suggested that the first amendment might protect defamatory remarks from state civil tort actions. Yet, this case resembled a criminal prosecution for seditious libel: the government, through the institution of the state courts, sought to punish the press for criticizing a public official, the police commissioner. In response, a unanimous Court reversed and issued one of its most vigorous defenses of free expression. Writing for seven other justices, Brennan invoked both the self-governance and search-for-truth rationales as well as the tradition of dissent. "[W]e consider this case against the background of a profound national commitment to the principle that debate on public issues should be uninhibited, robust, and wide-open, and that it may well include vehement, caustic, and sometimes unpleasantly sharp attacks on government and public officials." With this foundation, Brennan turned to history, to "the great controversy over the Sedition Act of 1798, which first crystallized a national awareness of the central meaning of the First Amendment." In an exceptional retroactive decision, Brennan pronounced that, in accordance with "the court of history," the justices agreed that this "dead" statute violated the first amendment. The Court now deemed governmental prosecution of seditious libel unconstitutional. Furthermore, if a state could not constitutionally punish criticisms of the government and public officials through a criminal prosecution, Brennan reasoned, then it should not be able to impose punishment through a civil defamation action. Even if newspapers could survive such civil suits, editors would self-censor their publications for fear of liability. The Court, therefore, articulated the highly speech-protective actual-malice standard for determining when a public official could recover damages in a civil suit against the press. A "public official" can recover "damages for a defamatory falsehood relating to his official conduct" only if "he proves that the statement was made with 'actual malice'—that is, with knowledge that it was false or with reckless disregard of whether it was false or not."[49]

Sullivan enunciated a strong conception of a free press, and of course, the press celebrated the decision. But *Sullivan* was "a race case first and foremost." It not only protected the expression of black civil rights leaders but also assured that news media, like the *Times,* could continue to report the atrocities visited on civil rights activists in the South. As the Reverend Ralph Abernathy, one of the leaders of the Southern Christian Leadership Conference, explained, the defamation suits were "part of a concerted, calculated program to carry out a policy of punishing, intimidating and silencing all who criticize and seek to change Alabama's notorious political system of enforced segregation." The Court's protection of the civil rights leaders *and* the press went hand in hand; news reporting, particularly on television, had helped nurture a national political coalition pushing for civil rights reform. This coalition, recall, had begun to develop as a Cold War response to the nation's needs to stimulate the southern economy and to align with emerging Third World countries populated by people of color. Thus, *Sullivan* did not show the Court baldly and boldly protecting a peripheral group's constitutional rights regardless of the political fallout. To the contrary, *Sullivan* manifested the Court's compliance with a dominant national political coalition that would, perhaps, reach the crest of its power later that year when Congress would pass the Civil Rights Act of 1964.[50]

When outsiders raise constitutional claims that do not converge with predominant interests and values — or even worse, that threaten predominant interests and values — the likelihood of success diminishes precipitously. Once again, the civil rights movement illustrates. During the 1960s, the Court confronted several cases arising from the prosecutions of civil rights protesters—protesters who often had provoked angry reactions from hostile audiences or onlookers. The protesters often were ensnared in a catch-22. If, on the one hand, they were peaceful, law abiding, and non-disruptive, they generally were ineffective and sometimes even ignored. In such cases, though, the Court tended to enforce the first amendment vigorously. If, on the other hand, the protesters were more aggressive, if they impeded "business as usual," if they raised their voices boisterously, then they could not be so easily disregarded. They required "the self-interested attention of those persons in power." But in such cases, the Court tended to allow the protesters' convictions to be upheld.[51]

In *Edwards v. South Carolina*, 187 African American students had marched to the statehouse grounds to protest racial discrimination. Approximately two to three hundred white onlookers gathered nearby. After arriving at the statehouse, the protesters sang patriotic songs and, when asked to disperse, refused to do so. They then were arrested and convicted for the common law crime of breach of the peace. In an eight-to-one decision handed down in 1963, during the halcyon days of the civil rights movement, the Court held that the convictions violated the first amendment. Stewart's majority opinion described the protest as archetypical protected expression: "The circumstances in this case reflect an exercise of these basic constitutional rights in their most pristine and classic form." The Court emphasized that the protesters had "peaceably assembled" and had "peaceably expressed their grievances." In particular, "[t]here was no violence or threat of violence on their part, or on the part of any member of the crowd watching them."[52]

Cox v. Louisiana, decided two years later, arose in the context of civil rights protests as well. Police had arrested twenty-three students from Southern University, a historically black college, "for picketing stores that maintained segregated lunch counters." In response, approximately two thousand more students marched peacefully along the sidewalks from the state capitol to the vicinity of the courthouse. Near the courthouse, between one and three hundred whites gathered to observe. The students held picket signs, sang songs, prayed, and listened to a speech by Elton Cox, a leader for the Congress of Racial Equality. Police arrested Cox after he urged the students to sit in at segregated lunch counters. He was convicted for disturbing the peace, obstructing public passages (the sidewalk), and picketing before a courthouse. The Court reversed all the convictions, but the justices nonetheless revealed a growing anxiety about civil rights protesters. "The rights of free speech and assembly, while fundamental in our democratic society, still do not mean that everyone with opinions or beliefs to express may address a group at any public place and at any time," wrote Goldberg for a five-justice majority. Thus, the Court refused to recognize any constitutional "right of protest." The first amendment might protect "pure speech," Goldberg reasoned, but whenever a protest involved "conduct such as patrolling, marching, and picketing"—precisely the type of conduct likely to be part of a political protest—the government could punish the protesters. The Court even suggested that the protesters, by picketing at a courthouse, had become a "mob," and "mob law is the very antithesis of due process." Democratic government, Goldberg maintained, requires peaceful expressions of grievance; disruptive protests go beyond constitutional protections. "There is a proper time and place for even the most peaceful protest and a plain duty and responsibility on the part of all citizens to obey all valid laws and regulations."[53]

In the summer of 1965, the politics of civil rights turned dramatically. In August, mere days after the signing of the Voting Rights Act, a traffic stop of a young African American in the Watts section of Los Angeles sparked the first major urban race riot since World War II. Lasting nearly a week, the riot left thirty-four people dead and millions of dollars in property destroyed. Similar riots exploded during the next two summers in Detroit, Newark, and other cities, and when a sniper assassinated Martin Luther King, Jr., on April 4, 1968, a new wave of riots erupted. In the midst of these race riots, during the summer of 1966, Stokely Carmichael was arrested (for the twenty-seventh time) while participating in a voter registration march through Tennessee and Mississippi. When released on bail, he declared he would not return to jail. Instead, he boomed, "We want black power!" The slogan resonated with many blacks who sought economic and social change, not solely legal rights. Between the constant news reports of urban riots and the transmogrification of the integrationist civil rights movement into the more segregationist and aggressive black power movement, white support for civil rights dissipated. From 1964 to late 1966, the percentage of white Americans who believed that African Americans "were demanding 'too much'" skyrocketed from 34 to 85 percent![54]

The Court decided *Adderley v. Florida* on November 14, 1966. Similar to *Cox,* a group of college students, here two hundred in number, marched from their school to a jail to protest the prior arrest of other students, who had also protested racial segregation. When the sheriff asked the protesters to disperse, some did so, but many remained. Consequently, 107 protesters were arrested and prosecuted for trespassing on jail premises. This time the Court swung five to four to uphold the convictions. The purported first-amendment absolutist, Black, wrote the majority opinion. He deflected the free-expression claim by reasoning that this case presented a simple trespass (on jail grounds). No constitutional right to protest exists: because of the protesters' conduct, and regardless of the content of the their message, the state could apply its general law proscribing trespasses. From Black's standpoint, it seemed, the protesters were not sufficiently subservient to governmental officials. The sheriff controlled the jail, "and when he said leave, that was it." According to the dissenting Douglas, Black had eviscerated first-amendment protections by permitting "this 'petition for redress of grievances' to be turned into a trespass action." In protest cases, Douglas emphasized, the government always claimed to apply some general criminal law proscribing trespass, breach of the peace, or the like. And the government always claimed that the content of the expression was irrelevant to the prosecution. But if one acknowledged the political nature of the defendants' expression, then the jailhouse appeared to be the perfect location for the protest. The defendants, after all, had sought to spotlight the unconstitutional detention of political prisoners (other civil rights protesters), held inside the jail.[55]

The next year, 1967, the Court reviewed a criminal contempt conviction of Martin Luther King, Jr. *Walker v. Birmingham* dated back to events occurring in 1963, when King sought to organize protest demonstrations in Birmingham, Alabama, for Good Friday and Easter Sunday. Refusing to issue the requisite parade permit, the notorious racist public safety commissioner, Eugene "Bull" Connor, seethed, "'No you will not get a permit in Birmingham, Alabama to picket. I will picket you over to the City Jail.'" A second permit request was again "summarily denied." The city then sought an injunction to prevent the planned demonstrations. A state court issued the injunction, but King, believing it constitutionally invalid, led the marches as planned. The state court promptly convicted King and seven other leaders for criminal contempt for violating the injunction. The Supreme Court upheld the conviction without reaching the first-amendment issue. Writing for a five-justice majority, Stewart applied the collateral-bar rule. The petitioners, including King, had not followed the proper procedures for challenging the constitutionality of the injunction, Stewart explained. They should have worked through the state court system to dissolve or modify the injunctive order. Once they had violated the injunction, it was too late to question its validity; they were precluded from challenging its constitutionality during the criminal contempt prosecution, a collateral proceeding.[56]

Stewart reiterated that no constitutional right to protest exists. The

government can punish conduct like "'patrolling, marching, and picketing,'" even if it cannot punish "'pure speech.'" The Court mandated that
King and the other petitioners follow the rule of law—the Birmingham
parade ordinance and the injunction—even though the justices admitted
that the ordinance appeared facially unconstitutional. Stewart pedanti-
cally lectured: "The rule of law that Alabama followed in this case reflects
a belief that in the fair administration of justice no man can be judge in his
own case, however exalted his station, however righteous his motives, and
irrespective of his race, color, politics, or religion. One may sympathize
with the petitioners' impatient commitment to their cause. But respect
for judicial process is a small price to pay for the civilizing hand of law."
Stewart's description of King's "commitment" to civil rights as *"impatient"*
belied King's long struggle for equality, liberty, and justice—a struggle
against governmental officials like Bull Connor, who relished unleashing
attack dogs and fire hose bursts in frenzied assaults on demonstrators, including children. Stewart's insistence that King show more *"respect"* for the
law demeaned an individual who had spent his seven days of imprisonment,
because of the contempt conviction, writing his famous "Letter from the
Birmingham City Jail," a meditation on social change, nonviolent action,
and the relation between injustice and law. "[A]n individual who breaks a
law that conscience tells him is unjust," King posited, "and willingly accepts the penalty by staying in jail to arouse the conscience of the community over its injustice, is in reality expressing the very highest respect
for law."[57]

This series of civil rights cases demonstrates three points. First, when
taken together, the cases suggest that if first-amendment claimants generally adhere to the status quo, then they maximize their chances for judicial success—though, perhaps, diminishing the chances for generating
social change. In such cases, the justices themselves might opportunisti-
cally laud the judicial process for its protection of minorities. But if the
claimants step too far outside the mainstream, if they challenge settled
values and interests, then the Court is unlikely to provide shelter. The
Court became less protective of civil rights protesters when many white
Americans, in reaction to urban race riots, began to believe that blacks
demanded too much social change too fast. Second, the Court's attitude
toward civil rights protesters turned cold during an era often deemed the
most liberal in Supreme Court history. After Frankfurter resigned in 1962,
the Warren Court entered a second and more liberal phase. Yet even the
later Warren Court refused to recognize a constitutional right to protest
and repeatedly reminded civil rights protesters that they should remain

polite, that they should obey the law, and that their conduct could always be punished. Third, the Court could invoke a variety of legal mechanisms to allow protesters' convictions to stand. In *Walker,* the Court reviewed the case but relied on the collateral-bar rule to skirt the free-expression claim. More often, especially in cases where the protesters had been too disruptive, the Court simply denied petitions for certiorari, summarily affirmed lower court judgments, or dismissed certiorari petitions as improvidently granted. Given that regardless of Supreme Court rulings, state and lower federal courts consistently ruled against civil rights protesters, "[t]he civil rights forces actually lost many, if not a majority, of these suits."[58]

While many cases, such as those involving civil rights protesters, turned on the convergence or lack of convergence of interests between outsider-claimants and the mainstream or elites, other cases have more baldly presented the justices with an opportunity to protect predominant interests and values. These cases typically translate the expenditure or protection of wealth into a first-amendment right. For instance, *First National Bank of Boston v. Bellotti,* involved a first-amendment challenge to a Massachusetts law that prohibited business corporations from spending money to influence voters in referendum elections. Writing for a five-justice majority, Justice Lewis F. Powell emphasized the self-governance rationale. Expression commenting on a proposed referendum "is the type of speech indispensable to decisionmaking in a democracy, and this is no less true because the speech comes from a corporation rather than an individual." Powell allowed, though, that the state could overcome this societal interest in the first amendment, but only if doing so were necessary to achieve a compelling interest, such as preserving "the integrity of the electoral process." The Court thus held the law unconstitutional because Massachusetts could not satisfy this strict scrutiny (or skewed balancing) test.[59]

Although Powell insisted that the restriction on corporate spending would undermine self-government, the state's purpose in passing the law was, of course, precisely to promote self-government, as Justice Byron White argued in dissent. Corporate money, the state legislature believed, could warp the politics of referendum decisions. While wealth might justly empower one to purchase consumer goods, wealth should not necessarily empower an individual or a business entity to shape political debates or control political outcomes. The year before the Court decided *Bellotti,* the political scientist and economist Charles Lindblom published a best-selling book, *Politics and Markets,* which described the role of business corporations in pluralist (or "polyarchal") democracy. As explained by Lindblom, democracy is a competition among interest groups, and business interests win "disproportionately." Why? Because business leaders enjoy "extraordinary sources of funds" and thus "easily command . . . the services of printing and broadcasting." Empirical evidence showed that "the scale of corporate spending dwarfs political spending by all other groups," and that corporate advertising and media campaigns successfully molded personal "volitions." Corporate business leaders indoctrinated "citizens so that they think they want what businessmen want." Corporate leaders purposefully sought "to dominate" politics to their own advantage, and because of their "privileged position," they consistently achieved "greatly disproportionate influence."[60]

PREDICTABLY, THE COURT'S first-amendment jurisprudence — the simultaneous celebration of free expression as constitutional lodestar and the interpretation of the first amendment in accordance with predominant interests and values — has engendered both numerous encomiums to the "worthy tradition" of free expression, "almost an absolute," and numerous bitter denunciations of the Court's decisions. One commentator applauds: "[T]he Court, from the time of Holmes and Brandeis, has understood and accepted the basic values and functions of freedom of expression and has often eloquently expounded on them to the country." But another commentator renounces: "Current First Amendment law is . . . skewed. Examination of the many 'exceptions' to First Amendment protection discloses that the large majority favor the interests of the powerful. . . . This one-sidedness of free-speech doctrine makes the First Amendment much more valuable to the majority than to the minority." This schizophrenic quality of first-amendment jurisprudence reminds us that Supreme Court doctrine coexists with two opposed traditions: the tradition of dissent and the tradition of suppression. Without doubt, free-expression doctrine under pluralist democracy corresponds more closely with the tradition of dissent, while under republican democracy, the doctrine corresponded more closely with the tradition of suppression. Yet, as was true under the republican regime, both traditions have remained vigorous under the pluralist regime.[61]

CHAPTER **12**

The Traditions of Dissent and Suppression in the Pluralist Democratic Regime

Under both the republican and pluralist democratic regimes, times of political crises such as wars have tended to provoke strong expressions of dissent and suppression. After the transition to pluralist democracy, three such periods arose in rapid succession: World War II, the Red Scare, and the Vietnam War. Each period was unique, with different degrees and types of dissent, official suppression, and unofficial suppression.[1]

WORLD WAR II

The degree of free expression turns as much on the interplay of the traditions of dissent and suppression as on legal doctrine. At the outset of World War II in Europe, Grenville Clark declared: "the maintenance of free expression ultimately depends . . . upon the traditions, the 'feel' or inner conviction of the people at large." In fact, prosecutions for dissident expression in World War II numbered far fewer than those in World War I. The transition to pluralist democracy relieved some of the pressures that had generated suppression during the First World War, fought during an era when immigration (along with industrialization and urbanization) strained the seams of republican democracy. Even *before* that war, many old-stock Americans had worried about the potential effects of the immigrant "outsiders." The coming of the war, then, inflamed those xenophobic fears and provided a rationalization for denouncing the outsiders' supposedly un-American habits and ideas. By the time World War II arrived, however, the dynamics of democracy had radically changed. Many immigrant outsiders had been absorbed into the national political system; they had become supporters of the New Deal; and they had helped usher in the transition to pluralist democracy. The American people who approached the Second War stood far more united, regardless of their attitudes toward the war itself. And then, the attack on Pearl Harbor and the atrocities committed by the Nazis in Europe bonded Americans from diverse backgrounds "in a grand orgy of patriotism" as they focused on battling a common enemy. The Second World War was the Good War; few Americans contemplated resisting the draft or protesting the war.[2]

Given the Second World War's proximity in time to the First, many key governmental officials remembered the Espionage Act prosecutions. They had personally experienced the events of the First War; they did not learn about them as history. Many officials believed the government had unjustly abused civil liberties and now included themselves in the civil libertarian political coalition. This support for civil liberties was most important at the Department of Justice. From 1939 (when the war started in Europe) to 1945, four different attorneys general headed Justice. The first three of them came into the job possessing strong civil libertarian credentials. Frank Murphy served as attorney general in 1939. He had previously garnered renown when, as governor of Michigan in 1937, he had refused to use force against workers during the massive sit-down strike against GM. Shortly after Murphy became attorney general, he created the Department's Civil Liberties Unit. When FDR appointed Murphy to the Supreme Court on January 4, 1940, the president asked the solicitor general, Robert Jackson, to become attorney general. Before World War I, Jackson had been castigated as "pro-German" for opposing U.S. participation, and during the postwar Red Scare, the American Legion had accused Jackson of un-Americanism. Ever since, he had remained wary of official and unofficial pressures to conform to orthodox viewpoints. Shortly before Roosevelt appointed him as attorney general, Jackson told the president that the Justice Department should prosecute based solely "on criminal acts, not merely on reprehensible attitudes or opinions." When FDR nominated Jackson for the Supreme Court, in June 1941, the president again chose his solicitor general, now Francis Biddle, to become the next attorney general. A member of both the ACLU and the NAACP, Biddle had clerked for Holmes and was personal friends with Roger Baldwin, still the ACLU director. Speaking at a conference ten days before he would become acting attorney general, Biddle reminded his audience about World War I. "The biased juries, the brutally long sentences, race prejudice, executive usurpations — we know these things followed in the wake of the last war, and our memories are still fresh from those perversions of justice." Biddle remained as attorney general until mere weeks before the end of the war, when President Harry Truman replaced him with Tom Clark, whose commitment to civil liberties was questionable.[3]

With the civil libertarian backgrounds of the wartime attorneys general, the national government's hesitancy to prosecute dissenters was unsurprising. Indeed, FDR vacillated before appointing Biddle as attorney general exactly because he feared Biddle was so concerned with protecting civil liberties that he would not "get tough with the subversive element." Shortly after Biddle's confirmation as attorney general, he told the *New York Times* that, even during wartime, "civil liberties are the essence of the democracy we are pledged to protect." Biddle therefore intended "to see that . . . we do not again fall into the disgraceful hysteria of witch hunts, strike-breakings and minority persecutions which were such a dark chapter in our record of the last World War." Throughout the war, first Jackson and then Biddle, in particular, attempted to ensure that the government follow the proper procedures of criminal justice. Most important, the government would not encourage or acquiesce in vigilantism. The government itself might suppress dissent, but it would not allow groups like the American Protective League from World War I to act in the government's stead. FDR, relatively unconcerned about civil liberties, especially during the war, nonetheless explained: "The common defense . . . should be through the normal channels of local, state and national law enforcement. . . . We must be vigilant, always on guard, and swift to act. But we must also be wise and cool-headed, and must not express our activities in the cruel stupidities of the vigilante."[4]

DESPITE THE DIFFERENCES between the two world wars, and despite the attitudes of Jackson and Biddle, governmental efforts to suppress dissent during World War II were extensive. In fact, considering the "paucity of opposition to the war," governmental suppression might even be described as "extraordinary" or "monumental." As totalitarian governments in Europe solidified their power during the 1930s, fears of subversion in this country intensified. In May 1938, the House of Representatives succumbed to pressure from a conservative Texas Democrat, Martin Dies, and created the House Committee on Un-American Activities (HUAC). The

Dies Committee focused on possible left-wing or Communist subversion, though it also investigated fascist groups; by the end of that year, 74 percent of Americans who knew of the Committee favored "continuing the investigation." Dies tried purposefully to spark hysteria, while also undermining FDR, by accusing the secretary of the interior, the secretary of labor, the works progress administrator, and the First Lady, Eleanor Roosevelt, of comporting with Communists. When Nazi Germany and the Soviet Union signed a nonaggression pact in August 1939, prompting the emboldened Germany to initiate the European War by invading Poland, American fears grew. Many citizens, polls showed, favored taking "repressive measures" against Communists. In 1939 and 1940, Congress responded by enacting three anti-Communist statutes, including the Alien Registration (or Smith) Act, which among other things, prohibited advocating the "propriety of overthrowing or destroying any government in the United States by force or violence." Moreover, in 1940, Congress reenacted the Espionage Act of 1917, ominously increasing the penalties and amending it to apply during peace as well as war time.[5]

Once the European War had begun, Attorney General Murphy initiated prosecutions, partly in response to Dies and Roosevelt, who did not want the administration to appear soft. The Department of Justice, for instance, indicted seventeen members of the Christian Front, virulent anti-Semitic fascists. Although FBI Director Hoover claimed that they "planned to 'knock off about a dozen Congressman' and 'blow up the goddam Police Department,'" the evidence was weak; confiscated weapons were an 1873 Springfield rifle and an old cavalry saber. None of the defendants would be convicted. During Jackson's brief stint as attorney general, he restrained the Department's prosecutors, but he could not slow Hoover. Authorized by Roosevelt to spy on dissidents, particularly Communists and Fascists, Hoover investigated anyone "believed to be unpatriotic, including pacifists, religious groups, labor unions, and unpopular political factions." This suppression sparked dissent, as often happens. The "conservative *Milwaukee Journal*" feared that the FBI acted as if it were "'a Gestapo that can haul citizens off to prison and court in ignominy, imposing any kind of conditions the captors wish without accountability.... Is it that Chief Hoover and his men want to create a wartime hysteria in this country?'" The *New Republic* worried in February 1940 that Hoover, by manipulating the media, had "made himself much too powerful to be easily curbed by a superior." He had requested that "local authorities notify [the FBI] of every permit issued anywhere in this country for any public assemblage, 'before the meeting starts.'"[6]

Yet, even staunch liberals, like the editors of the *Nation,* acknowledged that some suppression would be necessary during wartime. Jackson himself suspected that Communists might be undermining the nation's preparation for war. Thus, albeit under pressure from Hoover and others, Jackson initiated deportation proceedings against Harry Bridges, a radical union leader and purported Communist. Before the Bridges case was resolved, Jackson moved on to the Supreme Court, and Biddle took command at Justice. Within ten days of becoming acting attorney general, Biddle sent a memorandum to FDR explaining that he believed the prosecution of Communists under the Smith Act might "have some salutary effect," even if convictions would prove elusive. As of April 1941, 78 percent of Americans thought Communists responsible for strikes in defense industries. But world events suddenly forced Americans to reconsider their attitudes toward Communists. On June 22, 1941, Hitler attacked the Soviet Union, previously his ally. The United States extended aid to the Soviets, and the Communist Party of the United States of America (CPUSA) began supporting the Roosevelt administration and the arms buildup. As before, the defense industry continued to suffer from occasional labor strikes, but few Americans now blamed Communists. Even so, in July 1941, the government indicted twenty-nine members of the Socialist Workers party under the Smith Act for encouraging work stoppages in Minneapolis defense industries (eigthteen would be convicted).[7]

WITHIN THREE DAYS after Japan bombed Pearl Harbor, on December 7, 1941, the federal government had arrested more than three thousand "alien enemies," citizens of nations at war with the United States, though many other individuals were swept up in the mass arrests. But even as war fever raced across the country, Biddle reiterated his commitment to civil liberties. Among those initially arrested were several individuals who would be charged with violating the Espionage Act for uttering pro-Germany and pro-Japan statements. Biddle ordered these charges dismissed; he wanted prosecutions "only when public safety was directly imperiled." Partly because of the widespread popular support for the war, the few dissenters, mostly rabid fascists, seemed distinctly grating though not dangerous, like fingernails scratching across a blackboard. Nonetheless, public pressure on Biddle to prosecute seditionists and other dissenters intensified. Roosevelt, especially, pressed Biddle to act. In Biddle's words, the president "wanted this anti-war talk stopped." First, in memoranda, FDR asked Biddle how he planned to thwart the administration's critics, and then, during weekly

Cabinet meetings, Roosevelt would ask, "When are you going to indict the seditionists?" FDR was particularly incensed that Biddle had not indicted William Dudley Pelley, founder of the pro-Nazi Silver Shirts. With the nation initially faring poorly in the war, the pressure on Biddle mounted until he relented at the end of March 1942, when he began arresting dissenters. *Time* magazine proclaimed that the "milquetoast" attorney general had at last gotten "muscles."[8]

Even before this springtime burst of suppression, the national government had begun to force all persons of Japanese ancestry, aliens and citizens alike, who lived on the West Coast to leave their homes and to move to "relocation" centers, which Roosevelt inadvertently referred to as "concentration camps." FDR authorized the forced evacuation by executive order, issued on February 19, 1942, and then Congress followed with a statute, signed into law on March 21. Pursuant to the executive order, "the right of any person to enter, remain in, or leave shall be subject to whatever restrictions . . . the appropriate Military Commander may impose in his discretion." Three factors induced the government to act: fear of sabotage, racism, and economic greed. No evidence supported the fear of sabotage. While the government might justifiably have been concerned about Japanese enemy aliens, the same could not be said about Japanese American citizens. California Attorney General Earl Warren revealed the extent to which racial stereotypes shaped attitudes: "When we are dealing with the Caucasian race we have methods that will test the loyalty of them. . . . But when we deal with the Japanese we are in an entirely different field, and we cannot form any opinion that we believe to be sound." Army General John DeWitt, in charge of the Western Defense Command, declared: "A Jap's a Jap. . . . It makes no difference whether he is an American citizen or not. . . . I don't want any of them." With regard to economics, some members of California's white business establishment envied "the success of Japanese-Americans in their business and farming enterprises"; a Grower-Shipper Vegetable Association leader openly admitted "wanting to get rid of the Japs for selfish reasons." By the fall of 1942, the government had forcibly moved 115,000 people, including more than 70,000 citizens. When the constitutionality of the internment was challenged, the Army insisted that it had acted because of "military necessity." To support this assertion, the Army provided questionable facts; Justice Department attorneys called them "lies." For instance, the Army claimed that one FBI raid netted "more than 60,000 rounds of ammunition and many rifles, shotguns and maps"—items suggesting preparedness for subversive activities—but in truth, the FBI had confiscated these materials from a sporting goods store. Regardless, in *Korematsu v. United States,* a six-to-three decision, the Supreme Court accepted the government's claim that "military imperative" had necessitated the relocations. Concluding that the government had not violated equal protection guarantees, the Court approved one of the most egregious infringements of civil liberties since the end of slavery. In dissent, Justice Murphy denounced the governmental action as falling "into the ugly abyss of racism."[9]

Meanwhile, the Justice Department proceeded against opponents of the war effort. Biddle developed a plan with the postmaster general to invoke the Espionage Act's nonmailability provisions. Whereas prosecuting dissenters was likely to be time consuming and difficult — due process criminal procedures would have to be followed — denying publications access to the mails could be accomplished more expeditiously through administrative proceedings. Within months, the government had banned between thirty and seventy publications; throughout the course of the war, in an extraordinary expenditure of energy, the Postal Service would consider denying access to more than 17,000 publications. Restricted publications included Pelley's *Galilean,* a magazine selling between 3,500 and 5,000 copies per issue, and *Social Justice,* published by Father Charles Coughlin, rabidly anti-Semitic and fanatically anti-Roosevelt, with a circulation of 200,000. At FDR's urging, the government considered denying mail access to more mainstream though right-wing "isolationist, Roosevelt-hating, 'divisionist' publishers," including William Randolph Hearst, Robert McCormick of the *Chicago Tribune,* Joseph Patterson of the *New York Daily News,* and Eleanor (Cissy) Patterson of the *Washington Times-Herald.* Ultimately, the Postal Service decided not to act against these publishers as well as most others. The limited degree of postal censorship might not, however, have been due to first-amendment principles; rather, the Postal Service realized that fascist anti-Semitic sentiments were too common, not much beyond the American mainstream. As one antifascist journalist reported, "many Middle-town businessmen actually advertise" in these publications, and racist and anti-Semitic remarks could be found by flipping through the *Congressional Record.*[10]

From the government's perspective, the black press presented a special problem. As was true before the war, African American newspaper publishers and editors dutifully reported on racial discrimination in the United States. In January 1942, the editors of the NAACP's periodical, the *Crisis,* commented: "[N]ow is the time not to be silent about the breaches of democracy here in our own land. Now is the time to speak out, not in disloyalty, but in the truest patriotism." The editors emphasized that "black

Americans are loyal Americans," but they are loyal "to the democratic ideal [and] not . . . to many of the practices which have been — and are still — in vogue." In effect, the editors pushed for "Double V" (or Double Victory): victory over the totalitarian enemy overseas and victory over the racial caste system at home. Despite the black press's protestations of loyalty, many white Americans, including governmental officials, condemned such criticisms of American discriminatory practices as seditious. Consequently, at various times, the Justice Department, the FBI, the Postal Service, and numerous other governmental agencies investigated the black press. The War Production Board cut supplies of ink and paper to papers to discourage antidiscrimination articles. Hoover was intent on suppression, compiling a 714-page report on African Americans and the Communist party. In early 1942, in an attempt at intimidation, FBI agents visited several black publishers and accused them of printing subversive articles. On March 14, the largest black paper, the *Pittsburgh Courier,* responded angrily: "This sort of thing is an obvious effort to cow the Negro press into soft-pedaling its criticism and ending its forthright exposure of the outrageous discrimination to which Negroes have been subjected." In June 1942, Biddle met with the founder of the Negro Newspaper Publishers Association, John Sengstacke, to accuse the black press of sedition and to threaten suppression. By the end of the meeting, however, Sengstacke had convinced Biddle that the government's position was unjust. The black press supported the war effort, Sengstacke explained, but it must also continue reporting as it had for decades: exposing and denouncing racial discrimination. Thereafter, Biddle staunchly defended black publishers against the continuing entreaties to suppress, whether from the FBI or others.[11]

One month after the government denied Pelley's *Galilean* access to the mails, Justice indicted him under the Espionage Act for making false statements. The Seventh Circuit Court of Appeals eventually upheld his conviction; he would serve ten years in prison. By June 1943, the government had convicted forty-six individuals under the Espionage Act and another ninety-five for conspiring to obstruct the Selective Service Act; by the end of the war, Justice had prosecuted approximately two hundred individuals. On July 23, 1942, Justice indicted twenty-eight fascists for conspiring "to undermine the loyalty, morale, and discipline of the armed forces" in violation of the Espionage and Smith Acts. The defendants' fascist sympathies were incontrovertible, yet indicting all together for conspiracy was a questionable strategy. Concerned that indictments and convictions might be difficult to obtain in the defendants' respective local communities, Justice Department attorneys believed they might increase the likelihood of success by prosecuting the group together in Washington, D.C. In truth, many of the defendants had little connection to each other despite their "shared hatred of Jews, communism, and Roosevelt and a general faith in the principles of fascism." The initial indictment, nevertheless, was a "public relations coup." The next day the front page of the *New York Times* announced the indictments, and a second *Times* article detailed the identities of the defendants; the proceeding would be called the "Great Sedition Trial." Yet, from Biddle's perspective, the trial "was destined to drag through a shockingly dreary and degrading experience." It did not begin until April 1944, then stretched on for eight months, often taking on the "dimension of a riot." In court, "the defendants wore Halloween masks, 'moaned, groaned, laughed aloud, cheered and clamored,' [and] 'wailed' that it was all a 'Jewish-Communist plot to curb their freedom of speech.'" The presiding judge cited the defense lawyers for contempt five times. But when the judge died — Biddle thought the trial had "exhausted and . . . killed him" — a mistrial was declared, and Justice decided to dismiss the indictments.[12]

OVERALL, WORLD WAR II saw relatively little dissent because of its wide popularity. Given the minimal dissent, the public did not press strongly for suppression. Yet, within those rough parameters, the war can be divided into three time periods vis-à-vis free expression. First, before Pearl Harbor, the attorneys general, especially Jackson and Biddle, somewhat successfully imposed their civil libertarian views on the government and minimized suppression. Second, when the United States first entered the war, suppression surged. During the early months of 1942, the United States and its Allies suffered "an unbroken series of setbacks," causing "American morale and tolerance" to plummet. As reported at the time, the "war in the Pacific has . . . brought nothing but defeats," while in Europe, Americans needed to look realistically "at Axis achievements" to gain a "full appreciation of the extremely serious position" of the United States. The *New Republic* editors warned, "[T]here is a chance we shall lose the war." With the outlook so bleak, even a strong and able civil libertarian like Biddle prosecuted dissenters. His capitulation testifies to the difficulty of resisting the tradition of suppression during periods of political crisis, particularly wartime. True, the United States enjoys a great tradition of dissent; true, under pluralist democracy, first-amendment doctrine had shifted to become more consonant with that tradition; but, in the end, the pressure to suppress dissident expression during wartime proved too powerful. Even though Biddle did not see tangible benefits flowing from the prosecutions, he recognized the symbolic value and political merit of stifling the fascists' blatantly anti-American rhetoric.[13]

Third, the Allies' fortunes in battle turned both in the Pacific and in Europe during late 1942 and early 1943. As Germany and Japan began slow slides backward toward defeat, American confidence swelled. Periodicals reported on "German reverses" and "retreat," and even exclaimed that "the tide of Allied victory is rising inexorably." From a political standpoint, suppression of dissenters became far less important. The number of articles urging suppression of the fascist press plunged. After the "Great Sedition Trial" ended in a mistrial, Biddle admitted that the result was unimportant. Merely by bringing the indictments earlier in the war, "the prosecution had accomplished the purpose which the President had in mind." During the throes of national pessimism, the government had acted to quell fascist rhetoric, but when national optimism rose, suppression became unnecessary. This sanguine atmosphere animated the Supreme Court when it decided most of its World War II dissident-speech cases. To be sure, even as the nation rolled toward victory, the justices did not inevitably protect civil liberties. The Court decided *Korematsu* and upheld the internment of Japanese Americans after the war had turned in the Allies' favor. But *Korematsu* revolved around civil rights in general and equality more specifically; as the dissenters emphasized, the internment was fundamentally about "racial discrimination." Meanwhile, free expression was not just a civil right; it was *the* constitutional lodestar. It was integral to pluralist democratic government, and democracy separated *us* from *them*. By 1943, with victory in sight, the Court could afford to proclaim that the nation stood for free speech, a free press, and democratic self-government.[14]

The Court's free-expression decisions running from June 1940 through June 1943 reflected the national shift from fearful defensiveness to confident assertiveness. On June 3, 1940, the Court decided *Gobitis,* upholding compulsory flag salutes. Local school boards not only could compel students to salute the flag, they also could expel dissenters. Counting *Gobitis,* the Court in short order rejected five free-expression claims, the last coming in *Jones v. Opelika,* decided on June 8, 1942. *Jones* upheld convictions of Jehovah's Witnesses who had refused to pay license fees for the privilege of distributing religious literature. Once the course of the war had changed, the Court became more protective of free expression, especially that of Jehovah's Witnesses. On May 3, 1943, the Court vacated its decision in *Jones* and held the license fees unconstitutional. Further demonstrating its sudden change in direction, the Court decided *Barnette* on June 14, 1943, overruling *Gobitis* and holding that a compulsory flag-salute violated the first amendment. That same day, the Court decided *Taylor v. Mississippi,* the only World War II state sedition prosecution to reach the Supreme Court. The Court invalidated the convictions of Jehovah's Witnesses for encouraging disloyalty to the state and national governments as well as for teaching resistance to compelled flag salutes. Reasoning that individuals cannot be punished for expressing "beliefs and opinions concerning domestic measures and trends in national and world affairs," the Court stressed that the defendants had not "threatened any clear and present danger to our institutions or our government."[15]

Even though the Court swiftly returned to its endorsement of free expression as constitutional lodestar, the war had long-lasting repercussions for free expression. The wartime pressure to suppress had led the Court to end its post-1937 string of decisions protecting free expression; this break in first-amendment cases was in and of itself important. The justices might still call free expression the "fixed star in our constitutional constellation," as they did in *Barnette,* but they nonetheless could and sometimes would conclude that the Constitution did not protect expression. The war caused the political forces pressing on the justices in free-expression cases to shift in the long term. The political coalition supporting civil liberties in general and free expression in particular lost momentum and then unraveled. Indicative of this change, in 1942, the ABA ceased publishing the *Bill of Rights Review* after only two volumes. Meanwhile, liberal supporters of the ACLU split during the war. One group sided with ACLU Director Roger Baldwin and maintained that the Constitution protected even fascist expression. The other group insisted on "no tolerance for the intolerant" because racist and anti-Semitic rhetoric undermined the civil liberties of the attacked minorities. Struggling to straddle the divide between these two groups, the ACLU ultimately resolved: "Recognizing that our military enemies are now using techniques of propaganda which may involve an attempt to pervert the Bill of Rights to serve the enemy rather than the people of the United States, the [ACLU] will not participate . . . in cases where, after investigation, there are grounds for a belief that the defendant is cooperating with or acting on behalf of the enemy, even though the particular charge against the defendant might otherwise be appropriate for intervention by the Union." Unquestionably, this wartime resolution represented a retreat from the normal ACLU advocacy of "free speech for everyone." The ACLU would not intervene on behalf of American fascists and Nazis. After the war, the ACLU readily returned to its strict principled position. Its 1949 annual report stressed "that civil rights are indivisible; what goes for one cause goes for all." But the ACLU would not so readily recover the broad-based political support it had enjoyed before World War II. A June 1949 poll revealed that 92 percent of Americans believed they understood "the term 'freedom of speech,'" and of those, 45 percent believed that the freedom should be "qualified" — they did not "believe in freedom of speech for everybody."[16]

While a new coalition supporting civil rights specifically for African Americans would start to build in the late 1940s, a broad-based civil libertarian coalition supporting free expression in the abstract would not again crystallize. Many Americans would politically favor civil rights in certain situations without supporting expansive free-expression rights. In the mid-1950s, 67 percent of Americans believed Communists should not be allowed to make public speeches, but 71 percent of nonsouthern whites approved of *Brown v. Board of Education,* holding racially segregated public schools to be unconstitutional. In mid-1964, 74 percent of Americans believed that protest demonstrations "hurt" the "cause for racial equality," yet 60 percent preferred a candidate supporting civil rights. Political support for African American civil rights did not translate into widespread support for free expression or for the ACLU. By the late 1960s, many Americans viewed the ACLU as no more than one interest group competing against others. Moreover, Americans tended to view the ACLU less favorably than other organizations, including the American Cancer Society, the National Organization for Women, the National Rifle Association, the National Right to Life Committee, and the Planned Parenthood Foundation.[17]

RED SCARE

The post–World War II Red Scare was a period, like World War I, when the normal balance between the traditions of dissent and suppression faltered. Suppression by both governmental and nongovernmental actors became so frenzied that many Americans were frightened into silence, too scared to dissent. Merely questioning the justice of suppression itself could be denounced as un-American. The ACLU's 1949 annual report was entitled *In the Shadow of Fear.* How fearful were Americans? When a reporter asked people on July 4, 1951, to sign a petition expressing support for the Declaration of Independence, 99 percent refused. The politics of anti-Communism provided the impetus for the surge in suppression. Politics and suppression rolled together to form a muddy snowball, tumbling down a mountain of slushy crimson dirt. Red baiting proved a useful means of political advance, which led to suppression, which led to even more vociferous anti-Communism (anyone defending the rights of Communists must be a Red), which led to more suppression, and on and on.[18]

The roots of the Red Scare traced back to before World War II, though the wartime alliance with the Soviet Union temporarily dampened anti-Communist sentiments. Even before the end of the war, however, relations between the United States and the Soviets deteriorated. In a conference held in Yalta, Russia, in early February 1945—nearly three months before Germany would surrender—the Allied leaders, Roosevelt, Winston Churchill, and Joseph Stalin, attempted to sketch the contours for the coming postwar peace. While they agreed on some terms, such as the establishment of a world organization, which would become the United Nations, they failed to reach a consensus on many important issues. For political reasons, though, Roosevelt led the American people, including Vice President Truman, to believe that the Soviets had committed to establishing democratic governments in former German-controlled nations, but as the president realized, the Soviets had committed only to consult in the future on the fate of these countries. Even so, by late March, FDR had grown frustrated with Stalin for refusing to allow free elections in Poland and Romania. Whatever solution Roosevelt might have hoped to forge in the future, his unexpected death on April 12, 1945, intervened, thrusting Truman into the White House to confront the Soviets. Less than two weeks later, Truman met with the Soviet foreign minister and brazenly told him that the Soviet Union had broken the Yalta arrangement. "Carry out your agreements," Truman practically mandated. Truman's brashness did not faze Stalin, determined to control the nations bordering the Soviet Union in Europe.[19]

From that point, relations between the United States and the Soviets worsened rapidly. Germany surrendered on May 7, 1945, and Japan offered a peace settlement on August 10, the day after the United States had dropped the second atomic bomb. But the nation plunged into the Cold War. By April 1946, the secretary of the navy had declared that "[t]he ultimate aim of Soviet foreign policy is Russian domination of a communist world." With the fall 1946 midterm elections looming, Republicans "experimented" with anti-Communism as a political sword wielded against Democratic incumbents and the New Deal. Truman and the Democrats, Republicans charged, were too soft on Communism. Thirty-three-year-old Richard Nixon won a congressional seat in California after contending his opponent had ties with a "communist-dominated" labor union and had voted "the 'Moscow' line." The relatively obscure Joseph McCarthy won a Senate seat in Wisconsin in a similar fashion. Nebraska Senator Hugh Butler encapsulated the Republican strategy when he proclaimed: "if the New Deal is still in control of Congress after the election, it will owe that control to the Communist Party."[20]

The Republican strategy succeeded stunningly. By capturing an additional twelve seats in the Senate and fifty-five seats in the House, the Republicans gained control of Congress for the first time since 1931. Such a heady political triumph ensured that Red baiting would become a staple of Republican rhetoric. Almost immediately after taking control, the Republicans reinvigorated HUAC and promised to "ferret out" Communists and their sympathizers. Truman, now, stood in difficult political straits. On his right, the Republicans battered him for being too soft on Communism, and on his left, some Democrats believed he had too readily abandoned Roosevelt's conciliatory posture toward the Soviets. Meanwhile, Truman discovered that few in Congress would support his efforts for the economic reconstruction of Europe, which would become the core of the Marshall Plan (named for Secretary of State George Marshall), unless it entwined with the fight against Communism. Given Truman's own distrust of Stalin and the extreme political pressure from congressional Republicans, Truman took dramatic steps to prove his toughness against the Soviets. If those to his left insisted on protesting, he could brand them as subversives.[21]

On March 12, 1947, Truman articulated a policy — the Truman Doctrine — that committed the United States to aid democratic nations resisting Communist takeovers. "At the present moment in world history nearly every nation must choose between alternative ways of life," explained Truman. The American way of life "is based upon the will of the majority, and is distinguished by free institutions, representative government, free elections, guarantees of individual liberty, freedom of speech and religion, and freedom from political oppression." The alternative is based on minority rule. "It relies upon terror and oppression, a controlled press and radio; fixed elections, and the suppression of personal freedoms." But what did Truman mean, at this point, by freedom of speech? Nine days after proclaiming the Truman Doctrine, the president issued an executive order establishing a loyalty program for federal employees. "There shall be a loyalty investigation of every person entering the civilian employment of any department or agency of the executive branch of the Federal Government." An individual could be declared disloyal and denied or discharged from federal employment for "[a]dvocacy of revolution or force or violence to alter the constitutional form of government of the United States." More important, disloyalty could be established merely by a showing of "[m]embership in, affiliation with or sympathetic association with" any Communist or subversive organization.[22]

The loyalty program covered current and prospective federal employees; in 1947, more than two million people worked for the government. The executive order mandated that each employee be subject to a preliminary investigation. An initial investigation that uncovered "derogatory information" triggered "a full field investigation," which entailed federal (usually FBI) agents interviewing "the individual's current and former friends, neighbors, teachers, coworkers, employers, and employees in an effort to learn what they thought of his loyalty, what organizations he had joined, what journals and books he had read, and what sentiments he had expressed." The government subsequently conducted forty thousand full field investigations! The FBI passed the information to loyalty review boards, which would then conduct full hearings if "reasonable grounds" existed "for belief that the person involved is disloyal." The accused had certain procedural rights at these hearings, such as a right to counsel, but did not have a "right to confront the witnesses against him or, more important, even to learn their identity." If unable to rebut the review board's assertion of reasonable grounds to suspect disloyalty, the accused would be denied or discharged from employment.[23]

The entire process resembled a "medieval inquisition." Individuals were charged with disloyalty for reasons such as the following. "You have during most of your life been under the influence of your father, who . . . was an active member of the Communist Party." "Communist literature was observed in the book shelves and Communist art was seen on the walls of your residence." "A confidential informant . . . was present when [you, the employee, were] engaged in conversations with other individuals at which time [you] advocated the Communist Party line, such as favoring peace and civil liberties. . . . Another informant [was] of the opinion that [your] convictions concerning equal rights for all races and classes extend slightly beyond the normal feeling of the average individual and for this reason informant would be reluctant to vouch for the employee's loyalty." During loyalty hearings, the review boards would ask maddening questions. "Have you ever had Negroes in your homes?" "There is a suspicion in the record that you are in sympathy with the underprivileged. Is this true?" "Do you read Howard Fast? Tom Paine? Upton Sinclair?" When reviewing the credentials of a job applicant, apparently of superior intellect, a federal security officer worried that "intelligent people are very likely to be attracted to Communism." Meanwhile, a loyalty review board member observed: "Of course the fact that a person believes in racial equality doesn't *prove* that he's a communist, but it certainly makes you look twice, doesn't it?"[24]

Truman's executive order creating the loyalty program required the attorney general to generate a list of subversive organizations. The executive order did not require the attorney general to publish the list, but he did so anyway, to ruinous effect. The list effectively spread the loyalty program beyond governmental employees and removed the albeit limited procedural protections of the loyalty hearings. The attorney general could identify an organization as subversive without affording a chance for a hearing and without specifying the reasons for the listing. The attorney general's list became an "official black list," authoritatively providing "*the* definitive report on subversive organizations." Any listed organization faced probable demise, with contributions and membership rolls shriveling to nothingness. Given this, the government purposefully used the list to suppress dissident expression and to destroy organizations that would not conform to predominant opinions and policies. The initial list contained 78 organizations; by November 1950, it numbered 197; and eventually, it climbed over 250 organizations. Many Americans simply stopped joining voluntary organizations and refrained from any conduct or expression that might be interpreted as unusual. As one federal employee admitted, "If Communists like apple pie and I do, I see no reason why I should stop eating it. But I would."[25]

Regardless of the Truman administration's actions, the Republican-controlled Congress would not concede the anti-Communism issue. The Taft-Hartley Act, enacted in 1947, not only countered many of the NLRA's prounion provisions but also repressed Communism, requiring each union officer to attest that "he is not a member of the Communist Party or affiliated with such party." The House increased appropriations to HUAC, doubling the amount between 1945 and 1947, from $50,000 to $100,000, then doubling it again in 1948, to $200,000. The number of days devoted to public hearings jumped from three in 1946 to twenty-seven in 1947, to thirty-five in 1948, and seventy-seven in 1950. In the spring of 1947, HUAC discovered that a Hollywood composer, Gerhart Eisler, had spied for the Communist International party. This revelation sparked a full-fledged probe into the motion picture industry. Such an investigation had natural media appeal, especially for "fledgling television broadcasters." HUAC members could promote their anti-Communist cause and simultaneously rocket-boost their own political careers. With HUAC preparing to launch its investigation, Representative John Rankin, a Mississippi Democrat, advertised that Hollywood hid "the greatest hotbed of subversive activities in the United States." In October 1947, HUAC began its hearings. The testimony from Hollywood insiders, actors, directors, producers, and writers, "ranged all the way from intelligent penetrating analysis . . . to the strange, the bitter and the stupid." Gary Cooper testified as if he were playing one of his movie roles, the plain-speaking average American imbued with common sense. He "didn't like communism, because 'from what I hear, it isn't on the level.'" He had rejected scripts because they contained communist ideas, but he could not remember them specifically "'because most of the scripts I read at night.'" Over the first several days of the hearings, twenty-two witnesses, including Ronald Reagan, Jack Warner, and Louis Mayer, denounced more than a hundred of their film-industry colleagues as Communists.[26]

When HUAC called screenwriter John Howard Lawson, it asked him, "Are you now, or have you ever been a member of the Communist Party of the United States?" Lawson, president of the Screen Writers Guild, refused to answer. Nine subsequent witnesses, all screenwriters and directors, including such luminaries as Dalton Trumbo and Ring Lardner, Jr., were asked and refused to answer the same question. Based on information supplied by the FBI, HUAC condemned the "Hollywood Ten" as Communist party members and then imprisoned them for contempt of Congress. The major Hollywood studios, fearful of public reaction, voiced their support for HUAC's investigation. "[A]n exposed Communist is an unarmed Communist," the studios' attorney declared. To discourage possible boycotts of films — and lost profits — the studios publicly pledged not to "knowingly employ a Communist." Thus, the studios created a blacklist of writers, directors, and actors that would grow from the original Hollywood Ten to approximately 250 individuals; more would be banned from television. Dissent did not perish, but it became increasingly dangerous. Even before the Hollywood Ten hearings had begun, a group of stars, including Lucille Ball, Humphrey Bogart, Katherine Hepburn, Danny Kaye, and Frank Sinatra, formed a Committee for the First Amendment (CFA) to publicize the importance of protecting constitutional rights. After the hearings, a group of 208 members of the motion picture industry signed an amicus brief filed on behalf of Alexander Meiklejohn and the "Cultural Workers in Motion Pictures." The brief argued that the HUAC hearings and contempt convictions of the Hollywood Ten constituted censorship violating the first amendment. Such resistance invited retributive suppression. Eventually, the American Legion submitted a list of the CFA members to the studios, which then demanded members to write letters pledging their innocence and loyalty. Meanwhile, eighty-four of the individuals who signed the amicus brief were themselves blacklisted.[27]

The anti-Communist hysteria continued to snowball. The Hollywood Ten had not merely asserted their constitutional rights at the hearings. They had shouted at and insulted HUAC members, and in doing so, they had alienated many Americans, who already distrusted Communists. By the end of the 1940s, the American public strongly supported the repression of Communists. In 1949, only 9 percent of those Americans aware of HUAC believed that it had abused citizens' rights, and only 11 percent thought HUAC should be abolished. That same year, 68 percent of Americans expressed a belief that membership in the Communist party should be legally forbidden, and 77 percent favored the enactment of a law requiring Communists to register with the government. More than 70 percent believed Communists should not be allowed to teach in higher education. World events only exacerbated anti-Communist sentiments. In September 1949, Americans learned that the Soviets had successfully exploded an atomic bomb. In October, Mao Tse-tung's Chinese Communists triumphed over Chiang Kai-shek's Nationalist government. American fears that Communists aimed at world conquest seemed justified.[28]

Meanwhile, the Alger Hiss affair splashed all over the headlines. In August 1948, HUAC questioned Whittaker Chambers, who claimed to be a former Communist, reformed in 1939 to "'live an industrious and God-fearing life,' fighting 'communism constantly by act and written word.'" Chambers, a *Time* magazine editor, testified that one of the Communists he had worked with in the 1930s was Hiss. Hiss had graduated from Johns Hopkins University and Harvard Law School, where he studied under Felix Frankfurter. After graduation, Hiss clerked for Justice Holmes at the Supreme Court. During the 1930s, he worked in the New Deal, eventually moving into the State Department. Rising in the ranks, he attended the Yalta Conference, near the close of World War II. In 1947, he left government service to become director of the Carnegie Endowment for International Peace. Handsome and eloquent, Hiss "gave you a sense of absolute command and absolute grace," as one columnist phrased it. But in the eyes of conservative Republicans, Hiss epitomized the "rich, elitist, well-educated, eastern, Establishmentarian New Dealish government officials" who had plagued the country since the early thirties.[29]

Hiss insisted upon his innocence. "I am not and never have been a member of the Communist party," he testified before HUAC (by his request). "I do not and never have adhered to the tenets of the Communist party. I am not and never have been a member of any Communist 'front' organization. . . . To the best of my knowledge none of my friends is a Communist." Hiss denounced Chambers as "'a self-confessed liar, spy and traitor,' and 'questioned his sanity.'" Chambers retorted by saying that Hiss had led "a pre-war 'elite' Communist underground." Hiss dared Chambers to reiterate his charges in another venue, where Chambers would not be protected by HUAC's grant of immunity. Chambers complied, repeating on radio his "accusation that Mr. Hiss had been a Communist, [and] adding that 'he may be one now.'" Hiss promptly sued for slander. Most of the HUAC members believed Hiss, and Truman expressed his support. Nixon, however, remained suspicious, and with FBI assistance, he continued to challenge Hiss's denials. In November 1948, Chambers elaborated his charge, asserting that Hiss not only was a Communist but also had spied for the Soviets, passing them confidential government documents in the late 1930s. Chambers produced microfilmed documents that he claimed Hiss had given him years earlier; Chambers had supposedly secreted the documents inside of a "scooped-out pumpkin." The so-called pumpkin papers called Hiss's veracity into question and gave HUAC's investigation "a new lease on life." The government indicted Hiss for perjury in mid-December 1948. After a first trial ended with a hung jury, a second trial produced a conviction in January 1950. Hiss served three years in prison, though he always maintained his innocence.[30]

For Republicans, the Hiss affair was like manna from heaven. They had been sorely disappointed in November 1948 when Thomas E. Dewey unexpectedly lost the presidential election to Truman. Now, they could gleefully castigate the Democrats. Combined with the loss of China, the Hiss affair spurred Republican claims that the Democrats were soft on Communism and, even worse, were themselves often "spies, 'pinks,' and 'Commie sympathizers.'" HUAC member Karl Mundt exclaimed: "For eighteen years, [the nation has] been run by New Dealers, Fair Dealers, Misdealers and Hiss dealers who have shuttled back and forth between Freedom and Red Fascism like a pendulum on a Kukoo clock." Nixon catapulted onto the national stage and soon would land in the vice presidency under Dwight D. Eisenhower, who would become president in 1953. But perhaps no politician relied more on Red baiting than Senator Joseph McCarthy.[31]

On February 9, 1950, McCarthy spoke to the Women's Club of Wheeling, West Virginia. "I cannot take the time to name all the men in the State Department who have been named as active members of the Communist Party and members of a spy ring," McCarthy prevaricated. But "I have here in my hand a list of 205 — a list of names that were made known to the

Secretary of State as being members of the Communist Party and who nevertheless are still working on and shaping policy in the State Department." The State Department immediately issued an "unqualified denial," stating that McCarthy's charges were "entirely without foundation." In fact, McCarthy had lied; he "had no such list." When pressed, he refused to provide details and altered the numbers. Just three days after his speech, the *New York Times* reported that McCarthy had sent a letter to Truman claiming "there were fifty-seven Communists working in the State Department." Regardless, by the springtime, McCarthy had appeared on the covers of both *Newsweek* and *Time*.[32]

An alcoholic and bald-faced liar, McCarthy claimed to have been called "Tail Gunner Joe" during World War II, to have flown thirty combat missions, and to have been wounded with shrapnel. In reality, he had not been a tail gunner and had created the name himself. He had seen little combat and had not been wounded. He had not researched the American Communist party and its activities, but believed that subversives were "'homos' and 'pretty boys.'" He brazenly and persistently repeated his charges that Communists had infiltrated the government. Denouncing "'egg-sucking phony liberals'" and brandishing documents pulled from his briefcase, he would claim to possess proof supporting his accusations but would refuse to show it because of confidentiality. In one speech, McCarthy "charged that a group of 'whining, whimpering, craven appeasers' was preaching a gospel of fear." He particularly targeted Secretary of Defense George Marshall and Secretary of State Dean Acheson, whom he called the "'Red Dean of Fashion.'" McCarthy insisted that "'regardless of how high-pitched becomes the squealing and screaming of those left-wing, bleeding heart phony liberals, this battle is to go on.'" He refused to be dissuaded by the "'bleeding heart elements of press and radio,'" and attributed his own "'roughness in fighting the enemy to [his] training in the Marine Corps. . . . We weren't taught to wear lace panties.'"[33]

Other events continued to compound the Red Scare hysteria. In late June 1950, Communist North Korea attacked South Korea. Within two days, the United Nations had condemned the attack and called on member nations to assist South Korea. Truman quickly informed the American people: "I have ordered United States air and sea forces to give the Korean Government troops cover and support." China, though, sent three hundred thousand troops to Korea, and America was back at war, now against the Communists. The conflict would last three years, with more than thirty thousand Americans dying. Meanwhile, in early 1950, the British arrested Klaus Fuchs, a physicist who had worked on the Manhattan (atomic bomb) Project, for passing the Soviets secrets about the A-bomb. Fuchs's confession led to the arrest of several Americans, including Ethel and Julius Rosenberg. In March 1951, the Rosenbergs would be convicted of conspiracy to commit espionage, sentenced to death, and in 1953 executed. In the midst of these developments, many Republicans happily supported McCarthy and his exploits, despite his demagogic bombast. Senator Homer Capehart asked, "How much more are we going to have to take? Fuchs and Acheson and Hiss and hydrogen bombs threatening outside and New Dealism eating away at the vitals of the nation! In the name of Heaven, is this the best America can do?" Senator Robert Taft, known as "Mr. Republican," encouraged McCarthy to continue pressing his accusations. "[I]f one case doesn't work out, he should proceed with another one." While McCarthy and his cohorts' Red baiting cowed most Americans into submission, a few Democratic leaders with the (apparent) political clout to withstand McCarthy's barbs fought back. Soon after McCarthy's Wheeling speech, the Senate appointed a special subcommittee to investigate his charge that Communists had infiltrated the State Department. Chaired by Millard Tydings, a conservative Democrat from Maryland, the subcommittee issued on July 14, 1950, a report signed by three Democrats that unflinchingly impugned McCarthy's honesty. McCarthy's accusations "represent perhaps the most nefarious campaign of half-truths and untruth in the history of this Republic." Tydings, though, had miscalculated his own political strength. He hoped to thwart McCarthy, but Tydings himself could not withstand the Republicans' retributory attacks. McCarthy blustered that the "most loyal stooges of the Kremlin could not have done a better job of giving a clean bill of health to Stalin's fifth column in this country." The subcommittee report, according to McCarthy, was "gigantic in its fraud and deep in its deceit." Later that year, McCarthy circulated a fraudulent (composite) photograph of Tydings with a leader of the Communist party that helped seal Tydings's reelection defeat.[34]

In an archetypal manifestation of the tradition of dissent, a handful of Republicans also challenged McCarthy, despite having to buck against "the party hierarchy." Led by Senator Margaret Chase Smith, seven Republicans issued a Declaration of Conscience on June 1, 1950. With McCarthy sitting "white and silent hardly three feet behind her," Smith introduced the Declaration. She explained that McCarthy and his colleagues, by "words and acts, ignore some of the basic principles of Americanism — the right to criticize, the right to hold unpopular beliefs, the right to protest, the right to independent thought." She lamented that "[f]reedom of speech is not what it used to be in America." The Declaration condemned those

Republican senators who had resorted to "political smears" in the hope of riding "to victory through the selfish political exploitation of fear, bigotry, ignorance and intolerance."[35]

Truman himself, invoking the tradition of dissent, called McCarthy a "pathological liar." In an August 1951 speech, Truman denounced "the scaremongers and hatemongers" who had "created such a wave of fear and uncertainty that their attacks upon our liberties go almost unchallenged." McCarthy and his supporters were "already curbing free speech and . . . threatening all our other freedoms." Yet, Truman stood on shaky moral ground when attacking McCarthy. At one moment, Truman would condemn McCarthy's smear tactics, then the next moment, he would seek to parade his own anti-Communist epaulets. The Truman administration's saber rattling was most evident in its prosecution of numerous American Communists under the Smith Act. In July 1948, pressed by the FBI's Hoover, the federal government indicted Eugene Dennis and eleven other leaders of the CPUSA for conspiring both to organize the Communist party and to advocate the violent overthrow of the government. The trial ran from January to October 1949, "the longest criminal trial in American legal history," with convictions announced on October 14. Each defendant was sentenced to five years imprisonment. Significantly, the government attorneys prosecuted the defendants because of their ideas, not their conduct. The government did not seek to prove that the defendants had conspired to overthrow the government or had already acted to initiate the government's downfall. Instead, the prosecutors proved that the defendants taught Marxist-Leninist doctrine, as developed in books like Marx and Engels's *Communist Manifesto,* and that such doctrine predicted the demise of capitalism and encouraged the overthrow of government. "There could be no doubt what was on trial — the economic and political theories of Marx and Lenin." But did the Constitution protect the advocacy of such ideas?[36]

A unanimous three-judge panel on the Second Circuit Court of Appeals concluded that the first amendment did not protect the expression. The venerable Judge Learned Hand, now seventy-nine years old, wrote the court's opinion, handed down on August 1, 1950. Had Hand's commitment to the judicial protection of free expression wavered since World War I, when he had authored the highly speech-protective opinion of *Masses Publishing Company v. Patten?* In *Masses,* Hand had suggested that only direct advocacy or incitement of an overt act of unlawful conduct lay beyond first-amendment protections. In letters written in the early 1950s, Hand disparaged the Supreme Court's clear and present danger test and suggested that his *Masses* approach remained preferable. He also expressed an unequivocal belief that the prosecution of Communists was an ill-conceived policy. Nonetheless, in the aftershocks of the court-packing crisis of 1937, Hand himself had advocated for a restrained judicial role in protecting individual liberties, even those specified in the Bill of Rights. How, then, did Hand weave together these various threads in his *Dennis* opinion? He explained, albeit ambiguously (and unpersuasively), that his *Masses* test, if applied, would lead to the conclusion that the defendants' expression would be unprotected. More important, Hand acknowledged that application of his *Masses* test was hypothetical because Supreme Court precedent compelled him to apply the clear and present danger standard. And clear and present danger, Hand stressed, was "not a slogan or a shibboleth to be applied as though it carried its own meaning," but rather required a judicial balancing of interests. "In each case [courts] must ask whether the gravity of the 'evil,' discounted by its improbability, justifies such invasion of free speech as is necessary to avoid the danger." Under this interpretation of the clear and present danger test, Hand concluded, the defendants' expression was unprotected.[37]

On June 4, 1951, in a six-to-two decision, the Supreme Court affirmed the Second Circuit. Adopting the precise language of Hand's reformulated clear and present danger test, Vinson's plurality opinion reasoned that the justices must balance competing interests because "all concepts are relative." In this particular case, the advocated evil — the violent overthrow of the government — was so grave as to overcome its improbability. Even though the Communist revolution would be at some uncertain time in the future — when "a propitious occasion appeared" — its advocacy was constitutionally unprotected. Clear and present danger "cannot mean that before the Government may act, it must wait until the putsch is about to be executed, the plans have been laid and the signal is awaited." Maybe so, but the Court's *Dennis* decision "set in motion," in the words of the *Nation*'s Freda Kirchwey, a "chain-reaction process." Little more than two weeks after the Court handed down *Dennis*, the Truman administration began arresting lower-level CPUSA functionaries. Within three months, the government had arrested 41 Communists; by 1957, 145 had been indicted. And the purge extended far beyond CPUSA members. The administration implemented a new standard for the national loyalty program — now the government could deny employment merely because of "reasonable doubt" over an individual's loyalty — and thus the government reopened more than 2,500 cases of people already cleared under the old standard. Other governmental entities, not just the national executive branch, widened the scope of repression. In the end, more than 11,000 individuals lost their jobs as teachers, professors, doctors, lawyers, and so on because of suspected subversiveness or disloyalty.[38]

Despite the political benefits to be gained from Red baiting—as of November 1953, only 29 percent of Americans believed Communists should be free to make speeches in their towns or cities—McCarthy eventually overreached. He was not politically astute enough to recognize that his harangues became less useful to the Republican party once Eisenhower had secured the White House. Moreover, McCarthy blundered politically by attacking the Army. Eisenhower had long disliked McCarthy—he once said, "I will not get into the gutter with that guy"—but Eisenhower had been willing to tolerate him because of the political benefits. Eisenhower, however, would not acquiesce when McCarthy turned on the Army. Eisenhower had not merely been an Army general, he had been supreme commander of the Allied Forces during World War II and then Army chief of staff. Ultimately, the McCarthy-Army confrontation broke McCarthy and deflated the Red Scare hysteria.[39]

The dispute began in the fall of 1953, with McCarthy questioning whether Communists had infiltrated the Army. Tempers heated up, though, in early 1954 when McCarthy accused the Army of honorably discharging a Communist dentist rather than court-martialing him. McCarthy interrogated General Ralph Zwicker, the dentist's former commander. Zwicker had been a "regimental commander in Europe in World War II," the *New York Times* reported. "He has thirteen combat decorations, including the Purple Heart." Nonetheless, McCarthy fumed about Zwicker's evasive answers. "You are a disgrace to the uniform," McCarthy huffed. "You're shielding Communist conspirators. . . . You're not fit to be an officer. You're ignorant." On top of this, McCarthy accused Secretary of the Army Robert Stevens of "coddling Communists." Stevens responded initially by instructing his officers not to testify before McCarthy's subcommittee. He would not allow McCarthy to heap "unwarranted abuse [on] our loyal officers." Although Eisenhower ostensibly "gave 100 per cent backing" to Stevens, the administration, worried about the appearance of Republican infighting, pressured Stevens to soften his position. When he did so, McCarthy crowed that Stevens "could not have given in 'more abjectly if he had got down on his knees.'"[40]

Still, Eisenhower attempted to avoid directly confronting McCarthy. Eisenhower explained that the "ultimate responsibility for the conduct of all parts of the Executive Branch . . . rests with the President." Simultaneously, Eisenhower recognized a "Congressional right to inquire and investigate into every phase of our public operations." But how should such investigations be conducted? "[E]very governmental employe in the Executive Branch . . . is expected to respond cheerfully and completely to requests of the Congress. . . . In doing so it is, of course, assumed that they will be accorded the same respect and courtesy that I require that they show to the members of the legislative body." McCarthy replied less diplomatically: "If a stupid, arrogant or witless man in a position of power appears before our committee and is found aiding the Communist party, he will be exposed. The fact that he might be a general places him in no special class so far as I am concerned." As James Reston of the *New York Times* described this exchange, "President Eisenhower turned the other cheek today, and Senator Joseph R. McCarthy, always an obliging fellow, struck him about as hard as the position of the President will allow."[41]

Finally, the administration fought back. McCarthy relied heavily on his chief counsel, Roy Cohn, and Cohn's friend, G. David Schine, an unpaid staffer. In November 1953, around the time that McCarthy had begun investigating the Army, Schine was drafted. On March 11, 1954, the Army issued a report detailing how McCarthy and Cohn had requested that Schine be commissioned as an officer, assigned to certain activities, and accorded reduced duties. When the Army personnel had deflected these requests for "preferential treatment," McCarthy and Cohn had replied with threats. In response, McCarthy claimed the Army's report was "blackmail" in retribution for his investigations. Amid continuing charges and countercharges, the Senate designated a special subcommittee, chaired by a Republican, to investigate the dispute. Democratic Senator Lyndon B. Johnson arranged for television coverage, hoping the American people would "see firsthand 'what the bastard was up to.'" Johnson's hopes were fulfilled. The televised Army-McCarthy hearings attracted up to twenty million viewers each day, and as Cohn later admitted, McCarthy made "the perfect stock villain," with "his easily erupting temper, his menacing monotone, his unsmiling mien, [and] his perpetual 5 o'clock shadow." Once the hearings began on April 22, 1954, Stevens testified that McCarthy "had falsified . . . charges against Army officials," while McCarthy himself made a mockery of the proceedings by constantly interrupting to call for a "point of order."[42]

McCarthy's final undoing came on June 9. The special counsel for the Army, Joseph Welch, a private attorney from a prestigious Boston firm, was cross-examining Cohn. As McCarthy had done throughout the hearings, he interrupted, charging that one of Welch's law firm associates, Frederick Fisher, had "been for a number of years a member of an organization [the National Lawyers Guild] which was named — oh, years and years ago — as the legal bulwark of the Communist party." Welch asked the chair for a "personal privilege" so that he could respond. "Until this moment Senator," Welch said plaintively, "I think I never really gauged your cruelty or your recklessness." Welch admitted that Fisher had belonged to the Guild during law school and briefly afterward, but added that Fisher now served as secretary of the Young Republicans' League. Welch continued, "Little did I dream you could be so reckless and so cruel as to do an injury to that lad." McCarthy, like a bulldog, insisted that Fisher's record was relevant. Welch snapped, "Senator, may we not drop this? We know he belonged to the Lawyers' Guild." McCarthy demanded to continue, but Welch intervened, "Let us not assassinate this lad further, Senator. You've done enough. Have you no sense of decency, sir? At long last, have you left no sense of decency?" Still, McCarthy persisted, until Welch declared, "Mr. McCarthy, I will not discuss this further with you." As millions watched on television, the "crowded hearing room burst into applause for Mr. Welch." Leaving the chamber, Welch wiped tears from his face. "I don't see how in the name of God you can fight anybody like that," he said to reporters. "I never saw such cruelty . . . such arrogance."[43]

The hearings ended just over a week later, and the subcommittee issued a report on September 1 vindicating the Army's position. The Senate, voting sixty-seven to twenty-two, condemned McCarthy for "reprehensible . . . contemptuous [and] highly improper" conduct. McCarthy's popularity nosedived, as many members of his own party, including Eisenhower and Nixon, ostracized him. He drank more heavily until, while still a senator, he died from liver disease on May 2, 1957, only forty-seven years old.[44]

TO MANY AMERICANS, McCarthy's fall from grace in 1954 might have appeared to mark a political turning point. In early 1953, just slightly more than 20 percent of Americans viewed McCarthy unfavorably, but by July 1954, the number had jumped over 50 percent. Many Americans registered "intense disapproval" of McCarthy. Additional events mitigated fears of Communism. A cease-fire ended the Korean War in July 1953. Earlier that year, Stalin died, and Nikita Khrushchev became the Soviet leader. In less than three years, Khrushchev had condemned many of Stalin's dictatorial practices. To be sure, then, during the mid-1950s, the intensity of the Red Scare diminished, but just as surely, anti-Communist sentiments did not abate. The Cold War continued. Yet, the shifting tectonics of anti-Communism affected the Supreme Court justices, just as it affected other

Americans. Through the early 1950s, the Court had consistently deferred to governmental efforts at Communist repression and, in so doing, had interpreted the first amendment narrowly—reformulating the clear and present danger test in *Dennis* so that grave danger, such as government overthrow, could obviate the need for imminence. In the mid-1950s, the Court began to change.[45]

The first sign came in *Peters v. Hobby,* decided in 1955. John Peters, a professor at the Yale Medical School, worked part-time for the Public Health Service (PHS), a federal agency. In 1947, the national government instituted its loyalty program, and in 1949, the government subjected Peters to an investigation after "derogatory information" had called his loyalty into question. Nonetheless, the PHS's Agency (Loyalty Review) Board concluded that "no reasonable grounds existed for belief that petitioner was disloyal." After the administration modified the loyalty program with the new standard, the government reopened Peters's case. Even though the Agency Board considered evidence supplied by unidentified informants, it again found in Peters's favor. This time, however, the centralized Loyalty Review Board reviewed the Agency Board's decision and reached a contrary result: "on all the evidence, there is a reasonable doubt as to Dr. Peters' loyalty to the Government of the United States." Peters was barred from government employment. On appeal to the Supreme Court, Peters argued that the government violated the first amendment by discharging him because of his political opinions and violated due process by not affording him "any opportunity to confront and cross-examine his secret accusers." The Court held for Peters but did not reach these constitutional issues. Instead, in a majority opinion written by Warren, the Court reasoned that the Loyalty Review Board had exceeded its delegated powers under the executive order. This decision cut in two ways. On the one hand, the case signified in the justices a new-found willingness to scrutinize the government's suppression of alleged Communists. On the other hand, the Court's avoidance of the constitutional questions left the loyalty program largely intact. The government could continue to condemn individuals through "Kafkaesque" procedures that often relied on a "Faceless Informer," in Douglas's words.[46]

The following year, 1956, the Court decided its domestic security cases inconsistently, but still demonstrated that the *Peters* decision was not anomalous. The Court upheld one federal conviction while holding against the federal and state governments in four other cases. In the course of these 1956 decisions, Warren drifted left so that he appeared to join Black and Douglas on the liberal side of the Court, favoring the vigorous protection of free expression. Then, before the beginning of the next Supreme Court term, Justice Sherman Minton announced his retirement. Eisenhower asked his attorney general, Herbert Brownell, to recommend possible replacements, with an eye toward Eisenhower's upcoming reelection bid. In particular, Eisenhower hoped to find a conservative Catholic (to fill the Court's so-called Catholic seat — the last Catholic justice having been Murphy, who died in 1949), an experienced jurist (to counter criticisms of Warren, who had never been a judge before Eisenhower appointed him chief justice), and a Democrat (to show that Eisenhower truly wanted a nonpartisan Court). The administration quickly focused on William J. Brennan, whose liberal political views were somehow overlooked even though he had never disguised them. Eisenhower gave Brennan a recess appointment to the Court in mid-October, and Brennan immediately joined Black, Douglas, and Warren in creating a solid liberal bloc. In any particular case, they could form a majority by attracting just one more vote, usually from among either Frankfurter, John M. Harlan (a moderate appointed by Eisenhower in 1955), or Tom Clark (the former attorney general appointed to the Court by Truman in 1949).[47]

In the Supreme Court term beginning in October 1956, the Court heard twelve cases involvingw alleged Communists. Remarkably, the Court decided every one against the government. In a single day, June 17, 1957, called "Red Monday," the Court handed down four of the decisions. Even in these cases, the Court managed to avoid relying directly on the first amendment, though all had free-expression undertones — especially *Yates v. United States,* which might be understood as a sequel to *Dennis. Yates* arose from the convictions of fourteen second-level American Communist leaders under the Smith Act. The charges resembled those in *Dennis:* conspiring both to organize the Communist party and to advocate the violent overthrow of the government. In a six-to-one decision, with a majority opinion by Harlan, the Court acquitted or remanded each conviction (the government then dismissed the charges). Although Harlan did not reach the constitutionality of the convictions per se, he interpreted the Smith Act to follow the contours of first-amendment protections. Harlan reasoned that Congress must have intended to distinguish "between the advocacy or teaching of abstract doctrine and the advocacy or teaching of action." While the government could punish an individual for the "advocacy of action for the overthrow of government by force and violence," it could not punish for the "advocacy and teaching of forcible overthrow as an abstract principle." Harlan emphasized that his *Yates* opinion harmonized with *Dennis.* Putting the cases together, the advocacy of ideas or doctrine would be fully protected, while the advocacy of action, even at some uncertain future time, would trigger the *Dennis* reformulated clear and present danger test, balancing the gravity and the probability of the danger. The government could punish a defendant for advocating conduct even if it was highly unlikely to occur, so long as the advocated conduct was sufficiently grave, such as the violent overthrow of government.[48]

The justices' 1956 and 1957 decisions possibly reflected their perceptions that the Red Scare had diminished significantly. The Court softened its anti-Communist stance just as other Americans appeared to relax, to become less worried about Communists infiltrating the United States and conquering the world. If true, if the Court responded to changing American attitudes, then the justices misread the political signs. Americans were less anxious about Communism, but they were still concerned. The Red Scare might be over, but the Cold War continued. The Court had turned onto the same path that most Americans had begun to walk, but the justices traveled too fast and too far. Calls for political reprisals against the Court started after its 1956 decisions. Many white southerners still smarted from the Court's 1954 *Brown* decision, and after the 1956 cases, "national security conservatives" were ready to join these southerners in attacking the Court. *Time* magazine reported that many Court observers charged Warren with plotting "a deliberate course to the left." As a result, the Court "was under its heaviest fire in a decade." Congressmen introduced more than seventy bills aimed at reducing the Court's power and jurisdiction.[49]

After the following Supreme Court term, with its Red Monday, the "heaviest fire in a decade" became even heavier. True, the justices had decided the 1957 cases with technical felicity, yet the Court had been, in a sense, too clever for its own good. In *Yates,* for example, Harlan masterfully narrowed the reach of the Smith Act and, in doing so, implicitly expanded first-amendment protections — without relying on the Constitution per se. But the Court's adroit evasion of explicit first-amendment holdings did not deflect retributive political attacks. Eisenhower, without openly criticizing the Court, asserted that among its "recent decisions were 'some that each of us has very great trouble understanding.'" The president of the National Association of Attorneys General declared that, if the Court's decisions were allowed to stand, they would "completely destroy . . . the power of Congressional and state committees to compel answers to relevant questions in the field of sedition and subversive activities." The Association promptly passed a resolution requesting Congress to enact palliative or counteractive legislation. Congress responded, with senators and representatives introducing bills that would strip away parts of the Court's appellate jurisdiction and prevent the Court from deciding cases related to internal security. Republican Senator William Jenner proclaimed that the nation needed to restrict the judicial power because the Court had undermined "efforts of the peoples' representatives at both the national and state levels to meet and master the Communist plot." Some members of Congress called for even more drastic action. Democratic Senator Strom Thurmond of South Carolina denounced the Court as a "'great menace' [that] had 'jeopardized the security' of the nation," and demanded that the justices be impeached. He was not alone.[50]

Nonetheless, as the *New York Times* predicted, the Court's critics would largely "have to content themselves with grumbling." Many observers applauded the Court's decisions. The same day Thurmond called for impeachment, Senator Thomas Hennings, chair of the Senate Constitutional Rights subcommittee, declared that "the court should be praised for fulfilling its function as the ultimate guardian of human rights and freedom in our society." In fact, most of the anti-Court legislative proposals would die quiet deaths in committees. Even so, the *Times* added presciently, the Court never took "very long to catch up with the political philosophy of a large popular majority." While the Court would not completely reverse direction and return to its early 1950s deferential stance, it would "retreat," becoming far friendlier to the government. Two 1958 cases, for example, narrowed one of the 1956 decisions to the point that "it was rendered useless." The government, in effect, could again discharge employees merely because they had invoked the fifth-amendment privilege against self-incrimination and refused to testify in loyalty hearings. Unsurprisingly, when the 1960 term produced seven more cases involving domestic security, the government won six times.[51]

In conclusion, throughout the late 1940s and the 1950s, the national, state, and local governments actively repressed alleged Communists and fellow travelers, often without substantial evidence and frequently without affording the accused a reasonable opportunity at defense. Governmental institutions themselves discharged or denied employment to thousands of individuals through various mechanisms, such as loyalty programs. Moreover, the government artfully used public exposure — through, for instance, legislative investigations — to elicit manifestations of the tradition of suppression. Mere allegations of Communist affiliation could trigger ostracism and blacklisting. Finally, many such allegations, particularly those made by Senator McCarthy, were baseless. Nevertheless, it should be added, the 1990s release in the United States and Russia of the so-called Comintern and Venona documents revealed that at least some American Communists "had engaged in substantial espionage activity" for the Soviet Union. The

CPUSA was not "simply another political party." Yet, to appreciate the implications of the Comintern and Venona documents for free expression, one must distinguish espionage from advocacy. Espionage is unlawful conduct: "the clandestine transfer of classified or otherwise secret governmental information to agents of a foreign power." The Comintern and Venona documents provided retrospective evidence of espionage, yet the government rarely prosecuted or otherwise repressed alleged Communists for spying. In those unusual espionage cases, free expression was, at most, tenuously implicated. In the vast majority of instances, the government repressed based on mere membership in Communist organizations or on advocacy of abstract Communist doctrines. These governmental actions were inextricably entwined with free expression. Given that in such cases the government did not prosecute for illegal acts of espionage, the Comintern and Venona documents cannot retroactively illuminate the justice or injustice of the suppression. Advocacy is not equivalent to espionage.[52]

VIETNAM WAR

The Vietnam War can be understood as another stage in the Cold War. The nation's entry into open warfare in Vietnam culminated a series of policy decisions and actions that began during the Red Scare in the early 1950s. In 1950, the National Security Council articulated the domino theory: if a substantial part of Indochina, including Vietnam, were to become Communist, all of Southeast Asia would likely follow. Partly for this reason, the United States began supporting first the French colonial government, which fell in 1954, and then South Vietnam's government, controlled by Ngo Dinh Diem. This support took various forms, including supplies, advisers, and clandestine military and propaganda activities. It was grounded not on admiration for the French or Diem, a corrupt despot, but rather on opposition to the North's Communist leader, Ho Chi Minh, and the Communist Vietcong insurrectionists in the South (the National Liberation Front). At the outset of Kennedy's presidency in January 1961, a thousand advisers were stationed in Vietnam. By the end of the year, more than three thousand American troops were there; by October 1963, more than fifteen thousand. Even so, Kennedy explained that "[i]n the final analysis, it is [the South Vietnamese's] war. They are the ones who will have to win it or lose it." He then ordered that a thousand advisers be brought home by the end of the year. Indeed, Kennedy had always been guarded about overcommitting troops, but he also was leery about withdrawing and possibly losing Vietnam to the Communists. Then, on November 1, 1963, Diem was ousted through a coup, ironically encouraged by the United States. American policy remained unsettled when Kennedy was assassinated on November 22.[53]

Regardless of Kennedy's uncertain plans for Vietnam, President Lyndon B. Johnson sent an additional six thousand troops in 1964. During the first part of that year, the United States continued to carry out clandestine missions, including air and naval strikes, and the Joint Chiefs of Staff developed a list of bombing targets in North Vietnam. Like Kennedy, Johnson feared allowing "Southeast Asia [to] go the way China went"; moreover, LBJ believed the nation's support for the coup solidified the American commitment to the Vietnamese people. From a political vantage, he worried that his domestic Great Society program would suffer if he appeared "soft" on Communism. On August 2, 1964, an American destroyer, stationed off the North Vietnamese coast in the Gulf of Tonkin, exchanged gunfire with North Vietnamese PT (or patrol and torpedo) boats. In response, Johnson ordered another destroyer to the Gulf. On the morning of August 4, the Pentagon received reports of an attack against the two destroyers. That evening, Johnson spoke to the American people: "The initial attack on the destroyer . . . was repeated today by a number of hostile vessels attacking [the] two U.S. destroyers with torpedoes." As the Defense Department phrased it, the North Vietnamese had made a "deliberate attack" against the American destroyers. Consequently, Johnson explained, he had been "required . . . to order the military forces of the United States to take action in reply." As the president spoke, American planes were bombing North Vietnamese naval bases and oil supplies. LBJ immediately ordered more troops and supplies to be sent to Vietnam and requested that Congress pass a resolution supporting his actions. On August 7, Congress adopted the Tonkin Gulf Resolution, authorizing "the President, as Commander in Chief, to take all necessary measures to repel any armed attack against the forces of the United States and to prevent further aggression." This resolution would be interpreted as sanctioning all future military actions in Vietnam.[54]

Many have doubted the integrity of Johnson and his officials during the Tonkin Gulf crisis. While the administration prepared the execution order for the retaliatory bombing raids, Secretary of Defense Robert Mc-Namara learned that "there was now confusion over whether an attack on the destroyers had actually taken place." Nonetheless, before confirmation of an attack, "the formal execution order for the reprisals was transmitted." Still, the attack would not begin for another 2.5 hours, and before that time, McNamara and the Joint Chiefs decided that the attack had been genuine. Subsequent evidence would show, however, that the confusion concerning the attack came from one of the destroyer commanders in the Tonkin Gulf. Although his sonar operator had seen radar blips suggesting a possible attack, the commander had been uncertain; weather conditions or even the ship's own propellers might have produced the blips. In fact, "[n]o American ships were hit, no men wounded or killed." Moreover, when Johnson went to Congress to request the Tonkin Gulf Resolution, he failed to disclose that the United States had recently, on July 30 and August 3, participated in covert raids, and that the North Vietnamese, if they had indeed attacked, might have been responding to those provocations. As Congress debated the Resolution, McNamara testified during a secret session of the Senate Foreign Relations Committee and, when questioned, expressly denied any American involvement in the raids.[55]

In the midst of the 1964 presidential campaign, LBJ had anxiously sought a "pretext" for an attack to demonstrate his toughness and to counter Republican Barry Goldwater's claimed puissance. Whether Tonkin Gulf was pretext or not, the Johnson administration waited until after the president's reelection and then rapidly escalated American involvement. By the end of 1965, 184,000 Americans were in Vietnam, and the number continued to grow; by early 1968, more than a half million troops were there. With escalation came protest, and with protest came suppression. In this regard, the Vietnam War differed significantly from the post–World War II Red Scare; the tradition of suppression did not overwhelm the tradition of dissent. Instead, from the mid-1960s to the early 1970s, Americans engaged in an orgy of dissent *and* suppression. The two competing traditions battled against each other with ever-increasing intensity. As the war effort mounted, the government simultaneously increased efforts at suppression. Protestors thus began to hold more demonstrations. Then, suppression increased. The protests became more frequent and violent. Suppression became more aggressive. Like sharks thrashing in frenzied battle, dissent and suppression fed off each other's blood.[56]

Already in the spring of 1965, college professors and students were holding "teach-ins" in reaction against the war. On one October weekend in 1965, antiwar protests "were held in scores of cities." There were "marches on military installations, sit-ins, burning of draft cards and seminars on ways of avoiding military service." The protesters were dubbed "Vietniks"; *Time* magazine denigrated them as a "ragtag collection of the unshaven and unscrubbed." Even so, twelve thousand marched in Berkeley, California, and ten thousand protested in New York City. In response, as reported in the *New York Times* on October 21, "[p]arades, rallies, information programs, blood donations — even the sending of gifts to combat units — were being planned across the country yesterday as a show of support for the United States' military commitment in Vietnam." Many critics of the protesters reacted more violently. During antiwar demonstrations, fights erupted, some protesters "were pelted with raw eggs," and others "got doused with red paint." Still, the protests continued to grow. On Thanksgiving 1965, from thirty to forty thousand protesters descended on Washington to march and to deliberate about various methods of resistance. But while protesters chanted, "Hey, hey, L.B.J.! How many kids did you kill today?" many other Americans only nodded toward the tradition of dissent while simultaneously advocating suppression. *Time* magazine editors wrote that "[d]issent and disagreement are the essence of democracy and one of its greatest strengths." But they quickly added that "[t]he outer limits of dissent . . . are reached and breached by draft-card burning and other practices clearly against the laws of the land." Senator Thomas Dodd stressed the need to uphold free expression but declared: "We have to draw a line, and draw it soon, and draw it hard, between the right of free speech and assembly and the right to perpetrate treason." In Boston, a small protest in April 1966 drew a larger crowd of prowar supporters, who yelled, "Kill them! Shoot them! Commie!" The crowd then "surged forward, knocking some of the demonstrators to the ground and slugging and kicking them." Eventually, the police stopped the attack, with one officer explaining, "Anyone foolish enough to commit such an unpatriotic gesture . . . can only expect what these people got." Later, the *protesters* were convicted of loitering because of an earlier demonstration.[57]

At least from 1965 through the end of 1967, public opinion supported the war effort and opposed the protest demonstrations. In the fall of 1965, only 21 percent of Americans believed the United States had made a mistake by sending troops to Vietnam. In the springtimes of the following two years, this percentage remained low, hovering at just over 35 percent. In April 1967, 59 percent of Americans believed the nation's role in Vietnam was "morally justified," though by the end of the year, the percentage who thought involvement had been a mistake had risen slightly, to 45 percent. Despite the early popularity of the war, the protest movement expanded. Membership in the Students for a Democratic Society, a prominent antiwar organization, increased from approximately 1,500 in January 1965 to 10,000 in October 1965 and then to 80,000 in November 1968. In February 1967, 10,000 protesters braved a "driving rain" in Atlanta to participate in the "first in a nationwide series of rallies" against the war. In April of that year, between 200,000 and 300,000 protesters joined in New York and San Francisco. In 1969, more than 600,000 traveled to Washington to participate in one demonstration. During the 1966–67 academic year, students and faculty staged 400 campus demonstrations; in 1967–68, the number jumped to 3,400; and by 1969–70, there were 9,408. The number of violent protests also increased. For instance, during the spring of 1968, ten bombings hit college campuses; in the spring of 1969, the number increased to eighty-four.[58]

Throughout most of this period, opposition to war protesters remained strong. A November 1965 poll found that 32 percent of Americans believed people did not have a right to conduct peaceful demonstrations against the war. In May 1967, 29 percent still believed there was no right to protest. Fifty-six percent of Americans approved of how the Chicago police had handled protesters at the Democratic presidential convention in August 1968. The police, encouraged by Mayor Richard Daley, had repeatedly disrupted demonstrations by using tear gas and clubs — "Gestapo tactics," according to Senator Abraham Ribicoff. The national government purposefully stirred the cauldron of suppression. In 1966, in a typical governmental assertion, HUAC reported a "widespread and well-organized" Communist effort to oppose the war and create a "communist totalitarian dictatorship." Furthermore, the government did not merely encourage opposition to protesters — by labeling them Communists, for example — but aggressively sought to suppress dissent. The Selective Service sometimes withdrew deferments from students who participated in antiwar demonstrations. In 1965, Congress amended the Universal Military Training and Service (or Selective Service) Act. As Mendel Rivers explained in the House, the amendment would expressly allow the government to punish anyone who "knowingly destroys [or] knowingly mutilates" a draft card. Congress did not disguise the purpose behind the statutory amendment: "It is a straightforward clear answer to those who would make a mockery of our efforts in South Vietnam," Rivers declared. Congress wanted to prevent individuals from protesting against the war by burning their draft cards. Congressmen denounced the protesters as "a filthy, sleazy beatnik gang" — "a vocal minority [who would] thumb their noses at their own Government."[59]

In *United States v. O'Brien*, decided in 1968, the Court reviewed the convictions of David Paul O'Brien and three companions for violating the amended Selective Service Act. O'Brien had burned his draft card to protest the war and "to influence others to adopt his antiwar beliefs." Because he had engaged in "symbolic speech" — burning his draft card to express ideas, particularly his political views — O'Brien argued that the conviction

violated the first amendment. The Court disagreed, in a seven-to-one decision, with Warren writing the majority opinion. Warren reasoned that
"when 'speech' and 'nonspeech' elements are combined in the same course
of conduct," then the Court must apply a balancing test. "[A] government
regulation is sufficiently justified if it is within the constitutional power of
the Government; if it furthers an important or substantial governmental
interest; if the governmental interest is unrelated to the suppression of free
expression; and if the incidental restriction on alleged First Amendment
freedoms is no greater than is essential to the furtherance of that interest."
In applying this four-part test, Warren emphasized that Congress possesses
"broad and sweeping" power "to raise and support armies," a power that encompassed the congressional enactment of the Selective Service Act. The
bulk of Warren's opinion, then, focused on how the Act (though not necessarily the amendment proscribing draft-card burning) furthered substantial
governmental interests. Most important, the Act facilitated "the smooth
and proper functioning of the system that Congress has established to raise
armies." But what about the third prong of the test: was the governmental
interest unrelated to the suppression of free expression? O'Brien argued,
quite reasonably, that "the 'purpose' of Congress was 'to suppress freedom
of speech.'" Warren sidestepped this issue with two quick maneuvers.
First, he reasoned that the statutory amendment and O'Brien's conviction
were "limited to the noncommunicative aspect of O'Brien's conduct." The
government, Warren suggested, sought to punish O'Brien because he had
burned his draft card, not because he had expressed his political views.
Second, Warren asserted that "[i]t is a familiar principle of constitutional
law" for the Court not to inquire into congressional motives or purposes.
This assertion, however, was "flatly wrong." The Court, in prior cases, had
questioned congressional motives and purposes to determine whether facially constitutional laws were invalid, and the Court would do so repeatedly in the future.[60]

When *O'Brien* was argued, in January 1968, the justices apparently
shared the same mood as most other Americans. They disliked antiwar protesters and believed that many, including draft-card burners, had exceeded
the bounds of reasonable dissent. But during that year, American public
opinion started to shift perceptibly. No single moment marked a turn in
direction, but gradually, and for a variety of reasons, Americans had begun
to view the Vietnam War less favorably. It had already dragged on longer
than expected, and the television news brought the nightmare directly into
the nation's living rooms. In one haunting clip, a South Vietnamese general cold-bloodedly shot a Vietcong prisoner in the head. And the public

could not disregard the mounting numbers of American casualties. When the government changed the draft deferment rules in the spring of 1968, rendering many graduate students and recent college graduates draft eligible, middle- and upper-class families confronted the prospect of having their sons perish in Southeast Asia. By the end of 1968, one could discern clear evidence of a change in public opinion. In the midst of that year and for the first time during the war, the number of Americans who characterized themselves as doves (favoring peace) exceeded the number who self-identified as hawks (favoring war). Even so, toward the end of 1968, even after Johnson's approval rating had plummeted, less than 50 percent of Americans believed that involvement in Vietnam had been a mistake from the outset. In January 1969, though, the percentage jumped up over 50 (to 52 percent). And it continued to climb, to 56 percent in May 1970, and up over 60 percent in May 1971. In late 1970, 61 percent of Americans thought the United States should withdraw all troops from Vietnam by the end of the next year.[61]

Attitudes toward the antiwar protesters also shifted, albeit more slowly. At the end of 1969, approximately 75 percent of Americans viewed antiwar demonstrations unfavorably. But in a sign of change, 57 percent disagreed that "protesters are just a bunch of hippy, long-haired, irresponsible young people who ought to be cracked down on." Even more to the point, 82 percent agreed that while the antiwar protesters may not have been "entirely right," they nonetheless raised "real questions which ought to be discussed and answered." The following year, slightly more than 50 percent believed that student demonstrations and other public discussions of the war were "not a good thing." How should one understand these statistics? American attitudes toward the war might have shifted sharply, but many Americans remained politically conservative. After all, the people elected Richard Nixon twice during this time. So even as attitudes toward antiwar protesters softened, a disdain for their methods persisted. After National Guardsmen killed four and wounded nine students during a May 1970 demonstration at Kent State University in Ohio, 58 percent of Americans blamed the students rather than the National Guard (even though two of the dead students had merely been walking to class).[62]

As public opinion toward Vietnam and the protesters changed, so did the Court's reaction to war-related cases. In *Cohen v. California*, decided in 1971, the Court held that Paul Robert Cohen's conviction for disturbing the peace violated the first amendment. Police arrested Cohen in a Los Angeles courthouse for wearing a jacket inscribed with the message, "Fuck the Draft." According to Cohen, he had worn the jacket "as a means of informing the public of the depth of his feelings against the Vietnam War and the draft." The Court's treatment of the free-expression claim differed markedly from that in *O'Brien*. While the *O'Brien* Court emphasized the "noncommunicative aspect of O'Brien's conduct," the *Cohen* Court emphasized Cohen's intent to communicate. Writing for a five-justice majority, Harlan not only categorized Cohen's wearing of his jacket as "solely . . . 'speech,'" but also labeled it political, representing Cohen's "position on the inutility or immorality of the draft." The state, therefore, could not punish Cohen's expression unless it fell into a low-value (unprotected) category. In rejecting this possibility, Harlan tied free expression to pluralist democracy. "The constitutional right of free expression is powerful medicine in a society as diverse and populous as ours. It is designed [to put] the decision as to what views shall be voiced [in public discussions] largely into the hands of each of us, in the . . . belief that no other approach would comport with the premise of individual dignity and choice upon which our political system rests." Harlan acknowledged that the freedom to urge diverse viewpoints in the democratic arena can produce "verbal tumult, discord, and even offensive utterance." Yet, given the nature of pluralist democracy, a "verbal cacophony is . . . not a sign of weakness but of strength."[63]

Between 1968, when the Court decided *O'Brien,* and 1971, when the Court decided *Cohen,* the nation had not become more committed to pluralist democracy, which had been entrenched for decades. Hence, like the *Cohen* Court, the *O'Brien* Court *could* have celebrated diversity; it *could* have emphasized that discordant political views signify democratic strength. Or vice versa, the *Cohen* Court, similar to the *O'Brien* Court, *could* have sidestepped the crux of the free-expression issue by declaring that wearing a jacket is conduct and not speech. Indeed, Blackmun's dissent stressed this precise point. But the Court decided *Cohen* three years after *O'Brien,* and during those years, the mood of the country had swung. In 1967 and early 1968, the majority of Americans still strongly supported the war and abhorred the protesters. By 1971, the people largely opposed the war and sympathized with the goals of protesters. Given this prevalent political view, the *Cohen* Court readily reasoned that Americans might need to suffer a protester's occasional crudity.[64]

WHILE THE COURT ADJUSTED to the changed political climate, the Nixon administration pursued suppression as if it were 1965, or even worse, as if it were 1951 during the Red Scare. Convinced he was "surrounded by enemies," Nixon suffered from a "siege mentality." Partly for this reason, his administration "had a mind-set more hostile to basic concepts of civil liberty than any administration in American history." During the Nixon years, agencies such as the FBI, the Central Intelligence Agency (CIA), and the Internal Revenue Service (IRS) dramatically expanded their domestic surveillance activities (often regardless of illegality). More than 250,000 Americans were kept under "'active surveillance,' while 'hundreds of thousands more had information about their lawful political activity included in intelligence agency files.'" Domestic surveillance agencies "regularly collected information" about organizations and individuals, including the "intimate details" of personal lives, even though the government frequently did not suspect the targeted organizations and individuals of criminal activity. Besides such extensive surveillance, the Nixon administration also openly sought to suppress dissident expression. The administration "prosecuted virtually every prominent anti-war leader" on various charges, though most of the prosecutions eventually failed because the government had gathered evidence illegally (the administration loved to use bugs and wiretaps).[65]

Nixon and his aides also directed an extensive program of covert repression. In this regard, Nixon went beyond his predecessors. Ever since the development of the FBI after World War I, administrations had used federal agencies to carry on domestic surveillance of Americans. Such practices were rampant during the Johnson administration. Furthermore, prior administrations had overtly suppressed dissidents through legal channels, by prosecuting or threatening to prosecute. Nixon zealously continued and expanded these forms of repression, but still, they were not enough for him. From the White House, the Nixon administration created and administered "its own political surveillance and operations network." In 1969, the White House hired two former New York City police officers to spy on prominent Democrats, reporters, and even a comedian, Richard M. Dixon, who parodied the president. Nixon's staff compiled a roster of "opponents" whom they would exclude from White House "invitation lists" and also developed an official "Enemies List," including journalists, academics, entertainers, and of course, Democratic supporters. As White House counsel John Dean explained in an August 1971 memorandum, the administration ought to "use the available federal machinery to screw our political enemies." White House staff members were to "determine what sorts of dealings these individuals have with the federal government and how we can best screw them (e.g., grant availability, federal contracts, litigation, prosecution, etc.)." So, for instance, when a newspaper article criticized one of Nixon's close friends, Dean arranged to have the IRS audit the writers.[66]

The Vietnam War, Nixon's siege mentality, and his desire to be reelected combined to lead to his downfall. The people first elected Nixon president in November 1968 based partly on his campaign declaration that he had a "secret plan" to end the war. His administration's approval rating for the handling of Vietnam stood initially at 65 percent, but by February 1971, as the war dragged on, it had dropped to 41 percent. By mid-1972, 79 percent of Americans wanted to bring home all troops. As the November 1972 election approached, Nixon pressed for a cease-fire, making important concessions, such as allowing the North Vietnamese to keep troops in the South. While the final cease-fire agreement was not reached until January 1973, Nixon accomplished his political goal, depicting himself as committed to peace. In the midst of these developments, Daniel Ellsberg leaked a secret Department of Defense study on the war to the *New York Times*. In June 1967, Secretary of Defense McNamara had commissioned the study of American involvement in Vietnam running from 1945 to May 1968. During the early 1960s, Ellsberg had worked for the Defense Department; then in 1965 he volunteered to serve in Vietnam as a member of the State Department. At the time, he strongly supported the war, but his attitude changed when he witnessed events firsthand. He returned to the United States in 1967 and worked for the Rand Corporation, a nonprofit research institution focusing on national security issues. The government had given Rand a copy of the Defense Department study, called the "Pentagon Papers," and Ellsberg began reading through the forty-seven volumes (approximately seven thousand pages). Eventually, he decided to divulge the contents of the study to the public. In the fall of 1969, Ellsberg and a former Rand Associate began photocopying the entire study. In March 1971, Ellsberg gave the *New York Times* a redacted copy of the Pentagon Papers. After reviewing the documents for three months, the *Times* published a first installment on June 13, 1971, with nine subsequent installments to follow on a daily basis. The next day, Attorney General John Mitchell asked the *Times* to cease publication of the Pentagon study, but the newspaper refused. On June 15, after the *Times* had published three installments, a court granted the government a temporary restraining order enjoining further publication. On June 26, the Supreme Court heard arguments in the case, and on June 30, the Court predictably held against the government, reasoning in a *per curiam* opinion that an injunction amounted to an unconstitutional prior restraint. Even during the era of republican democracy, the Court had stated that the first amendment proscribed prior restraints. And while republican democratic courts had usually not categorized injunctions as prior restraints, pluralist democratic courts had consistently done so. Moreover, given the judicial hostility toward prior restraints, the political context of the Pentagon Papers case almost assured the outcome. The American people had turned against the war (the Court had decided *Cohen* earlier that June), and the Pentagon Papers concurrences suggested that some of the justices had already grown disgusted with the Nixon administration's repressive practices.[67]

However predictable the Court's decision might have been, it angered the White House. Nixon fumed even more, though, about how Ellsberg had been able to leak the Pentagon study in the first place. Nixon ordered his closest aides to create a "program" to control "leaking information." It had to be run from "right here in the White House." Hence, in July 1971, they established a White House Special Investigations Unit. "Have them get off their tails," Nixon decreed, "and find out what's going on and figure out how to stop it." Because it was to plug leaks, the covert group became known as the "plumbers." On Labor Day weekend, following the instructions of John Ehrlichman, one of Nixon's top aides, the plumbers broke into the office of Ellsberg's psychiatrist in a quest for damaging information about Ellsberg. By the middle of the next year, the Committee to Re-elect the President (CREEP), headed by former Attorney General Mitchell, decided to use the plumbers to help facilitate Nixon's reelection. On May 27, 1972, they broke into the offices of the Democratic National Committee, located in the Watergate building, and tapped the phones of the Committee chair, Lawrence O'Brien. When the tap malfunctioned, CREEP sent another group of plumbers back to the Watergate, on June 17. This time, however, a security guard caught them in the midst of the break-in.[68]

Nixon, at this point, decided to cover up the administration's involvement in the break-in — a seemingly inevitable decision given his personality and his administration's prior practices. Nixon instructed his chief of staff, H. R. Haldeman, to "[p]lay it tough," and Nixon's press secretary dismissed the break-in as a "third-rate burglary attempt." White House staff pressured the plumber-burglars to lie about their connections to the administration. One of the plumbers, James McCord, admitted being offered "funds, a future job and possible clemency in return for continued silence." But one cover-up led to another cover-up, which led to another, with Nixon tottering unsteadily on top, until the whole house of lies came crashing down. In mid-July 1973, a former White House aide, testifying before the Senate Select Committee investigating the Watergate break-in (the Ervin Committee, named for its chair, Sam Ervin), revealed that Nixon had "routinely" taped conversations in the White House's Oval Office. "Most participants in conversations with the President did not know they were being taped," the witness added. With this revelation, the Ervin Committee, the presiding judge in the prosecution of the plumber-burglars (Judge John Sirica), and the special prosecutor investigating Watergate (Harvard law professor Archibald Cox), all demanded access to the tapes, which might contain a "smoking gun" linking Nixon directly to the break-in. Nixon declined, claiming executive privilege, and instead ordered Attorney General Elliot Richardson to fire Cox, whom Nixon had been pressured to appoint as special prosecutor. Richardson refused, resigning instead. Deputy Attorney General William Ruckelshaus did the same. But the Solicitor General Robert Bork, now the acting attorney general, complied with Nixon's demand and fired Cox. After this "Saturday Night Massacre," occurring on October 20, 1973, Nixon tried to pacify his critics by releasing a portion of the tapes to Judge Sirica. But the Ervin Committee, Sirica, and the new special prosecutor, Leon Jaworski, all wanted more. Suspicions about Nixon's possible criminal activities spread uncontrollably when Sirica discovered in the released tapes an 18.5-minute gap from three days after the Watergate break-in.[69]

In early February 1974, the House Judiciary Committee began deliberating about articles of impeachment. On July 24, the Supreme Court unanimously held that executive privilege did not shield the president from a subpoena duces tecum demanding the tapes. By the end of July, the House Judiciary Committee had voted to impeach Nixon for "high crimes and misdemeanors," including obstruction of justice. Meanwhile, Nixon's lawyers had begun listening to the tapes and realized there was, in fact, a "smoking gun." Six days after the break-in, Nixon had told Haldeman to get the CIA to stop the FBI from investigating the break-in; if the FBI uncovered the connection between the White House and the plumber-burglars, the administration would be politically devastated. Given this evidence, Nixon's lawyers encouraged him to resign. At first he resisted, but he finally relented and announced his resignation on August 8, 1974.[70]

NIXON'S RESIGNATION LOWERED the curtain on perhaps the most intense period of suppression and dissent in American history. The pressure to suppress dissident expression is always strong during wartime. The Vietnam War was no different from other wars in this regard. Yet, factors unique to the 1960s rendered Vietnam distinct. Recall that Vietnam was a stage in the Cold War and that Cold War anti-Communist sentiments had generated mass suppression during the 1950s Red Scare. Given this, when Vietnam first exploded into open conflict, the normal patriotic fervor of warfare readily sparked latent anti-Communist fears into fires of suppression. Yet, exactly because of the Vietnam War's proximity in time to the Red Scare, many governmental officials hesitated before acting in ways reminiscent of McCarthyism. LBJ wanted to suppress dissent, but he had never supported Red baiting during the 1950s and was wary of fanning another outburst. Regardless of Johnson's ambivalence, dissent seemed inevitable because of the war's nebulous goals. If one did not accept Vietnam as a Cold War imperative, as necessary to stop the dominoes from falling for the Communist side, then the reasons for the nation's aggressive actions became difficult to comprehend, especially given the eventual length and magnitude of the conflict; 58,000 Americans and more than 1,400,000 Vietnamese died, while the United States dropped more than twice the bombs (in tonnage) than the Allies had dropped during all of World War II.[71]

This problem of justification became magnified because the Vietnam War happened to begin in the mid-1960s. Dissent, of course, had always been endemic to the American people, but the 1960s saw the tradition of dissent flourish in numerous contexts. As the baby boom generation came of age, the ostensible consensus of the 1950s shattered. The antiwar protesters were not the only societal group to speak out against prevalent practices and values; there was a civil rights movement, a women's movement, a consumers' movement, and so on. Protest was in the air, and the antiwar demonstrators believed they represented a righteous cause. But as might be expected, dissent during the Vietnam War enhanced the prowar advocates' desires to suppress. Having built his career on Red baiting during the Red Scare, Nixon fervently sought to intensify suppression when he took office. Yet, by that time, the protest movement had become too powerful to pummel into submission. If anything, the protesters helped swing the political winds enough so that Nixon ran both times as a peace candidate. Ultimately, from a political standpoint, Nixon's grossest error lay not in his desire to suppress but in his decision to turn the techniques of suppression against a "mainstream" group, the Democratic party. When the government had previously applied such methods — "wiretapping, burglary, massive political intelligence operations and harassment" — to suppress peripheral or ostensibly "extremist" groups, few Americans had resisted. But when Nixon was caught using the apparatus of suppression against the Democrats, the American people became sufficiently outraged to force him from office.[72]

CHAPTER 13

Open Questions

The legal doctrines and theories of free expression under pluralist democracy remain in flux. In the realm of free-expression doctrine, at least three major questions persist. First, should the Court eliminate the two-level approach, which presumes that expression is constitutionally protected unless it falls into a low-value category, like obscenity or fighting words? Second, assuming that the Court retains the two-level doctrine, should the justices recognize additional low-value categories, thus placing more expression outside of first-amendment protections? Third, should the Court elaborate the two-level doctrine so that it becomes a trilevel or multilevel approach?

Over the years, numerous scholars have criticized the Court's two-level doctrine. Harry Kalven and Thomas Emerson emphasized that, while the first amendment proscribes the government from evaluating the merits of ideas and propositions, the two-level approach requires the justices to render precisely such judgments, labeling certain types of expression as low value. The Court, in other words, draws first-amendment boundaries based on the content of the disputed expression. Even so, the Court has never repudiated the two-level doctrine, though individual justices, particularly Douglas and Black, have denigrated it. Moreover, in several cases, various justices have suggested that an overarching balancing approach might supersede the two-level doctrine in importance. For example, in *Turner Broadcast System v. Federal Communications Commission*, decided in 1994, the Court reviewed the constitutionality of "must-carry" statutory provisions that required "cable operators to carry the signals of a specified number of local broadcast television stations." Justice Anthony Kennedy, writing for an eight-justice majority, briefly adverted to the low-value categories, but then devoted the bulk of his opinion to a balancing approach. Kennedy suggested that a content-based restriction might be valid, regardless of the low-value categories, if the government satisfied a strict scrutiny test, showing that the restriction was necessary to achieve a compelling state interest. Content-neutral burdens on expression, such as the disputed must-carry provisions, would be subject to intermediate-level scrutiny: the law must promote "a substantial government interest" that could not "be achieved less effectively absent the regulation."[1]

While the low-value categories are historically rooted in the defunct republican democratic regime, balancing accords better with pluralist democracy. Nonetheless, the Court has not jettisoned the two-level approach (and does not seem likely to do so in the near future). Given this, should the Court recognize additional low-value categories? For more than two decades, scholars have advocated that the government should restrict racist hate speech. Hate speech, these scholars argue, constitute "words that wound," inflicting "concrete psychological and physical harm." Besides experiencing intense fear, victims have suffered from "rapid pulse rate and difficulty in breathing, nightmares, post-traumatic stress disorder, hypertension, psychosis, and suicide." Consequently, some victims "quit jobs, forgo education, [and] avoid certain public places." Because hate speech causes these serious harms, it is argued, the government should deter and punish its expression. In fact, many universities and colleges, including more than 350 public institutions, adopted anti–hate-speech codes. The University of Michigan, for one, adopted a code punishing expression that "stigmatizes or victimizes an individual on the basis of race" while creating "an intimidating, hostile, or demeaning environment for educational pursuits [or] extra-curricular activities."[2]

Critics of such anti–hate-speech codes immediately protest: "What about the first amendment? No matter how despicable we might find racist hate speech, doesn't the first amendment protect it?" If we find hate speech to be offensive or injurious, the proper response should not be suppression but counterspeech — expressing ideas that oppose hate speech. Anti–hate-speech codes are, from this perspective, simply another form of censorship. In reply, proponents of anti–hate-speech codes emphasize that the first amendment is not an absolute. The two-level approach to free expression places several categories of low-value expression beyond first-amendment protections; hate speech should be added to the list. The Court's observations about fighting words would seem to fit hate speech equally well: "such utterances are no essential part of any exposition of ideas." Partly for that reason, counterspeech seems an inefficacious remedy for hate speech; racists who spout epithets are not likely to be persuaded by rational argument. The Court itself has avoided definitively resolving whether hate speech should be a low-value category. Predictably, the justices seem as irresolute as other Americans, who in recent years have become less tolerant of hate speech while remaining ambivalent about governmental proscriptions.[3]

Might the justices augment the two-level doctrine by adding more levels (rather than more low-value categories) to create a trilevel or multilevel doctrine? Not all expression, then, would be either fully protected or completely unprotected. Instead, some speech and writing would fall somewhere between those extremes. To a degree, the Court has already taken this step, with commercial expression being a prime example. In *Valentine v. Chrestensen,* decided slightly more than a month after *Chaplinsky* in 1942, the Court held that commercial advertising was a low-value category and therefore constitutionally unprotected. In a brief unanimous opinion, the Court considered advertising — the distribution of handbills, in this instance — to be more in the nature of economic than expressive activity. And since the case arose only five years after the 1937 turn, the justices readily deferred to the disputed ordinance as an economic regulation.[4]

In those early years of the pluralist democratic regime, political speech provided the prototype of protected expression, as underscored by the self-governance rationale. Commercial advertising seemed too distant from political activity to be accorded first-amendment protection. But as the mass-consumer culture infused more deeply into pluralist democracy after World War II, the importance of commercial expression grew. American democracy became a consumers' democracy: if advertising was part of commercial consumption, then it was also part of democracy. For most postwar Americans, economic consumption appeared to provide the path to self-fulfillment, and commercial speech became at least as important as political speech. Regardless of how political and constitutional theorists might harp on the centrality of political expression to democracy, commercial advertising provided the grist for the everyday grinding of personal decisions.

Partly because of this evolution of pluralist democracy, the Court changed its approach to commercial expression during the mid-1970s. In a 1976 case, *Virginia State Board of Pharmacy v. Virginia Citizens Consumer Council,* the Court invalidated a prohibition on price advertising for prescription drugs. Writing for an eight-justice majority, Blackmun reasoned that, given the connections between commercial expression and (the consumers') pluralist democracy, the first amendment protects advertising.

Democracy is ultimately about the allocation of resources in society, but most resource-allocation decisions are made "through numerous private economic decisions" in the marketplace. "Advertising, however tasteless and excessive it sometimes may seem, is nonetheless dissemination of information as to who is producing and selling what product, for what reason, and at what price." Nevertheless, Blackmun added, the first amendment shields advertising to "a different degree" than fully protected expression. And ever since *Virginia Pharmacy,* the justices have disputed the precise extent of protection. The Court applies a balancing test that requires the government to justify a commercial regulation with a substantial (rather than compelling) interest, but the justices persistently differ about the degree of deference owed the government.[5]

THE UNCERTAINTIES CONCERNING commercial expression manifest the ambiguities inherent in both the evolving practices of pluralist democracy and the theories of free expression. The self-governance rationale — asserting that free speech and writing are necessary for pluralist democracy — has remained one of the predominant theories of free expression ever since World War II. "The heart of a free society is the right . . . of the citizens to discuss politics and to criticize the government," one constitutional scholar wrote in 2002. Yet, as the Supreme Court broadened the scope of free expression under pluralist democracy, the limits of the self-governance rationale became apparent. What could justify the more expansive first amendment? Some justices and scholars opted to stretch the concept of political expression encompassed within the self-governance rationale. Hence, the *Virginia Pharmacy* Court attempted to show that commercial advertising was essential to the operation of pluralist democracy. If advertising could be categorized as political expression, then presumably, the self-governance rationale justified its constitutional protection.[6]

But such efforts to shoehorn in commercial expression bulged the self-governance box to near breaking. If the justices could deem any speech or writing — even straightforward price advertising aimed at increasing sales — to be political expression, then the self-governance rationale became meaningless. As articulated by Meiklejohn and his followers, the self-governance rationale explained that political expression, distinct from other types of speech and writing, deserved strong judicial protection because of its function within democracy. If the Court recategorized all or most expression as political, then political speech and writing would no longer be special. Dissenting in *Virginia Pharmacy,* Rehnquist stressed that the first amendment relates primarily "to public decisionmaking as to political, social, and other public issues, rather than the decision of a particular individual as to whether to purchase one or another kind of shampoo." Partly because of these problems, some first-amendment scholars questioned the coherence of the self-governance rationale itself. Early Meiklejohnians assumed that citizens engaged in a vigorous and ongoing dialogue about issues of widespread importance. Pluralist democracy supposedly depended on full and fair political participation, and free expression was prerequisite to such participation. But as the consumers' democracy developed, a growing chasm gaped between the reality and the theorization of democracy. Not only did disparities of wealth and power consistently skew opportunities to influence democratic decision making, but the people did not use free expression in accordance with the self-governance rationale. Americans, for the most part, did not devote their words and thoughts to rational deliberation on pressing political problems. As the *Virginia Pharmacy* Court recognized, most Americans cared more about everyday commercial transactions than about even "the day's most urgent" political issues. In the consumers' democracy, the emphasis lay on consumption rather than democracy.[7]

Many other scholars still accepted the self-governance rationale while also recognizing its inherent limits. Insisting that the first amendment extends beyond political expression to protect other types of speech and writing, these scholars explored alternative free-expression theories. As in the past, periods of official suppression, like the Vietnam War, sparked outbursts of theorizing about the importance of dissent and the doctrinal protection of speech and writing. If anything, this tendency, to theorize in response to suppression, became stronger after the transition to pluralist democracy because free expression became a constitutional lodestar (plus, the expanding legal academy of the 1960s and 1970s engendered more law professors writing about constitutional law). Scholars and justices still persistently reiterated the search-for-truth theory, which Holmes relied upon in his *Abrams* dissent when he first advocated for the protection of expression. "It is the purpose of the First Amendment," a unanimous Court wrote, "to preserve an uninhibited marketplace of ideas in which truth will ultimately prevail." The abiding appeal of this theory is obvious: in our consumers' democracy, the marketplace metaphor has become all pervasive. Buying products evinces our acquisitive or possessive interests in the economic marketplace. Voting for candidates and referenda evinces our political interests in the democratic marketplace. Shouldn't we also understand speech and writing to evince our interests in a marketplace of ideas?

Moreover, if the primary objection to the self-governance rationale is its narrowness — it justifies the protection of only political expression — the marketplace approach provides a possible solution. It broadly justifies the constitutional protection of any speech or writing that might contribute to the identification of truth. Given the elusiveness of truth — or even the meaning of "truth" — the marketplace theory can be stretched to cover any expression that does not lead to immediate violence (which would preclude further debate about the truth). One can easily justify, for example, the protection of commercial expression by arguing that advertising contributes to the individual's quest to identify a preferred product (the truth).[8]

Many scholars, though, have criticized the search-for-truth rationale. C. Edwin Baker has questioned "the plausibility of the belief that the marketplace leads to truth, or even to the best or most desirable decision." The marketplace-of-ideas theory assumes that people will rationally assess ideas and be persuaded by the force of the best (or most truthful) ones. But many factors other than rationality might influence people to latch onto certain ideas. Individuals might evaluate ideas based on preexisting biases or emotional reactions. Also, as Laurence Tribe emphasized, disparate wealth can skew the marketplace because of unequal "access to the most potent media of communication." And even if truth were to emerge in the long run, many people might follow false and harmful ideas for years or even decades beforehand. How many people believed slavery was justifiable? Given such problems, many critics have concluded that the marketplace of ideas is a misleading metaphor for a questionable and potentially dangerous theory.[9]

During the post–World War II era, scholars also developed a self-fulfillment rationale. In 1963, Thomas Emerson began with "the widely accepted premise of Western thought that the proper end of man is the realization of his character and potentialities as a human being." From this premise, Emerson reasoned that "every man — in the development of his own personality — has the right to form his own beliefs and opinions." Moreover, it "follows that he has the right to express these beliefs and opinions." Free expression, in other words, is necessary to avoid stunting personal development. It allows the individual "to realize his potentiality as a human being." While Emerson might have been the first scholar of the pluralist democratic era to articulate the self-fulfillment rationale, his argument resonated with the republican democratic past. During the 1798 Sedition Act crisis, George Hay and John Thomson had developed libertarian theories of expression. Hay, in particular, had described a liberty of expression grounded on an inherent right of the autonomous individual to do as he or she pleases, free of governmental constraints. During the late-nineteenth and early-twentieth centuries, John Burgess, Ernst Freund, and especially Theodore Schroeder had articulated libertarian theories of free expression that echoed the tradition of dissent, with its emphasis on speaking one's mind. Although Emerson did not cite any of these intellectual predecessors, his (re)introduction of the self-fulfillment–libertarian approach proved influential. Numerous other scholars would reiterate and elaborate the theory. Several traced the concern for self-fulfillment to Immanuel Kant's moral philosophy, with its emphasis on individual dignity and autonomy. The justices, too, have invoked the self-fulfillment rationale. "[T]he fundamental rule of protection under the First Amendment," David Souter wrote in 1995, "[is] that a speaker has the autonomy to choose the content of his own message."[10]

Three factors attracted scholars and justices to the self-fulfillment rationale. First, its emphasis on individual fulfillment conformed with the intellectual trends of mid-twentieth-century modernism, which emphasized the assertion of individual sovereignty (or power). Emerson perceived that expression must be "an integral part of the development of ideas, of mental exploration and of the affirmation of self." Second, the major alternatives, the self-governance and search-for-truth rationales, invest free expression with value for instrumental purposes. Speech and writing should be constitutionally protected because they help achieve other goals: either democratic self-government or the identification of truth. But if speech and writing are valued for instrumental reasons, sometimes other means might better accomplish those ends, even if expression must be suppressed. The self-fulfillment rationale eschews such an instrumental approach. Instead, it recognizes an inherent value in free speech and writing. Free expression is "an end in itself" because it constitutes an essential element of the individual's assertion of dignified selfhood. Third, partly because it is not instrumental, the self-fulfillment rationale justifies an expansive concept of free expression. The thrust of the self-fulfillment rationale is "express yourself." If you want to say something, then say it, because that's how you become "all you can be." As Thurgood Marshall phrased it, free expression "serves . . . the needs of . . . the human spirit — a spirit that demands self-expression."[11]

Despite the strong appeal of the self-fulfillment theory, numerous critics have attacked it. The emergence of the self-fulfillment rationale coincided with the development and entrenchment of the mass-consumer culture in postwar America. In the late 1940s and after, Americans became ever-more intent on personal satisfaction in the economic marketplace, on self-fulfillment in and through their purchases of products. As capitalist economic principles penetrated more deeply into pluralist democracy, a free-expression theory grounded on self-fulfillment seemed to follow naturally. Given this background, the primary criticism of this theory also seemed to follow naturally: the self-fulfillment rationale was too indiscriminate. The theory appeared to justify any expression at all, so long as the speaker (or writer) or listener (or reader) found the production or perception of the material to be fulfilling. But, obviously, not all expression is equally valuable to other individuals or to society. Expression nurturing a speaker's self-fulfillment might, for instance, diminish the self-fulfillment of a listener. A white supremacist might find the expression of racist epithets personally fulfilling, but such statements might injure the targeted individuals. Furthermore, many types of activities might seem as self-fulfilling as speech and writing, but the Constitution does not preclude the government from regulating any number of those activities. "An individual may develop his faculties or derive pleasure from trading on the stock market, following his profession as a river port pilot, [or] working as a barmaid," wrote Robert Bork. The self-fulfillment rationale did not adequately "distinguish speech from any other human activity."[12]

HAS FREE EXPRESSION in America progressed? Do we have "more" freedom of speech and writing today than we did in 1930, in 1875, or in 1798? If one focuses on legal doctrine, the answer seems unequivocal: doctrine since World War II has become more protective of expression. Compare the bad tendency test, used in cases involving the encouragement of unlawful conduct during World War I, with the *Brandenburg* test, articulated in 1969. Under the former, the government could punish any expression likely to generate harmful conduct. Under the latter, only expression specifically intended to incite imminent unlawful action and likely to produce such unlawful action imminently lay beyond first-amendment protection. The various doctrinal rules that the Court invokes today—whether the presumption favoring protection of expression; the limited number of low-value categories; or the balancing tests skewed toward protection—all seem to stretch the scope of the first amendment beyond that enjoyed under the formerly predominant and ecumenical bad tendency test.

Yet, legal doctrine comprises only part of a complex story. In specific cases, contemporary political sentiments always influence judicial interpretations of doctrine. Consider *Cohen v. California,* decided in 1971, when the majority of Americans wanted the troops home from Vietnam. In that political climate, the Court concluded that the first amendment protected an individual wearing a jacket inscribed with the message, "Fuck the Draft." If *Cohen* had arisen earlier, let's say in 1965, at the height of the Vietnam War's popularity, the result likely would have been different. The justices would have concluded that the expression-action either fell into a low-value category (and therefore was unprotected) or was merely conduct outside the scope of first-amendment protections. More broadly, the Court's development of more protective free-expression doctrine followed in the wake of the transition from republican to pluralist democracy. Under republican democracy, the Court would allow the government to punish speech and writing with bad tendencies because such expression contravened the common good. After the 1937 turn, the Court realized the bad tendency test did not comport with the new pluralist democratic regime. The justices, then, did not render first-amendment doctrine more protective of expression merely to fulfill a latent principle of free expression. Rather, they grappled with the ramifications of the paradigm change from republican to pluralist democracy, and in so doing, they developed new approaches to judicial review, including specific doctrines for resolving free-expression disputes.[13]

As pluralist democracy continues to evolve, partly in response to political forces, free-expression doctrine will also continue to change. Besides the overarching doctrinal and theoretical issues already discussed — such as the vitality of the two-level approach — the immediate politics of current issues will press the Court to mold specific doctrinal responses. For instance, changes in communication technology — in particular, the rise of the internet — have spurred some to declare that Americans could more widely and actively participate in democracy by somehow directly registering their preferences online. While such changes in democracy are conjectural, online communications have already begun to present novel free-expression issues. Should the government, for example, be able to restrict online content that might be viewed by children? So far, the Court has limited governmental power to impose content-based restrictions on the internet, though the justices have emphasized that the law remains unsettled because of the rapidly changing technology. Meanwhile, given the history of governmental actions during prior times of crisis, the "War on Terror" has predictably generated governmental policies that threaten individual rights. The justices, to this point, have been reluctant to confront these issues, mixing national security and individual liberties, though the Court has held that the executive branch will not be given free rein to restrict civil liberties without judicial oversight.[14]

The degree to which Americans enjoy a freedom to express themselves unhampered by others — by the government or otherwise — depends not only on first-amendment doctrine but also on the traditions of suppression and dissent. As a general matter, legal doctrine under republican democracy comported more closely with the tradition of suppression, while doctrine under pluralist democracy has veered closer to the tradition of dissent. Yet if American history teaches a lesson that reliably portends the future, it is that dissent and suppression will both persist, despite legal doctrine. A recent poll demonstrated the vitality of both traditions. While 75 percent of Americans viewed "the right to speak freely" as "essential," less than 50 percent believed the first amendment should protect the display of "potentially offensive art." Of course, depending on current political controversies, such percentages will vary year to year — or day to day — revealing ebbs and flows in the popular support for both dissent and suppression. Americans will continue to speak their minds while struggling to stop others from doing the same.[15]

Notes

ON THE FORMAT OF THE NOTES

Whenever feasible, I append one note for an entire paragraph, rather than using multiple notes within individual paragraphs. If a paragraph contains multiple quotations (but only one note), I cite the source of the first quotation first, the source of the second quotation next, and so on. If, however, a subsequent quotation in the paragraph is derived from a source previously cited in the same note, then I add the page number to the earlier citation of that source (without repeating the entire citation). After citing the sources for all quotations, I sometimes cite additional materials, whether primary or secondary, that provide supplemental support and information. If I have already cited one of those additional primary or secondary sources in that particular note — because it was the source of a quotation — then I include the additional page numbers in the original citation (so I do not need to cite the same source more than once in any note).

CHAPTER ONE

1. Alexander Meiklejohn, Free Speech: And Its Relation to Self-Government 26–27 (1948); e.g., Frederick Schauer, *Free Speech and the Argument from Democracy, in* Liberal Democracy: Nomos XXV 241, 241–42 (J. Roland Pennock & John W. Chapman, eds., 1983).

2. Halter v. State, 74 Neb. 757, 105 N.W. 298, 299–300 (1905); 205 U.S. 34, 39 n.††, 42–43 (1907); *see* Brief for Plaintiffs in Error, at 26–49, Halter v. Nebraska, 205 U.S. 34 (1907) (Oct. term, 1906, No. 174).

3. Texas v. Johnson, 491 U.S. 397, 405, 410, 414 (1989).

4. *Id.* at 419.

5. G. Edward White, *The First Amendment Comes of Age,* 95 Mich. L. Rev. 299, 300–301 (1996). Helpful sources on the history of free expression include Larry D.

Eldridge, A Distant Heritage (1994); Leonard W. Levy, Emergence of a Free Press (1985); Bernard Schwartz, The Great Rights of Mankind (1977) [hereinafter Rights]; Philip Hamburger, *The Development of the Law of Seditious Libel and the Control of the Press*, 37 Stan. L. Rev. 661 (1985); The Founders' Constitution (Philip B. Kurland & Ralph Lerner eds., 1987) [hereinafter Founders]; The English Libertarian Heritage (David L. Jacobson ed., 1994 ed.) [hereinafter Libertarian]; The Federal and State Constitutions, Colonial Charters, and other Organic Laws of the United States (Ben Perley Poore ed., 2d ed. 1878) [hereinafter Poore]; The Bill of Rights: A Documentary History (Bernard Schwartz ed., 1971) [hereinafter Documentary].

6. *Cf.* Nancey Murphy, Anglo-American Postmodernity 8, 40–41 (1997); Dennis Patterson, *Postmodernism/Feminism/Law,* 77 Cornell L. Rev. 254, 262–69 (1992).

7. Mark Tushnet, A Court Divided 130, 180 (2005); Arthur M. Schlesinger, Jr., The Disuniting of America (1992 ed.).

8. The First Charter of Virginia (1606), *reprinted in* 2 Poore, *supra* note 5, at 1888, 1891–92; E.P. Thompson, The Making of English Working Class 78 (1963); Magna Carta (1215), *reprinted in* Documentary, *supra* note 5, at 8, 12; Gordon S. Wood, The Radicalism of the American Revolution 14 (1991) (quoting the Prince of Wales, "soon to be George III").

9. Fredrick Seaton Siebert, Freedom of the Press in England 21–164 (1952); Hamburger, *supra* note 5, at 674–75, 714–15, 725–26.

10. John Milton, *Areopagitica* (1644); Rights, *supra* note 5, at 10 (quoting King James); The Commons Protestation (Dec. 18, 1621); Levy, *supra* note 5, at 91–92; Siebert, *supra* note 9, at 120–26, 166–67; *see* An Agreement of the Free People of England (May 1, 1649).

11. An Act for Preventing the Frequent Abuses in Printing Seditious Treasonable and Unlicensed Books and Pamphlets and for Regulating Printing and Printing Presses, 14 Chas. 2, c. 33 (1662), *reprinted in* 5 Founders, *supra* note 5, at 112; Trial of John Twyn, *reprinted in* Thomas Bayly Howell, A Complete Collection of State Trials and Proceedings for High Treason 535–36 (1816); Levy, *supra* note 5, at 6–9; Rights, *supra* note 5, at 24–25; Siebert, *supra* note 9, at 165–267.

12. Bill of Rights (1689), *reprinted in* Documentary, *supra* note 5, at 41, 43; John Locke, *A Letter Concerning Toleration* (1689), *in* Four Letters on Toleration 2 (7th ed. 1758; 1870 ed.); Siebert, *supra* note 9, at 260–63; Hamburger, *supra* note 5, at 714–15, 725–26.

13. William Blackstone, 4 Commentaries on the Laws of England 150–53 (1769), *reprinted in* 5 Founders, *supra* note 5, at 119.

14. *Of Freedom of Speech* (Feb. 4, 1720), *reprinted in* Libertarian, *supra* note 5, at 38 (Thomas Gordon); *see Discourse upon Libels* (Oct. 27, 1722), *reprinted in id.* at 230–32 (John Trenchard); Bernard Bailyn, The Ideological Origins of the American Revolution 22–54 (1967).

15. Milton, *supra* note 10; David Hume, *Of the Liberty of the Press* (1742), *reprinted in* 5 Founders, *supra* note 5, at 117; Libertarian, *supra* note 5, at xl–xli; Levy, *supra* note 5, at 93–96.

16. Eldridge, *supra* note 5, at 25, 43–44 (quoting Baltimore and Lee); The Funda-

mental Constitutions of Carolina (1669), *reprinted in* 2 Poore, *supra* note 5, at 1397, 1405; Norman L. Rosenberg, Protecting the Best Men 17–18, 26 (1986).

17. Massachusetts Body of Liberties, *reprinted in* Documentary, *supra* note 5, at 71, 73; Maryland Act for the Liberties of the People (1639), *reprinted in id.* at 68; New York Charter of Libertyes and Privileges (1683), *reprinted in id.* at 163; Pennsylvania Charter of Privileges (1701), *reprinted in id.* at 170; Eldridge, *supra* note 5, at 131; Rights, *supra* note 5, at 36–37; David M. Rabban, *The Ahistorical Historian,* 37 Stan. L. Rev. 795, 823–24 (1985).

18. Levy, *supra* note 5, at 26; Sydney E. Ahlstrom, A Religious History of the American People 121–329 (1972); Eldridge, *supra* note 5, at 139–42.

19. Eldridge, *supra* note 5, at 134; Levy, *supra* note 5, at 37–45; Melvin I. Urofsky & Paul Finkelman, 1 Documents of American Constitutional and Legal History 22–27 (2d ed. 2002).

20. Melvin I. Urofsky & Paul Finkelman, 1 A March of Liberty 36 (2d ed. 2002); Levy, *supra* note 5, at 38, 121, 128 (quoting *American Weekly Mercury,* Apr. 6, 1732; *Philadelphia Gazette,* May 18, 1738); Michael Kent Curtis, Free Speech, "The People's Darling Privilege" 46 (2000); Eldridge, *supra* note 5, at 65.

21. Kai T. Erikson, Wayward Puritans 86, 93 (1966) (quoting Winthrop); Eldridge, *supra* note 5, at 9; Witness to America 47–53 (Henry Steele Commager & Allan Nevins eds., 1949); Levy, *supra* note 5, at 17–18; Leonard W. Levy, Blasphemy 238–61 (1993).

CHAPTER TWO

1. Helpful sources on the development of democracy include Willi Paul Adams, The First American Constitutions (2001); Joyce Appleby, Capitalism and a New Social Order (1984); Erik W. Austin, Political Facts of the United States since 1789 (1986); Bernard Bailyn, The Ideological Origins of the American Revolution (1967); Samuel H. Beer, To Make a Nation (1993); Stanley Elkins & Eric McKitrick, The Age of Federalism (1993); Joseph J. Ellis, Founding Brothers (2000); John Gerring, Party Ideologies in America (1998); Howard Gillman, The Constitution Besieged (1993); Richard Hofstadter, The American Political Tradition (1948); James Willard Hurst, Law and the Conditions of Freedom in the Nineteenth-Century United States (1956); Alexander Keyssar, The Right to Vote (2000); Michael E. McGerr, The Decline of Popular Politics (1986); Douglas T. Miller, The Birth of Modern America 1820–1850 (1970); Edmund S. Morgan, Inventing the People (1988); Jennifer Nedelsky, Private Property and the Limits of American Constitutionalism (1990); William J. Novak, The People's Welfare (1996); Edward Pessen, Jacksonian America (rev. ed. 1985); J.G.A. Pocock, The Machiavellian Moment (1975); Jack N. Rakove, Original Meanings (1996); James Roger Sharp, American Politics in the Early Republic (1993); Rogers M. Smith, Civic Ideals (1997); Herbert J. Storing, What the Anti-Federalists Were For (1981); Frank Tariello, Jr., The Reconstruction of American Political Ideology (1982); Stephan Thernstrom, A History of the American People (2d ed. 1989); Alexis de Tocqueville, Democracy in America (Henry

Reeve text, Francis Bowen revision, Phillips Bradley ed.; Vintage Books ed. 1990; French publication, 1835 & 1840); Harry L. Watson, Liberty and Power (1990); Morton White, Philosophy, The Federalist, and the Constitution (1987); Sean Wilentz, The Rise of American Democracy (2005) [hereinafter Rise]; Sean Wilentz, Chants Democratic (2004 ed.) [hereinafter Chants]; Gordon S. Wood, The Radicalism of the American Revolution (1991) [hereinafter Radicalism]; Gordon S. Wood, The Creation of the American Republic, 1776–1787 (1969) [hereinafter Creation]; Michael Les Benedict, *Laissez-Faire and Liberty,* 3 Law & Hist. Rev. 293 (1985); Larry D. Kramer, *Foreword: We the Court,* 115 Harv. L. Rev. 4 (2001); Harry N. Scheiber, *Private Rights and Public Power,* 107 Yale L.J. 823 (1997); Documents of American History (Henry Steele Commager ed., 9th ed. 1973) [hereinafter Commager]; The Records of the Federal Convention of 1787 (Max Farrand ed., 1966 reprint of 1937 rev. ed.) [hereinafter Farrand]; Great Issues in American History (Richard Hofstadter ed., 1982) [hereinafter Great]; The Founders' Constitution (Philip B. Kurland & Ralph Lerner eds., 1987) [hereinafter Founders]; The Federal and State Constitutions, Colonial Charters, and other Organic Laws of the United States (Ben Perley Poore ed., 2d ed. 1878) [hereinafter Poore]; The Anti-Federalist (Herbert J. Storing ed., 1-vol. abridgment, Murray Dry ed., 1985) [hereinafter, Abridgment].

2. Freeborn American, *Messiers Edes & Gill, Please to Insert Following,* Boston Gazette, Apr. 27, 1767; The Declaration of Independence (July 4, 1776), *reprinted in* 2 Great, *supra* note 1, at 70; John Locke, 2 Two Treatises of Government §§ 208, 222 (Peter Laslett ed., rev. ed. 1963); Radicalism, *supra* note 1, at 174–75; Creation, *supra* note 1, at 14–17, 33–45.

3. Creation, *supra* note 1, at 59, 98, 100 (quoting Josiah Quincy); Constitution of Massachusetts (1780), *reprinted in* 1 Poore, *supra* note 1, at 956–58, 970; Virginia Bill of Rights (1776), *reprinted in* 2 Poore, *supra* note 1, at 1908–9; Edmund S. Morgan, The Birth of the Republic 7 (rev. ed. 1977).

4. Constitution of New Hampshire (1784), Constitution of North Carolina (1776), *both reprinted in* 2 Poore, *supra* note 1, at 1280, 1409; Adams, *supra* note 1, at 104 (quoting *Providence Gazette,* Aug. 9, 1777); Aristotle, The Politics, at bk. III, ch. 7 (Carnes Lord trans., 1984); Morgan, *supra* note 1, at 235–306; Creation, *supra* note 1, at 344–90. As the passage from the *Providence Gazette* suggests, the Revolutionary generation often did not precisely define republicanism, democracy, or the differences between the two. Adams, *supra* note 1, at 96–110.

5. Constitution of Massachusetts (1780), *reprinted in* 1 Poore, *supra* note 1, at 956, 958; Virginia Bill of Rights (1776), *reprinted in* 2 Poore, *supra* note 1, at 1908; Resolutions of the Stamp Act Congress (Oct. 19, 1765), *reprinted in* 2 Great, *supra* note 1, at 7–10; *see* Keyssar, *supra* note 1, at 8–24, 340–41; Morgan, *supra* note 1, at 149–306.

6. Beer, *supra* note 1, at 276; Letter from John Jay to George Washington (June 27, 1786), *reprinted in* 2 Great, *supra* note 1, at 80, 81; *Political Problems,* Essex J., Dec. 27, 1786, at 3 (Shays's Rebellion was "political problem"); James Madison, *Vices of the Political System of the United States* (Apr. 1787), *reprinted in* James Madison: Writings 69 (Library of America 1999) [hereinafter Writings] (for his own use, Madison outlined before the Constitutional Convention the problems encountered under the

Articles of Confederation); Shays' Rebellion (1786), *in* 1 Commager, *supra* note 1, at 126; Pocock, *supra* note 1, at 516–17; Rise, *supra* note 1, at 31; Creation, *supra* note 1, at 410–13.

7. Virginia Bill of Rights (1776), *reprinted in* 2 Poore, *supra* note 1, at 1908; Madison, *Memorial and Remonstrance Against Religious Assessments* (June 20, 1785), *reprinted in* Writings, *supra* note 6, at 29, 31; Adams, *supra* note 1, at 124; Creation, *supra* note 1, at 24, 413–25, 608–9; *see* Constitution of Pennsylvania (1776), *reprinted in* 2 Poore, *supra* note 1, at 1540.

8. John Locke, The Second Treatise of Government 4–5, 17–18, 44, 70–74, 82, 119, 139 (Thomas P. Peardon ed., 1952); Creation, *supra* note 1, 282–91; *see* Nedelsky, *supra* note 1, at 1–3; Tariello, *supra* note 1, 6–14; Ellen Meiksins Wood & Neal Wood, A Trumpet of Sedition 115–34 (1997); David N. Mayer, *The English Radical Whig Origins of American Constitutionalism,* 70 Wash. U.L.Q. 131, 138–39 (1992); Jeffrey C. Isaac, *Republicanism vs. Liberalism? A Reconsideration,* 9 Hist. of Pol. Thought 349 (1988). On the influence of Enlightenment thinking, see Stephen M. Feldman, Please Don't Wish Me a Merry Christmas 148, 155 (1997); Jeffery A. Smith, Printers and Press Freedom 42–53 (1988).

9. The Federalist No. 39, at 241 (James Madison) (Clinton Rossiter ed., 1961) [hereinafter Federalist]; Beer, *supra* note 1, at 362; James Wilson, The Works of James Wilson 77 (1804; 1967 ed.); Daniel T. Rodgers, *Republicanism,* 79 J. Am. Hist. 11, 36 (1992); Federalist No. 1, at 33 (Alexander Hamilton); Federalist No. 10, at 79, 83–84 (Madison). James Madison, Alexander Hamilton, and John Jay, writing under the pseudonym Publius, first published the essays of the *Federalist Papers* in newspapers to advocate for ratification of the proposed Constitution. Wilson delivered his *Lectures on Law* in 1790–91, though they were not published until after his death in 1804. Wilson, *supra,* at 49, 59.

10. Federalist No. 17, at 120 (Hamilton); Federalist No. 71, at 432 (Hamilton); Federalist No. 17, at 120 (Hamilton); 1 Farrand, *supra* note 1, at 135–36 (June 6, 1787); Federalist No. 10, at 78 (Madison); *see* Madison, *In Virginia Convention* (June 5, 1788), *reprinted in* The Complete Madison: His Basic Writings 46, 46 (Saul K. Padover ed., 1953) [hereinafter Complete]; White, *supra* note 1, at 125–27.

11. Madison, *Letter to James Monroe* (Oct. 5, 1786), *reprinted in* Complete, *supra* note 10, at 45; Federalist No. 10, at 82 (Madison); Federalist No. 37, at 231 (Madison); *see* Federalist No. 6, at 54 (Hamilton); Federalist No. 2, at 40 (John Jay); Letter from James Madison to Thomas Jefferson (Oct. 24, 1787) *reprinted in* 1 Founders, *supra* note 1, at 644, 647.

12. Federalist No. 57, at 350 (Madison); Federalist No. 6, at 54 (Hamilton); John Adams, *Defence of the Constitutions of Government of the United States* (1787), *reprinted in* 1 Founders, *supra* note 1, at 59, 59; Federalist No. 10, at 78–79 (Madison); Noah Webster, *An Examination into the Leading Principles of the Federal Constitution,* Oct. 10, 1787, *reprinted in* 1 Founders, *supra* note 1, at 596, 597; Federalist No. 48, at 309 (Madison); *see* Rakove, *supra* note 1, at 322–24.

13. Federalist No. 51, at 322–25 (Madison); Federalist No. 10, at 81–83 (Madison); *see* Beer, *supra* note 1, at 270–76; Ellis, *supra* note 1, at 53–54.

14. Madison, *Parties,* National Gazette (Jan. 23, 1792), *Memorial and Remonstrance Against Religious Assessments* (June 20, 1785), *both reprinted in* Writings, *supra* note 6, at 29, 31, 504; Federalist No. 51, at 322–23 (Madison); U.S. Const. art. I, § 8 (enumerated powers); Federalist No. 84, at 510–15 (Hamilton); Madison, *Letter to Jacob de la Motta* (Aug., 1820), *reprinted in* Complete, *supra* note 10, at 310, 311.

15. Federalist No. 10, at 80 (Madison); Constitution of Maryland (1776), *reprinted in* 1 Poore, *supra* note 1, at 817, 821; Keyssar, *supra* note 1, at 5, 9–24, 340–41; Adams, *supra* note 1, at 315–27; Novak, *supra* note 1, at 9–11; *e.g.,* Madison, *In First Congress* (Apr. 9, 1789), *reprinted in* Complete, *supra* note 10, at 269–72 [hereinafter First] (emphasizing free market and governmental assistance); *see* Feldman, *supra* note 8, at 119–254; Tariello, *supra* note 1, at 25–26; Chants, *supra* note 1, at 23–103. The one state without a property or wealth requirement in its constitution was Vermont, not officially admitted to the Union until 1791. Constitution of Vermont (1777), *reprinted in* 2 Poore, *supra* note 1, at 1857.

16. Federalist No. 2, at 38 (Jay); Brutus, *To the Citizens of the State of New York* (Oct. 18, 1787), *reprinted in* Abridgment, *supra* note 1, at 108, 114; Aristotle, *supra* note 4, at bk. I, ch. 5; Keyssar, *supra* note 1, at 24, 54–60; Storing, *supra* note 1, at 19–21; Leslie Paul Thiele, Thinking Politics 87 (1997); *see* Smith, *supra* note 1, at 471; White, *supra* note 1, at 266–67. Not all framers accepted all of the contemporary exclusions from the polity. Rakove, *supra* note 1, at 87 (some framers opposed slavery); Creation, *supra* note 1, at 182–83 (some Americans supported universal suffrage during Revolution).

17. Thomas J. Curry, The First Freedoms 219 (1986); A Watchman, *Letter From a Bostonian* (Feb. 4, 1788), *in* 4 The Complete Anti-Federalist 229 (Herbert J. Storing ed., 1981); 4 The Debates in the Several State Conventions on the Adoption of the Federal Constitution 192–94 (Jonathan Elliot ed., 1836); First, *supra* note 15, at 276; Feldman, *supra* note 8, at 145–74; Morgan, *supra* note 1, at 293; 1 Thernstrom, *supra* note 1, at 236–38; Robert A. Williams, The American Indian in Western Legal Thought (1990); Radicalism, *supra* note 1, at 123, 232–33; *see* Constitution of Pennsylvania (1776), *reprinted in* 2 Poore, *supra* note 1, at 1540–43 (religiously slanted oath); Morton Borden, Jews, Turks, and Infidels 11–15 (1984); Winthrop S. Hudson & John Corrigan, Religion in America 129–30 (5th ed. 1992); Martin E. Marty, Protestantism in the United States 169 (2d ed. 1986). Helpful discussions of religion include Sydney E. Ahlstrom, A Religious History of the American People (1972); Jon Butler, Awash in a Sea of Faith (1990); Nathan O. Hatch, The Democratization of American Christianity (1989).

18. Tariello, *supra* note 1, at 21 (quoting Paine).

19. First, *supra* note 15, at 276; Madison, *Letter to Dr. Thomas Cooper* (Mar. 22, 1824), *reprinted in* Complete, *supra* note 10, at 273; Gillman, *supra* note 1, at 61–62; Smith, *supra* note 1, at 14–19; Radicalism, *supra* note 1, at 229–369.

20. Elkins & McKitrick, *supra* note 1, at 77–89; Sharp, *supra* note 1, at 7–10, 69–76; *see* Ellis, *supra* note 1, at 44.

21. Federalist No. 78, at 464, 467–68 (Hamilton); Madison, *Letter to Edward Everett* (Aug. 28, 1830), *reprinted in* Writings, *supra* note 6, at 842, 847; *e.g.,* Calder v.

Bull, 3 U.S. (3 Dall.) 386, 398 (1798) (Iredell, J.) (Connecticut legislature previously exercised a "superintending power" over the state courts); *see* Nedelsky, *supra* note 1, at 188–99; Sylvia Snowiss, Judicial Review and the Law of the Constitution (1990); Radicalism, *supra* note 1, at 325; Kramer, *supra* note 1, at 77–83, 90–100. On early judicial review, see Gordon S. Wood, *Judicial Review in the Era of the Founding, in* Is the Supreme Court the Guardian of the Constitution? 153 (Robert A. Licht ed., 1993); William Michael Treanor, *Judicial Review Before* Marbury, 58 Stan. L. Rev. 455 (2005).

22. G. Edward White, The Constitution and the New Deal 36 (2000); James Kent, 2 Commentaries on American Law 276 (1827; Legal Classics Library Reprint). "The boundary of the police power beyond which its exercise becomes an invasion of the guaranty of liberty under the Fifth and Fourteenth Amendments to the Constitutions is not easy to mark. Our court has been laboriously engaged in pricking out a line in successive cases." Adkins v. Children's Hosp., 261 U.S. 525, 562 (1923) (Taft, C.J., dissenting).

23. Calder v. Bull, 3 U.S. (3 Dall.) 386, 388, 394 (1798) (Chase, J.); *see* VanHorne's Lessee v. Dorrance, 28 F. Cas. 1012 (C.C. Pa. 1795).

24. Goshen v. Stonington, 4 Conn. 209, 221 (1822); Taylor v. Porter & Ford, 4 Hill 140, 40 Am. Dec. 274 (1848); Gillman, *supra* note 1, at 10–15; Novak, *supra* note 1, at 24; *e.g.,* Billings v. Hall, 7 Cal. 1, 14 (1857); Gaines v. Gaines's Executor, 48 Ky. 295 (1848); Eakin v. Raub, 12 Serg. & Rawle 330 (Pa. 1825).

25. Fletcher v. Peck, 10 U.S. (6 Cranch) 87, 135 (1810); Vanzant v. Waddel, 10 Tenn. 260 (1829) (Catron, J.); *Cooper,* 10 Tenn. 599 (1831) (Green, J.); Baggs's Appeal, 43 Pa. 512 (1862); *see* James W. Ely, Jr., *The Oxymoron Reconsidered,* 16 Const. Comment. 315, 332–38 (1999); *e.g.,* Constitution of New York (1821), *reprinted in* 1 Poore, *supra* note 1, at 1341, 1347 ("due process of law"); Constitution of North Carolina (1776), *reprinted in* 2 Poore, *supra* note 1, at 1409, 1410 ("law of the land").

26. Vanderbilt v. Adams, 7 Cow. 349, 351–52 (N.Y. 1827); Commonwealth v. Alger, 61 Mass. 53, 7 Cush. 53, 84–85 (1851); Novak, *supra* note 1, at 44; Thorpe v. Rutland & Burlington R.R. Co., 27 Vt. 140, 149 (1855); *e.g.,* State v. Glen, 52 N.C. 321, 327 (1859); Panton v. Norton, 18 Ill. 496, 501 (1857). *Sic utere tuo* was associated with another maxim, *salus populi:* "the welfare of the people is the supreme law." Novak, *supra* note 1, at 45; *e.g.,* Donahoe v. Richards, 38 Me. 379, 412 (1854). *Salus populi* stressed the government's affirmative obligation to act for the common good, while *sic utere tuo* "recognized the social, relative nature of rights." Novak, *supra* note 1, at 70.

27. Vandine's Case, 23 Mass. 187, 191–93 (1828); *see* Commonwealth v. Rice, 9 Met. 253, 50 Mass. 253 (1845).

28. Commonwealth v. Alger, 61 Mass. 53, 7 Cush. 53, 85–86 (1851); *Thorpe,* 27 Vt. at 156 n.a1; Novak, *supra* note 1, at 51–233.

29. Pingrey v. Washburn, 1 Aik. 264, 15 Am. Dec. 676 (1826); *Cooper,* 10 Tenn. (Green, J.); *see* Gillman, *supra* note 1, at 54; Stephen A. Siegel, *Lochner Era Jurisprudence and the American Constitutional Tradition,* 70 N.C. L. Rev. 1, 60 (1991). Many pre–Civil War jurists nonetheless interpreted the formal categories in accord with an instrumental support for commercial progress. Stephen M. Feldman, American

Legal Thought from Premodernism to Postmodernism 74–82 (2000); *e.g.,* Swift v. Tyson, 41 U.S. (16 Pet.) 1 (1842), overruled by Erie R. Co. v. Tompkins, 304 U.S. 64 (1938).

30. Appleby, *supra* note 1, at 14–15; Radicalism, *supra* note 1, at 230; Thomas Hobbes, Leviathan 186 (1651; C.B. Macpherson ed., 1968); *see* Chants, *supra* note 1, at 14–15.

31. McGerr, *supra* note 1, at 13 (quoting *Philadelphia Inquirer*); Elkins & McKitrick, *supra* note 1, at 263–66, 753; Richard Hofstadter, The Idea of a Party System 208–13, 251–59 (1969); Pessen, *supra* note 1, at 160–61, 197–232; Sharp, *supra* note 1, at 285–88; Melvin I. Urofsky, Money and Free Speech 6 (2005); Watson, *supra* note 1, at 66–72, 172–74; Sean Wilentz, *On Class and Politics in Jacksonian America,* 10 Revs. in Am. Hist. 45, 55–56 (1982).

32. Storing, *supra* note 1, at 20–21, 30–31, 73 (quoting Cato); Radicalism, *supra* note 1, at 218, 269–70 (quoting Rush); George Sidney Camp, Democracy 88 (1841).

33. Hofstadter, *supra* note 1, at 32–41; Tocqueville, *supra* note 1, at 157; Miller, *supra* note 1, at 28–30; Novak, *supra* note 1, at 115–48; Pessen, *supra* note 1, at 120–21.

34. Miller, *supra* note 1, at 21 (quoting Kent); 2 Tocqueville, *supra* note 1, at 156–57; 1 Thernstrom, *supra* note 1, at 236–38, 251–53; Chants, *supra* note 1, at 4–6; Radicalism, *supra* note 1, at 308–47.

35. Tunis Wortman, A Treatise Concerning Political Enquiry, and the Liberty of the Press 128 (1800; 1970 reprint ed.); Radicalism, *supra* note 1, at 340; Andrew Jackson, *Bank Veto Message* (July 10, 1832), *reprinted in* 2 Great, *supra* note 1, at 291, 294; *see* 1 Tocqueville, *supra* note 1, at 98–105.

36. Ralph Waldo Emerson, *Self-Reliance* (1841), *reprinted in* Selected Writings of Ralph Waldo Emerson 257, 263 (1965); Confession of the Free-Will Baptists (1834, 1868), *reprinted in* 3 The Creeds of Christendom 749–53 (Philip Schaff ed., 3d ed. 1877) [hereinafter Schaff]; Robert Monk & Joseph Stamey, Exploring Christianity 94 (2d ed. 1990) (quoting Finney); Butler, *supra* note 17, at 256; Hatch, *supra* note 17, at 3; Hudson & Corrigan, *supra* note 17, at 129–30; Marty, *supra* note 17, at 169.

37. Hudson & Corrigan, *supra* note 17, at 28, 136, 162, 182 (quoting Noah Webster; John McGee); Hatch, *supra* note 17, at 9, 172; The Doctrinal Basis of the Evangelical Alliance (1846), *reprinted in* Schaff, *supra* note 36, at 827.

38. Wortman, *supra* note 35, at 49; Appleby, *supra* note 1, at 3; Hofstadter, *supra* note 1, at 14–15, 154–55; Andrew Jackson, First State of the Nation Address (Dec. 1829); *see* Richard Hofstadter, Anti-Intellectualism in American Life (1962).

39. Watson, *supra* note 1, at 80 (quoting Jackson); Austin, *supra* note 1, at 378; McGerr, *supra* note 1, at 5, 22–29; Pessen, *supra* note 1, at 132; Smith, *supra* note 1, at 170–73; Radicalism, *supra* note 1, at 294; Kramer, *supra* note 1, at 101–4, 112–13.

40. Pessen, *supra* note 1, at 42–43, 49–50; Smith, *supra* note 1, at 173–86, 195–96; Watson, *supra* note 1, at 13–14; Jacob D. Wheeler, A Practical Treatise on the Law of Slavery 190–200 (1837; 1968 reprint ed.). Some states diminished the rights of African Americans and women early in the nineteenth century. Watson, *supra* note 1, at 51–53.

41. 2 Tocqueville, *supra* note 1, at 6; Philip Hamburger, Separation of Church

and State 213, 220 (2002); Austin, *supra* note 1, at 472; John Higham, Strangers in the Land 5–6 (1992 ed.); David Tyack & Elisabeth Hansot, Managers of Virtue 21 (1982); Rise, *supra* note 1, at 450.

42. Higham, *supra* note 41, at 6; Pessen, *supra* note 1, at 37 (quoting diary of Strong); Smith, *supra* note 1, at 209 (quoting Morse).

43. Higham, *supra* note 41, at 4 (quoting 1855 Know-Nothing journal); Hofstadter, *supra* note 1, at 102 (quoting letter from Lincoln to Joshua F. Speed, Aug. 24, 1855); Ahlstrom, *supra* note 17, at 562, 565; Keyssar, *supra* note 1, at 84–85.

44. Radicalism, *supra* note 1, at 318–20; Morton J. Horwitz, The Transformation of American Law 116–17 (1977); Miller, *supra* note 1, at 23; Novak, *supra* note 1, at 105–06; *see* Herbert Hovenkamp, Enterprise and American Law 36 (1991) [hereinafter Enterprise]; Herbert Hovenkamp, *The Classical Corporation in American Legal Thought*, 76 Geo. L.J. 1593, 1634 (1988) [hereinafter Classical].

45. Hurst, *supra* note 1, at 7, 15; Radicalism, *supra* note 1, at 320–21; Horwitz, *supra* note 44, at 112–13.

46. Dartmouth College v. Woodward, 17 U.S. (4 Wheat.) 518, 624–28 (1819); *id.* at 675, 702 (Story, J., concurring); Novak, *supra* note 1, at 296 n.123 (quoting Laws of Massachusetts, 1809); U.S. Const. art. I, § 10, cl. 1; G. Edward White, The Marshall Court and Cultural Change 612–28 (1991).

47. Charles River Bridge v. Warren Bridge Company, 36 U.S. (11 Pet.) 420, 547–48 (1837).

48. Hurst, *supra* note 1, at 21, 27; Gillman, *supra* note 1, at 34–36; Hofstadter, *supra* note 1, at 64–65; Classical, *supra* note 44, at 1634–35.

49. Benedict, *supra* note 1, at 320; 1 Tocqueville, *supra* note 1, at 252; Enterprise, *supra* note 44, at 3 (quoting Sedgwick); *see* Gillman, *supra* note 1, at 38.

50. Wynehamer v. The People, 13 N.Y. 378, 387 (1856); Hurst, *supra* note 1, at 11; Haywood v. Mayor and Aldermen of Savannah, 12 Ga. 404 (1853); Morton Keller, *Powers and Rights*, 74 J. Amn. Hist. 675, 681 (1987).

51. Pessen, *supra* note 1, at 81–87; Watson, *supra* note 1, at 33.

52. James M. McPherson, Ordeal By Fire 44, 111–12, 313 (1982) (quoting Greeley); *The Slavery Issue*, N.Y. Daily Times, June 5, 1856, at 4; Richard H. Sewell, Ballots for Freedom 292–93, 306–7 (1976) (quoting *Pennsylvania Weekly Telegraph*, June 20, 1860); *How Shall We Vote*, N.Y. Daily Times, Oct. 21, 1856, at 2; *Free Labor and the Press*, N.Y. Daily Times, June 5, 1856, at 4; Eric Foner, Reconstruction 28–29 (1988) (quoting Lincoln); William E. Forbath, *The Ambiguities of Free Labor*, 1985 Wis. L. Rev. 767, 773–76; *see* Eric Foner, Free Soil, Free Labor, Free Men 11–39 (1970).

CHAPTER THREE

1. Benjamin Franklin, *An Apology for Printers*, Pa. Gazette (June 10, 1731), *reprinted in* Freedom of the Press from Zenger to Jefferson 4, 5–6, 9 (Leonard W. Levy ed., 1996) [hereinafter Freedom]; *see* Leonard W. Levy, Emergence of a Free Press 86–87 (1985); Norman L. Rosenberg, Protecting the Best Men 30–31, 41 (1986). Additional helpful sources on the history of free expression include Arthur M. Schlesinger,

Prelude to Independence (1958); Bernard Schwartz, The Great Rights of Mankind (1977) [hereinafter Rights]; David A. Anderson, *The Origins of the Press Clause,* 30 U.C.L.A. L. Rev. 455 (1983); David N. Mayer, *The English Radical Whig Origins of American Constitutionalism,* 70 Wash. U. L.Q. 131 (1992); David M. Rabban, *The Ahistorical Historian,* 37 Stan. L. Rev. 795 (1985); The Complete Bill of Rights: The Drafts, Debates, Sources, and Origins (Neil H. Cogan ed., 1997) [hereinafter Cogan]; The Founders' Constitution (Philip B. Kurland & Ralph Lerner eds., 1987) [hereinafter Founders]; The Bill of Rights: A Documentary History (Bernard Schwartz ed., 1971) [hereinafter Documentary].

Other helpful sources include Willi Paul Adams, The First American Constitutions (2001); Joseph J. Ellis, Founding Brothers (2000); Edmund S. Morgan, Inventing the People (1988); Jack N. Rakove, Original Meanings (1996); Documents of American History (Henry Steele Commager ed., 9th ed. 1973) [hereinafter Commager]; The Records of the Federal Convention of 1787 (Max Farrand ed., 1966 reprint of 1937 rev. ed.) [hereinafter Farrand]; Great Issues in American History (Richard Hofstadter ed., 1982) [hereinafter Great]; The Federal and State Constitutions, Colonial Charters, and other Organic Laws of the United States (Ben Perley Poore ed., 2d ed. 1878) [hereinafter Poore]; The Anti-Federalist (Herbert J. Storing ed., 1-vol. abridgment, Murray Dry ed., 1985) [hereinafter Storing, Abridgment].

2. Jeremy Black, A History of the British Isles 178 (1997) (quoting George III); Michael Kent Curtis, Free Speech, "The People's Darling Privilege" 42–44 (2000) (quoting Wilkes); E.P. Thompson, The Making of English Working Class 69–71 (1963); Robert Hargreaves, The First Freedom 118–42 (2002).

3. Declaratory Act (Mar. 18, 1766), *reprinted in* 1 Commager, *supra* note 1, at 60, 61; The Stamp Act (Mar. 22, 1765), *reprinted in id.* at 53, 53–55; Resolutions of the Stamp Act Congress (Oct. 19, 1765), *reprinted in* 2 Great, *supra* note 1, at 7–10; Soame Jenyns, *The Objections to the Taxation . . . Consider'd* (1765), *reprinted in id.* at 10 (member of Parliament arguing Americans were virtually represented); Levy, *supra* note 1, at 87; Morgan, *supra* note 1, at 239–40; Schlesinger, *supra* note 1, at 68–70.

4. Declaration and Resolves of the First Continental Congress (Oct. 14, 1774), *reprinted in* 2 Great, *supra* note 1, at 26–29; The Boston Port Act (Mar. 31, 1774), *reprinted in* 1 Commager, *supra* note 1, at 71.

5. Schlesinger, *supra* note 1, at 145, 147, 214–17 (quoting *Massachusetts Spy,* Sept. 10, 1772; *Boston Gazette,* May 18, 1772; *Boston Gazette,* Jan. 6, 1772; *Boston Gazette,* Mar. 16, 1772); Levy, *supra* note 1, at 63, 87–88 (quoting Quincy).

6. Rosenberg, *supra* note 1, at 45 (quoting Hutchinson); Populus (Adams), *To the Printers,* Boston Gazette & Country J., Mar. 14, 1768, at 2; Schlesinger, *supra* note 1, at 95, 148 (quoting Thomas, Oct. 8, 1772).

7. Schlesinger, *supra* note 1, at 210–12, 216 (quoting *Pennsylvania Journal,* Feb. 22, 1775; May 17, 1775); Wilbur H. Siebert, The Loyalists of Pennsylvania 22–23 (1920); Claude H. Van Tyne, The Loyalists in the American Revolution 62–65 (1902); Robert W.T. Martin, The Free and Open Press 74–89 (2001).

8. Ellis, *supra* note 1, at 5; Rosenberg, *supra* note 1, at 52.

9. Freeborn American, *Messiers Edes & Gill, Please to Insert Following,* Boston Gazette, Mar. 9, 1767; Levy, *supra* note 1, at 155–56, 170.

10. Levy, *supra* note 1, at 176 (quoting Adams); Schlesinger, *supra* note 1, at 298 (quoting Hopkinson); William Bollan, *On Liberty of the Press* (excerpt from *The Freedom of Speech. . . ,* 1766), *reprinted in* Freedom, *supra* note 1, at 84–93.

11. Virginia Bill of Rights (1776), *reprinted in* 2 Poore, *supra* note 1, at 1908, 1909; Constitution of Pennsylvania (1776), *reprinted in id.* at 1540, 1542, 1547; Rights, *supra* note 1, at 71–73.

12. Constitution of Vermont (1777), *reprinted in* 2 Poore, *supra* note 1, at 1857, 1860; Levy, *supra* note 1, at 186–88; Dwight L. Teeter, *Press Freedom and the Public Printing,* 45 Journalism Q. 445, 446 (1968); The Federalist No. 84, at 510, 514–15 (Hamilton) (Clinton Rossiter ed., 1961) [hereinafter Federalist]; Rights, *supra* note 1, at 87.

13. Schlesinger, *supra* note 1, at 210; *Address to the Inhabitants of Quebec, reprinted in* Documentary, *supra* note 1, at 221, 223; 2 Great, *supra* note 1, at 26–27; Rights, *supra* note 1, at 87.

14. Delaware Declaration of Rights (1776), *reprinted in* Documentary, *supra* note 1, at 276, 278; Maryland Declaration of Rights (1776), *reprinted in id.* at 279, 284; Constitution of Massachusetts (1780), *reprinted in* 1 Poore, *supra* note 1, at 956, 959; Rights, *supra* note 1, at 87.

15. Van Tyne, *supra* note 7, at 327–29; Levy, *supra* note 1, at 177–82; Thomas Jefferson, *Notes on the State of Virginia* (1787; written in 1781–82), *reprinted in* Jefferson: Writings 123, 281 (Library of America 1984) [hereinafter Writings].

16. Levy, *supra* note 1, at 207, 209 (quoting *Independent Gazetteer,* Oct. 1, 1782; Oct. 15, 1782); Rabban, *supra* note 1, at 816; Dwight L. Teeter, *The Printer and the Chief Justice,* 45 Journalism Q. 235, 239 (1968); Respublica v. Oswald, 1 Dall. 319 (Pa. 1788), *reprinted in* 5 Founders, *supra* note 1, at 124 (reprinting Oswald's writing).

17. *Respublica,* 1 Dall., *reprinted in* 5 Founders, *supra* note 1, at 127; Levy, *supra* note 1, at 210–11; Rosenberg, *supra* note 1, at 62–63.

18. Constitution of Pennsylvania (1790), *reprinted in* 2 Poore, *supra* note 1, at 1548, 1554; Levy, *supra* note 1, at 211–12; Rosenberg, *supra* note 1, at 64–65.

19. James Wilson, The Works of James Wilson 278–80, 287, 313–14, 395–97 (James DeWitt Andrews ed., 1895 ed.).

20. Constitution of Massachusetts (1780), *reprinted in* 1 Poore, *supra* note 1, at 956, 959; Letter from William Cushing to John Adams (Feb. 18, 1789), *reprinted in* Freedom, *supra* note 1, at 147, 148–51; Letter from John Adams to William Cushing (Mar. 7, 1789), *reprinted in id.* at 152, 153; Levy, *supra* note 1, at 198–201; Rosenberg, *supra* note 1, at 67–68.

21. James Burgh, *Political Disquisitions* (1775), *reprinted in* 5 Founders, *supra* note 1, at 120; Bernard Bailyn, The Ideological Origins of the American Revolution 40–42, 132–33 (1967); Caroline Robbins, The Eighteenth-Century Commonwealthmen (1959); Mayer, *supra* note 1, at 169–74; Morgan, *supra* note 1, at 232.

22. Benjamin Franklin, An Account of the Supremest Court of Judicature in Pennsylvania, viz., The Court of the Press (Sept. 12, 1789), *reprinted in* 5 Founders, *supra* note 1, at 130–31.

23. Mark David Hall, The Political and Legal Philosophy of James Wilson 107–9 (1997).

24. 3 Farrand, *supra* note 1, at 599; 2 Farrand, *supra* note 1, at 334, 341–42, 587–88, 617–18.

25. U.S. Const. art. I, § 6, cl. 1; Constitution of Maryland (1776), *reprinted in* 1 Poore, *supra* note 1, at 817, 818; The Articles of Confederation, art. V. (1781).

26. Cincinnatus, No. 2, to James Wilson (Nov. 8, 1787), *reprinted in* 5 Founders, *supra* note 1, at 122; Herbert J. Storing, What the Anti-Federalists Were For 64–70 (1981); Akhil Reed Amar, *The Bill of Rights as a Constitution,* 100 Yale L.J. 1131–33, 1203–5 (1991); *e.g.,* Centinel, No. 2 (Oct. 24, 1787), *reprinted in* Cogan, *supra* note 1, at 103–4.

27. Federalist No. 84, at 513–14 (Hamilton); James Wilson, Speech at a Meeting in Philadelphia (Oct. 6, 1787), *reprinted in* Cogan, *supra* note 1, at 102; *see* Ellis, *supra* note 1, at 22, 60; Rakove, *supra* note 1, at 144.

28. Federal Farmer No. 4 (Oct. 12, 1787), Federal Farmer No. 16 (Jan. 20, 1788), *both reprinted in* Storing, Abridgment, *supra* note 1, at 54, 59, 79, 86.

29. Letters of a Countryman (Nov. 22, 1787), *reprinted in* Documentary, *supra* note 1, at 538, 539; Federalist No. 84, at 510–14 (Hamilton); A Citizen of New-York: An Address to the People of the State of New York (Apr. 15, 1787), *reprinted in* Cogan, *supra* note 1, at 101, 102.

30. Centinel, No. 2 (Oct. 24, 1787), *reprinted in* Cogan, *supra* note 1, at 103; *e.g.,* Mr. Dawson at Virginia Ratification Convention (June 24, 1788), *reprinted in id.* at 101; Patrick Henry at Virginia Ratification Convention (June 14, 1788), *reprinted in* Documentary, *supra* note 1, at 800.

31. Federal Farmer, No. 6 (Dec. 25, 1787), *reprinted in* Storing, Abridgment, *supra* note 1, at 65, 71.

32. Proposal by Madison in House (June 8, 1789), *reprinted in* Cogan, *supra* note 1, at 83; Congress, Amendments to the Constitution (June 8, 1789), *reprinted in* 5 Founders, *supra* note 1, at 128; Cogan, *supra* note 1, at 92–93; Levy, *supra* note 1, at 257, 261–62; Lucas A. Powe, Jr., The Fourth Estate and the Constitution 22–23 (1991). Madison admitted during the ratification debates that seeking amendments after ratification would be prudent. Letter from James Madison to Alexander Hamilton (June 22, 1788), *reprinted in* Documentary, *supra* note 1, at 848; *see* James Madison, Speech in the Virginia Ratifying Convention on Ratification and Amendments (June 24, 1788), *reprinted in* James Madison: Writings 401, 406–7 (Library of America 1999) [hereinafter Writings]. Only after ratification, however, did Madison promise to pursue amendments, and he did so partly to generate support in his Virginia campaign for a seat in the first House of Representatives. Letter from James Madison to George Eve (Jan. 2, 1789), *reprinted in* Writings, *supra,* at 427, 428; Paul Finkelman, *James Madison and the Bill of Rights,* 1990 S. Ct. 301, 322–36.

33. Constitution of Pennsylvania (1776), *reprinted in* 2 Poore, *supra* note 1, at 1540, 1542; Virginia Ratifying Convention (June 25, 1788), *reprinted in* Documentary, *supra* note 1, at 838–39.

34. House of Representatives, Amendments to the Constitution (June 8,

1789), *reprinted in* 5 Founders, *supra* note 1, at 20, 22, 26; Letter from Fisher Ames to Thomas Dwight (June 11, 1789), *reprinted in* Cogan, *supra* note 1, at 117, 117; House of Representatives, Amendments to the Constitution (Aug. 15, 1789), *reprinted in* 5 Founders, *supra* note 1, at 204.

35. Documentary, *supra* note 1, at 627–28, 658–73; Cogan, *supra* note 1, at 92–93; Anderson, *supra* note 1, at 471–72; Rabban, *supra* note 1, at 842.

36. Gordon S. Wood, The Creation of the American Republic 227 (1969); House of Representatives, Amendments to the Constitution (June 8, 1789), *reprinted in* 5 Founders, *supra* note 1, at 20, 26; Virginia Ratifying Convention, *reprinted in* Documentary, *supra* note 1, at 766, 818–19 (June 4, 1788; June 24, 1788).

37. House of Representatives, Amendments to the Constitution (June 8, 1789), *reprinted in* 5 Founders, *supra* note 1, at 20, 21–22; Letter from Abraham Baldwin to Joel Barlow (June 14, 1789), Letter from Pierce Butler to James Iredell (Aug. 11, 1789), *both reprinted in* Cogan, *supra* note 1, at 118.

38. House of Representatives, Amendments to the Constitution (Aug. 15, 1789), *reprinted in* 5 Founders, *supra* note 1, at 128–29, 200–204; Cogan, *supra* note 1, at 83–92; Rights, *supra* note 1, at 231–46; Documentary, *supra* note 1, at 1050; Anderson, *supra* note 1, at 478.

39. Congress, Amendments to the Constitution (June 8, 1789; Aug. 17, 1789), *reprinted in* 5 Founders, *supra* note 1, at 128–29; House Committee of Eleven Report (July 28, 1789), House Resolution (Aug. 24, 1789), Senate Resolution (Sept. 9, 1789), Agreed Resolution (Sept. 25, 1789), *all reprinted in* Cogan, *supra* note 1, at 84–87, 92; Documentary, *supra* note 1, at 1006, 1159; Anderson, *supra* note 1, at 483–85.

40. Senate Journal (Sept. 1789), *reprinted in* Documentary, *supra* note 1, at 1163–65; Levy, *supra* note 1, at 263–66; Documentary, *supra* note 1, at 1171–1203.

41. Levy, *supra* note 1, at 266 (quoting Jefferson); Federal Farmer, No. 6 (Dec. 25, 1787), *reprinted in* Storing, Abridgment, *supra* note 1, 65, 67; Letter from James Madison to George Eve (Jan. 2, 1789), *reprinted in* Writings, *supra* note 32, at 427, 428; Letter from Thomas Jefferson to James Madison (Mar. 15, 1789), *reprinted in* Writings, *supra* note 15, at 942, 943.

CHAPTER FOUR

1. James Roger Sharp, American Politics in the Early Republic 8, 40–41 (1993); *see* Stanley Elkins & Eric McKitrick, The Age of Federalism 68 (1993); Richard Hofstadter, The American Political Tradition 33 (1948). Other helpful sources on the development of democracy include Joyce Appleby, Capitalism and a New Social Order (1984); Erik W. Austin, Political Facts of the United States since 1789 (1986); Joseph J. Ellis, Founding Brothers (2000); Colleen A. Sheehan, *Madison v. Hamilton,* 98 Am. Pol. Sci. Rev. 405 (2004).

2. *See* Letter from Thomas Jefferson to John Taylor (June 4, 1798), *reprinted in* Thomas Jefferson: Writings 1048–49 (Library of America, 1984) [hereinafter Writings]; Sheehan, *supra* note 1, at 405. Helpful sources on the history of free expression include Michael Kent Curtis, Free Speech, "The People's Darling Privilege" (2000)

[hereinafter Free]; Robert Hargreaves, The First Freedom (2002); Leonard W. Levy, Emergence of a Free Press (1985); John C. Miller, Crisis in Freedom (1952); Norman L. Rosenberg, Protecting the Best Men (1986); James M. Smith, Freedom's Fetters (1956); David A. Anderson, *The Origins of the Press Clause,* 30 U.C.L.A. L. Rev. 455 (1983); James P. Martin, *When Repression Is Democratic and Constitutional,* 66 U. Chi. L. Rev. 117 (1999); Documents of American History (Henry Steele Commager ed., 9th ed. 1973) [hereinafter Commager]; The Founders' Constitution (Philip B. Kurland & Ralph Lerner eds., 1987) [hereinafter Founders]; Great Issues in American History (Richard Hofstadter ed., 1982) [hereinafter Great].

3. Elkins & McKitrick, *supra* note 1, at 93, 229; Thomas Jefferson, *Opinion on the Constitutionality of a National Bank* (Feb. 15, 1791), *reprinted in* Writings, *supra* note 2, at 416, 418; Hofstadter, *supra* note 1, at 14–15; Sharp, *supra* note 1, at 33–41; Sheehan, *supra* note 1, at 409–12.

4. Alexander Hamilton, *Opinion on the Constitutionality of the Bank* (Feb. 23, 1791), *reprinted in* 2 Great, *supra* note 2, at 164–69; *see* McCulloch v. Maryland, 17 U.S. (4 Wheat.) 316, 421 (1819) (upholding Congress's power to charter second national bank).

5. Sharp, *supra* note 1, at 95; Annals of Congress of the United States, 1793–1795, 3d Cong., 2d Sess. 789 (Nov. 1794) [hereinafter Annals]; Elkins & McKitrick, *supra* note 1, at 461–74; Sharp, *supra* note 1, at 93–98.

6. Sharp, *supra* note 1, at 86–87, 97 (quoting *General Advertiser,* Jan. 18, 1794); *Deodatus, No. II,* Columbian Centinel, Sept. 27, 1794, at 1; Annals, 1793–1795, 3d Cong., 2d Sess. 788 (Nov. 1794) (President Washington's address to both houses of Congress); Appleby, *supra* note 1, at 63; Elkins & McKitrick, *supra* note 1, at 451–61; Martin, *supra* note 2, at 124–38, 147–48, 156–57, 165.

7. Martin, *supra* note 2, at 139 n.71 (quoting *New York Gazette and General Advertiser,* Nov. 13, 1798); Respublica v. Montgomery, 1 Yeates 419 (Pa. 1795); Robert W.T. Martin, The Free and Open Press 139–41 (2001); Rosenberg, *supra* note 2, at 72–73; Sharp, *supra* note 1, at 100–103.

8. *Gracchus, No. II,* Indep. Gazetteer, July 26, 1794, at 1; *Gracchus, No. I,* Aurora Gen. Advertiser, Sept. 4, 1795, at 3; *Atticus, Letter VI, to the Freemen of the United States,* Indep. Gazetteer, Aug. 12, 1795, at 2; *Gracchus, No. II,* Aurora Gen. Advertiser, Sept. 9, 1795, at 2; Rosenberg, *supra* note 2, at 73–75; Sharp, *supra* note 1, at 123–24; Donald H. Stewart, The Opposition Press of the Federalist Period (1969); Anderson, *supra* note 2, at 507.

9. Sharp, *supra* note 1, at 70–74, 80, 113–39; *Gracchus, No. III,* Aurora Gen. Advertiser, Sept. 18, 1795, at 2 (reprinting essay from the *Petersburgh Intelligencer*); *Washington's Proclamation of Neutrality* (Apr. 22, 1793), *reprinted in* 1 Commager, *supra* note 2, at 162; *The Jay Treaty* (Nov. 19, 1794), *reprinted in id.,* at 165; Elkins & McKitrick, *supra* note 1, at 237, 308–11, 330–36, 388–96, 415–49.

10. Elkins & McKitrick, *supra* note 1, at 537–57, 571–75; Ellis, *supra* note 1, at 177–85, 195; Sharp, *supra* note 1, at 161–66, 171.

11. Elkins & McKitrick, *supra* note 1, at 571–75, 588–89, 597–99, 643–62; Sharp,

supra note 1, at 171–72; Smith, *supra* note 2, at 7–9; *see* Annals, 1797–1799, 5th Cong., 2d Sess. 1370–71, 1374–75 (Apr. 1798).

12. Elkins & McKitrick, *supra* note 1, at 605, 615–17 (quoting Gerry's Minutes of a Conference with the President, Mar. 26, 1799); Sharp, *supra* note 1, at 181, 239–40; *see Congress of the United States: House of Representatives Important Debate,* Fed. Gazette & Baltimore Daily Advertiser, Jan. 31, 1800, at 2.

13. Levy, *supra* note 2, at 213 (quoting McKean).

14. Smith, *supra* note 2, at 21 (quoting Sedwick, Mar. 7, 1798); Levy, *supra* note 2, at 280, 298–300 (quoting Hopkinson, 1798; Dwight, 1798; *Columbian Centinel,* Oct. 5, 1798); Rosenberg, *supra* note 2, at 75–78.

15. Annals, 1797–1799, 5th Cong., 2d Sess. 1991 (June 1798); Sharp, *supra* note 1, at 177 (quoting Hamilton); John Marshall to a Freeholder (Sept. 20, 1798), *reprinted in* 5 Founders, *supra* note 2, at 131; Annals, 1797–1799, 5th Cong., 2d Sess. 2016–18 (June 1798) (statements of John Wilkes Kittera and Harrison Gray Otis); Smith, *supra* note 2, at 105–11, 151.

16. Annals, 1797–1799, 5th Cong., 1st Sess. 429–30 (July 1797); An Act Respecting Alien Enemies (July 6, 1798), 1 Stat. 577–78; The Alien Friends Act (June 25, 1798), 1 Stat. 570; Naturalization Act of 1798 (June 18, 1798), 1 Stat. 566; Annals, 1797–1799, 5th Cong., 2d Sess. 1570–71, 1580, 1778 (May 1798).

17. The Sedition Act of 1798 (July 14, 1798), 1 Stat. 596–97.

18. Free, *supra* note 2, at 62; Smith, *supra* note 2, at 94–155; Geoffrey R. Stone, Perilous Times 15–78 (2004); Anderson, *supra* note 2, at 519–21; *see* Smith, *supra* note 2, at 21 (Hamilton equating Republicans with Tories).

19. Elkins & McKitrick, *supra* note 1, at 590–93; Levy, *supra* note 2, at 202, 280; Anderson, *supra* note 2, at 520–21.

20. Annals, 1797–1799, 5th Cong., 2d Sess. 2093–94 (July 1798).

21. Letter from Thomas Jefferson to John Taylor (June 4, 1798), *reprinted in* Writings, *supra* note 2, at 1048–50; Smith, *supra* note 2, at 101 (quoting Letter from Jefferson to Madison, June 7, 1798); Annals, 1797–1799, 5th Cong., 2d Sess. 2110 (July 1798). A sedition bill had been mentioned as early as April 1798. Smith, *supra* note 2, at 95–99, 131.

22. Annals, 1797–1799, 5th Cong., 2d Sess. 2110 (July 1798); Ellis, *supra* note 1, at 186, 198–99; Richard Hofstadter, The Idea of a Party System 209–10 (1969).

23. Annals, 1797–1799, 5th Cong., 2d Sess. 2139, 2151, 2153 (July 1798).

24. *Id.* at 2110, 2139, 2162, 2164; Levy, *supra* note 2, at 291. Throughout the 1790s, the masthead of the *Boston Gazette,* published by Benjamin Edes, stated: "A free Press maintains the Majesty of the People." *E.g.,* Boston Gazette & Country J., May 18, 1795, at 1. The term, "the Fourth Estate," did not emerge until 1820s England. David Lange, *The Speech and Press Clauses,* 23 U.C.L.A. L. Rev. 77, 89–91 & n.79 (1975).

25. Kentucky Resolutions (Nov. 10, 1798; Nov. 14, 1799), *reprinted in* 5 Founders, *supra* note 2, at 131, 131–33; *see* Thomas Jefferson, *Draft of the Kentucky Resolutions* (Oct. 1798), *reprinted in* Writings, *supra* note 2, at 449, 453 (language omitted from

the state resolution); Wayne D. Moore, Constitutional Rights and Powers of the People 241–42 (1996); Sharp, *supra* note 1, at 196–97.

26. Virginia Resolutions (Dec. 21, 1798), *reprinted in* 5 Founders, *supra* note 2, at 135–36; Sharp, *supra* note 1, at 196–98.

27. John Marshall, Report of the Minority on the Virginia Resolutions (Jan. 22, 1799), *reprinted in* 5 Founders, *supra* note 2, at 136–38. The editor of the online Founders' Constitution recently changed the designated author of the minority report from Marshall to Henry Lee. Kurt T. Lash & Alicia Harrison, *Minority Report: John Marshall and the Defense of the Alien and Sedition Acts,* 68 Ohio St. L.J. 435, 439 n.17 (2007). Nevertheless, a recent article shows that Marshall most likely wrote the report. *Id.* at 438–43.

28. The Legislature of Rhode Island on the Virginia Resolutions (Feb. 1799), *reprinted in* 2 Great, *supra* note 2, at 184–85; Sharp, *supra* note 1, at 200.

29. Elkins & McKitrick, *supra* note 1, at 703–11; Levy, *supra* note 2, at 203; Rosenberg, *supra* note 2, at 87–88; Smith, *supra* note 2, at 184–86; Anderson, *supra* note 2, at 515 & n.343.

30. Miller, *supra* note 2, at 104–5 (quoting *Porcupine's Gazette,* Jan. 10, 1799); Elkins & McKitrick, *supra* note 1, at 706–10; Smith, *supra* note 2, at 221–31 & nn.14–15; Free, *supra* note 2, at 80–82; *see* Hargreaves, *supra* note 2, at 185–86 (Federalists planned to prosecute first a renowned Republican publisher); Smith, *supra* note 2, at 231–32 (two attorneys were to represent Lyon, but inclement weather delayed them).

31. Miller, *supra* note 2, at 104–11 (quoting *Greenleaf's New Daily Advertiser,* Feb. 21, 1799); Elkins & McKitrick, *supra* note 1, at 710–11; Smith, *supra* note 2, at 225, 236–44.

32. United States v. Cooper, 25 F. Cas. 631, 632 (1800); Smith, *supra* note 2, at 185–86, 308–16; Anderson, *supra* note 2, at 519–21.

33. 25 F. Cas. at 634–38; Free, *supra* note 2, at 90; Smith, *supra* note 2, at 319–24.

34. 25 F. Cas. at 639–44; Smith, *supra* note 2, at 326–27; *see* Case of Fries, 9 F. Cas. 826, 829–30, 838–39 (C.C.D. Pa. 1799) (Iredell, J.).

35. James Madison, Address of the General Assembly to the People of the Commonwealth of Virginia (Jan. 23, 1799), reprinted in 5 Founders, *supra* note 2, at 139–40.

36. James Madison, *Report on the Alien and Sedition Acts* (Jan. 7, 1800), *reprinted in* James Madison: Writings 608, 619, 642–58 (Library of America 1999).

37. *Id.* at 647, 651; *see* Levy, *supra* note 2, at 197–98, 311–20; Rosenberg, *supra* note 2, at 93–94.

38. Hargreaves, *supra* note 2, at 180–81; Levy, *supra* note 2, at 297, 301.

39. The Sedition Act of 1798 (July 14, 1798), 1 Stat. 596–97; 25 F. Cas. at 642–43; Free, *supra* note 2, at 106; Levy, *supra* note 2, at 128, 201; Rosenberg, *supra* note 2, at 87–89; Smith, *supra* note 2, at 185–87, 417.

40. George Hay, An Essay on the Liberty of the Press (1799), *reprinted in* Two Essays on the Liberty of the Press 5, 21–25 (1803; 1970 reprint ed.) [hereinafter Hay, 1799]; Annals, 1797–1799, 5th Cong., 3d Sess. 3005–7, 3014 (Feb. 1799); *see* George Hay, An Essay on the Liberty of the Press (1803), *reprinted in* Two Essays

on the Liberty of the Press 28 (1803; 1970 reprint ed.); Rosenberg, *supra* note 2, at 87–88 (at least three state common law prosecutions occurred during the Sedition Act era).

41. Hay, 1799, *supra* note 40, at 23–24; Levy, *supra* note 2, at 313–14; Rosenberg, *supra* note 2, at 93–94.

42. Tunis Wortman, A Treatise Concerning Political Enquiry, and the Liberty of the Press 48, 118–19, 146 (1800; 1970 reprint ed.); *see id.* at 54 (linking antielitist individualism with the doctrine of moral sense).

43. *Id.* at 121, 157–58.

44. *Id.* at 36, 153–60, 168, 170, 177, 205, 253–60; *see* Levy, *supra* note 2, 331; Rosenberg, *supra* note 2, at 94.

45. Wortman, *supra* note 42, at 118–19, 199–202, 262.

46. John Thomson, An Enquiry Concerning the Liberty and Licentiousness of the Press 19–21, 60–61 (1801, 1970 reprint ed.); U.S. Const. art. I, § 6, cl. 1.

47. Thomson, *supra* note 46, at 11–12.

48. *Id.* at 16, 68, 79–84.

49. Elkins & McKitrick, *supra* note 1, at 647.

50. Smith, *supra* note 2, at 324 (quoting prosecutor's speech); Elkins & McKitrick, *supra* note 1, at 4, 77–79, 92–93, 547; Rosenberg, *supra* note 2, at 83–84.

51. Austin, *supra* note 1, at 53.

CHAPTER FIVE

1. Helpful sources on the history of free speech include Michael Kent Curtis, Free Speech, "The People's Darling Privilege" (2000) [hereinafter Free]; Donna L. Dickerson, The Course of Tolerance (1990); Leonard W. Levy, Emergence of a Free Press (1985); Norman L. Rosenberg, Protecting the Best Men (1986); Michael Kent Curtis, *Lincoln, Vallandigham, and Anti-War Speech in the Civil War,* 7 Wm. & Mary Bill Rts. J. 105 (1998) [hereinafter Lincoln]; Michael Kent Curtis, *The 1837 Killing of Elijah Lovejoy by an Anti-Abolition Mob,* 44 UCLA L. Rev. 1109 (1997) [hereinafter Lovejoy]; Michael Kent Curtis, *The Curious History of Attempts to Suppress Antislavery Speech, Press, and Petition in 1835–37,* 89 Nw. U. L. Rev. 785 (1995) [hereinafter Curious]; Michael Kent Curtis, *The 1859 Crisis over Hinton Helper's Book,* The Impending Crisis, 68 Chi.-Kent L. Rev. 1113 (1993) [hereinafter Hinton]; Gregory A. Mark, *Forgotten Constitutional History,* 97 Mich. L. Rev. 1673 (1999); Geoffrey R. Stone, *Abraham Lincoln's First Amendment,* 78 N.Y.U. L. Rev. 1 (2003); Documents of American History (Henry Steele Commager ed., 9th ed. 1973) [hereinafter Commager]; The Founders' Constitution (Philip B. Kurland & Ralph Lerner eds., 1987) [hereinafter Founders]; Freedom of the Press from Zenger to Jefferson (Leonard W. Levy ed., 1996) [hereinafter Freedom]; Freedom of the Press from Hamilton to the Warren Court (Harold L. Nelson ed., 1967) [hereinafter Nelson].

2. Helpful sources on the development of democracy in America include Erik W. Austin, Political Facts of the United States since 1789 (1986); Stanley Elkins & Eric McKitrick, The Age of Federalism (1993); William J. Novak, The People's Welfare

(1996); Edward Pessen, Jacksonian America (rev. ed. 1985); James Roger Sharp, American Politics in the Early Republic (1993); Alexis de Tocqueville, Democracy in America (Henry Reeve text, Francis Bowen revision, Phillips Bradley ed.; Vintage Books ed. 1990; French publication, 1835 & 1840); Harry L. Watson, Liberty and Power (1990); Gordon S. Wood, The Radicalism of the American Revolution (1991); The Federal and State Constitutions, Colonial Charters, and other Organic Laws of the United States (Ben Perley Poore ed., 2d ed. 1878) [hereinafter Poore].

3. Annals of Congress of the United States, 1799–1801, 6th Cong., 1st Sess. 409 (Jan. 1800) [hereinafter Annals].

4. Austin, *supra* note 2, at 53; Elkins & McKitrick, *supra* note 2, at 746–47; Sharp, *supra* note 2, at 247, 256.

5. Elkins & McKitrick, *supra* note 2, at 747–50 (quoting Sedgwick letter, Jan. 10, 1801; Hamilton letter, Jan. 16, 1801); Annals, 1799–1801, 6th Cong., 2d Sess. 1028–29 (Feb. 1801); Sharp, *supra* note 2, at 267–73.

6. James Monroe, Second Inaugural Address (Mar. 5, 1821); *cf.* Austin, *supra* note 2, at 53.

7. St. George Tucker, Blackstone's Commentaries: With Notes of Reference to the Constitution and Laws, of the Federal Government of the United States; and of the Commonwealth of Virginia (1803) [hereinafter Tucker]; James Madison, *Report on the Alien and Sedition Acts* (Jan. 7, 1800), *reprinted in* James Madison: Writings 608 (Library of America 1999); Paul Finkelman & David Cobin, *Introduction, in* 1 Tucker, *supra,* at i, xiii. Tucker explained his views on free expression in Appendix, Note D, and Appendix, Note G. St. George Tucker, Blackstone's Commentaries (1803), *reprinted in* 5 Founders, *supra* note 1, at 152, 157 n.* [hereinafter Tucker in Founders].

8. Tucker in Founders, *supra* note 7, at 152–57.

9. *Id.* at 157–58; Levy, *supra* note 1, at 326–27.

10. Thomas Jefferson, *First Inaugural Address* (Mar. 4, 1801), *reprinted in* Thomas Jefferson: Writings 492–93 (Library of America, 1984) [hereinafter Writings]; Letter from Thomas Jefferson to Abigail Adams (July 22, 1804), *reprinted in* Freedom, *supra* note 1, at 365 (on pardons); Zechariah Chafee, Jr., Freedom of Speech 29–30 (1920); Michael T. Gibson, *The Supreme Court and Freedom of Expression from 1791 to 1917,* 55 Fordham L. Rev. 263, 275 (1986).

11. Letter from Thomas Jefferson to Levi Lincoln (Mar. 24, 1802), *reprinted in* Freedom, *supra* note 1, at 360; Rosenberg, *supra* note 1, at 103–4.

12. Letter from Thomas Jefferson to Thomas McKean (Feb. 23, 1803), *reprinted in* Freedom, *supra* note 1, at 364.

13. Thomas Jefferson, *Second Inaugural Address* (Mar. 4, 1805), *reprinted in* Writings, *supra* note 10, at 518–22; Letter from Thomas Jefferson to Abigail Adams (Sept. 11, 1804), *reprinted in* Freedom, *supra* note 1, at 366, 367; Rosenberg, *supra* note 1, at 105.

14. Annals, 1799–1801, 6th Cong., 2d Sess. 939–40 (Jan. 1801); Rosenberg, *supra* note 1, at 103.

15. People v. Croswell, 3 Johns. Cas. 337 (N.Y. Sup. Ct. 1804), *reprinted in* 5 Founders, *supra* note 1, at 158, 158–59; Levy, *supra* note 1, at 338.

16. *Croswell,* 3 Johns. Cas. at 349; Dickerson, *supra* note 1, at 23–24.

17. *Croswell, reprinted in* 5 Founders, *supra* note 1, at 160; Rosenberg, *supra* note 1, at 112 (calling this the "truth-plus" approach).

18. 5 Founders, *supra* note 1, at 169; William Blackstone, 4 Commentaries on the Laws of England 150–53 (1769), *reprinted in* 5 Founders, *supra* note 1, at 119; Rosenberg, *supra* note 1, at 112. Kent did not carry a clear majority of the judges in *Croswell,* and ultimately, the prosecution was dropped. Free, *supra* note 1, at 113–14.

19. Letter from Thomas Jefferson to Thomas Seymour (Feb. 11, 1807), *reprinted in* Freedom, *supra* note 1, at 369; United States v. Hudson & Goodwin, 11 U.S. (7 Cranch) 32 (1812); Levy, *supra* note 1, at 274–79, 343–45; Rosenberg, *supra* note 1, at 104. The Republicans had also sought to use federal law to suppress the Federalists through the impeachment of Federalist judges, including most famously Supreme Court Justice Samuel Chase. Melvin I. Urofsky & Paul Finkelman, 1 A March of Liberty 199–201 (2d ed. 2002) (the House impeached, but the Senate acquitted).

20. Constitution of New York (1821), *reprinted in* 2 Poore, *supra* note 2, at 1341, 1347; Levy, *supra* note 1, at 339–40; Rosenberg, *supra* note 1, at 115–18. State constitutions with relatively clear language included Constitution of Ohio (1851), *reprinted in* 2 Poore, *supra* note 2, at 1465, 1466; Constitution of California (1849), *reprinted in* 1 Poore, *supra* note 2, at 195. Ambiguous constitutional provisions included Constitution of Arkansas (1836), Constitution of Illinois (1848), *both reprinted in id.* at 101–2, 449, 467; *see* Rosenberg, *supra* note 1, at 301 n.37, 302 n.43. For cases following *Croswell,* see Castle v. Houston, 19 Kan. 417 (1877); Perkins v. Mitchell, 31 Barb. 461 (N.Y. Sup. 1860); Commonwealth v. Morris, 3 Va. 176 (1811).

21. Updegraph v. Commonwealth, 11 Serg. & Rawle 394 (Pa. 1824), *reprinted in* 5 Founders, *supra* note 1, at 170, 173; *see* Respublica v. Dennie, 4 Yeates 267 (1805); Constitution of Pennsylvania (1790), *reprinted in* 2 Poore, *supra* note 2, at 1548, 1554.

22. Commonwealth v. Blanding, 3 Pick. 304 (Mass. 1825), *reprinted in* 5 Founders, *supra* note 1, at 176–78; *see* Commonwealth v. Clap, 4 Mass. 163, 168–70 (1808).

23. Constitution of New York (1821), Constitution of New Jersey (1844), *both reprinted in* 2 Poore, *supra* note 2, at 1314, 1341, 1347; Constitution of Arkansas (1836), Constitution of California (1849), *both reprinted in* 1 Poore, *supra* note 2, at 101–2, 195; *Blanding,* 3 Pick. at 315 n.1 (reporting postcase legislation); Levy, *supra* note 1, at 342–43; Rosenberg, *supra* note 1, at 108; Margaret A. Blanchard, *Filling in the Void, in* The First Amendment Reconsidered 14, 18–19 (Bill F. Chamberlin & Charlene J. Brown eds., 1982).

24. James Kent, 2 Commentaries on American Law 13–14, 19–22 (1827; Legal Classics Library Reprint).

25. Joseph Story, 3 Commentaries on the Constitution §§ 1874–86 (1833), *reprinted in* 5 Founders, *supra* note 1, at 182–83.

26. *Id.* at 184. For similar views, see Nathaniel Chipman, Principles of Government; A Treatise on Free Institutions 104–5 (1833); William Rawle, A View of the Constitution of the United States of America 124 (2d ed. 1829).

27. 1 Tocqueville, *supra* note 2, at 184; Williams Printing Co. v. Saunders, 73 N.E.

472, 475 (Va. 1912); *Morris,* 3 Va.; Free, *supra* note 1, at 111; Dickerson, *supra* note 1, at 34; Rosenberg, *supra* note 1, at 120, 140–42.

28. Cincinnati Gazette Co. v. Timberlake, 10 Ohio St. 548, 555 (1860); Dickerson, *supra* note 1, at 57–61; Rosenberg, *supra* note 1, at 120–34.

29. Mark A. Graber, *Antebellum Perspectives on Free Speech,* 10 Wm. & Mary Bill Rts. J. 779, 781–86 (2002); Mark, *supra* note 1, at 1688–90.

30. Rosenberg, *supra* note 1, at 130 (quoting Duane, July 4, 1834); 1 Tocqueville, *supra* note 2, at 183 (quoting *Vincenne's Gazette*); James M. Smith, Freedom's Fetters 277–306 (1956); Watson, *supra* note 2, at 13.

31. Alfred Stunt v. The Steamboat Ohio, 3 Ohio Dec. Rep. 362 (1855); Ex Parte Hickey, 12 Miss. 751, 758–59 (1845).

32. 1 Tocqueville, *supra* note 2, at 263–64; Dickerson, *supra* note 1, at 43–46.

33. Constitution of Ohio (1851), *reprinted in* 2 Poore, *supra* note 2, at 1465, 1465 n.*; Constitution of California (1849), *reprinted in* 1 Poore, *supra* note 2, at 195, 195 n.*.

34. Final Form of the "Jew Bill" (1826), *reprinted in* The Jews of the United States, 1790–1840, A Documentary History 53 (Joseph Blau & Salo Barron eds., 1963); State v. Chandler, 2 Del. 553, 555 (1837); Constitution of Maryland (1776), *reprinted in* 1 Poore, *supra* note 2, at 817, 820; Jon Butler, Awash in a Sea of Faith 284–85 (1990); Pessen, *supra* note 2, at 33–52; Rogers M. Smith, Civic Ideals 173–96 (1997). On blasphemy, see City Council of Charleston v. Benjamin, 33 S.C.L. 508 (1848); Commonwealth v. Kneeland, 37 Mass. 206 (1838); People v. Ruggles, 8 Johns. R. 290 (N.Y. 1811); Leonard W. Levy, Blasphemy 400–23 (1993).

35. Bryan v. Walton, 14 Ga. 185, 206–7 (1853); Bob v. State, 32 Ala. 560, 565 (1858); *Dred Scott,* 60 U.S. (19 How.) 393, 404–5 (1857); Jacob D. Wheeler, A Practical Treatise on the Law of Slavery 190–200 (1837; 1968 reprint ed.); *see* Mark V. Tushnet, The American Law of Slavery, 1810–1860 (1981). Other helpful sources regarding slavery and abolition include Clement Eaton, Freedom of Thought in the Old South (1940; 1951 reprint); Paul Finkelman, Slavery in the Courtroom (1985) [hereinafter Courtroom]; William W. Freehling, The Road to Disunion (1990); William Lee Miller, Arguing about Slavery (1996); Russel B. Nye, Fettered Freedom (1972 ed.); W. Sherman Savage, The Controversy over the Distribution of Abolition Literature (1938; 1968 reprint); Richard H. Sewell, Ballots for Freedom (1976); James Brewer Stewart, Holy Warriors (1976); Larry E. Tise, Proslavery (1987). Helpful accounts of the Civil War include Robert S. Harper, Lincoln and the Press (1951); Frank L. Klement, The Limits of Dissent (1970); James M. McPherson, Battle Cry of Freedom (1988); Peter J. Parish, The American Civil War (1975).

36. Tise, *supra* note 35, at 286; The American Anti-Slavery Society: Constitution (Dec. 4, 1833), *reprinted in* 1 Commager, *supra* note 1, at 278, 279; Ferenc M. Szasz, *Antebellum Appeals to the "Higher Law,"* 110 Essex Inst. Hist. Collections 33, 45 (1974) (quoting Garrison); Stewart, *supra* note 35, at 11–12, 23–29, 35–51, 78–81; *e.g.,* Thomas Jefferson, *Notes on the State of Virginia* (1787), *reprinted in* Writings, *supra* note 10, at 123, 288–89; 2 Tucker, *supra* note 7, Appendix, Note H, at 31–85; *see* Nye, *supra* note 35, at 199–200; Wood, *supra* note 2, at 186–87.

37. Dickerson, *supra* note 1, at xiv (quoting *Commercial Advertiser*); McPherson,

supra note 35, at 8; Miller, *supra* note 35, at 29; Parish, *supra* note 35, at 28–31. For contemporary essays for and against abolition and slavery, see Agitation for Freedom (Donald G. Mathews ed., 1972) [hereinafter Agitation]; Abolitionism (Bernard A. Weisberger ed., 1963); Cotton is King and Pro-Slavery Arguments (E.N. Elliott, ed., 1860; 1968 reprint ed.); Slavery Defended (Eric L. McKitrick ed., 1963). *See generally* Tise, *supra* note 35 (emphasizing Northern responsibility for proslavery arguments).

38. James G. Birney, *Narrative of the Late Riotous Proceedings Against the Liberty of the Press, in Cincinnati* (1836), *reprinted in* Nelson, *supra* note 1, at 179, 183–84; Dickerson, *supra* note 1, at 115–17; Nye, *supra* note 35, at 194–204; Stewart, *supra* note 35, at 64–66.

39. Nye, *supra* note 35, at 129–31, 193–94 (quoting the *Republican*); Birney, *supra* note 38, at 181–82; Dickerson, *supra* note 1, at 118–19.

40. Birney, *supra* note 38, at 188–90.

41. Stewart, *supra* note 35, at 84; Birney, *supra* note 38, at 192–93; *cf.* Derrick A. Bell, *Brown v. Board of Education and the Interest-Convergence Dilemma,* 93 Harv. L. Rev. 518 (1980).

42. Nye, *supra* note 35, at 145–47 & n.93; Dickerson, *supra* note 1, at 122–25; Courtroom, *supra* note 35, at 147–48; *see* Lovejoy, *supra* note 1, at 1110.

43. Dickerson, *supra* note 1, at 128; Lovejoy, *supra* note 1, at 1145–46, 1157; Courtroom, *supra* note 35, at 149; *see, e.g., The Alton Murderers,* New Bedford Mercury, Nov. 24, 1837, at 2.

44. *From New York American,* Hudson River Chron., Nov. 28, 1837, at 2; Lovejoy, *supra* note 1, at 1145–59; Stewart, *supra* note 35, at 72–76 (quoting Phillips); *From New York Observer,* Farmer's Cabinet, Dec. 1, 1837, at 3 (Lovejoy defended "liberty of the press" and "personal freedom"); Nye, *supra* note 35, at 152–53.

45. Courtroom, *supra* note 35, at 149; Dickerson, *supra* note 1, at 128–33; Lovejoy, *supra* note 1, at 1146–47; *e.g., Office of the Missouri Argus, Nov. 9, 1837,* Richmond Enquirer, Nov. 21, 1837, at 2.

46. *Horrible Outrage Mob Law and Bloodshed,* Barre Gazette, Nov. 24, 1837, at 2; Dickerson, *supra* note 1, at 92, 131–32; Virginia Laws of 1832, 1836, 1848, *reprinted in* Nelson, *supra* note 1, at 173–77; From a Letter Signed "Appomattox," Richmond Enquirer (Feb. 4, 1832), *reprinted in id.* at 170, 171; Nye, *supra* note 35, at 153–59, 177, 179; Freehling, *supra* note 35, at 99.

47. Stewart, *supra* note 35, at 68–70; Dickerson, *supra* note 1, at 86–87; Letter of Kendall to Huger (Aug. 4, 1835), *reprinted in* Nelson, *supra* note 1, at 212–13; Courtroom, *supra* note 35, at 171; Miller, *supra* note 35, at 93–94.

48. William Leggett, No Twopenny Postmaster Should Judge What Should be Circulated (Aug. 12, 1835), Andrew Jackson, Mailing Inflammatory Appeals to the Passions of Slaves Should be Stopped by Law (Dec. 7, 1835), *both reprinted in* Nelson, *supra* note 1, at 211–17; Dickerson, *supra* note 1, at 88 (quoting Jackson); Miller, *supra* note 35, at 97–98; Nye, *supra* note 35, at 69–70; Pessen, *supra* note 2, at 172; Stephan Thernstrom, 1 A History of the American People 323 (2d ed. 1989).

49. Motion and Remarks on that Portion of the President's Message Concern-

ing the Incendiary Publications of the Abolitionists (Dec. 21, 1835), *reprinted in* XIII The Papers of John C. Calhoun 7, 8 (Clyde N. Wilson ed., 1980); Miller, *supra* note 35, at 98; Watson, *supra* note 2, at 116–22; Curious, *supra* note 1, at 823–24.

50. Report from the Select Committee on the Circulation of Incendiary Publications (Feb. 4, 1836), *reprinted in* XIII The Papers of John C. Calhoun 53–60 (Clyde N. Wilson ed., 1980); Bill from the Select Committee on the Circulation of Incendiary Publications (Feb. 4, 1836), *reprinted in id.* at 67–68; *see* Cong. Globe, 24th Cong., 1st Sess. 165 (Feb. 4, 1836).

51. South Carolina Resolutions on Abolitionist Propaganda (Dec. 16, 1835), *reprinted in* 1 Commager, *supra* note 1, at 280; Dickerson, *supra* note 1, at 93–94, 104–7; Miller, *supra* note 35, at 103–5; Nye, *supra* note 35, at 80–84; Curious, *supra* note 1, at 813–16, 837.

52. Alvan Stewart, *Response to the Message of Governor Marcy* (Feb. 1836), *reprinted in* Writings and Speeches of Alvan Stewart on Slavery 59 (1860); Curious, *supra* note 1, at 839–44; Freehling, *supra* note 35, at 294; Nye, *supra* note 35, at 72–74.

53. Freehling, *supra* note 35, at 310, 321; Miller, *supra* note 35, at 65–93, 105–8, 306–9; Nye, *supra* note 35, at 42–43, 47; Stewart, *supra* note 35, at 81–83; Mark, *supra* note 1, at 1694.

54. Cong. Globe, 24th Cong., 1st Sess. 24–25 (Dec. 16, 1835).

55. *Id.* at 27 (Dec. 18, 1835).

56. *Id.* at 75 (Jan. 7, 1836); Freehling, *supra* note 35, at 312–13; 12 Cong. Deb. 10 (Jan. 11, 1836); *id.* at 478–79, 482 (Feb. 12, 1836); Miller, *supra* note 35, at 31–32.

57. 12 Cong. Deb. 10 479, 482 (Feb. 12, 1836); Cong. Globe, 24th Cong., 1st Sess. 247–48 (Mar. 11, 1836); *see id.* at 239 (Mar. 9, 1836); Freehling, *supra* note 35, at 325; Miller, *supra* note 35, at 119.

58. Cong. Globe, 24th Cong., 1st Sess. 165 (Feb. 4, 1836); *id.* at 171–72 (Feb. 8, 1836); Freehling, *supra* note 35, at 328–29; Miller, *supra* note 35, at 142–43, 204.

59. Cong. Globe, 24th Cong., 1st Sess. 469 (May 18, 1836); Freehling, *supra* note 35, at 329–30, 332 (quoting Virginian Henry Wise); Miller, *supra* note 35, at 144–46, 221–22.

60. Miller, *supra* note 35, at 199 (quoting Adams, Feb. 20, 1832); Cong. Globe, 24th Cong., 1st Sess. 39–40 (Dec. 21, 1835); Mark, *supra* note 1, at 1694; *see* Cong. Globe, 27th Cong., 2d Sess. 202 (Feb. 2, 1842) (Adams opposing abolitionism).

61. Cong. Globe, 24th Cong., 1st Sess. 498–99 (May 25, 1836); *id.* at 505–6 (May 26, 1836).

62. Cong. Globe, 26th Cong., 1st Sess. 150 (Jan. 28, 1840); *id.* at 130 (Jan. 20, 1840); *id.* at 133 (Jan. 22, 1840); *id.* at 151 (Jan. 28, 1840); Freehling, *supra* note 35, at 343–49; Miller, *supra* note 35, at 369–70.

63. Cong. Globe, 27th Cong., 2d Sess. 168 (Jan. 24, 1842).

64. *Id.* at 168 (Jan. 24, 1842); *id.* at 169 (Jan. 25, 1842); Miller, *supra* note 35, at 431.

65. Miller, *supra* note 35, at 433–34, 443–44 (quoting Weld); Cong. Globe, 27th Cong., 2d Sess. 205 (Feb. 3, 1842); *id.* at 214–15 (Feb. 7, 1842); *id.* at 170 (Jan. 25, 1842); *id.* at 200 (Feb. 2, 1842). The House rescinded the gag rule on December 3, 1844, partly because Northern Democrats now aligned more with other Northerners

rather than with Southern Democrats. Cong. Globe, 28th Cong., 2d Sess. 7 (Dec. 3, 1844); Miller, *supra* note 35, at 480–82.

66. Hinton Rowan Helper, The Impending Crisis of the South (1857; George M. Fredrickson ed., 1968); Eaton, *supra* note 35, at 223–24; Courtroom, *supra* note 35, at 188–91; Sewell, *supra* note 35, at 317–18; Hinton, *supra* note 1, at 1142–64.

67. Nelson, *supra* note 1, at 229; Harper, *supra* note 35, at 117 (quoting *New York Daily News,* May 1864); *Freedom of the Press,* American Annual Cyclopaedia and Register of Important Events (1867), *reprinted in* Nelson, *supra* note 1, at 222–23; Dickerson, *supra* note 1, at 141–86; Harper, *supra* note 35, at 229–32; *see* McPherson, *supra* note 35, at 287–90 (Lincoln's suspension of habeas corpus).

68. Lincoln, *supra* note 1, at 119.

69. Stone, *supra* note 1, at 5, 9–16 (quoting Burnside); Ex parte Vallandigham, 28 F. Cas. 874, 875, 921, 925 (C.C.D. Ohio 1863); Klement, *supra* note 35, at 150; *see* Lincoln, *supra* note 1, at 129 (Burnside's and Vallandigham's counsels "either assumed the President had not suspended the [habeas] writ in Ohio or did not rely on its suspension").

70. Stone, *supra* note 1, at 14–18 (quoting *Chicago Times,* May 27, 1863); Burnside Orders and President Lincoln Remands the Suppression of the *Chicago Times* (1863), *reprinted in* Nelson, *supra* note 1, at 230, 231 [hereinafter Burnside]; Klement, *supra* note 35, at 178–81; Lincoln, *supra* note 1, at 136–37, 145, 155 (quoting *Cincinnati Commercial,* May 6, 1863; *New York Evening Post,* May 16, 1863); Harper, *supra* note 35, at 259–61; McPherson, *supra* note 35, at 597; Lincoln, *supra* note 1, at 132–45.

71. Lincoln, *supra* note 1, at 142; Klement, *supra* note 35, at 181 (quoting *Harper's Weekly,* May 30, 1863); Burnside, *supra* note 70, at 231; Stone, *supra* note 1, at 19 (quoting Letter from Lincoln to Erastus Corning and Others, June 12, 1863); President Lincoln Commands the Arrest and Imprisonment of Proprietors of the *New York World* and *New York Journal of Commerce* (1864), *reprinted in* Nelson, *supra* note 1, at 232–47.

72. Dickerson, *supra* note 1, at 88; Sewell, *supra* note 35, at 284; Hinton, *supra* note 1, at 1147, 1151.

73. Nelson, *supra* note 1, at 4; Nye, *supra* note 35, at 227; 12 Cong. Deb. 1152 (Apr. 2, 1836); *id.* at 1108 (Apr. 7, 1836); Eaton, *supra* note 35, at 25–26.

74. Freehling, *supra* note 35, at 342–43 (quoting Adams); Pessen, *supra* note 2, at 165–67; Watson, *supra* note 2, at 87–92; Sean Wilentz, The Rise of American Democracy 294–95 (2005).

75. Cong. Globe, 26th Cong., 1st Sess. 150 (Jan. 28, 1840); John C. Calhoun, *Speech On the Reception of Abolition Petitions, Delivered in the Senate* (Feb. 6, 1837), *in* 2 The Works of John C. Calhoun 625, 630–32 (1851).

76. John C. Calhoun, *A Disquisition on Government, in* 1 The Works of John C. Calhoun 1–2, 54–59 (1854).

77. Theodore Dwight Weld, *American Slavery as It Is* (1839), *reprinted in* Agitation, *supra* note 37, at 54–66.

78. Lovejoy, *supra* note 1, at 1143 (quoting Channing, 1835); *see* Alvan Stewart, *Response to the Message of Governor Marcy* (Feb. 1836), *reprinted in* Writings and Speeches

of Alvan Stewart on Slavery 59–85 (1860) (abolitionist arguing that mob violence contravened republican democratic government).

79. Letter from William Ellery Channing to James G. Birney (Nov. 1, 1836), *reprinted in* Nelson, *supra* note 1, at 193–97.

80. *Id.* at 199–200.

81. Frederick Grimke, The Nature and Tendency of Free Institutions 396–400, 436 (1848; 1968 ed., John William Ward ed.); John William Ward, *Introduction, in* Grimke, *supra,* at 2–4; Rosenberg, *supra* note 1, at 145. When George Sidney Camp published his book *Democracy* in 1841, the publisher and the author both claimed it was the first theoretical explanation of democracy written by an American. George Sidney Camp, Democracy iii, 11 (1841). Camp did not explicitly discuss free expression.

82. *Cf.* Morris R. Cohen, Law and the Social Order 196 (1933).

83. Andrew Jackson, First State of the Nation Address (Dec. 1829). During the petition crisis, Massachusetts representative Caleb Cushing relied on republican democracy to argue for a broad free expression. 12 Cong. Deb. 2326–31 (Jan. 25, 1836); *see id.* at 2334–36 (Virginian James Garland responding to Cushing); *cf.* T.R. Sullivan, Letters Against the Immediate Abolition of Slavery 41–42 (Boston 1835) (William Sullivan relying on republican democracy to argue for a narrow free expression).

CHAPTER SIX

1. Bruce Ackerman, We the People: Transformations 161, 455 n.3 (1998); William Lee Miller, Arguing about Slavery 8 (1996). Helpful sources on the postbellum development of democracy and related issues include Erik W. Austin, Political Facts of the United States since 1789 (1986); Lynn Dumenil, The Modern Temper (1995); John Gerring, Party Ideologies in America, 1828–1996 (1998); Howard Gillman, The Constitution Besieged (1993); Richard Hofstadter, The American Political Tradition (1948); Morton Keller, Affairs of State (1977); Alexander Keyssar, The Right to Vote (2000); Samuel Lubell, The Future of American Politics (3d ed., revised, 1965); Michael E. McGerr, The Decline of Popular Politics (1986); William Preston, Jr., Aliens and Dissenters (1963); Rogers M. Smith, Civic Ideals (1997); Stephen Steinberg, The Ethnic Myth (1989 ed.); Frank Tariello, Jr., The Reconstruction of American Political Ideology, 1865–1917 (1982); Stephan Thernstrom, A History of the American People (2d ed. 1989); Robert H. Wiebe, Self-Rule (1995) [hereinafter Rule]; Robert H. Wiebe, The Search for Order, 1877–1920 (1967) [hereinafter Order]; William M. Wiecek, The Lost World of Classical Legal Thought (1998); Dorothy Ross, *The Liberal Tradition Revisited and the Republican Tradition Addressed, in* New Directions in American Intellectual History 116 (John Higham & Paul K. Conkin eds., 1979); Documents of American History (Henry Steele Commager ed., 9th ed. 1973) [hereinafter Commager]; Great Issues in American History (Richard Hofstadter ed., 1982) [hereinafter Great]; The Statistical History of the United States from Colonial Times to the Present (1965) [hereinafter Statistical].

2. Arthur Bestor, *The American Civil War as a Constitutional Crisis,* 69 Am. Hist. Rev. 327, 348 (1964) (quoting Douglas); Pamela Brandwein, Reconstructing Recon-

struction 26–29, 39 (1999) [hereinafter Reconstructing]; Eric Foner, Reconstruction 231–32, 242 (1988); James M. McPherson, Battle Cry of Freedom 213–16 (1988); William E. Nelson, The Fourteenth Amendment 61 (1988); Pamela Brandwein, *Slavery as an Interpretive Issue in the Reconstruction Congresses,* 34 Law & Soc'y Rev. 315, 328–29, 350–51 (2000) [hereinafter Slavery]; Robert J. Kaczorowski, *Revolutionary Constitutionalism in the Era of the Civil War and Reconstruction,* 61 N.Y.U. L. Rev. 863, 877–78 (1986); *see* Eric Foner, Free Soil, Free Labor, Free Men 156–57 (1970) [hereinafter Free]; James M. McPherson, Ordeal by Fire (1982) [hereinafter Ordeal]; Richard M. Valelly, The Two Reconstructions (2004).

3. Nelson, *supra* note 2, at 123–45; Reconstructing, *supra* note 2, at 23.

4. Foner, *supra* note 2, at 28–29, 231, 234, 242–44 (quoting Greeley); The Civil Rights Act (Apr. 9, 1866), § 1, 14 Stat. 27; Slavery, *supra* note 2, at 326, 342; Black Code of Mississippi (1865), *reprinted in* 1 Commager, *supra* note 1, at 452; Free, *supra* note 2, at 11–39; Charles W. McCurdy, *The "Liberty of Contract" Regime in American Law, in* The State and Freedom of Contract 161, 167–68 (Harry N. Scheiber ed., 1998); Herbert Hovenkamp, *The Political Economy of Substantive Due Process,* 40 Stan. L. Rev. 379, 395 (1988) [hereinafter Political]. Other helpful sources discussing labor, liberty of contract, industrialization, and related issues include Richard F. Bensel, The Political Economy of American Industrialization, 1877–1900 (2000); Melvyn Dubofsky, The State and Labor in Modern America (1994); Philip S. Foner, I History of the Labor Movement in the United States (1947); John A. Garraty, The New Commonwealth (1968); Samuel P. Hays, The Response to Industrialism, 1885–1914 (1957); Paul Le Blanc, A Short History of the U.S. Working Class (1999); Karen Orren, Belated Feudalism (1991); Kim Voss, The Making of American Exceptionalism (1993); Michael Les Benedict, *Laissez-Faire and Liberty,* 3 Law & Hist. Rev. 293 (1985); David E. Bernstein, *Lochner Era Revisionism, Revised,* 92 Geo. L.J. 1 (2003); William E. Forbath, *The Shaping of the American Labor Movement,* 102 Harv. L. Rev. 1109 (1989) [hereinafter Shaping]; William E. Forbath, *The Ambiguities of Free Labor,* 1985 Wis. L. Rev. 767 [hereinafter Ambiguities]; Howard Gillman, *How Political Parties Can Use the Courts to Advance Their Agendas,* 96 Am. Pol. Sci. Rev. 511 (2002); Arthur F. McEvoy, *Freedom of Contract, Labor, and the Administrative State, in* The State and Freedom of Contract 198 (Harry N. Scheiber ed., 1998).

5. Nelson, *supra* note 2, at 68 (quoting Martindale); Cong. Globe, 39th Cong., 1st Sess. 2766 (May 23, 1866); Andrew Johnson, State of the Union (Dec. 4, 1865); Gillman, *supra* note 1, at 8–9, 59.

6. Thomas M. Cooley, The General Principles of Constitutional Law in the United States of America 202 (1880); Nelson, *supra* note 2, at 8–10, 82–91, 104–9, 150–51.

7. McCurdy, *supra* note 4, at 168.

8. U.S. Const. amend. XIV, § 1; Cong. Globe, 39th Cong., 1st Sess. 1757 (Apr. 4, 1866); *id.* at 1781 (Apr. 5, 1866); Cong. Globe, 40th Cong., 2d Sess. Appendix 352 (June 11, 1868) (Yates); *id.* at 2463 (May 14, 1868) (Bingham); Cong. Globe, 39th Cong., 1st Sess. 2542 (May 10, 1866) (Bingham); Foner, *supra* note 2, at 231, 245.

9. Cong. Globe, 39th Cong., 1st Sess. 1151 (Mar. 2, 1866); Cong. Globe, 39th Cong., 2d Sess. 252 (Jan. 3, 1867); Foner, *supra* note 2, at 231–37, 246, 409; McPherson, *supra*

note 2, at 841–42; Smith, *supra* note 1, at 299–304; Valelly, *supra* note 2, at 25–26; McCurdy, *supra* note 4, at 168.

10. Cong. Globe, 40th Cong., 3d Sess. 1299 (Feb. 17, 1869); Plessy v. Ferguson, 163 U.S. 537, 544 (1896); *id.* at 552 (Harlan, J., dissenting); Smith, *supra* note 1, at 303–4; Steinberg, *supra* note 1, at 173–76, 191–99; Herbert Hovenkamp, *The Cultural Crises of the Fuller Court,* 104 Yale L.J. 2309, 2337–43 (1995).

11. The Reconstruction Act (Mar. 2, 1867), § 5, 14 Stat. 428; Cong. Globe, 39th Cong., 2d Sess. 252 (Jan. 3, 1867) (Stevens); Foner, *supra* note 2, at 231, 277, 448; Valelly, *supra* note 2, at 23–24.

12. Cong. Globe, 40th Cong., 3d Sess. 1623–26 (Feb. 26, 1869); *id.* at 979 (Feb. 8, 1869); Foner, *supra* note 2, at 448–49.

13. Foner, *supra* note 2, at 426–27, 446–48; Keyssar, *supra* note 1, at 106, 363–89; Ordeal, *supra* note 2, at 543–46.

14. The Ku Klux Klan Act (Apr. 20, 1871), § 1, 17 Stat. 13; Austin, *supra* note 1, at 53, 54; Foner, *supra* note 2, at 512; Keller, *supra* note 1, at 181; Ordeal, *supra* note 2, at 585–86.

15. Gillman, *supra* note 4, at 516; Keller, *supra* note 1, at 146–47, 559 (quoting 1881 Maryland Republican platform); Richard F. Bensel, Yankee Leviathan 11 (1991); Derrick Bell, Race, Racism, and American Law 34–44 (2d ed. 1980); Foner, *supra* note 2, at 486–87, 496–99, 524–29; Gerring, *supra* note 1, at 15.

16. Keyssar, *supra* note 1, at 106–8; Foner, *supra* note 2, at 444, 570, 577; William Cohen & Jonathan D. Varat, Constitutional Law 1160 (11th ed. 2001); Ordeal, *supra* note 2, at 594.

17. Foner, *supra* note 2, at 575–82; Ordeal, *supra* note 2, at 599–604.

18. Foner, *supra* note 2, at 584, 587 (quoting *Philadelphia Evening Bulletin,* Jan. 11, 1882); Civil Rights Cases, 109 U.S. 3, 10–12, 25 (1883).

19. Keyssar, *supra* note 1, at 112–15 (quoting future Senator Carter Glass); Smith, *supra* note 1, at 383, 605 n.110; Valelly, *supra* note 2, at 121–48; *see, e.g.,* Austin, *supra* note 1, at 244–357.

20. Keyssar, *supra* note 1, at 178–79, 186; Smith, *supra* note 1, at 314–16, 339–41.

21. McGerr, *supra* note 1, at 45–51 (quoting Adams; Shearman); Keyssar, *supra* note 1, at 45–46, 105–29 (quoting Parkham); Smith, *supra* note 1, at 347–409.

22. McGerr, *supra* note 1, at 52–65 (quoting Adams, 1876; Theodore Dwight Woolsey, 1878); Foner, *supra* note 2, at 527; Austin, *supra* note 1, at 378; Hofstadter, *supra* note 1, at 176–79.

23. Austin, *supra* note 1, at 378–79; John Higham, Strangers in the Land 97–98 (1992 ed.); Keyssar, *supra* note 1, at 138; McGerr, *supra* note 1, at 63; *see* Lubell, *supra* note 1, at 51.

24. Ambiguities, *supra* note 4, at 807; Wiecek, *supra* note 1, at 10.

25. Gillman, *supra* note 1, at 63; Manufactures of the United States in 1860; Compiled From the Original Returns of the Eighth Census 729 (1865); Ordeal, *supra* note 2, at 24, 183, 372–73.

26. Bensel, *supra* note 4, at xviii–xix, 5–10; Garraty, *supra* note 4, at 9; Wiecek,

supra note 1, at 71; *see* Theda Skocpol, Protecting Soldiers and Mothers 1–2, 7, 65 (1992).

27. Gillman, *supra* note 4, at 516; Dubofsky, *supra* note 4, at 2; Statistical, *supra* note 1, at 415; Garraty, *supra* note 4, at 89, 90–95, 181; Hays, *supra* note 4, at 11, 48–49; Thernstrom, *supra* note 1, at 433; Wiecek, *supra* note 1, at 65; Herbert Hovenkamp, *The Classical Corporation in American Legal Thought*, 76 Geo. L.J. 1593, 1641–42 (1988).

28. Bensel, *supra* note 4, at 314–15, 320; Statistical, *supra* note 1, at 139, 428, 480–81, 483–84, 572; Garraty, *supra* note 4, at 81, 86; Hays, *supra* note 4, at 7–8.

29. Statistical, *supra* note 1, at 74, 401–2, 409; The Statistics of the Wealth and Industry of the United States; Compiled From the Original Returns of the Ninth Census 392 (1872); Compiled From 1900 Census; Bensel, *supra* note 4, at 19–100.

30. Garraty, *supra* note 4, at 78 (quoting David A. Wells, Economic Changes (1889)); Statistical, *supra* note 1, at 7, 14; *see* Frederick Jackson Turner, *The Significance of the Frontier in American History* (July 12, 1893).

31. Bensel, *supra* note 4, at 207–8; Steinberg, *supra* note 1, at 36–38. Additional sources on xenophobia, nativism, and immigration include E.P. Hutchinson, Legislative History of American Immigration Policy, 1798–1965 (1981); Matthew Frye Jacobson, Whiteness of a Different Color (1998); Desmond King, Making Americans (2000).

32. U.S. Immigration Commission (Chair: Senator William P. Dillingham), *Dictionary of Races or Peoples* 33 (Dec. 5, 1910) (printed 1911) [hereinafter Dictionary]; Austin, *supra* note 1, at 470; Robert T. Handy, A History of the Churches in the United States and Canada 312 (1977); Higham, *supra* note 23, at 59–61.

33. Turner v. Williams, 194 U.S. 279, 291, 294 (1904); Act of Mar. 3, 1875, 18 Stat. 477; U.S. Bureau of Immigration, Annual Report of the Commissioner-General of Immigration (1923), *reprinted in* 2 Commager, *supra* note 1, at 315; Hutchinson, *supra* note 31, at 405–7, 478–81; Jacobson, *supra* note 31, at 41–43; Preston, *supra* note 1, at 4, 23.

34. Dictionary, *supra* note 32, at 2, 74, 82–83, 100, 129; Jacobson, *supra* note 31, at 21 (quoting Laughlin); Howard M. Sachar, A History of the Jews in America 321, 324 (1992) (quoting Coolidge); Immigration Act of Feb. 5, 1917, 39 Stat. 874; Hutchinson, *supra* note 31, at 167.

35. Higham, *supra* note 23, at 235; King, *supra* note 31, at 89, 91 (quoting Wilson, 1916; America First Campaign, 1917); Steinberg, *supra* note 1, at 44–48.

36. Horace M. Kallen, *Democracy versus the Melting Pot*, Nation, Feb. 25, 1915; King, *supra* note 31, at 27, 124 (quoting Wilson); Higham, *supra* note 23, at 235–63.

37. Richard T. Ely, Studies in the Evolution of Industrial Society 18 (1903; 1971 reprint ed.); Keller, *supra* note 1, at 373; *see* Rule, *supra* note 1, at 134; Wiecek, *supra* note 1, at 71.

38. 2 Cong. Rec., Appendix at 393, 43d Cong., 1st Sess., (June 9, 1874); Free, *supra* note 2, at 19 (quoting Henry C. Carey).

39. George E. McNeill, *Progress of the Movement From 1861 to 1886*, *in* The Labor

Movement 124, 161 (George E. McNeill ed., 1887; 1971 reprint) [hereinafter Today]; Ambiguities, *supra* note 4, at 768–69 & n.3, 805–8; *Co-operative Stories in New York,* N.Y. Times, Aug. 13, 1867, at 2; Dubofsky, *supra* note 4, at 1–35.

40. Terence V. Powderly, *The Organization of Labor,* 135 N. Am. Rev. 118, 125–26 (1882); Le Blanc, *supra* note 4, at 47 (quoting Knights' executive board, 1886); Preamble of the Constitution of the Knights of Labor (Jan. 1, 1878), *reprinted in* 1 Commager, *supra* note 1, at 546, 547; *Co-operative Stories in New York,* N.Y. Times, Aug. 13, 1867, at 2; Shaping, *supra* note 4, at 1121–22, 1204–5; Dubofsky, *supra* note 4, at 4, 14; Foner, *supra* note 4, at 433–38; Hays, *supra* note 4, at 36–37; Voss, *supra* note 4, at 187–228.

41. Dubofsky, *supra* note 4, at 4; Statistical, *supra* note 1, at 99; Gillman, *supra* note 1, at 84; Le Blanc, *supra* note 4, at 46; Wiecek, *supra* note 1, at 75.

42. Wiecek, *supra* note 1, at 85–86 (quoting Brewer, 1893); Le Blanc, *supra* note 4, at 48–49; Preston, *supra* note 1, at 25–26; Voss, *supra* note 4, at 78–79; Howard Zinn, A People's History of the United States 263–66 (1980).

43. Le Blanc, *supra* note 4, at 48–51 (quoting *Preamble;* Gompers); Philip S. Foner, III History of the Labor Movement in the United States 195–281 (1964); Hays, *supra* note 4, at 63–65; Keller, *supra* note 1, at 396–97; Shaping, *supra* note 4, at 1122–24, 1205.

44. Charles Darwin, The Origin of Species (1859); Theodore Dwight Bozeman, Protestants in an Age of Science 172 (1977); Richard Hofstadter, Social Darwinism in American Thought 24–30 (1944; 1992 ed.) [hereinafter Darwinism]; Robert Scoon, *The Rise and Impact of Evolutionary Ideas, in* Evolutionary Thought in America 4, 19 (Stow Persons ed., 1956).

45. Laurence R. Veysey, The Emergence of the American University 9, 12, 58 (1965); Political, *supra* note 4, at 381; Robert Stevens, Law School 40 (1983) (quoting James Barr Ames); Stephen M. Feldman, American Legal Thought from Premodernism to Postmodernism 83–105 (2000); *e.g.,* C.C. Langdell, Cases on Contracts (2d ed. 1879).

46. G. Edward White, The Marshall Court and Cultural Change 6 (1991); Dorothy Ross, *Modernist Social Science in the Land of the New/Old, in* Modernist Impulses in the Human Sciences 171, 177 (Dorothy Ross ed., 1994); Ely, *supra* note 37, at 4, 10–11.

47. Leading postbellum constitutional law treatise writers dealt ambivalently with natural rights. Thomas M. Cooley, A Treatise on the Constitutional Limitations Which Rest Upon the Legislative Power of the States of the American Union 21–25, 35 (1868; Da Capo Press reprint ed. 1972) (natural rights protected only if adopted as positive law); Feldman, *supra* note 45, at 101–5.

48. Cooley, *supra* note 47, at 28, 160, 168, 353–54, 573–74 (quoting Webster).

49. *Id.* at 129, 175, 391–93; *see* People v. Salem, 20 Mich. 452 (1870) (Judge Cooley).

50. Andrew Jackson, *Bank Veto Message* (July 10, 1832), *reprinted in* 2 Great, *supra* note 1, at 291, 294–95; Robert S. McElvaine, The Great Depression 198–99 (1984); Skocpol, *supra* note 26, at 18–21.

51. Gillman, *supra* note 1, at 63–64; Rule, *supra* note 1, at 115–16.

52. 15 The American and English Encyclopaedia of Law 969 (David S. Garland & Lucius P. McGehee eds., 2d ed. 1900); 17 Cong. Rec., 49th Cong., 1st Sess. 8030 (Aug. 5, 1886).

53. Grover Cleveland, Fourth Annual Message (Dec. 3, 1888); Benjamin Harrison, First Annual Message (Dec. 3, 1889), *reprinted in* 1 The Legislative History of the Federal Antitrust Laws and Related Statutes 60 (Earl W. Winter ed., 1978); George E. McNeill, *The Problem of To-day, in* Today, *supra* note 39, at 454, 462; Dubofsky, *supra* note 4, at 21.

54. George E. McNeill, *Labor Legislation, in* Today, *supra* note 39, at 172, 173–79; Shaping, *supra* note 4, at 1219–20, 1237–43; McCurdy, *supra* note 4, at 173.

55. The Interstate Commerce Act (Feb. 4, 1887), 24 Stat. 379; 17 Cong. Rec., Appendix at 458, 49th Cong., 1st Sess., (July 21, 1886); 21 Cong. Rec., 51st Cong., 1st Sess. 2457, 2462 (Mar. 21, 1890); The Sherman Anti-Trust Act (July 2, 1890), 26 Stat. 209; Wabash, St. Louis & Pac. Ry. Co. v. Illinois, 118 U.S. 557 (1886); Garraty, *supra* note 4, at 115–20; Keller, *supra* note 1, at 422–29.

56. Cong. Globe, 39th Cong., 1st Sess. 2783 (May 23, 1866); Benedict, *supra* note 4, at 309 (quoting Wells, 1875; Tribune, 1891); 17 Cong. Rec., 49th Cong., 1st Sess. 3762–63 (Apr. 23, 1886); 20 Cong. Rec., 50th Cong., 2d Sess. 1459 (Feb. 4, 1889).

57. Darwinism, *supra* note 44, at 45 (quoting Rockefeller).

58. William Graham Sumner, What the Social Classes Owe To Each Other 47, 103–4 (1883; 1966 ed.); Charles Dunbar, *Economic Science in America,* 122 N. Am. Rev. 124, 129 (Jan. 1876); Amasa Walker, *Labor and Capital in Manufactures,* 4 Scribners Monthly 460, 463, 465 (Aug. 1872); F.W. Taussig, 2 Principles of Economics 429 (2d ed. 1915); Francis Bowen, American Political Economy 19, 85–86 (1890); Mike Hawkins, Social Darwinism in European and American Thought 115 (1997); Darwinism, *supra* note 44, at 48–49, 61–62; Wiecek, *supra* note 1, at 74–76; Political, *supra* note 4, at 385–90, 418–19.

59. Cooley, *supra* note 47, at 165, 393; Gillman, *supra* note 1, at 55–59; *see* Cooley, Constitutional Limitations (4th ed. 1878).

60. Christopher G. Tiedeman, A Treatise on the Limitations of Police Power in the United States vi–vii, 4, 10 (1886; Da Capo Press ed. 1971). Francis Wharton leaned closer to Tiedeman's than Cooley's views on laissez-faire. Francis Wharton, Commentaries on Law 681, 711–13 (1884; 2001 reprint ed.).

61. Benedict, *supra* note 4, at 301; Ambiguities, *supra* note 4, at 790–91.

62. Statistical, *supra* note 1, at 572; Jerold S. Auerbach, Labor and Liberty 15 (1966); Orren, *supra* note 4, at 2–4, 15–16, 112; Skocpol, *supra* note 26, at 1, 7, 65; Benedict, *supra* note 4, at 301–2; McEvoy, *supra* note 4, at 205, 223.

63. Taussig, *supra* note 58, at 163, 166.

64. Wiecek, *supra* note 1, at 187; Richard Hofstadter, The Age of Reform 7–8 (1955); Michael Kazin, The Populist Persuasion 33 (1995); American Populism xvi, 85–86 (George McKenna ed., 1974) [hereinafter McKenna]. Other helpful sources on Populism and Progressivism include Maxwell Bloomfield, Peaceful Revolution (2000); John Chambers, The Tyranny of Change (2d ed. 1992); Charles Forcey, The

Crossroads of Liberalism (1961); William E. Leuchtenburg, The Perils of Prosperity, 1914–1932 (1958); Arthur S. Link & Richard L. McCormick, Progressivism (1983); James R. Hackney, Jr., *The Intellectual Origins of American Strict Products Liability,* 39 Am. J. Legal Hist. 443 (1995).

65. Hofstadter, *supra* note 64, at 64; People's Party Platform (1892), *reprinted in* McKenna, *supra* note 64, at 88, 92 [hereinafter Platform]; Kazin, *supra* note 64, at 27–28, 33, 38, 40; Link & McCormick, *supra* note 64, at 17.

66. Platform, *supra* note 65, at 89–90; Hofstadter, *supra* note 64, at 62; Kazin, *supra* note 64, at 17–25; McKenna, *supra* note 64, at 86.

67. Platform, *supra* note 65, at 91; Chambers, *supra* note 64, at 42; Kazin, *supra* note 64, at 30–32, 42; Order, *supra* note 1, at 97–102.

68. William Jennings Bryan, The Cross of Gold, *reprinted in* McKenna, *supra* note 64, at 130–32; Hofstadter, *supra* note 64, at 83, 104–9 (quoting Watson); Kazin, *supra* note 64, at 33–43; Chambers, *supra* note 64, at 147–48; Gerring, *supra* note 1, at 193, 204–6, 221–31; Order, *supra* note 1, at 98–105.

69. Herbert Croly, The Promise of American Life 138 (1909); Lincoln Steffens, *Shame of the Cities* (1904), *reprinted in* Great, *supra* note 1, at 237, 239; Statistical, *supra* note 1, at 500; Hofstadter, *supra* note 64, at 198–214.

70. Walter Lippmann, Drift and Mastery 82, 147–51 (1914; 1961 reprint ed.) [hereinafter Drift]; Croly, *supra* note 69, at 22; Walter Lippmann, A Preface to Politics 12, 42–44 (1914; 1962 reprint).

71. Roscoe Pound, *Mechanical Jurisprudence,* 8 Colum. L. Rev. 605 (1908); Roscoe Pound, *A Theory of Social Interests,* 15 Am. Soc. Soc'y 16, 32–33, 44–45 (1920); Ely, *supra* note 37, at 405–11; Drift, *supra* note 70, at 99; *The Progressive Party Platform* (Aug. 5, 1912), *reprinted in* 2 Commager, *supra* note 1, at 73–75 [hereinafter Party]; Hackney, *supra* note 64, at 462–63.

72. Hofstadter, *supra* note 64, at 142–43, 164 (quoting Brandeis); Croly, *supra* note 69, at 20, 199; Walter E. Weyl, The New Democracy 237–38 (1912); Forcey, *supra* note 64, at xiii.

73. Thorstein Veblen, The Theory of Business Enterprise 28–29 (1904); Woodrow Wilson, *First Inaugural Address* (Mar. 4, 1913), *reprinted in* 2 Commager, *supra* note 1, at 82, 83; Hofstadter, *supra* note 1, at 254 (quoting Wilson, 1912); Roscoe Pound, *Liberty of Contract,* 18 Yale L.J. 454, 466 (1909); Ernst Freund, Standards of American Legislation 68 (1917); Roscoe Pound, *Common Law and Legislation,* 21 Harv. L. Rev. 383, 384 (1908) [hereinafter Common]; Ely, *supra* note 37, at 408.

74. Ely, *supra* note 37, at 404–5; Croly, *supra* note 69, at 24; *see* Clayton Anti-Trust Act (Oct. 15, 1914), 38 Stat. 730; Chambers, *supra* note 64, at 71, 181, 194–97, 288.

75. Theodore Roosevelt, *Speech before the Ohio Constitutional Convention* (Feb. 21, 1912), *reprinted in* 2 Commager, *supra* note 1, at 66, 67; Editors, The New Republic, Nov. 9, 1914, at 3 (vol. 1, no. 1); Forcey, *supra* note 64, at 3–4, 188.

76. Ely, *supra* note 37, at 12; Croly, *supra* note 69, at 4, 199; Hofstadter, *supra* note 1, at 174–86, 229 (quoting Roosevelt); Wilson, *supra* note 73, at 83; Winthrop S. Hudson & John Corrigan, Religion in America 303 (5th ed. 1992) (Roosevelt at

convention); Chambers, *supra* note 64, at 17–19, 105–9; Link & McCormick, *supra* note 64, at 23–47.

77. Josiah Strong, *Our Country* (1886), *reprinted in* William G. McLoughlin, The American Evangelicals 194, 205 (1968); Chambers, *supra* note 64, at 144–45; Joseph R. Gusfield, Symbolic Crusade (1963).

78. Party, *supra* note 71, at 74; Dumenil, *supra* note 1, at 53; *see* Edward A. Ross, The Old World in the New (1914) (Progressive condemnation of immigrants); William Allen White, The Old Order Changeth 12–31 (1910) (on city machines).

79. *The New Party*, N.Y. Times, July 22, 1910, at 6; Keyssar, *supra* note 1, at 197–200 (quoting Olympia Brown); Link & McCormick, *supra* note 64, at 35–36, 53–55.

80. Dred Scott v. Sandford, 60 U.S. (19 How.) 393 (1857); *e.g.,* Cong. Globe, 39th Cong., 1st Sess. 41–42 (Dec. 13, 1865); *see* Foner, *supra* note 2, at 258; Nelson, *supra* note 2, at 122.

81. Foner, *supra* note 2, at 232 (quoting Sumner); Cong. Globe, 39th Cong., 1st Sess. 342 (Jan. 22, 1866); *id.* at 2538 (May 10, 1866); Nelson, *supra* note 2, at 104–9.

82. Cooley, Constitutional Limitations 334 (3d ed. 1874); Ku Klux Klan Act (Apr. 20, 1871), 17 Stat. 13; Habeas Corpus Act (Feb. 5, 1867), 14 Stat. 385; Habeas Corpus Act (May 11, 1866), 14 Stat. 46; Civil Rights Act (Apr. 9, 1866), 14 Stat. 27; Gillman, *supra* note 1, at 62, 69; Shaping, *supra* note 4, at 1129–30; Gillman, *supra* note 4, at 512–19.

83. The Removal Act (Mar. 3, 1875), 18 Stat. 470; Austin, *supra* note 1, at 10–11, 50–54; Deborah J. Barrow et al., The Federal Judiciary and Institutional Change 28–30 (1996); Gillman, *supra* note 4, at 513–20.

84. G. Edward White, The Constitution and the New Deal 36 (2000); Niagara Fire Ins. Co. v. Cornell, 110 F. 816, 821–25 (D. Neb. 1901); Lawton v. Steele, 152 U.S. 133, 137 (1894) (means-ends nexus); Gillman, *supra* note 1, at 54–55; Shaping, *supra* note 4, at 1221; Stephen A. Siegel, *Lochner Era Jurisprudence and the American Constitutional Tradition,* 70 N.C. L. Rev. 1, 60–62 (1991).

85. *Slaughterhouse,* 83 U.S. (16 Wall.) 36, 61–64, 71–81 (1873); Slavery, *supra* note 2, at 353–55.

86. *Slaughterhouse,* 83 U.S. at 87, 101, 109–10 (Field, J., dissenting).

87. *Id.* at 110 & n.* (Field, J., dissenting) (quoting Smith, 1776); Benedict, *supra* note 4, at 318–19; Slavery, *supra* note 2, at 356.

88. *Slaughterhouse,* 83 U.S. at 116 (Bradley, J., dissenting); *id.* at 124–28 (Swayne, J., dissenting); Nelson, *supra* note 2, at 160–64.

89. *Butchers' Union,* 111 U.S. 746, 751 (1883); *id.* at 757, 759 (Field, J., concurring); *id.* at 762 (Bradley, J., concurring); Nelson, *supra* note 2, at 165–77; McEvoy, *supra* note 4, at 211.

90. *In re Jacobs,* 98 N.Y. 98, 104–7, 115 (1885); Godcharles v. Wigeman, 113 Pa. 431, 437 (1886).

91. *Allgeyer,* 165 U.S. 578, 589–91 (1897) (quoting Powell v. Pennsylvania, 127 U.S. 678, 684 (1888)).

92. Lochner v. New York, 198 U.S. 45, 53–64 (1905); *id.* at 67–73 (Harlan, J., dis-

senting); *id.* at 75–76 (Holmes, J., dissenting); Gillman, *supra* note 1, at 127–29; White, *supra* note 84, at 246–51; Bernstein, *supra* note 4, at 23–26.

93. *Chicago, Burlington, & Quincy Ry.,* 200 U.S. 561, 584–85 (1906); *Adair,* 208 U.S. 161, 175 (1908); Bunting v. Oregon, 244 U.S. 590 (1917); Owen M. Fiss, Troubled Beginnings of the Modern State 15–19 (1993).

94. Gillman, *supra* note 4, at 512; James B. Thayer, *The Origin and Scope of the American Doctrine of Constitutional Law,* 7 Harv. L. Rev. 129, 144 (1893); Wiecek, *supra* note 1, at 135, 158.

95. Shaping, *supra* note 4, at 1133, 1154–55, 1220–22, 1237–49; *see* Orren, *supra* note 4, at 112; McCurdy, *supra* note 4, at 165–67.

96. *Lochner,* 198 U.S. 45, 59 (1905); Brief for Defendant in Error, at 1–113, Muller v. Oregon, 208 U.S. 412 (1908), *reprinted in* 16 Landmark Briefs and Arguments of the Supreme Court of the United States: Constitutional Law 63–178; Party, *supra* note 71, at 74; *see* Common, *supra* note 73, at 404.

CHAPTER SEVEN

1. Helpful sources on the history of free expression during this period include Margaret A. Blanchard, Revolutionary Sparks (1992) [hereinafter Sparks]; Mark A. Graber, Transforming Free Speech (1991); William Preston, Jr., Aliens and Dissenters (1963); David M. Rabban, Free Speech in Its Forgotten Years (1997) [hereinafter Forgotten]; Norman L. Rosenberg, Protecting the Best Men (1986); Howard Zinn, A People's History of the United States (1980); Margaret A. Blanchard, *Filling in the Void, in* The First Amendment Reconsidered 14 (Bill F. Chamberlin & Charlene J. Brown eds., 1982) [hereinafter Void]; Michael T. Gibson, *The Supreme Court and Freedom of Expression from 1791 to 1917,* 55 Fordham L. Rev. 263 (1986); David M. Rabban, *The IWW Free Speech Fights and Popular Conceptions of Free Expression before World War I,* 80 Va. L. Rev. 1055 (1994) [hereinafter Fights]; David M. Rabban, *The Free Speech League, the ACLU, and Changing Conceptions of Free Speech in American History,* 45 Stan. L. Rev. 47 (1992) [hereinafter League]; G. Edward White, *Justice Holmes and the Modernization of Free Speech Jurisprudence,* 80 Cal. L. Rev. 391 (1992); Freedom of the Press from Hamilton to the Warren Court (Harold L. Nelson ed., 1967) [hereinafter Nelson]; The Federal and State Constitutions, Colonial Charters, and other Organic Laws of the United States (Ben Perley Poore ed., 2d ed. 1878) [hereinafter Poore].

2. Cong. Globe, 39th Cong., 1st Sess. 1066 (Feb. 27, 1866) (Iowa Republican Hiram Price); *Slaughterhouse,* 83 U.S. (16 Wall.) 36, 123 (1873) (Bradley, J., dissenting); *Cruikshank,* 25 F. Cas. 707, 714–15 (C.C.D. La. 1874) (Bradley, Circuit Justice), aff'd, 92 U.S. (2 Otto) 542, 552–55 (1876); Cong. Globe, 39th Cong., 1st Sess. 2765 (May 23, 1866) (Senator Jacob Howard saying proposed fourteenth amendment would apply Bill of Rights to states); Pamela Brandwein, Reconstructing Reconstruction 12, 68–74 (1999); *see* Bryan H. Wildenthal, *The Lost Compromise,* 61 Ohio St. L.J. 1051 (2000).

3. William W. Van Alstyne, *A Critical Guide to* Ex Parte McCardle, 15 Ariz. L. Rev.

229, 236 n.42 (1973) (quoting *Vicksburg Times,* Nov. 6, 1867); An Act to Amend (Feb. 5, 1867), § 1, 14 Stat. 385, 386; An Act to Amend (Mar. 27, 1868), § 2, 15 Stat. 44; Ex parte McCardle, 74 U.S. (7 Wall.) 506 (1869); Mark A. Graber, *Antebellum Perspectives on Free Speech,* 10 Wm. & Mary Bill Rts. J. 779, 795–96 (2002); *e.g.,* Constitution of Texas (1868), *reprinted in* 1 Poore, *supra* note 1, at 1801; Morton v. State, 3 Tex. App. 510 (1878).

4. Nicola Beisel, Imperiled Innocents 3–12 (1998); Donna I. Dennis, *Obscenity Law and the Conditions of Freedom in the Nineteenth-Century United States,* 27 Law & Soc. Inquiry 369, 371–76, 384, 393–95 (2002); League, *supra* note 1, at 55–57; *see* Paul S. Boyer, Purity in Print (1968); William J. Novak, The People's Welfare 149–89 (1996); Frederick F. Schauer, The Law of Obscenity 10–12 (1976); *e.g.,* 2 Mich. Laws 1542, ch. 185, § 5868 (1857); Code of Va. 740, title 54, ch. 192, § 11 (1873).

5. Beisel, *supra* note 4, at 3; Sparks, *supra* note 1, at 15–18; Boyer, *supra* note 4, at 2–8; Heywood Broun & Margaret Leech, Anthony Comstock 36–40 (1927); Forgotten, *supra* note 1, at 28.

6. An Act for the Suppression of Trade in, and Circulation of, Obscene Literature and Articles of Immoral Use (Mar. 3, 1873), 17 Stat. 598, §§ 1–2; Beisel, *supra* note 4, at 25–48; Alison M. Parker, Purifying America (1997); Dennis, *supra* note 4, at 384–85. Congress amended the statute in 1876 to strengthen the proscription against mailing obscene materials. 19 Stat. 90 (July 12, 1876).

7. Anthony Comstock, Traps for the Young 131–36 (1883; 1967 reprint ed.); Forgotten, *supra* note 1, at 27–31; Boyer, *supra* note 4, at 12, 16–17; Sparks, *supra* note 1, at 16–22; League, *supra* note 1, at 89, 93.

8. Commonwealth v. Sharpless, 2 Serg. & R. 91, 102 (Pa. 1815); Commonwealth v. Landis, 8 Phila. 453 (1870), *reprinted in* Edward De Grazia, Censorship Landmarks 41, 42 (1969); People v. Muller, 96 N.Y. 408, 410–13 (1884) (citing *Hicklin,* 3 L.R.-Q.B. 360 (1868)); Commonwealth v. Holmes, 17 Mass. 336 (1821) (upholding common law obscenity indictment); Novak, *supra* note 4, at 149–89; Dennis, *supra* note 4, at 382–83; *cf.,* Lynn Dumenil, The Modern Temper 144 (1995) (on "the Victorian worldview").

9. Knowles v. United States, 170 F. 409, 411–12 (8th Cir. 1909); *see* Ex parte Jackson, 96 U.S. 727 (1878) (upholding federal statute restricting mailing of lottery advertisements and, in dictum, approving Comstock Act); United States v. Britton, 7 F. 731, 733 (S.D. Ohio 1883) (bad tendency test).

10. Strohm v. People, 160 Ill. 582, 585, 43 N.E. 622 (1896) (upholding indictment; not requiring detailed specification of obscenity); Commonwealth v. McCance, 164 Mass. 162, 165–66 (1895) (quashing indictment for lack of specificity); United States v. Bennett, 24 F. Cas. 1093, 1094 (C.C.S.D. N.Y. 1879) (public record should not reproduce obscenity); Boyer, *supra* note 4, at 10; Forgotten, *supra* note 1, at 30–31.

11. Thomas M. Cooley, Constitutional Limitations 422, 438–39 (1868; Da Capo Press reprint ed. 1972). Among treatise writers, neither Theodore Schroeder nor Francis Wharton became professors. *See* Herbert Hovenkamp, *The Political Economy of Substantive Due Process,* 40 Stan. L. Rev. 379, 396 (1988). Original sources related to

free expression include John W. Burgess, Political Science and Comparative Constitutional Law (1890); Ernst Freund, The Police Power (1904); Theodore Schroeder, "Obscene" Literature and Constitutional Law (1911; 1972 reprint ed.); Theodore Schroeder, Free Speech for Radicals (1916) [hereinafter Radicals]; Christopher G. Tiedeman, A Treatise on the Limitations of Police Power in the United States (1886; Da Capo Press reprint ed. 1971); Francis Wharton, Commentaries on Law, Embracing Chapters on the Nature, the Source, and the History of Law; on International Law, Public and Private; and on Constitutional and Statutory Law (1884; 2001 reprint ed.); John W. Burgess, *Private Corporations From the Point of View of Political Science*, 13 Pol. Sci. Q. 201 (1898) [hereinafter Private]; Henry Schofield, *Freedom of the Press in the United States* (1915), *reprinted in* Nelson, *supra* note 1, at 42; Theodore Schroeder, *Liberty of Conscience, Speech, and Press* (1906), *reprinted in id.* at 279 [hereinafter Liberty].

12. Cooley, *supra* note 11, at 429, 464; Atkinson v. Detroit Free Press, 46 Mich. 341, 376, 9 N.W. 501, 520 (1881) (Cooley, J., dissenting); MacLean v. Scripps, 52 Mich. 214, 18 N.W. 209 (1884); Bathrick v. Detroit Post & Trib. Co., 50 Mich. 629, 16 N.W. 172 (1883); Rosenberg, *supra* note 1, at 167, 179–82; *see* Thomas M. Cooley, The General Principles of Constitutional Law 272–82 (1880) (more consistently asserting a broad free expression); George Chase, *Criticism of Public Officers and Candidates for Office,* 23 Am. L. Rev. 346, 370 (1889) (broad free expression based on the "public weal").

13. Tiedeman, *supra* note 11, at 189–93; Wharton, *supra* note 11, at 635–36, 642.

14. Schofield, *supra* note 11, at 59–60; Freund, *supra* note 11, at 506–10; John W. Burgess, The Reconciliation of Government with Liberty 358–83 (1915); 1 Burgess, *supra* note 11, at 86–89, 178; John W. Burgess, *The Ideal of the American Commonwealth,* 10 Pol. Sci. Q. 404, 412–17 (1895); *see* Graber, *supra* note 1, at 18 (on conservative libertarians).

15. Schroeder, *supra* note 11, at 12–13, 92–93; Liberty, *supra* note 11, at 282, 285.

16. Schroeder, *supra* note 11, at 8, 81, 206, 286; Liberty, *supra* note 11, at 285–86, 289; Graber, *supra* note 1, at 38–39.

17. Schroeder, *supra* note 11, at 14, 101, 103; Liberty, *supra* note 11, at 285.

18. Schroeder, *supra* note 11, at 87, 89; *see id.* at 229 n.24 (citing Wortman); Free Press Anthology (Theodore Schroeder ed., 1909) (referring to Wortman and Thomson); League, *supra* note 1, at 52–55 (distinguishing civil, conservative, and radical libertarianisms).

19. Jerold Auerbach, *Introduction, in* Schroeder, *supra* note 11, at v; League, *supra* note 1, at 72, 89 (quoting *By the Way,* Lucifer: The Light-Bearer, May 15, 1902, at 139–40; Letter from Theodore Schroeder to P.L. Pendleton, Aug. 24, 1916); Lincoln Steffens, *An Answer and an Answer,* 25 Everybody's Mag. 717, 717–20 (1911); Turner v. Williams, 194 U.S. 279 (1904); An Act to Regulate the Immigration of Aliens into the United States, 32 Stat. 1213 (Mar. 3, 1903); Sparks, *supra* note 1, at 18–19, 34–39; Donna L. Dickerson, The Course of Tolerance 232–36 (1990); Preston, *supra* note 1, at 30–32; Forgotten, *supra* note 1, at 23–25, 64–69.

20. Beisel, *supra* note 4, at 87–91 (quoting Heywood); Comstock, *supra* note 7, at 163–66; Forgotten, *supra* note 1, at 32–36 (quoting Heywood); Sparks, *supra* note 1, at 17–18.

21. *Bennett,* 24 F. Cas. at 1094, 1099, 1103–4.

22. Coleman v. MacLennan, 78 Kan. 711, 98 P. 281, 283–86 (1908) (quoting Cooley, A Treatise on the Constitutional Limitations 603–4 (7th ed. 1903)); Sparks, *supra* note 1, at 23–24; Rosenberg, *supra* note 1, at 132–33, 179, 184, 200–202.

23. Commonwealth v. Karvonen, 219 Mass. 30, 32–33, 106 N.E. 556 (1914); Moody v. State, 10 So. 670, 670, 94 Ala. 42 (1892); Sparks, *supra* note 1, at 27; Rosenberg, *supra* note 1, at 156, 177–82, 197; Void, *supra* note 1, at 33–34; Clyde Spillenger, *David M. Rabban and the Libertarian Tradition That Time Forgot,* 26 Law & Soc. Inquiry 209, 221–22 (2001); *e.g.,* Atwater v. Morning News Co., 67 Conn. 504 (1896); Riley v. Lee, 88 Ky. 603 (1889).

24. People v. Most, 128 N.Y. 108, 115 (1891); People v. Most, 171 N.Y. 423, 426, 431 (1902); Forgotten, *supra* note 1, at 142–44; David Yassky, *Eras of the First Amendment,* 91 Colum. L. Rev. 1699, 1717–18 (1991).

25. Special Message of the President to Congress, *The Charges Are a Libel* (Dec. 15, 1908), *reprinted in* Nelson, *supra* note 1, at 121, 124; Sparks, *supra* note 1, at 60 (quoting *New York World,* Dec. 16, 1908); United States v. Smith, 173 F. 227, 230 (D. Ind. 1909); Rosenberg, *supra* note 1, at 197–98.

26. State v. Howell, 80 Conn. 668, 69 A. 1057, 1058–59 (1908); Sparks, *supra* note 1, at 67; *see* State v. Tugwell, 19 Wash. 238, 251–56, 52 P. 1056 (1898); Void, *supra* note 1, at 35.

27. *Atkinson,* 46 Mich. at 376, 9 N.W. at 520 (Cooley, J., dissenting); Graber, *supra* note 1, at 8, 18–21, 34.

28. Schroeder, *supra* note 11, at 13–14, 346, 353.

29. 1 Burgess, *supra* note 11, at 86–89, 178; Private, *supra* note 11, at 210–11.

30. McAuliffe v. New Bedford, 155 Mass. 216, 220 (1892); Commonwealth v. Davis, 162 Mass. 510, 511 (1895), *aff'd, sub nom.* Davis v. Massachusetts, 167 U.S. 43 (1897).

31. William E. Forbath, *The Shaping of the American Labor Movement,* 102 Harv. L. Rev. 1109, 1185, 1212–13, 1249 (1989) (quoting *More Abuse of the Injunction,* 8 Am. Federationist 216, 217 (1901); Debs); Jerold S. Auerbach, Labor and Liberty 14–15 (1966); Chi., B. & Q. Ry. Co. v. Burlington, C.R. & N. Ry. Co., 34 F. 481 (1888); Gibson, *supra* note 1, at 319; *see* Melvyn Dubofsky, The State and Labor in Modern America (1994); Philip S. Foner, 4 History of the Labor Movement in the United States (1965).

32. Forbath, *supra* note 31, at 1213; Arthur v. Oakes, 63 F. 310, 328–29 (1894); William Howard Taft, *The Injunction in Labor Disputes* (extract from Inaugural Address, Mar. 4, 1909), *reprinted in* 2 Documents of American History 53, 53–54 (Henry Steele Commager ed., 9th ed. 1973); *e.g.,* Brief and Argument for Petitioners, at 3, 72–78, 94–95, In re Debs, 158 U.S. 564 (1895), *reprinted in* 11 Landmark Briefs and Arguments of the Supreme Court of the United States: Constitutional Law 267, 270, 339–45, 361–62 (Philip B. Kurland & Gerhard Casper eds., 1975).

33. Zinn, *supra* note 1, at 322–23, 330 (quoting Haywood); Eugene V. Debs, *Unionism and Socialism* (1904), *reprinted in* American Labor 66, 70 (Jerold S. Auerbach ed. 1969); Preston, *supra* note 1, at 41–50 (quoting Haywood); Foner, *supra* note 31, at 13–39, 115–23, 391–414; Fights, *supra* note 1, at 1066–68.

34. Foner, *supra* note 31, at 134–40, 179, 182; Forgotten, *supra* note 1, at 77, 83–84; Zinn, *supra* note 1, at 323–24.

35. Radicals, *supra* note 11, at vi, 39, 162; Forgotten, *supra* note 1, at 70, 92, 101 (quoting Ross; Creel).

36. Forgotten, *supra* note 1, at 81, 86–87 (quoting *Industrial Worker,* Nov. 17, 1909, Dec. 14, 1911; *Solidarity,* Dec. 7, 1912); Paul L. Murphy, World War I and the Origin of Civil Liberties in the United States 139–40 (1979).

37. Foner, *supra* note 31, at 184, 403–14; Fights, *supra* note 1, at 1063–67, 1093–94 (quoting Debs); Preston, *supra* note 1, at 48–49; Zinn, *supra* note 1, at 324.

38. *Good for Paterson,* N.Y. Times, Sept. 14, 1915, at 10; Auerbach, *supra* note 31, at 16–17 (quoting *San Diego Tribune,* Mar. 4, 1912); Radicals, *supra* note 11, at 132–33 (quoting Wobbly).

39. Auerbach, *supra* note 31, at 16; Foner, *supra* note 31, at 147; Preston, *supra* note 1, at 44, 55; Zinn, *supra* note 1, at 324; Fights, *supra* note 1, at 1061–62; *see* Philip S. Foner, 3 History of the Labor Movement in the United States (1964).

40. 18 The American and English Encyclopaedia of Law 1125 (David S. Garland & Lucius P. McGehee eds., 2d ed. 1901); *e.g.,* Tilton v. Maley, 186 Ill. App. 187 (1914); In re Fite, 76 S.E. 397, 418 (Ga. App. 1912).

41. *Davis,* 167 U.S. 43 (1897); Mutual Film Corp. v. Ohio Industr. Comm'n, 236 U.S. 230, 242, 244 (1915); Forgotten, *supra* note 1, at 173–75; White, *supra* note 1, at 404–5.

42. Gompers v. Bucks Stove & Range Co., 221 U.S. 418, 436–39 (1911); Dubofsky, *supra* note 31, at 29–31, 45–47; Gibson, *supra* note 1, at 319–21; White, *supra* note 1, at 403–5; *see* Loewe v. Lawlor, 208 U.S. 274 (1908) (upholding labor injunction in Danbury Hatters boycott); In re Debs, 158 U.S. 564 (1895) (upholding injunction against strike and boycott of the Pullman Company).

43. Roberston v. Baldwin, 165 U.S. 275, 280–81 (1897).

44. Halter v. Nebraska, 205 U.S. 34, 39–42 (1907).

45. Patterson v. Colorado, 205 U.S. 454, 458–59, 462 (1907) (quoting Commonwealth v. Blanding, 3 Pick. 304, 313–14 (Mass. 1825)); Forgotten, *supra* note 1, at 132–35; White, *supra* note 1, at 399.

46. *Patterson,* 205 U.S. at 463–65 (Harlan, J., dissenting); *see* Adair v. United States, 208 U.S. 161, 174 (1908).

47. Fox v. Washington, 236 U.S. 273, 275–77 (1915); Forgotten, *supra* note 1, at 138–40.

48. *Fox,* 236 U.S. at 276–77; White, *supra* note 1, at 402.

49. Contemporary legal commentators recognized the anomaly between the granting of labor injunctions and the proscription of prior restraints. *E.g.,* Roscoe Pound, *Equitable Relief against Defamation and Injuries to Personality,* 29 Harv. L. Rev. 640, 651–52 n.29 (1916).

CHAPTER EIGHT

1. Helpful sources on the history of free expression during this period include Margaret A. Blanchard, Revolutionary Sparks (1992); Mark A. Graber, Transforming Free Speech (1991); William E. Leuchtenburg, The Perils of Prosperity (1958); Paul L. Murphy, World War I and the Origin of Civil Liberties in the United States (1979); Richard Polenberg, Fighting Faiths (1987); William Preston, Jr., Aliens and Dissenters (1963); David M. Rabban, Free Speech in Its Forgotten Years (1997) [hereinafter Forgotten]; Geoffrey R. Stone, Perilous Times (2004); Patrick S. Washburn, A Question of Sedition (1986); Howard Zinn, A People's History of the United States (1980); Thomas A. Lawrence, *Eclipse of Liberty,* 21 Wayne L. Rev. 33 (1974); David M. Rabban, *Free Speech in Progressive Social Thought,* 74 Tex. L. Rev. 951 (1996) [hereinafter Progressive]; David M. Rabban, *The Free Speech League, the ACLU, and Changing Conceptions of Free Speech in American History,* 45 Stan. L. Rev. 47 (1992) [hereinafter League]; David M. Rabban, *The Emergence of Modern First Amendment Doctrine,* 50 U. Chi. L. Rev. 1205 (1983) [hereinafter Emergence]; Geoffrey R. Stone, *Judge Learned Hand and the Espionage Act of 1917,* 70 U. Chi. L. Rev. 335 (2003) [hereinafter Espionage]; Geoffrey R. Stone, *The Origins of the "Bad Tendency" Test,* 2002 Sup. Ct. Rev. 411 [hereinafter Origins]; Christina E. Wells, *Discussing the First Amendment,* 101 Mich. L. Rev. 1566 (2003); G. Edward White, *Justice Holmes and the Modernization of Free Speech Jurisprudence: The Human Dimension,* 80 Cal. L. Rev. 391 (1992) [hereinafter Human]; Documents of American History (Henry Steele Commager ed., 9th ed. 1973) [hereinafter Commager]; Landmark Briefs and Arguments of the Supreme Court of the United States: Constitutional Law (Philip B. Kurland & Gerhard Casper eds., 1975) [hereinafter Landmark].

2. Wilson's Appeal for Neutrality (Aug. 19, 1914), *reprinted in* 2 Commager, *supra* note 1, at 96; Address of President Wilson to the U.S. Senate (Jan. 22, 1917), *reprinted in id.* at 125–26; Wilson's Speech for Declaration of War against Germany (Apr. 2, 1917), *reprinted in id.* at 128, 131.

3. 55 Cong. Rec., 65th Cong., 1st Sess. 3144 (May 31, 1917) (quoting Letter from Wilson to Representative Webb, May 22, 1917); Emergence, *supra* note 1, at 1217–18, 1223–24 (quoting Warren); 55 Cong. Rec., 65th Cong., 1st Sess. 1824–34 (May 4, 1917); Blanchard, *supra* note 1, at 76; Murphy, *supra* note 1, at 52–58.

4. H.R. 291, tit. I, §4, *in* 55 Cong. Rec., 65th Cong., 1st Sess. 1695 (May 2, 1917); 55 Cong. Rec., 65th Cong., 1st Sess. 3137 (May 31, 1917); *id.* at 1713 (May 2, 1917); *id.* at 1773 (May 3, 1917); *The Espionage Bill,* N.Y. Times, Apr. 13, 1913, at 12; 55 Cong. Rec., 65th Cong., 1st Sess. 1167 (Apr. 26, 1917); Espionage, *supra* note 1, at 346–47.

5. 55 Cong. Rec., 65th Cong., 1st Sess. 1595, 1603 (Apr. 30, 1917); *id.* at 1820, 1835–36 (May 4, 1917).

6. An Act to Punish Acts of Interference with the Foreign Relations, the Neutrality, and the Foreign Commerce of the United States, to Punish Espionage, and Better to Enforce the Criminal Laws of the United States, Title XII (Use of Mails) (June 15, 1917), 40 Stat. 230; 55 Cong. Rec., 65th Cong., 1st Sess. 3129–30 (May 31, 1917); Espionage, *supra* note 1, at 350.

7. Espionage, *supra* note 1, at 353–54; 55 Cong. Rec., 65th Cong., 1st Sess. 1780 (May 3, 1917); *id.* at 1695 (May 2, 1917).

8. Emergence, *supra* note 1, at 1217 n.44, 1223 (quoting Wilson; Warren); 55 Cong. Rec., 65th Cong., 1st Sess. 1695, 1700–1701 (May 2, 1917); *id.* at 3143 (May 31, 1917).

9. 55 Cong. Rec., 65th Cong., 1st Sess. 1594 (Apr. 30, 1917); An Act to Punish Acts of Interference with the Foreign Relations, the Neutrality, and the Foreign Commerce of the United States, to Punish Espionage, and Better to Enforce the Criminal Laws of the United States, Title I (Espionage), § 3 (June 15, 1917), 40 Stat. 217, 219; Forgotten, *supra* note 1, at 250, 254.

10. John Dewey, *Conscience and Compulsion,* The New Republic (TNR), July 14, 1917, at 297; Lawrence, *supra* note 1, at 42; U.S. CPI, War Cyclopedia 101 (Frederic L. Paxson et al. eds., 1918); Origins, *supra* note 1, at 413.

11. John Higham, Strangers in the Land 204–12 (1992 ed.); Lawrence, *supra* note 1, at 54; ADS, *History, Purpose and Accomplishments* 2, 18, 26–27 (1918); Murphy, *supra* note 1, at 87–90, 123.

12. William T. Hornaday, Awake! America 9, 106–15, 124, 139–44, 180–81 (1918).

13. Higham, *supra* note 11, at 206–11; Origins, *supra* note 1, at 413; Murphy, *supra* note 1, at 87, 94–95; *Kahn Would Silence Sedition with Rope,* N.Y. Times, Mar. 25, 1918, at 8; ADS, *History, Purpose and Accomplishments* 26–27 (1918); Lawrence, *supra* note 1, at 58–59.

14. Origins, *supra* note 1, at 413; Shaffer v. United States, 255 F. 886, 886–89 (9th Cir. 1919); Wells, *supra* note 1, at 1582; *see* Zechariah Chafee, Jr., Freedom of Speech 387–94 (1920). Chafee's other key writings on free expression during World War I include Zechariah Chafee, *Freedom of Speech in War Time,* 32 Harv. L. Rev. 932 (1919) [hereinafter War]; Zechariah Chafee, Jr., *A Contemporary State Trial — The United States versus Jacob Abrams et al.,* 33 Harv. L. Rev. 747 (1920) [hereinafter Contemporary]; Zechariah Chafee, Jr., *Freedom of Speech,* TNR, Nov. 16, 1918, at 66 [hereinafter Speech]; Zechariah Chafee, Jr., *Legislation against Anarchy,* TNR, July 23, 1919, at 379 [hereinafter Anarchy].

15. Masses Publ'g Co. v. Patten, 244 F. 535, 540–43 (S.D.N.Y. 1917), *reversed,* 246 F. 24 (2d Cir. 1917); Forgotten, *supra* note 1, at 261–65.

16. United States v. Hall, 248 F. 150, 152–53 (D. Mont. 1918); *see* United States v. Schutte, 252 F. 212 (D. N.D. 1918) (Judge Amidon reading Act narrowly); Origins, *supra* note 1, at 423–25.

17. 56 Cong. Rec., 65th Cong., 2d Sess. 4559–61 (Apr. 4, 1918); *id.* at 4824 (Apr. 9, 1918); *id.* at 6183 (May 7, 1918); An Act to Amend Section Three, Title One of the Espionage Act (May 16, 1918), 40 Stat. 553 (Sedition Act); Masses Publ'g Co. v. Patten, 246 F. 24, 38 (2d Cir. 1917); Polenberg, *supra* note 1, at 28–33.

18. Chafee, *supra* note 14, at 57–63; Espionage, *supra* note 1, at 337; Murphy, *supra* note 1, at 16; Washburn, *supra* note 1, at 13; Wells, *supra* note 1, at 1582–83.

19. Higham, *supra* note 11, at 219–20, 247–49; Murphy, *supra* note 1, at 271; *see* Joyce Mendelsohn, The Lower East Side 45 (2001); Lawrence, *supra* note 1, at 88.

20. 55 Cong. Rec., 65th Cong., Appendix at 332–34, 1st Sess. (June 15, 1917);

Polenberg, *supra* note 1, at 72; Blanchard, *supra* note 1, at 80, 87–88, 503 n.44 (quoting Landis); Murphy, *supra* note 1, at 141–43; Preston, *supra* note 1, at 118–41; Washburn, *supra* note 1, at 13; Zinn, *supra* note 1, at 355–59, 364.

21. Preston, *supra* note 1, at 97–98; Higham, *supra* note 11, at 215; Melvyn Dubofsky, The State and Labor in Modern America 61–81 (1994).

22. Maxwell Bloomfield, Peaceful Revolution 52 (2000); Richard Hofstadter, The Age of Reform 277–81 (1955); Arthur S. Link & Richard L. McCormick, Progressivism 107–8 (1983); Murphy, *supra* note 1, at 25–26; Charles Hirschfeld, *The Transformation of American Life, in* World War I 63, 72 (Jack J. Roth ed., 1967).

23. Samuel Walker, In Defense of American Liberties 16 (1990); Donald Johnson, The Challenge to American Freedoms 63 (1963); Polenberg, *supra* note 1, at 165; Donald L. Smith, Zechariah Chafee, Jr. 43 (1986).

24. Editors, *Editorial Notes,* TNR, Sept. 29, 1917, at 227, 228 (Croly); Editors, *Public Opinion in War Time,* TNR, Sept. 22, 1917, at 204 (Croly); Graber, *supra* note 1, at 25–27, 83–84; Emergence, *supra* note 1, at 1215–16.

25. John Dewey, *The Future of Pacificism,* TNR, July 28, 1917, at 358; John Dewey, *What America Will Fight For,* TNR, Aug. 18, 1917, at 68–69; John Dewey, *Conscription of Thought,* TNR, Sept. 1, 1917, at 128–29.

26. William R. Vance, *Freedom of Speech and Press,* 2 Minn. L. Rev. 239, 241, 255, 259 (1918); *see* Henry J. Fletcher, *The Civilian and the War Power,* 2 Minn. L. Rev. 110 (1918).

27. Randolph S. Bourne, *Twilight of Idols,* Seven Arts, Oct. 1917, *reprinted in* The Radical Will 336–38 (1977); Lillian Schlissel, *Introduction, in* Randolph S. Bourne, The World of Randolph Bourne xv–xxvii; Progressive, *supra* note 1, at 1007–10; *see* Editors, *Civil Liberty Dead,* Nation, Sept. 14, 1918, at 282 (opposing suppression).

28. Walker, *supra* note 23, at 11–20, 38; Murphy, *supra* note 1, at 153–60, 174 (quoting Baldwin); Forgotten, *supra* note 1, at 306–7; *see* Peggy Lamson, Roger Baldwin 111–12 (1976); League, *supra* note 1, at 100.

29. Editors, *War Propaganda,* TNR, Oct. 6, 1917, at 255–57 (Croly); John Dewey, *In Explanation of Our Lapse,* TNR, Nov. 3, 1917, at 17–18; Smith, *supra* note 23, at 16–17; Progressive, *supra* note 1, at 1010, 1017–18.

30. Speech, *supra* note 14, at 66–68. Published more than a year earlier than Chafee's essay, Herbert L. Stewart, *Freedom of Speech in War Time,* Nation, Aug. 30, 1917, at 219, argued from a Miltonian standpoint that free expression served a social interest that must be balanced against other social interests. But unlike Chafee, Stewart did not accord free expression special weight in the balance.

31. Schenck v. United States, 249 U.S. 47, 51–52 (1919); *Patterson,* 205 U.S. 454, 462 (1907).

32. *Schenck,* 249 U.S. at 52; Oliver Wendell Holmes, Jr., The Common Law 66, 68 (1881, Dover ed. 1991); Letter from Holmes to Chafee, June 12, 1922, *responding to* Letter from Chafee to Holmes, June 9, 1922, *both quoted in* David S. Bogen, *The Free Speech Metamorphosis of Mr. Justice Holmes,* 11 Hofstra L. Rev. 97, 99–100 (1982); *see* Graber, *supra* note 1, at 110; Emergence, *supra* note 1, at 1260–61, 1271–78; Fred D. Ragan, *Justice Oliver Wendell Holmes, Jr., Zechariah Chafee, Jr., and the Clear and Pres-*

ent Danger Test for Free Speech, 58 J. Am. Hist. 24, 34–36 (1971); Human, *supra* note 1, at 414–19.

Primary sources include Holmes-Laski Letters: The Correspondence of Mr. Justice Holmes and Harold J. Laski (1953) [hereinafter Holmes-Laski]; Holmes-Pollock Letters: The Correspondence of Mr. Justice Holmes and Sir Frederick Pollock, 1874–1932 (1941) [hereinafter Holmes-Pollock]. Secondary sources include Albert W. Alschuler, Law without Values: The Life, Work, and Legacy of Justice Holmes (2000); Vincent Blasi, *Holmes and the Marketplace of Ideas,* 2004 Sup. Ct. Rev. 1; Gerald Caplan, *Searching for Holmes among the Biographers,* 70 Geo. Wash. L. Rev. 769 (2002); Gerald Gunther, *Learned Hand and the Origins of Modern First Amendment Doctrine,* 27 Stan. L. Rev. 719 (1975); Sheldon M. Novick, *The Unrevised Holmes and Freedom of Expression,* 1991 Sup. Ct. Rev. 303; Yosal Rogat & James M. O'Fallon, *Mr. Justice Holmes,* 36 Stan. L. Rev. 1349 (1984).

33. Sugarman v. United States, 249 U.S. 182, 183, 185 (1919); Human, *supra* note 1, at 413 n.123.

34. Frohwerk v. United States, 249 U.S. 204, 206–9 (1919); Forgotten, *supra* note 1, at 282–83; Stone, *supra* note 1, at 195–96; Human, *supra* note 1, at 416–19.

35. Walker, *supra* note 23, at 41 (quoting Debs); *Debs,* 249 U.S. 211, 213–16 (1919).

36. Rogat & O'Fallon, *supra* note 32, at 1378 (quoting Harry Kalven, Jr.); McAuliffe v. New Bedford, 155 Mass. 216, 220 (1892); Letter from Holmes to Hand, June 24, 1918, *reprinted in* Gunther, *supra* note 32, at 756–57; *Schenck,* 249 U.S. at 52; Selective Draft Law (May 18, 1917), 40 Stat. 76; *see* Goldman v. United States, 245 U.S. 474 (1918); Emergence, *supra* note 1, at 1244–46.

37. Letter from Holmes to Laski, Mar. 16, 1919, *in* 1 Holmes-Laski, *supra* note 32, at 189, 190; Letter from Hand to Holmes, late Mar., 1919, *reprinted in* Gunther, *supra* note 32, at 758, 759; Letter from Holmes to Hand, Apr. 3, 1919, *reprinted in id.* at 759–60.

38. Baltzer v. United States, No. 320 (U.S. S. Ct., Oct. term, 1918), *reprinted in* Novick, *supra* note 32, at 388–90; *Baltzer,* 248 U.S. 593 (1918); *see* Novick, *supra* note 32, at 331–33.

39. Letter from Holmes to Pollock, Apr. 23, 1910, *in* 1 Holmes-Pollock, *supra* note 32, at 163; Howard Gillman, *Preferred Freedoms,* 47 Pol. Res. Q. 623, 640 (1994).

40. Lawrence, *supra* note 1, at 61–62; Letter from Holmes to Laski, Mar. 16, 1919, *in* 1 Holmes-Laski, *supra* note 32, at 189, 190; Letter from Hand to Chafee, Jan. 2, 1921, *reprinted in* Gunther, *supra* note 32, at 769, 770.

41. Emergence, *supra* note 1, at 1313; Higham, *supra* note 11, at 222–32, 277–99 (quoting Ford); Editors, *Danger Ahead,* Nation, Feb. 8, 1919, at 186; *see* The Statistical History of the United States from Colonial Times to the Present 127 (1965); Leuchtenburg, *supra* note 1, at 66–83; Washburn, *supra* note 1, at 14–23.

42. Leuchtenburg, *supra* note 1, at 50–65; Emergence, *supra* note 1, at 1216, 1313; Progressive, *supra* note 1, at 954–56; *see* The Defeat of the League of Nations, *reprinted in* 2 Commager, *supra* note 1, at 160.

43. Ernst Freund, *The Debs Case and Freedom of Speech,* TNR, May 3, 1919, at 13–15; *Anarchy, supra* note 14, at 379, 384.

44. Graber, *supra* note 1, at 75–121.

45. War, *supra* note 14, at 938, 956–60, 967.

46. *Id.* at 960–68; Chafee, *supra* note 14, at 34–38, 158.

47. Roscoe Pound, *Interests in Personality (Part I),* 28 Harv. L. Rev. 343–49 (1915); Roscoe Pound, *Interests in Personality (Part II),* 28 Harv. L. Rev. 445, 454–56 (1915); Smith, *supra* note 23, at 6, 86.

48. War, *supra* note 14, at 957–59.

49. Letter from Holmes to Einstein (Aug. 12, 1916), *quoted in* Bogen, *supra* note 32, at 132; Emergence, *supra* note 1, at 1280 n.459; *see* Alschuler, *supra* note 32, at 78–79, 181–84; Bogen, *supra* note 32, at 131–33; Human, *supra* note 1, at 408–12.

50. Letter from Hand to Holmes, June 22, 1918, *reprinted in* Gunther, *supra* note 32, at 755–56; Letter from Hand to Holmes, late Mar., 1919, *reprinted in id.* at 758–59; Ragan, *supra* note 32, at 43 (quoting Laski to Chafee); Smith, *supra* note 23, at 30 (quoting Chafee to Amidon); Polenberg, *supra* note 1, at 223–27; Human, *supra* note 1, at 430–31.

51. Letter from Holmes to Pollock, Apr. 5, 1919, *in* 2 Holmes-Pollock, *supra* note 32, at 7; Letter from Holmes to Laski, May 13, 1919, *in* 1 Holmes-Laski, *supra* note 32, at 202–3; Smith, *supra* note 23, at 32; Letter from Holmes to Laski, Mar. 16, 1919, *in* 1 Holmes-Laski, *supra* note 32, at 189–90; Human, *supra* note 1, at 420–21.

52. Human, *supra* note 1, at 411.

53. Polenberg, *supra* note 1, at 43–50, 66–72, 88–91, 145; Chafee, *supra* note 14, at 137; *Long Prison Terms for the Bolsheviki,* N.Y. Times, Oct. 26, 1918, at 18.

54. Abrams v. United States, 250 U.S. 616, 627–29 (Holmes, J., dissenting). Holmes and Brandeis previously dissented together in *Toledo Newspaper Co. v. United States,* upholding a contempt order against a newspaper. Holmes's dissent focused on interpreting the applicable contempt statute. 247 U.S. 402, 422–23 (1918) (Holmes, J., dissenting), *overruled by* Nye v. United States, 313 U.S. 33 (1941).

55. *Abrams,* 250 U.S. at 630 (Holmes, J., dissenting).

56. Letter from Holmes to Laski, Dec. 17, 1920, *in* 1 Holmes-Laski, *supra* note 32, at 297; Human, *supra* note 1, at 431.

57. *Abrams,* 250 U.S. at 630 (Holmes, J., dissenting); War, *supra* note 14, at 956; John Stuart Mill, On Liberty 21–27 (1859; Liberal Arts Press ed. 1956); Human, *supra* note 1, at 439–40; *see* Letter from Holmes to Laski, Feb. 28, 1919, *in* 1 Holmes-Laski, *supra* note 32, at 186, 187; Letter from Holmes to Laski, Mar. 11, 1922, *in id.* 1 at 409, 410; Walter Bagehot, *The Metaphysical Basis of Toleration* (Apr. 1874), *reprinted in* 14 The Collected Works of Walter Bagehot 58, 61, 72–73 (Norman St. John-Stevas ed., 1986). Holmes did not use the precise phrase, "marketplace of ideas." Blasi, *supra* note 32, at 13, 24.

58. Bogen, *supra* note 32, at 99–100 (quoting Letter from Holmes to Chafee, June 12, 1922); Letter from Holmes to Laski, Oct. 26, 1919, *in* 1 Holmes-Laski, *supra* note 32, at 217; Letter from Holmes to Pollock, Oct. 26, 1919, *in* 2 Holmes-Pollock, *supra* note 32, at 27, 29; Letter from Holmes to Pollock, Nov. 6, 1919, *in id.* at 29; *Abrams,*

250 U.S. at 627; Letter from Holmes to Pollock, Dec. 14, 1919, *in* 2 Holmes-Pollock, *supra* note 32, at 32; Emergence, *supra* note 1, at 1267.

59. Letter from Holmes to Pollock, Oct. 26, 1919, *in* 2 Holmes-Pollock, *supra* note 32, at 27, 28; Letter from Holmes to Hand, June 24, 1918, *reprinted in* Gunther, *supra* note 32, at 756–57; Letter from Holmes to Laski, July 7, 1918, *in* 1 Holmes-Laski, *supra* note 32, at 160–61.

60. Letter from Laski to Holmes, Nov. 12, 1919, *in* 1 Holmes-Laski, *supra* note 32, at 220; Letter from Felix Frankfurter to Oliver Wendell Holmes (Nov. 12, 1919), *reprinted in* White, *supra* note 1, at 441; Contemporary, *supra* note 14, at 769; Editors, *The Call to Toleration,* TNR, Nov. 26, 1919, at 360–61.

61. Schaefer v. United States, 251 U.S. 466, 482, 486 (1920) (Brandeis, J., dissenting).

62. Pierce v. United States, 252 U.S. 239, 267–73 (1920) (Brandeis, J., dissenting).

63. Milwaukee Soc. Democratic Publ'g Co. v. Burleson, 255 U.S. 407, 417–36 (1921) (Brandeis, J., dissenting); *id.* at 436 (Holmes, J., dissenting).

64. Gilbert v. Minnesota, 254 U.S. 325, 326–27, 333 (1920); *id.* at 337–38, 342 (Brandeis, J., dissenting).

65. *Id.* at 334 (Holmes, J., concurring in judgment); *Pierce,* 252 U.S. at 273 (1920) (Brandeis, J., dissenting).

66. *Abrams,* 250 U.S. at 629 (Holmes, J., dissenting); Graber, *supra* note 1, at 111–12; Lawrence, *supra* note 1, at 103; *see* Letter from Holmes to Pollock, Dec. 14, 1919, *in* 2 Holmes-Pollock, *supra* note 32, at 32.

67. Letter from Holmes to Laski, Dec. 3, 1917, *in* 1 Holmes-Laski, *supra* note 32, at 115–16; Letter from Holmes to Hand, June 24, 1918, *reprinted in* Gunther, *supra* note 32, at 756, 757; *e.g.,* Oliver Wendell Holmes, Jr., *The Path of the Law,* 10 Harv. L. Rev. 457 (1897).

68. Emergence, *supra* note 1, at 1319; Polenberg, *supra* note 1, at 211 (quoting Nov. 17, 1915, letter).

69. *Schaefer,* 251 U.S. at 493–95 (Brandeis, J., dissenting); Emergence, *supra* note 1, at 1321, 1329; *see* Alschuler, *supra* note 32, at 41–51; Philippa Strum, Louis D. Brandeis 309–38 (1984).

70. Blanchard, *supra* note 1, at 120 (quoting Speaker Thaddeus Sweet); Higham, *supra* note 11, at 230–31; Johnson, *supra* note 23, at 136–45; Leuchtenburg, *supra* note 1, at 77–79; Preston, *supra* note 1, at 220–22.

71. Walker, *supra* note 23, at 44; Leuchtenburg, *supra* note 1, at 79; Preston, *supra* note 1, at 221–22; Smith, *supra* note 23, at 48.

72. Polenberg, *supra* note 1, at 272, 280; Smith, *supra* note 23, at 37–39, 51–55; Emergence, *supra* note 1, at 1314–15.

73. James Parker Hall, *Free Speech in War Time,* 21 Colum. L. Rev. 526, 528 (1921); Johnson, *supra* note 23, at 66–67; Smith, *supra* note 23, at 1–12; Walker, *supra* note 23, at 45–47; Thomas G. Barnes, *Introduction, in* Chafee, *supra* note 14, at 9–10; Emergence, *supra* note 1, at 1215–16; Origins, *supra* note 1, at 450.

74. Chafee, *supra* note 14, at 2; Johnson, *supra* note 23, at 147; Walker, *supra* note 23, at 44–53; League, *supra* note 1, at 100–110.

75. *Reds by the Thousands,* N.Y. Times, Jan. 5, 1920, at 10; *The Red Assassins,* Wash. Post, Jan. 4, 1920, at 26.

76. Edward S. Corwin, Freedom of Speech and Press under the First Amendment, 30 Yale L.J. 48, 55 (1920).

77. Wigmore, 14 Ill. L. Rev. 539, 543–58 (1920).

78. Johnson, *supra* note 23, at 197; Murphy, *supra* note 1, at 31.

CHAPTER NINE

1. Warren G. Harding, *A Return to Normalcy* (May 14, 1920); Warren G. Harding, *The Return to Normalcy* (Apr. 12, 1921); David M. Kennedy, Freedom from Fear 29–30 (1999) (quoting Coolidge); William E. Leuchtenburg, The Perils of Prosperity 87–88, 126 (1958) [hereinafter Perils]; Erik W. Austin, Political Facts of the United States since 1789, at 450 (1986); The Statistical History of the United States from Colonial Times to the Present 711 (1965) [hereinafter Statistical]. Other sources on the development of democracy and related issues include Jerold S. Auerbach, Labor and Liberty (1966); Anthony J. Badger, The New Deal (1989); Daniel Bell, The Cultural Contradictions of Capitalism (1978); Lizabeth Cohen, A Consumers' Republic (2003) [hereinafter Republic]; Lizabeth Cohen, Making a New Deal (1990) [hereinafter Making]; Gary Cross, An All-Consuming Century (2000); Marc Dollinger, Quest for Inclusion (2000); Melvyn Dubofsky, The State and Labor in Modern America (1994); Lynn Dumenil, The Modern Temper (1995); George H. Gallup, The Gallup Poll: Public Opinion 1935–1971 (1972) [hereinafter Gallup]; John Gerring, Party Ideologies in America (1998); John Higham, Strangers in the Land (1992 ed.); Richard Hofstadter, The Age of Reform (1955); Matthew Frye Jacobson, Whiteness of a Different Color (1998); Alexander Keyssar, The Right to Vote (2000); Desmond King, Making Americans (2000); William E. Leuchtenburg, Franklin D. Roosevelt and the New Deal (1963) [hereinafter Deal]; Donald R. McCoy, Coming of Age (1973); Robert S. McElvaine, The Great Depression (1984); Frances Fox Piven & Richard A. Cloward, Poor People's Movements (1977); Robert D. Putnam, Bowling Alone (2000); David R. Roediger, Working toward Whiteness (2005); Arthur M. Schlesinger, Jr., The Crisis of the Old Order (1988 ed.); Paul Starr, The Creation of the Media (2004); Stephen Steinberg, The Ethnic Myth (1989 ed.); Thomas J. Sugrue, The Origins of the Urban Crisis (1996); Robert H. Wiebe, Self-Rule (1995); William M. Wiecek, The Lost World of Classical Legal Thought (1998); 2 Who Built America? (Stephen Brier, supervising ed., 1992) [hereinafter Built]; Barry Friedman, *The History of the Countermajoritarian Difficulty, Part Four,* 148 U. Pa. L. Rev. 971 (2000); American Labor (Jerold S. Auerbach ed., 1969) [hereinafter Labor]; Documents of American History (Henry Steele Commager ed., 9th ed. 1973) [hereinafter Commager]; Great Issues in American History (Richard Hofstadter ed., 1982) [hereinafter Great].

2. Making, *supra* note 1, at 103–4; Kennedy, *supra* note 1, at 35–36; McCoy, *supra* note 1, at 24, 116; Statistical, *supra* note 1, at 73, 139, 179, 409.

3. Dumenil, *supra* note 1, at 35–37; Warren G. Harding, *The Return to Normalcy*

(Apr. 12, 1921); Kennedy, *supra* note 1, at 33 (quoting Coolidge); Perils, *supra* note 1, at 103; Schlesinger, *supra* note 1, at 61–70; Wiecek, *supra* note 1, at 200–201.

4. Making, *supra* note 1, at 103–4; Auerbach, *supra* note 1, at 6 (quoting Taft, 1922); Dubofsky, *supra* note 1, at 76–79, 88–89; Kennedy, *supra* note 1, at 25–27; Built, *supra* note 1, at 298; Wiebe, *supra* note 1, at 124–25; Statistical, *supra* note 1, at 91–93, 167.

5. Gerring, *supra* note 1, at 86 (quoting Coolidge); Dumenil, *supra* note 1, at 202, 212; Austin, *supra* note 1, at 470.

6. Perils, *supra* note 1, at 208–12; Dumenil, *supra* note 1, at 211, 235–44.

7. McCoy, *supra* note 1, at 99–100; Dumenil, *supra* note 1, at 201–2, 239.

8. Dumenil, *supra* note 1, at 211, 213; Making, *supra* note 1, at 211; Leonard Dinnerstein, Antisemitism in America 80–82 (1994).

9. Congressional Committee on Immigration, *Temporary Suspension of Immigration* (1920), *reprinted in* The Jew in the Modern World 405, 406–7 (Paul R. Mendes-Flohr & Jehuda Reinharz eds., 1980); E.P. Hutchinson, Legislative History of American Immigration Policy 175–76, 187–92, 484–85 (1981); Immigration Act of 1924, *reprinted in* 2 Commager, *supra* note 1, at 372; Perils, *supra* note 1, at 206–8; Howard M. Sachar, A History of the Jews in America 319–24 (1992).

10. Making, *supra* note 1, at 5, 55–83, 104–16; Dumenil, *supra* note 1, at 255, 267–68; Starr, *supra* note 1, at 367.

11. Higham, *supra* note 1, at 324–27.

12. Dumenil, *supra* note 1, at 8, 11; Horace M. Kallen, *Democracy versus the Melting Pot,* Nation, Feb. 25, 1915, at 3–4; Making, *supra* note 1, at 149–50; Statistical, *supra* note 1, at 14.

13. Built, *supra* note 1, at 279–81, 291; Making, *supra* note 1, at 100; Cross, *supra* note 1, at 20–26; Andrew Heinze, *From Scarcity to Abundance, in* Consumer Society in American History 190 (Lawrence B. Glickman ed., 1999) [hereinafter Glickman].

14. Ronald K.L. Collins & David M. Skover, *Commerce and Communication,* 71 Tex. L. Rev. 697, 700–703 (1993); Dumenil, *supra* note 1, at 89–90.

15. Making, *supra* note 1, at 138–41; Cross, *supra* note 1, at 34, 49–50, 77; Perils, *supra* note 1, at 196; Starr, *supra* note 1, at 337–67; Built, *supra* note 1, at 283–86.

16. Built, *supra* note 1, at 285; Cross, *supra* note 1, at 31–35, 65; John Dewey, Individualism, Old and New 42–43 (1930); Making, *supra* note 1, at 116–28.

17. Cross, *supra* note 1, at 37; Built, *supra* note 1, at 285; Jacobson, *supra* note 1, at 95; Dumenil, *supra* note 1, at 81–82; Higham, *supra* note 1, at 327; Roediger, *supra* note 1, at 145–56; Wiebe, *supra* note 1, at 197–98.

18. Jacobson, *supra* note 1, at 95; King, *supra* note 1, at 103 (quoting James Davis, 1923); Cross, *supra* note 1, at 34–35, 59; Dumenil, *supra* note 1, at 78–85, 266–67; Starr, *supra* note 1, at 369.

19. Lizabeth Cohen, *Encountering Mass Culture at the Grassroots, in* Glickman, *supra* note 13, at 147, 162–63; Making, *supra* note 1, at 157–74, 201–11; Hofstadter, *supra* note 1, at 182–83, 298–99; William Allen White, The Old Order Changeth 12–31 (1910).

20. Allan J. Lichtman, Prejudice and the Old Politics 10, 25, 77 (1979); Samuel

Lubell, The Future of American Politics 48–52 (3d ed., revised, 1965); Austin, *supra* note 1, at 379; Hofstadter, *supra* note 1, at 299–301; Perils, *supra* note 1, at 235–36.

21. Dumenil, *supra* note 1, at 40–47, 276–77; Lichtman, *supra* note 20, at 93; Arthur S. Link & Richard L. McCormick, Progressivism 56–57 (1983).

22. Lichtman, *supra* note 20, at 71; Perils, *supra* note 1, at 234–39; Austin, *supra* note 1, at 97; Lubell, *supra* note 20, at 55.

23. Lichtman, *supra* note 20, at 10–15, 75–76; Dumenil, *supra* note 1, at 48–50 (quoting Oliver McKee, *North American Review*); Perils, *supra* note 1, at 231.

24. Perils, *supra* note 1, at 217–24; Constitution of Tennessee (1870), *reprinted in* 2 The Federal and State Constitutions, Colonial Charters, and other Organic Laws of the United States 1694, 1695, 1706 (Ben Perley Poore ed., 2d ed. 1878); Paul K. Conkin, When All the Gods Trembled 99 (1998); Dumenil, *supra* note 1, at 185–87.

25. Perils, *supra* note 1, at 219, 223; Ray Ginger, Six Days or Forever? (1958).

26. Kennedy, *supra* note 1, at 35–38; Perils, *supra* note 1, at 243–44; McCoy, *supra* note 1, at 168–77.

27. Studs Terkel, Hard Times 104 (1970) (quoting Clifford Burke); Badger, *supra* note 1, at 12; Making, *supra* note 1, at 240–43; Kennedy, *supra* note 1, at 86–87; McElvaine, *supra* note 1, at 187; Piven & Cloward, *supra* note 1, at 60; Statistical, *supra* note 1, at 73, 92, 95, 139, 278, 409.

28. Making, *supra* note 1, at 249; Joseph Torrio, *Job Hunting* (Apr. 19, 1934), *reprinted in* Labor, *supra* note 1, at 231, 232; Piven & Cloward, *supra* note 1, at 49–60.

29. Maxwell Bloomfield, Peaceful Revolution 99–123 (2000); Hofstadter, *supra* note 1, at 307 n.4; McCoy, *supra* note 1, at 192; McElvaine, *supra* note 1, at 172–73; Friedman, *supra* note 1, at 1004–6.

30. Stephen M. Feldman, American Legal Thought from Premodernism to Postmodernism 91–101 (2000); Peter Novick, That Noble Dream 16, 31 (1988); Dorothy Ross, The Origins of American Social Science 62 (1991); *e.g.,* C.C. Langdell, Summary of the Law of Contracts (2d ed. 1880). Additional sources on intellectual history and related issues include John G. Gunnell, The Descent of Political Theory (1993); Edward A. Purcell, Jr., The Crisis of Democratic Theory (1973); G. Edward White, The Constitution and the New Deal (2000); James R. Hackney, Jr., *Law and Neoclassical Economics,* 15 Law & Hist. Rev. 275 (1997); G. Edward White, *The Arrival of History in Constitutional Scholarship,* 88 Va. L. Rev. 485 (2002) [hereinafter Arrival].

31. Ross, *supra* note 30, at xv, 3–4; Feldman, *supra* note 30, at 105–15; White, *supra* note 30, at 5–6; Arrival, *supra* note 30, at 506–19.

32. Purcell, *supra* note 30, at 17–19; Charles E. Merriam, *Preface to the First Edition* (1925), *in* New Aspects of Politics 49, 55 (3d ed. 1970); Walter Wheeler Cook, The Logical and Legal Basis of the Conflict of Laws 4 (1942); Felix Cohen, *Transcendental Nonsense and the Functional Approach,* 35 Colum. L. Rev. 809 (1935); Karl N. Llewellyn, The Bramble Bush 12 (1930); Walter Wheeler Cook, *Legal Logic,* 31 Colum. L. Rev. 108, 113 (1931); Herbert Hovenkamp, *Labor Conspiracies in American Law,* 66 Tex. L. Rev. 919, 936–37 (1988); Charles E. Merriam & Harold F. Gosnell, Non-Voting (1924); Underhill Moore & Gilbert Sussman, *Legal and Institutional Methods Ap-*

plied to the Debiting of Direct Discounts— III. The Connecticut Studies, 40 Yale L.J. 752 (1931); Mark Blaug, Economic Theory in Retrospect 593–95 (5th ed. 1996); Edwin Mansfield, Economics 476–77 (1974); Ross, *supra* note 30, at 414–20; Hackney, *supra* note 30, at 288–91.

33. Walter Lippmann, A Preface to Morals 3–4, 8 (1929); Antony Flew, A Dictionary of Philosophy 214 (rev. 2d ed. 1979); A.J. Ayer, Language, Truth, and Logic (1936; 1952 Dover reprint ed.); Rudolf Carnap, *The Rejection of Metaphysics* (1935), *in* Morton White, The Age of Analysis 209, 212–18 (1955); Purcell, *supra* note 30, at 40–42, 69–73; Ross, *supra* note 30, at 314–15; Hackney, *supra* note 30, at 280–82.

34. Lippmann, *supra* note 33, at 267; Charles E. Merriam, *Preface to the Second Edition* (1931), *in* New Aspects of Politics 39 (3d ed. 1970); John Dewey, *"America"—By Formula,* The New Republic (TNR), Sept. 18, 1929, at 117, 118; John Dewey, *Toward a New Individualism,* TNR, Feb. 19, 1930, at 13–15.

35. Purcell, *supra* note 30, at 103 (quoting Lasswell, 1930); Dumenil, *supra* note 1, at 146–47.

36. Wiebe, *supra* note 1, at 176 (quoting Dewey, 1927); Walter Lippmann, The Phantom Public 30, 147, 155–56 (1925); Lippmann, *supra* note 33, at 278; Charles E. Merriam, Political Power 4 (1934); Llewellyn, *supra* note 32, at 12; Jerome Frank, *Mr. Justice Holmes and Non-Euclidean Legal Thinking,* 17 Cornell L.Q. 568, 571, 580 (1932); Jerome Frank, Law and the Modern Mind (1930); Feldman, *supra* note 30, at 109–15.

37. Ross, *supra* note 30, at 330–39; Keyssar, *supra* note 1, at 226–228 (quoting Munro); *New Literacy Test Adopted by State,* N.Y. Times, Aug. 9, 1923, at 30; Purcell, *supra* note 30, at 119–27 (quoting Dewey); Walter J. Shepard, *Democracy in Transition,* 29 Am. Pol. Sci. Rev. 1, 6–19 (1935); Arthur F. Bentley, The Process of Government (1908); Charles Beard, An Economic Interpretation of the Constitution (1913); *The Literacy Law,* N.Y. Times, Mar. 28, 1931, at 15; Gunnell, *supra* note 30, at 84, 105; Schlesinger, *supra* note 1, at 145–52; Wiecek, *supra* note 1, at 256–57.

38. Hofstadter, *supra* note 1, at 301, 307; Badger, *supra* note 1, at 58.

39. Franklin D. Roosevelt, *The Forgotten Man* (Radio Address, Apr. 7, 1932).

40. Deal, *supra* note 1, at 5 (quoting Smith); Franklin D. Roosevelt, *Commonwealth Club Speech* (Sept. 23, 1932), *reprinted in* 3 Great, *supra* note 1, at 335, 341–42; Franklin D. Roosevelt, *First Inaugural Address* (Mar. 4, 1933), *reprinted in id.* at 343, 346; Dollinger, *supra* note 1, at 24–25.

41. Badger, *supra* note 1, at 61–65; Kennedy, *supra* note 1, at 119–24.

42. Deal, *supra* note 1, at 339 (quoting Tugwell, 1935); Starr, *supra* note 1, at 374–75.

43. Deal, *supra* note 1, at 41–62, 85–86, 146–47, 184, 347; Kennedy, *supra* note 1, at 133–53, 378–79; Jerold S. Auerbach, Unequal Justice (1976); Badger, *supra* note 1, at 249; Sachar, *supra* note 9, at 446–50; G. Edward White, *Recapturing New Deal Lawyers,* 102 Harv. L. Rev. 489, 514–15 (1988).

44. Deal, *supra* note 1, at 89–90, 147–48; *see* Herbert Hoover, *This Challenge to Liberty, reprinted in* 3 Great, *supra* note 1, at 349.

45. Piven & Cloward, *supra* note 1, at 130–31 (quoting Moley); Franklin D.

Roosevelt, *We Have Only Just Begun to Fight* (Radio Address, Oct. 31, 1936); Americans All, Immigrants All (1938–39), http://americanradioworks.publicradio.org/features/jim_crow/americansall.html (accessed Oct. 20, 2005); Deal, *supra* note 1, at 85; Starr, *supra* note 1, at 375.

46. Piven & Cloward, *supra* note 1, at 96–97, 120–31; Deal, *supra* note 1, at 7, 106–8; National Industrial Recovery Act (July 5, 1935), § 7(a), 49 Stat. 449; Auerbach, *supra* note 1, at 51–53; Dubofsky, *supra* note 1, at 110–24; McElvaine, *supra* note 1, at 225–26.

47. Dubofsky, *supra* note 1, at 119–28; Labor, *supra* note 1, at 365; Schechter Poultry Corp. v. United States, 295 U.S. 495 (1935); The National Labor Relations Act (July 5, 1935), 49 Stat. 449; Kennedy, *supra* note 1, at 296–98; Deal, *supra* note 1, at 150–52; Geoffrey D. Berman, *A New Deal for Free Speech,* 80 Va. L. Rev. 291, 305 n.92 (1994).

48. NLRB, Legislative History of the National Labor Relations Act, 1935, at 446, 2361, 2367, 2414–15, 3228 (1985 Commemorative ed.) [hereinafter History]; Badger, *supra* note 1, at 4; Dubofsky, *supra* note 1, at 127–28; Deal, *supra* note 1, at 89.

49. Deal, *supra* note 1, at 109–11; Piven & Cloward, *supra* note 1, at 115–19; Christopher Tomlins, The State and the Unions 140–45 (1985); Statistical, *supra* note 1, at 98.

50. Kennedy, *supra* note 1, at 308–15; Dubofsky, *supra* note 1, at 132–43 (quoting *Fortune,* Oct. 1938); Deal, *supra* note 1, at 239–41; Piven & Cloward, *supra* note 1, at 133–47; *see* Herbert G. Gutman, Work, Culture, and Society in Industrializing America xii, 10–11 (1976).

51. Louis L. Jaffe, *Law Making by Private Groups,* 51 Harv. L. Rev. 201–3 (1937); History, *supra* note 48, at 1620–21; Making, *supra* note 1, at 362; Dumenil, *supra* note 1, at 49–52; Wiebe, *supra* note 1, at 197–203; Statistical, *supra* note 1, at 491.

52. Making, *supra* note 1, at 333, 355, 362; Kennedy, *supra* note 1, at 284–85, 315; Deal, *supra* note 1, at 185–89; Austin, *supra* note 1, at 379; Badger, *supra* note 1, at 191, 248–49; Dubofsky, *supra* note 1, at 133–35; Lubell, *supra* note 20, at 49.

53. Deal, *supra* note 1, at 157–58, 189–90; Austin, *supra* note 1, at 97; Kennedy, *supra* note 1, at 252; Lichtman, *supra* note 20, at 210–11.

54. Making, *supra* note 1, at 355, 362; Deal, *supra* note 1, at 125–26, 335. The expansion of national power did not diminish state governmental power. William E. Leuchtenburg, The Supreme Court Reborn 225–27 (1995); Stephen Gardbaum, *New Deal Constitutionalism and the Unshackling of the States,* 64 U. Chi. L. Rev. 483 (1997).

55. Steinberg, *supra* note 1, at 53; Irving Howe, World of Our Fathers 228 (1976); Auerbach, *supra* note 43, at 186.

56. Arthur F. McEvoy, *Freedom of Contract, Labor, and the Administrative State, in* The State and Freedom of Contract 198, 225–26 (Harry N. Scheiber ed., 1998); Making, *supra* note 1, at 252–53; Dubofsky, *supra* note 1, at 110–11; Piven & Cloward, *supra* note 1, at 32, 81–82, 96–97.

57. Stephen M. Feldman, Please Don't Wish Me a Merry Christmas 213 (1997); Gerring, *supra* note 1, at 145 (quoting Wilkie); Auerbach, *supra* note 43, at 186.

58. Ira Katznelson, When Affirmative Action Was White 22, 43–46 (2005);

Michael K. Brown, et al., Whitewashing Race 28–30, 193–94 (2003); McElvaine, *supra* note 1, at 193; Kennedy, *supra* note 1, at 378; Deal, *supra* note 1, at 185–87; Roediger, *supra* note 1, at 203–11; *see* Keyssar, *supra* note 1, at 226–37, 249–55; Manning Marable, The Great Wells of Democracy (2002).

59. Kennedy, *supra* note 1, at 350–61; Austin, *supra* note 1, at 52–55; Deal, *supra* note 1, at 243–50, 272.

60. Robert Brooks, *Reflections on the "World Revolution" of 1940*, 35 Am. Pol. Sci. Rev. 1, 3, 21 (1941); John E. Mulder, *Democracy Must Introspect*, 1 Bill Rts. Rev. 259, 260 (1941); Gallup, *supra* note 1, at 186 (Oct. 23, 1939); Kennedy, *supra* note 1, at 361, 415–27.

61. Geoffrey R. Stone, *Free Speech in World War II*, 2 Int'l J. Const. L. 334 (2004); Purcell, *supra* note 30, at 117–58; Gunnell, *supra* note 30, at 127–33.

62. Charles E. Merriam, The New Democracy and the New Despotism v, 4, 252 (1939); Walter Lippmann, An Inquiry into the Principles of the Good Society xii, 112 (1937).

63. Lippmann, *supra* note 62, at 286; Carl J. Friedrich, The New Belief in the Common Man 41 (1945); *see* John Dewey & James H. Tufts, Ethics (1932 ed.), *reprinted in* John Dewey, 7 The Later Works 1, 359 (Jo Ann Boydston ed., 1985); John Dewey, Freedom and Culture (1939) [hereinafter Freedom].

64. Joseph A. Schumpeter, Capitalism, Socialism, and Democracy 250–51, 269, 283, 286 (1942; 3d ed. 1950); Freedom, *supra* note 63, at 175–76; Friedrich, *supra* note 63, at 41; Lippmann, *supra* note 62, at 286.

65. Freedom, *supra* note 63, at 134; Robert H. Jackson, *Messages on the Launching of the "Bill of Rights Review*," 1 Bill Rts. Rev. 34, 36 (1940); Mulder, *supra* note 60, at 260; Lippmann, *supra* note 62, at 283.

66. C. Herman Pritchett, The Roosevelt Court xi, 16, 136 (1948); Leo Strauss, Natural Right and History (1953); Eric Voegelin, The New Science of Politics (1952); *see* Gunnell, *supra* note 30, at 155–56, 195–205, 237–40.

67. Wilfred E. Binkley & Malcolm C. Moos, A Grammar of American Politics 7, 9 (1949); David B. Truman, The Governmental Process 505–6 (1951); *see* Theodore J. Lowi, The End of Liberalism (1969).

68. Henry M. Hart, Jr. & Albert Sacks, The Legal Process: Basic Problems in the Making and Application of Law 4, 164–67 (Tentative ed. 1958); *see* Feldman, *supra* note 30, at 105–23; Henry M. Hart, Jr., *Holmes' Positivism — An Addendum*, 64 Harv. L. Rev. 929, 934 (1951); John Dickinson, *Legal Rules*, 79 U. Pa. L. Rev. 833 (1931).

69. Robert A. Dahl, A Preface to Democratic Theory 6, 143 (1956); Robert A. Dahl, Democracy and Its Critics 106, 109, 169–75 (1989).

70. Lowi, *supra* note 67, at 74; Cross, *supra* note 1, at 82–84; Republic, *supra* note 1, at 65, 85 (quoting Gordon); Statistical, *supra* note 1, at 139, 178.

71. John E. Mulder, *Civil Liberty — 1917–1942*, 2 Bill Rts. Rev. 83 (1942); Dollinger, *supra* note 1, at 63; Roediger, *supra* note 1, at 134–38; Sugrue, *supra* note 1, at 19.

72. Brown, *supra* note 58, at 71; Badger, *supra* note 1, at 310–11; Sugrue, *supra* note 1, at 26–27.

73. Sugrue, *supra* note 1, at 28–29, 218; Republic, *supra* note 1, at 93–94; Dinner-

stein, *supra* note 8, at 131; Dollinger, *supra* note 1, at 78; Executive Order 9066, Authorizing the Secretary of War to Prescribe Military Areas (Feb. 19, 1942), 7 Fed. Reg. 1407; An Act to Provide a Penalty for Violation of Military Restrictions (Mar. 21, 1942), 56 Stat. 173.

74. Bell, *supra* note 1, at 70; Republic, *supra* note 1, at 119; Cross, *supra* note 1, at 86; Statistical, *supra* note 1, at 139, 178.

75. Katznelson, *supra* note 58, at 113; Servicemen's Readjustment Act of 1944 (June 22, 1944), 58 Stat. 284–301; Republic, *supra* note 1, at 139–40.

76. Republic, *supra* note 1, at 118–24; Cross, *supra* note 1, at 87; David Halberstam, The Fifties 142 (1993); Statistical, *supra* note 1, at 379, 393.

77. Halberstam, *supra* note 76, at 496, 587; Will Herberg, Protestant-Catholic-Jew 87–89, 167 (1955); *see* Brown, *supra* note 58, at 74; Dollinger, *supra* note 1, at 130.

78. Cross, *supra* note 1, at 100–103; Halberstam, *supra* note 76, at 197, 509–10; Starr, *supra* note 1, at 382–84; Statistical, *supra* note 1, at 491, 500b; *see* James T. Patterson, Grand Expectations 343–74 (1996).

79. Republic, *supra* note 1, at 7–9, 126, 332–41; Collins & Skover, *supra* note 14, at 724–25; *see* Bell, *supra* note 1, at 23–24.

80. Charles L. Black, Jr., Structure and Relationship in Constitutional Law 54 (1969); Austin, *supra* note 1, at 379; *see* Isaac Kramnick & R. Laurence Moore, The Godless Constitution 204 (2005); Deal, *supra* note 1, at 347; Putnam, *supra* note 1, at 31–47; *e.g.,* Frank Michelman, *Foreword: Traces of Self-Government,* 100 Harv. L. Rev. 4 (1986).

81. Cross, *supra* note 1, at 176; Republic, *supra* note 1, at 331–44; Collins & Skover, *supra* note 14, at 705–7.

82. Taft-Hartley Act (June 23, 1947), *reprinted in* 2 Commager, *supra* note 1, at 537; Dubofksy, *supra* note 1, at xii–xiii; Austin, *supra* note 1, at 50–55; Republic, *supra* note 1, at 342, 366–67; Statistical, *supra* note 1, at 98, 100c; *see* Inequality and American Democracy (Lawrence R. Jacobs & Theda Skocpol eds., 2005).

83. Republic, *supra* note 1, at 155, 169–71; Piven & Cloward, *supra* note 1, at 184; Brown, *supra* note 58, at 75–77; Halberstam, *supra* note 76, at 446–49; Sugrue, *supra* note 1, at 38–44, 91–123, 275–78.

84. Katznelson, *supra* note 58, at 114–15, 122–29, 164; Brown, *supra* note 58, at 72; Republic, *supra* note 1, at 171, 217; Halberstam, *supra* note 76, at 135.

85. Jerome A. Chanes, *Antisemitism and Jewish Security in America Today, in* Antisemitism in America Today 3, 24 (Jerome A. Chanes ed., 1995); To Secure These Rights: The Report of President Harry S. Truman's Committee on Civil Rights 176–77 (1947; 2004 reprint) [hereinafter Secure]; Dinnerstein, *supra* note 8, at 150–74; Kennedy, *supra* note 1, at 773; Sachar, *supra* note 9, at 791.

86. Richard Kluger, Simple Justice (1975); Secure, *supra* note 85, at 158–67; Mary L. Dudziak, Cold War Civil Rights (2000); Derrick A. Bell, *Brown v. Board of Education and the Interest-Convergence Dilemma,* 93 Harv. L. Rev. 518 (1980).

87. Keyssar, *supra* note 1, at 258, 263 (quoting Johnson); Malcolm X, *The Ballot or the Bullet* (Apr. 3, 1964), *in* Malcolm X Speaks 23–44 (George Breitman ed., 1965); Gallup, *supra* note 1, at 1863 (Feb. 2, 1964).

88. Keyssar, *supra* note 1, at 281–82; Voting Rights Act of 1965, 79 Stat. 437; Civil Rights Act of 1964, 78 Stat. 241; Brown, *supra* note 58, at 194–95; Marable, *supra* note 58, at 71; Lucas A. Powe, Jr., The Warren Court and American Politics 239–40 (2000).

89. Martin Luther King, Jr., *Where Do We Go from Here?* (1967), *in* A Testament of Hope 555, 558 (James M. Washington ed., 1986); Civil Rights Act of 1964, Title II, 78 Stat. 241; Brown, *supra* note 58, at 73; David J. Garrow, Bearing the Cross 481–525 (1986); Sugrue, *supra* note 1, at 176–77; Robert Weisbrot, Freedom Bound 196–221 (1990).

90. Marable, *supra* note 58, at 153; The Sentencing Project, *Losing the Vote* 8, 12–13 (1998); Ryan S. King, The Sentencing Project, *A Decade of Reform* 2, 18 (2006); Daniel S. Goldman, *The Modern-Day Literacy Test?*, 57 Stan. L. Rev. 611, 633 (2004).

CHAPTER TEN

1. Adkins v. Children's Hospital, 261 U.S. 525, 557, 559, (1923). Sources on judicial review include Barry Cushman, Rethinking the New Deal Court (1998); Howard Gillman, The Constitution Besieged (1993); Ken I. Kersch, Constructing Civil Liberties (2004); William E. Leuchtenburg, The Supreme Court Reborn (1995); G. Edward White, The Constitution and the New Deal (2000); T. Alexander Aleinikoff, *Constitutional Law in the Age of Balancing,* 96 Yale L.J. 943 (1987); David E. Bernstein, *Lochner Era Revisionism, Revised,* 92 Geo. L.J. 1 (2003); Barry Friedman, *The History of the Countermajoritarian Difficulty, Part Four,* 148 U. Pa. L. Rev. 971 (2000); Richard D. Friedman, *Switching Time and Other Thought Experiments,* 142 U. Pa. L. Rev. 1891 (1994) [hereinafter Switching]; Stephen Gardbaum, *New Deal Constitutionalism and the Unshackling of the States,* 64 U. Chi. L. Rev. 483 (1997); James A. Henretta, *Charles Evan Hughes and the Strange Death of Liberal America,* 24 Law & Hist. Rev. 115 (2006). Other helpful sources include Jerold S. Auerbach, Labor and Liberty (1966); Erik W. Austin, Political Facts of the United States since 1789 (1986); Lucas A. Powe, Jr., The Warren Court and American Politics (2000); William M. Wiecek, The Lost World of Classical Legal Thought (1998); Documents of American History (Henry Steele Commager ed., 9th ed. 1973) [hereinafter Commager]; Landmark Briefs and Arguments of the Supreme Court of the United States: Constitutional Law (Philip B. Kurland & Gerhard Casper eds., 1975) [hereinafter Landmark].

2. *Blaisdell,* 290 U.S. 398 (1934); *Nebbia,* 291 U.S. 502, 536 (1934); Stromberg v. California, 283 U.S. 359, 368–70 (1931); Bernstein, *supra* note 1, at 51; Switching, *supra* note 1, at 1900–1903.

3. *R.R. Retirement Bd.,* 295 U.S. 330, 368, 374 (1935); *Carter,* 298 U.S. 238, 304 (1936); *see* Morehead v. New York ex rel. Tipaldo, 298 U.S. 587 (1936) (state minimum wage law for women); Leuchtenburg, *supra* note 1, at 214–15.

4. *Butler,* 297 U.S. 1, 78–88 (1936) (Stone, J., dissenting); *Schechter,* 295 U.S. 495 (1935). Stone followed sociological jurisprudence in *The Common Law in the United States,* 50 Harv. L. Rev. 4 (1936), after previously criticizing it. *Some Aspects of the*

Problem of Law Simplification, 23 Colum. L. Rev. 319, 327–28 (1923); *Book Review,* 22 Colum. L. Rev. 382, 384 (1922).

5. Robert L. Hale, *Force and the State,* 35 Colum. L. Rev. 149, 168, 198–201 (1935); Morris Cohen, *The Basis of Contract,* 46 Harv. L. Rev. 553 (1933); *see* Louis Boudin, Government by Judiciary (1932) (Court frustrated democratic will).

6. Felix Cohen, *Transcendental Nonsense and the Functional Approach,* 35 Colum. L. Rev. 809, 839–40 (1935).

7. Leuchtenburg, *supra* note 1, at 96–97, 119; Drew Pearson & Robert S. Allen, The Nine Old Men 2–3, 28–40 (1936); *Triple A Plowed Under,* N.Y. Times, Jan. 12, 1936, at E1; Austin, *supra* note 1, at 97; Friedman, *supra* note 1, at 1011–19; *see* Barry Cushman, *Mr. Dooley and Mr. Gallup: Public Opinion and Constitutional Change in the 1930s,* 50 Buff. L. Rev. 7, 19–58 (2002) (polls showed that most Americans supported New Deal in general but did not always support specific New Deal programs as strongly).

8. Congress or the Supreme Court: Which Shall Rule America? 414, 416 (Egbert Ray Nichols ed., 1935) (attributing this idea to Corwin); 81 Cong. Rec., Appendix at 469–71, 75th Cong., 1st Sess. (Mar. 10, 1937); 81 Cong. Rec., 75th Cong., 1st Sess. 877–79 (Feb. 5, 1937); Leuchtenburg, *supra* note 1, at 114–31; Wiecek, *supra* note 1, at 200–01; Friedman, *supra* note 1, at 1019–23; Henretta, *supra* note 1, at 166.

9. See *Three Senators Score Court Plan Here as Peril to Nation,* N.Y. Times, Mar. 13, 1937, at 1; Robert C. Albright, *Congressional Factions Unite in Hailing Wagner Decisions,* Wash. Post, Apr. 13, 1937, at 1; Thomas Reed Powell, *Authority and Freedom in a Democratic Society,* 44 Colum. L. Rev. 473, 484 (1944); Cushman, *supra* note 1, at 18–19; Leuchtenburg, *supra* note 1, at 142–44, 177; Friedman, *supra* note 1, at 1038–44.

10. *West Coast Hotel,* 300 U.S. 379, 391–92, 398–400 (1937); *id.* at 411–12 (Sutherland, J., dissenting).

11. *Jones & Laughlin,* 301 U.S. 1, 34–37, 41–42 (1937).

12. *Id.* at 33, 43–46; *see* Kersch, *supra* note 1, at 178. In *Associated Press v. NLRB,* 301 U.S. 103 (1937), decided the same day as *Jones and Laughlin,* the Court reiterated that the NLRA did not exceed Congress's commerce power and held that the first amendment did not insulate the AP from the NLRA. *See* Lauf v. Shinner, 303 U.S. 323 (1938) (interpreting pre–New Deal Norris-LaGuardia Act); Senn v. Tile Layers Union, 301 U.S. 468 (1937) (upholding state labor law, reinforcing the right of workers to unionize and to press their claims).

13. *See* Steward Mach. Co. v. Davis, 301 U.S. 548, 583–89, 594 (1937) (upholding Social Security Act of 1935 sections providing for unemployment benefits).

14. *Supreme Court Upholds Wagner Labor Law; Hailed by Friends and Foes of Bench Change,* N.Y. Times, Apr. 13, 1917, at 1; Franklyn Waltman, *Politics and People: Wagner Labor Act Decisions Seen as Turning Point in United States History,* Wash. Post, Apr. 13, 1937, at 2; Albright, *supra* note 9, at 1; *Butler,* 297 U.S. at 62; Franklyn Waltman, *Roberts Switch Strengthens U.S. Control in Industry,* Wash. Post, Apr. 13, 1937, 1, 4; see Cushman, *supra* note 1, at 31, 177–78; Leuchtenburg, *supra* note 1, at 142–43; Switching, *supra* note 1, at 1897–98; Eugene V. Rostow, *Book Review,* 56 Yale L.J. 1469, 1472 (1947) (the Court "died, and was reborn, in 1937").

15. *Roosevelt to Quit in 1940, Creel Says,* N.Y. Times, Nov. 30, 1936, at 4; *Highlights of Today's Polls,* Wash. Post, Dec. 13, 1936, at B1; Cushman, *supra* note 1, at 18; Leuchtenburg, *supra* note 1, at 114–31, 143, 310–11 n.17.

16. Cushman, *supra* note 1, at 42; Gillman, *supra* note 1, at 147–93.

17. C. Herman Pritchett, The Roosevelt Court (1948); Cushman, *supra* note 1, at 175–76, 187–89; Leuchtenburg, *supra* note 1, at 180–85.

18. *Wickard,* 317 U.S. 111, 118, 120, 129 (1942); Cushman, *supra* note 1, at 31.

19. Stephen M. Feldman, American Legal Thought from Premodernism to Postmodernism 91 (2000); G. Edward White, *The Arrival of History in Constitutional Scholarship,* 88 Va. L. Rev. 485, 536–37 (2002).

20. Alexander M. Bickel, The Least Dangerous Branch 16 (1962; 2d ed. 1986); *Jackson Calls Court Curb on Democracy,* N.Y. Times, Oct. 13, 1937, at 6; Powell, *supra* note 9, at 484; Wiecek, *supra* note 1, at 241; Friedman, *supra* note 1, at 1000–1001.

21. Learned Hand, *The Contribution of an Independent Judiciary to Civilization* (1942), *reprinted in* The Spirit of Liberty 118–25 (Irving Dilliard ed., 1959 ed.) [hereinafter Contribution]; Learned Hand, The Bill of Rights (1958) (elaborating these views).

22. Eugene V. Rostow, *The Democratic Character of Judicial Review,* 66 Harv. L. Rev. 193, 205 (1952).

23. G. Edward White, *Historicizing Judicial Scrutiny,* 57 S.C. L. Rev. 1, 53 (2005) (citing David P. Brewer, 1893).

24. Pritchett, *supra* note 17, at xiii; Fowler Harper & Edwin Etherington, *Lobbyists before the Court,* 101 U. Pa. L. Rev. 1172, 1173 (1953); Wilfred Binkley & Malcolm Moos, A Grammar of American Politics 525–26 (1949); C. Herman Pritchett, *Dissent on the Supreme Court, 1943–44,* 39 Am. Pol. Sci. Rev. 42 (1945); *see* Henry Steele Commager, Majority Rule and Minority Rights 43 (1943; 1950 reprint); Lee Epstein & Jack Knight, *Mapping Out the Strategic Terrain, in* Supreme Court Decision-Making 215, 221–22 (Cornell W. Clayton & Howard Gillman eds., 1999); Samuel Krislov, *The Amicus Brief,* 72 Yale L.J. 694, 713–17 (1963).

25. United States v. Carolene Prods. Co., 304 U.S. 144, 152 (1938). The only possible exception to the assertion that the Court rubber-stamped economic regulations was *Hartford Steam Boiler I. & Ins. Co. v. Harrison,* 301 U.S. 459 (1937), decided less than six weeks after *Jones and Laughlin* and before FDR had replaced any of the Four Horsemen. Hughes joined the Horsemen in holding that a state police power law differentiating between stock and mutual insurance companies violated equal protection. Barry Cushman, *Regime Theory and Unenumerated Rights: A Cautionary Note,* 9 U. Pa. J. Const. L. 263, 277 (2006).

26. Auerbach, *supra* note 1, at 1, 75; Committee on Education and Labor, 76th Cong., 1st Sess. Report No. 6, Pt. 3 (1939), *reprinted in* American Labor 254, 258 (Jerold S. Auerbach ed., 1969); Robert H. Wiebe, Self-Rule 223 (1995).

27. *Martin,* 319 U.S. 141, 146–47 (1943); *id.* at 150 (Murphy, J., concurring); ABA Committee on the Bill of Rights, *Activities of the Bar Association Committees,* 1 Bill

Rts. Rev. 63–65 (1940); Geoffrey D. Berman, *A New Deal for Free Speech*, 80 Va. L. Rev. 291, 321 (1994).

28. Berman, *supra* note 27, at 305 (quoting ACLU report); Grenville Clark, *The Prospects for Civil Liberty*, 24 A.B.A. J. 833, 836 (1938).

29. Richard W. Steele, Free Speech in the Good War 11 (1999) (Hogan); Grenville Clark, *Conservatism and Civil Liberty*, 24 A.B.A. J. 640–44 (1938); Ran Hirschl, *The Political Origins of Judicial Empowerment through Constitutionalization*, 25 Law & Soc. Inquiry 91, 95–103 (2000); *cf.*, Kersch, *supra* note 1, at 112–17.

30. NLRB v. Va. Elec. & Power Co., 314 U.S. 469, 477 (1941); Editors, *Employers' Right of Free Speech*, 2 Bill Rts. Rev. 144 (1942).

31. The Supreme Court in Conference 404 (Del Dickson ed., 2001); Everson v. Bd. of Educ., 330 U.S. 1 (1947); Cantwell v. Connecticut, 310 U.S. 296 (1940); Robert T. Handy, A History of the Churches in the United States and Canada 312 (1977); Geoffrey R. Stone et al., Constitutional Law 1494–1503 (2d ed. 1991).

32. West Va. State Bd. of Ed. v. Barnette, 319 U.S. 624, 639 (1943); White, *supra* note 1, at 149–52.

33. *Carolene Products*, 304 U.S. at 152–53 n.4 (1938); Louis Lusky, *Footnote Redux*, 82 Colum. L. Rev. 1093 (1982).

34. *Colegrove*, 328 U.S. 549, 553–56 (1946).

35. *Id.* at 569–71 (Black, J., dissenting).

36. Williamson v. Lee Optical of Okla., Inc., 348 U.S. 483, 488 (1955); John H. Ely, Democracy and Distrust 106 (1980).

37. Schneider v. State, 308 U.S. 147, 161 (1939); *Pike*, 397 U.S. 137, 142 (1970); Aleinikoff, *supra* note 1, at 963–64; Julian Eule, *Laying the Dormant Commerce Clause to Rest*, 91 Yale L.J. 425 (1982); *cf.*, Ronald Dworkin, Taking Rights Seriously 194, 269 (1978) (arguing rights and interests are philosophically distinct).

38. *Carolene Products*, 304 U.S. at 152–53 n.4; *Murdock*, 319 U.S. 105, 111, 115 (1943); *Palko*, 302 U.S. 319, 325 (1937); *see* Thomas v. Collins, 323 U.S. 516, 529–30 (1945); White, *supra* note 19, at 144, 157–58; Howard Gillman, *Preferred Freedoms*, 47 Pol. Res. Q. 623, 640–45 (1994).

39. *Barnette*, 319 U.S. at 638; Mark A. Graber, Transforming Free Speech 181 (1991) (quoting Black); Hugo L. Black, *The Bill of Rights*, 35 N.Y.U. L. Rev. 865 (1960).

40. Korematsu v. United States, 323 U.S. 214, 216 (1944); Sherbert v. Verner, 374 U.S. 398 (1963); Skinner v. Oklahoma, 316 U.S. 535, 541 (1942) (first time majority used precise phrase, "strict scrutiny").

41. Contribution, *supra* note 21, at 123; Aleinikoff, *supra* note 1, at 972–95.

42. Sweezy v. New Hampshire, 354 U.S. 234, 267 (1957) (Frankfurter, J., concurring in result); Aleinikoff, *supra* note 1, at 962–63.

43. *Thomas*, 323 U.S. at 557 (Roberts, J., dissenting).

44. *Gobitis*, 310 U.S. 586, 592, 599–600 (1940); *id.* at 605–6 (Stone, J., dissenting); *overruled*, *Barnette*, 319 U.S.

45. *Barnette*, 319 U.S. at 638, 641 (1943); *id.* at 670–71 (Frankfurter, J., dissenting); Shawn Peters, Judging Jehovah's Witnesses 72–95 (2000); William McAninch,

A Catalyst for the Evolution of Constitutional Law, 55 U. Cin. L. Rev. 997, 1018–21 & n.147 (1987).

46. *Brown,* 347 U.S. 483, 493, 495 (1954); Powe, *supra* note 1, at 209–17, 487–99; Ely, *supra* note 36, at 121.

47. *Gomillion,* 364 U.S. 339, 340–41, 347 (1960); *Baker,* 369 U.S. 186, 208–37 (1962); *id.* at 301 (Frankfurter, J., dissenting).

48. *Wesberry,* 376 U.S. 1, 7–8 (1964) ; Ely, *supra* note 36, at 117, 120–21; *Suit Pushed Here,* N.Y. Times, Mar. 27, 1962, at 1; William N. Eskridge, *Channeling,* 150 U. Pa. L. Rev. 419, 423, 510 (2001); *Reynolds,* 377 U.S. 533 (1964).

49. *Griswold,* 381 U.S. 479, 482 (1965); *Roe,* 410 U.S. 113, 116 (1973); Robert H. Bork, *Neutral Principles and Some First Amendment Problems,* 47 Ind. L.J. 1, 1–9, 17, 22–23 (1971); Robert Bork, The Tempting of America 112–16 (1990); David J. Garrow, Liberty and Sexuality (1994).

50. Norman L. Rosenberg, *Another History of Free Speech,* 7 L. & Inequality 333, 341 (1989).

51. James T. Patterson, Restless Giant 36 (2005); Brief of Synagogue Council of America and National Community Relations Advisory Council as *Amici Curiae,* Engel v. Vitale, 370 U.S. 421 (1962) (1961 Term, No. 468), at 26; Brief for Appellants, Braunfeld v. Gibbons, *aff'd sub nom.* Braunfeld v. Brown, 366 U.S. 599 (1961) (1960 Term, No. 67), at 10; *see* Gallagher v. Crown Kosher Super Mkt., 366 U.S. 617, 619–20 (1961); Ronald Dworkin, Law's Empire 223 (1986); Kimberle Crenshaw, *Race, Reform, and Retrenchment,* 101 Harv. L. Rev. 1331 (1988); Stephen M. Feldman, *Empiricism, Religion, and Judicial Decision Making,* 15 Wm. & Mary Bill Rts. J. 43 (2006).

52. Robert A. Dahl, *Decision-Making in a Democracy,* 6 J. Pub. L. 279, 284, 293 (1957); *see* Gerald N. Rosenberg, The Hollow Hope (1991); Barry Friedman, *The Counter-Majoritarian Problem and the Pathology of Constitutional Scholarship,* 95 Nw. U. L. Rev. 933 (2001); Mark A. Graber, *Constitutional Politics and Constitutional Theory,* 27 Law & Soc. Inquiry 309 (2002); Terri Peretti, *An Empirical Analysis of Alexander Bickel's The Least Dangerous Branch, in* The Judiciary and American Democracy 123 (Kenneth D. Ward & Cecilia R. Castillo eds., 2005).

CHAPTER ELEVEN

1. Helpful sources on the history of free expression during this period include Robert Justin Goldstein, Political Repression in Modern America (2001); Mark A. Graber, Transforming Free Speech (1991); Lucas A. Powe, Jr., The Warren Court and American Politics (2000); David M. Rabban, Free Speech in Its Forgotten Years (1997); Paul Starr, The Creation of the Media (2004); Geoffrey R. Stone, Perilous Times (2004); G. Edward White, The Constitution and the New Deal (2000); Geoffrey D. Berman, *A New Deal for Free Speech,* 80 Va. L. Rev. 291 (1994); William N. Eskridge, *Some Effects of Identity-Based Social Movements on Constitutional Law in the Twentieth Century,* 100 Mich. L. Rev. 2062 (2002).

General histories and other helpful resources include Erik W. Austin, Political

Facts of the United States since 1789 (1986); George H. Gallup, The Gallup Poll (1972; in 3 vols.); James T. Patterson, Grand Expectations (1996); Documents of American History (Henry Steele Commager ed., 9th ed. 1973) [hereinafter Commager]; Landmark Briefs and Arguments of the Supreme Court of the United States: Constitutional Law (Philip B. Kurland & Gerhard Casper eds., 1975) [hereinafter Landmark].

2. Gitlow v. New York, 268 U.S. 652, 666–71 (1925). The lower courts also continued to apply republican democratic principles. Thomas v. Indianapolis, 195 Ind. 440, 145 N.E. 550, 553 (1924); Robison v. Hotel & Rest. Employees, Local 782, 35 Idaho 418, 207 P. 132, 135 (1922); Margaret A. Blanchard, *Filling in the Void, in* The First Amendment Reconsidered 14, 27–29 (Bill F. Chamberlin & Charlene J. Brown eds., 1982).

3. *Gitlow,* 268 U.S. at 672–73 (Holmes, J., dissenting).

4. Whitney v. California, 274 U.S. 357, 359–60, 371 (1927).

5. *Id.* at 374–80 (Brandeis, J., concurring in judgment). For emphases on individual dignity and self-fulfillment, see C. Edwin Baker, Human Liberty and Freedom of Speech 47–69 (1989); Thomas I. Emerson, The System of Freedom of Expression 6–7 (1970). Other free-expression theorists include Harry Kalven, Jr., A Worthy Tradition (1988); Alexander Meiklejohn, Free Speech and Its Relation to Self-Government (1948); Steven H. Shiffrin, Dissent, Injustice, and the Meanings of America (1999); Robert Post, *Reconciling Theory and Doctrine in First Amendment Jurisprudence,* 88 Calif. L. Rev. 2353 (2000); Frederick Schauer, *Free Speech and the Argument from Democracy, in* Liberal Democracy: Nomos XXV 241 (J. Roland Pennock & John W. Chapman, eds., 1983).

6. *Whitney,* 274 U.S. at 377–78 (Brandeis, J., concurring in judgment).

7. Fiske v. Kansas, 274 U.S. 380, 382–87 (1927); Schwimmer v. United States, 279 U.S. 644, 646–48, 652 (1929), *overruled by* Girouard v. United States, 328 U.S. 61 (1946); *see* Burns v. United States, 274 U.S. 328 (1927) (sufficient evidence supported federal conviction of Wobbly organizer under California syndicalism statute); Turner v. Williams, 194 U.S. 279, 294 (1904) (aliens lack first-amendment rights). For other remote free-expression cases where the Court favored first-amendment values, see Pierce v. Soc'y of Sisters, 268 U.S. 510 (1925); Bartels v. Iowa, 262 U.S. 404 (1923); Meyer v. Nebraska, 262 U.S. 390 (1923); G. Edward White, *Justice Holmes and the Modernization of Free Speech Jurisprudence,* 80 Cal. L. Rev. 391, 445–59 (1992).

8. *Schwimmer,* 279 U.S. at 654–55 (Holmes, J., dissenting).

9. Stromberg v. California, 283 U.S. 359, 361, 368–70 (1931).

10. Kalven, *supra* note 5, at 167; *see* Erwin Chemerinsky, Constitutional Law 910–12 (2d ed. 2002) (vagueness).

11. Near v. Minnesota, 283 U.S. 697, 701–2, 707–8, 713–14 (1931); *id.* at 735–36 (Butler, J., dissenting); Starr, *supra* note 1, at 291–92.

12. Grosjean v. American Press Company, 297 U.S. 233, 240, 243, 249–50 (1936). Between *Near* and *Grosjean,* the Court rejected a free-expression claim, but not on the merits. Herndon v. Georgia, 295 U.S. 441 (1935).

13. De Jonge v. Oregon, 299 U.S. 353, 362–65 (1937).

14. Associated Press v. NLRB, 301 U.S. 103 (1937).

15. Kalven, *supra* note 5, at 170; Herndon v. Lowry, 301 U.S. 242, 246 n.2 (1937).

16. *Herndon,* 301 U.S. at 257–64.

17. *Id.* at 258; *Schneider,* 308 U.S. 147, 160–61 (1939).

18. *Hague,* 307 U.S. 496, 515 (1939); *Cantwell,* 310 U.S. 296, 303 (1940); *Thornhill,* 310 U.S. 88 (1940); *Carlson,* 310 U.S. 106 (1940); *Schneider,* 308 U.S.; *Lovell,* 303 U.S. 444 (1938).

19. G. Edward White, *The First Amendment Comes of Age,* 95 Mich. L. Rev. 299, 300–301 (1996); Palko v. Connecticut, 302 U.S. 319, 326–27 (1937); *Hague,* 307 U.S. at 524 (Stone, J., concurring).

20. Chaplinsky v. New Hampshire, 315 U.S. 568, 572 (1942); Zechariah Chafee, Jr., Free Speech in the United States 31–35, 559–61 (1941); *see* Baker, *supra* note 5, at 7–12.

21. Martin H. Redish, The Logic of Persecution 9 (2005); Graber, *supra* note 1, at 165–69; Post, *supra* note 5, at 2367–69.

22. *Thornhill,* 310 U.S. at 95–96; W. Va. State Bd. of Educ. v. Barnette, 319 U.S. 624, 641–42 (1943); Martin v. City of Struthers, 319 U.S. 141, 150 (1943) (Murphy, J., concurring); Terminiello v. Chicago, 337 U.S. 1, 4 (1949).

23. *Terminiello,* 337 U.S. at 4; *id.* at 24 (Jackson, J., dissenting).

24. *E.g.,* John E. Mulder, *Civil Liberty — 1917–1942,* 2 Bill Rts. Rev. 83, 85 (1942).

25. Grenville Clark, *The Limits of Free Expression,* 73 U.S. L. Rev. 392, 394–95 (1939); Meiklejohn, *supra* note 5, at 38–46.

26. Meiklejohn, *supra* note 5, at 18–27, 45–46, 90.

27. *Id.* at 89, 96–97; Jürgen Habermas, Communication and the Evolution of Society 27, 65–66 (1979); Stephen M. Feldman, *The Problem of Critique,* 4 Contemp. Pol. Theory 296 (2005).

28. Meiklejohn, *supra* note 5, at 3, 97; Norman L. Rosenberg, *Another History of Free Speech,* 7 L. & Inequality 333, 361 (1989).

29. Meiklejohn, *supra* note 5, at x, 6, 13, 90; *see* White, *supra* note 1, at 155–56; Schauer, *supra* note 5, at 246; Post, *supra* note 5, at 2367–69.

30. Harry Kalven, Jr., *The New York Times Case,* 1964 Sup. Ct. Rev. 191, 208 (quoting N.Y. Times v. Sullivan, 376 U.S. 254, 273 (1964)); Schauer, *supra* note 5, at 241; Robert A. Dahl, Democracy and Its Critics 109, 169–170 (1989); *see* Edmond Cahn, *The Firstness of the First Amendment,* 65 Yale L.J. 464, 480 (1956); Owen M. Fiss, *Free Speech and Social Structure,* 71 Iowa L. Rev. 1405 (1986).

31. Bridges v. California, 314 U.S. 252, 263–71 (1941).

32. Thomas v. Collins, 323 U.S. 516, 529–30 (1945).

33. *Martin,* 319 U.S. at 143; *Schneider,* 308 U.S. at 161. Ironically, Black wrote the *Martin* opinion using a balancing approach, though he would become renowned as a first-amendment absolutist. Hugo L. Black, *The Bill of Rights,* 35 N.Y.U. L. Rev. 865 (1960).

34. *Thornhill,* 310 U.S. at 96, 105; *Bridges,* 314 U.S. at 263; *Barnette,* 319 U.S. at 633. *Compare* Konigsberg v. State Bar of Cal., 366 U.S. 36, 50 & n.11 (1961) (Harlan rea-

soning that clear and present danger was balancing test) *with id.* at 62–63 (Black, J., dissenting) (clear and present danger did not invite judicial balancing).

35. Zechariah Chafee, Jr., *Book Review,* 62 Harv. L. Rev. 891, 894–900 (1949).

36. *Chaplinsky,* 315 U.S. at 571–72. According to Harry Kalven, he coined the phrase, the "two-level" theory. Kalven, *supra* note 31, at 217 n.111; Harry Kalven, Jr., *The Metaphysics of the Law of Obscenity,* 1960 S. Ct. Rev. 1, 10–11, 18–19, 41. The distinction between content-based and content-neutral time-place-or-manner restrictions vis-à-vis the balancing and two-level approaches was not rigid. In *Thornhill,* the Court balanced interests to determine the constitutionality of a content-based statutory restriction on labor picketing.

37. Roth v. United States, 354 U.S. 476, 482–89 (1957); *id.* at 495 (Warren, C.J., concurring in the result).

38. Jacobellis v. Ohio, 378 U.S. 184, 197 (1964) (Stewart, J., concurring); Paris Adult Theatre I v. Slaton, 413 U.S. 49, 82 & n.8 (1973) (Brennan, J., dissenting); *Miller,* 413 U.S. 15, 24 (1973); Redrup v. New York, 386 U.S. 767 (1967); *see* Pope v. Illinois, 481 U.S. 497 (1987).

39. Melville Nimmer, Nimmer on Freedom of Speech § 2.03 (1984); *Roth,* 354 U.S. at 484; Dennis v. United States, 341 U.S. 494, 510 (1951) (quoting United States v. Dennis, 183 F.2d 201, 212 (2d Cir. 1950)).

40. *Miller,* 413 U.S. at 44 (Douglas, J., dissenting); *Barnette,* 319 U.S. 624, 642.

41. Richard W. Steele, Free Speech in the Good War 9–11, 70 (1999); John Dewey & James H. Tufts, Ethics 398–99 (1936 ed.); Franklin D. Roosevelt, *Four Freedoms Speech* (Jan. 6, 1941), *reprinted in* 2 Commager, *supra* note 1, at 446, 449; ABA Committee on the Bill of Rights, *Activities of the Bar Association Committees,* 1 Bill Rts. Rev. 63, 65 (1940); *e.g.,* Brief of ACLU as Amicus Curiae, *Barnette,* 319 U.S. , *reprinted in* 40 Landmark, *supra* note 1, at 151; *see* Rabban, *supra* note 1, at 335–38; Rosenberg, *supra* note 29, at 357, 360; Berman, *supra* note 1, at 317–18.

42. Berman, *supra* note 1, at 301–2 (quoting ACLU annual report, 1923; citing ACLU annual report, 1930–31); *see Thomas,* 323 U.S. at 546 (Jackson, J., concurring); *Bridges,* 314 U.S.; *Thornhill,* 310 U.S.; *Hague,* 307 U.S..

43. *Gobitis,* 310 U.S. 586 (1940), *overruled by Barnette,* 319 U.S.; *Cox,* 312 U.S. 569 (1941); *Milk Wagon,* 312 U.S. 287 (1941); *Chaplinsky,* 315 U.S..

44. Mark A. Graber, *Constitutional Politics and Constitutional Theory,* 27 Law & Soc. Inquiry 309, 310–11 (2002); Douglas v. City of Jeannette, 319 U.S. 167, 167, 171, 180 (1943) (*Douglas 2*) (Jackson, J., dissenting from *Murdock*); *Murdock,* 319 U.S. 105 (1943); *Cantwell,* 310 U.S. at 302–3, 309; Shiffrin, *supra* note 5, at 110.

45. *Terminiello,* 337 U.S. at 20–22 (Jackson, J., dissenting); Feiner v. New York, 340 U.S. 315, 317 (1951); *id.* at 324 & n.5 (Black, J., dissenting); Brief of the American Jewish Congress as Amicus Curiae, at 9–21, *Terminiello,* 337 U.S. (Oct. term, 1948, No. 272).

46. Stone, *supra* note 1, at 522; Gerald Gunther, *Learned Hand and the Origins of Modern First Amendment Doctrine,* 27 Stan. L. Rev. 719, 754–55 (1975); Brandenburg v. Ohio, 395 U.S. 444, 444–47 (1969).

47. *Brandenburg,* 395 U.S. at 445–46 & n.1; *Martin,* 319 U.S. at 145–46; Derrick A. Bell, *Brown v. Board of Education and the Interest-Convergence Dilemma,* 93 Harv. L. Rev. 518 (1980).

48. Thomas L. Tedford, Freedom of Speech in the United States 87 (3d ed. 1997); N.Y. Times v. Sullivan, 376 U.S. 254, 256–59 (1964); Kalven, *supra* note 5, at 228.

49. *Sullivan,* 376 U.S. at 269–70, 276–80; Powe, *supra* note 1, at 308.

50. Powe, *supra* note 1, at 309–10; Civil Rights Act of 1964, 78 Stat. 241 (July 2, 1964); Norman L. Rosenberg, Protecting the Best Men 235–37 (1986).

51. Charles R. Lawrence, *If He Hollers Let Him Go,* 1990 Duke L.J. 431, 466; Derrick Bell, Race, Racism, and American Law 280–85 (2d ed. 1980).

52. Edwards v. South Carolina, 372 U.S. 229, 235–36 (1963).

53. Cox v. Louisiana, 379 U.S. 536, 538, 550, 554–55 (1965); Cox v. Louisiana, 379 U.S. 559, 562, 574 (1965); Bell, *supra* note 51, at 287.

54. Patterson, *supra* note 1, at 656 (quoting Carmichael); Stephan Thernstrom, 2 A History of the American People 850 (2d ed. 1989); David J. Garrow, Bearing the Cross 481–525 (1986); Godfrey Hodgson, America in Our Time 224, 265–67, 361–62 (1976); Powe, *supra* note 1, at 275; Robert Weisbrot, Freedom Bound 196–221 (1990); *see* Gallup, *supra* note 1, at 2076 (Aug. 16, 1967).

55. Adderley v. Florida, 385 U.S. 39, 46–48 (1966); *id.* at 48–50, 52, 56 (Douglas, J., dissenting); Powe, *supra* note 1, at 278.

56. Walker v. Birmingham, 388 U.S. 307, 315–16 (1967); *id.* at 325 (Warren, C.J., dissenting).

57. *Id.* at 316, 320–21; Martin Luther King, Jr., *Letter from Birmingham City Jail* (Apr. 16, 1963), *in* A Testament of Hope 289, 294 (James M. Washington ed., 1986); Powe, *supra* note 1, at 223–25, 279–80; *see* Patterson, *supra* note 1, at 478–79.

58. Bell, *supra* note 51, at 295–302; *e.g.,* McLaurin v. Greenville, 385 U.S. 1011 (1967) (denying cert.); Wells v. Reynolds, 382 U.S. 39 (1965) (affirming summarily); *see* NAACP v. Button, 371 U.S. 415, 430 (1963) ("litigation may well be the sole practicable avenue open to a minority to petition for redress of grievances"); Powe, *supra* note 1, at 209–17, 280; Lawrence, *supra* note 51, at 466–70. Even after the political winds shifted, civil rights protesters did not lose every Supreme Court case. *E.g.,* Gregory v. Chicago, 394 U.S. 111, 111–13 (1969) (reversing disorderly conduct conviction).

59. First National Bank of Boston v. Bellotti, 435 U.S. 765, 776–77, 788–92 (1978).

60. Charles E. Lindblom, Politics and Markets 5, 131, 194–207 (1977); *Bellotti,* 435 U.S. at 803–4 (White, J., dissenting); Graber, *supra* note 1, at 186, 227–34; Michael Walzer, Spheres of Justices 119–23, 310–11 (1983).

61. Kalven, *supra* note 5, at xxii; Emerson, *supra* note 5, at 720; Richard Delgado & Jean Stefancic, *Images of the Outsider in American Law and Culture,* 77 Cornell L. Rev. 1258, 1285–86 (1992). "The first amendment has replaced the due process clause as the primary guarantor of the privileged." Mark Tushnet, *An Essay on Rights,* 62 Tex. L. Rev. 1363, 1387 (1984).

CHAPTER TWELVE

1. Helpful sources on the history of free expression during this period include Margaret A. Blanchard, Revolutionary Sparks (1992); Robert Justin Goldstein, Political Repression in Modern America (2001); Lucas A. Powe, Jr., The Warren Court and American Politics (2000); Martin H. Redish, The Logic of Persecution (2005); Richard W. Steele, Free Speech in the Good War (1999); Geoffrey R. Stone, Perilous Times (2004); Geoffrey R. Stone, *Free Speech in the Age of McCarthy,* 93 Cal. L. Rev. 1387 (2005) [hereinafter Age]. Other helpful resources include George H. Gallup, The Gallup Poll (1972; in 3 vols.); Godfrey Hodgson, America in Our Time (1976); David M. Kennedy, Freedom from Fear (1999); James T. Patterson, Grand Expectations (1996); Richard Polenberg, War and Society (1972); Documents of American History (Henry Steele Commager ed., 9th ed. 1973) [hereinafter Commager].

2. Grenville Clark, *The Limits of Free Expression,* 73 U.S. L. Rev. 392, 403 (1939); Blanchard, *supra* note 1, at 216, 225; *see* ACLU, Freedom in Wartime (June 1943) [hereinafter Report].

3. Steele, *supra* note 1, at 12, 22–23, 55–56, 120, 229 (quoting Jackson); Francis Biddle, *Civil Rights in Times of Stress,* 2 Bill Rts. Rev. 13, 15 (1941); John E. Mulder, *Civil Liberty — 1917–1942,* 2 Bill Rts. Rev. 83 (1942); William E. Leuchtenburg, Franklin D. Roosevelt and the New Deal 242 (1963); Kennedy, *supra* note 1, at 310–12.

4. Steele, *supra* note 1, at 123 (quoting FDR); Cabell Phillips, *No Witch Hunts,* N.Y. Times, Sept. 21, 1941, at SM8; Biddle, *supra* note 3, at 16 (quoting FDR).

5. Steele, *supra* note 1, at 1; Goldstein, *supra* note 1, at 240–42; Gallup, *supra* note 1, at 128 (Dec. 11, 1938); *id.* at 277 (May 5, 1941) (favoring "repressive measures"); Alien Registration Act § 2 (June 28, 1940), 54 Stat. 670, 671; Espionage and Other Crimes (Mar. 28, 1940), 54 Stat. 79; Blanchard, *supra* note 1, at 158; Stone, *supra* note 1, at 250–52.

6. Stone, *supra* note 1, at 253; Steele, *supra* note 1, at 44–47, 64; *American Ogpu,* The New Republic (TNR) (Feb. 19, 1940), at 230–31 (quoting *Milwaukee Journal*).

7. Steele, *supra* note 1, at 99–112, 130–34; Kennedy, *supra* note 1, at 482–85; Stone, *supra* note 1, at 255; Dunne v. United States, 138 F.2d 137 (8th Cir. 1943), *cert. denied,* 320 U.S. 790 (1943); Gallup, *supra* note 1, at 277 (May 5, 1941); *e.g.,* Charles Malcolmson, *Mr. Jackson's Dilemma,* Nation (June 8, 1940), at 699.

8. Francis Biddle, In Brief Authority 235–38 (1962); Washburn, *supra* note 1, at 77; Goldstein, *supra* note 1, at 264–71; Steele, *supra* note 1, at 147–49, 206; Stone, *supra* note 1, at 256–63.

9. Goldstein, *supra* note 1, at 267–68; Kennedy, *supra* note 1, at 750–60; Korematsu v. United States, 323 U.S. 214, 219 (1944); *id.* at 233 (Murphy, J., dissenting); Executive Order 9066, Authorizing the Secretary of War to Prescribe Military Areas (Feb. 19, 1942), 7 Fed. Reg. 1407; An Act to Provide a Penalty for Violation of Military Restrictions (Mar. 21, 1942), 56 Stat. 173; Report, *supra* note 2, at 24. While even Japanese American citizens were relocated, Biddle ceased in the fall 1942 "all

restrictions on enemy aliens of Italian nationality, some 600,000." Report, *supra* note 2, at 46.

10. Kennedy, *supra* note 1, at 410; Steele, *supra* note 1, at 161–72; Goldstein, *supra* note 1, at 268; Stone, *supra* note 1, at 275–77; Washburn, *supra* note 1, at 60; *see* United States v. Pelley, 132 F.2d 170, 176 (7th Cir. 1942); Howard M. Sachar, A History of the Jews in America 454 (1992).

11. Washburn, *supra* note 1, at 6–8, 53, 81–100, 167; Steele, *supra* note 1, at 176; Polenberg, *supra* note 1, at 101–2.

12. Steele, *supra* note 1, at 211, 213, 223; Stone, *supra* note 1, at 264–66, 273–75; Biddle, *supra* note 8, at 241, 243; Goldstein, *supra* note 1, at 268–69; *28 Are Indicted on Sedition Charge*, N.Y. Times, July 24, 1942, at 1; *Named in Sedition Indictment*, N.Y. Times, July 24, 1942, at 8; *Pelley*, 132 F.2d 170; Report, *supra* note 2, at 33.

13. Steele, *supra* note 1, at 149–50; Donald W. Mitchell, *How to Lose the War*, Nation (Jan. 24, 1942), at 85; Editors, *We Can Lose This War*, Nation (Feb. 14, 1942), at 179; Editors, *Grim Days Ahead*, TNR (Feb. 16, 1942), at 215.

14. Donald W. Mitchell, *The Axis Cornered*, Nation (Nov. 27, 1943), at 603; Editors, *The Fronts*, TNR (Nov. 8, 1943), at 631; Biddle, *supra* note 8, at 243; *Korematsu*, 323 U.S. at 246 (Jackson, J., dissenting); Thomas Bailey et al., The American Pageant 860–63 (11th ed. 1998); Steele, *supra* note 1, at 219, 230–31.

15. *Taylor*, 319 U.S. 583, 589–90 (1943); *Barnette*, 319 U.S. 624 (1943); *Jones*, 316 U.S. 584 (1942); Chaplinsky v. New Hampshire, 315 U.S. 568 (1942); Cox v. New Hampshire, 312 U.S. 569 (1941); Milk Wagon Drivers Union v. Meadowmoor Dairies, Inc., 312 U.S. 287 (1941); *Gobitis*, 310 U.S. 586 (1940); *see* Hartzel v. United States, 322 U.S. 680 (1944) (reversing conviction for insufficient evidence in Court's only Espionage Act decision). In overturning *Jones*, the Court handed down several decisions: Douglas v. City of Jeannette, 319 U.S. 157 (1943); Murdock v. Pennsylvania, 319 U.S. 105 (1943); Jones v. Opelika, 319 U.S. 103 (1943). Two decisions rendered the revocation of naturalization more difficult. Baumgartner v. United States, 322 U.S. 665 (1944); Schneiderman v. United States, 320 U.S. 118 (1943).

16. *Barnette*, 319 U.S. at 642; Steele, *supra* note 1, at 155–59, 231; Report, *supra* note 2, at 34; ACLU, In the Shadow of Fear 6 (Aug. 1949); Gallup, *supra* note 1, at 855 (reported Sept. 30, 1949); Samuel Walker, In Defense of American Liberties 317–18 (1990).

17. Gallup, *supra* note 1, at 1191 (Dec. 5, 1953); *id.* at 1401 (Feb. 27, 1955); *id.* at 1884 (June 7, 1964); *id.* at 1884 (June 10, 1964). Among nine organizations, Americans viewed only Handgun Control, Inc., at 46 percent, and the Tobacco Institute, at 24 percent, less favorably than the ACLU (52 percent). *Interest Groups*, The Gallup Poll (May 1989), at 25–27.

18. ACLU, In the Shadow of Fear (Aug. 1949); Stone, *supra* note 1, at 419.

19. Patterson, *supra* note 1, at 85–86, 93, 105–13; Yalta Conference (Feb. 1945), *in* 2 Commager, *supra* note 1, at 487; Goldstein, *supra* note 1, at 291–92.

20. Patterson, *supra* note 1, at 113; Goldstein, *supra* note 1, at 295; Age, *supra* note 1, at 1388–89.

21. Goldstein, *supra* note 1, at 296–99; Age, *supra* note 1, at 1389; Erik W. Austin,

Political Facts of the United States since 1789, at 50–55 (1986); The Marshall Plan (June 5, 1947), *reprinted in* 2 Commager, *supra* note 1, at 532.

22. The Truman Doctrine (Mar. 12, 1947), *reprinted in* 2 Commager, *supra* note 1, at 525, 527; Truman Loyalty Order (Mar. 21, 1947), *reprinted in id.* at 529, 532 [hereinafter Loyalty].

23. Loyalty, *supra* note 22, at 529–32; Age, *supra* note 1, at 1392; Goldstein, *supra* note 1, at 300–302; *see* The Statistical History of the United States from Colonial Times to the Present 709 (1965).

24. Goldstein, *supra* note 1, at 302–4; Stone, *supra* note 1, at 345–46.

25. Goldstein, *supra* note 1, at 308–11; Age, *supra* note 1, at 1392–93.

26. Redish, *supra* note 1, at 139; Goldstein, *supra* note 1, at 289–90, 307–8; Taft-Hartley Act (June 23, 1947), *reprinted in* 2 Commager, *supra* note 1, at 537, 539; Patterson, *supra* note 1, at 46–51; *see* Am. Commc'ns Association v. Douds, 339 U.S. 382 (1950) (upholding Taft-Hartley affidavit requirement); Telford Taylor, *The Issue Is Not TV, but Fair Play,* N.Y. Times, Apr. 15, 1951, at 12.

27. Goldstein, *supra* note 1, at 307; Redish, *supra* note 1, at 139–41; Ellen Schrecker, Many Are the Crimes 324, 330 (1998); Stone, *supra* note 1, at 363–66; *see* Alfred E. Clark, *TV "Blacklist" Cited by Susskind in Faulk's Suit,* N.Y. Times, Apr. 28, 1962, at 12; Brief of Alexander Meiklejohn, of Cultural Workers in Motion Pictures and Other Arts, and of Members of the Professions, as Amici Curiae, at 2–5, Lawson v. United States, 339 U.S. 934 (1950) (Oct. term, 1949, No. 248).

28. Goldstein, *supra* note 1, at 317; Patterson, *supra* note 1, at 169–70, 190; Gallup, *supra* note 1, at 787 (Jan. 31, 1949); *id.* at 873–74 (Dec. 16, 1949); *id.* at 853 (Sept. 21, 1949).

29. Stone, *supra* note 1, at 370; Patterson, *supra* note 1, at 194–95; e.g., C.P. Trussell, *Red "Underground" in Federal Posts Alleged by Editor,* N.Y. Times, Aug. 4, 1948, at 1; *Hiss Sues Chambers for Slander; Calls Communist Charge "False,"* N.Y. Times, Sept. 28, 1948, at 1.

30. C.P. Trussell, *President Is Blunt,* N.Y. Times, Aug. 6, 1948, at 1; C.P. Trussell, *Hiss and Chambers Meet Face to Face,* N.Y. Times, Aug. 26, 1948, at 1; John D. Morris, *Hiss-Chambers Farm Tie Studied,* N.Y. Times, Aug. 28, 1948, at 1, 5; *Who Did What?* N.Y. Times, Dec. 12, 1948, at E1; Alexander Feinberg, *Grand Jury to Get Secret Microfilms,* N.Y. Times, Dec. 12, 1948, at 1, 65; Patterson, *supra* note 1, at 179, 193–95; Goldstein, *supra* note 1, at 316–17; Stone, *supra* note 1, at 328, 370–72. *Compare* Schrecker, *supra* note 27, at 174–75 (questioning Hiss's guilt) *with* John Earl Haynes & Harvey Klehr, In Denial 141–62 (2003) (evidence shows Hiss's guilt).

31. Patterson, *supra* note 1, at 171–72, 195.

32. Stone, *supra* note 1, at 331; Patterson, *supra* note 1, at 196, 199; *M'Carthy Insists Truman Oust Reds,* N.Y. Times, Feb. 12, 1950, at 5; *see Excerpts from Text of Majority Report on Charges by Senator McCarthy,* N.Y. Times, July 18, 1950, at 16.

33. Patterson, *supra* note 1, at 196–98; *M'Carthy Labels Marshall "Unfit,"* N.Y. Times, Apr. 21, 1950, at 3; *M'Carthy Scores "Appeaser" Group,* N.Y. Times, June 17, 1951, at 3; *M'Carthy Attacks Cheered by V.F.W.,* N.Y. Times, Aug. 31, 1951, at 9; Stone, *supra* note 1, at 374–75.

34. *Truman's Statement of the Korean War* (June 27, 1950), *reprinted in* 2 Commager, *supra* note 1, at 553, 553; Patterson, *supra* note 1, at 179, 202–8, 263; *Excerpts from Text of Majority Report on Charges by Senator McCarthy,* N.Y. Times, July 18, 1950, at 16, 17; *Text of McCarthy Reply,* N.Y. Times, July 18, 1950, at 16; James P. Connolly, *Maryland: "M'Carthyism,"* N.Y. Times, Nov. 12, 1950, at 154 (composite photo); *Tydings Charges Election Fraud,* N.Y. Times, Dec. 17, 1950, at 48; Blanchard, *supra* note 1, at 245–47; Goldstein, *supra* note 1, at 321–26; Stone, *supra* note 1, at 331–37, 377–79.

35. William S. White, *Seven G.O.P. Senators Decry "Smear" Tactics of McCarthy,* N.Y. Times, June 2, 1950, at 1, 11; Blanchard, *supra* note 1, at 247–48.

36. *Text of Truman Address to Legion Denouncing McCarthy Attacks,* N.Y. Times, Aug. 15, 1951, at 12; Stone, *supra* note 1, at 396, 398, 408; Redish, *supra* note 1, at 83–84 (quoting Peter L. Steinberg, The Great "Red Menace" 160 (1984)); Goldstein, *supra* note 1, at 329–30; *see* Dennis v. United States, 341 U.S. 494, 581–82 (1951) (Douglas, J., dissenting). The government indicted twelve defendants, but one, William Z. Foster, had his trial severed and deferred because of ill health. United States v. Foster, 80 F. Supp. 479 (S.D.N.Y. 1948).

37. United States v. Dennis, 183 F.2d 201, 207–8, 212 (2d Cir. 1950); Learned Hand, *The Contribution of an Independent Judiciary to Civilization* (1942), *reprinted in* The Spirit of Liberty 118 (Irving Dilliard ed., 1959 ed.); Gerald Gunther, Learned Hand 598–612 (1994); Stone, *supra* note 1, at 398–402.

38. *Dennis,* 341 U.S. at 497, 508–10; Freda Kirchwey, *The Shape of Things,* Nation, Jan. 31, 1953, at 89; *Truman Sharpens Loyalty Standard,* N.Y. Times, Apr. 29, 1951, at 1, 24; Goldstein, *supra* note 1, at 329–33; Patterson, *supra* note 1, at 185, 193, 204, 362–63; Redish, *supra* note 1, at 172–74; Stone, *supra* note 1, at 337, 372, 411, 421–23; *e.g.,* Adler v. Bd. of Educ., 342 U.S. 485 (1952) (teacher); Barsky v. Bd. of Regents, 347 U.S. 442 (1954) (doctor). In 1950, the Senate created the Senate Internal Security Subcommittee, which conducted investigations similar to those of HUAC. Goldstein, *supra* note 1, at 326.

39. Patterson, *supra* note 1, at 265–66; Gallup, *supra* note 1, at 1191 (Dec. 5, 1953); Goldstein, *supra* note 1, at 334; David Halberstam, The Fifties 250 (1993).

40. *M'Carthy Repeats Demands on Army,* N.Y. Times, Feb. 21, 1954, at 2; *McCarthy v. Army,* N.Y. Times, Feb. 21, 1954, at E1; James Reston, *Officers Ordered to Defy M'Carthy and Not Testify,* N.Y. Times, Feb. 21, 1954, at 1; W.H. Lawrence, *M'Carthy Asserts He Has a New "Red" To Link to Army,* N.Y. Times, Feb. 23, 1954, at 1; W.H. Lawrence, *A Day of Parleys,* N.Y. Times, Feb. 26, 1954, at 1; James Reston, *Stevens Case Stuns Capital; Pentagon Bitter and Gloomy,* N.Y. Times, Feb. 26, 1954, at 1, 12; Stone, *supra* note 1, at 383–85.

41. *Texts of Statements by President and Senator McCarthy's Reply,* N.Y. Times, Mar. 4, 1954, at 12; James Reston, *Other Cheek Is Struck,* N.Y. Times, Mar. 4, 1954, at 14.

42. W.H. Lawrence, *Stevens a Target,* N.Y. Times, Mar. 12, 1954, at 1; *Text of Army Report Charging Threats by McCarthy and Cohn in Interceding for Schine,* N.Y. Times, Mar. 12, 1954, at A9; *M'Carthy and the Army,* N.Y. Times, Mar. 13, 1954, at 14; W.H. Lawrence, *M'Carthy Charges Army "Blackmail," Says Stevens Sought Deal with Him,* N.Y. Times, Mar. 13, 1954, at 1; W.H. Lawrence, *Stevens Swears M'Carthy Falsified,*

Lays "Perversion of Power" to Him, N.Y. Times, Apr. 23, 1954, at 1; W.H. Lawrence, *Senator Is Irate,* N.Y. Times, May 18, 1954, at 1, 24; Stone, *supra* note 1, at 386–88 & n.*; Patterson, *supra* note 1, at 267.

43. *Excerpts From 30th Day of Testimony in Senate Hearings on Army-McCarthy Dispute,* N.Y. Times, June 10, 1954, at 14; W.H. Lawrence, *Exchange Bitter,* N.Y. Times, June 10, 1954, at 1; *Calls Fisher a "Fine Kid,"* N.Y. Times, June 10, 1954, at 17; Patterson, *supra* note 1, at 268–69; Stone, *supra* note 1, at 387.

44. *Judgment on Mr. M'Carthy,* N.Y. Times, Sept. 28, 1954, at 28; *McCarthy Is the Fourth Member to Draw Senate Disciplinary Vote,* N.Y. Times, Dec. 3, 1954, at 13; W.H. Lawrence, *M'Carthy Is Dead of Liver Ailment at the Age of 47,* N.Y. Times, May 3, 1957, at 1; Patterson, *supra* note 1, at 269–70; Stone, *supra* note 1, at 389–91; see High Type v. Tintype, Time Archives, Oct. 15, 1956 (Nixon snubbing McCarthy).

45. Gallup, *supra* note 1, at 1135 (Apr. 13, 1953); *id.* at 1246 (Aug. 22, 1954); *id.* at 1246 (June 23, 1954) (intense disapproval); Powe, *supra* note 1, at 80, 90; Stone, *supra* note 1, at 413; *see The Crisis in Communism,* Time Archives, Nov. 5, 1956 (diminishing Soviet power).

46. Peters v. Hobby, 349 U.S. 331, 335–49 (1955); Powe, *supra* note 1, at 80–82.

47. Cole v. Young, 351 U.S. 536 (1956); Communist Party v. Subversive Activities Control Bd., 351 U.S. 115 (1956); Slochower v. Bd. of Educ., 350 U.S. 551 (1956); Pennsylvania v. Nelson, 350 U.S. 497 (1956); Ullmann v. United States, 350 U.S. 422 (1956) (upholding conviction); Powe, *supra* note 1, at 82–90; Bernard Schwartz, A History of the Supreme Court 269–75 (1993).

48. Yates v. United States, 354 U.S. 298, 318–25 (1957); Powe, *supra* note 1, at 90–99; Stone, *supra* note 1, at 413–15.

49. Powe, *supra* note 1, at 85; *Ends a Busy Term, Draws a Heavy Fire,* Time Archives, June 25, 1956; *see* C. Herman Pritchett, Congress versus the Supreme Court 15–24 (1961); C. Dickerman Williams, *The Law of the Land,* Nat'l Rev., June 20, 1956, at 14.

50. William S. White, *President Asks Respect for Court,* N.Y. Times, June 27, 1957, at 10; Lawrence E. Davies, *High Court Views Upset Law Group,* N.Y. Times, June 24, 1957, at 19; *Impeach Justices, Thurmond Urges,* N.Y. Times, July 8, 1957, at 15; *Jenner Would Curb High Court's Power,* N.Y. Times, July 27, 1957, at 21; Powe, *supra* note 1, at 99–102; Philip P. Frickey, *Getting from Joe to Gene (McCarthy),* 93 Cal. L. Rev. 397, 424–25 (2005); *see* Pritchett, *supra* note 49, at 41–116; *Dr. Corwin on the Jenner Bill,* Nat'l Rev., Mar. 29, 1958, at 292.

51. Arthur Krock, *High Court's Critics Grumble but Conform,* N.Y. Times, June 30, 1957, at 135; *Impeach Justices, Thurmond Urges,* N.Y. Times, July 8, 1957, at 15 (quoting Hennings); Pritchett, *supra* note 49, at 14; Powe, *supra* note 1, at 135–56; Lerner v. Casey, 357 U.S. 468 (1958); Beilan v. Bd. of Educ., 357 U.S. 399 (1958); *Slochower,* 350 U.S..

52. Redish, *supra* note 1, at 63–65, 73; *see* John Earl Haynes & Harvey Klehr, Venona (1999); Age, *supra* note 1, at 1404.

53. Patterson, *supra* note 1, at 515; *see* The Pentagon Papers 1–157 (1971) [hereinafter Papers]; Hodgson, *supra* note 1, at 175–77; Patterson, *supra* note 1, at 509–17; Stone, *supra* note 1, at 428–30.

54. Hodgson, *supra* note 1, at 176; *The President's Address,* N.Y. Times, Aug. 5, 1964, at 1; Arnold H. Lubasch, *Reds Driven Off,* N.Y. Times, Aug. 5, 1964, at 1; Joint Resolution of Congress, H.J. Res. 1145 (Aug. 7, 1964), *reprinted in* 2 Commager, *supra* note 1, at 690; *see* Papers, *supra* note 53, at 259–70.

55. Papers, *supra* note 53, at 262; Patterson, *supra* note 1, at 603–4.

56. Patterson, *supra* note 1, at 595–603; Papers, *supra* note 53, at 240, 310, 312; *see* Goldstein, *supra* note 1, at 430–49; Stone, *supra* note 1, at 436–37.

57. *The Vietniks: Self-Defeating Dissent,* Time Archives, Oct. 29, 1965; *Show of Support on Vietnam Gains Strength in U.S.,* N.Y. Times, Oct. 21, 1965, at 1; *And Now the Vietnik,* Time Archives, Oct. 22, 1965; *The Wrong Place,* Time Archives, Apr. 8, 1966; Andrew Kipkind, *Radicals on the March,* TNR, Dec. 11, 1965, at 15; *see* Goldstein, *supra* note 1, at 430; Patterson, *supra* note 1, at 598.

58. Gene Roberts, *10,000 Rally in Atlanta Rain to Back Vietnam Policy,* N.Y. Times, Feb. 13, 1966, at 2; Gallup, *supra* note 1, at 1971 (Nov. 21, 1965); *id.* at 2010 (June 3, 1966) (36 percent); *id.* at 2063 (May 14, 1967) (37 percent); *id.* at 2074 (July 30, 1967) (41 percent); *id.* at 2099 (Jan. 3, 1968) (45 percent); Goldstein, *supra* note 1, at 430–31; Patterson, *supra* note 1, at 624–25, 753; *The Dilemma of Dissent,* Time Archives, Apr. 21, 1967.

59. Patterson, *supra* note 1, at 694–97; Goldstein, *supra* note 1, at 437; 111 Cong. Rec., 89th Cong., 1st Sess. 19,871 (Aug. 10, 1965); An Act to Amend the Universal Military Training and Service Act of 1951, as amended (Aug. 30, 1965), 79 Stat. 586; Carl Cohen, *Punishment by Conscription,* Nation, Dec. 27, 1965, at 520; Survey Collection: Harris/1561 (Nov. 1965), http://cgi.irss.unc.edu/tempdocs/11:15:54:2.htm (accessed June 9, 2006); Survey Collection: Harris/1735 (May 1967); Gallup, *supra* note 1, at 2160 (Sept. 18, 1968).

60. United States v. O'Brien, 391 U.S. 367, 370, 376–77, 381–83 (1968); Powe, *supra* note 1, at 325; *e.g.,* Turner Broad. Sys. v. FCC, 512 U.S. 622, 645–47 (1994); Washington v. Davis, 426 U.S. 229 (1976).

61. Gallup, *supra* note 1, at 2099 (Jan. 3, 1968); *id.* at 2189 (Mar. 23, 1969); *id.* at 2254 (June 28, 1970); *id.* at 2309 (June 6, 1971) (61 percent); *id.* at 2271 (Nov. 8, 1970); Blanchard, *supra* note 1, at 320; Hodgson, *supra* note 1, at 356–57, 384; Patterson, *supra* note 1, at 629–32.

62. Survey Collection: Harris/1970 (Oct. 1969); The Harris Survey Yearbook of Public Opinion, 1970, at 277 (1971); Gallup, *supra* note 1, at 2224–25 (Nov. 27, 1969); *see* Hodgson, *supra* note 1, at 412–28, 484–85.

63. Cohen v. California, 403 U.S. 15, 16–26 (1971).

64. *Id.* at 27 (Blackmun, J., dissenting); *see* Stone, *supra* note 1, at 519–21.

65. Patterson, *supra* note 1, at 718, 742; Goldstein, *supra* note 1, at 462–67, 487; Stone, *supra* note 1, at 492–96.

66. Goldstein, *supra* note 1, at 462–63, 500–502; The Senate Watergate Report: The Final Report of the Senate Select Committee on Presidential Campaign Activities (The Ervin Committee) 58–60, 211–12 (June 1974; 2005 abridged ed.) [hereinafter Watergate]; Patterson, *supra* note 1, at 742; Stone, *supra* note 1, at 493.

67. Patterson, *supra* note 1, at 701, 743, 749, 758–66; N.Y. Times v. United States,

403 U.S. 713 (1971); Survey Collection: Harris/2221 (May 1972); Gallup, *supra* note 1, at 2236 (Jan. 29, 1970); *id.* at 2291 (Mar. 7, 1971); Blanchard, *supra* note 1, at 368–72; Stone, *supra* note 1, at 501–2; Papers, *supra* note 53, at ix.

68. Stone, *supra* note 1, at 514; Patterson, *supra* note 1, at 757, 772–73; *see* Watergate, *supra* note 66, at 196–202; Alfred E. Lewis, *5 Held in Plot to Bug Democrats' Office Here*, Wash. Post, June 18, 1972, at A1.

69. Walter Pincus, *The Latest Cover-up*, TNR, June 30, 1973, at 14–15; Tad Szulc, *Ex-G.O.P. Aide Linked to Political Raid*, N.Y. Times, June 20, 1972, at 1, 24; Lawrence Meyer, *President Taped Talks, Phone Calls*, Wash. Post, July 17, 1973, at A1; Patterson, *supra* note 1, at 775–76.

70. United States v. Nixon, 418 U.S. 683 (1974); John Herbers, *Tapes Released*, N.Y. Times, Aug. 6, 1974, at 1; Carroll Kilpatrick, *Nixon Resigns*, Wash. Post, Aug. 9, 1974, at A1; Patterson, *supra* note 1, at 777–78.

71. Patterson, *supra* note 1, at 595–97; Stone, *supra* note 1, at 4–13, 441.

72. Goldstein, *supra* note 1, at 461, 463, 501; *see* Hodgson, *supra* note 1, at 306–25, 401–11.

CHAPTER THIRTEEN

1. Turner Broad. Sys. v. FCC, 512 U.S. 622, 630, 662 (1994); *e.g.*, Texas v. Johnson, 491 U.S. 397, 412 (1989); Roth v. United States, 354 U.S. 476, 511–14 (1957) (Douglas, J., dissenting); Thomas I. Emerson, The System of Freedom of Expression 326 (1970); Harry Kalven, Jr., *The Metaphysics of the Law of Obscenity*, 1960 S. Ct. Rev. 1; *see* Erwin Chemerinsky, Constitutional Law: Principles and Policies 932–34 (3d ed. 2006).

2. Richard Delgado, *Words That Wound*, 17 Harv. C.R.-C.L. L. Rev. 133 (1982); Toni M. Massaro, *Equality and Freedom of Expression*, 32 Wm. & Mary L. Rev. 211, 221 (1991); Mari Matsuda, *Public Response to Racist Speech*, 87 Mich. L. Rev. 2320, 2336–37 (1989); *see* Doe v. Univ. of Mich., 721 F. Supp. 852 (E.D. Mich. 1989).

3. Chaplinsky v. New Hampshire, 315 U.S. 568, 572 (1942); Jon B. Gould, Speak No Evil 177–78 (2005); Jon B. Gould, *The Precedent That Wasn't*, 35 L. & Soc'y Rev. 345, 384 (2001); *see* Richard Delgado & Jean Stefancic, *Images of the Outsider in American Law and Culture*, 77 Cornell L. Rev. 1258 (1992); Steven G. Gey, *The Case against Postmodern Censorship Theory*, 145 U. Pa. L. Rev. 193 (1996); *e.g.*, Virginia v. Black, 538 U.S. 343 (2003); R.A.V. v. City of St. Paul, Minn., 505 U.S. 377 (1992).

4. Valentine v. Chrestensen, 316 U.S. 52, 54–55 (1942); Laurence H. Tribe, American Constitutional Law 930 (2d ed. 1988).

5. Va. State Bd. of Pharmacy v. Va. Citizens Consumer Council, 425 U.S. 748, 765 (1976); Central Hudson Gas & Elec. Corp. v. Public Serv. Comm'n, 447 U.S. 557, 566 (1980); Bd. of Trustees of SUNY v. Fox, 492 U.S. 469, 480 (1989).

6. Paul Finkelman, *Speech, Press, and Democracy*, 10 Wm. & Mary Bill Rts. J. 813, 813–14 (2002); *see* Martin H. Redish, *The First Amendment in the Marketplace*, 39 Geo. Wash. L. Rev. 429 (1971).

7. *Va. Pharmacy*, 425 U.S. at 763; *id.* at 787 (Rehnquist, J., dissenting); C. Edwin Baker, Human Liberty and Freedom of Speech 194–224 (1989); Ronald K.L. Collins

& David M. Skover, *Pissing in the Snow,* 45 Stan. L. Rev. 783, 785 (1993); Owen M. Fiss, *Free Speech and Social Structure,* 71 Iowa L. Rev. 1405, 1425 (1986).

8. Red Lion Broad. v. FCC, 395 U.S. 367, 390 (1969); Mark A. Graber, Transforming Free Speech 227–34 (1991); Sylvia Law, *Addiction, Autonomy, and Advertising,* 77 Iowa L. Rev. 909, 929 (1992).

9. Baker, *supra* note 7, at 12; Tribe, *supra* note 4, at 786; Harry Wellington, *On Freedom of Expression,* 88 Yale L.J. 1105, 1130–32 (1979).

10. Thomas I. Emerson, *Toward a General Theory of the First Amendment,* 72 Yale L.J. 877, 879 (1963); Hurley v. Irish-Am. Gay, Lesbian and Bisexual Group of Boston, 515 U.S. 557, 573 (1995); Charles Fried, *The New First Amendment Jurisprudence,* 59 U. Chi. L. Rev. 225, 233 (1992); Christina E. Wells, *Reinvigorating Autonomy,* 32 Harv. C.R.-C.L. L. Rev. 159, 161–70 (1997).

11. Emerson, *supra* note 10, at 879; Tribe, *supra* note 4, at 788; Procunier v. Martinez, 416 U.S. 396, 427 (1974) (Marshall, J., concurring); Frederick Schauer, Free Speech 47–72 (1982); G. Edward White, *The First Amendment Comes of Age,* 95 Mich. L. Rev. 299, 303–8, 352–57 (1996).

12. Robert H. Bork, Neutral Principles and Some First Amendment Problems, 47 Ind. L.J. 1, 25 (1971); Thomas Scanlon, Freedom of Expression and Categories of Expression, 40 U. Pitt. L. Rev. 519, 531–34 (1979).

13. Cohen v. California, 403 U.S. 15 (1971).

14. Hamdan v. Rumsfeld, 126 S.Ct. 2749 (2006); Ashcroft v. ACLU, 542 U.S. 656 (2004); Reno v. ACLU, 521 U.S. 844 (1997).

15. First Amendment Center, State of the First Amendment 10–32 (2002).

Index

Adderley v. Florida, 415–16
Address to the Inhabitants of Quebec, 53–54
Adkins v. Children's Hospital, 349, 354, 479n22
administrative agencies, 316–17, 325
ADS, 246–47
advertising, 299–300, 336, 465–66; and free expression, 465–66; and irrationality, 312; and politics, 340, 342; and radio, 300; and television, 340; types of, 299. *See also* commercial expression
AFL. *See* American Federation of Labor
African Americans, 5, 24, 38, 100, 105, 171, 294, 368, 411; and *Americans All, Immigrants All*, 318; antebellum rights of free blacks, 38, 480n40; black cabinet, 328; and black nationalism, 298; black power movement, 341, 347, 415; and Caucasians, 301; citizenship, 121, 197; and civic virtue, 5; and civil rights movement, 345–48, 377–78, 412–18, 431, 530n58; and communism, 393, 427; comprehensive suppression, 121; and defamation, 413; as discrete and insular minority, 368; disenfranchisement, 197; and Double Victory, 427; and economic opportunities, 347; elected to Congress, 347; and felony disenfranchisement, 348; and GI Bill of Rights, 343–45; and immigrants, 301; and imprisonment, 348; leave South, 298; and mass-consumer culture, 298; and New Deal, 327–28; during 1930s, 308; and pluralist democracy, 328–29, 341, 344–48; and politics of suffrage, 158; post-Reconstruction

disenfranchisement, 163; post-Reconstruction exclusion, 163; Reconstruction and, 154–64; and Republicans, 328; rights denied, 121; rights differentiated during Reconstruction, 156–58, 163; and riots, 337; segregation, 154, 157–58, 198, 302; suffrage and, 158–61, 163, 328; suppression of black press during World War II, 426–27; and thirteenth amendment, 156; and wealth inequality, 343–44, 348; and World War II, 336–37. *See also* civil rights and liberties; racism
agrarian economy, 24, 35; commercial development, 34–35; during Great Depression, 308; transition to manufacturing, 169; in Virginia, 70
Agricultural Adjustment Act, 317–18, 351
AJCommittee, 301, 303, 305
Alabama, 121, 160, 163, 224, 304, 358, 377, 413
A.L.A. Schechter Poultry Corporation v. United States, 351
Albany, New York, 141
Albany Resolves, 141
Alexandria Gazette, 128
Alger, Horatio, 193
Alien and Sedition Acts, 26, 77–81, 83–89; Alien Laws and republican democratic exclusion, 78; consequences of Sedition Act prosecutions, 89–100; Hamilton, Alexander, urges caution, 78; jurisdictional attack, 82, 84, 90, 92, 106, 112, 131; jurisdictional attack as federalism argument, 83; political calculations, 77–78, 98; public sentiment condemns, 119; Sedition Act of 1798, 79–82, 84–87, 98–101, 111–12, 142, 147, 150, 216, 254, 268, 412, 468, 487n21, 488n30;

Chicago Times, 140–42, 225
Chicago Tribune, 330, 426
Chicago World's Fair of 1893, 207
China, 437–39
Chinese, 301
Christian Century, 304
Christian Front, 423
Christians, as interest group, 341
Churchill, Winston, 432
CIA, 458, 461
Cincinnati, 123, 148
Cincinnati Commercial, 141
Cincinnati Gazette, 118
Cincinnati Whig, 128
CIO, 321, 323–25
cities. *See* urbanization
civic republicanism, 15, 17, 65, 94,
    476n4
civic virtue, 3, 32, 97; and African
    Americans, 5; changing definition
    of, 32–40, 180; excuse for
    exclusion, 293, 341; free labor
    and, 154; and immigrants, 295;
    immigrants criticized as lacking,
    164; individualism increases, 35–36,
    118; and political deliberation, 386,
    396; Populists question capitalists',
    188; private virtue contrasted, 32;
    and Progressives, 194; Revolution
    and, 15; situs changes, 36–37, 151;
    wealth and property, 15, 23, 33–34;
    Wilson, James and, 56
Civilian Conservation Corps, 317
civil libertarians, 285, 421; Brandeis
    supports, 284; distinguish
    economic and expressive liberties,
    268–72; Holmes not one, 284;
    movement emerges after World
    War I, 267–74, 280, 284–90, 364;
    movement strengthened, 389.
    See also civil rights and liberties
Civil Liberties Bureau, 257
Civil Liberties Unit, 364, 421
Civil Rights Act of 1866, 154, 156–57,
    198

Civil Rights Act of 1871, 198
Civil Rights Act of 1875, 163
Civil Rights Act of 1964, 346–47, 377,
    413
civil rights and liberties, 267, 361,
    364; as American creed, 364; Bill
    of Rights Committee, 364; Civil
    Liberties Unit, 364; civil rights
    movement, 345–46, 377, 412–18,
    431, 462; civil rights movement
    dissipates, 347, 415, 530n58; Cold
    War and civil rights movement,
    346; Congress and, 364; and
    conservatives, 366–67; and court
    packing, 354; and defamation,
    413; economic development
    and civil rights movement, 345;
    and expanding governmental
    power, 365; and La Follette Civil
    Liberties Committee, 364; and
    labor, 364; no right of protest,
    415–17, 454, 530n58; not a political
    issue during World War I, 257;
    political coalition, 377, 408, 421;
    political coalition dissipates during
    World War II, 430–31; and public
    opinion, 288; and self-fulfillment,
    364; Supreme Court and civil
    rights movement, 418. *See also* civil
    libertarians
Civil Rights Cases, 163
civil rights movement. *See* civil rights
    and liberties
Civil War, 14, 38, 121, 139–40, 142, 151,
    153, 163, 180, 209, 211; pensions,
    167, 186
Clark, Grenville, 365–66, 397, 420
Clark, Tom, 422, 447
Clarke, John H., 275
classical economics, 311
classical political economy, 191, 202
class legislation, 155, 183, 192, 199–208,
    380; arbitrary or unreasonable
    laws, 155, 199, 384; concept
    repudiated under pluralist

333–35; voters as consumers, 340,
342; and voting, 341, 396; and
wartime suppression, 421; wealth
and power, 327–28, 342, 344,
347–48, 366, 467. *See also* judicial
review under pluralist democracy;
relativism
Poland, 296, 329, 423, 432
police powers, 21, 31, 155, 201–6, 240,
385, 388; Congress not granted, 62;
defined, 30
political economists, 184, 188, 191, 202
political machines, 170, 180, 194–95,
297, 302; and Roosevelt, Franklin,
315
political parties, 38; development
of, 33; Protestant elites
attack two-party system, 165;
proto-parties, 70; two-party
system, 104, 117, 224; two-party
system and voter turnout, 165;
two-party system in Jacksonian
era, 149–51; two-party system
lacking in 1790s, 82, 99, 109
political question doctrine, 369, 377
political science, 227, 311, 351, 358, 381;
and legal realism, 363
Politics and Markets, 418
Polk, James, 137
Pollock, Frederick, 265, 273, 279–80,
283
popular sovereignty. *See* sovereignty of
the people
population, 169–70, 173, 303
Populism, 187–90, 224; aims to
resuscitate republican democracy,
188; alienates Catholics and Jews,
189; alienates urbanites, 189; free
silver and, 189; policies, 189; and
societal divisions, 188
Portland Journal, 231
positivism, 178
Pound, Roscoe, 191, 193, 207, 271–72,
286; and balancing interests, 271

Powell, Lewis F., 418
Powell, Thomas Reed, 361
pragmatism, 333
preferred freedoms, 371, 402
premodernism, 178, 305, 307, 309, 360
press. *See* freedom of expression;
publishers
Price, Richard, 59
Priestly, Joseph, 59
printers. *See* freedom of expression;
publishers
printing press, 6, 38, 129
prior restraints, 55–56, 77, 86, 90–91,
216, 234, 236–37, 240, 242, 256,
258–59, 390, 394, 410, 459;
Blackstone and, 8; and injunctions,
229, 389–90, 459; and labor
injunctions, 229, 508n49; licensing
in England, 6–7
Pritchett, C. Herman, 333, 359, 362–63
private sphere. *See* republican
democracy
private virtue, 32, 34, 45, 154, 180, 183,
322; capital versus labor, 180
privileges or immunities, 201, 282
Proclamation of Neutrality, 241
progress. *See* modernism
Progressive historians, 313
Progressive Party Platform of 1912, 191,
195
Progressivism, 187, 190–97, 207–8, 220,
385; adjust republican democratic
procedures, 195; at-large (or
multi-member) elections,
196; best men, 192, 195–96;
and Bourne, Randolph S., 256;
centralization of governmental
power and World War I, 253, 268,
291; and civic virtue, 194; and
class legislation, 192; common
good pursued, 191–92; diminish
immigrant political strength, 195;
disappointment after World War I,
267–68; dissipates, 291; and Ely,

slander. *See* defamation
Slaughterhouse Cases, The, 200, 203, 209
slave power, 125
slavery, 5, 45, 100, 144, 372; American
  Anti-Slavery Society, 122; and
  Great Slavepower Conspiracy, 134;
  legal disabilities, 121; and popular
  sovereignty, 153; pro-slavery
  advocacy, 122; slave trade, 122;
  Southern economy depends on,
  122; Southerners admit temporary
  evil, 122; theoretical defenses,
  144–46, 492–93n37; thirteenth
  amendment ends, 156. *See also*
  abolition
Slavs, and *Americans All, Immigrants
  All,* 318
Smith, Adam, 202–3
Smith, Al, 294, 303–5, 341; condemns
  Roosevelt's *Forgotten Man* address,
  315
Smith, Margaret Chase, 440
Smith Act, 423–24, 427, 447–48;
  prosecutions of Communists,
  441–43, 447, 450
social Darwinism, 184–85, 188, 206;
  justifying wealth disparity, 187
social engineering, 191
Social Gospel, 195
Socialists, 176, 223, 230, 232, 243–44,
  246–47, 250, 252, 255, 257, 259,
  261–62, 264–66, 268, 287, 424; in
  New York legislature, 286; strength
  of party, 252
Social Justice, 426
Social Security Act, 320; blacks and,
  328
Social Statics, 206
social virtue. *See* private virtue
sociological jurisprudence, 191, 193,
  207–8, 271, 351–52, 374, 522n4;
  Brandeis brief, 208; empirical
  evidence of common good, 208,
  271, 351, 374; reforming republican

democracy, 271; and Supreme
  Court, 351
Souter, David, 469
South Carolina, 9, 60, 78, 131–32,
  134–35, 138, 149, 162, 359, 449;
  campaign to limit black voting,
  161; Committee of Safety, 129
South Carolina College, 143
South Dakota, 264
Southern Christian Leadership
  Conference, 413
Southerners: in agriculture, 166;
  black exodus, 298; black
  representatives from South, 347;
  blacks as consumers, 345; blacks
  post–Civil War, 156, 158, 160–61,
  164; constitutions post–Civil War,
  210; and GI Bill of Rights, 344–45;
  and New Deal, 328; plantations,
  122–23, 157; and pre–Civil War
  Democrats, 153; readmission of
  Confederate states, 158; resent
  Hamilton's financial plan, 37,
  71; and secession, 84; slavery
  and abolition, 5, 122–23, 125,
  128–30, 132–36, 138–39, 143–44,
  146–47; and suffrage, 328; and
  suffrage of Confederates, 160;
  and Taft-Hartley Act, 342; whites
  enjoy disproportionate political
  power, 164; whites minimize
  black political power, 161, 163;
  whites oppose change, 346; whites
  post–Civil War, 154, 158, 162
Southern University, 414
sovereignty of the people, 15, 35,
  330–31, 334, 376, 396–97, 400; and
  Cooley, Thomas, 179; expanding,
  38; freedom of expression and, 55,
  58–59; and free expression, 91, 97;
  Lippmann doubts existence of
  "The People," 313; mob contrasted,
  147; petitioning representatives,
  133; Revolution and, 48; and